Heirs and Graces

ELEANOR DOUGHTY

Heirs and Graces

A History of the Modern British Aristocracy

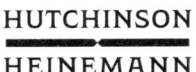
HUTCHINSON
HEINEMANN

HUTCHINSON HEINEMANN

UK | USA | Canada | Ireland | Australia
India | New Zealand | South Africa

Hutchinson Heinemann is part of the Penguin Random House group of companies
whose addresses can be found at global.penguinrandomhouse.com

Penguin Random House UK,
One Embassy Gardens, 8 Viaduct Gardens, London SW11 7BW

penguin.co.uk

Penguin
Random House
UK

First published 2025
002

Set in 11/15pt Sabon LT Std
Typeset by Six Red Marbles UK, Thetford, Norfolk

Printed and bound in Great Britain by Clays Ltd, Elcograf S.p.A.

The authorised representative in the EEA is Penguin Random House Ireland,
Morrison Chambers, 32 Nassau Street, Dublin D02 YH68

A CIP catalogue record for this book is available from the British Library

ISBN: 978-1-529-15304-0

*In memory of Peter and Obby Fitzwilliam,
and to their daughter Lady Juliet Tadgell*

'Happy families are all alike; every unhappy family is unhappy in its own way'

—Leo Tolstoy

Contents

CONTENTS

Dramatis Personae

The peerage bristles with numbered dukes, marquesses and earls, many of whom appear to or do have similar names. To help the reader negotiate the various generations of those families whose names appear most frequently in the text, a biographical list of dynasties is included below.

Ailesbury, Marquesses of

Michael Sydney Cedric Brudenell-Bruce, 8th Marquess (1926–2024), eldest son of the 7th Marquess. He was thrice married and had five children, the eldest of whom succeeded him in the marquessate. The 30th Hereditary Warden of Savernake Forest, he sold the family's ancient ivory horn, traditionally blown when the sovereign passed through the forest, in 1975. He was a keen betting man.

David Michael James Brudenell-Bruce, 9th Marquess (1952–), only son of the 8th Marquess. He has married twice and has three children, the eldest of whom, Thomas, Earl of Cardigan, will succeed him in the marquessate. In 1985, he was a witness to the Battle of the Beanfield, when local police stopped New Age travellers setting up that year's Stonehenge Free Festival.

Ailsa, Marquesses of

Archibald Angus *Charles* Kennedy, 8th Marquess (1956–2015), eldest son of the 7th Marquess. He married and had two daughters, and was succeeded by his younger brother. In 2011, he sold Ailsa Craig, the 240-acre island in the Firth of Clyde owned by the Kennedys since 1548.

David Thomas Kennedy, 9th Marquess (1958–), younger brother of the 8th Marquess. He married Anne Kelly and has two children, the second of whom, Archie, Earl of Cassillis, will succeed him in the marquessate. In 2015 he bought back Ailsa Craig.

Anglesey, Marquesses of
(Surname pronounced 'Paj-it')

Henry Cyril 'Toppy' Paget, 5th Marquess (1875–1905), only son of the 4th Marquess. He married his cousin Lilian Chetwynd but the marriage was childless and he was therefore succeeded by another cousin. He was dubbed 'the dancing marquess' owing to his butterfly-style dancing. He was declared bankrupt in 1904.

Lieutenant-Colonel Charles 'Charley' Henry Alexander Paget, GCVO, DL, 6th Marquess (1885–1947), eldest son of Lord Alexander Paget (1839–1896) and first cousin of the 5th Marquess. He married Lady Marjorie Manners, with whom he had six children, the fifth of whom succeeded him in the marquessate. In 1936, he commissioned the artist Rex Whistler to paint *Capriccio*, the artist's largest mural, at his Anglesey home, Plas Newydd.

Major George Charles *Henry* Victor Paget, DL, 7th Marquess (1922–2013), only son of the 6th Marquess. He married Shirley Morgan, the daughter of two novelists, and had five children, the second of whom succeeded him in the marquessate. He wrote eight volumes on the history of the British cavalry, 1816–1919, and gave Plas Newydd to the National Trust in 1976.

Charles *Alexander* Vaughan Paget, 8th Marquess (1950–), eldest son of the 7th Marquess. He has married twice and has two children, the elder of whom, Ben, Earl of Uxbridge, will succeed him in the marquessate. He carried the standard of Wales at Charles III's coronation and, as Alex Uxbridge, works as an artist.

Antrim, Earls of

Alexander Randal Mark McDonnell, 9th Earl (1935–2021), eldest son of the 8th Earl. He married twice and had four children, the third of whom succeeded him in the earldom. He was keeper of conservation at the Tate Gallery for twenty years, and the first to identify Bankside Power Station as a possible site for Tate Modern.

Randal Alexander McDonnell, 10th Earl (1967–), only son of the 9th Earl. He married Aurora Gunn, with whom he has two children; the elder, Alexander, Viscount Dunluce, will succeed him. He goes by 'Randal Dunluce' in civilian life, and commutes to his ancestral home, Glenarm Castle, County Antrim, at the weekends.

Argyll, Dukes of

Captain Ian Douglas Campbell, 11th Duke (1903–1973), only son of Douglas Campbell (1877–1926) and first cousin once removed of the 10th Duke. He married four times and had three children, the second of whom succeeded him as duke. He loved bird-watching and gardening.

Ian Campbell, DL, 12th Duke (1937–2001), elder son of the 11th Duke. He married Iona Colquhoun, the daughter of a Scottish baronet, with whom he had two children, the first succeeding him in the dukedom. With his wife he rebuilt his ancestral home, Inveraray Castle, after a fire there in 1975.

Torquhil Ian Campbell, 13th Duke (1968–), only son of the 12th Duke. He married Eleanor Cadbury, of the famed chocolate family, with whom he has three children. The eldest, Archie, Marquess of Lorne, will succeed him as duke. He once served as captain of Scotland's national elephant polo team.

Bath, Marquesses of
(Surname pronounced 'Thin')

Lieutenant-Colonel Thomas Henry Thynne, KG, CB, 5th Marquess (1862–1946), eldest son of the 4th Marquess. He married Violet Mordaunt, whose parentage was disputed, and had five children. His eldest son was killed in the First World War and he was succeeded in the marquessate by his second son. He was chairman of Wiltshire County Council for forty years, and spent the Second World War at his ancestral home, Longleat, with his Great Dane, Stephen, who followed him around like a witch's familiar.

Major Henry Frederick Thynne, 6th Marquess (1905–1992), only surviving son of the 5th Marquess. He was twice married, first to the writer Daphne Fielding (née Vivian), and had six surviving children, the second of whom succeeded him in the marquessate. He opened Longleat to the public in 1949, and its safari park in 1966. In later life he collected paintings by Adolf Hitler.

Alexander George Thynn, 7th Marquess (1932–2020), eldest son of the 6th Marquess. He married Hungarian-born Anna Gyarmathy, with whom he had two children; the second succeeded him in the marquessate. He had a number of mistresses, known to him as 'wifelets', some of whom lived on the Longleat estate. He adopted an alternative spelling of the family name in 1976, and decorated rooms at Longleat with erotic scenes from the Kama Sutra.

Ceawlin Henry Laszlo Thynn, 8th Marquess (1974–), only son of the 7th Marquess. He married Emma McQuiston, with whom he has two sons. The elder son, John, Viscount Weymouth, will succeed him. His Christian name derives from that of an ancient king of Wessex. He has been a donor to the Liberal Democrats.

Beauchamp, Earls
(Title pronounced 'Beecham'; surname pronounced 'Liggon')
William Lygon, KG, KCMG, CB, 7th Earl (1872–1938), eldest son of the 6th Earl. He married Lady Lettice Grosvenor and had seven children, the eldest of whom succeeded him. His family is generally considered to be the model for the Flyte family in Evelyn Waugh's magnum opus *Brideshead Revisited* (1945).
William Lygon, DL, 8th Earl (1903–1979), eldest son of the 7th Earl. He married Else 'Mona' Schiwe, a Dane. The marriage produced no children, and since both of his brothers had predeceased him, the earldom became extinct after his death. He was a very large man.

Beaufort, Dukes of
Henry 'Master' Hugh Arthur FitzRoy Somerset, KG, GCVO, 10th Duke (1900–1984), only son of the 9th Duke. He married Lady Mary Cambridge but the marriage was childless and he was therefore succeeded by his first cousin twice removed. He was known from the age of eleven as 'Master' after his father gave him a pack of harriers, of which he became master.
David Robert Somerset, 11th Duke (1928–2017), eldest surviving son of Captain Henry Somerset (1898–1965) and first cousin twice removed of the 10th Duke. He was twice married, first to Lady Caroline Thynne, with whom he had four children, the eldest of whom succeeded him as duke. Just as his predecessor had loved the company of women, he was described as 'the great woman slayer' by his friend Woodrow Wyatt.
Henry 'Bunter' John FitzRoy Somerset, 12th Duke (1952–), eldest son of the 11th Duke. He has been twice married, first to Tracy Ward, with whom he has three children. The eldest, Bobby, Marquess of Worcester, will succeed him as duke. He was the singer and songwriter of the rock group The Listening Device.

Bedford, Dukes of
Colonel Herbrand Arthur Russell, KG, KBE, DL, 11th Duke (1858–1940), younger brother of the 10th Duke. Married Mary Du Caurroy Tribe,

the daughter of an archdeacon of Lahore, with whom he had a son, who succeeded him in the dukedom. He was president of the Zoological Society of London for thirty-seven years, and responsible for saving Père David's deer from extinction: he kept a herd of them at his ancestral home of Woburn Abbey.

Hastings William Sackville Russell, 12th Duke (1888–1953), only son of the 11th Duke. Married Louisa Whitwell, the daughter of a medievalist, and had three children, the eldest of whom succeeded him in the dukedom. He was involved in far-right politics in the 1930s, and despite being a competent shot, died from injuries sustained from a shotgun.

John *Ian* Robert Russell, 13th Duke (1917–2002), eldest son of the 12th Duke. He was thrice married and had three children; his eldest son succeeded him as duke for only seven and a half months. He opened Woburn Abbey to the public in 1955, and established its safari park in 1970, following a short-lived career as a fruit farmer in South Africa.

Henry *Robin* Ian Russell, DL, 14th Duke (1940–2003), eldest son of the 13th Duke. He married Henrietta Tiarks, the daughter of a merchant banker, and had three sons, the eldest of whom succeeded him. He met his wife when they were children. She remembered asking him about his ambitions and receiving the reply: 'The only thing I want to be is a very good duke.'

Andrew Ian Henry Russell, 15th Duke (1962–), eldest son of the 14th Duke. He married Louisa Crammond and has two children, the younger of whom, Henry, Marquess of Tavistock, will succeed him in the dukedom. He lives at Woburn with his family, and has said that if he could save only one object from the house, it would be the Armada Portrait of Elizabeth I.

Bradford, Earls of

Lieutenant-Colonel Orlando 'Laddo' Bridgeman, DL, 5th Earl (1873–1957), eldest son of the 4th Earl. He married the Hon. Margaret 'Daisy' Bruce and had four children who survived infancy. The second of these succeeded him in the earldom. He fought in both the Second Boer War and the First World War, and also served as a government whip in the House of Lords.

Captain Gerald Michael Orlando Bridgeman, DL, 6th Earl (1911–1981), only son of the 5th Earl. He married the linguist Mary Montgomery, with whom he had four children, the eldest of whom succeeded him in the earldom. He served with the Shropshire Yeomanry during the Second

World War, and was said to have been written up for a Military Cross after Monte Cassino but declined it.

Richard Thomas Orlando Bridgeman, 7th Earl (1947–), eldest son of the 6th Earl. He has been married twice and has four children, the eldest of whom, Alexander, Viscount Newport, will succeed him in the earldom. He can count three dukes as his second cousins.

Bristol, Marquesses of
(Surname pronounced 'Harvy')

Rear-Admiral Frederick William Fane Hervey, MVO, 4th Marquess (1863–1951), eldest surviving son of Lord Augustus Hervey (1837–1875) and nephew of the 3rd Marquess. He married the heiress Dora Wythes, with whom he had two daughters; he was succeeded in the marquessate by his younger brother. He was considered peculiar by one of his grandsons who suggested that this was because he lived in relative isolation – in the middle of a park, at Ickworth, which is nine miles in circumference.

Herbert Arthur Robert Hervey, 5th Marquess (1870–1960), younger brother of the 4th Marquess. He was twice married, first to Lady Jean Cochrane, with whom he had a son who succeeded him in the marquessate. He was known in the family as 'Poor Old Herbert' or 'P.O.H.'. He served with the consular service.

Victor Frederick Cochrane Hervey, 6th Marquess (1915–1985), only son of the 5th Marquess. He was thrice married, on the second occasion to Lady Juliet Fitzwilliam; in total, he had five children who survived to adulthood, the eldest of whom succeeded him in the marquessate. He was a fantasist and a criminal, and in later life became a tax exile in Monaco.

Frederick William *John* Augustus Hervey, 7th Marquess (1954–1999), eldest son of the 6th Marquess. He married Francesca Fisher but their union was childless, and he was succeeded in the marquessate by his younger half-brother. He was a drug addict and died penniless, having spent his fortune.

Frederick William Augustus Hervey, 8th Marquess (1979–), younger half-brother of the 7th Marquess. He married the American art consultant Meredith Dunn with whom he has two children; the younger, Frederick, Earl Jermyn, will succeed him in the marquessate. He works in property management and previously managed a pan-Baltic property fund in Estonia.

Buccleuch and Queensberry, Dukes of
(Title pronounced 'Buckloo and Queensberry')

Lieutenant John Charles Montagu Douglas Scott RN, KT, GCVO, 7th Duke (1864–1935), eldest surviving son of the 6th Duke. He married Lady Margaret 'Molly' Bridgeman and had eight children, the second of whom succeeded him as duke. He despised pretension, though perhaps not comfort. Asked to open an event in Edinburgh, he instructed his chauffeur to drop him off from his Rolls-Royce at a tram stop, so that he could be seen to arrive by public transport.

Captain Walter John Montagu Douglas Scott, KT, GCVO, 8th Duke (1894–1973), eldest son of the 7th Duke. He married Mary 'Mollie' Lascelles, and had three children, the second of whom succeeded him as duke. His experiences with the Grenadier Guards during the First World War caused him to dread a further war with Germany to the extent that he became an advocate of appeasement in the years leading up to the Second World War.

Lieutenant-Commander Walter Francis John 'Johnny' Montagu Douglas Scott, 9th Duke (1923–2007), only son of the 8th Duke. He married the model Jane McNeill, and had four children, the eldest of whom succeeded him as duke. He was paralysed from the chest down in a hunting accident in 1971.

Richard Walter John Montagu Douglas Scott, 10th Duke (1954–), eldest son of the 9th Duke. He married Lady Elizabeth 'Bizza' Kerr and has four children, the eldest of whom, Walter, Earl of Dalkeith, will succeed him. In 2023 he was made Chancellor of the Order of the Thistle, and a week after his wife's death carried the Sceptre with Cross at Charles III's coronation.

Caledon, Earls of
(Title pronounced 'Cal-le-don', as in 'the Caledonian Ball')

Major Erik James Desmond Alexander, 5th Earl (1885–1968), eldest son of the 4th Earl. He was dominated by his imperious mother, Lady Elizabeth Graham-Toler, and never married. His nephew succeeded him in the earldom. His first name, like those given to his three brothers, derives from his mother's predilection for all things Scandinavian. He was fined multiple times for reckless driving.

Major Denis James Alexander, DL, 6th Earl (1920–1980), only son of Lieutenant-Colonel the Hon. Herbrand Alexander (1888–1965) and nephew of the 5th Earl. He was thrice married and had three children, the second of whom succeeded him in the earldom. After the Second World War, during which he served with the Irish Guards, he worked for BP as an engineer, before inheriting his uncle's estate in the borderlands of County Tyrone.

Nicholas James Alexander, KCVO, 7th Earl (1955–), only son of the 6th Earl. Thrice married, he has two children, the elder of whom, Frederick, Viscount Alexander, will succeed him in the earldom. He has served as Lord-Lieutenant of County Armagh since 1989.

Carlisle, Earls of

George James Howard, 9th Earl (1843–1911), only son of the Hon. Charles Howard (1814–1879) and nephew of the 8th Earl. He married the Hon. Rosalind Stanley, a follower of the Temperance Movement, and had ten children who survived infancy. He was a painter, a member of the Cambridge Apostles and the last Earl of Carlisle to own Castle Howard.

Captain Charles 'Charley' James Stanley Howard, DL, 10th Earl (1867–1912), eldest son of the 9th Earl. He married Rhoda L'Estrange, the daughter of an army officer, and had four children, the eldest of whom succeeded him. He was ill for a long period at the end of his life and predeceased his mother, setting in motion great changes in the settlement of the family estates.

Lieutenant-Commander George Josslyn L'Estrange Howard, 11th Earl (1895–1963), only son of the 10th Earl. He was married twice, first to Bridget 'Biddy' Hore-Ruthven, later 11th Lady Ruthven of Freeland, and had three children, the second of whom succeeded him in the earldom. He did not inherit his ancestral home of Castle Howard as might have been expected.

Charles 'Charlie' James Ruthven Howard, MC, DL, 12th Earl (1923–1994), only son of the 11th Earl. He married the Hon. Ela Beaumont and had four children, the eldest of whom succeeded him in the earldom. He served with the Rifle Brigade during the Second World War and was badly injured in 1944, writing home to his father: 'Had slight accident with mine. Lost my leg. Left arm completely paralysed, but I think it will be OK so don't worry.' He later became an expert on trees and wildfowl.

Major George William Beaumont Howard, 13th Earl (1949–), eldest son of the 12th Earl. He is unmarried. He served for twenty years in the 9th/12th Royal Lancers, and in 2011 stood as a Liberal Democrat candidate in elections to the House of Lords. His title will probably pass to his brother, the Hon. Philip Howard (1963–).

Carrington, Barons

Major Peter Alexander Rupert Carington, KG, GCMG, CH, MC, 6th Baron (1919–2018), only son of the 5th Baron. He married Iona McClean and had three children, the youngest of whom succeeded him in the barony. Having inherited his title aged nineteen, during the Second World War, he served as an active peer in the House of Lords until his death in 2018, aged ninety-nine. With his wife he painstakingly restored the house and gardens on the family's Buckinghamshire estate.

Rupert Francis John Carington, DL, 7th Baron (1948–), only son of the 6th Baron. He married Daniela Diotallevi and has three children; his only son, the Hon. Robert Carington, will succeed him in the barony. A merchant banker, in 2022 he became Lord Great Chamberlain of England.

Castle Stewart, Earls

Major Arthur Stuart, MC, 7th Earl (1889–1961), third son of the 6th Earl, whom he succeeded after his two brothers were killed in the First World War. He married Eleanor Guggenheim, daughter of the art collector Solomon Guggenheim, and had four sons, two of whom were killed in the Second World War. He was succeeded by his third son, Patrick. He worked briefly as a schoolmaster and took his own life in 1961.

Arthur *Patrick* Avondale Stuart, 8th Earl (1928–2023), third son of the 7th Earl. Twice married, he had two children, the elder of whom succeeded him in the earldom. He was a passionate forester and planted many trees on his Northern Irish estate, which was bombed by the IRA in 1972.

Andrew Richard Charles Stuart, 9th Earl (1953–), only son of the 8th Earl. Twice married, he has a daughter. He lives in Somerset and enjoys bell-ringing, cycling and sailing. His heir is his first cousin Thomas Stuart.

Cawdor, Earls

Lieutenant-Colonel John 'Jack' Duncan Vaughan Campbell, 5th Earl (1900–1970), eldest son of the 4th Earl. He married Wilma Vickers, the daughter of a rich industrialist, and had three children, the second of whom succeeded him in the earldom. His father contracted syphilis in Japan and spent his last years in a sanatorium. Perhaps as a result of this, Jack found it easiest to communicate with his own family by letter.

Hugh John Vaughan Campbell, 6th Earl (1932–1993), eldest son of the 5th Earl. He married twice and had five children, the third of whom succeeded him in the earldom. He was an aficionado of alcohol and fast cars.

Colin Robert Vaughan Campbell, DL, 7th Earl Cawdor (1962–), elder son of the 6th Earl. He married the sometime fashion editor Lady Isabella Stanhope and has four children, the second of whom, James, Viscount Emlyn, will succeed him in the earldom. He trained as an architect.

Chichester, Earls of

Captain John Buxton Pelham, 8th Earl (1912–1944), younger brother of the 7th Earl, who bore the title for only eight days. He married Ursula von Pannwitz, the daughter of a German lawyer and art collector, whose mother was a friend of the former German kaiser, Wilhelm II. They had two children, but he lived to see the birth of only one. He was killed in a car accident on the A1 during the Second World War.

John Nicholas Pelham, 9th Earl (1944–), only son of the 8th Earl, born posthumously. He married June Wells, with whom he has a daughter. While studying music in Austria, he lodged with Hermann Göring's sister, Olga Rigele, though he didn't realise that at the time. His heir is his second cousin once removed, Duncan Pelham.

Crathorne, Barons

Major Thomas Lionel Dugdale, 1st Baron (1897–1977), son of Captain James Lionel Dugdale (1862–1941), created Baron Crathorne in 1959. He married Nancy Tennant, with whom he had two sons; the elder succeeded him in the barony. He served with the Scots Greys in the First World War and the Yorkshire Hussars during the Second World War, and was for thirty years a Conservative MP.

Charles *James* Dugdale KCVO, 2nd Baron (1939–), elder son of the 1st Baron. He married Sylvia Montgomery, with whom he had three children, the second of whom, the Hon. Thomas Dugdale, will succeed him in the barony. He has been a working hereditary peer since he succeeded his father in 1977 and remained an active member after the expulsion of the bulk of hereditary peers in 1999.

Derby, Earls of

Edward 'Eddy' George Villiers Stanley, KG, GCB, GCVO, 17th Earl (1865–1948), eldest son of the 16th Earl. He married Lady Alice Montagu and had three children, two of whom predeceased him; he was succeeded by his grandson. He was active in British politics for over fifty years, serving as ambassador to France and secretary of state for war, and was known as the king of Lancashire.

Major Edward *John* Stanley, MC, 18th Earl (1918–1994), eldest son of Captain Edward Stanley, Lord Stanley, MC (1894–1938) and grandson of the 17th Earl. He married Lady Isobel Milles-Lade, but the marriage produced no children and he was therefore succeeded by his nephew. He served with the Grenadier Guards during the Second World War, and enjoyed gambling – though only at cards, and not on the racehorses that he dearly loved.

Edward 'Teddy' Richard William Stanley, DL, 19th Earl (1962–), son of Hugh Stanley (1926–1971) and nephew of the 18th Earl. He married the Hon. Caroline 'Cazzy' Neville and has three children, the second of whom, Edward, Lord Stanley, will succeed him in the earldom. A former merchant banker, he runs the Knowsley Hall estate on Merseyside and is active on the racing scene; his mare Ouija Board won the Oaks in 2004.

Devon, Earls of

Captain Charles *Christopher* Courtenay, 17th Earl (1916–1998), only surviving son of the 16th Earl. He married Venetia, Countess of Cottenham, and had two children, the younger of whom succeeded him in the earldom. Between 1927 and 1935, both of his uncles and his father died, each having succeeded to the earldom. He therefore inherited Powderham Castle with triple death duties.

Hugh Rupert Courtenay, DL, 18th Earl (1942–2015), only son of the 17th Earl. He married Diana Watherston, whom he met at a Pony Club camp in the Scottish Borders, and had four children, the youngest of whom succeeded him in the earldom. He was born in the state bed at Powderham shortly after Exeter was bombed during the Luftwaffe's Baedeker raids, while his father was serving in North Africa.

Charles Peregrine Courtenay, 19th Earl (1975–), only son of the 18th Earl. He married the actor Allison-Joy 'AJ' Langer, with whom he has two children, the second of whom, Jack, Lord Courtenay, will succeed him in the earldom. In 2018 he was elected as a crossbench member of the House of Lords. He works as a barrister specialising in intellectual property.

Devonshire, Dukes of

Major Victor Christian William Cavendish, KG, GCMG, GCVO, 9th Duke (1868–1938), eldest son of Lord Edward Cavendish (1838–1891) and nephew of the 8th Duke. He married Lady Evelyn Petty-Fitzmaurice and had seven children, the eldest of whom succeeded him as duke. As well as a landowner, he was an active politician, serving as secretary of state for the colonies, and as Governor General of Canada. He was appointed a Knight of the Garter in 1916.

Lieutenant-Colonel Edward 'Eddy' William Spencer Cavendish, KG, MBE, 10th Duke (1895–1950), eldest son of the 9th Duke. He married Lady Mary 'Moucher' Gascoyne-Cecil and had four children who survived infancy. His second son succeeded him as duke after his elder brother was killed in the Second World War. He was an active freemason and at the time of his death, from a heart attack, grand master of the United Grand Lodge of England.

Major Andrew Robert Buxton Cavendish, KG, MC, 11th Duke (1920–2004), only surviving son of the 10th Duke. He married the Hon. Deborah 'Debo' Freeman-Mitford, with whom he had three surviving children; the second of these succeeded him as duke. With his wife he transformed his ancestral home of Chatsworth House into one of the country's most successful visitor attractions, having conquered his alcoholism in the 1980s.

Peregrine 'Stoker' Andrew Morny Cavendish, KCVO, CBE, DL, 12th Duke (1944–), only surviving son of the 11th Duke. He married Amanda Heywood-Lonsdale, the daughter of a naval officer, and has three children, the eldest of whom, William, Earl of Burlington, will succeed him as duke. He has been deputy chairman of Sotheby's since 1996, and is the owner of Heywood Hill, the bookshop his aunt Nancy Mitford worked at during the Second World War.

Donoughmore, Earls of
(Title pronounced 'Donomore')
Colonel John 'Ordy' Michael Henry Hely Hutchinson, 7th Earl (1902–1981), eldest son of the 6th Earl. He married Jean Hotham and they had three children, the eldest of whom succeeded him in the earldom. His younger son, the Hon. Mark Hely Hutchinson, was chief executive of the Bank of Ireland. With his wife, he was kidnapped from his home, Knocklofty House, County Tipperary, and held by an IRA unit in 1974.

Richard *Michael* 'Mick' John Hely Hutchinson, 8th Earl (1927–2025), eldest son of the 7th Earl. Twice married, he had four children, the eldest of whom succeeded him in the earldom. He studied medicine at Oxford University and served in the Royal Army Medical Corps.

John Michael James Hely Hutchinson, 9th Earl (1952–), eldest son of the 8th Earl. He married Marie-Claire van den Driessche and has three children, the second of whom, Richard, Viscount Suirdale, will succeed him in the earldom.

Downe, Viscounts

Colonel Richard Dawnay, OBE, DL, 10th Viscount (1903–1965), eldest son of the 9th Viscount. He married Margaret Bahnsen, whom he met in the United States while working as a banker, and had two sons, the elder of whom succeeded him in the viscountcy. He was Page of Honour to George V 1917–1919, and with his wife kept a pair of brown bear cubs, Bruin and Teddy.

John Christian George Dawnay, DL, 11th Viscount (1935–2002), elder son of the 10th Viscount. He married Diana Sconce, with whom he had a son and daughter; the former succeeded him in the viscountcy. A shy man, he ran a private laboratory at Wykeham Abbey near Scarborough. He collected Aston Martin cars, the first of which he bought as an undergraduate.

Richard Henry Dawnay, 12th Viscount (1967–), only son of the 11th Viscount. He is unmarried and divides his time between Wykeham and London. He studied chemistry at Durham University rather than learning the ropes of estate management as many of his peers have done, and afterwards worked for HSBC for twenty years. Despite his father's one-time extensive car collection, he does not drive. The heir to the title is his first cousin, Tom Dawnay.

Durham, Earls of

Antony 'Tony' Claud Frederick Lambton, 6th Earl but disclaimed in 1970 (1922–2006), eldest surviving son of the 5th Earl. He married Belinda 'Bindy' Blew-Jones and had six children; his only son succeeded him in the earldom, and did not disclaim it. He often wore his trademark round, dark glasses and was involved in a sex scandal in 1973 after which he left parliament, having served as a Conservative MP for twenty-two years.

Edward 'Ned' Richard Lambton, 7th Earl (1961–), only son of the 6th Earl, who disclaimed his title. He is thrice married and has five children. His eldest son Frederick, Viscount Lambton, will succeed him in the title. One of his godparents was former prime minister Sir Anthony Eden. With his third wife Marina Hanbury, he divides his time between London and Cetinale, the Italian villa his father bought in 1978.

Erroll, Earls of

Captain Josslyn Victor Hay, 22nd Earl (1901–1941), eldest son of the 21st Earl. He was twice married, firstly to the much-married Lady Idina Sackville, the inspiration for 'The Bolter' in Nancy Mitford's 1945 novel *The Pursuit of Love*. They had a daughter, Diana, who succeeded him in the title. He moved to Kenya in 1924, became a member of the 'Happy Valley Set', and was murdered. Sir Henry 'Jock' Delves Broughton, 11th Baronet, was accused of killing him, tried and ultimately acquitted. He took his own life a year later.

Diana Denyse Hay, 23rd Countess (1926–1978), only child of the 22nd Earl. She married Sir Iain Moncreiffe of that Ilk, Chief of Clan Moncreiffe, and had three children, the eldest of whom succeeded her. After her parents' divorce she was raised in England by her Sackville relations. She took her seat in the House of Lords following 1963 legislation that allowed female hereditary peers to do so for the first time.

Merlin Sereld Victor Gilbert Hay, 24th Earl (1948–), eldest son of the 23rd Countess. He married Isabelle Hohler, who was born in Brussels, the daughter of a banker, and has four children, the eldest of whom, Harry, Lord Hay, will succeed him in the earldom. He is a member of the Royal Company of Archers, the monarch's bodyguard in Scotland, and has worked as a computer consultant.

Exeter, Marquesses of
(Surname pronounced 'Cissel')

Colonel William Thomas Brownlow Cecil, KG, CMG, 5th Marquess (1876–1956), only son of the 4th Marquess. He married the Hon. Myra Orde-Powlett and had four children: both of his sons ultimately became successive Marquesses of Exeter. He lived at his ancestral home, Burghley House, Lincolnshire, for his whole life, and was appointed a Knight of the Garter in 1937.

Lieutenant-Colonel David George Brownlow Cecil, KCMG, DL, 6th Marquess (1905–1981), eldest son of the 5th Marquess. He was twice married: first to Lady Mary Montagu Douglas Scott, with whom he had three surviving children, and then to Diana Henderson, with whom he had a fourth daughter. He won the gold medal in the 400-metre hurdles at the 1928 Olympic Games in Amsterdam, and went on to become chairman of the British Olympic Association. His brother Lord Martin Cecil succeeded him in the marquessate, and he established a charitable trust to look after Burghley House.

William *Martin* Alleyne Cecil, 7th Marquess (1909–1988), younger
brother of the 6th Marquess. Twice married, he had two surviving
children, the elder of whom succeeded him as marquess. He moved to
Canada aged twenty-one to live and work on the ranch in British Columbia that his father had bought. In later life he became head of the
intentional community the Emissaries of Divine Light.

William *Michael* Anthony Cecil, 8th Marquess (1935–), only son of the
7th Marquess. Twice married, he has two children, the elder of whom,
Anthony, Lord Burghley, will inherit the marquessate. He lives, as his
father did, in North America, but remains keenly interested in what goes
on at Burghley House, his ancestral home in Lincolnshire.

Fife, Dukes of

James 'Jamie' George Alexander Bannerman Carnegie, 3rd Duke (1929–
2015), only son of the 11th Earl of Southesk (1893–1992) and nephew
of the 2nd Duchess. He married the Hon. Caroline Dewar and had two
children; they divorced in 1966. His only son succeeded him in the dukedom. As a toddler in 1932, he spat on Queen Mary, his great-aunt, when
she offered her hand to him to kiss. It did not put her off him: later,
when he was in Malaya with the Scots Guards, she would send him food
parcels.

David Charles Carnegie, 4th Duke (1961–), only son of the 3rd Duke. He
married the horse-loving Caroline Bunting and together they have three
sons, the eldest of whom, Charlie, Earl of Southesk, will succeed him in
the dukedom. The Fifes live at Kinnaird Castle in Angus and are building
a town on the Elsick estate just outside Aberdeen.

Fitzwilliam, Earls

William Thomas Spencer Wentworth-Fitzwilliam, KG, DL, 6th Earl (1815–
1902), eldest surviving son of the 5th Earl. He married Lady Frances
'Fanny' Douglas, and had twelve children who survived infancy. Both
his wife and five of his children died in his lifetime, including his heir,
William, Viscount Milton, whose own son Billy succeeded him in the
earldom. A painting of a fox hunt hangs in an office at his ancestral
home of Wentworth Woodhouse: he used to say that he had bred everything in it – not just two of his daughters, as well as the horses and
hounds, but the huntsman, and a member of the hunt staff too.

Major William 'Billy' Charles de Meuron Wentworth-Fitzwilliam, KCVO,
CBE, DSO, 7th Earl (1872–1943), only son of William Wentworth-

Fitzwilliam, Viscount Milton (1839–1877), and grandson of the 6th Earl. He married Lady Maud Dundas and had five children; his only son succeeded him in the earldom. His middle name of 'de Meuron' derives from the location on the Kaministiquia River in Canada at which he was born. His birth was not reported in *The Times* until he was two months old.

Captain William Henry Lawrence *Peter* Wentworth-Fitzwilliam, DSC, 8th Earl (1910–1948), only son of the 7th Earl. He married Olive 'Obby' Plunket, the daughter of Benjamin Plunket, Bishop of Meath, and they had a daughter, Lady Juliet (1935–). He was succeeded by his second cousin once removed. He served in the Second World War with the Grenadier Guards, 8 Commando, and with the Special Operations Executive. He and his wife referred to each other, respectively, as 'Mrs Pod' and 'Mr Pod'.

Eric Spencer Wentworth-Fitzwilliam, 9th Earl (1883–1952), son of Captain Sir William Wentworth-Fitzwilliam (1848–1925) and first cousin once removed of the 8th Earl. He married Jessica Rowlands but the marriage was dissolved without issue. He lived at Barnsdale Hall on Rutland Water and spent most of his time drinking. He succeeded to the title after the 8th Earl's death in a plane crash.

Captain William *Thomas* George Wentworth-Fitzwilliam, DL, 10th Earl (1904–1979), younger son of George Wentworth-Fitzwilliam (1866–1935) and second cousin of the 9th Earl. He married Joyce Langdale, formerly Viscountess FitzAlan, and had no legitimate children; together they had a daughter before they were married. He inherited the earldom from his second cousin following a court case that determined whether or not his elder brother Toby was legitimate; the court ruled that he was not. Upon his death, with no male heirs, the earldom became extinct.

Hailsham, Viscounts

Major Quintin McGarel Hogg, KG, CH, 2nd Viscount but disclaimed in 1963 (1907–2001), elder son of the 1st Viscount. Thrice married, he had five children with his second wife, Mary Martin, the eldest of whom succeeded him in the viscountcy. He was a Conservative politician and served as Lord Chancellor under both Edward Heath and Margaret Thatcher, having disclaimed his hereditary title in order to stay in the House of Commons. He was created a life peer as Baron Hailsham of St Marylebone in 1970.

Douglas Martin Hogg, KC, 3rd Viscount (1945–), eldest son of the 2nd Viscount, who disclaimed his title. He married the Hon. Sarah

Boyd-Carpenter, with whom he has two children, the younger of whom, the Hon. Quintin Hogg, will succeed him in the viscountcy. His wife was created a life peer in 1995 and as such the Hailshams are among the few married couples both to hold titles in their own right. In 2009, the *Telegraph* reported that, as MP for Sleaford and North Hykeham, he claimed expenses for the cleaning of his moat, at Kettlethorpe Hall, Lincolnshire.

Hertford, Marquesses of
(Title pronounced 'Harford'; surname pronounced 'Seamer')

Hugh Edward Conway Seymour, DL, 8th Marquess (1930–1997), only son of Brigadier-General Lord Henry Seymour (1878–1939) and nephew of the 7th Marquess. He married Louise de Caraman, Princesse de Chimay, and had four children, the eldest of whom succeeded him in the marquessate. He inherited the title at the age of nine, having read in the newspaper that a young boy of his age had succeeded his uncle – and to his surprise discovered that he was the young boy.

Henry 'Harry' Jocelyn Seymour, DL, 9th Marquess (1958–), only son of the 8th Marquess. He married the Brazilian Beatriz Karam and has four children, the eldest of whom, William, Earl of Yarmouth, will succeed him in the marquessate. His first job was working for Johnny Buccleuch at Boughton as a shepherd. William Yarmouth married Kelsey Wells and has two sons, the elder of whom is second in line to inherit the Hertford marquessate.

Home, Earls of
(Title and surname pronounced 'Hume')

Alexander 'Alec' Frederick Douglas-Home, KT, DL, 14th Earl but disclaimed in 1963 (1903–1995), eldest son of the 13th Earl. He married Elizabeth Alington, the daughter of his Eton headmaster, and had four children, the youngest of whom succeeded him in the earldom that he disclaimed. As Lord Dunglass he accompanied Neville Chamberlain to his final meeting with Adolf Hitler in Munich in September 1938.

David Alexander Cospatrick Douglas-Home, KT, CVO, CBE, 15th Earl (1943–2022), only son of the 14th Earl who disclaimed his title. He married Jane Williams-Wynne and had three children, the youngest of whom succeeded him in the earldom. He was at Christ Church, Oxford as Lord Dunglass when his father disclaimed his peerage, and shortly after word was given that the act had been completed, the college porters went around swapping the painted words 'Lord Dunglass' for 'The Hon. David Douglas-Home'.

Michael David Alexander Douglas-Home, 16th Earl (1987–), only son of the 15th Earl. He married Sally Underhill, the daughter of an RAF officer, and has three children, the youngest of whom, Leo, Lord Dunglass, will succeed him in the earldom. He was a Page of Honour to Elizabeth II, 1997–2000.

Kimberley, Earls of
(Surname pronounced 'Woodhouse')

John Wodehouse, 2nd Earl (1848–1932), eldest son of the 1st Earl. He married Isabel Stracey, the daughter of a baronet, and had four children. Two of his sons were killed in or from injuries sustained during the First World War, and he was succeeded in the earldom by his eldest and only surviving son. He was the first member of the Labour Party in the House of Lords and became known as the 'Labour Earl'.

Captain John 'Jack' Wodehouse, CBE, MC, 3rd Earl (1883–1941), eldest son of the 2nd Earl. He married the socialite Margaret Irby and had one son, who succeeded him in the earldom. He represented his country playing polo at both the 1908 London and 1920 Antwerp Olympics. Until his death in the Blitz, he was the Other Man of Geordie Sutherland's wife Eileen.

John Wodehouse, 4th Earl (1924–2002), only son of the 3rd Earl. He was married six times, and had four sons, the eldest of whom succeeded him in the earldom. His godfather was his third cousin thrice removed, P. G. Wodehouse. His mother did not discourage him in his infidelities, and he described his first marriage as a kind of insurance: 'While I was married to her, I couldn't be married to anyone else.'

John Armine Wodehouse, 5th Earl (1951–), eldest son of the 4th Earl. He married the Hon. Carol Palmer and has two children, the younger of whom, David, Lord Wodehouse, will succeed him in the earldom. He is a chemist and worked for GlaxoSmithKline for almost forty years.

Kinloss, Ladies

Beatrice *Mary* Freeman-Grenville, 12th Lady (1922–2012), eldest daughter of Luis Morgan-Grenville, Master of Kinloss (1889–1944) and granddaughter of the 11th Lady. She married Dr Greville Freeman and had three children. Her son and heir the Hon. Bevil Freeman-Grenville died suddenly nine months before her and she was succeeded by her eldest daughter. While her husband was working for the Aden Protectorate, she lived there as an ordinary housewife, before returning to the UK and taking up her seat in the House of Lords in early 1964.

Teresa Mary Nugent Freeman-Grenville, 13th Lady (1957–), eldest daughter of the 12th Lady. She is unmarried and the heir to her title is her sister, the Hon. Hester Haworth, Mistress of Kinloss. She was born in what was then Tanganyika, and has worked for the National Milk Records since 1992.

Lansdowne, Marquesses of

Henry 'Clan' Charles Keith Petty-Fitzmaurice, KG, GCSI, GCMG, GCIE, 5th Marquess (1845–1927), eldest son of the 4th Marquess. He married Lady Maud Hamilton, daughter of the Duke of Abercorn, and had four children, the second of whom succeeded him in the marquessate. His younger son was killed in the First World War. He served in many political roles – as Governor General of Canada, Viceroy of India, secretary of state for war and foreign secretary. His nickname comes from his courtesy title Viscount Clanmaurice.

Lieutenant-Colonel Henry 'Kerry' William Edmund Petty-Fitzmaurice, DSO, MVO, 6th Marquess (1872–1936), eldest son of the 5th Marquess. He married Elizabeth 'Elsie' Hope and had five children, the second of whom would have succeeded him but for his death in 1933. He was instead succeeded by his middle son in the marquessate. He was known as 'Kerry' throughout his life, owing to his courtesy title Earl of Kerry.

Captain Charles Hope Petty-Fitzmaurice, 7th Marquess (1917–1944), eldest surviving son of the 6th Marquess. He never married and was killed in Italy during the Second World War while serving with the Royal Wiltshire Yeomanry. He has no known grave and is commemorated on the memorial at Monte Cassino. His younger brother was killed nine days before him in Normandy. He was succeeded by his first cousin, Captain George Mercer Nairne.

Major George John Charles Mercer Nairne Petty-Fitzmaurice, DL, 8th Marquis (1912–1999), only son of Lord Charles Fitzmaurice, MVO (1874–1914) and first cousin of the 7th Marquess. He married four times and had four children from his first marriage to Barbara Chase, the daughter of an American businessman whom he met in California. As his father had been equerry to George V, the king was his godfather.

Charles Maurice Petty-Fitzmaurice, LVO, DL, 9th Marquis (1941–), eldest son of the 8th Marquess. Twice married, he has four children, the third of whom, Simon, Earl of Kerry, will succeed him in the marquessate. He inherited Bowood House and opened it to the public in 1975. He served for eleven years as a member of the Council of the Duchy of Cornwall.

Latymer, Barons
Hugo Nevill Money-Coutts, 8th Baron (1926–2003), only son of the 7th Baron. He was twice married and had six children; his eldest son succeeded him in the barony. At Eton he rowed in the VIII and afterwards worked as a merchant banker before sailing to Australia via the Panama Canal. He settled in Majorca with his second wife.
Crispin James Alan Nevill Money-Coutts, 9th Baron (1955–), eldest son of the 8th Baron. Twice married, first to the Hon. Lucy Deedes, daughter of the journalist Bill Deedes, he has three children, the second of whom, the Hon. Drummond Money-Coutts, a magician, will succeed him in the barony. Like his father he is a keen rower, and represented Oxford University in the Boat Race in both 1975 and 1977.

Leeds, Dukes of
George Godolphin Osborne, 10th Duke (1862–1927), eldest surviving son of the 9th Duke. He married Lady Katherine Lambton and they had five children; his only son succeeded him in the dukedom. He was a keen yachtsman, a member of the Ancient Order of Druids and was sometime MFH, Bedale Hunt.
John Francis Godolphin Osborne, 11th Duke (1901–1963), only son of the 10th Duke. He was thrice married and had a daughter, Lady Camilla (1950–); he was succeeded in the dukedom by his second cousin once removed. He sold his ancestral home of Hornby Castle in 1930, partly to pay off his father's gambling debts, and became a tax exile on Jersey.
Francis *D'Arcy* Godolphin Osborne, KCMG, 12th Duke (1884–1964), eldest son of Sidney Osborne (1835–1903) and second cousin once removed of the 11th Duke. He never married and upon his death, with no remaining male heirs, the dukedom became extinct. He served as British Ambassador to the Holy See for eleven years and was a friend of Queen Elizabeth, the Queen Mother.

Linlithgow, Marquesses of

Colonel Victor Alexander John Hope, KG, KT, GCSI, GCIE, OBE, 2nd Marquess (1887–1952), eldest son of the 1st Marquess. He married Doreen Milner, the daughter of a baronet and Conservative MP, and had five children, including twin boys. His eldest twin son succeeded him in the marquessate. He served as Viceroy of India in the pre-war period and until 1943.

Captain Charles William Frederick Hope, MC, 3rd Marquess (1912–1987), eldest twin son of the 2nd Marquess. He was twice married and had two children from his first marriage to Vivien Kenyon-Slaney, the younger of whom succeeded him in the marquessate. He was captured in 1940 and later held as a prisoner-of-war at Oflag IV-C at Colditz Castle, Saxony, where he turned his hand to amateur dramatics, and played Ernest in a two-night production of Oscar Wilde's *The Importance of Being Earnest*.

Adrian John Charles Hope, 4th Marquess (1946–), only son of the 3rd Marquess. He has been thrice married and has four children; his eldest son, Andrew, Earl of Hopetoun, will succeed him in the marquessate. He has worked as a stockbroker.

Londonderry, Marquesses of

Major Charles Stewart Henry Vane-Tempest-Stewart, KG, MVO, 7th Marquess (1878–1949), eldest son of the 6th Marquess. He married the Hon. Edith 'Circe' Chaplin and had five children, the second of whom succeeded him in the marquessate. He served as secretary of state for air for four years; owing to his German sympathies he acquired the unfortunate nickname of the 'Londonderry Herr'. On the mantelpiece of his study at Mount Stewart, County Down, he kept a small porcelain statue of an SS man carrying a Nazi flag, given to him by Joachim von Ribbentrop in 1936.

Edward Charles Stewart Robert 'Robin' Vane-Tempest-Stewart, DL, 8th Marquess (1902–1955), only son of the 7th Marquess, from whom he was long estranged. He married Romaine Combe, the daughter of an army officer, and had three children, the youngest of whom succeeded him in the marquessate. After his wife's death, depressed and lonely, he became an alcoholic and eventually drank himself to death.

Alexander 'Alastair' Charles Robert Vane-Tempest-Stewart, 9th Marquess (1937–2012), only son of the 8th Marquess. He married twice and had four children, the third of whom succeeded him in the marquessate. He sold the Londonderrys' remaining seat, Wynyard Hall, in 1987. He was an accomplished pianist and an authority on the Hungarian composer Franz Liszt.

Frederick Aubrey Vane-Tempest-Stewart, 10th Marquess (1972–), eldest son of the 9th Marquess. He married the artist Rita Nowak in 2022; his brother Lord Reginald, a photographer, is his heir. He works as a sculptor and has the most beautiful handwriting.

Longford, Earls of

(Surname pronounced 'Pack-en'um')

Francis 'Frank' Aungier Pakenham, KG, 7th Earl (1905–2001), younger brother of the 6th Earl. He married Elizabeth Harman, who became a celebrated writer and historian, and with her had eight children, the second of whom succeeded him in the earldom. His eldest daughter Lady Antonia (1932–) also became a historian. He was a member of the Labour Party and served in various ministerial roles during both Clement Attlee's and Harold Wilson's governments. He befriended the murderer Myra Hindley whose release he campaigned for, earning him the soubriquet 'Lord Wrongford'.

Thomas Francis Dermot Pakenham, 8th Earl (1933–), eldest son of the 7th Earl. He married the writer Valerie Scott and has four children, the third of whom, Ned Pakenham, will succeed him in the earldom. Like his late wife, he is a writer. He does not use his title and as his earldom is an Irish peerage it cannot be disclaimed.

Lonsdale, Earls of

Lieutenant-Colonel Hugh Cecil Lowther, KG, GCVO, DL, 5th Earl (1857–1944), younger brother of the 4th Earl. Despite her parents' opposition, he married Lady Grace Gordon. After she fell and had a miscarriage out hunting, she found herself unable to have children. He was succeeded in the earldom by his younger brother. He was the first president of the Automobile Association (AA), and travelled between his houses with a twenty-five-piece private orchestra.

Captain Lancelot Edward Lowther, OBE, DL, 6th Earl (1867–1953), younger brother of the 5th Earl. He married Gwendoline Sheffield, the daughter of a baronet, and had three children. His only son, Anthony, Viscount Lowther, predeceased him and he was succeeded in the earldom by his grandson. Thanks to his brother's over-spending, he was forced to sell the contents of Lowther Castle in 1947.

Captain James Hugh William Lowther, 7th Earl (1922–2006), eldest son of Anthony, Viscount Lowther (1896–1949) and grandson of the 6th Earl. He married four times and had eight children, the second and fourth of whom successively succeeded him in the earldom. He took the roof off Lowther Castle in 1957, leaving it a romantic ruin, and for years resisted being included in the *Sunday Times* Rich List on the grounds that he was penniless. He subsequently appeared in the 2006 List with an estimated wealth of £80 million.

Hugh Clayton Lowther, 8th Earl (1949–2021), eldest son of the 7th Earl. He married thrice, and had one adopted son who could not inherit the earldom. He was succeeded by his half-brother. Following an accident in his teenage years he was unable to walk for long periods of time but enjoyed his ancestral lands from the air, in a microlight.

William Lowther, 9th Earl (1957–), half-brother of the 8th Earl. He married Angela Tinker; they have no children. His heir is his half-brother, the Hon. James 'Jim' Lowther, who with his wife runs Lowther Castle as a popular visitor attraction.

Lothian, Marquesses of
(Surname pronounced 'Car')

Philip Henry Kerr, KT, CH, DL, 11th Marquess (1882–1940), eldest son of Major-General Lord Ralph Kerr (1837–1916) and first cousin of the 10th Marquess. He never married and was succeeded by his first cousin. As a young man he maintained a fairly untidy appearance and seems to have been wholly unselfconscious, as was demonstrated when in 1917, upon arrival at a country house in Lancashire to join David Lloyd George, he was mistaken by the butler for the prime minister's valet and directed to the back entrance. At the time of his death he was British Ambassador to the US.

Peter Francis Walter Kerr, KCVO, DL, 12th Marquess (1922–2004), eldest son of Captain Andrew Kerr (1877–1929) and first cousin of the 11th Marquess. He married the writer Antonella 'Tony' Newland, and had six children, the second of whom succeeded him in the marquessate. He was a devout Roman Catholic and in 1979 returned the Franciscan monastery of San Damiano, which he had inherited, to the Franciscan Friars Minor.

Michael Andrew Foster Jude Kerr, KC, 13th Marquess (1945–2024), eldest son of the 12th Marquess. He married Lady Jane Fitzalan Howard, from 2017 16th Lady Herries of Terregles, and had three daughters. He was succeeded in the marquessate by his younger brother. He was a barrister and sometime deputy leader of the Conservative Party, known to his friends as 'Crumb' following an incident at a party in the 1960s when he introduced himself as 'Lord Ancram', his then-title, and the butler announced him as 'Mr Norman Crumb'.

Ralph William Francis Joseph Kerr, 14th Marquess (1957–), younger brother of the 13th Marquess. Twice married, he has six children with his second wife, the artist Marie-Claire Black. His eldest son Johnnie, Earl of Ancram, will succeed him in the marquessate.

Lovat, Lords
(Title pronounced 'Luvvut')

Brigadier Simon 'Shimi' Christopher Joseph Fraser, DSO, MC, DL, 15th Lord (1911–1995), eldest son of the 14th Lord. He married Rosamond Broughton, daughter of Sir 'Jock' Delves Broughton, 11th Baronet, and had six children. Two of his four sons predeceased him, and he was succeeded in the title by his grandson. He ordered his personal piper, Bill Millin, to pipe him off the landing ramp at Sword Beach in Normandy on D-Day.

Simon Christopher Joseph Fraser, 16th Lord (1977–), elder son of Simon Fraser, Master of Lovat (1939–1994) and grandson of the 15th Lord. He married the Hon. Petra Palumbo and has two daughters. Currently his heir is his younger brother Jack, Master of Lovat. He manages the Lovat Estates in Inverness-shire, some of which were sold by his father in the 1990s.

Lucan, Earls of

Colonel George Charles Patrick 'Pat' Bingham, MC, 6th Earl (1898–1964), eldest son of the 5th Earl. He married fellow socialist Kaitlin Dawson and had four children, the eldest of whom succeeded him in the earldom. He was a proud Labour member of the House of Lords and served as opposition chief whip.

Richard *John* Bingham, 7th Earl (1934–?), eldest son of the 6th Earl. He married Veronica Duncan with whom he had three children. His only son succeeded him in the earldom in 2016, forty-two years after he disappeared following the murder of Sandra Rivett, his children's nanny. He gave up a short-lived career in banking to focus on gambling with cards, at which he was proficient.

George Charles Bingham, 8th Earl (1967–), only son of the 7th Earl. He married the Danish heiress Anne-Sofie Foghsgaard and has two children, the younger of whom, Charles, Lord Bingham, will succeed him in the earldom.

Mancroft, Barons

Lieutenant-Colonel Stormont Mancroft Samuel, KBE, 2nd Baron (1914–1987), only son of the 1st Baron. He married Diana Lloyd, the daughter of an army officer, and had three children, the youngest of whom succeeded him in the barony. He wrote humorous articles for *Punch* magazine. His father changed his name by deed poll, from Samuel to Mancroft, so that he could attend Winchester College with a less conspicuously Jewish name, to avoid him being bullied. This did not work.

Benjamin Lloyd Stormont Mancroft, 3rd Baron (1957–), only son of the 2nd Baron. He married Emma Peart and has three children, the second of whom, Captain the Hon. Arthur Mancroft, will succeed him in the barony. As a result of his father's experience at Winchester, he was sent to Eton instead.

Mansfield, Earls of

Major Mungo David Malcolm Murray, DL, 7th Earl (1900–1971), only son of the 6th Earl. He married Dorothea Carnegie, the daughter of a diplomat, and had three children, the eldest of whom succeeded him in the earldom. He was the founding chairman of the British Trust for Ornithology.

William David Mungo James Murray, DL, 8th Earl (1930–2015), only son of the 7th Earl. He married Pamela Foster, the daughter of an oil executive, and they had three children, the eldest of whom succeeded him in the earldom. He was a loving but determined father, with very clear ideas as to the paths he wished his children to take.

Alexander David *Mungo* Murray, 9th Earl (1956–), eldest son of the 8th Earl. He married Sophia 'Sophy' Ashbrook and they have four children, the second of whom, William, Viscount Stormont, will succeed him in the earldom. As a teenager he worked as a tour guide at his family home of Scone Palace when it opened to the public.

Mar, Earls of

James Clifton of Mar, 30th Earl (1914–1975), eldest son of Charles Lane (1882–1956) and first cousin once removed of the 29th Earl. He married twice and had three children from his first marriage. His son predeceased him and he was succeeded in the earldom by his eldest daughter. He was a farmer in Kenya.

Margaret Alison of Mar, 31st Countess (1940–), eldest daughter of the 30th Earl. She has been married thrice, and has a daughter from her first marriage, who will succeed her in the title. She worked for British Telecom before turning her hand to farming; in 1989, she fell ill after being poisoned by the chemicals she was using to dip her sheep.

Marlborough, Dukes of
(Title pronounced 'Maulbro')

George Charles Spencer-Churchill, DL, 8th Duke (1844–1892), eldest son of the 7th Duke. He was twice married, first to Lady Albertha 'Goosie' Hamilton, with whom he had four children, the second succeeding him as duke. He had a son from an extra-marital relationship with the Countess of Aylesford, and was said to care more for him than for his legitimate children – something they noted. The Prince of Wales declared him 'the greatest blackguard alive' for his role in what became known as the Aylesford Scandal.

Lieutenant-Colonel Charles 'Sunny' Richard John Spencer-Churchill, KG, 9th Duke (1871–1934), only legitimate son of the 8th Duke. Twice married, he had two sons with his first wife, the American heiress Consuelo Vanderbilt, the first of whom succeeded him in the dukedom. On one occasion he gave each of his grandchildren a gift of a hard-boiled plover's egg.

Lieutenant-Colonel John Albert 'Bert' Edward William Spencer-Churchill, DL, 10th Duke (1897–1972), elder son of the 9th Duke. He was married twice, first to the Hon. Mary Cadogan, and had five children, the third of whom succeeded him in the dukedom. Upon his birth he displaced his first cousin, the future prime minister Winston Churchill, in the ducal line of succession.

Captain John George 'Sunny' Vanderbilt Henry Spencer-Churchill, DL, 11th Duke (1926–2014), eldest son of the 10th Duke. He married four times and had six children, four of whom survived into adulthood. His eldest surviving son succeeded him in the dukedom. His nickname was derived not from his cheery disposition but from his courtesy title Earl of Sunderland.

Charles *James* Spencer-Churchill, 12th Duke (1955–), eldest surviving son of the 11th Duke. Twice married, he has three children, the eldest of whom, George, Marquess of Blandford, will succeed him in the dukedom. He is one of the few of today's peers to have spent time in prison.

Middleton, Barons

Captain Digby Wentworth Bayard Willoughby, DL, 9th Baron (1844–1922), eldest son of the 8th Baron. He married Eliza 'Eisa' Gordon-Cumming, daughter of a Scottish baronet, but the marriage was childless and he was succeeded in the barony by his younger brother. He was MFH East Riding Fox Hounds, Lord Middleton's Hunt, for forty-three years, and wholeheartedly took on the role of local dignitary.

Captain Godfrey *Ernest* Willoughby, 10th Baron (1847–1924), younger brother of the 9th Baron. He married Ida Ross and had eight children, two of whom predeceased him. He was succeeded in the barony by his second son. He served in both the navy and the army – as a midshipman on HMS *Liffey* in the West Indies, and later in the 9th Lancers.

Colonel Michael *Guy* Percival Willoughby, KG, MC, 11th Baron (1887–1970), eldest surviving son of the 10th Baron. He married Angela Hall and had four children, the eldest of whom succeeded him in the barony. He was known to have advertised for a clergyman for one of his church livings in the pages of *Horse & Hound*.

Major Digby *Michael* Godfrey John Willoughby, MC, DL, 12th Baron (1921–2011), eldest son of the 11th Baron. He married Janet Marshall-Cornwall, the daughter of a general, and had three sons, the eldest of whom succeeded him in the barony. He lived for seventy of his ninety years at Birdsall, near Malton; his wife worked for MI6.

Michael Charles James Willoughby, DL, 13th Baron (1948–), eldest son of the 12th Baron. He married the Hon. Lucy Sidney, daughter of William 'Bill' Sidney, 1st Viscount De L'Isle, VC, and has five children, the eldest of whom, the Hon. James Willoughby, will succeed him in the barony. He was master of the Middleton Hunt for four years.

Milford, Barons

Laurence Richard Philipps, 1st Baron (1874–1962), sixth son of Reverend Sir James Philipps, 12th Baronet (1824–1912), created Baron Milford in 1939. He married Ethel Speke, the daughter of a clergyman, and had six children, the eldest of whom succeeded him in the barony. He founded the shipping company Court Line, in which business he made his money.

Wogan Philipps, 2nd Baron (1902–1993), eldest son of the 1st Baron. He was thrice married, first to the writer Rosamond Lehmann, with whom he had a son and a daughter; the former succeeded him in the barony. He was the only member of the Communist Party to sit in the House of Lords, having found inspiration for radical left-wing politics while observing the General Strike.

Hugo John Laurence Philipps, 3rd Baron (1929–1999), only son of the 2nd Baron. He was thrice married and had five children, the second of whom succeeded him in the barony. He spent much of his time at Cambridge on the river in boats; parties were often given in honour of his mother Rosamond whenever she came to visit.

Guy Wogan Philipps, KC, 4th Baron (1961–), eldest son of the 3rd Baron. He married Alice Sherwood and has two sons, the elder of whom, the Hon. Archie Philipps, will succeed him in the barony. In 1988 he edited an anthology of atrociousness, having been given an anthology of goodness in his younger years, and believing that the world was in need of a contrary volume.

Montagu of Beaulieu, Barons
(Title pronounced 'Montagu of Bewly')

Edward John Barrington Douglas-Scott-Montagu, 3rd Baron (1926–2015), only son of the 2nd Baron. He married twice, and had three children, the eldest of whom succeeded him in the barony. He founded the National Motor Museum at his Beaulieu estate in Hampshire.

Ralph Douglas-Scott-Montagu, 4th Baron (1961–), eldest son of the 3rd Baron. He married Ailsa Camm; his heir is his younger half-brother, the Hon. Jonathan Douglas-Scott-Montagu. He works as a graphic designer and as head of heritage at the *Radio Times*, alongside managing Beaulieu.

Moray, Earls of
(Title pronounced 'Murry')

Captain Francis Douglas Stuart, MC, 18th Earl (1892–1943), eldest son of the 17th Earl. He married Barbara Murray, an American, and the daughter of a lawyer, in Paris, and had three daughters. He was succeeded in the earldom by his younger brother. He was awarded the Military Cross during the First World War for shooting down a German Fokker.

Lieutenant-Commander Archibald *John* Morton Stuart, 19th Earl (1894–1974), younger brother of the 18th Earl. He married Mabel Wilson, the daughter of a pioneer who worked for Cecil Rhodes, whom he met in Bulawayo, modern-day Zimbabwe. They had four children, the second of whom succeeded him in the earldom. On the family ranch, he bought an Airspeed Oxford plane and built a hangar for it out of corrugated i. When one day his daughter Hermione had an attack of appendicitis, he su er life by flying her to Johannesburg.

Douglas John Moray Stuart, 20th Earl (1928–2011), eldest son of the 19th Earl. He married Lady Malvina Murray and had two children, the elder of whom succeeded him in the earldom. He began collecting cars in 1953, and in 1970 opened his collection as the Doune Motor Museum; it included, variously, a 1905 Rolls-Royce, the second-oldest in the world, a 1938 Bugatti 57C, and a 1973 Ferrari Dino.

John Douglas Stuart, 21st Earl (1966–), only son of the 20th Earl. He married Cathy Lawson and has three sons, the eldest of whom, James, Lord Doune, will succeed him in the earldom. When *Monty Python and the Holy Grail* was being filmed at the Morays' Doune Castle in 1974, he went to watch.

Moyne, Barons

Major Bryan Walter Guinness, 2nd Baron (1905–1992), eldest son of the 1st Baron. He was married twice, first to the Hon. Diana Freeman-Mitford, and had two sons, the first of whom succeeded him in the barony. He had a further nine children with his second wife. He qualified for the bar in 1930 but struggled for cases due to the fact that he was supposed to be – and was – incredibly rich and did not need the work.

Jonathan Bryan Guinness, 3rd Baron (1930–), elder son of the 2nd Baron. He has been married twice and has eight children. His eldest son predeceased him and he will be succeeded in the barony by his second son, the Hon. Valentine Guinness. His mother didn't like the term 'Daddy' and so he called his father 'Bryan' his whole life.

Norfolk, Dukes of

Major Bernard Marmaduke Fitzalan Howard, KG, GCVO, GBE, 16th Duke (1908–1975), eldest surviving son of the 15th Duke. He married the Hon. Lavinia Strutt and had four daughters; he was succeeded in the dukedom, and as Earl Marshal, by his second cousin once removed. While on a tour of Australia as manager of the England cricket team in the 1960s, he told reporters that he hoped this would be an informal tour, and that they should address him merely as 'Sir' rather than 'Your Grace'. He inherited the dukedom at the age of nine.

Major-General Miles Francis Stapleton Fitzalan Howard, KG, GCVO, CB, CBE, MC, DL, 17th Duke (1915–2002), eldest son of Bernard Fitzalan Howard, 3rd Baron Howard of Glossop (1885–1972), and second cousin once removed of the 16th Duke. He married Anne Constable-Maxwell and had five children, the fourth of whom succeeded him in the dukedom. All eight of his siblings had Christian names beginning with the letter 'M'.

Edward William Fitzalan Howard, GCVO, DL, 18th Duke (1956–), eldest son of the 17th Duke. He has been twice married, with five children from his first marriage, the eldest of whom, Henry, Earl of Arundel, will succeed him in the dukedom and as Earl Marshal. In recent years he has successfully embarked on a project to save the grey partridge on his West Sussex estate.

Northumberland, Dukes of
Captain Alan Ian Percy, KG, CBE, MVO, 8th Duke (1880–1930), eldest surviving son of the 7th Duke. He married Lady Helen Gordon Lennox, daughter of the 7th Duke of Richmond, and had six children, the eldest of whom succeeded him as duke. He was a radical right-wing writer and newspaper proprietor, in addition to having numerous landed interests in Northumberland.

Henry *George* Alan Percy, 9th Duke (1912–1940), eldest son of the 8th Duke. He was killed in action in Belgium during the retreat to Dunkirk while serving with the Grenadier Guards. He never married though was considered one of the country's most eligible bachelors. He was succeeded in the dukedom by his younger brother.

Captain Hugh 'Hughie' Algernon Percy, KG, GCVO, 10th Duke (1914–1988), younger brother of the 9th Duke. He married Lady Elizabeth Montagu Douglas Scott, daughter of the Duke of Buccleuch, having proposed to her after riding all the way from Alnwick Castle in Northumberland to Drumlanrig Castle in Dumfriesshire. They had seven children, the fourth of whom succeeded him as duke. He served as master of the Percy Hunt for forty-eight years.

Henry 'Harry' Alan Walter Richard Percy, 11th Duke (1953–1995), eldest son of the 10th Duke. He never married and was succeeded in the dukedom by his younger brother. A godson of Elizabeth II, he suffered badly with depression.

Ralph George Algernon Percy, DL, 12th Duke (1956–), younger brother of the 11th Duke. He married Jane Richard, the daughter of a stockbroker, and has four children, the second of whom, George, Earl Percy, will succeed him in the dukedom and in the running of Northumberland Estates. He has a black cocker spaniel called Hector.

Onslow, Earls of
William Hillier Onslow, GCMG, DL, 4th Earl (1853–1911), only son of George Onslow (1813–1855) and great-nephew of the 3rd Earl. He

married the Hon. Florence Gardner and had four children, the second of whom succeeded him in the earldom. He was Governor of New Zealand 1889–1892 and gave his youngest son a Maori name.

Major Richard 'Cranley' William Alan Onslow, GBE, 5th Earl (1876–1945), eldest son of the 4th Earl. He married the Hon. Violet Bampfylde and had two children, the second of whom succeeded him in the earldom. In 1927, he gave six acres of land in Guildford for the site on which Guildford Cathedral was built.

Captain William *Arthur* Bampfylde Onslow, KBE, MC, 6th Earl (1913–1971), only son of the 5th Earl. He was married twice and had two children, the elder of whom succeeded him in the earldom. He was awarded the Military Cross while serving in North Africa during the Second World War. Shortly after, he led a group of tanks into action while standing on top of a scout car and waving them on with his handkerchief. Later, he was taken prisoner.

Michael William Coplestone Dillon Onslow, 7th Earl (1938–2011), only son of the 6th Earl. He married Robin Bullard, an American, and had three children, the eldest of whom succeeded him in the earldom. He was a popular member of the House of Lords with a penchant for bow ties. He appeared on *Have I Got News for You* twice and presented a five-part series on Radio 3 during which he would announce, 'It's time to get trippin' with me, Lord Onslow.'

Rupert Charles William Bullard Onslow, 8th Earl (1967–), only son of the 7th Earl. He married Leigh Jones-Fenleigh and has a daughter, Lady Olympia (2003–). His heir is his fourth cousin once removed Anthony Onslow. He works in fine art underwriting and is a keen equestrian.

Peel, Earls

Arthur William Ashton Peel, 2nd Earl (1901–1969), only son of the 1st Earl. He married Kathleen McGrath and had two sons, the elder succeeding him in the earldom. He was a keen shot and loved traditional folk songs as well as the music of Gilbert and Sullivan.

William James Robert Peel, GCVO, DL, 3rd Earl (1947–), elder son of the 2nd Earl. He has married twice and has three children, the eldest of whom, Ashton, Viscount Clanfield, will inherit the earldom. He loves music – before his father died he ran a mobile discotheque in Italy. His favourite band is the Steve Miller Band.

Richmond and Gordon, Dukes of

Charles Henry Gordon Lennox, KG, GCVO, CB, 7th Duke (1845–1928), eldest son of the 6th Duke. He married twice, was widowed twice, and had seven children, the eldest of whom succeeded him as duke. After his first wife, Amy Ricardo, died in 1879, the light went out of his life, and his sister Caroline took over the parenting of his five young children.

Lieutenant-Colonel Charles 'Set' Henry Gordon Lennox, DSO, MVO, 8th Duke (1870–1935), eldest son of the 7th Duke. He married Hilda Brassey, granddaughter of railway contractor Thomas Brassey, who, by 1847, had built a third of the railways in Britain. They had five children: his eldest son, Charlie, Lord Settrington, was killed in the months following the end of the First World War while fighting with the White Russians, and he was succeeded in the dukedom by his second son. He contracted polio in 1915 and was paralysed from the waist down as a result.

Frederick Charles Gordon Lennox, 9th Duke (1904–1989), eldest surviving son of the 8th Duke. He married Elizabeth Hudson and they had two sons, the elder of whom succeeded him in the dukedom. He dropped out of Oxford to work at Bentley Motors in north London as 'Mr Settrington', and later established his Goodwood estate as a centre of motor racing.

Charles Henry Gordon Lennox, DL, 10th Duke (1929–2017), eldest son of the 9th Duke. He married Susan Grenville-Grey and had five children, the eldest of whom succeeded him in the dukedom. He was a liberal man who was not interested in possessions.

Charles Henry Gordon Lennox, CBE, DL, 11th Duke (1955–), only son of the 10th Duke. He has married twice and has five children, the second of whom, Charlie, Earl of March, will succeed him in the dukedom. He left Eton early and went to work as a stills photographer for the film director Stanley Kubrick.

Rosebery, Earls of

Archibald Philip Primrose, KG, KT, 5th Earl (1847–1929), eldest son of Archibald, Lord Dalmeny (1809–1851) and grandson of the 4th Earl. He married the heiress Hannah de Rothschild; Benjamin Disraeli gave her away at their wedding. They had four children, the third of whom succeeded him in the earldom. He was prime minister for fifteen months from March 1894, and was fascinated by Napoleon Bonaparte.

Albert Edward *Harry* Meyer Archibald Primrose, KT, DSO, MC, 6th Earl (1882–1974), eldest son of the 5th Earl. He married twice and had three children who survived infancy. His eldest son predeceased him and he was succeeded in the earldom by his younger son. He was a keen cricketer and racehorse owner, and won the Derby with two of his horses, Blue Peter and Ocean Swell.

Neil Archibald Primrose, DL, 7th Earl (1929–2024), eldest surviving son of the 6th Earl. He married Deirdre Reid and had five children, the youngest of whom succeeded him in the earldom. He was an early adopter of computers and bought a mainframe computer which he nursed well beyond its lifespan. When his family contacted the manufacturer to ask for help with it, they received the reply, 'There's a man in Scotland who is really good on these computers – he's called Lord Rosebery . . .'

Harry Ronald Neil Primrose, DL, 8th Earl (1967–), only son of the 7th Earl. He has married twice and has five children, the youngest of whom, Caspian, Lord Dalmeny, will succeed him in the earldom. One of his life's ambitions is to ride the Cresta Run in under fifty seconds.

Rossmore, Barons

William 'Paddy' Warner Westenra, 7th Baron (1931–2021), only son of the 6th Baron. He married Valerie Tobin and had a son, who succeeded him in the barony. He worked as a photographer and was prone to wearing old clothes with holes in them. In the 1960s he had a relationship with the singer Marianne Faithfull.

Benedict William Westenra, 8th Baron (1983–), only son of the 7th Baron. He is unmarried and there is no heir to the title. He has worked as a composer and music teacher.

Roxburghe, Dukes of

(Title pronounced 'Roxborough'; surname pronounced 'Innez Car')

Henry 'Kelso' John Innes Ker, KT, MVO (1876–1932), 8th Duke, eldest son of the 7th Duke. He married Mary 'May' Goelet, the daughter of a New York real estate magnate. They had a son who succeeded him in the dukedom. He was badly injured at Roulers in October 1914 while serving with the Royal Horse Guards and was thereafter unable to ride. This was a severe blow for him as a keen huntsman and polo player.

Major George 'Bobo' Victor Robert John Innes Ker, 9th Duke (1913–1974), only son of the 8th Duke. He married Lady Mary Crewe-Milnes, but the marriage ended in divorce after he had attempted to evict her from Floors Castle. He remarried and had two sons, the first of whom succeeded him in the dukedom. His valet, Charles Chandler, returned to Floors after the Second World War, having been taken prisoner by the Japanese; Bobo left him £1,000 in his will.

Guy David Innes Ker, 10th Duke (1954–2019), elder son of the 9th Duke. He married twice and had five children, the second of whom succeeded him in the dukedom. He was awarded Sword of Honour for being the best cadet at the Royal Military Academy, Sandhurst in 1974.

Captain Charles Robert George Innes Ker, 11th Duke (1981–), eldest son of the 10th Duke. He has married twice and has two children, the younger of whom, Frederick, Marquess of Bowmont and Cessford, will succeed him in the dukedom. Only two Roxburghe dukes since 1707 have lived beyond the age of sixty-four, perhaps because of what is known by some as the 'Roxburghe Curse'. The story goes that the 5th Duke assaulted a gypsy woman from the village of Yetholm, seven miles south of Floors, so bringing a curse upon the family that no duke would live to see his first-born son's first-born son.

Rutland, Dukes of

Captain Henry John Brinsley Manners, KG, 8th Duke (1852–1925), eldest son of the 7th Duke. He married the artist Violet Lindsay and had five children, at least one of whom was not his biologically. His elder son, Robert, Lord Haddon, predeceased him and he was succeeded in the dukedom by his second son. He and his wife were publicly and almost professionally unfaithful to one another. His interests were largely fishing and sex.

Captain John Henry Montagu Manners, 9th Duke (1886–1940), eldest surviving son of the 8th Duke. He married Kathleen 'Kakoo' Tennant, granddaughter of the industrialist Sir Charles Tennant, 1st Baronet, and had five children, the third of whom succeeded him in the dukedom. He was an authority on medieval art. When in 1933 his eldest daughter Lady Ursula was seventeen, he escorted her to Drummond's Bank to open her first account, wearing a frock coat with a gardenia in his buttonhole.

Captain Charles John Robert Manners, CBE, DL, 10th Duke (1919–1999), eldest son of the 9th Duke. He was married twice, secondly to Frances Sweeny, and had five children, the second of whom succeeded him in the dukedom. He served on Leicestershire County Council for forty years.

David Charles Robert Manners, 11th Duke (1959–), eldest son of the 10th Duke. He married Emma Watkins, from whom he is legally separated, and has five children, the fourth of whom, Charles, Marquess of Granby, will succeed him in the dukedom. He inherited his great-grandfather's 1908 Renault and in 2008 drove it to Dieppe from his home, Belvoir Castle, for a festival of classic cars from around the world.

Sackville, Barons

Lionel Edward Sackville-West, DL, 3rd Baron (1867–1928), eldest son of the Hon. William Sackville-West (1830–1905) and nephew of the 2nd Baron. He married his first cousin Victoria Sackville-West, and had a daughter, the writer Vita Sackville-West. Upon his death, his body was put into a lead coffin in the chapel at Knole.

Major-General Charles 'Charlie' John Sackville-West, KBE, CB, CMG, 4th Baron (1870–1962), younger brother of the 3rd Baron. He married twice and had two children, the first of whom succeeded him in the barony. He served in the Anglo-Manipur War, the Second Boer War and the First World War, and was wounded at the Somme. He was evacuated back to Britain, and then posted back to the Western Front, where he was promptly wounded again. He ended his wartime service working for Field Marshal Sir Henry Wilson at Versailles.

Edward 'Eddy' Charles Sackville-West, 5th Baron (1901–1965), only son of the 4th Baron. He never married and was succeeded in the barony by his first cousin. He was a writer and music critic, and the model for Uncle Davey in Nancy Mitford's 1945 novel *The Pursuit of Love*.

Captain Lionel Bertrand Sackville-West, 6th Baron (1913–2004), elder son of the Hon. Bertrand Sackville-West (1872–1959) and first cousin of the 5th Baron. He was thrice married with five daughters, and was succeeded in the barony by his nephew. During the First World War he wrote to George V asking when the war would be over, since he missed his father and having sugar in his porridge. The king replied saying that he missed having sugar in his porridge, too.

Robert Bertrand Sackville-West, DL, 7th Baron (1958–), elder son of Hugh Sackville-West (1919–2001) and nephew of the 6th Baron. He has married twice and has three children, the second of whom, the Hon. Arthur Sackville-West, will succeed him in the barony. He has written two books on the Sackville-Wests and Knole.

St Albans, Dukes of
(Surname pronounced 'Bo-clare')
Colonel Charles Frederick Aubrey de Vere Beauclerk, OBE, 13th Duke (1915–1988), only son of Aubrey Beauclerk (1850–1933) and second

cousin of the 12th Duke. He married twice and had five surviving children, the eldest of whom succeeded him in the dukedom. He grew up understanding that he would one day be duke and took the family history seriously, restoring the Beauclerk mausoleum in Lincolnshire.

Murray de Vere Beauclerk, 14th Duke (1939–), eldest son of the 13th Duke. He has been married three times and has two children, the second of whom, Charles, Earl of Burford, will succeed him in the dukedom. A member of the Drapers' Company, he is a qualified accountant and lives in Chelsea.

Salisbury, Marquesses of
(Surname pronounced 'Gascoyne-Cissel')

Robert Arthur Talbot Gascoyne-Cecil, KG, GCVO, DL, 3rd Marquess (1830–1903), eldest surviving son of the 2nd Marquess. He married Georgina Alderson, the daughter of a judge, and had seven children who survived infancy, the third of whom succeeded him in the marquessate. He took no interest in clothes and was once, as prime minister, refused entrance to a casino in Monte Carlo for being inappropriately dressed.

Lieutenant-Colonel James 'Jem' Edward Hubert Gascoyne-Cecil, KG, GCVO, 4th Marquess (1861–1947), eldest son of the 3rd Marquess. He married Lady Alice Gore and had four children, the eldest of whom succeeded him in the marquessate. He was the smallest and frailest of the five boys in his family and his poor health often caused him to be laid up for weeks on end.

Robert 'Bobbety' Arthur James Gascoyne-Cecil, KG, 5th Marquess (1893–1972), eldest son of the 4th Marquess. He married Elizabeth 'Betty' Cavendish and had three sons, two of whom predeceased both their parents. His eldest son succeeded him in the marquessate. He had a lisp, but his grandchildren still loved the fact that he read to them when they were little.

Captain Robert Edward Peter Gascoyne-Cecil, DL, 6th Marquess (1916–2003), eldest son of the 5th Marquess. He married the gardener Marjorie 'Mollie' Wyndham-Quin and had six surviving children, the eldest of whom succeeded him in the marquessate. His second son Lord Richard Cecil, a freelance journalist, was killed in Rhodesia (now Zimbabwe) in 1978.

Robert Michael James Gascoyne-Cecil, KG, KCVO, 7th Marquess of Salisbury (1946–), eldest son of the 6th Marquess. He married Hannah Stirling, daughter of the SAS commander Bill Stirling, and has five children, the eldest of whom, Ned, Viscount Cranborne, will succeed him in the marquessate. He negotiated the deal for ninety-two hereditary peers to remain in the House of Lords in 1999.

Sandwich, Earls of

George Charles Montagu, 9th Earl (1874–1962), only son of Rear-Admiral the Hon. Victor Montagu (1841–1915) and nephew of the 8th Earl. He was twice married, first to the American heiress Alberta Sturges, and had four children, the eldest of whom succeeded him in the earldom. He was the author of several books, including one on locomotives.

Alexander *Victor* 'Hinch' Edward Paulet Montagu, 10th Earl but disclaimed in 1964 (1906–1995), eldest son of the 9th Earl. He was twice married, first to the artist Rosemary Peto, and had six surviving children, the fourth of whom succeeded him in the earldom that he disclaimed in order to remain a Conservative MP. In the end, he failed to win a seat in the 1964 general election and was therefore left without a place in either the House of Commons or the Lords. His nickname derived from his courtesy title Viscount Hinchingbrooke.

John Edward Hollister Montagu, 11th Earl (1943–2025), eldest son of the 10th Earl who disclaimed his title. He married Caroline Hayman and had three children, the eldest of whom succeeded him in the earldom. As a little boy he picked primroses from the garden at Hinchingbrooke House to sell to the visiting public.

Luke Timothy Charles Montagu, 12th Earl (1969–), eldest son of the 11th Earl. He married the American yoga instructor and entrepreneur Julie Fisher and has two sons, the elder of whom, William, Viscount Hinchingbrooke, will succeed him in the earldom. With his wife he runs a successful YouTube channel documenting their life at Mapperton House in Dorset.

Shaftesbury, Earls of

Anthony Ashley-Cooper, 10th Earl (1938–2004), only son of Major Anthony Ashley-Cooper, Lord Ashley (1900–1947), and grandson of the 9th Earl. He was thrice married and had two sons, the elder of whom succeeded him in the earldom. His third wife admitted that her brother had murdered him in Cannes and later dumped his body.

Anthony Nils Christian Ashley-Cooper, 11th Earl (1977–2005), elder son of the 10th Earl. He was unmarried and died while visiting his brother in New York City, six weeks after inheriting the title.

Nicholas Edmund Anthony Ashley-Cooper, DL, 12th Earl (1979–), younger brother of the 11th Earl. He married the German veterinary surgeon Dinah Streifeneder and has three children, the eldest of whom, Anthony, Lord Ashley, will succeed him in the earldom. He proposed to his wife in front of St Giles House, his family's ancestral home in Dorset.

Shrewsbury, Earls of

Major Charles Henry John Chetwynd-Talbot, KCVO, 20th Earl (1860–1921), only son of the 19th Earl. He married Ellen Palmer-Morewood and had two children. His only son predeceased him and he was succeeded in the earldom by his grandson. He founded and ran his own hansom cab business.

Captain John George Chetwynd-Talbot, 21st Earl (1914–1980), only son of Charles, Viscount Ingestre (1882–1915) and grandson of the 20th Earl. He was twice married: his first marriage resulted in six children and culminated in a divorce that was both extremely public and extremely expensive. His eldest son succeeded him in the earldom.

Charles Henry John Benedict Crofton Chetwynd Chetwynd-Talbot, 22nd Earl (1952–), eldest son of the 21st Earl. He married Deborah Hutchinson and has three children, the second of whom, James, Viscount Ingestre, will succeed him in the earldom. He left school at sixteen and went to work at a racing stables, becoming an amateur jockey.

Shuttleworth, Barons

Ughtred James Kay-Shuttleworth, DL, 1st Baron (1844–1939), eldest son of the social reformer Sir James Kay-Shuttleworth, 1st Baronet (1804–1877), created Baron Shuttleworth in 1902. He married Blanche Parish, the daughter of a diplomat, and had six children. Both of his sons were killed during the First World War, and he was therefore succeeded by his grandson. He was proud of having been the last survivor of Gladstone's last government, and regarded this as a personal triumph.

Richard Ughtred Paul Kay-Shuttleworth, 2nd Baron (1913–1940), eldest son of Captain the Hon. Lawrence Kay-Shuttleworth (1887–1917) and grandson of the 1st Baron. He never married and was succeeded by his younger brother. He learned to fly at Cambridge before the Second World War and was killed during the Battle of Britain while flying a Hurricane.

Captain Ronald Orlando Lawrence Kay-Shuttleworth, 3rd Baron (1917–1942), younger brother of the 2nd Baron. He was killed in North Africa while serving with the Royal Artillery. He never married and was succeeded in the barony by his nephew.

Captain Charles 'Tom' Ughtred John Kay-Shuttleworth, MC, DL, 4th Baron (1917–1975), only son of the Hon. Edward 'Ted' Kay-Shuttleworth (1890–1917) and nephew of the 3rd Baron. He married Anne Phillips and had four children, the eldest of whom succeeded him in the barony. He lost one and a half legs during the Second World War, but nevertheless persisted in going shooting, aided by his shooting stick. He was a Freemason.

Charles Geoffrey Nicholas Kay-Shuttleworth, KG, KCVO, 5th Baron (1948–), eldest son of the 4th Baron. He married Ann Whatman and has three sons, the eldest of whom, the Hon. Tom Kay-Shuttleworth, will succeed him in the barony. He was appointed a Knight of the Garter in 2016.

Sligo, Marquesses of

Denis Edward Browne, 10th Marquess (1908–1991), eldest son of Captain Lord Alfred Browne, DSO (1878–1918), nephew of the 9th Marquess, and, incredibly, grandson of the 5th Marquess. Both of his parents died before he was ten, and he was brought up by his maternal grandparents. His father was posthumously awarded the DSO and young Denis went to Buckingham Palace to receive the medal from George V on his father's behalf. He married the artist José Gauche and had a son who succeeded him in the marquessate.

Jeremy Ulick Browne, 11th Marquess (1939–2014), only son of the 10th Marquess. He married Jennifer Cooper and had five daughters; he was succeeded by his first cousin. He did not use the title and changed his name by deed poll to 'Jeremy Ulick Browne Altamont' in 1986. With his father he opened his ancestral home, Westport House in County Mayo, to the public in 1960.

Sebastian Ulick Browne, 12th Marquess (1964–), only son of Lord Ulick Browne (1915–1979) and first cousin of the 11th Marquess. He has married twice and has two children, the second of whom, Christopher, Earl of Altamont, will succeed him in the marquessate. He emigrated to Australia in 1997.

Stafford, Barons

Basil Francis Nicholas Fitzherbert, DL, 14th Baron (1926–1986), elder son of Captain the Hon. Thomas Fitzherbert (1869–1937) and nephew of the 13th Baron. He married Morag Campbell and had six children, the second of whom succeeded him in the barony. In 1962 he was described as 'a peer with mud on his boots', not just because he was a farmer but because he played for and was president of Stafford Rugby Club.

Francis Melfort William Fitzherbert, DL, 15th Baron (1954–), eldest son of the 14th Baron. He married Katie Codrington and has four children, the eldest of whom, the Hon. Ben Fitzherbert, will succeed him in the barony. Despite having left Reading University without a degree, he served for a decade as chancellor of Staffordshire University, in which role he presented thousands of degrees. Unusually, there are two men in the peerage called Lord Stafford – Francis Stafford and the Duke of Sutherland's eldest son the Marquis of Stafford.

Stansgate, Viscounts

Air Commodore William Wedgwood Benn, DSO, DFC, 1st Viscount (1877–1960), second son of Sir John Benn, 1st Baronet (1850–1922), created Viscount Stansgate in 1942. He married Margaret Holmes, daughter of a Scottish Liberal MP, and had three surviving sons, the second of whom succeeded him in the viscountcy but soon after disclaimed the title. Since he had fought in the First World War, his wife was rather surprised when, at the outbreak of the Second, he met her one day at St James's Park underground station wearing his pilot officer's uniform. When she asked who would look after his constituency while he was away, he replied that he hoped she would do that.

Anthony 'Tony' Neil Wedgwood Benn, 2nd Viscount but disclaimed in 1963 (1925–2014), eldest surviving son of the 1st Viscount. He married the American Caroline DeCamp, to whom he proposed on a bench in Oxford, and had four children, the eldest succeeding him in the viscountcy that he disclaimed. He later bought the bench from Oxford City Council and placed it in the family garden in Holland Park. He was teetotal and a vegetarian.

Stephen Michael Wedgwood Benn, 3rd Viscount (1951–), eldest son of the 2nd Viscount, who disclaimed his title. He married Ashika Bowes and has two children, the second of whom, the Hon. Daniel Benn, will succeed him in the viscountcy. He was elected a Labour hereditary peer in the House of Lords in July 2021 and made his maiden speech later that year.

Suffolk and Berkshire, Earls of

Major Henry Molyneux Paget Howard, 19th Earl (1877–1917), eldest son of the 18th Earl. He married Margaret 'Daisy' Leiter, an American heiress, and had three children, the eldest of whom succeeded him in the earldom. He was killed near Baghdad while serving with the Royal Field Artillery during the First World War. He was a keen amateur dramatist.

Charles 'Jack' Henry George Howard, GC, 20th Earl (1906–1941), eldest son of the 19th Earl. He married the actress Minnie 'Mimi' Forde-Pigott and had three sons, the eldest of whom succeeded him in the earldom. His mother did not approve of his choice of wife and began auctioning items from Charlton Park, the family's ancestral home, to force him to buy back his inheritance. A civilian bomb disposal expert, he was killed in the line of duty during the Second World War on Erith Marshes, Kent.

Michael 'Mickey' John James George Robert Howard, 21st Earl (1935–2022), eldest son of the 20th Earl. He was thrice married and had four surviving children, the second of whom succeeded him in the earldom. He was one of the models for the novelist Jilly Cooper's lothario protagonist Rupert Campbell-Black.

Alexander Charles Michael Winston Robsahm Howard, 22nd Earl (1974–), only son of the 21st Earl. He married Victoria Hamilton and has two children; they divorced in 2018. His son Arthur, Viscount Andover, will succeed him in the earldom. He enjoys driving and owning fast cars.

Sutherland, Dukes of

(Surnames pronounced 'Loosun-Gore' and 'Edger-ton')

Commander George 'Geordie' Granville Sutherland-Leveson-Gower, KT, 5th Duke (1888–1963), eldest son of the 4th Duke. He was twice married, first to Lady Eileen Butler, but neither marriage produced any children. He was succeeded in the dukedom by his third cousin once removed and in his identically named earldom by his niece. He served as Lord Steward of the Household for his friend Edward VIII, but found the role dull, uninspiring and routine.

Captain John Sutherland Egerton, DL, 6th Duke (1915–2000), only son of John Egerton, 4th Earl of Ellesmere (1872–1944), and third cousin once removed of the 5th Duke. He married twice but had no children and was succeeded in the dukedom by his first cousin once removed. He was taken prisoner during the Second World War and became one of the Prominente in Colditz. Post-war, he became a county councillor in Berwickshire.

Francis Ronald Egerton, 7th Duke (1940–), only son of Cyril Egerton (1905–1992) and first cousin once removed of the 6th Duke. He married

Victoria Williams and had two sons, the elder of whom, James, Marquis of Stafford, will succeed him in the dukedom. Both of his sons have only daughters.

Westminster, Dukes of

Hugh Lupus Grosvenor, KG, 1st Duke (1825–1899), eldest surviving son of Richard Grosvenor, 2nd Marquess of Westminster (1795–1869), created Duke of Westminster in 1874. He married twice, was widowed once, and had twelve children who survived infancy. His eldest son predeceased him and he was succeeded in the dukedom by his grandson. When he died he was thought to be the wealthiest man in Britain. A keen racing enthusiast, his horses won the Derby on four occasions.

Colonel Hugh 'Bend'Or' Richard Arthur Grosvenor, GCVO, DSO, 2nd Duke (1879–1953), only son of Victor Grosvenor, Earl Grosvenor (1853–1884), and grandson of the 1st Duke. He married four times and had three children; his only son died in childhood and he was succeeded in the dukedom by his first cousin. He was politically right-wing and prone to anti-Semitic rants. He had an affair with the fashion designer Gabrielle 'Coco' Chanel for a decade.

William Grosvenor, 3rd Duke (1894–1963), only son of Lord Henry Grosvenor (1861–1914) and first cousin of the 2nd Duke. He never married and was succeeded in the dukedom by his first cousin. He was brain-damaged at birth and known in the family as 'Mad Billy'. He bred ducks and was not involved with the running of his family's empire.

Lieutenant-Colonel Gerald Hugh Grosvenor, DSO, 4th Duke (1907–1967), eldest son of Lord Hugh Grosvenor (1884–1914) and first cousin of the 3rd Duke. He married Sally Perry but the marriage produced no children and he was succeeded in the dukedom by his younger brother. In 1963 he demolished the Alfred Waterhouse-designed family home of Eaton Hall in Cheshire and had a new building constructed by John Dennys.

Lieutenant-Colonel Robert George Grosvenor, DL, 5th Duke (1910–1979), younger brother of the 4th Duke. He married his second cousin the Hon. Viola Lyttelton and had three children, the second of whom succeeded him in the dukedom. He was known as 'Pud'.

Major-General Gerald Cavendish Grosvenor, KG, CB, CVO, OBE, 6th Duke (1951–2016), only son of the 5th Duke. He married Natalia Phillips and had four children, the third of whom succeeded him as duke. He took on a huge number of charitable obligations, and at one time had in excess of 150 patronages.

Hugh Richard Louis Grosvenor, DL, 7th Duke (1991–), only son of the 6th Duke. He married Olivia Henson in 2024. He is a godfather to Prince George.

Winchester, Marquesses of

Nigel George Paulet, 18th Marquess (1941–2016), eldest son of Cecil Paulet (1905–1961) and first cousin once removed of the 17th Marquess. He married Rosemary Hilton and had three children, the eldest of whom succeeded him in the marquessate. He moved his family from Rhodesia (now Zimbabwe) to South Africa in the early 1980s. Most of his contributions to House of Lords business focused on Africa. He was a humble man.

Christopher John Hilton Paulet, 19th Marquess (1969–), eldest son of the 18th Marquess. He married Christine Town and has two children, the second of whom, Michael, Earl of Wiltshire, will succeed him in the marquessate. He formerly played in a heavy metal band.

Zetland, Marquesses of

Lawrence Dundas, KT, 1st Marquess, (1844–1929), eldest surviving son of the Hon. John Dundas (1808–1866), created Marquess of Zetland in 1892. He married Lady Lilian Lumley and had four surviving children, the second of whom succeeded him in the marquessate. He served as Lord-Lieutenant of Ireland. 'Zetland' is an old spelling of 'Shetland'.

Major Lawrence John Lumley Dundas, KG, 2nd Marquess (1876–1961), eldest son of the 1st Marquess. He married Cicely Archdale and had five children, the eldest of whom succeeded him in the marquessate. He was appointed a Knight of the Garter in 1942 and was chairman of the National Trust for thirteen years from 1932.

Major Lawrence Aldred Mervyn Dundas, DL, 3rd Marquess (1908–1989), eldest son of the 2nd Marquess. He married Katherine Pike and had four children, the eldest of whom succeeded him as marquess. He played tennis at Wimbledon in the 1940s.

Lawrence Mark Dundas, DL, 4th Marquess (1937–), eldest son of the 3rd Marquess. He married Susan Chamberlain and had four children, the eldest of whom, Robin, Earl of Ronaldshay, will succeed him in the marquessate. He was a founding member of the British Horseracing Board.

Introduction

The turning circle is raked and the door open when I arrive at Lady Rosemary Muir's house, off a winding country lane outside Windsor Great Park. She directs me to a suitable spot to park my car; I try hard not to reverse into anything – or her. She is a sprightly ninety-two, tall, smiling, with a firm handshake. We go to the sitting room, just off the hall, where a portrait of her grandmother Consuelo Vanderbilt is displayed on an easel. The ticking of a clock is all that disturbs the hushed atmosphere. Later, her dog will come in from her kennel, craving fuss. It will be politely denied her.

Rosemary Muir is one of the last survivors of the old aristocratic world – one of butlers and French chefs, of dressing gongs sounded before dinner, of deference and *noblesse oblige*. Today all that sounds almost impossibly remote. To her, though, it is just how things were and how things were done not so long ago.

She was born Lady Rosemary Mildred Spencer-Churchill on 24 July 1929, the fourth child and third daughter of John 'Bert' Spencer-Churchill, Marquess of Blandford, a godson of Edward VII, and his wife the Hon. Mary Cadogan. Mary, a granddaughter of George Cadogan, 5th Earl Cadogan, the owner of the Cadogan estate in London's Chelsea, came from a line of society women.[1] Known as 'the General' by her husband and regarded as someone who could pass 'for the great [first Duke of] Marlborough himself', she proved to be a distant mother but an efficient, ruthless organiser of people and things – a 'typical English rose even down to the thorns'.[2] Bert was the son of Charles 'Sunny' Spencer-Churchill, 9th Duke of Marlborough,[3] and his first wife, the American heiress Consuelo Vanderbilt, who had been pushed by her mother into what turned out to be a very unhappy marriage. 'I know she was very rich but she had wonderful taste and she was fantastic-looking,' says Rosemary of her grandmother. 'I remember meeting an old woman who told me that Consuelo used to come down in a carriage dressed in fur from top to bottom, and they thought a saint had arrived. She was worshipped.'

Sunny, for his part, was a model duke of the paternalistic variety. A member of the Privy Council, sometime Mayor of Woodstock, and Lord-Lieutenant of Oxfordshire for almost twenty years, he was generous in his response to a continuous flow of requests for help and money, despite the fact that, although they were dukes, the Marlboroughs were not exactly flush with funds.[4] But he was also a difficult man – a loner wont to stalk around the house in a white suit, damaged by his unhappy childhood and weighed down by his ducal inheritance.[5] One day in the early 1930s, he arranged for his grandchildren to line up in the hall at his home, Blenheim Palace in Oxfordshire, to receive a present. They were, naturally, excited. In the event Sunny didn't appear. Instead, he sent his butler down with a silver salver on which lay four small eggs. '"With His Grace's compliments," said the butler, solemnly handing each child one hard-boiled plover's egg.'[6] When Bert was born in 1897 – displacing his first cousin once removed, the future prime minister Winston Churchill, in the line of ducal succession – Sunny commissioned a life-size bronze of the baby, gave a ball at Blenheim and ordered a salute to be fired from the palace roof. Bert would grow up to be very tall: 'in scale to the great Palace and park at Blenheim', as a friend put it, writing in *The Times*, following his death in 1972.[7] He would also acquire a tendency to end every other sentence with the word 'what'.

While Bert and Mary awaited their promotion to the dukedom and Blenheim, they made their lives at Lowesby Hall, a Queen Anne house near Leicester, and it was here that their daughter

Rosemary spent her early years. It was a regimented, if comfortable life. Regular fire drills were held, during which dogs, nannies and children were shot down a canvas chute to the grass below. 'Somebody stood at the top saying "you're next", so nobody could refuse to go down,' Rosemary remembers. Contact with her parents was restricted to brief encounters in the morning and after tea. While the adults entertained guests – including the Prince of Wales in 1925 – or hunted with the Quorn, the children roamed the countryside or visited the home farm. Rosemary recalls that this – and indeed, the estate as a whole – was run by an Irishman called Charlie Clarke,[8] a friend of Bert and Mary's who was wont to make up poems. One of them was about Bert: 'scratching his bottom and picking his nose, always a marquess wherever he goes'. Rosemary was given a donkey, 'with one of those old-fashioned saddles, a box that you sat in'.

The family spent time in London, too, and their town residence from April 1928 was 27 Hill Street, a large house on the corner of Chesterfield Hill in Mayfair. Here Mary would host committee meetings for her various charitable endeavours. The family dogs – usually lurchers – joined them from Lowesby. Rosemary recalls visits to Hyde Park with her nanny, during which the dogs would chase rabbits. 'When we went back to Hill Street, Nanny used to say to the policeman, "The dogs are still in the park," and he'd say, "That's alright, Nanny, I'll see that they cross the road." He'd stop the traffic to let them across.' Dogs loomed large in the Blandford family's life. Rosemary recalls an occasion at Lowesby when she spotted a footman with a towel on his arm and a dish in his hand, heading towards one of the dogs, Chaz, who had given birth to puppies in the hollow of a tree about a hundred yards from the front of the house. 'I must have said to him, "Where are you going with that dish?" and he said, "I'm going to feed Chaz." We traipsed down there together and there was Chaz with her puppies. He gave her her dinner and then we came back again. The dog didn't come to the house, you took the dog's dinner down to the dog.'

In 1934, when Rosemary was four years old, her grandfather Sunny Marlborough died, and the Blandfords left Lowesby for Blenheim, morphing into the Marlboroughs as they did so.[9] 'It was rather a shock, I'll admit,' Bert recalled later. 'I'd known it would come to me, but the suddenness was disturbing, to say the least.'[10] He was self-conscious about his position, acutely aware of the weight of the legacy. He also knew that times were changing. 'He gave a speech at the beginning of the war saying things will never be the same again, and he was right,' says his daughter. 'I was too young then to understand, but there was always the worry of what was going to happen. He knew that he was the incumbent for his life and he shouldn't be the one that was going to get rid of it – and anyway he couldn't, as there has to be an Act of Parliament before you can sell Blenheim[11] – so all of that hung very heavily on him. He realised that everybody wanted better housing and better living standards, and all of that had to be paid for somehow. There just wasn't enough money on an estate like Blenheim to do that.'

In the meantime, life continued in the strictly organised way it had done for decades. 'Everything was done to the minute,' Rosemary remembers. 'When I came in from riding with my father, the butler would be standing in the hall ready to ring the gong, and I would say, "Please, Mr Taylor, don't ring the gong until I come downstairs," and he would say, "I ring the gong at quarter-past one, m'lady, and that's it." I used to go into the nursery where Nanny would be having her lunch on a tray, and I would say, "Nanny, will you help me pull off my jodhpurs?" And she'd say, "I certainly will not. Pull them off yourself, I'm having my lunch." I'd struggle with these things and literally did my skirt up coming down the stairs. You would never have gone down for lunch in your riding stuff, never! You would have been sent straight back upstairs to change.'

As at Lowesby, contact with her parents was limited – certainly by the standards of today. When one of the governesses the family had successively engaged left during the war, Rosemary remembers, 'My mother and father had completely forgotten that I even

existed. I appeared after measles or something, having been isolated somewhere, and they thought, what are we going to do with
Rosemary?' Their immediate solution was to send her to Wych-
wood School in Oxford – one that involved her having to cycle
part of the way (with gas mask to hand) and then catch a bus. She
lasted a term before her mother 'pulled herself together' and found
another governess. Back at home she learned to observe air-raid
checklists, typed on wartime thirty-gram Blenheim writing paper.

As for Mary Marlborough – who on one occasion during the
war was mistaken by a visiting Polish general for an English one,
before she surprised him by taking out a powder puff and some
lipstick – she generally started the day with breakfast in bed.
There she would go through the Blenheim menu for the day. When
Rosemary came in to say good morning, her mother would greet
her with a remark such as: 'You look like an owl sitting in an
ivy bush,' and would then dispatch her post haste to take 'the
book' to the chef. The food, she recalls, was 'delicious but plain –
English cooking, none of this froth, with nasturtiums on top. It's
so unnecessary. We had roast beef on Sunday and cottage pie on
Monday, like seventy-five per cent of the rest of the populace.'
Did the family ever cook for themselves? 'Cooking! You must be
joking! My mother didn't know how to boil an egg, she wouldn't
have known what to do with it.' Even the meals the family ate on
their caravanning holidays relied on catering staff: 'I've got a picture of the footmen loading the caravans,' Rosemary says. Mary
Marlborough's great indulgence was the Crunchie bar, which Rosemary reckons her sister must have introduced her to, since Mary
herself, she points out, 'wouldn't have been into a sweet shop'. In
the years before Mary's death in 1961, the holiday caravan was
often stuffed with them.

* * *

That, of course, was then – in the days when the aristocracy
boasted prime ministers, generals and thought-leaders among

their number, when they enjoyed privilege and wealth, when they didn't have to work for a living – or, at least, didn't have to take paid employment. Today, they are less the owners of vast estates than the managers of them. They are also financiers, entrepreneurs, businesspeople and lawyers. Rosemary's parents wouldn't have thought of concealing their noble lineage and were proud of it. Today's aristocrats, by contrast, are more guarded. They often hide away from their titles – or, at least, disguise them – insisting they be called by their first names. 'It is slowly happening that society will care about class far less,' says Archie Kennedy, Earl of Cassillis, the heir of David Kennedy, 9th Marquess of Ailsa. 'My [future] children could call themselves whatever they like and not feel slightly guilty and like they're being snobs because people would understand that people are just people . . . I don't really feel like I deserve a place in the annals of history just because I have a title,' he adds. 'I don't think there is necessarily a role to fill just because you have a title.'

That doesn't mean, though, that the hereditary peerage – who range from ancient Plantagenet-era families, through the descendants of Victorian industrialists, to the more recently ennobled – have parted company altogether with the privileged lifestyle of their ancestors. Even today, there remain those who can afford to live in a manner their forebears would have approved of, with a large country house, drivers and housekeepers, staff who call them by their titles, and estates where they can indulge their love of field sports. As former *Tatler* editor Kate Reardon says, 'There is still a large percentage of the current aristocracy leading broadly Edwardian lives, people who would still, when they were in town, have lunch at White's or Wilton's.' As a class they may not have the money and the influence they once enjoyed, but money and influence – if concealed – are nevertheless still there. There may have been a decline, but there has not yet been a fall.

As I hope to show in the chapters that follow, there is also still a definably aristocratic way of approaching the world, whether it's in the nature of their family life, the choice of school for their children, or in their political outlook. And that 'aristocratic way' has proved remarkably resilient and slow to alter. I've met modern-day peers who, to all intents and purposes, tick in much the same way as their parents and grandparents. I have encountered stories about aristocrats from the recent past that read like echoes of a much earlier age. Changes there have definitely been, and continue to be, but not at the same pace – and often not at the same intensity – as the changes that society as a whole has experienced.

My guiding principle has been to focus on the hereditary peerage from the end of the Second World War to the present day. Inevitably, though, it's sometimes been necessary to dig further into the past: to show, for example, when and why aristocratic estates started to decline or how particular family crises came about. Throughout, I have observed the work of earlier historians of the peerage, but I have also drawn heavily on the hundreds of interviews that contemporary peers and members of their families have been kind enough to give me. These have filled out and immeasurably enriched the various aspects of the peerage that I have sought to explore and understand: their changing relationships with their houses and estates, the shifting nature of their influence on society, and their social and inner lives.

* * *

Before I go any further, it's probably as well to say a little about *who* the aristocracy are.

At the time of writing, the hereditary peerage comprises 793 families possessing titles that can be passed down to the next generation. (This book does not incorporate the hereditary knights of the baronetage, another 983 families.[12]) Not all of those I interviewed regard themselves as aristocrats. Robin Byron, 13th Baron Byron, for example, argued that he doesn't fit the definition since: '[T]he aristocracy are only those peers who still have land and a historic estate, and those people who don't really need to work. They may work, and they may have very successful careers, but they also have a few thousand acres in the background.' The fact remains, though, that his title was created in 1643, and he is the thirteenth possessor of it, so, unwilling though he may feel to be regarded as a *landed* aristocrat, he remains, in my view, an aristocrat.

At the top of the pyramid are the twenty-four dukes. After them come the thirty-four marquesses, and then the 188 earls, the 108 viscounts, and the 439 barons. The vast majority of these titles can pass only through the male line, for reasons I shall explain later.

The title 'duke' derives from the Latin *dux* ('leader') and was originally the preserve of the sovereign: indeed, William the Conqueror was also Duke of Normandy. The first use of duke as a peerage title came in 1337 when Edward III made his son, the Black Prince, Duke of Cornwall. A century later, in 1448, Sir William de la Pole, 1st Marquess of Suffolk, became the first duke not to be a member of, or closely related to, the royal family when he was promoted to his dukedom. The ducal heyday came much later, in the eighteenth and nineteenth centuries. By this time, dukes were, and were expected to be, major forces in the land with lifestyles to match – alarmingly and ruinously so in some cases. The journalist Ernest Sackville Turner described how a ducal title during this era '. . . unmistakably conveyed that here was a man who owned Belgravia, or Eastbourne or Ben Lomond . . . There he was, a most puissant and most excellent prince, and it was necessary to make the best of it. He had inherited a string of boroughs and was responsible for the votes of those who lived in them . . . If there was a forest going a-begging, he would surely wish to be made ranger of it, with a free house, and the privilege of presenting a buck now and then to his friends, and no questions asked if he helped himself to the timber from time to time. If his leanings were political, he would expect to be offered a government post sooner or later. And since he was a duke, he was liberally qualified to govern Ireland as Viceroy or to represent his country in Paris.'[13] His seat had to be a mansion, castle, or palace, '. . . supporting at least a hundred servants reached by a drive a mile long through a walled park with a thousand head of deer. The dwelling would be on a slight eminence, reflected in water, with its outlook unimpaired by ugly villages.'[14]

Marquesses form the second rank of the peerage, the first English marquess (albeit only for life) being Richard II's favourite, Robert de Vere, 9th Earl of Oxford, who was raised to this rank in 1385. Perhaps because the title (which derives from the Middle Latin *marcha*) was once used on the continent to delineate counts who guarded the marches, or borders, it's sometimes been regarded as a little too European, and therefore suspect. When, for example, early in the twentieth century, Queen Mary's brother Adolphus 'Dolly' Cambridge, formerly Prince Adolphus of Teck (and then Duke of Teck), swapped the family name for Cambridge in 1917, becoming Marquess of Cambridge, he complained that 'Marquess sounded French'.[15] Henry Lascelles, Viscount Lascelles, later 6th Earl of Harewood, who married Princess Mary, daughter of George V and Queen Mary, and who was encouraged by his father-in-law to accept a marquessate in 1922, had a different objection. As his son remembered: '[H]e told me once that the king had wanted to follow precedent over the husband of a monarch's daughter and make him a marquess, but he refused on the grounds that marquisates [sic] died out quicker than any other title and he was keen to provide himself and his ancestors with heirs!'[16] The last marquessate created was in 1936 for Freeman Freeman-Thomas, 1st Earl of Willingdon, following the end of his viceregal tenure of India.

Earls possess the oldest titles in the peerage, the Old English *earl* being 'a man of noble birth or rank', according to the *Oxford English Dictionary*. After the Norman Conquest earls assumed a rank equivalent to that of the continental count in England, while in Scotland the title of earl incorporated the idea of the Gaelic *mormaer*, second in theory only to the King of Scots. After them come the viscounts: a bunch of titles that are either very ancient (Gormanston, the oldest, was created in 1478) or very recent (Whitelaw, for the former home secretary, was created in 1983). Over 60 per cent of them were created before 1900. As Roy Perrott put it in his 1968 book *The Aristocrats*, the viscounts are

'. . . mostly politicians, retired and elevated from the House of Commons . . . most of all they suffer from the cloak of anonymity which a title casts upon a man who was once reasonably well known.'[17] Finally there are the barons, possessors of a mixed bag of very old and very new titles – the oldest dating from 1264 (de Ros) and the newest from 1965 (Margadale). In England, barons were originally those who held land by the feudal tenure of 'barony' and were entitled to attend what became the English Parliament.

Inevitably, as the aristocracy has declined in importance, so the once jealously guarded distinctions between those five degrees of rank have largely vanished. Most non-aristocrats probably regard them as virtually interchangeable. For one peer who shall remain nameless, it is enough that when he starts his car it greets him with the salutation, 'Good morning, Your Lordship.'

Most male members of the population stick to one name over the course of their lifetime. Among the hereditary peerage, however, names shift constantly, thanks to the convention of courtesy titles – ranks that are lower than the one held by the top tier of the family and that can be used by the heir and his eldest son (and occasionally daughter). Dukedoms can come with marquessates, earldoms, viscountcies and baronies too – though not always the whole set – and so those titles trickle down until barons just have 'the Honourable' to offer their children. The Duke of Buccleuch's eldest son is traditionally styled Earl of Dalkeith, for example. But not '*the* Earl of Dalkeith'. You only get the 'the' when you are top of your family pyramid. The current Duke of Marlborough was born James Spencer-Churchill, Earl of Sunderland. He was promoted to Marquess of Blandford in 1972 when his grandfather Bert Marlborough died. In 2014 when his father John 'Sunny' Spencer-Churchill, 11th Duke of Marlborough, died he became the 12th Duke. His eldest son George is now styled Marquess of Blandford, and his younger son and daughter Lord Caspar and Lady Araminta Spencer-Churchill, since daughters of earls, marquesses and dukes are styled 'Lady Jane Bloggs' by courtesy.

Younger sons of marquesses and dukes are styled 'Lord Joe

Bloggs' by courtesy, while younger sons of earls have to make do with 'The Honourable', abbreviated in practical usage to 'The Hon.', as do both sons and daughters of viscounts and barons. A mistake often made in the press – and, worse, by the titleholders themselves – is calling life peers 'Lord Joe Bloggs', especially when they have been known before their ennobling as Joe Bloggs. They are Lord Bloggs, or Lord (Joe) Bloggs, or even just Joe Bloggs. Anything will do in this case except Lord Joe Bloggs. This is what Lady Celestria Hales, daughter of Anthony Noel, 5th Earl of Gainsborough, calls 'Lady Diana Mosley syndrome' – 'She is always called "Lady Diana Mosley" and you can never convince people that she was not. Names are got wrong ten times a day, nobody understands how to get it right anymore.'

To avoid confusion, I have opted to refer to people by the name by which they were known at the specific period in their life I happen to be writing about. If the name changes as the story progresses – which it will – I seek to make that clear. I have chosen to use individuals' full names, including their surnames on first mention, as in some cases the family name is more familiar than the title name, and helps with context. Subsequently, peers become known by their Christian name and their title. When referring to women of the peerage who are ladies by courtesy, I use their title on the first mention but drop it thereafter. Thus Ralph Percy, 12th Duke of Northumberland, becomes Ralph Northumberland, while Lady Violet Manners becomes Violet Manners on second and all future mentions. This should not be taken as over-familiarity on my part, but an attempt to make things easier to follow. Where generations of a family have shared a first name, I have tended to use their nicknames or middle names (where they exist) to distinguish grandfathers from fathers and fathers from sons. Thus Edward Stanley, 17th Earl of Derby, becomes Eddy Derby, and Edward Stanley, 19th Earl of Derby, becomes Teddy Derby.[18]

* * *

Before I take my leave of Rosemary Muir, I ask her to reflect on the ways in which society has changed since her childhood. 'People were rather more deferential fifty years ago than they are now,' she says. 'I think nowadays titles and things don't mean anything to anyone anymore, which is right, really. I think it's better probably to do away with the aristocracy completely.' To abolish it? 'I would somehow let it die a natural death. "Abolish" is rather a strong word. I don't know how you deal with it really. Somebody has got to manage these houses. A lot of people find it very hard because the money just isn't there. You can't defend the idea of aristocracy now, but on the other hand, how do you look after these places?'

Blenheim is now run by her nephew James Marlborough, who inherited the dukedom from his father in 2014. James Marlborough has three children, including a son, George Blandford, who will one day inherit Blenheim. The family do not live there all the time and the house and park are open to the public 364 days a year. There's a children's adventure playground in the walled garden, a café in the stables, and a restaurant in the orangery. Rosemary still visits Blenheim, but inevitably it's not the same as it was in what she regards as its heyday, '. . . with the wonderful flowers that my mother did and all the furniture, beautifully arranged and polished, and the people who came . . . It was all on a much higher echelon,' she maintains. 'Now, it's a municipal building that people go and look at because it's a rather extraordinary place. The real beauty of the place was when it was in private hands. It felt like a home, even though it was huge.'

Are people intimidated by her illustrious background? 'They shouldn't be,' she says. 'But how do you stop that? You are what you are.'

PART ONE

A Household of Gentlefolks

Houses and Estates

I

Unconditional Surrender

The Decline of the Great Estates

It's April 1946, and Peter Wentworth-Fitzwilliam, 8th Earl Fitzwilliam, is standing on the south terrace of the park that surrounds his ancestral home, Wentworth Woodhouse, near Rotherham, surveying the scene of total devastation that lies before him. The ornamental eighteenth-century garden temple is still clearly visible in the background. But where, until just a few days ago, he would have looked out onto beautifully manicured lawns and carefully tended flowerbeds, trees and shrubs, his eyes are now met by a sea of churned mud, the scars of trenches and the track marks of bull-dozers. Rose bushes have been uprooted from flowerbeds. There are great tears in the ground where bulldozers have dragged the poles required for electricity cables. German prisoners-of-war have erected fences to contain the requisitioned area, slashing down shrubs and bushes in the process. Soon, an excavator capable of shifting 130 tons of earth an hour will scoop out the topsoil. The gardens, recognised as being among England's most beautiful, had been a green oasis of tranquillity in the middle of South York-shire's industrial heartland. Now they are rapidly becoming a desert – ripped up to enable the exploitation of the coal seam that lies beneath them.

In itself the demolition of a large part of a significant estate in the middle years of the twentieth century was nothing particularly newsworthy. After all, members of the aristocracy had for decades been selling off land and houses to consolidate their landholdings, increase their wealth or to raise cash. But the scale of the destruction at Wentworth Woodhouse in April 1946 was a very different matter. Previous disposals of land and property might sometimes have been forced on their aristocratic owners by financial necessity, but they had always been sanctioned by them. At Wentworth, by contrast, the decision to carve away at the estate in order to exploit its natural minerals was taken not by its owner, but by the Labour minister of fuel and power, Emanuel 'Manny' Shinwell. The Fitzwilliams fought a desperate rearguard action. Peter and his agent appealed directly to Shinwell. Their words fell on deaf ears. They commissioned a group of mining engineers from the department of fuel technology at Sheffield University to undertake a feasibility study. To no avail. Peter even asked the prime minister, Clement Attlee, to intervene. The premier deigned to see him, but no gentlemen's agreement, no knowing nod of the head of the sort that men in Peter's position had long expected, was forthcoming.

Shinwell's unwavering argument was that only by turning the gardens at Wentworth into an open-cast mine could Britain's post-war fuel shortage be mitigated. It's hard to avoid the suspicion, though, that he also relished the prospect of bringing the aristocracy down a peg or two. The extent to which the destruction at Wentworth would boost Britain's coal production was open to debate. What was unquestionably true was that it would mark the end of the Fitzwilliams' aristocratic world of hunt meets, country house parties and aristocratic paternalism, and signalled a new era when the grip on wealth, power and influence formerly enjoyed by the peerage was finally, and irrevocably, broken.

* * *

Barely fifty years before things had seemed so different. As earls, the Fitzw   might not have sat at the top of the aristocratic tree. But their estates in England and Ireland totalled well over 100,000 acres and they employed a veritable army of staff in their various houses: chauffeurs, valets, maids, gamekeepers – even, in living memory, a bearkeeper – all drawn from Britain's servant class that at that time totalled over 1.5 million people. The Fitzwilliams were also mayors and members of parliament, Knights of the Garter, lord-lieutenants and proud possessors of various aristocratic titles: a barony created in 1620, an Irish earldom created in 1716 and, better still, a British one created in 1746, which entitled the head of the family to a seat in the House of Lords.

In addition, they were staggeringly wealthy coal magnates. By 1856 the family employed 869 miners across seven collieries. By 1910 those mines were producing 300,000 tons of coal a year. When William Wentworth-Fitzwilliam, 6th Earl Fitzwilliam, died in 1902, he left £2.95 million[1] in his will. Based on his gross rental income in 1883 of £138,801 and including his personal assets, he was probably worth over £4.1 million,[2] a figure that has been calculated to have represented around 0.38 per cent of the then £1.075 billion net national income.[3]

As for the Fitzwilliams' houses, these were extraordinary affairs, filled with exquisite furniture and works of art, with paintings by Sir Anthony Van Dyck, Sir Joshua Reynolds and George Stubbs. At Wentworth, there were camellias that had originally been imported from China – each said to have cost the equivalent of a housemaid's annual wage – in a specially built camellia house. There were carefully tended beds that kept the house supplied with flowers, as well as greenhouses, a kitchen garden, a Japanese garden and, nearby, the bear pit. Beyond the gardens were estates that extended for miles, peopled by tenants and workers whose finances depended on the patronage of the Fitzwilliams. A circular, Fitzwilliam-centric economy, built on paternalism, operated. Much of the local workforce was employed in Fitzwilliam mines, lived in Fitzwilliam-built houses, drank in Fitzwilliam-controlled pubs, sent their children to the schools the Fitzwilliams funded, and bought groceries in Fitzwilliam-owned shops.

The Fitzwilliams' 'big house', Wentworth Woodhouse, was not just big, it was enormous – one of the two largest in England (the

other being Stowe, formerly the home of the Dukes of Bucking-
ham and Chandos[4]). It owed its origins to a family feud. When
William Wentworth, 2nd Earl of Strafford, son of an adviser to
Charles I, died in 1695, he left his Wentworth estate to his nephew
Thomas Watson, rather than his male-line heir, his first cousin
once removed, Thomas Wentworth. Inheriting the junior title of
Lord Raby, Thomas Wentworth was so outraged by this treatment
that he set out to outdo his cousin, who now assumed the name
Thomas Watson-Wentworth. Having bought Stainborough Hall
near Barnsley in 1709, Raby renamed it Wentworth Castle, turned
it into a continental-style baroque palace, and set about buying up
land around the Wentworth estate he had been denied.

Thomas Watson-Wentworth died in 1723, and was succeeded
by his son, also called Thomas, who was created 1st Marquess of
Rockingham in 1746. Taking up the gauntlet thrown down by Raby,
he began building a west-facing, nine-bay baroque brick mansion
at Wentworth on the site of an old Jacobean house in 1725, only
to find, on its completion, that architectural taste had changed over
the years of its construction. What had seemed the height of fashion
when work had started was now viewed as dated and, thanks to
its association with continental Catholic tradition, somewhat suspect. A baroque house, Thomas Rockingham realised, was the sort
of edifice that a Catholic – and a Tory – like Raby would favour.
He needed something of which his Whig friends would approve.
And so he built a new, Palladian house on the back of the existing west-facing house, conceived on a far more ambitious scale.
It had a nineteen-bay central block, two wings – a service wing
to the north and a bachelor wing, 'Bedlam', to the south, either
of which would serve as a substantial country house today – and
a pavilion to each end. In total, the east front extended for 606
feet. When Thomas Rockingham died in 1750, Wentworth – by
then complete with a sixty-foot square marble hall – passed to his
son, Charles Watson-Wentworth, 2nd Marquess of Rockingham,
a powerful Whig politician, who served twice as prime minister.
Charles Rockingham continued to add to Wentworth. In 1768, he

commissioned the leading North of England architect John Carr to build him an eighty-four-horse stable block so monumental that visitors to Wentworth today sometimes mistake it for the main house. When Charles Rockingham died in 1782, Wentworth passed to his nephew William Fitzwilliam, 4th Earl Fitzwilliam, and so began the Fitzwilliam reign in South Yorkshire.

Wentworth was built as, and remains, a lavish piece of architectural theatre. Until the contents were separated from the house in the 1940s, the state rooms, filled with breathtaking objects, were a testament to the family's generations of power and wealth. Treasures could be found everywhere. On the wall between the billiard room and the blue dressing room hung a framed Eton College charter from Henry VI; in the pillared hall, positioned between marble statues, were displayed buffalo heads and several 'royal' – twelve-point – stags' heads. In the Whistlejacket Room there was a Sèvres vase, almost three feet in height, standing on a fluted gilt pedestal, a gilt console table inlaid with marble, and two ten-foot sofas upholstered in blue velvet. All of these served as sideshows to the main event, for which the room was named: George Stubbs' 1762 life-size portrait of Charles Rockingham's great, albeit temperamental, stallion. There were more paintings by Stubbs at Wentworth than by any other artist – thirteen in all, seven of which were in the billiard room. Anthony Van Dyck, the nearest runner up, was represented by eleven paintings displayed around the house, of which there were four in the appropriately named room.

No one is quite sure how many rooms there are at Wentworth. The number usually given is 365, but this notion of a room for each day of the year seems a little too convenient. The estate agent who sold Wentworth in 1986 suggested that there were 189 rooms above ground. That begs the question, however: what is a room? At Wentworth, there are dozens of spaces that could serve as rooms but aren't counted as such. 'We've got a cupboard we keep light-bulbs in that's bigger than my bedroom,' says the house's archivist David Allott. 'We've got alcoves which could be the kitchen in a London flat.'

So bewilderingly huge is the house that when the German scientist Justus von Liebig visited in the mid-nineteenth century, '[H]e insisted on being provided with a packet of wafers, so that by dropping them in a continuous line from the smoking room to his bedroom he might the next morning find his way back again.'[5] After his stay, the family took to dishing out confetti to guests so that they could lay a path back to their rooms; when Margaret Sweeny, future Duchess of Argyll, went to stay at Wentworth over Christmas in the late 1930s, a footman unwound a ball of string to help her find her way around. At the turn of the century, guests were advised to bring with them treble the ordinary number of hats, to save them the trouble of '. . . walking about a quarter of a mile from one entrance to another in order to fetch the hat which they may have left at another'.[6] One story relates how two friends only realised that they had both been weekend guests at Wentworth when they bumped into each other at Doncaster railway station on their way home. Scores of staff were required to look after the many dozens of rooms – or spaces – and the family and friends who stayed in them. Over the course of a weekend in September 1854 when twelve family members were in residence, their needs were tended to by sixty-four people, who included among their number a battalion of maids, two under-butlers and two confectioners.

Wentworth and its 22,000-acre estate may have been the centre of the Fitzwilliam universe, but it was by no means the family's only property. They also owned Milton Hall near Peterborough, a Fitzwilliam home since 1502, which at the turn of the century was occupied by a junior branch of the family. There were houses in London – 4 Grosvenor Square and, later, 10 Chesterfield Street – along with *Shemara*, a 588-ton steam yacht. Then there was Coollattin, an 89,000-acre estate in County Wicklow. The original pretty five-bay house there, which was built in the 1790s for the 4th Earl, was burned down during the 1798 rebellion against English rule; its replacement was completed in 1807. During the Irish War of Independence in the early 1920s, Coollattin again seemed to be at risk. It was spared, so it is said, because the house's agent, Dermot Doyne, persuaded republican forces that were it to be destroyed, hundreds of families dependent on Coollattin would be left destitute.

The man destined to lose the battle against Manny Shinwell for control of the gardens at Wentworth Woodhouse – William Henry Lawrence Peter Wentworth-Fitzwilliam, for the first thirty-two years of his life styled Viscount Milton – was born just over a decade before the republicans agreed to spare Coollattin, on New Year's Eve 1910. His father was William 'Billy' Wentworth-Fitzwilliam, 7th Earl Fitzwilliam, grandson of the exceedingly rich 6th Earl.[7] His mother, Lady Maud Dundas, was the daughter of the former Lord-Lieutenant of Ireland Lawrence Dundas, 1st Marquess of Zetland.[8] She was a keen sportswoman and, by all accounts, devoted to her family and close to her three siblings. Her elder brother Lawrence was a particularly frequent visitor to Wentworth, as he reflected in a comment he left in the house's visitors' book in May 1942, following his third stay there that month: 'What? Not again!'.

Peter's birth was much anticipated and much longed for. Billy and Maud's first four children had all been daughters – first Elfreda or Elfin; then Joan; then Donatia, known as Pickles; and finally Helena, nicknamed Boodley. Because custom dictated that only a son could inherit the earldom and the estate that went with it, Maud was fully prepared to keep on giving birth until she had a boy – as she made clear in 1951, when giving testimony about the legitimacy of a member of the family. In the event, however, a less arduous tactic proved effective.

When Boodley was born in 1907, she was given the middle names Marie Gabrielle,[9] on the grounds, as she later explained, that, '[I]f you call a baby Marie Gabrielle the next one is a boy.'[10] It worked. Three years later, Peter was born, the first direct heir to an Earl Fitzwilliam in seventy-one years.[11] Billy expressed his delight in the only way that a man of his standing and wealth could: publicly and on a massive scale, extending invitations to tens of thousands of guests to attend a celebratory 1,000-rocket firework display to mark Peter's christening in February 1911. They duly munched their way through 32,000 sandwiches and 20,000 meat patties, and consumed 2,000 gallons of beer.

Growing up, Peter's status as son and heir was constantly put on display. On 13 November 1913, six weeks before his third birthday, he was dispatched to turn the first sod of a new colliery at Greasbrough near Rotherham. Billy informed the crowd that he intended '. . . to let his son go through the mill as he went through it, in order that he might take an interest in mining'.[12] When Peter was not quite three and a half, he presented a silver cup to a point-to-point winner at Wentworth. Eighteen months later, he was, according to the *Penistone, Stocksbridge and Hoyland Express*, 'naturally an object of great interest' as he inspected a euphonium at a Wentworth fete, with a boater jammed on his head.[13] A few days after the Armistice was signed in November 1918, Peter lit a large bonfire in front of Wentworth; the following summer, after a bout of scarlet fever, he presented a goat to a woman who had won it by guessing its name. Each occasion demanded an appropriate outfit, as the photographs in Maud's album for him reveal. Aged eighteen months, and with long, fair hair, he posed for the camera in a white cotton gown; at two and a half, the gown had given way to a buttoned cotton play suit. Another early photograph shows him holding the whip and reins to a small carriage, pulled by a pair of goats. Aged four – now with the smart right-hand parting in his hair that he kept into adulthood – he was trussed up in a First World War officer's battledress complete with Sam Browne belt, shorts and calf-length white socks.

After attending prep school at Ludgrove, then in Cockfosters – where his then name, Viscount Milton, is displayed among those of all former old boys in the dining room – Peter went to Eton College in 1924. Initially, he joined the cricketer Cyril Wells' house at Westbury, and then, when he was in his third year, the Classics master Hugh Howson's at Corner House.[14] A keen player of association football, the young Peter Milton co-founded a junior eleven, which quickly showed 'quite good form'. '[W]ith further practice,' the *Eton College Chronicle* pontificated, '[they] should develop into good players in the future.'[15] Academically, though, he proved undistinguished, and left school in 1929 to join the Royal Scots Greys.

It was not long after he had embarked on his career as a cavalry officer that he met the woman who would become his wife. Olive Plunket – generally known as 'Obby', sometimes spelled 'Obbie' – was the second daughter of the Hon. Benjamin Plunket, sometime Bishop of Tuam and later of Meath, and his wife Dorothea Butler, the daughter of an Irish baronet. Benjamin Plunket's mother, Anne Lee Guinness, could trace her ancestry on both sides back to the famous brewery's founding father. In 1915, her son inherited St Anne's, an Italian Renaissance-style palazzo in Dublin, from his childless uncle, the philanthropist Arthur Guinness, 1st (and last) Baron Ardilaun, and it was at St Anne's that Obby and her three siblings grew up. Theirs was, without doubt, a life of ample privilege, even if it was not quite on the same scale as that of the Fitzwilliams at Wentworth. After all, Benjamin Plunket was a bishop, not a coal magnate. Obby was, by all accounts, a horsey, doggy, country girl, with a mischievous sense of humour. Her nephew Charles Plunket – son of her brother Benjamin – recalls a story his father told him about life at St Anne's. 'A new secretary arrived for my grandfather, and she was terribly nervous. They went into lunch, and it was globe artichokes. My father and Obby winked at each other and started to put the leaves in their mouth and pretend to chew them up and swallow them. This poor woman was watching, and my grandfather suddenly saw her trying to chew the leaves and took pity on her, saying to pay no attention to those horrible children of his. I don't think she quite choked but she wasn't far off it.'

In May 1929 Obby, wearing a dress made by Knightsbridge designer Éve Valère, was presented at Court. Soon afterwards, she hot-footed it back to Ireland and in December that year became engaged to the Westmorland landowner Peter Brougham, 4th

Baron Brougham and Vaux. Their engagement photograph, published in *Tatler*, shows them sitting in a boat on the Thames.

The wedding, however, never took place. An entry in the Coollattin visitors' book for August 1930 helps to explain why. It reads, quite simply, '21–23 August – Olive D. Plunket'. On 24 August 1930 a broken-hearted Peter Brougham wrote to Obby to say how devastated he was to learn that she wouldn't be attending his coming-of-age party in October. Two days after that she received a letter from Peter Milton.

'How is my love-ely bum (meaning you not Hippo),' he wrote ['bum' being his pet name for Obby; Hippo was one of the Plunkets' dogs]. 'Well Obbs do you still miss me? My sweetheart I miss you more than words can say.' On 13 September 1930 a notice appeared in the *Irish Times*, informing the public at large that: '[T]he marriage arranged between Lord Brougham and Vaux and Miss Olive Plunket will not take place.'[16] The following December, Peter Milton's coming of age was celebrated at Wentworth with a party for thousands of guests and tenants that featured the roasting of a whole ox, and a fireworks portrait of the birthday boy. Obby was a guest at Coollattin for the Irish version that followed four months later and that involved decking out Shillelagh village with black and yellow scrolls inscribed 'Long live Lord Milton'. Three weeks later, shortly after her twenty-first birthday, the couple's engagement was announced.

The wedding was held the following spring at St Patrick's Cathedral in Dublin, on Primrose Day, 19 April 1933. The *Dundee Evening Telegraph* declared it 'the most important Irish wedding of the year'.[17] A photograph taken outside the cathedral shows crowds twenty deep; as many as 7,000 people lined the streets nearby, with more than 2,000 inside. The Plunkets had a hand in every detail: the choir sang music chosen by Dorothea Plunket, and Obby was married by her father in the cathedral restored by her great-grandfather Sir Benjamin Guinness.

The bride, accompanied by her brother David, or 'Dig' as she called him, wore an ice blue satin gown embroidered with pearls and diamonds, with a veil to match that was held in place by a pearl and orange blossom wreath. The groom was nervous; his 'I will' was scarcely audible even up close. As Obby and Peter, the new Viscount and Viscountess Milton, signed the register, the choir sang the anthem that extols the congregation to 'Love one another with a pure heart, fervently', and then the organ played Mendelssohn's 'Wedding March'.

Alongside the requisite society names there was a group of 112 Fitzwilliam tenants from Yorkshire. Wearing the primrose yellow, black and green badge of Peter's racing colours in their buttonholes, they were keen to wish Peter and Obby their best, and as the couple walked up the aisle after the ceremony, the tenants formed a guard of honour. The youngest of their number was thirteen-year-old Ray Chinnery, a Wolf Cub from Wentworth, who gave the salute. George Fitzpatrick, former huntsman of the Wentworth pack, said he was going to dance on the boat all the way home. 'You must always dance at a wedding, and a fine wedding like this. I'm so happy, I'm to dance all the night.'[18]

Once the festivities had come to an end, Obby and Peter departed for their honeymoon, motoring through Italy and Spain, and finishing up in the south of France. On their return, they visited Wentworth, where a 'Welcome Home' sign had been erected at the entrance to the deer park by Peacock Lodge. They arrived ceremoniously in a carriage and were pulled the final few feet to the front of the house by estate workers wearing flat caps and puttees. Peter, dressed in a double-breasted suit, stood on the steps of the east front, where refreshments had been organised, looking, as family photographs show, rather pleased.

The newlyweds settled into life as Fitzwilliam heirs in North Yorkshire, living at 'Chateau Milton', a pretty farmhouse better known as The Croft, and taking their place as representatives of aristocratic society around Malton. Peter became president of the Yorkshire Flower Show, and vice-president of Malton Cricket Club. When he announced his intention to stand as master of the Derwent Hunt, he was elected unanimously. To get some practical work experience of a potentially more useful sort, he took up a placement at the Yorkshire Insurance Company's office in York. 'I don't expect to learn all there is about insurance,' he said, 'but it will give me some insight into commercial life, and I cannot therefore fail to be better equipped for the duties which will devolve upon me in connection with the management of my father's estate.' He adopted his family's passion for racing and in August 1935 became the youngest owner to win the Gimcrack Stakes at York, with his colt Paul Beg.

Obby got stuck in to her new role as well, presenting prizes at whist drives, crowning queens at carnivals and opening church fetes. 'One of the most popular bazaar openers for miles around,' she threw herself 'with gay enthusiasm into the communal life of the North Yorkshire villages about her home'.[19] 'Yorkshire and Lady Milton met only a few months ago, but they took to each other on sight and are the best of friends,' the *Yorkshire Post* declared in October 1934 when she hosted an exhibition in aid of the Soldiers' and Sailors' Mutual Association.[20] This was, of course, all part of the deal: marry into the Fitzwilliam family and you were required to take up your responsibilities to the wider community.

On 24 January 1935, to the couple's great delight, Obby gave birth to a little girl, Ann Juliet Dorothea Maud, always known as Juliet. 'My parents certainly wanted more children,' says their daughter, now Lady Juliet Tadgell. 'I think they would have liked several children – if not six, perhaps a family of four. My mother had two miscarriages that I know about. [With] one of them, she went riding when she shouldn't have and had a fall and lost that child. Both of them wanted a son, obviously.'

* * *

The background of Peter's nemesis, Manny Shinwell, could not have been more different. His grandfather Levy Shinwell, a master baker, had fled to England as a refugee from Russian-occupied Poland in 1868 and had settled in Leeds. His son Samuel came to

London at the age of twelve and later married a fellow member of the Jewish diaspora with Dutch origins, Rosetta Königswinter, setting up home in two tiny rooms in a house in the shadow of Spitalfields fruit market. Samuel was a keen agitator for better wages and conditions in a poverty-stricken part of London where people were 'quarrelsome, hot-tempered, loyal to their ideals and any master they acknowledged'.[21] With the economy in dire straits during Manny's early years, Samuel was forced to leave London to find work, travelling from Nottingham to Leicester and on to Newcastle. Only rarely could he send any money down to Rosetta, who had a job cooking for infants attending two East End ragged schools. Manny, the eldest of her thirteen children, stood by her side as she served platters of porridge to the hungry children – 'a sop to the poor', as he later described it.[22]

Aged eleven he went to work for his father in Glasgow, running errands, and then got a job with Smith's tobacco firm as a van-boy. A keen reader, he spent his wages on books and joined the library, where he gorged himself on literature and became attracted, for a while, to Marxism. Soon, he was spending every Saturday afternoon testing himself on what he had learned. In 1928, aged forty-three, he was elected MP for Linlithgowshire, and two years later was appointed secretary for mines. When Clement Attlee's Labour Party won the election in July 1945, he was appointed minister of fuel and power. A current Labour peer, asked to place Manny Shinwell on today's political compass, describes him as a traditional Labour loyalist – 'not old Labour nor New Labour, but real Labour'.

During the war, Shinwell had gained a reputation as a passionate backbench critic of Winston Churchill, forming an unlikely alliance with the similarly minded and similarly cantankerous Edward Turnour, 6th Earl Winterton (who, as an Irish peer, was able to sit as an MP in the Commons). At Christmas 1942, a popular black comedy called *Arsenic and Old Lace* by Joseph Kesselring opened at the Strand Theatre, and Shinwell and Winterton – 'the agitator and the aristocrat', as Harold Macmillan put it – became known by this joint nickname. Winterton was 'gaunt, awkward, [and] angular', with a 'long record of undistinguished administration in minor positions', and a 'curious, almost childish' egotism. 'He would stroll through the lobbies,' Macmillan added, 'with Shinwell running at his feet', bringing to mind Don Quixote and Sancho Panza.[23] Despite this alliance across the political divide, Shinwell's suspicion of wealth and dislike of privilege nevertheless remained steadfast. In 1943, in his book *The Britain I Want*, he declared inherited titles such as Winterton's useless. 'Can anyone say why all titles should not die with their present holders? . . . To make any earldom or baronetcy hereditary is just plain illogicality; it is frequently a thoroughly ridiculous procedure.'[24]

Manny Shinwell and Peter Milton's paths first crossed that September, when Peter, who, on his father's death five months earlier, had become 8th Earl Fitzwilliam, bought a filly at Newmarket for 8,000 guineas. It was almost, but not quite, a wartime record. The previous year, he had had the misfortune to get a fly in his eye while attending a sale there. His action in removing it 'drew the attention of the auctioneer, who thought it was a bid and accordingly made a deal'.[25] Whether or not the 1943 purchase involved a similar misunderstanding, Shinwell was deeply unimpressed by the wealth it so clearly demonstrated. 'Surely you are not so dull that you cannot appreciate that whatever misery you may have endured,' he wrote sarcastically in his 1944 pamphlet *When the Men Come Home*, 'everything is as it should be in a country where at the recent yearling sales at Newmarket a filly was sold for 8,000 guineas.'[26]

While Shinwell sharpened his political attacks on Churchill and on the aristocracy, Peter spent the first year of his war with No. 8 (Guards) Commando, part of a new formation organised after the British Expeditionary Force's evacuation from Dunkirk in 1940. It was a socially rather grand unit, with an officer class drawn largely from the Household Cavalry and the Brigade of Guards and consisting predominantly of members of the exclusive gentlemen's club White's. Its commanding officer, the Old Etonian Royal

Horse Guards officer Captain Robert 'Bob' Laycock, later immortalised as Tommy Backhouse in Evelyn Waugh's Sword of Honour trilogy, was certainly no stranger to such a rarified world. A member of White's himself, his father Brigadier-General Sir Joe Laycock had shared a mistress with the future Edward VII.

Among the officers invited by Laycock to join 8 Commando, following casually conducted interviews on the ground floor of 32 Cadogan Square, home of the Hon. Ursula Nicholson, were Ursula's brother Richard 'Bones' Hanbury-Tracy, 6th Baron Sudeley; Harry Fox-Strangways, Lord Stavordale, heir to the Ilchester earldom, an estate in Dorset with its own swannery, and the west London mansion Holland House; the prime minister's son Randolph Churchill, an inveterate gambler; and Robin Campbell, the son of the ambassador to Portugal and a former Reuters correspondent, who had been inspired to join the Commandos after reading Ernest Hemingway's For Whom the Bell Tolls at his desk in the Army Propaganda Bureau. Others included Philip Dunne, a fox-hunting Old Etonian Blues officer and the son of a Liberal politician, who later appeared in Sword of Honour as Ivor Claire, 'the fine flower of them all. He was quintessential England, the man Hitler had not taken into account'; [27] the future baronet Godfrey Nicholson, 'a most unsoldierly figure';[28] and David Stirling, the younger son of a Scottish laird, 'a gentleman obsessed by the pleasures of chance', who 'rarely appears before dinner'.[29]

In some ways this motley collection of upper-class males confirmed every prejudice that Manny Shinwell must have entertained about them. Randolph Churchill's wife Pamela assessed Laycock's officers as 'absolutely unemployable', knowing 'nothing but the inside of White's'.[30] Waugh, who joined them from the Royal Marines in November 1940, was equally dismissive. 'The indolence and ignorance of the officers seemed remarkable,' he wrote in his diary: 'No one even pretended to work outside working hours . . . officers took leave when their troops were not allowed it'.[31] One troop leader couldn't even read a compass. And yet this bunch of gentlemen amateurs included figures who, by the end of the war, would have more than proved themselves. David Stirling went on to found the Special Air Service. George Jellicoe commanded the Special Boat Service. Philip Dunne and Ralph 'Toby' Milbanke[32] were both awarded the Military Cross. Robin Campbell, who lost a leg in combat and spent two years in a German prisoner-of-war camp, won the Distinguished Service Order.

Peter travelled to Cairo with 8 Commando on HMS *Glenroy* in early 1941. Once there, he lived up to Shinwell's jaded view of the aristocracy, firing his revolver at a passing pigeon on one occasion, while lying in bed at Shepheard's Hotel, shattering the window in the process and hitting a house on the other side of the road. The incident caused '. . . a minor disturbance both in the hotel and at GHQ'. Those around him were similarly lax and chaotic. Harry Stavordale, as acting adjutant, took it on himself to eschew the approved signal network in favour of the Egyptian State Railways Telegraph system on the grounds that it was quicker. His decision prompted a senior officer at GHQ to protest in a memo: '[A] great deal of disorganisation and disorder is being created at the present time by Commanders . . . flagrantly disregarding orders.'[33]

But like so many of his upper-class friends, Peter was also a very brave man. Shortly after Billy Fitzwilliam died, in February 1943, and 8 Commando had been disbanded, he was approached by former Arctic explorer Sir George Binney, to join what became Operation Bridford – a blockade-running mission to the Swedish port of Lysekil to bring back ball bearings required for aircraft manufacture. Binney had worked for the Canadian fur-trading business the Hudson's Bay Company in the Arctic, and for the Ministry of Supply in the iron and steel control department. He knew the northern waters and their dangers well. Assembling a volunteer crew, most of whom came from Hull, and who became known as merchant navy commandos, Binney's team sailed on high-speed motorboats disguised as merchant naval vessels through the Skagerrak eight times in the winter of 1943–4. Peter, the new Earl Fitzwilliam, adopted the name 'Peter Lawrence' for his role as chief officer of MV *Hopewell*. Later, he told his sister Elfin that the yachting they had all done as children with their parents had proved invaluable. He was duly awarded the Distinguished Service Cross in 1944, for 'distinguished services in a special operation'.[34]

Back home, meanwhile, Wentworth was undergoing a wartime transformation. Billy and Maud, with their granddaughter Juliet and, at different stages during the war, various other children of family members, retreated to about a quarter of the house, while dozens of other rooms were requisitioned by the Intelligence Corps. The army's shop, the NAAFI, was set up in the riding school, while Obby divided her time between London, Wentworth and Ireland, working for a while in a munitions factory. Juliet recalls the war years as 'oddly enough very happy for me'. Because of the local supply of logs and coal, the house was always warm, she says, and there was always plenty to do. Maud had had the foresight to buy '. . . literally tonnes of sugar, partly to make crab apple jelly because we had a lot of crab apple trees, but just to store against eventualities, I suppose'. Juliet's third cousin Jane Pidcock, née Doyne, also spent part of the war at Wentworth. She has fond memories of Maud, whom she remembered smelling of lavender and mothballs. 'She had the knack with children, she never patronised them. When a bomb, probably dropped on the way home from Sheffield, came down near Wentworth, she sat down and talked to my brother Nigel about it like a grown-up – she debriefed him, asking him what he had made of it, was he bothered by it. She had a deep understanding of people.'

* * *

During the final years of the war, Peter had agreed with Manny Shinwell's predecessor, the Conservative minister for fuel and power Major Gwilym Lloyd George, the former prime minister's son, that the coal fields around Wentworth could be worked for the nation. They struck a deal that allowed for the extraction of over one million tons from fields outside the park boundary. They also agreed that the park and garden would not be touched except in an emergency.

All went well with this arrangement until the war's end. Following Labour's overwhelming victory in the July 1945 general election, prime minister Clement Attlee appointed Shinwell to the fuel ministry. The following month, the new minister made a speech in County Durham, in which he stated how essential it was that eight million more tons of coal should be mined nationally between October and the following spring than was currently being extracted. Some of this additional supply, he added, would have to come from further seams at Wentworth. His proposal was that the government should seize 110 acres of Fitzwilliam land for open-cast mining that would yield a much-needed 345,000 tons – a move that would necessitate the destruction of twenty acres of gardens on the west front of the house, just beyond the back door.

Peter wrote to Shinwell to protest; after all, the minister's proposal was contrary to the gentlemen's agreement that had been struck with Lloyd George. He didn't get very far: Shinwell was not a man who believed in gentlemen's agreements. The future Conservative MP Roger Gresham Cooke also expressed his opposition. In a letter he wrote in October 1945 to the editor of the weekly newspaper *Truth*, he pointed out that while the public were under the impression that additional coal supplies the government were now promising were to 'come from improved working in the coal mines', the fact was that the areas selected by the Ministry of Fuel and Power '. . . include woodlands and plantations, as well as large parts of the private gardens and the historic terrace wall at Wentworth Woodhouse.' Gresham Cooke was worried for the future of Wentworth. 'The gigantic American machinery employed for these operations uproots trees, smashes buildings and walls and, although the land may be levelled at the end, what was previously a beautiful countryside becomes a desolate wilderness. Whether the need for coal is worth this destruction the public ought to have an opportunity for judging.'[35]

Joe Hall, president of the Yorkshire branch of the National Union of Mineworkers, also argued that the gardens should be preserved. His argument was that the coal Shinwell had his eyes on was of an inferior grade. '[T]he miners of Yorkshire will give you more and better additional coal in quicker time than you will get from this stretch of open-cast mine,' he pledged.[36] 'These are among the most beautiful gardens in the country,' he wrote to Attlee a week later, adding: 'I am confident now that there is no necessity for this mining here. In six months a greater quantity of cleaner coal could be won more economically by drifting methods without the least defacement of the surface.'[37]

In early March 1946, Peter's agent Colonel Jim Landon wrote to Shinwell, asking him to reconsider the decision to open-cast mine in Wentworth's park, gardens and woodlands. He accused the minister of not understanding the full picture. 'We suggest that it is very easy for people in Whitehall to make decisions while looking at a plan, but I do not think they can realise fully what will be involved, and its effect on those who live in this district. I plead therefore, on behalf of the majority of the residents, not only of this parish but of the surrounding districts, that serious consideration should be given to this.'[38]

A month later, Shinwell visited Wentworth and walked through the gardens, then ablaze with daffodils and primroses. He conceded how charming it looked. Landon presented him with a red camellia from the camellia house: 'You chose the right colour,' Shinwell replied, fastening it to his coat. He then told Landon that the gardens would be used as a forty-foot-high dump for spoil. Landon objected that this would obscure the view from the back of the house, and that the dump would inevitably overspill, sweeping away trees, rhododendrons and other shrubs in the process. Shinwell was unmoved. 'It would be no great loss if they were pulled up,' he said. As for the Fitzwilliams losing their view of the gardens, his was that: '[T]he people who are living in the centre of Sheffield look out on worse things.'[39]

After the visit, Jim Landon described Manny Shinwell as 'a Labour dictator' and 'not a Labour democrat'. 'Some of his remarks were not what is expected from a Minister of the Crown,' he complained.[40] Rotherham Alderman George Caine also voiced his objections, pointing out that it wasn't just the Fitzwilliams who would suffer. Local people would be affected, too. And whereas the Fitzwilliams could move elsewhere if they wanted, '[W]e can't go elsewhere. We are fixed here, and it is not merely the rights of the family, but the rights and privileges of the people, which are due to the Fitzwilliam family, that we are really fighting for.'[41] An official from the Council for the Preservation of Rural England concluded that Shinwell's mind was made up before he had even visited Wentworth. A few weeks later, speaking in Newcastle, Shinwell defended his decision. 'We shall restore the land after we have finished and make it even better than before.'[42]

Peter managed to secure a meeting with Attlee on 15 April. The night before, he and Obby walked through the gardens. 'We are grasping at every possibility and I have an alternative scheme to put before the Prime Minister. I am hoping that it will give us one last chance,' he said.[43] 'There is a slight possibility of a reprieve. I am grasping at any last straw.'[44]

The next morning, while Peter was en route to Downing Street, preliminary work got underway. An excavator scooped off the topsoil, revealing the ten-foot seam of coal stretching through the park, and by two o'clock in the afternoon, more than a thousand tons had been exposed. In ten minutes, twenty-eight tons were carted off, leaving an ugly scar. Bulldozers broke through the wall separating the paddock from the gardens, churning up the turf, ploughing across the beds in front of the camellia house, and sweeping away rhododendrons, trees and shrubs just coming into bud. Bulbs were crushed to a pulp. Some were rescued by a man who spent his lunch break digging up as many as he could and taking them for his own garden.

In the afternoon, a bulldozer burst out of the wood onto a path fifty yards from the house. Swinging round, it 'charged full tilt at a beautiful copse of holly trees. They fell like nine-pins and were contemptuously pushed along the turf out of the way.'[45] Obby stepped out from the house to see the bulldozer demolish a group of trees that had stood on the edge of the lawn for eighty years. She watched for a moment and then left to go back inside.

Peter's appeal to the prime minister was not successful. He therefore turned to the National Trust. They could have the house, 200 acres of park and sixty acres of gardens, provided he could keep some of the rooms for the family. On 26 May 1946, the Trust's James Lees-Milne and Michael Parsons, 6th Earl of Rosse, visited Wentworth. Lees-Milne found it 'certainly the most enormous private house I have ever beheld. Strange to think that up till 1939 one man lived in the whole of it.'[46] He found the contents stored, and the pictures outside their frames. The interior was dirty. To the exterior, the immediate vicinity, where the surface had been worked, was pure chaos; it was, Michael Rosse remarked, worse than the French battlefields after D-Day.

The National Trust might initially have been minded to take on Wentworth, but ultimately they were dissuaded by a civil servant at the Ministry of Town and Country Planning who warned of the dangers of getting drawn in to a messy political controversy. It's hard not to think that there was a strongly ideological element to Shinwell's ostensibly industrial and economic decision. Juliet Tadgell, for one, views him as a 'class warrior'. 'Some of the ministers were decent people, but Shinwell was not. He was extremely rude to our agent who had to take him around the garden. He was a marvellous man and Shinwell treated him as scum, which he thought not only the aristocracy were, but the people who worked for them. Of course,' she concludes, 'that was a lot of people, so Shinwell was very unpopular, not only with us but with everyone.'

* * *

Alderman George Caine's observation that, if push came to shove, the Fitzwilliams could simply move, proved to be well founded. Peter, Obby and Juliet relocated to Coollattin where they were joined by their agent and Peter's second cousin Mervyn Doyne, his wife Ella, and their three children Nigel, Jane and Sara. Jane (now Pidcock) recalls an idyllic childhood there, in which hunting played a major part. 'Whenever I went for a ride, I'd stop for a bit and think, I'm so lucky. It was a glorious place to live. Cousin Obby would stroll out with her dogs all around her in the gardens, with her pugs yipping, and everyone wishing they could give one a passing kick. She would say good morning to everybody, and she never forgot people's names.' Obby took Jane to the races in her Sunbeam, while the chauffeur drove the rest of the party in the family's Chevrolet. 'Every time she got to a crossroads she'd drive into the back of the Chevrolet and bump it,' Jane remembers. 'She told me that she once did it twenty times, and said, "I thought he might leave!" At one point on that journey [the chauffeur] got out of the car and said, "Stop doing that, will you, m'lady, I can't drive safely if you keep bashing me." I remember at one particular cross- roads she gave it quite a whack.'

The Fitzwilliams were sociable people who constantly invited guests to stay at Coollattin. Among them was the younger sister of John F. Kennedy, Kathleen 'Kick' Cavendish, Marchioness of Hartington. She is said to have first visited the house in November 1946 with her sister Eunice while they were on a sight-seeing tour of Ireland, though, puzzlingly, the Coollattin visitors' book, which appears to be complete, records only her five-day visit from 9 June 1947, and doesn't mention Eunice at all.

Kick had come to London in 1938 when her father, Joseph P. Kennedy Sr., was made American ambassador to the UK. There she had caught the eye of Billy Cavendish, Marquess of Har- tington, eldest son and heir of Eddy Cavendish, 10th Duke of Devonshire. The couple had married at Chelsea Town Hall in May 1944, but four months later, Billy was shot dead by a sniper in Belgium. Post-war, the widowed Kick took up the chairmanship of the Commandos' Ball committee, of which Obby was president. It was at their ball on 12 June 1946 that Kick and Peter first met and danced together.

Soon afterwards Kick declared that she had never previously experienced feelings like the ones she now had for Peter. He made her forget herself, she said. He was her *Gone with the Wind* hero Rhett Butler. Returning to America in 1948, she told her family and friends that she intended to marry him. Her friend Charlotte McDonnell pronounced her hysterical; her mother, Rose, threatened to disown her if she went ahead with her plans.

There is no evidence to suggest that Peter ever countenanced divorcing Obby and marrying Kick. For a start, as one member of the family points out, Kick was Catholic, and as late as the 1960s Fitzwilliam family members were shunning Catholics as suitable partners. In any case, divorce would not have been regarded as the 'done thing' – Maud, for one, would have disapproved. 'Family history never related that [Peter and Kick] were going to get married,' says Peter's great-nephew Willie Gething. 'Peter must have been an extraordinarily romantic and attractive catch. He was probably exactly her idea of an English war hero. She turned his head but that doesn't mean they were going to get married.' Juliet agrees. Obby 'liked to believe that he would come back home, as it were, and keep Kathleen in the background. I think that is [a] likely outcome. I think she'd have told me eventually if he'd asked for a divorce. She never did, so I don't think he had.'

Over Whitsun 1948, Kick and Peter planned a weekend away together. They stayed for two days at Wentworth, before stopping off at Milton to see Peter's cousin Tom Fitzwilliam. The next morning, Thursday 13 May, the couple boarded a de Havilland Dove to Paris, which after refuelling, and despite the weather taking a bad turn, set off to fly on to Cannes. A little while later it crashed in the Ardèche. Everyone on board was killed.

That day, Obby had planned to go to Newmarket for the races. When news of the accident arrived, she crossed out 'Newmarket' in her diary and wrote below it: '6pm my loverly [*sic*] bum taken. He has gone. Plane crash in S. France.' The next day, she added: 'Oh darling – what have you done.' Juliet was thirteen when her father was killed. 'Life changed, obviously,' she says. 'To say I missed him is an understatement. I still do miss him. I would love him to be around, and often try and think what would be happening if he were and what he would say. I have very happy memories of him which I treasure.'

Three weeks later, a memorial service was held at St Patrick's Cathedral in Dublin, where fifteen years previously Peter and Obby had wed. 'Lovely service,' Obby wrote in her diary.

The entry for 19 April 1949 consists of a single sentence: 'Our wedding anniversary 1933, 16 years.' And then, on the first anniversary of Peter's death: 'To-day last year my whole life went with my loverly [sic].'

After his death, Charles Plunket remembers, Peter was scarcely mentioned at Coollattin. 'Obby kept a portrait of Peter in his hunting coat, but I can't remember seeing any photographs of him. It makes me wonder if she drew a line under that side of her life. She never talked about him.' Peter was, remembered Paddy Behan, a former head groom at Coollattin, '. . . a very decent man, and after a very heavy week, he would come out with a ten-shilling note for each of us stable men and personally thank us for all the extra work.'[47] When the news of his death came, '[I]t was like a bomb had fallen on the village and the surrounding areas. I was absolutely crestfallen with the sheer shock and sadness of his death.'[48]

* * *

As Peter and Obby had not produced a male heir, Peter was succeeded by his first cousin once removed Eric Wentworth-Fitzwilliam, a bachelor twenty-seven years his senior. Eric nominally moved into Wentworth, but spent most of his time at Barnsdale Hall, his house on Rutland Water. 'He was known as "Eric or Bottle by Bottle", instead of "little by little", that Victorian book about a child who was dying of consumption,' remembers Juliet Tadgell. 'I think he was probably an alcoholic, and he was very eccentric.'

When Eric died in April 1952, the earldom passed to his second cousin Tom, twenty-one years his junior, the younger son of George Fitzwilliam, a grandson of the 5th Earl and his wife Evie, a former

Gaiety Girl, who lived at Milton. Tom had an elder brother, Toby, who had grown up believing that he was the legitimate child of his parents and so, potentially, the future Earl Fitzwilliam. But it turned out that George and Evie's supposed marriage in autumn 1886, two years before Toby was born, had been invalid, and so, despite a second marriage ceremony after his birth – for which George had to resign his Royal Horse Guards commission, since the regiment's officers were not permitted to marry actresses – Toby was never in line to inherit. His parents concealed his illegitimacy and continued to do so after his younger brother was born in 1904.

Toby may not have known the true circumstances of his birth, but plenty of other Fitzwilliams did. The 6th Earl is supposed to have said: 'I don't want that child in the house,' when Toby was born. 'He was probably suspicious that Grandfather was illegitimate – in those days you didn't have children before having an enormous wedding, if [a man like George] is the father,' says Toby's grandson Robin Fitzwilliam. Maud Fitzwilliam was fully aware, too. Even so, a year before Eric died, Tom and Toby went to court to determine who should be the next Earl Fitzwilliam. 'There was a question mark,' says Robin Fitzwilliam. 'Everybody knew that my great-grandparents got married after Toby was born, so legally he *was* illegitimate. Eric said he didn't mind who inherited, but he wanted to get the matter sorted out because it would come up anyway on his death.' Tom won the case, and on Eric's death became 10th Earl Fitzwilliam accordingly.[49]

Four years later, he married Joyce Fitzalan Howard, whom he had long pined after. The former wife of Henry 'Boydy' Fitzalan Howard, from 1947 2nd Viscount Fitzalan of Derwent, Joyce was a friend of Billy and Maud's. With her husband she had holidayed with them on *Shemara* and had spent Christmas 1937 with them at Wentworth. In April 1933, it was Tom with whom Joyce came as a guest to Coollattin for Peter and Obby's wedding. The following January, Joyce had a baby, whom she named Elizabeth-Anne. A photograph taken soon after shows the baby in her mother's arms and alongside Maud. Lizzie-Anne, as she was known, 'was a darling – she and I got on very well,' says Juliet. Her paternity was a poorly kept secret. 'She was most certainly Tom's daughter, she looked very like him.'

It was a cruel irony for the Fitzwilliams that the illegitimate Toby, not the legitimate Tom, went on to have a son. When Tom died aged seventy-five in September 1979, thirty-one years after Peter's death, the Fitzwilliam earldom became extinct. Had the case gone Toby's way, when he died in 1955, his son Richard would have become the 11th Earl, and when Richard died in 1987, Robin Fitzwilliam would have become the 12th. Robin has a son, Michael, and a grandson, Tom. But the Fitzwilliam earls are no more.

* * *

The fall of one of England's premier families was spectacular but scarcely unique. It was emblematic of the wider phenomenon of aristocratic decline that took root in the late nineteenth century and accelerated in the years after the Second World War. And, as at Wentworth, that decline achieved its most visible form in the struggle for survival of the country house and the country estate.

Up until late-Victorian times, most estates owned by Britain's upper class had been reasonably stable, passing relatively smoothly to direct or indirect heirs and only occasionally being sold off or split up. So powerful did the grip of the landed class seem, indeed, that it became something of a political hot potato. The 1861 census returns, which suggested that the United Kingdom was in the hands of a mere 30,000 landowners, caused outrage among many in the population at large and defensiveness in establishment ranks. The result was a debate over what became known as the Land Question, though, as the historian David Spring suggests, it 'might equally well have been called the Aristocracy Question', since those who were anti-landowner were by default anti-aristocrat, and particularly opposed to the great landowners who wielded huge influence.[50] The Liberal and Radical MP John Bright, for example, both deplored the 'practical monopoly of land' that the census suggested and proposed reversing it by abolishing the mechanisms by which the aristocracy kept their estates intact – notably the principle of inheritance through primogeniture.

Speaking in the House of Lords on 19 February 1872, Edward Stanley, 15th Earl of Derby, son of the former prime minister, sought to defend the position of the landed class by expressing his doubts as to the accuracy of the figures being bandied about. The census data, he argued, were misleading, since only those who chose to describe themselves as landowners were labelled as such. His own view was that there were surely far more landowners than 30,000 – perhaps ten times as many. A few months before, in September 1871, when he had been addressing the annual dinner of the Manchester and Liverpool Agricultural Society, he had wondered aloud, 'Is it impossible to get at the facts? Is a Domesday Book more difficult now than in the days of the Conqueror?'[51] Now he asked whether the government had any intention of 'ascertaining accurately the number of proprietors of land or houses in the United Kingdom, with the quantity of land owned by each'. He accepted that the issue was a matter of public interest but argued that there had been the 'wildest and most reckless exaggerations and misstatement of fact' surrounding the subject.[52]

By chance, precisely the same question had been raised the previous August by the statistician F. P. Fellowes in an address to the Statistical Section of the British Association for the Advancement of Science. His proposed solution, mentioned in passing, was a modern-day Domesday Book, and that was what duly appeared in 1873 in the form of a Return of Owners of Land survey. The first audit of English landownership since 1086, it demonstrated that Edward Derby was right to say that there were more than 30,000 landowners in the British Isles – in fact, there were over a million. Unfortunately, from Derby's point of view, it also showed that four-fifths of the landmass was owned by just over 700 people, 710 to be precise. His uncomfortable Thirty Thousand had been replaced by the significantly more uncomfortable Seven Hundred. In March 1876, the Liberal publication the *Spectator* labelled these titled and untitled landowners the 'territorialists', pointing out that they owned '. . . immediately or in reversion, one-seventh of the entire rental of the Kingdom, a proportion which, if London could be included, would be very greatly increased'. John Bright, the magazine concluded, may have been wrong to suggest that Englishmen 'have been divorced from the soil', but there was no doubt that he was right to believe that vast swathes of land were in the hands of a very small group of men.[53]

The *Spectator* suggested that enemies of the landed aristocracy might want to do some further work on the subject. In the event, though, it was not a Bright radical, but a Tory country gentleman with a Cambridge education who decided to take up the gauntlet. John Bateman was a landowner, with almost 3,000 acres in County Mayo as well as a 1,400-acre estate at Brightlingsea in Essex. As such, he appeared in his own survey. Though little is known about him, he appears to have been a conventional Victorian squire who took his public responsibilities seriously, as a member of Essex County Council and Brightlingsea Urban District Council, chairman of the local Conservative Association and a justice of the peace. He was not a professional writer or researcher, but from 1876 he began to publish, over three editions, what would eventually become *The Great Landowners of Great Britain and Ireland* – a life's work and a far more detailed survey than the New Domesday Book. Not only did it list all landowners who possessed 3,000 acres or more and were worth £3,000 gross or more a year, but it gave their names, addresses, education, clubs, dates of birth and marriage details, too. It was a *Debrett's Peerage* of the land.

Bateman's endeavours revealed that in the early 1880s, 482 peers collectively owned 16,018,719 acres worth over £12 million gross per annum. Inevitably, the extent of individual holdings varied hugely, from Eyre Massey, 4th Baron Clarina's 2,012 acres in County Limerick, to George Sutherland-Leveson-Gower, 3rd Duke of Sutherland's 1,358,545 acres, mostly in his titular county. In all, 138 peers were in possession of more than 30,000 acres.

The value of these holdings ranged widely, too, from Frederick Lambart, 8th Earl of Cavan's £2,099 for his 2,731 acres in County Mayo, Somerset and Hertfordshire, to Walter Montagu Douglas Scott, 5th Duke of Buccleuch's £217,163 for his 460,108 mostly Scottish acres. Bateman concluded that the top ten largest landowners were in possession of 4,075,686 acres, and that seven of them were dukes.

Within a decade or so, though, the picture began to change dramatically, transformed by two economic events. The first was an agricultural depression, caused by the influx of cheap wheat from the American prairies that began in the 1870s and persisted until the late 1890s. As it took hold, the countryside underwent severe depopulation and aristocratic incomes fell significantly. Between 1880 and 1914 the number of British millionaires who were landowners dropped from 88 per cent to 33 per cent. As former Conservative prime minister Arthur Balfour observed in 1909: '[T]he bulk of the great fortunes now are in a highly liquid state.'[54] The patrician class were ceasing to be 'lords of the earth'.[55]

The second key event was the introduction in 1894 of death duties – then called estate duty – by the chancellor of the exchequer Sir William Harcourt. His Finance Act represented the first considered attempt to tax the rich in any kind of systematic way, replacing a complex system of probate, account and succession duties, as well as an estate duty introduced in 1889, which was due to expire two years after his budget. As Harcourt pointed out in his Budget speech:

[E]ven without the pressure of immediate necessity, it would be a mere act of financial justice to redress inequalities which have too long existed. It is difficult to understand how the intolerable injustice of the relations between the taxation of various kinds of property under the death duties has been so long endured ... The whole system is admittedly difficult and complicated. The death duties have grown up piecemeal ... they have never been established upon any general principles, and they present an extraordinary specimen of tessellated legislation. Various measures have been made at different times to redress some of their inequalities. Here a patch and there a patch, but each successive modification has only left confusion worse compounded.[56]

Harcourt's reforms were cautious. Even the biggest estates – those whose value exceeded £1 million – attracted only an 8 per cent duty. But they represented just the first twist of the vice. Over the next decades, death duties would be continually ratcheted up until, by 1946, they had reached a 75 per cent levy on taxable amounts over £2 million. Careful tax planning became *de rigueur*, but good luck was often required, too. Eddy Devonshire, for example, recalling the £500,000 tax bill that his father Victor Cavendish, 9th Duke of Devonshire, had had to pay in 1908 on the death of his uncle (in part settlement of which it had been necessary to sell Devonshire House on Piccadilly), planned ahead by transferring most of his (many) assets to his younger but only surviving son Andrew in 1946. All he then had to do for that transfer to remain tax-free was to survive five years. As Andrew Devonshire later recalled, '[M]y father went to church virtually every Sunday and used to tell me that it was then he ticked off another week.' Unfortunately, Eddy Devonshire died prematurely in 1950, fourteen weeks before the five years was up, and, at a stroke, Andrew found himself burdened with £4.72 million in death duties – 80 per cent of the value of the Devonshire estates – with interest payable at £1,000 a week. 'There was very little public sympathy at the time for tax planning which failed,' the new duke remembered, noting, too, that it took him almost twenty-five years to pay off the debt.[57] Eddy Devonshire's daughter-in-law Debo Devonshire felt that, '[I]t seemed strange to me that the family of a man who had given a lifetime of public service should have to pay such a vast fine on his death.'[58]

The fate of the Willoughby family is representative – if in an extreme form – of the challenges so many old landed families faced in the early years of the twentieth century. Back in 1883 they owned 99,576 acres in England and Scotland, and at the turn of the century five stately homes: Wollaton Hall, near Nottingham; Middleton Hall, near Tamworth, which had been in the family since the fifteenth century; Applecross, in Wester Ross; and both Settrington House and Birdsall, near Malton.

Everything changed after the First World War. Digby Willoughby, 9th Baron Middleton, had no sons himself, but his brother Ernest had four, so the line of succession was straightforward, at least on paper. However, a wave of deaths wreaked havoc with any carefully laid plans the family might have devised. First, two of Ernest's sons died in action: Captain Bobby Willoughby at Hooge in August 1915, and nine months later, his older brother Commander Digby Willoughby aboard HMS *Indefatigable* during the Battle of Jutland. Then, in 1922, Digby and his wife Eliza 'Eisa' Middleton died within a few weeks of each other, followed barely two years later by Ernest and his wife. Their surviving middle son Guy now became 11th Baron Middleton but found himself saddled with death duties that amounted to 80 per cent of the assets he had inherited.

Faced with financial ruin, he bowed to the inevitable and began to dispose of the Middleton estates. First to go, in 1924, was Wollaton, built by the architect Robert Smythson for Sir Francis Willoughby between 1580 and 1588, on land that had been acquired by the Willoughbys in about 1314. Guy had hoped to save the house for the family by getting permission from Nottingham Corporation to build new housing in the park. They, however, refused, at which point Guy agreed to sell the house and park to them for £200,000. The Corporation went on to build the housing that Guy had suggested, and within two years had made their money back. 'The family needn't have sold Wollaton,' says Lady Cara Willoughby, Guy Middleton's great-granddaughter-in-law. 'There is still a regret that there wasn't a better conversation at that point.'

One by one, the family houses were sold off until only Birdsall was left, piled high with the contents of the houses Guy had been forced to let go.[59] The sales destroyed him. Even today the family feels a profound sense of loss. 'The Willoughby family tree goes back to 1066, so relatively speaking it's only happened in the last five minutes,' says Cara. 'Wollaton was a Willoughby family home for 340 of its 440 years, and the reason it's there is all Willoughby. No other family has taken it on so the evolution has stopped there. It's in Willoughby aspic.' When Guy died in 1970, and his son Michael took over, a determination grew that 'this is never going to happen again'.

* * *

Other families facing similar scales of financial challenge sought safety through marriage alliances. The Leveson-Gower family, created Dukes of Sutherland in 1833, for example, made canny unions with other British landowning families, and in doing so became, for a time, the most powerful family in the land. Others looked further afield. Between 1870 and 1914, sixty peers married American women and, more often than not, American women with money. The 'most superior person', sometime foreign secretary George Curzon, from 1921 1st Marquess Curzon of Kedleston, for example, wedded the retail heiress Mary Leiter, who came with a $200,000 dowry, in 1895.[60] After Mary's death in 1906, Curzon married another even richer American, Grace Hinds, the daughter of a Union soldier, who had inherited an $18 million fortune from her first, Irish–Argentinian, husband, Alfredo Duggan. Mary Leiter's younger sister Margaret, known as 'Daisy', was another of the so-called 'dollar princesses'. In December 1904, she married Henry Howard, the am-dram-acting, tiger-shooting 19th Earl of Suffolk and Berkshire, Curzon's aide-de-camp. Daisy spent £225,000 of her own money modernising the Suffolks' Wiltshire home of Charlton Park, near Malmesbury – not much in itself, perhaps, considering that her share of her father's fortune was £50 million, but certainly enough to sort out the plumbing.

Daisy and Henry's charmed life didn't last long; when war came, he was given command of the Wiltshire Battery of the 3rd Wessex

Brigade, Royal Field Artillery, and in April 1917 was killed near Baghdad, aged thirty-nine. Daisy was devastated. Henry's death, she wrote to her niece Lady Cynthia 'Cimmie' Mosley, '... has nearly killed me so I am less able to struggle through these cruel days, tho' I long to find courage to fight my battle as bravely as he did all of his.'[61] She left Charlton Park in 1934 for Arizona, where she bought a citrus grove and built a modern house with the then new-fangled invention of air-conditioning.

Not all transatlantic unions were successful. In 1879, the Hon. Jim Roche, the future 3rd Baron Fermoy, was introduced to Frances 'Fanny' Work by fellow American Jennie Spencer-Churchill (née Jerome) while she was visiting London. A belle of 1870s New York, Fanny was the daughter of self-made millionaire stock-broker Frank Work, who had little time for penniless Englishmen. He decreed that Fanny and Jim's twin sons, Maurice and Francis, were to inherit nothing of the Work fortune unless they became American citizens, took Work as their surname, and maintained a permanent residence in the US. In the event, Fanny and Jim, a keen gambler, who had spent a fair amount of his wife's money, divorced in 1891. The twins, however, did eventually receive their share of Frank Work's $15 million fortune, and in 1920 Maurice became 4th Baron Fermoy. His daughter Frances married Johnnie Spencer, the future 8th Earl Spencer; their daughter Lady Diana married the Prince of Wales in 1981, making Fanny Work great-great-grandmother of the future King of England.

A happier marriage was made by Mary 'May' Goelet and Henry 'Kelso' Innes Ker, 8th Duke of Roxburghe. Her father, a New York landlord, had inherited $50 million, and left his daughter $20 million (which was kept in trust until she was twenty-five) on his death in 1897. Once she had married Kelso in 1903, two months before her twenty-fifth birthday, May used her money to update the interior decoration of the Roxburghes' Floors Castle in the Scottish Borders, installing a selection of seventeenth-century Flemish tapestries, and beginning a collection of twentieth-century art, with works by Henri Matisse, Augustus John and Pierre Bonnard.

Much of what was already there was removed; the story goes that May had the Victorian furniture taken outside onto the lawn and burned, so that she could install her preferred continental furniture. The same fate likely struck a large number of card tables, which mysteriously vanished from Floors, disapproved of by May, never to be seen again.

After the Second World War, May's only son George who was always known as 'Bobo', by then 9th Duke of Roxburghe, had to dispose of the family's lease of 2 Carlton House Terrace, and the family's Dunbar estate Broxmouth Park, as well as a collection of family furniture, porcelain and tapestries, but there's no doubt that May saved the family. In 1883, the Roxburghes had been in possession of 60,418 acres; in 2023, their estates comprised 52,000 acres, a remarkable victory over social change and events – in large part thanks to May's legacy. As her great-grandson Lord Ted Innes Ker says: 'For one hundred years Floors hadn't been touched because May had spent such a lot of money and such a lot of time filling it. To this day, walking around, she's there. Without May, we would be in a much more difficult financial position, there's no doubt about it.'

The most famous American heiress to enter the British aristocracy was Consuelo Vanderbilt, who we met a little earlier, scion of a family of Dutch origin that had made its home in the US back in 1650 and that owed its extraordinary wealth to the railroad business. In 1895, with the help of her ambitious mother, Consuelo married Sunny Marlborough, the son of the philandering 8th Duke, George Marlborough. George had also married American money; after divorcing his first wife Lady Albertha 'Goosie' Hamilton, daughter of James Hamilton, 1st Duke of Abercorn, he had promptly headed across the Atlantic and latched himself onto Lily Hamersley, who had been widowed five years previously with an annual income of $150,000.

The Marlboroughs were certainly among those who were adversely affected by the agricultural depression of the latter years of Queen Victoria's reign. They were also architects of their own financial problems. In the early nineteenth century, the 5th Duke, a rare plant collector, spent £50,000 building extensive gardens at Blenheim, and another £10,000 on plants. His life has been rightly described as 'a fantastic farrago of luxury and squalor',[62] and he has equally justifiably been termed 'the most thriftless and the most extravagant' of the Marlborough dukes. Before he inherited in 1817, he described how the 'immense fortune of my family will be frittered away; but I can't help it.' 'I must live,' he went on. 'My father inherited £500,000 in ready money and £70,000 a year in land; and in all probability when it comes to my turn to live at Blenheim I shall have nothing left but the annuity of £5,000 a year on the Post Office.'[63] By the time he died in 1840, he had sold many of Blenheim's treasures; as a peer and not a 'trader', he could not be declared bankrupt, but he had become in effect penniless. His grandson, the church-reforming, priggish, Tory 7th Duke, continued the spoliation of the Blenheim collection. In 1875, on his quest to bring in some much-needed cash, he sold the Marlborough gems that had been collected by the 4th Duke, for 35,000 guineas. '[O]nly Blenheim was [left] the poorer,' concluded the historian A. L. Rowse.[64]

By the last decades of the nineteenth century, the Marlboroughs were struggling – at least relative to their fellow aristocrats. Algernon Percy, 6th Duke of Northumberland, had over £160,000 a year revenue coming in from his titular county and Walter Montagu Douglas Scott, 5th Duke of Buccleuch, over £170,000 from his Scottish estates alone (and another £45,000 from his English estates besides), while Francis Russell, 9th Duke of Bedford, enjoyed £120,000 from his rural estates, excluding the monies raised from those in London. By comparison, the Marlboroughs were earning under £36,000 a year from their Oxfordshire estate of 25,511 acres, and just over £5,000 from their small Buckinghamshire estate. After the 3rd, 4th, 5th and 7th Dukes were all unsuccessful in securing an heiress, Blenheim was broke and increasingly pinched; the 7th Duke had eight surviving children: six daughters and two extravagant sons, 'addicted to society with all its expensive allurements'.[65]

When George Marlborough died in 1892, his son Sunny,

psychologically scarred by an unhappy childhood, now just shy of his majority, realised that in order to save Blenheim, he needed to find a lot of money very quickly. Initially, he had his heart set on the shipping heiress Muriel Wilson, whose millionaire father Arthur Wilson had played host to the Prince of Wales at his home Tranby Croft in 1890, the scene of the baccarat scandal of September 1890, when the Scottish landowner Sir William Gordon-Cumming had been accused of cheating and subsequently ostracised from society. But it was thought, at least by Sunny's odious cousin Ivor Guest, later 1st Viscount Wimborne,[66] that Muriel wasn't rich enough. 'You must marry some money,' he urged: 'Perhaps are you in love because you are living at Blenheim and bored with life? You seem to be in a cul-de-sac and you grasp eagerly at any ray of light which shines through the dull wall which blocks your immediate prospect of advance.'[67] Later that year, concerned he had been too forward with his cousin, Guest wound back, writing to Sunny: 'I wish you would disassociate from yourself the idea of "selling yourself". Don't marry for money but go where money is in moderation.'[68] Sunny did not take this latter piece of advice.

Having decided that Consuelo would do, Sunny proposed to her in September 1895 and was accepted, even though her brother Harold, for one, knew that this would be a marriage of convenience rather than one of love. Sunny's uncle Henry 'Clan' Petty-Fitzmaurice, 5th Marquess of Lansdowne, put matters a little more delicately in a letter to Sunny in September 1895: 'I would not for the world have you marry for money but it was essential that your wife should contribute something to the "menage" and the problem was to find one who should do this and also be attractive.'[69]

Consuelo dressed for her wedding feeling 'like an automaton'.[70] Glancing at Sunny as bride and groom stood side by side inside St Thomas Church at 53rd Street and Fifth Avenue in New York City, she saw that his eyes were 'fixed in space'.[71] When they arrived at Blenheim, after their honeymoon in Europe, she found the house depressing: '[W]e slept in small rooms with high ceilings; we dined in dark rooms with high ceilings; we dressed in closets without ventilation; we sat in long galleries or painted saloons. Had they been finely proportioned or beautifully decorated I would not so greatly have minded sacrificing comfort to elegance. But alas, Vanbrugh [the architect] appears to have subscribed more readily to the canons of dramatic art than to those of architecture.'[72] The Marlborough family proved cold comfort. Consuelo's account of her first meeting with Sunny's grandmother Fanny, Duchess of Marlborough, is worth repeating. 'She was,' Consuelo remembered, 'a formidable old lady of the Queen Anne type . . . An English Duchess to her was the highest position any woman not of royal birth could reach, and like Sarah Jennings, 1st Duchess of Marlborough, she felt capable of matching her wits against any queen's.'[73] She received Consuelo at her house in Grosvenor Square, where she '. . . bestowed a welcoming kiss in the manner of a deposed sovereign greeting her successor'. And then she said the now infamous words to Consuelo: 'Your first duty is to have a child and it must be a son, because it would be intolerable to have that little upstart Winston become Duke. Are you in the family way?'[74]

In September 1897, Consuelo produced the required son, Bert. The following October, Consuelo and Sunny's second son Lord Ivor Spencer-Churchill was born.[75] Consuelo felt she had done her duty. The Marlboroughs separated in 1906, and finally divorced in 1921, when she wanted to marry the French balloonist Jacques Balsan.

Just as May Goelet ensured the survival of the Roxburghes, so Consuelo saved the Marlboroughs. At the time she married Sunny it cost £100,000 a year to keep Blenheim going. The coal bill alone was £2,500. Upon the Marlboroughs' marriage, Consuelo's father William Kissam 'W. K.' Vanderbilt gave his son-in-law $2.5 million in the form of 50,000 shares of Beech Creek Railroad Company stock, and also presented the couple with an annual dividend of $100,000 dollars. By the time their marriage had run its course, W. K. Vanderbilt had put about $10 million into the Marlborough dukedom. The couple's divorce represented a disappointing return on his investment.[76] For Sunny, by contrast, the marriage had been a financial triumph. Vanderbilt money paid for the dredging of the lake, the refilling of the library, the replanting of the Grand Avenue in the park, and the building of a new formal garden at Blenheim. As the former editor of *Burke's Peerage* Hugh Montgomery-Massingberd put it: 'Caddish he may have been to continue to accept Consuelo's cash, but without it Blenheim could have been ruined.'[77] Later, when Bert was asked about his father's motives in marrying Consuelo, he would only say, 'Everyone was doing it. Everyone just then was marrying an American heiress.'[78]

* * *

At the same time as many members of the traditional aristocracy were becomingly increasingly financially squeezed, their ranks were being augmented and reinforced by the newly ennobled. In the sixty-five years from 1880, 660 men were advanced through the peerage by nineteen prime ministers, who either elevated them to the House of Lords or raised their status from one rank of the peerage to another.[79] Previously, family prestige and the extent of their landholdings had been key. Now, increasingly, money became the determining factor. Of the 246 peers created between 1886 and 1924, only about a quarter were inheritors of landed estates. Of the fifteen men given titles by prime minister Herbert Asquith in 1910, five were major businessmen.

This new type of peer had its origins among the existing members of the super-wealthy landed peerage themselves – specifically George Leveson-Gower, 2nd Marquess of Stafford, the 'leviathan of wealth ... the richest individual who ever died,' who in 1833 had been advanced to Duke of Sutherland, a title he had long craved.[80] Once the principle of advancement because of wealth or prestige or both was established, it quickly became something of a norm. Asquith ennobled or advanced ninety-nine men as peers during his eight-year premiership. His successor, former chancellor David Lloyd George, the so-called 'Welsh Wizard', ennobled or advanced 115 men over his six-year premiership, almost 20 per cent of the total number of those promoted in the sixty-five years from 1880. Almost half of his peers were fresh creations, and a third of the promotions he sanctioned, including some of the most notable new peers of the day, followed to an extent Asquithian principles. Only ten of Lloyd George's new peers were sons or grandsons of existing peers who had held their titles for more than one generation. The same number were soldiers or admirals of household repute – among them Field Marshal Douglas Haig and Admiral of the Fleet David Beatty.

The largest single group comprised current or former politicians – from the long-standing speaker of the House of Commons James Lowther, who became Viscount Ullswater, to the sometime foreign secretary and Viceroy of India George Curzon, promoted from 1st Earl Curzon to 1st Marquess Curzon of Kedleston.[81] After the politicians, the next-largest group were businessmen of some kind or another: industrialists, shipowners, factory owners, newspaper proprietors, brewers and distillers.

Some of those wealthy businessmen were very wealthy indeed. William Waldorf Astor, born in New York City in 1848, and ennobled first as Baron Astor by Asquith in January 1916, in recognition of his charitable works, and advanced to Viscount Astor by Lloyd George in the following year, was the second-richest man in America in 1890. Marmaduke Furness, 2nd Baron Furness, created Viscount Furness in 1918 by Lloyd George, was a shipping magnate (and the son of Christopher Furness, 1st Baron Furness, who had been given his peerage in 1910 by Asquith). Edward Guinness, made 1st Viscount Iveagh in 1891 by Robert Gascoyne-Cecil, 3rd Marquess of Salisbury, and promoted to 1st Earl of Iveagh in September 1919, was a great-grandson of Arthur Guinness, founder of the eponymous brewery, and sometime the richest man in Ireland. Though the Astors had come to America from Germany in 1783, and Iveagh could trace his family history back to the first Arthur Guinness in the early eighteenth century, they were not from old families in the same way as George Sutherland, one of whose ancestors served as an MP in the early fourteenth century,

and his grandson-in-law the super-landlord Hugh Grosvenor, 1st
Duke of Westminster – whose family could trace its origin back to
the Norman Conquest, and who was himself advanced from 3rd
Marquess of Westminster to 1st Duke in 1874 – were. Edward
Iveagh was part of a group known disparagingly as the 'beerage',
a portmanteau of 'beer' and 'peerage' first recorded in Hansard on
19 April 1883, when Cobdenite Liberal MP Sir Wilfrid Lawson,
2nd Baronet, noting the changing nature of the times, lamented
that: 'Anybody might be made a peer now-a-days, and it did not
require a man to go into battle to be made a peer. He had only to
win two or three elections, to be a personal friend of the minister
or to brew enough beer; then he was raised from the beerage up
to the peerage.'[82]

By the time that William Buchan, 3rd Baron Tweedsmuir, went
up to Eton in 1929, the mix of old and new aristocracy was virtually complete. He recalled how, on the one hand, '. . . many of
my comrades were long-descended, quietly established on their
land; many bore names and titles so resounding as to seem too
heavy for the young shoulders of their bearers'; on the other hand,
he described how many, '. . . were descendants of Victorian and
Edwardian entrepreneurs, manufacturers, iron masters who, once
grown rich, had forsaken their former fields of action to enjoy a
gentleman's existence behind park gates and had seen to it that
their sons and grandsons should never have to soil their hands in
industry or commerce, except as owners of mines or directors of
shipping lines, breweries and banks.'[83]

In previous eras, land had bought wealth and influence. Now,
among the newly ennobled, wealth and influence went to buy land.
By 1920, over half of Lloyd George's new or promoted peers had
bought themselves country estates or large country houses. Seven
bought their estates in the year of their ennoblement or within a
few years of this. Nineteen already possessed an estate, having, for
the most part, acquired it at the time of their original promotion,
be this a knighthood or a junior peerage. Edward Iveagh was first
ennobled in 1891. Three years later he bought Elveden Hall in

Suffolk with its 17,000-acre estate for £159,000 from the executors of the will of the late Maharajah Duleep Singh, the last ruler of the Sikh Empire. This purchase – 'the greatest single *coup* affecting the Iveagh lifestyle' – marked his arrival as a landed peer.[84] He added a new wing to Elveden as well as a replica Taj Mahal, rebuilt the village in the manner of one whose family had lived in the area for centuries, laid out six miles of roads across the estate, and increased its acreage to 23,000. Clearing the heathland, previously only the playground of rabbits, he developed it into one of the best pheasant and partridge shoots in England, to rival even nearby Sandringham, which had been bought by his friend the Prince of Wales in 1862.

In a similar way, the whisky distiller Sir Thomas 'Tommy' Dewar, knighted in 1902 and created Baron Dewar by Lloyd George in May 1919, had, within five years of his first promotion, bought the medieval country house Homestall near East Grinstead in West Sussex, which he lavished money on, restoring it inside and out. Meanwhile in 1912, Sir Harold Harmsworth, co-founder of the *Daily Mail*, later to be created Baron Rothermere and then Viscount Rothermere, bought the 4,900-acre Hemsted Park estate in Kent, where he remodelled the house. Rothermere kept Hemsted for only twelve years before selling it. In 2000, his great-grandson Jonathan Harmsworth, 4th Viscount Rothermere, and his wife Claudia commissioned the classical architect Quinlan Terry to build them a brand new country house. This, Ferne Park in Wiltshire, is, as Kate Reardon found it in 2006, '. . . notable for what's missing: no leaky taps, no freezing damp sheets. Instead there are sofas that envelop you, luxurious linens, spruce bathrooms, piles of fluffy towels, and bath products that weren't pilfered from a hotel. There is sisal carpet, but with a fat, generous weave that doesn't hurt your bare feet.'[85]

* * *

Meanwhile, there were those among the old aristocracy who were finding the going tougher and were retrenching accordingly. In

Wales between 1910 and 1914, the historian David Cannadine notes, 'almost every major Welsh owner whose territorial identity was mainly within the Principality began to dispose of parts of their estates.' They included the Powises, the Harlechs, the Wimbornes and the Westminsters, while in 1915 Henry Somerset, 9th Duke of Beaufort, cut his family's ties with Wales with the sale of his 5,000-acre Brecon estate. In Scotland, where individual aristocratic landholdings were often larger than elsewhere but also less valuable, vast tracts of land were put on the market. In November 1918, the estate agents Knight Frank & Rutley announced that George 'Geordie' Sutherland-Leveson-Gower, 5th Duke of Sutherland, had disposed of 320,000 acres of his northern Scottish estates. The following month, they were instructed to sell another 90,000 acres of Sutherland's land – 'conveniently situated for railway communication', as they were quick to point out.[86] John Hamilton-Gordon, 1st Marquess of Aberdeen and Temair, Simon Fraser, 14th Lord Lovat, William Cavendish-Bentinck, 6th Duke of Portland, and Gavin Campbell, 1st Marquess of Breadalbane (in 1883 the third-biggest landowner in the country), also all reduced their holdings during this period. Indeed, between 1912 and 1920 Knight Frank & Rutley reckoned to have handled the sale of some 1.6 million acres in Scotland. Meanwhile in England, some 800,000 acres of land changed hands for about £20 million between 1909 and late 1914. Those with lands in Ireland also cut back on their holdings, though here the reasons were as much political as economic as successive administrations brought in legislation to help tenants buy the land they farmed.

Of those families who lost their ancestral homes altogether at this time, the Capell family, from 1661 the Earls of Essex, offer a poignant example. In 1910, *Country Life* had published an article on Cassiobury House in Watford – the Capells' home since 1627 – that celebrated the house and its 'grandly timbered park', gushing that: 'Therein is peace and quiet; the aloofness of the old-world country home far from the haunts of men reigns there still.'[87] But beneath the surface the Essexes were struggling. In 1893, following his grandfather's death the previous year, George Capell, 7th

Earl of Essex, had sold pictures, books, porcelain and furniture from Cassiobury's collection. His marriage in 1893 to the sociable New York railway heiress Adele Grant helped for a while, but from 1913 it had proved necessary to let Cassiobury to various tenants including Seymour 'Simon' and Brenda Egerton, 6th Earl and Countess of Wilton. The Essexes meanwhile decamped to London where, in January 1916, George Essex was run over by a taxi, dying a few months later aged fifty-eight. In June 1922 Cassiobury, its contents and its 870 acres went under the hammer, so ending a family association that had endured for 300 years. Adele's friend Nancy Astor's biographer Adrian Fort describes the decline of the Essexes as being '. . . sadly typical of the dramatic and swift change of fortune that befell so much of the top echelons of English society following the First World War, when political, social and financial upheaval almost entirely obliterated what had seemed only a few years previously to be set fair for ever.'[88] A month after the sale of Cassiobury, Adele Essex was found dead in the bath at her London home, 72 Brook Street. She was thought to have suffered a heart attack.

The Chetwynd-Talbot family, owners of Alton Towers near Stoke-on-Trent since 1406, and created Earls of Shrewsbury in 1442, suffered a similar fate. Their problems began in 1896 when Charles Chetwynd-Talbot, 20th Earl of Shrewsbury, and his wife Ellen separated. Ellen stayed at Alton, while her husband went to live at the family's other house, Ingestre Hall near Stafford. Charles Shrewsbury had blotted his copybook in any case by daring at the age of twenty-three to start his own hansom cab business.[89] His great-grandson Charles Chetwynd-Talbot, 22nd Earl of Shrewsbury, describes how what to us seems an impressive display of entrepreneurship ensured that he should have been 'ostracised from society': 'I have a wonderful letter from him to [his sister] great-aunt Viola, saying "Dear Viola, life in London has taken a change for the worst – we're no longer invited to smart parties because I have been perceived to have gone into trade."'

Then real tragedy struck. In 1915, the Shrewsburys' son Charles,

Viscount Ingestre, contracted pneumonia while training with the Royal Horse Guards on Salisbury Plain and died aged thirty-two. Six years later, Charles Shrewsbury followed his son to the grave. Alton, which he had put on the market in May 1922, was sold along with its contents. Ingestre was left to his companion Mrs Eleanor Brownlee, but Charley Paget, 6th Marquess of Anglesey, uncle and guardian of the new, seven-year-old earl John Shrewsbury, challenged the dead earl's will on the grounds that he was not of sound mind when he made it. Ironically, John Shrewsbury would go on to sell Ingestre in 1960 (see Chapter 8). As a result, the Shrewsburys now have no ancestral home.

The current earl, who lives ten miles from Alton Towers, right on the Derbyshire border, explains how it could all have been so different. 'Only in the last twenty years,' he says, 'has my grandfather been recognised as one of the war dead. He had been deemed unfit for action [owing to having varicose veins] but he was actually a serving soldier when he died. If they had recognised him at that stage as one of the war dead, it would probably be the case that the Ingestre and Alton Towers estates would still be together. He died seven years before my great-grandfather and they got hit for two lots of death duties.' 'My father didn't finish paying off his father and grandfather's death duties until the 1960s,' he adds.

Charley Anglesey, incidentally, also struggled with estate finances. Back in the 1880s the Angleseys' relatively modest 30,000-acre holdings in both England and Wales yielded an impressive annual income of £110,598, and they enjoyed the use of two stately homes – Plas Newydd on Anglesey and Beaudesert House in Staffordshire, which had been in the family since 1546. But when the 'tall, quite handsome, good-natured' Charley inherited the Anglesey marquessate in 1905, he also took on his predecessor Henry 'Toppy' Anglesey's £250,000 debts.[90] He managed to get things back on track and in due course set about painstakingly restoring Beaudesert with the help of his future mother-in-law Violet Manners, Duchess of Rutland's brother, Captain Harry Lindsay. But, as his grandson Alex Paget, 8th Marquess of Anglesey, explains, he

'. . . finally decided that he couldn't maintain it . . . They lived there 50–50 [with Plas Newydd] and he felt he had to decide [which one to keep]. He tried to sell it but it just never happened.' Charley Anglesey put Beaudesert on the market in 1924 but it failed to find a buyer. In 1935 it was sold to housebreakers and is now a romantic ruin, many of its bricks reused in the restoration of St James's Palace. After that, the Anglesey haul continued to drip away: their townhouse in Queen's Gate was sold and is now part of Imperial College; the brace of yachts was disposed of, as was the family home in France, later, by Henry Paget, 7th Marquess of Anglesey. All that was left was Plas Newydd – on which more later.

It is tempting to conclude from such tales of decline that by the 1970s the old landed aristocracy were heading for oblivion. Certainly, it was a not uncommon view at the time. In December 1924, the Hon. Edward Wood, future 1st Earl of Halifax, then minister of agriculture, speaking at a dinner of the Central and Associated Chambers of Agriculture and the Farmers' Club, at a restaurant in London,[91] claimed that a 'silent revolution' was in progress: '[W]e are, unless I mistake it,' he said, 'witnessing in England the gradual disappearance of the old landed class.'[92] The introduction to the 1919 *Year Book of Auction Sales*, a trade journal circulated to members of the Royal Institute of Chartered Surveyors, similarly described how 'with the continued breaking up of innumerable ancestral domains, all England seemed to be changing hands, every county being represented in the great revival and in the stupendous transactions.'[93] Two years later the *Estates Gazette*, the house journal of the land agent industry, noted that one London firm of agents alone had sold 1.776 million acres across the UK in the previous four years, and speculated that if this extraordinary activity was representative of estate agents as a whole, 'one quarter of England must have changed hands in four years.'[94] As F. M. L. Thompson in 1963 pointed out in his seminal book *English Landed Society in the Nineteenth Century*, if the *Estates Gazette*'s calculations were correct, 'such an enormous and rapid transfer of land had not been seen since the confiscations and sequestrations of the Civil War, such a permanent transfer not since the dissolution of the monasteries in the sixteenth century. Indeed, a transfer on this scale and in such a short space of time had probably not been equalled since the Norman Conquest.'[95]

A very loud note of caution needs to be sounded here, however. In the wake of a cataclysmic world war when the old order and old certainties seemed to be in irreversible retreat, individual stories of aristocrats selling up houses and land must, understandably, have seemed confirmation of a broader social revolution. As the historians Professor John Beckett and Dr Michael Turner put it – the former the author of *The Aristocracy in England 1660–1914* – there was, at the time, a '. . . temptation to emphasise the significance of what was happening, to interpret the figures in the worst possible light, and to suggest that doom and gloom was everywhere'.[96] But contemporary assertions and figures don't really stack up. In the course of his research, Thompson himself came to doubt the accuracy of the *Estates Gazette*'s numbers, and in a lecture to the Royal Historical Society in November 1989 he suggested that what took place in those early decades of the twentieth century amounted to 'something far short of the collapse or catastrophe which has been over-dramatised by many commentators'.[97] Beckett and Turner, following up on Thompson's research, dug back into the statistics that the *Estates Gazette* had referred to, and found that far from the 8 million acres that would have had to change hands to justify the *Estates Gazette*'s claim, 2.1 million acres were sold, equivalent to about 6.5 per cent of the total land area of England.[98] That was still a considerable figure. But it certainly didn't represent a collapse.

What would be more accurate to say is that those years before and after the First World War saw not a retreat but a certain retrenchment. Some aristocrats who owned vast tracts of land – and it's worth bearing in mind in this context that George Sutherland possessed 1.3 million acres in the 1880s – sold some but kept much. They remained territorial magnates, and a few still retain that status in 2025. Others may have sold or demolished ancestral homes, but they often did so not for reasons of economy but because they had their eye on something they preferred. In 1912, John Egerton, 4th Earl of Ellesmere, bought Mertoun House in the Scottish Borders for £256,000 – more than £24.5 million today. When, two years later, his immensely wealthy father[99] died, John Ellesmere saw fit to sell Worsley (New) Hall,[100] the family's Lancashire home since 1748, and took up permanent residence at Mertoun with his wife Violet. True, Worsley was sold for £3.3 million, but then Mertoun had hardly been cheap, and it wasn't John Ellesmere's only house. He also owned Stetchworth Park near Newmarket, and the enormous Bridgewater House in St James's. Worsley would be demolished after the Second World War, following damage caused both by fire and occupation by the military, but the Ellesmeres did not do badly out of the rest of the twentieth century. In 1963, John Ellesmere's son, also called John, who we will meet later, inherited the Sutherland dukedom from his third cousin once removed. In general terms, the staggeringly wealthy became the extremely wealthy, and the extremely wealthy either remained extremely wealthy or became merely wealthy.[101]

* * *

By the late 1940s, after another cataclysmic world war, Wentworth's glory days were well and truly over. In 1947, it was leased to West Riding County Council, in a fifty-year deal brokered by Billy Fitzwilliam's elder sister Mabel,[102] at Peter's request, and in 1950, it became home to the Lady Mabel College of Physical Education.

The college closed in 1979, and students from Sheffield City Polytechnic moved in. Breeze-block accommodation was built in the park, and the riding school was converted into a gymnasium. In 1988, the house and seventy acres surrounding it was bought by the businessman Wensley Haydon-Baillie. A decade later, it was sold again to the architect Clifford Newbold. After Newbold died in 2015, the Wentworth Woodhouse Preservation Trust was able to secure the house and gardens, following a grant of £7.6 million given by the then chancellor Philip Hammond in the November 2016 Budget. Since then, they have begun to restore it. Although open-cast mining at Wentworth Woodhouse came to an end in the early 1950s, the damage it caused is still writ large on the landscape. The meadow turns to bog every spring. Even so, it remains, in the words of head gardener Scott Jamieson, a '. . . plant person's garden'. 'Although we have lost those wonderful trees and pathways and history, we have been gifted an openness that the garden didn't have. Nature has embraced it,' he says. The green-flowered helleborine comes back every year, moving around the garden. 'They live in established woodland and they're not usually interlopers. I like to think that successive generations of gardeners and family members have seen it.'

Wentworth Woodhouse remains an extraordinary – and extraordinarily bewildering – house. The first time I tried to negotiate a path from the archive in the south tower to the ladies' loos, I ended up in the chapel. On my second attempt, I wandered along a freezing corridor, mounted some ancient stairs and found myself in the old earls' bedroom. Eventually, I perfected a route that involved opening and closing eight doors and took five minutes to complete. The house is cold and dusty and endless, a labyrinth of corridors and rooms that are empty and echoey. The Long Gallery, used by Billy and Maud as a living room of sorts, once contained fifty paintings. Now it has none. The Van Dyck Room is destitute of any Van Dycks, just a photograph to remind the visitor of its former glories. An enormous gap is conspicuous in the Whistlejacket Room. The Lower Hall, once hung with big game trophies, is now home to a reception desk. Where once visitors would have signed their name in a large leather-bound book, now they wear lanyards bearing paper badges that note their time of arrival or they have to pay to enter. Just occasionally, one catches a glimpse of what the house must have been like before its contents were sold off in the late 1940s. In the green bedroom there are tapestry-covered chairs dating from 1740, on loan from Juliet. Next door, a photograph of her grandmother Maud at 4 Grosvenor Square hangs on the wall, opposite a drawing of her father Peter Fitzwilliam by Philip de László. Otherwise, there's almost nothing.[103] But in a way that's what makes Wentworth such a moving place to visit: its life, its emotions, all visibly lie in the past.

The Fitzwilliams, though, are still around. The last Earl and Countess Fitzwilliam, Tom and Joyce's daughter Lizzie-Anne had a son, Philip, with her first husband Sir Vivyan Naylor-Leyland, 3rd Baronet. Sir Philip, who succeeded his father as 4th Baronet in 1987, owns the 15,000-acre estate around the house, where wild red deer and cattle graze, and lives at Milton. In 1980, he married Lady Isabella Lambton, daughter of Antony Lambton, the disclaimed 6th Earl of Durham, and with her has six children. Their eldest son Tom named his son Billy. Juliet Fitzwilliam eventually inherited a large part of her father's estate and the bulk of the Fitzwilliam collection, much of which is on display at her home in Kent. In 1997, she sold *Whistlejacket* to the National Gallery. She first married Victor Hervey, 6th Marquess of Bristol, with whom she had a son, Lord Nicholas Hervey. Her second husband Somerset de Chair, with whom she had a daughter, Helena, died in 1995, and two years later she married the architectural historian Dr Christopher Tadgell. Together they have travelled the world. She still has a home in Malton, where her earliest days were spent.

Robin Fitzwilliam, her fourth cousin, lives near Oban, in the West Highlands. Peter was his godfather, and he himself was christened at Wentworth. 'I knew my name from an early age but I didn't appreciate the relevance and importance, indirectly and historically, of the Fitzwilliam family until I was in my twenties,' he says. Even if he had become Earl Fitzwilliam, he believes that Wentworth would still have gone out of the family – what remained would have been lost by his father, Richard 'Fitz' Fitzwilliam, who in the 1950s ran a team of MGA racing cars. 'Money went through his hands like nobody's business.'

Robin first visited Wentworth in the 1980s. As he parked by the east front, a man came out and asked if he would mind moving his car. 'Then he stopped and said, "You're a Fitzwilliam, aren't you?"' Robin said he was. The man said, "'Sir, I'm terribly sorry, do come in."'

Of all of them, Robin is the only one to retain the family name, while Juliet is one of very few alive who can remember the magic of the old Fitzwilliam world. Their family stand out in the narrative of the British upper class in the years surrounding the Second World War. They had not had to marry American money to support themselves, nor were they forced to sell their worldly possessions to pay death duties. Conspicuous decline, beyond the predictable, necessary changing nature of life in big houses post-war, was not on the cards – until Manny Shinwell came along.

2

A Handful of Dust

The Country House under Threat

Rupert Onslow, 8th Earl of Onslow, was heading back home to Leicestershire on 29 April 2015 after a day at Royal Ascot when the call came. It was his mother Robin, Countess of Onslow. 'She said, "There's a fire at the house," and I said, "OK, well, the fire brigade will come and put it out." But she said again, "No, there's a *fire* at the house." Halfway to the M1, I turned around and came back.'

He arrived at Clandon Park, near Guildford, at about 7.30 p.m., and from then until midnight stood on the lawn watching the house burn. The fire, thought to have been caused by an electrical fault, had broken out at about 4 p.m. in the basement, and, on account of a disused lift shaft that acted as a wind tunnel and fanned the flames, had rapidly spread through the house and up onto the roof. Local residents reported hearing loud bangs coming from inside the building; others saw flames shooting up. Sixteen fire crews struggled to save what they could, but by the time the blaze was brought under control, 90 per cent of the contents had been lost, including porcelain and furniture bequeathed by the collector Hannah Gubbay, a set of 1640s Mortlake tapestries, and one of the footballs kicked across no-man's-land on the first day of the Battle of the Somme. The state bed, commissioned in 1710 and too heavy for firefighters to retrieve before the evacuation call came, was badly damaged. Ironically a fire evacuation and disaster drill had been held just a few weeks earlier.

Until the day of the fire, Clandon, a Palladian mansion designed by the Venetian architect Giacomo Leoni for Thomas Onslow, 2nd Baron Onslow, in the 1720s, had boasted among its many treasures a magnificent marble hall – white, bright, and dazzling. When I visited nine months later, the hall was a grey, tortured shell. Daylight was visible through the upstairs windows. Ash and debris lay everywhere. As Rupert Onslow put it to me, not long after, 'The house was alive and now she's dead.'

For the Onslows the catastrophic fire at Clandon Park was the final chapter in a story of decline that had begun a century before. Created barons in 1716 and earls in 1801, they had in their time been a significant political force in the land, boasting Whig politicians and lord-lieutenants, a chancellor of the exchequer and speaker of the House of Commons, while Onslow women had made canny marriages.[1] At 13,000 acres the family estate may not have been particularly large by aristocratic standards, but it was nevertheless significant. Yet by the early 1900s William Onslow, 4th Earl of Onslow, claimed to be feeling the financial pinch. In 1906, he sold his son-in-law Rupert Guinness, Viscount Elveden, 700 acres on which to build his own house, Pyrford Court, with views across the Surrey Downs. Three years later, in the wake of a Liberal Budget which sought to increase taxes to fund social reform, he announced at a lunch with his tenants in Guildford that land could now 'never be looked upon as an investment but only as a luxury', and that he had no choice but to put a considerable portion of his estate up for sale.[2]

Contemporary press reaction was scathing. 'Pity the sorrows of poor Lord Onslow! Listen to his tale of woe!' wrote a journalist in the *Boston Guardian*.[3] In the *Daily News*, the radical Liberal politician and land reform advocate R. L. Outhwaite mocked the peer for his attempt to conjure up '. . . a vision of ancestral acres being wrenched from an unwilling hand, of the coming of a day when Guildford should know an Onslow no more'.[4] The *Norfolk News* was equally damning – and at considerable length:

> We trust that the country will give as much attention as it can spare from other matters to consideration of the hard case of the Earl of Onslow [its correspondent wrote]. This nobleman is the Chairman of Committees in the House of Lords. He is a Conservative. He had, in fact, held salaried positions in Conservative administrations and colonial positions, likewise salaried . . . when the Liberal party came into power it might have appointed one of its own supporters to the post of Chairman of Committees in the House of Lords, but it did not do so. It left the Earl of Onslow in comfortable possession of a salary of between £2,000 and £3,000 a year. That was not ungenerous. It was even noble. The post of Chairman of Committees in the House of Lords is not absolutely a sinecure, but it is not onerous. The Chairman of Committees in the House of Commons is a frightfully overworked man in comparison with the Earl of Onslow, but it is the Earl of Onslow who, receiving a quite comfortable and even generous recompense for sitting on occasion in the same seat in the House of Lords, announces that he is being driven to sell part of his estates, and dismiss many of his labourers, because of the manner in which he is being oppressed by the Budget. It seems that the Budget is oppressing everybody . . .

The paper still hadn't finished.

> Lord Onslow's point of view is that of the other landed proprietor who announced the other day that in consequence of the Budget he might find it necessary to cease to give tips to his railway porters. It is about equally noble and dignified, and we are afraid that we must go to the length of saying that Lord Onslow's statements about the effects of the Budget are quite without substance behind them. There is nothing in the Budget which should make him desirous of selling his land or of dismissing his labourers.[5]

In fact, William Onslow made good on his threat, selling 1,740 acres in July 1909 (though, as the *Northern Daily Telegraph* caustically pointed out, '[I]t is interesting to note that the auctioneer yesterday declared that some of the land was offered by his firm four years ago and was not sold.'[6]). Then, the following spring, he suffered a seizure while speaking at a political meeting in Guildford and found it necessary to cut back on his public engagements. A year later, he gave notice to his employees at Clandon, some of whom had worked for the family for forty years. Only the gardeners were spared. The estate office, he announced, would shortly be closed, and the management of the estate undertaken by agents on behalf of his son Richard 'Cranley' Onslow, Viscount Cranley. William Onslow justified his actions in a letter to *The Times*: 'Agreeable as it is to have men who can do any estate work at a moment's notice and even upon occasion economical, in making that "stitch in time which saves nine", it cannot be denied that it is a luxury that is not indispensable. As time goes on and large slices of estates have to go to pay death duties only the "nouveau riches" and a few owners of very large estates will be able to maintain a staff to do nothing but work on the estate.' He sketched out – possibly a little tactlessly – the future of a landowner placed in this 'new and different position': 'With a clear conscience he can now spend his time and money as an absentee and escape the rigours of the English winter in the South of France living there on the proceeds of sale of part of his estate invested abroad, where Mr Lloyd George's taxes cannot reach him.'[7]

Two family tragedies followed. That summer, the Onslows' younger son Huia – born during his father's tenure as Governor of New Zealand and so given a Maori name – hit his head while diving in the Tyrol and was paralysed from the waist down. He would survive for a decade, dying aged thirty in 1922. Then, in October 1911, William Onslow himself died, two years before his sixtieth birthday. To many he had come across as the typical hard-hearted lord of the manor. His son-in-law, Edward Wood, however, remembered him as 'a most sympathetic and delightful father-in-law, full of vitality and interest in everything'.[8]

Clandon now passed to William Onslow's son, the diplomat Richard Cranley, and his wife the Hon. Violet Bampfylde. But by the 1930s it was clear that the burden of upkeep that Richard

Cranley's father had so publicly complained about was similarly becoming too much for them. The new Onslows found themselves living in a decaying mansion with carpets that were worn out, doors that desperately required repainting, and curtains in the dining rooms that had been left untouched since 1801. They were not the happiest of families, either. Cranley may have been a clever man, but he had a reputation for being somewhat dull and very untidy. Violet, according to socialite and social climber Sir Henry 'Chips' Channon, was 'rude, a bully and cruel to her children . . . generally loathed by all' – and a hypochondriac and heroin addict to boot.[9] She was also mean. While her son and heir Arthur was away during the Second World War, Violet evicted his wife Pamela from an estate house because a delay to the payment of his army salary had meant that she had been temporarily unable to pay the rent. Pamela's view of her mother-in-law was encapsulated in a vignette she related to Rupert Onslow many years later. One day, she said, members of the family had been swimming in the top lake on the estate on a glorious summer day. Then Violet came along, and 'it suddenly went cold'.

Realising how tenuous the Onslows' grip was on Clandon, Channon – Cranley and Violet's nephew-in-law and, thanks in part to his marriage into the Guinness family, a wealthy man – entertained hopes that he might one day be able to call the house his own. It was, he reflected post-war, 'that most satisfying of all country houses'.[10] But the Onslows clung on.

In June 1945, just as the war was ending, Cranley died aged sixty-eight, and Arthur, who after the Libyan campaign, during which he had won the Military Cross, had been taken prisoner-of-war in Normandy, succeeded to the earldom. He and Pamela did what they could to keep the house going – after all, it had long been the centre of the Onslows' universe, both public and private. They economised wherever possible and sold off the occasional treasure to cover the bills. A Chippendale cock-fighting table and a pair of George I chairs went in a sale in 1947. A collection of family silver was disposed of three years later. There was a further sale in 1951. But Clandon was a white elephant, designed for another age. Whatever money the family could raise, it was never enough.

By 1949, it had got too much for Arthur, who resorted increasingly to the bottle to keep his demons at bay. He had what would probably now be diagnosed as post-traumatic stress disorder; he had come through the war, just about, and returned home to find a broken family business at Clandon that no one had cared about for five years, and yet, as the facilitator of his local 'welfare state', the head of his community, was not able to show any weakness. When he died twenty-two years later, it was, says Rupert Onslow, courtesy of over-consumption, 'but it has to be put into perspective', given all he experienced. Desperate measures were required. And so the Onslows turned to the people who would be in charge of the house on the fateful day in April 2015 when fire broke out: the National Trust.

* * *

The National Trust for Places of Historic Interest or Natural Beauty was founded in 1895 by three individuals with a strong sense of mission: Sir Robert Hunter, a solicitor and countryside campaigner; Canon Hardwicke 'Hardie' Rawnsley, a poet and priest; and Octavia Hill, a social housing campaigner. All three had become concerned about the ruthless speed with which Victorian England was demolishing its old buildings and building on its fields and woodlands. All three felt that active steps needed to be taken if much of the nation's heritage was not to be swept away by developers.

The Trust's early acquisitions were modest ones. In 1895, a four-and-a-half-acre strip of coastal land overlooking Cardigan Bay and the Llŷn peninsula in west Wales, Dinas Oleu, became its first piece of property, thanks to a generous donation by local philanthropist Mrs Fanny Talbot. This was followed by the fourteenth-century Clergy House in Alfriston in East Sussex, bought for £10 in 1896. Soon after came the Joiners' Hall,

Salisbury in 1898, the Courthouse at Long Crendon, Buckingham-shire in 1900, and the Old Post Office at Tintagel in 1903, all of which were acquired by the Trust with help from the Society for the Preservation of Ancient Buildings (SPAB). In 1907, the year an act of parliament declared National Trust properties inalienable unless their disposal was sanctioned by a further act of parliament, the Trust launched into its most ambitious undertaking to date: the splendid but almost derelict Barrington Court in Somerset. It turned out to be almost a bridge too far. According to National Trust historian John Gaze, the years the house took to restore 'made such an impression on [Trust secretary] Nigel Bond that thirty years later he greeted any suggestion of preserving a house with, "We cannot possibly afford to take it on: remember Barrington!"'[11]

The cautionary tale of Barrington Court helps explain why few significant country houses should have been among the Trust's pre-war acquisitions.[12] But the fact is that, in any case, there weren't too many large houses that appeared to need saving. The late-nineteenth-century agricultural depression might have made times more difficult for many landowners, but while some had felt it necessary to sell land, few had reached the point where the prospect of having to ask for help was on the cards. Such aristocrats as were involved with the Trust in its first decades were not supplicants, but supporters. Its early presidents included both Hugh Westminster, thought to be the richest man in Britain, and Frederick Hamilton-Temple-Blackwood, 1st Marquess of Dufferin and Ava, former Viceroy of India and owner of an estate in County Down.

In the years that followed the First World War, however, things started to change, and with them the nature of the landed gentry's relationship with the Trust. In 1925, George Curzon, who had devoted years to restoring Tattershall Castle in Lincolnshire and Bodiam Castle in East Sussex, opted to leave both to the Trust. Six years later, thanks largely to the generosity of Ernest Cook, a grandson of the nineteenth-century travel operator Thomas Cook, Montacute House in Somerset, which had been the home of Phelips family since its construction in 1598 and which Gerard

Phelips had put on the market in 1929, also came the Trust's way. Over the same period, as financial pressures on the landed aristocracy increased, the benevolent National Trust figureheads of just a few years started to become more active participants. The historian George Macaulay 'G. M.' Trevelyan, younger brother of Sir Charles Trevelyan, 3rd Baronet, who owned Wallington Hall in Northumberland, became involved with the Trust in 1925, when he began campaigning for the Brownlow family's Ashridge estate in Hertfordshire to go to the National Trust rather than be sold for development. In 1927 he joined the Trust's estates committee, and the following year was appointed its chairman, being joined by Oliver Brett, 3rd Viscount Esher, owner of Watlington Park in Oxfordshire. In 1932, Lawrence Dundas, 2nd Marquess of Zetland, owner of Aske Hall in North Yorkshire and brother of Maud Fitzwilliam (see previous chapter), was appointed overall chairman.

Two years later Lawrence Zetland invited another landed peer, Philip Kerr, 11th Marquess of Lothian, to address the National Trust's annual general meeting on what was by now becoming a growing national problem of great houses in decline. Philip Lothian was well placed to talk about the issue. He had succeeded to his cousin Robert Lothian's title in 1930 and at a stroke had found himself both the proud owner of a 230-year-old marquessate and four country houses, as well as the one responsible for the payment of death duties of £250,000. In his view, he told the meeting, Britain's country houses 'represent a treasure of quiet beauty which is not only specially characteristic but quite unrivalled in any other land'; but they were being squeezed out of existence by death duties.[13] There was, however, a potential solution at hand. If a list could be drawn up of the most important houses, and the government could be pressed to grant these immunity from death duties provided they opened to the public, then the Trust could step in as custodians and save these treasures for the nation.

Lawrence Zetland was impressed by the proposal, and when he joined the cabinet as secretary of state for India the following year, raised the matter with chancellor of the exchequer Neville

Chamberlain. Galvanised by their lord and master, the Treasury duly devised two schemes. One, for those not wishing to hand over responsibility for their houses altogether, involved a low level of tax relief on death duties in return for an agreement to open their houses to the public. This proved to have little appeal to most stately home owners and was swiftly dropped. The other scheme – which did prove popular – allowed for the cancellation of death duties altogether provided that the property in question was donated to the National Trust, alongside a cheque for its upkeep. Essentially, owners were given a stark choice: 'hand over *in toto* or do nothing.'[14]

By the following spring, a list of 230 suitable houses had been drawn up, and the first negotiations were underway.

The man responsible for rounding up country house owners who might be interested in collaborating with the National Trust was not an aristocrat himself, though he certainly moved in aristocratic circles. James Lees-Milne (generally known as Jim), the son of a farmer and cotton manufacturer, had grown up at Wickhamford Manor in Worcestershire in the 1910s, and attended Eton and Oxford, from which he emerged with a third-class degree in history. He had found out about the job at the National Trust via a rather circuitous if cosy route. His friend and sometime lover, the writer and diplomat Harold Nicolson, was married to the writer Vita Sackville-West. She had had a relationship with the BBC producer Hilda Matheson, whose brother Donald was, at the time, secretary of the National Trust.

Despite the financial pressures that so many owners of big houses were experiencing, finding ones who were prepared to sign up to the new scheme proved to be hard work. Of the 225 contacted by the middle of October 1936, a mere forty-two took up Jim's invitation to an initial meeting; and by the time war broke out in 1939 only one country house had actually made its way into the Trust's possession: Wightwick Manor in Staffordshire, which had previously belonged to the Liberal MP Geoffrey Mander.

When war came in 1939, Jim applied to join the Irish Guards, but he was discharged in 1941, following a diagnosis of Jacksonian epilepsy, and in the November of that year returned to the Trust. A diary he started to keep the following January gives an indication of the delicate and protracted negotiations in which he became involved. Sometimes they led nowhere. His diary entry for 5 January 1942, for example, chronicles his trip to Althorp, the Northamptonshire home of Jack Spencer, 7th Earl Spencer. Things looked hopeful when Jack told Jim that he was the first National Trust person who had talked sense. But Jim sensed that, '[T]he difficulties will be infinite before we get it.'[15] In the end Althorp never made its way into National Trust hands and remains the home of the Earls Spencer.

Knole, on the other hand, first mentioned in Jim's diary on 8 December 1941, did come to the Trust. The Kentish home of the Sackville-West family since 1603, it has often been described as a 'calendar house', with fifty-two staircases, seven courtyards and 365 rooms, though today the Trust claims that there are in fact about 400 rooms. Knole had been the childhood home of Vita Sackville-West, but when her father Lionel Sackville-West, 3rd Baron Sackville, died in January 1928, the house passed to the nearest male heir, Vita's uncle Major-General Sir Charlie Sackville-West, who assumed the title of 4th Baron Sackville. A veteran of both the Boer War and the Somme, where he had sustained several injuries, he was now in his seventies, tired, and all too soon overwhelmed by a house that cost £7,900 a year to run, despite only a skeleton staff of butler, cook and a single housemaid. He had first considered the Trust as a possible custodian for Knole as early as 1935, before the country houses scheme had been formally launched, and had invited Donald Matheson to Knole to discuss how this might be achieved. Over lunch he had complained constantly about how expensive the house was to maintain, and how, unless a suitable scheme could be devised, he would be obliged to pass the burden of ownership to his rather uninterested son Eddy, and ultimately to Eddy's future sons. 'Eddy's obstructive unborn sons were to become a sick joke throughout the prolonged negotiations,' Jim remembered.[16] At first Charlie hoped to deal with the problem of Knole via the Trust's halfway scheme – the one that was ultimately scrapped. By the time Jim went to meet him at Martin's Bank in March 1943, it was clear that it was the Trust or nothing.

It took three years to complete negotiations for the house, during which Charlie felt horribly torn. He knew that he had neither the money nor the appetite to keep Knole going. At the same time, he was tortured by the alternative. As Jim put it, '[W]as an irreversible hand-over of his great inheritance of over three and a half centuries going to be worth the candle?'[17] Right up until the last minute he was constantly threatening to pull out of the deal. When it was finally done, the Trust took control of the house, while the family kept the park and most of the contents. Charlie also signed a 200-year lease on private apartments in the house.

Knole was preserved for the nation. But Charlie resented the means by which it had been saved. As Jim described it: '[H]e did not see himself in the role of willing benefactor to the National Trust to be accorded grateful thanks on a public stage. He saw himself as the inheritor of a glorious palace the burden of which he had been forced by a disabling new world to shift on to the shoulders of an alien organisation while retaining, as far as it were possible, the status granted him by the old world.'[18] He resisted requests by the Trust for an official, stage-managed handover organised by its publicity department, and became irritated when members of the public began ringing up to ask about entry times before Knole had officially opened. What he thought of the thousand visitors who came to Knole over Easter 1947, and the couple of thousand who visited during the spring bank holiday, is fortunately not recorded.

Jim Lees-Milne's negotiations with the Onslows for Clandon proved rather less fraught. In the opinion of Chips Channon, the discussions would have been wholly unnecessary had Violet Onslow been less mean: she had money of her own, some of which stemmed from her husband's unentailed fortune, and this would 'have been just enough to keep Clandon going'.[19] As it was, she refused to help. Her son and his wife were therefore left with no choice but to invite Jim to the house for a preliminary conversation in November 1949. He wolfed down the tea he was offered. The Onslows ate nothing, weighed down by the enormity of what they were about to commit themselves to.

A deal was thrashed out whereby the Trust would take custody of the house and its seven-acre garden, and the family would loan them the contents of the state rooms. The sting in the tail was that the family also had to offer an endowment of £40,500 to ensure the future upkeep of the house. Such an enormous sum of money, representing over £1 million today, was wholly beyond what they could afford. Of course, had they had it, they wouldn't have had to talk to the National Trust in the first place. One morning therefore, having consumed a large glass of whisky to provide herself with the necessary Dutch courage, Pamela Onslow drove to Woking to ask her husband's aunt, Gwendolen Iveagh, if she could help. She agreed. A year later, *The Times* announced: 'The Earl and Countess of Onslow have left Clandon Park and have taken up residence at Little Clandon, Clandon Park, Guildford.'[20] The transfer was completed in 1956. Arthur and Pamela Onslow divorced six years later.

Some houses came to the National Trust almost effortlessly: by 1946 Thomas Noel-Hill, 8th Baron Berwick's Attingham Park, Sir Henry Hoare's Stourhead, Philip Lothian's Blickling Hall, Colonel John Lutley's Brockhampton Manor and Sir George Vernon's Hanbury Hall had all been made over to it in their owners' wills. Sometimes, the Trust was the recipient of a mere shadow of what once had been: the big house at Clumber Park in Nottinghamshire, which since 1711 had been the home of the Pelham family – made Dukes of Newcastle in 1756 – had been devastated by fire in 1879 and then finally demolished in 1938 ('there is not one vestige of the house left, nor of the terraces, nor the foundations, so that you can barely tell where the house stood,' Jim Lees-Milne wrote in January 1946).[21] What came to the Trust that year, therefore, was 4,000 acres of a once notable estate. And at Gawthorpe Hall in Lancashire discussions became so protracted that they were not brought to a conclusion until decades after Jim had left the Trust.

The Kay-Shuttleworth family who owned Gawthorpe had experienced more than their fair share of misfortune, with four direct heirs to the estate all dying before their time: two during the First World War, two during the Second.[22] Charles 'Tom' Kay-Shuttleworth, MC, who became 4th Baron Shuttleworth in 1942, survived the war, but was badly scarred by it. An officer in the Royal Artillery, he had crossed the Channel before the Battle of France in 1940, and as his son Charles Kay-Shuttleworth, 5th Baron Shuttleworth, explains, '[W]ithin a few days he found himself serving in a make-shift anti-tank unit, equipped with obsolescent field guns.' On 26 May 1940, he defended a bridge near Béthune under heavy fire and was awarded the Military Cross. Two years later, fighting in the Battle of Gazala, he was wounded twice – so badly on the second occasion that he lost one leg, and the use of the other.

Returning home in 1944 as the new Lord Shuttleworth, he found his aunt Rachel Kay-Shuttleworth manning the ship at Gawthorpe. 'There you are,' she said, as she handed the house over to him. 'We made £26 profit last year.' In 1949, with almost no money in the family coffers and struggling with his severe physical injuries, Tom had little choice than to turn to the National Trust.

Jim Lees-Milne visited Gawthorpe that November, three weeks before his trip to Clandon. Tom's wife Anne greeted him in the drawing room: '[O]ne of the best Elizabethan rooms I have ever been inside.' Tom was there too, 'a rather stiff, too serious, but extremely gallant young man who . . . is filled with a sense of duty to the locality. He sits on committees, dispenses patronages and does what is required of him.'[23] But, he made clear, he couldn't live at Gawthorpe. Not only was it impractical and prohibitively expensive to run, but it was hemmed in by open-cast mines and was accordingly filthy. 'I can remember the horror of the coal dust from the open-cast which was within fifty yards of the back door and the front, and on both sides of the drive up to it,' recalls Charles Shuttleworth. 'There was just clouds and clouds of black dust. It wasn't a very nice place to live – the grass was covered in black slime.'

Even so, it was not until 1970 that the Shuttleworths finally handed Gawthorpe to the National Trust, with Lancashire County Council taking a ninety-nine-year lease on it. The delay had been caused by lack of funds. 'The only way that the National Trust would agree to take Gawthorpe on was if there was a public campaign to raise funds to put it in good order,' says Charles Shuttleworth. 'That was the alternative to the normal process in which people handed over the house and a large dollop of cash.' He imagines that giving up Gawthorpe must have been a wrench for his father, but '. . . he could hardly walk, and he was married with a young family, so an Elizabethan mansion was not really the right place to be living. The kitchen was in the basement, and the dining room up a circular stone staircase, which my father couldn't get down.' The house was cold, too. There was no central heating and Charles Shuttleworth reckons that it would have taken several servants to keep all the many fires that were needed going – servants the family could not possibly afford. Ultimately, painful though the decision was, the National Trust was the only option for Gawthorpe.

Not all those families who handed their ancestral homes over to the Trust felt, in retrospect, that they had made the right decision. There is, even today, lingering discontent among some of those who still retain a few rooms in houses where their ancestors had the full run. But Rupert Onslow, for one, believes that his grandparents had no choice. 'There was no net spendable income in those days, for anybody. Clandon isn't that big compared to other country houses, but it's still a 40,000-square-foot building.' As for Charlie Sackville-West's successor but two, the publisher Robert Sackville-West, 7th Baron Sackville, his view is that: '[H]ad the National Trust not acquired the house in the 1940s, or even in the 1950s, I don't think Knole would be anything like it is today. There's a good chance that quite a lot of it would be pretty ruinous. In retrospect I can't think of many viable alternatives.' Born in 1958, nine years after the Trust acquired Knole, he was brought up in the seven-up, seven-down north wing while his father Hugh worked as the land agent. 'I realised that I lived in a really big stately home, and that I was incredibly lucky,' he says. The apartment he now lives in with his family in the south wing has eight bedrooms, plenty of reception rooms and a private garden. On the whole, it is not overlooked. 'You just choose the bit where you know there isn't a window looking over,' he says. 'You always know that there are people not very far away.' It works for him because he wants it to. 'For everyone's sake one has to make it work. It could become a terrible place to live if you were in constant conflict.'

* * *

By December 1950, in what was Jim's last year full-time at the Trust as historic buildings secretary, the National Trust had seventy-six houses in its care. Of these, ten had been transferred from families within the hereditary peerage – 13 per cent of the total. Over the next twenty-two years, the Trust acquired sixty-nine more historic houses, of which almost 40 per cent came from aristocratic families. Not every one of them came to the Trust out of family necessity. Walter Montagu Douglas Scott, 8th Duke of Buccleuch, for example, remained in possession of four stately homes and nearly 300,000 acres in England and Scotland when he presented the Trust with the medieval tower known as Dalton Castle in 1965. But many did. In most cases it was probably just as well that they did.

It wasn't just that these grand edifices were so expensive to keep in good repair. They also required an army of staff to look after them. They had, after all, been built at a time when domestic labour was cheap and the ostentation they made possible was regarded as essential. An aristocratic house wasn't just a home, it was a theatre for display: 'a family headquarters, a historic headquarters, part of the nation's heritage', as one peer put it to me some years ago. They were, as F. M. L. Thompson described in

1989, places for lord-lieutenants to host county events, for royals to visit, '. . . designed as the stage setting for lives of public display of the aristocratic presence, fountains of honour, hospitality, paternalism, and local power'. When the role of the aristocracy declined, so did the need for a public display. The big house became a 'social white elephant'.[24]

By the post-war period the servants who made that public display possible were becoming rather scarcer than they had once been. Between 1900 and 1945 the number of people in domestic service fell by three-quarters to 400,000. Between 1945 and 1963, it fell again to just over 200,0000 – many of whom were daily helps.[25] Demand was dropping too, as a comparison of two sets of small ads columns in *The Times* twenty years apart makes abundantly clear. In its 1 January 1936 edition the paper featured eighty individual advertisements for everything from governesses, to between maids to cooks, and one for a gardener. The Hon. Lady (Alathea) Fry, Evelyn Waugh's sometime sister-in-law, sought two housemaids for Oare House in Wiltshire; Lady Evelyn Parker, the youngest of Thomas Parker, 6th Earl of Macclesfield's fifteen children, required a 'good cook; thoroughly reliable, not under 30; two ladies; four maids, including kitchen girl' and a 'well-trained House-Parlourmaid' for her Cotswolds home; a 'titled family, near Oxted, Surrey, with eight servants' offered a weekly salary of 25s for an upper housemaid.[26] *The Times* edition for 4 January 1956, by contrast, featured just twelve advertisements, including four for cooks and a maid for 'Lady W' (who already had 'two in staff') to carry out 'general housework' in her Mayfair flat.[27]

The 'servant problem' was something that Jim Lees-Milne noted several times in the course of the travels he undertook for the Trust. By October 1942 Sir Henry and Lady (Alda) Hoare had been reduced to the services of a cook and a butler at Stourhead in Wiltshire. Even then they counted themselves lucky, as Jim observed: 'The Duchess of Somerset at Maiden Bradley has to do all her own cooking,' Lady Hoare said.[28] Other contemporary diarists, including Chips Channon, made similar observations. Sir Bertie and Lady Diana Abdy, whom Channon visited at their Cornish home of Newton Ferrers for lunch in August 1943, were found to have no cook, just a nursery maid. Odd job men were in precipitous decline, too; Jeremy Musson, in his 2009 book on domestic staff in the country house, has described how the loss of the man 'who had once swept the gutters and cleared the drains was in many ways as significant as the loss of a steward or a butler'.[29]

Not all were equally affected. As Jim observed, the former Chief of the Imperial General Staff Field Marshal Sir Archie Montgomery-Massingberd and his wife Diana spent the war in 'easy austerity', leading a 'feudal existence on a modest scale'[30] with a butler, cook, pantry boy, two housemaids and a chauffeur, even if they did offer only a plain dinner to their guest (the wine and spirits having been put away for 'patriotic reasons', they said).[31] The Devonshires at Chatsworth lived an extraordinary life right up until the 1970s, 'surrounded by works of art of the greatest rarity, living in this enormous house, with old retainers, servants and butler and footman and private telephonist on duty all day and night; and providing access to the public practically the whole year round'. 'Long, long may it last,' said Jim.[32] Michael Flower, 11th Viscount Ashbrook, told me in 2019 that for upwards of a decade after the Second World War his family retained the services of a butler at Arley Hall ('He was a very nice man – he and I had a wonderful relationship'). After that, 'things changed', though the Ashbrooks still employed servants at the house into the 1960s, even if by then 'it was a little bit different'. William Sackville, 11th Earl De La Warr, remembers his father having a cook and a butler in the 1950s: '[H]e didn't earn that much money but nonetheless that much money was enough to employ a cook and a butler, and as a child we had a nanny and a nursery maid under the nanny. When the butler left there was another one too.' When David Lascelles, 8th Earl of Harewood, was growing up at Harewood House near Leeds in the 1950s, there were at one point a butler and two under-butlers.

Even so, the general servant trend was ever downwards. Many among the upper classes found it difficult to adapt. Encountering

Horatia Durant, a cousin of Henry 'Master' Somerset, 10th Duke of Beaufort, Jim Lees-Milne noted how she 'exuded [a] sour smell of unwashed clothes: in this respect,' he went on, 'upper-class old ladies are worse offenders these days than lower. Explanation presumably is that they have been accustomed to maids washing their clothes for them, and now they have none.'[33] And if some of the upper class suffered a decline in their personal hygiene, so too the houses in which they lived tended to become dirtier, more unkempt. When, for example, Jim visited the Leicester-Warren family at Tabley House in Cheshire in September 1945, he found them still in possession of a butler and 'some four indoor servants of sorts' but living in serious disarray: 'all the wallpapers are torn, the walls damp, and the woodwork in need of paint.' The Leicester-Warrens, he added, '... don't in the least know what to do with the place, and are too old to adapt themselves to a new form of life in it.'[34]

It's not surprising, therefore, that those families who either could not or did not wish to come to an accommodation with the National Trust, sometimes resorted to extreme measures with their ancestral homes. I've already described the destruction of Clumber Park in Nottinghamshire. It was not a unique instance. As the Second World War receded into the past, the number of houses acquired by the Trust was rapidly overtaken by the number of great houses abandoned altogether by their owners or subjected to the wrecking ball. In 1955 alone, at the peak of the destructive wave that hit post-war Britain, forty-eight notable houses were partly or wholly demolished.

The government was aware of the growing problem but felt that there was little it could do. A report by the civil servant Sir Ernest Gowers, commissioned to define what role the state should take vis-à-vis Britain's country house heritage and published in 1950, recommended that it should not actively seek to acquire struggling properties, since they were invariably then put to institutional use and so ceased to be homes; and that if owners could not afford to keep their houses any longer then they should turn to the National

Trust's country houses scheme, ideally negotiating an agreement whereby they could remain in residence. Gowers was nevertheless aware that such a solution was not always available, and he lamented the existential threat so many of the country's architectural treasures now faced. 'It is not too much to say that these houses represent an association of beauty, art and of nature, the achievement often of centuries of effort, which is irreplaceable and has seldom, if ever, been equalled in the history of civilisation,' he wrote. 'Certainly nowhere else is such richness and variety to be found within so narrow a compass.' He quoted an unspecified Duke of Wellington: 'The English country house is in fact the greatest contribution made by England to the visual arts.'[35]

The timing of Gowers' report proved prescient, for the following year wholesale destruction took place at one of England's most important architectural treasures, Bowood in Wiltshire, a house so large that it was actually two, known somewhat unimaginatively as the Big House and the Little House – Bowood major and minor. The Big House, built mostly by Henry Keene in the 1750s, and altered by Robert Adam in the late 1760s, was the showpiece, with its Diocletian Orangery – now an art gallery – screening the service courtyards, and its seven-bay Doric portico. The Little House, adjoining the Big House, was the service wing, complete with an Adam drawing room hung with family portraits.

Bowood had been home since 1754 to the Petty-Fitzmaurice family, created Marquesses of Lansdowne in 1784. By the time, a century later, that the fifth incumbent, Clan Lansdowne, took up post as Viceroy of India, they were in possession of just shy of 143,000 acres in England, Scotland and Ireland, with a house in each: Meikleour in Perthshire, Derreen in County Kerry and Bowood, the Lansdowne palace in Wiltshire. As well as these, until 1929, the Lansdownes had an eponymous house on London's Berkeley Square, 'the family's baroque héréditaire . . . a monument to their liberal tradition', with rooms by Robert Adam, marble floors and a sculpture gallery by Robert Smirke.[36]

To the public then, and to us today, the Lansdownes appear

eye-wateringly rich. In 1883, five years before he assumed his post in India, Clan Lansdowne was – on paper, at least – the sixth-wealthiest marquess in Britain of thirty-three, and the sixteenth-richest peer overall, whose 142,000 acres yielded £62,025 a year.[37] But this apparent wealth was something of an illusion. In reality, Clan was saddled with his father's substantial debts, and with estates that cost £20,000 a year to run. Bowood, he once said, 'is not a poor man's residence'; it never made any money and required constant support from his bank, Coutts.[38] Clan held on to Lansdowne House out of a sense of pride, but pride did not pay the bills. Anxious to reduce his overdraft, he would now and again discuss selling Derreen, or letting Bowood; in 1887 he joked that unless his eldest son Henry, Earl of Kerry – always known as Kerry – married into proper money, the family might have to 'migrate permanently to South Kensington'. Disliking the 'humiliation of living shabbily in a large house and receiving hospitality that he could not return', he threatened to sell Lansdowne House – as Kerry, who never did marry proper money, would do in 1929 – as this would clear his debts and allow him a better standard of living at Bowood.[39] It's said that Clan was relieved never to have been offered a dukedom as his grandfather had, for one simple reason: he couldn't have afforded it.[40]

As for many aristocratic families, the first half of the Lansdownes' twentieth century was marked by loss. Kerry's nineteen-year-old son and heir, Maurice, died after being hit by a tube train at Regent's Park underground station in 1933. On his death, his brother Lord Charlie Petty-Fitzmaurice – 'a gentle, sensitive boy who, being unjudgemental and observant, could fit in with anyone', according to his friend Clarissa Spencer-Churchill, who later married Anthony Eden – became heir to the marquessate and assumed the title Earl of Shelburne. Three years later, when Kerry died aged sixty-four, Charlie became 7th Marquess of Lansdowne.[41] When war came he joined the Royal Wiltshire Yeomanry, while his younger brother Ned became an officer in the Irish Guards. In the early stages of the Battle of El Alamein in 1942 Charlie was badly burned when his tank was set on fire, though Henry Thynne, Viscount Weymouth, writing home to his wife Daphne that November, reported that Charlie was 'making grand progress, is in cracking form – and should be out in three weeks' time without a scar on him.'[42]

In the second week of August 1944, Ned was deep in Sourdeval, a thickly wooded region of Normandy. His company attacked up a hill, and, crossing the crest of the Sourdeval Ridge – later described by the Irish Guards as 'this horrible place' – found they had no cover.[43] Fire came at them from every direction. German snipers picked off the commanders. Ned was fatally wounded while helping an injured comrade. He was twenty-two years old. Hearing of Ned's death, his cousin Eddy Devonshire sought to get Charlie home. Nine days later, the tank Charlie was commanding in Italy was hit by enemy fire. It was initially reported that he had been taken prisoner-of-war. Then, in January 1945, his mother Elsie learned of '. . . reports that point to the conclusion that he has been killed in action'.[44]

Ned was buried in a cemetery in France. Charlie has no known grave and is commemorated on the memorial at Monte Cassino. A joint memorial service was held for the two young men in July 1945 at Calne Parish Church. Over the course of eleven years, Elsie Lansdowne had lost her husband and all three of her sons. 'My mother', remembered her youngest daughter Elizabeth, 'had so much tragedy in her life. We had thought we might lose one of them in the war but never ever thought we would lose them both.' Elizabeth had adored Charlie and he had adored her, writing her regular letters while on combat duty. She responded to her brother's death by '. . . shutting it away inside me . . . some may have thought me uncaring but that was how I dealt with my loss.'[45]

With Charlie and Ned both dead, it was their first cousin Captain George Mercer Nairne, then working as private secretary to Duff Cooper, ambassador to France, who became head of the family, as 8th Marquis of Lansdowne. Cooper described how, when Charlie's death was confirmed in January 1945, George '. . . seemed rather stunned by the news himself although he must have been expecting it.'[46] He had inherited the Lansdownes' Scottish estate, Meikleour, complete with a 580-yard beech hedge that was said to be the longest in the world, from his father who was killed in the First World War. Now he had two more estates to contend with, and a title to assume.

George was, by all accounts, something of a free spirit: charming, worldly and attractive. He loved female company, and they loved his. A friend of the family said at his funeral: 'George loved women and he married some of them.' In the end, he married four times.

He met his first wife on a polo field in California in 1937, having left Oxford without a degree. The pair could not have come from more contrasting backgrounds. He was steeped in the heritage and values of the British aristocracy. Barbara Chase came from small-town America and Puritan stock. They married in March 1938 at the Chase family home in Santa Barbara, and then returned to Meikleour, George carrying Barbara over the threshold of her new home as the housekeeper, marking a Scottish wedding tradition, broke a bannock – a Scottish oatcake – over her head. Barbara soon fell pregnant, giving birth to their daughter Caroline the following January. Her eldest son Charlie was born in 1941 in California, where she had fled for safety when the Second World War broke out. There, while George served with the Scots Greys, she worked in the British Embassy's press office in Washington, returning home to Meikleour – by then being used as a maternity hospital – in 1944. In the following years, she had two more children, Robert and Georgina. The younger Mercer Nairnes were brought up in the nursery by their nanny, and did not know their mother well. Towards the end of her life, Lord Robert Mercer Nairne remembers, 'she was profoundly unhappy,' and she died on his eighteenth birthday. Not particularly close to his father during childhood, he got to know George quite well towards the end of his life, but, even so, they never talked about the early years. 'My parents fought the good fight, and I will always be grateful to both of them for having stuck it out as long as they did, thereby endowing me with two such rich traditions,' he says.

When the official announcement came in January 1945 that Charlie Lansdowne was dead, George and Barbara considered their options. Meikleour was their home, but the question of what to do with Bowood required their urgent attention.

During the early years of the war, the Big House had been used by Westonbirt School, while Elsie Lansdowne, her second husband Lord Colum Crichton-Stuart, her younger daughter Elizabeth, and her elder daughter Kitty Bigham with her husband the Hon. Edward Bigham, had lived in the Little House. Elizabeth had been allowed to join the girls from Westonbirt and they had lessons all over the house, including the Adam orangery. After Westonbirt left, the Big House was let to the Air Ministry, while the Bighams remained in the Little House (as they continued to do until 1951). On their arrival in Wiltshire, George and Barbara moved into Buckhill House, the old land agent's accommodation on the estate. They then camped in the nursery wing of the Little House while they considered what to do.

It wasn't easy. After all, they didn't *need* the house, and it was, in any case, riddled with dry rot. 'When the house was taken over by the Ministry of Defence shortly after the beginning of the war, my cousin refused to sign an agreement with them to fully restore the house in the event of any damage during their occupation – a costly mistake,' says their son Charlie Petty-Fitzmaurice, 9th Marquis of Lansdowne. 'The contents had been dispersed, so there was nothing in it.' The prospect of demolition began to raise its head.

What followed was some complicated horse trading. The Settled Land Act of 1925 that Clan Lansdowne had employed to ensure that his landholdings would pass to his successors had involved restrictions being placed on the resale of the land. Charlie Lansdowne had bequeathed most of his possessions, including Bowood's contents, to his sisters, Kitty and Elizabeth. Kitty and her husband were trustees of his will, so they decided which items should be designated 'heirlooms', to be placed in trust together with the house and gardens. It was agreed that Kitty would give many of Bowood's contents to George in exchange for the house and estate at Derreen. Kitty and Edward's middle son, the Hon. David Bigham, remembered how 'awful' it was to leave Bowood, 'but we were extremely lucky to have this wonderful place in Ireland to come to.'[47] 'It was a wonderful thing for George to agree to,' says Elizabeth's son Julian Lambton. 'Derreen is a place which we all love with all our hearts. It is the most beautiful place in the world. I would rather have Derreen than Bowood any day, and Mum was never happier than at Derreen.'

That left the question of what to do with Bowood. The answer, the family decided, was partial demolition: they would bulldoze the 100-room wing that had been built for Sir Orlando Bridgeman in about 1730. 'Lord Lansdowne feels that the change will improve Bowood both in appearance and as a residence,' *The Times* reported.[48] In anticipation, George sold off hundreds of architectural fixtures and fittings – marble fireplaces by Robert Adam, staircases, doorways, windows and mouldings. The south elevation, including the portico with its Doric columns, was offered as one lot.

Unsurprisingly, not everyone approved. A correspondent to *The Times*' letters pages, Miss Ann Webber, described Bowood as too important to be touched. 'Doubtless there are sound economic reasons why this famous house should be destroyed. But was it not in order to cope with a situation that has got beyond the resources of any one person that the Government set up in recent years the Historic Buildings Council, the advisory committee of the Ministry of Housing, and the whole rigmarole of scheduling, listing, and building preservation orders?'[49] George responded a few days later: 'No one would deny that in these days the reduction of some 90 to 100 rooms might be considered as a practical improvement to a private residence ... I was reluctantly driven to the decision that if anything was to be saved of Bowood as a habitation something would have to go.'[50]

Jim Lees-Milne then got involved. 'The responsibility of inheriting a great house today is most unenviable,' he conceded. 'Yet whatever Lord Lansdowne may imply, Bowood is one of England's great houses which should somehow have been preserved ... the block about to be destroyed contains a number of apartments as masterly and perfect as any Robert Adam created ... the dining room with its coved and coffered ceiling and its plaster panelled walls is a chef-d'oeuvre not excelled by this architect anywhere else.'[51]

George remained unmoved. Shortly after the sale of its fixtures, which raised £8,000, the Big House came down, and a vast 130,000-square-foot edifice was reduced to a very large 50,000-square-foot one. 'It was a very brave decision,' says Charlie Lansdowne. The event was judged to be mundane enough that he should stay at Eton the day the demolition crew came to Bowood, and not be present to see the wrecking ball in action. 'What it has resulted in is a house which is much softer and more liveable,' he says. 'The Big House was a typical Georgian house for mega entertaining. The one we live in now is the domestic element, the support element of that bigger house.' Like his father, he was relatively unfazed by the changes at Bowood. 'I was fourteen, and it didn't hit me very hard,' he says. 'It didn't send a shiver down my spine. Our home was at Meikleour. I had been to Bowood, but I'd never lived in it. We had lots of friends in Scotland and we had none at Bowood. It was awkward, an interruption in our lifestyle.'

In February 1973, thirty-one-year-old Charlie Lansdowne, then Earl of Shelburne, moved into Bowood when George Lansdowne left for Meikleour. 'I would have pursued a political career if this hadn't turned up,' he says. 'My father didn't want to have two places to run, and he said he would leave and go back to Scotland, where his heart was, and he would leave me to get on with this.' In early 1975, Charlie opened Bowood to the public.

By then, what might be termed the country house industry was in full swing.

3

Put Out More Flags

From Stately Home to Business Enterprise

On 15 April 1950, alongside a news story about meat rations, the following item appeared in *The Times*: 'In response to many requests *The Times* has compiled a list of English country houses of special interest which are now open to the public or are being prepared to receive visits from the public during the summer.'[1] There followed a list of fifty-four houses in twenty-six counties.

One of those mentioned was Longleat House in Wiltshire, for 383 years the home of the Thynne family. A prodigy house, built of Bath stone between 1568 and 1580 by Robert Smythson for Sir John Thynne, steward to Edward Seymour, 1st Duke of Somerset, it boasts 128 rooms, including an Elizabethan great hall and a vast library of 40,000 books. The surrounding parkland was designed in the eighteenth century by Lancelot 'Capability' Brown.[2]

The man responsible for opening Longleat to the public was born Lord Henry Thynne on 26 January 1905. As the younger son of Thomas Thynne, 5th Marquess of Bath, and his wife Violet Mordaunt, he had not initially been in line to inherit Longleat, but his destiny had changed at a stroke when his older brother John Thynne, Viscount Weymouth, was killed in France in February 1916. The news was imparted to Henry 'in a rather brief and off-hand fashion'. 'There was no family conclave at which I was told solemnly that I was now the heir,' he later recalled. 'Perhaps they thought I was too young to appreciate what had happened. But children are surprisingly sensitive ... I knew perfectly well that I was the only surviving male of the family and that the great house in which we lived would in due course be mine and that I would be responsible for it.' He walked to the front steps of Longleat and, gazing at the house, said to himself, '"I will never be able to look after you."' 'I was', he remembered, 'terrified of this enormous building.'[3]

His terror was understandable. Even in the middle of the First World War, when the world could not conceive of a second, nor of the social changes that were to come in the intervening years, Longleat, with its indoor regiment of forty-three servants, an expensive French chef, a company of fifty gardeners, and a platoon of fourteen stable staff – including a boy whose sole job was to polish the horses' bits – presented its next custodian with a mighty challenge. Thirty years later, on 9 June 1946, this challenge became Henry's personal burden, when his father Thomas Bath, who, accompanied by his Great Dane Stephen, had shared the house during the war years with the Royal School for Daughters of Officers of the Army, died aged eighty-three. Henry was now 6th Marquess of Bath.

Who needed a house like Longleat anymore? he wondered. Who required so many rooms and outbuildings? And who wanted to live in a house where the footmen still had their hair powdered for big house parties, as they had done during Henry's childhood? It all seemed so unnecessary and old-fashioned, not to mention over the top and staggeringly expensive in a country 'where our kind had rather lost our place' and where, in his view, 'the influence of the great families hardly counted anymore.'[4]

In the short term, Henry had to find a way to pay off the £600,000 in death duties that had come with his inheritance. Ignoring advice that he should sell his stocks and shares rather than his land, he quickly disposed of 280 acres at Church Stretton in Shropshire, where Sir John Thynne, the builder of Longleat, had been born in 1512. Further land sales followed over the next decade, bringing the total to 9,000 acres. In 1954 Henry presented the National Trust with the local landmark Cley Hill. By the time his sales spree was over, the Baths' landholdings were down to 1,000 acres of parkland at Longleat, and 9,000 acres contiguous to it.

Henry's actions were pragmatic. Rather than try to keep spinning so many plates, he opted to consolidate his possessions and his financial position. But even though he was now left with just one estate, that estate was more than large and money-hungry enough to defeat the average marquess.[5] Perhaps, he initially thought, he could offer the house to the cabinet as a country retreat, just as Chequers had been given to the nation for the prime minister's use by politician and co-founder of the Courtauld Institute Arthur Lee, 1st Viscount Lee of Fareham, in 1917. But somehow that didn't seem very satisfactory. Perhaps, given that Henry, his wife Daphne and their four surviving children preferred living in their Georgian manor house Sturford Mead, a few miles from Longleat, it might be worth seeing whether opening the house to the public could be made to pay its way. After all, the area was already a popular holiday destination. Longleat stands not too far from the Baths' Cheddar Gorge, the limestone landmark and Somerset beauty spot that had long attracted a steady stream of tourists and where a 9,000-year-old human skeleton had been unearthed in 1903. If he could put the house in order, get the furniture and pictures back in place, and make sure that the silver was polished, he could charge half-a-crown a head for a guided tour.

Over the next three years, Henry, Daphne and the wider Longleat family worked to make the house the sort of place that people would be prepared to pay to visit. The land agent Thomas Gill worked out a tour route through the house; Henry's elder sisters Kathleen Stanley and Emma Northampton restored the furniture to its pre-war layout, while Daphne wrote a guidebook for visitors. Henry had the Baths' nineteenth-century state coach placed in the entrance hall, surrounded by dummies dressed in the family livery to create a Tussaud-like tableau. As work neared conclusion, he began a recruitment drive, hiring guides, parking attendants and cleaners.

Finally, on 1 April 1949, Longleat opened to the public. Everyone in the family was given a job. Daphne and her daughter Lady Caroline conducted guided tours, while the Thynne boys Alexander, Viscount Weymouth, and his younger brothers Lords Christopher and Valentine, worked in the car park. Henry was the ringmaster and the focal point, who would happily stand on the front steps to greet people and sign autographs. In the first year the house was open, 115,000 people visited Longleat. Among them was a Mexican man who approached Henry and, waving his chequebook, offered him £2 million for the house. Henry declined.

The new Lord Bath became used to being gawped at by the public. 'I had to learn to live with the fact that as far as the visitors were concerned I was one of the more interesting pieces of furniture,' he remembered. 'I rather doubt whether I lived up to their expectations. Instead of standing at the top of the main staircase wearing a coronet and my father's Garter robes, I tended to drop in from my work round the estate dressed in my usual careless fashion of corduroy trousers and an old sports jacket.' Visitors would approach him to ask: 'Are you Lord Bath?' And when he admitted that he was they would turn to their companion and say: 'You've lost your bet.' Henry observed that 'people seem to have retained a conception of the aristocracy, that we have long since lost ourselves. When I was young it was still a matter of consequence to have a title, but all that has, largely, gone by the board.'[6]

What Henry and Daphne elected to do wasn't wholly novel. Owners of country houses had, since the eighteenth century, allowed members of the public to have a quick look around. But Longleat nevertheless marked an important departure. In previous eras visitors had usually only been admitted when the family weren't there – while they were staying at one of their other estates or at their house in town. The Hon. Rosalind Stanley, the tyrannical future Countess of Carlisle, had been none too happy when she and George Howard, the future 9th Earl of Carlisle, turned up at Naworth Castle in Cumberland on their honeymoon in 1864 to find it packed with tourists. 'The visitors to the castle are rather a nuisance,' she complained to her mother.[7]

Much of the appeal of visiting Longleat, by contrast, was to be welcomed and shown round by the family who owned it. There was another important point of difference from the past, too. In previous eras an excursion to see a great house had not involved money changing hands, apart from a token payment to the accompanying servant; it was seen as '. . . a cultural and political gesture on the part of both aristocratic hosts and the mass of guests'.[8] The opening of Longleat, however, was an avowedly commercial exercise.

* * *

Where the Baths led, the Marlboroughs soon followed, albeit initially in a rather amateur fashion. Bert Marlborough had employed only one professional guide when the house officially opened to the public on 1 April 1950, and the result, as the expectant crowd surged in, was total chaos. The rest of the family was swiftly pressed into service, as was Henry 'Porchy' Herbert, 6th Earl of Carnarvon, who was staying that weekend. Serial Marlborough biographer David Brontë Green, who was present that day and who had coached that single guide as best he could, recalled that it was as though 'every living soul west of the Iron Curtain was heading for Blenheim' on that first day.[9] 'Hordes of people suddenly arrived and the whole thing was completely out of control,' Rosemary Muir remembers. 'We thought there would be a few people from the village who might like to come and wander round, but there was a queue right down through Woodstock onto the main road – hundreds of people. It was the first time [the house] had been formally opened on that scale. We just didn't understand it at all.' It was too much for Bert who was found later that afternoon, slouched and with his eyes closed, in a leather chair in the Great Hall. 'Someone left a baby in the hall,' he said wearily. 'It cried for a solid hour.'[10]

The family soon got the hang of things, and by 1967 they were welcoming 170,000 visitors a year. Today, Blenheim Palace is the most-visited privately owned stately home in the country. According to the Association of Leading Visitor Attractions, it welcomed over 958,000 visitors in 2024.

The opening of Woburn Abbey in Bedfordshire to the public in 1955 proved an even greater challenge to the family who owned it. At least, as a child, Henry Bath had had an inkling of what his future destiny might be; and he had grown up, along with his youngest sister Mary and their nanny, on the top floor of the house whose doors he was to throw open to those prepared to pay their half-crown. Ian Russell, 13th Duke of Bedford, by contrast, claimed to have found out that he was related to a duke only by chance from a parlourmaid at Woburn in 1933, when he was sixteen.[11] 'It simply never occurred to me that my grandfather was a duke,' he remembered, 'and as there was a complete conspiracy of silence on the subject, there was no reason why it should.'[12]

His ignorance was scarcely surprising. His grandfather, the military-minded Herbrand Russell, 11th Duke of Bedford, had fallen out so badly with Ian's father, the pacifist turned far-right supporter Hastings 'Spinach' Russell, Marquess of Tavistock, that they did not speak for twenty years. Hastings, in turn, had become estranged from Ian when his son was twenty-one and had refused to support him financially. They had never been close. Like his own father, Hastings had lacked any paternal feeling and was incapable of expressing his emotions.[13] During family holidays fishing in Galloway, he had gone out of his way to make 'quite certain that there was nothing in the pool' before he allowed his wife Louisa and his three children to fish.[14] So poor were relationships between the generations, indeed, that during his father's thirteen-year tenure at Woburn, Ian was not allowed near. His return was made possible only by two family tragedies. First Herbrand Bedford died broken-hearted in August 1940, three years after his aviator wife Mary had perished in a plane crash in the North Sea. Then Hastings himself died in October 1953 when a shotgun he was carrying somehow discharged itself while he was out shooting on his Devon estate. Since his father was an accomplished shot, Ian found it

'... quite incredible that a man with that much experience could have had an accident with a gun'.[15]

The Woburn Ian returned to was a sad shadow of its former self. Home to the Political Warfare Executive during the Second World War, it had been found to suffer from dry rot and had, as a result, been subjected to a ruthless partial demolition job by Hastings Bedford. Ian recalled later that the house looked 'as if a bomb had fallen on it'. He found 'piles of stones and building materials lying in a haphazard fashion all over the place', while 'the courtyard in the centre of the house was full of Nissen huts. There were one or two workmen around, but otherwise the place was deserted.' Creepier still were the 'troop of Alsatian dogs, chained to long wires, [keeping] watch at most of the gates ... you could hear them barking and their chains rattling, like some eerie scene out of *The Hound of the Baskervilles*.' Inside, the house was freezing cold and had all the appearance of 'a series of bankrupt auction rooms'.[16] There were mounds of furniture everywhere, mostly uncovered by protective dust sheets. Linen baskets were piled high in the front hall. The whole place was dirty, unloved and stank of damp. Ian's understandable verdict was that his father had not 'paid any attention whatsoever to the details of upkeep'.[17]

At the time Ian inherited Woburn he was living in South Africa with his second wife Lydia Lyle, where they were making a living on a fruit farm. It was an open question, therefore, whether he should remain in the country he had now made his home and sell off the ancestral pile, or return to England and grapple with the challenges that Woburn posed. His inclination was to go with the former course of action, not least because, as he later recalled, '[W]hat with death duties and the inability to carry out one's responsibilities it seemed to me that there was no future for the aristocracy in England.'[18]

He wrote to his friend, the politician and owner of the *Daily Express* Max Aitken, 1st Baron Beaverbrook, to ask what he should do. Beaverbrook, he thought, would give him good advice: he was 'one of those people whom you may not see for five years, yet the contact remained as warm and friendly as if you met him every day'. Beaverbrook's reply surprised him: '[C]ome back and get on with the job you are supposed to do as Duke of Bedford.'[19] Ian duly returned to England in spring 1954.

The challenges he faced were immense. Not only was Woburn in a parlous state, but there were death duties to pay that amounted to a staggering £4.5 million. Gallingly, these could largely have been avoided had Hastings Bedford lived just two months longer. One option was to hand Woburn over to the National Trust, but Ian was unwilling to do this, his argument being that: '[I]f Woburn was sold or otherwise disposed of to the National Trust or some institution, something would have gone out of the family and indeed the history of England which could never possibly be replaced.'[20] That left him with only one course of action, so far as he was concerned: to open the house to the public and make it pay its way. His trustees were not convinced, telling him that it seemed highly unlikely that a venture of this sort would earn enough. But Ian was undeterred. The future of the Bedfords and their 'right to exist in the second half of the twentieth century', he said, 'were bound up with the reopening of Woburn'.[21]

Having been exposed to country house culture only briefly as a child, and having previously lived abroad, Ian was acutely aware that he had much to learn. He accordingly made a couple of incognito trips to other stately homes to see how things were done. He was unimpressed. Owners, he felt, were '. . . all doing it rather on the theory that the sooner the visitors were in, the sooner they would be gone, and the quicker you got the money the better, and good-bye'.[22] Such an approach held no appeal for him. 'I wanted to make people enjoy themselves,' he wrote later, 'give them service and value for money, and make sure they would come back again.' At the same time, he wanted Woburn to be the proper home of the Duke of Bedford again, and to give his three children somewhere to live '. . . where we could all be amused and enjoy ourselves, a place where every member and generation of the family could have something which gave him a central point of attraction in his life'.[23]

The task that lay before him was immense. Apart from a night watchman or two, and a handful of labourers, there were few estate workers he could call on for help. The house was a tottering shambles, strewn with miscellaneous furniture and uncatalogued paintings. But Ian found the challenge strangely liberating. There was no one around to hover over his shoulder and say: '[T]hat was not the way grandmother had it.'[24] He and Lydia could arrange things any way they liked. They proceeded to clean and clear one filthy room at a time, and then refurnish and redecorate according to their own taste, choosing what picture or *objet d'art* should go where. Ian focused on the pictures, which were all in the Long Gallery '... in rows about twelve feet deep from the wall, with their backs to us'. They had no idea what was what: was it a Van Dyck or was it 'my great-aunt painted by her sister'?[25] Lydia concentrated on the furnishings, 'much the hardest task' in Ian's view.[26] When she died in 2006, she was described as 'a good sport, ready to enter into the spirit of the age'.[27] Friends who pitched up at Woburn were immediately roped in to help. One day, the working party found an 800-piece set of Sèvres porcelain that had been given by Louis XV to Gertrude Bedford, wife of the 4th Duke, in loose boxes in one of the stable blocks. The Bedfords washed it up themselves.

The grand opening took place on Good Friday, 8 April 1955. In the first year, Woburn welcomed 181,000 people through its doors. But simply opening the house to the public wasn't enough. Ian had to advertise the fact, too, and never be too proud to turn down any commercial opportunity that came his way. 'He knew that he had to publicise the Abbey opening as much as he could,' says his grandson Andrew Russell, 15th Duke of Bedford, who took over at Woburn in 2003. 'In those days nearly a million people came to the house ... There were films [made] of people queuing outside, and him walking down the queue. It was the card he was dealt. It was an all in or bust situation.' Like Henry Bath, Ian Bedford became an attraction for those visiting his ancestral home, and as 'an old gossip' didn't mind indulging in some chat, particularly when he discovered that guidebook sales shot up if he was there to sell them. 'Everyone wants to shake me by the hand or have my photograph taken with mum, dad, and the kids,' he remembered. 'I had no idea until I started this sort of thing that one has separate muscles for smiling. At the end of the day my face ache[s] so much that I think if I grin once more I shall go crazy.'[28] He developed a habit of asking visitors what they liked best at Woburn and then noting it all down. He thrust himself unashamedly into the public eye. 'I have been accused of being undignified,' he said. 'That is quite true, I am . . . I don't think there is any point in being toffee-nosed or sticking your nose in the air and pretending you're something you are not. Being a showman is much more fun than sitting about in dignity or potting pheasants.'[29]

Andrew Bedford, a tall man, with a big brush of dark hair, who dresses in the ducal uniform of shirt and shooting jacket, and who works at the bloodstock auctioneers Tattersalls, has not adopted the public persona his grandfather felt obliged to assume. But, as he says, 'he just did things differently then'. Ian was: 'A personality. Nowadays, it's not about being a personality, it's about looking after the place, our team, and our visitors, and keeping the show on the road.' One might observe that these days, when people think of 'Bedford', they would say it's a place rather than a dukedom. After all, the ducal profiles have certainly diminished. Still, when I visited him at Woburn, I was told to call him 'Your Grace' and to stand up when he entered the room.

* * *

At Longleat, meanwhile, Henry Bath embarked on an ambitious new venture to attract yet more visitors: he introduced a safari park. Keeping exotic animals in the parks and gardens of a stately home was not in itself an innovation. As early as the eleventh century, members of the nobility had maintained menageries on their estates as prestige symbols. Not to be outdone, Henry III started a collection of animals at the Tower of London that, by his death in

1272, included lions, a polar bear and an elephant. In more recent times, Charles Lennox, 2nd Duke of Richmond, kept lions, tigers, monkeys and wolves at Goodwood in West Sussex in the eighteenth century; the Fitzwilliams at Wentworth not only had a bear and attendant bearkeeper, but a range of other wildlife that included antelope, an armadillo and an emu as late as the mid-nineteenth century. And at Woburn at the turn of the century, Herbrand Bedford, for thirty-seven years president of the Zoological Society of London, introduced a small number of Père David's deer, so ensuring the preservation of the species when it later became extinct in its native China. But as with allowing visitors into stately homes in the eighteenth and nineteenth centuries, no commercial considerations had been involved in making room for wild animals. Having an exotic beast or two on your estate was a bit like having a living, breathing and roaring version of an architectural folly. It was something to exhibit – and the more people who knew, the better – not to make money from.

At Longleat, though, this was about to change.

One day in 1964, Henry Bath's eldest son Alexander Weymouth received a telephone call from his friend David Booth-Jones of Hale Park, near Salisbury. Booth-Jones had, he said, been approached by the circus owner Jimmy Chipperfield who had asked if the Booth-Joneses would be interested in keeping lions in their park that the public could come to view. The family had discounted the idea, but they wondered whether the Baths might be interested.

Henry was initially a little sceptical, but he nevertheless agreed to meet Chipperfield that November. Later, the showman recalled his introduction to Longleat. 'I drove slowly down the long drive into his lovely park at Longleat, set among steeply-rolling hills and studded with ancient trees: if I owned this lot, I was thinking, I wouldn't have a dog walk in it, let alone a pack of lions and millions of people looking at them.'[30] It took a while for him to explain his idea to Henry, who initially thought that Chipperfield's plan involved building vast cages that drivers would pass through as they viewed the lions. No, Chipperfield explained: '[T]he lions won't be in any cage at all, except the fence round the outside. It's the people who'll be in the cages – in their cars.'[31]

Three weeks later, Henry told Chipperfield that they had a deal, and the two men ranged the park at Longleat to find a suitable spot for the lions. They alighted on an area that bore some resemblance to African lion country: Hazel Copse. Chipperfield then bought fifty lions – at a cost of £9,821 15s 7d[32] – while Henry got busy erecting special fencing, roads and entrance buildings, at a cost of £32,722 9s 7d.[33] Henry's trustees grumbled: it seemed such a gamble. But then, opening the house in 1949 had been a gamble, and that had paid off. They decided to give him the benefit of the doubt.

News that an enclosure for large, carnivorous mammals was being planned for Wiltshire soon got out and, not surprisingly, caused some alarm. One particularly concerned member of the public complained to the county council and their local MP, Lynch Maydon, and before Henry knew what was happening, the story had become national news. *The Times*, for one, was unimpressed by the plan. In a leading article on 2 September 1965, it took Henry severely to task. 'Sporting competition between owners to make their stately homes and broad-acred parks the mostest for visitors is all very well,' it opined, 'but there are limits, and in proposing to enlarge a pride of lions in a compound on his Wiltshire estate, the Marquess of Bath has overstepped them.'[34]

Henry carried on regardless, and on the morning of Tuesday 5 April 1966 was on hand at the safari-park gates to take the first motorist's pound note. By Good Friday, three days later, cars were arriving in a never-ending stream. Soon the roads between Warminster and Longleat became jammed. On Easter Sunday some visitors had to wait five or six hours to get in. By the end of the Easter weekend, 50,000 people had come to see the lions. By the season's end, the park had played host to 160,000 cars and nearly 2,000 coaches.

Later, Henry argued that the lions saved Longleat. Before the safari park opened, the greatest number of visitors the house had welcomed in any one year had been 135,000. At the end of the safari park's third year, it received 318,000. Chips Channon had predicted 'the end' for Longleat when Henry and Daphne's divorce had been filed in April 1953.[35] Now he was proved to have been comprehensively wrong.

Not surprisingly, where Henry Bath led, other stately home owners followed. In 1970, Ian Bedford opened Woburn Safari Park, and the following year, John Stanley, 18th Earl of Derby, threw open the gates of his own safari park at Knowsley Hall on Merseyside. All three safari parks remain open today.

* * *

For Henry Bath and Ian Bedford, opening a stately home to the paying public was a gamble that paid off. Freddie Gordon Lennox, 9th Duke of Richmond and Gordon's gamble was of a very different nature: to save his ancestral home, he opened a motor-racing track.

Born Lord Frederick Gordon Lennox in February 1904 at his family's home in Marylebone, Freddie was the second son of the future 8th Duke and Duchess of Richmond, Charles and Hilda Gordon Lennox, then Earl and Countess of March. Like Henry Bath, Freddie was the spare rather than the heir – and like Henry Bath, his destiny was transformed by family tragedy. In 1919 his brother Charlie, Lord Settrington, was killed aged twenty while fighting with the White Russians near Archangel. When the news reached the Richmonds at Gordon Castle in Moray, Freddie found his father staring into space. For a while, neither of them was able to speak. Then Charles March put out a hand, pulled his son close, kissed him on the forehead and said, 'Well, Fred, it's only you and me now.'[36] In honour of his dead brother, and after some family debate, Freddie became Lord Settrington. When his grandfather the 7th Duke died in 1928, he became Earl of March and Kinrara, and then in 1935 after his father's death, 9th Duke of Richmond. He is the only Duke of Richmond not to have been called Charles.

The founder of the line, Charles Lennox, 1st Duke of Richmond, was an illegitimate son of Charles II who bought a late-Elizabethan house at Goodwood in West Sussex in 1697. But the family's ascent to real wealth and influence came nearly a century later, in 1789, with the marriage of Charles Lennox, 4th Duke of Richmond, to Lady Charlotte Gordon, daughter of the Scottish magnate Alexander Gordon, 4th Duke of Gordon. In 1836, this association brought the Richmonds the Gordons' extensive Scottish holdings, and by 1883 they were veritable territorial magnates, possessing 286,411 acres across six counties, worth £79,683 a year.[37] Thanks to their Scottish estates, fishing became something of a raison d'être for male members of the family. When a suggestion was made that a swimming pool should be built at Gordon Castle, some expressed scepticism that any member of the family would ever want to use it. 'As far as I'm concerned,' said Freddie's uncle Lord Esmé Gordon Lennox, 'water is a thing you get fishes out of.'[38]

When Freddie became duke he inherited not only the vast Richmond landholdings, but death duties of £170,000, mortgages totalling £250,000, and a surplus of estates that he had no particular interest in. 'We'd got no money,' he later said, 'not a bob in the bank and no industrial shares. We had to make ourselves liquid and the only thing to do was to sell the Scottish property.'[39] Twelve thousand acres of the Huntly estate went first in 1925, raising £80,000 in the process. Gordon Castle, the monstrously large 'world of a house', was next.[40] After a year of protracted negotiations, the Crown Estate agreed to buy it for £525,000 – sufficient to clear Freddie's debts.[41] By 1956, with the sale of Glenfiddich, the 286,411 acres the family had owned at the turn of the century had shrunk to a mere 12,000 acres in Sussex.

But even the English estate posed an economic challenge. During the Second World War, when Freddie joined the Royal Air Force, Goodwood served as a hospital and part of the surrounding estate as an airfield. When hostilities ceased, Freddie decided to turn the airfield into a motor-racing track. He himself was a keen petrolhead: back in 1931 he had won the Junior Car Club's Double Twelve-hour Race at Brooklands in his MG Midget. On 18 September 1948, accordingly, Freddie drove out onto the new Goodwood Motor Circuit in his Bristol 400. The same year, horse racing on Goodwood's course, first launched in 1802, resumed, and in 1957, Freddie opened the aerodrome for the first time since the war, bringing all his sporting interests together.

The motor circuit operated at Goodwood until 1966, when Freddie felt compelled to close it as it was simply too dangerous for drivers and spectators alike. Three years later, aged sixty-five, he retired from running Goodwood and handed it over to his eldest son, Charles, Earl of March. The future Duke of Richmond immediately offered it to the National Trust. 'Don't give us another of those places!' came back the cry, unless the gift came with an endowment.[42] Since that simply wasn't possible, he cheerily responded that 'we'll have a go ourselves.' After all, he mused, why '... should the family surrender the ultimate control and perhaps even the value of these considerable assets (which in economic terms represented the family's final reserve) just because it was difficult to meet the maintenance and running expenses of the house?'[43]

Instead of retreating from Goodwood, Charles March and his wife Susan moved back into it, having first knocked down a thirty-room wing to make the house more manageable. The state rooms were kept open to the public. The first-floor accommodation became offices. Charles and Susan's eldest son, also Charles, now 11th Duke of Richmond, grew up playing in the pits at the motor circuit. He vowed to revive it, and in 1993, with his father, launched the Festival of Speed, a hill-climb race down the drive in front of the house and up the hill behind it. Five years later, he drove a Bristol 400 around the motor circuit and declared it open once more. This launched Goodwood Revival, an annual event themed around the years that the circuit had originally been open.

The result is that while Longleat and Woburn today are houses – visitor attractions and family homes – Goodwood is a luxury sporting brand, associated more with motor and horse racing than the bricks and mortar these activities help maintain. Its current custodian Charles Richmond, who took over running the estate in 1997, and succeeded his father as duke in 2017, freely acknowledges the fact. The house is filled with lovely paintings: Stubbs in the hallway, Van Dycks in the ballroom, Canalettos in the Long Hall. But as he acknowledges, '[U]nless you love English furniture and paintings, you're probably not going to come.' Contemplating the million or so people who visit Goodwood each year, he reckons that a desire to see the house is 'pretty high on the list, but it's not necessarily at the top of the list . . . Our mantra is horse racing, motor racing, golf, flying, shooting and cricket,' he says.

The Goodwood brand is an expensive one to maintain. The running costs of the estate – 'without staff, and we've got 800 staff' – amount to a seven-figure sum every month. Sporting membership, which 'opens the doors to companies who want to entertain their clients at the highest of levels and in a very special way', helps, of course. The former kennels are now a members' clubhouse, while Hound Lodge, a former luxury home for hounds, is now a luxury ten-bedroom lodge for humans. 'Whatever we do we want it to be connected to the place,' says Charles Richmond. 'We don't want to just dream something up, suddenly do a rock concert in the park or something. I'm very interested in the brand, I'm very interested in creating something really meaningful. It has to feel right for Goodwood.'

Charles Richmond's task, in common with many other estate owners, has been to make Goodwood a commercial prospect – a going concern that can be satisfactorily passed on, eventually, to the next generation. In this he has been successful. In 2022 the estate welcomed over one million visitors, with 100,000 of these travelling from outside the UK. The 2020 *Sunday Times* Rich List estimated the duke's wealth as £228 million. The family is flourishing. When I went to Goodwood to meet Charles Richmond, he sent a Rolls-Royce made at the factory on his estate to pick me up from the railway station. It was worth more than the price of the average UK home. Our conversation was held in the Large Library, a room bursting with sofas too deep to get out of elegantly, and a total of fourteen lamps. He has been described as looking like the actor Hugh Grant, but I detect more than a hint of Tony Blair and a touch of Richard E. Grant. He is a very modern duke.

* * *

Throughout the 1950s and into the 1960s, scores of stately home owners opened their doors to the general public in a bid to secure the much-needed funds that would keep their houses going. Some – the Bedfords, Baths and Richmonds among them – were extraordinarily successful. Some turned over just enough to make the exercise worthwhile. A few, however, struggled to make the books balance.

Among the last group were the Earls of Bradford, whose family seat was Weston Park in Shropshire, a pretty red-brick house built in 1671 for Elizabeth, Lady Wilbraham (often described as the first female architect). Weston had passed through the Wilbraham and Newport families before in 1762 it came to the Bridgemans, later to be created Earls of Bradford in 1815. They were a political family. Orlando Bridgeman, 3rd Earl of Bradford, served as Lord Chamberlain under Edward Smith-Stanley, 14th Earl of Derby, during his third premiership, and in 1884 married the Hon. Selina Weld-Forester, a close friend and confidante of Benjamin Disraeli, who fell deeply in unrequited love with her. In 1915, there was a change of patriarch when Orlando 'Laddo' Bridgeman inherited the Bradford earldom and embarked on his forty-year reign of Weston and its environs as 5th Earl. He quickly became, as was appropriate for the time, a prominent local figure: chairman of the church council, parish council, chair of governors of the local school, a magistrate and president of the cricket club. As the *Staffordshire Advertiser* put it, he was 'the cornerstone of village activity . . . always uppermost in the thoughts of its inhabitants'. Under the Bradfords, the newspaper went on, the village of Weston-under-Lizard was 'one big happy family . . . radiating throughout the village from the family at the Hall is a beneficent spirit. The people respond to it, and it's reflected in the village's character.' [44]

While Laddo Bradford was alive, three generations of the family lived at Weston. A widower after his wife Margaret 'Daisy' Bruce died in 1949, Laddo – or 'Fardy', as he was known in the family – ran his staff from the ground floor. Upstairs, on the nursery floor, lived his son Gerald, Viscount Newport, and his wife Mary,[45] alongside their four children – Richard, Serena, Caroline and Charles. The young Bridgeman children didn't see that much of Laddo, though Richard, now 7th Earl of Bradford, remembers that 'he had a television before we did'. He recalls watching the BBC News with his grandfather, as his father – who, he says, was written up for the Military Cross at Monte Cassino and had declined it, 'that's how honest a man he was' – blew up the remains of Tong Castle alongside the Territorial Army.[46]

At the time of Richard Bradford's birth in 1947, the family prospects looked bright. He was the required heir, and his brother Charles the spare. Then, when Richard was nine, his grandfather died. Gerald Newport became Gerald Bradford and took over Weston. Richard received a promotion in turn. 'I left school one term as Bridgeman,' he recalls, 'and came back the next term as Newport. I remember my mother changing the name labels over.' Later, when his own sons started school, as Viscount Newport and the Hon. Harry Bridgeman, they came home having discovered that in most families, boys don't change their surnames every thirty years. 'It's very strange,' they said to their mother, 'there's another pair of brothers in the school, and do you know, they've both got the same name!'[47]

Gerald and Mary dedicated the years immediately after Laddo's death to restoring Weston. In 1964 they opened it to the public. 'I often wonder what some of my more strait-laced forebears would think if they could see what we are doing today,' Gerald mused. 'Personally, I believe our decision to share our treasures is in keeping with the tradition of Weston.'[48] By 1967, the house was attracting 35,000 visitors a year. Unfortunately, their contribution was a drop in the ocean for a house and estate that was saddled with an enormous overdraft. Gerald was nevertheless determined to keep it going, describing it as '. . . a place I've always wanted to come back to, a place I couldn't think of abandoning'.[49] An active man, he loved field sports and the countryside in general, particularly trees; he reckoned he must have been bitten by a 'mad tree', and described how he suffered from acute dendrophilia. 'It's very, very catching. If I find I am feeling rather low or depressed I go out into the trees.'[50]

In the summer of 1981, just before England won the Ashes at Headingley, the hitherto healthy Gerald had a heart attack. Impatient with life as a convalescent he went back to work too quickly. That August he died, aged sixty-nine. The night of his death, Richard had phoned to tell him that his wife Joanne was pregnant again. 'My mother said that he danced into her bedroom, absolutely thrilled. The next morning she rang up and said that he'd died during the night.'

The onerous financial challenges the family already faced now became seemingly insurmountable ones. 'My father was never ill, and his father had lived to be eighty-three,' says Richard Bradford. 'Dad always seemed incredibly well, so we hadn't done any tax planning.' When Gerald died, Weston was costing the family about £150,000 a year to run and was only just about a going concern. With his death the estate became saddled with over £8 million in death duties. Richard was advised to sell up. Weston had been a millstone around his father's neck, he was told. That millstone was now big enough to sink the next generation.

At first, Richard tried to prove the pessimists wrong. Looking at Weston 'from the eyes of somebody who had worked in hospitality', having run his own restaurants, and who could see that it offered 'an amazing opportunity', he installed new bathrooms and opened the house as an 'exclusive-use space', which could be rented by the night (now a very popular way of making big houses pay). Within three years, the house was making a bottom-line profit. But that profit barely made a dent in the death duties the exchequer was demanding. Richard felt increasingly broken and depressed by it all. 'I just couldn't see a way out. I knew that I had to pay this money and while I wasn't paying I was being charged interest.'[51]

He gave up the family's home in London 'because there didn't seem to be much point in having it any longer' and devoted himself wholly to Weston. He even opted to be the chef there for a while. But ultimately, the mountain of debt was too much for him. He found himself having to make a stark choice: to 'lose the house and keep the estate, or lose the estate and keep the house'. He chose the former, and in 1986 gave Weston to the nation, along with the 900-acre park. 'I think I made the right decision from the family's point of view, although I will always regret it,' he says, almost forty years later. 'I feel that my son blames me for the fact that the family lost Weston. At least I ensured that the house is properly looked after.'

The following year, an £8,850,000 grant from the National Heritage Memorial Fund enabled Weston to pass into the hands of an independent charitable trust, the Weston Park Foundation, who now run the house. At first the relationship between former owner and new custodian went well. Then, Richard Bradford says, the foundation's chairman of trustees 'took against me'. 'He didn't like the fact that there were still people at Weston who looked to the family instead of kowtowing to him. He couldn't wait to get rid of me, and eventually he succeeded.'

As a result, Richard Bradford now has nothing to do with Weston. Asked what it represents to him today, he answers in one word: 'sadness'. He feels 'divorced' from it. 'People ask me things about Weston and I am unable to answer because I am not fully in touch with what is going on there.' 'For three hundred years, the Bradfords were integral to Weston,' but now, he says, 'everything has changed, it's not ours.' He no longer has much of a role in the county, either. His eldest son Alexander Bridgeman, Viscount Newport, and his wife run the estate, managing 145 residential properties and a farming and forestry business. It is they who are photographed presenting prizes and visiting schools. Richard Bradford lives three miles from Weston, in a rented farmhouse.

He once said that he had no regrets, and that, 'I'm just a bit soft about Weston.'[52] Now, he misses the house 'very much', but believes that his father would have supported his decision to transfer Weston to the nation. The idea that one could never sell a big house, just because it belonged to you, is 'pathetic', he says. 'People will sit in their dining room with buckets [to catch the drips], saying that they are staying here to preserve the house, but they're not. In that situation they should sell it to somebody who has the means to be able to look after it.' If his father had lived another seven months, he adds, the whole saga could have been avoided, with the arrival of chancellor Sir Geoffrey Howe's further reforms to capital transfer tax.

* * *

Weston may evoke a sense of unhappiness in the family that once owned it, but at least Richard Bradford was able to ensure that the house was preserved and maintained. Other houses were less fortunate. Throughout the post-war period, many estates became so ruinously expensive to maintain that their owners felt they had no choice but to allow them to be reduced to piles of dust by the wrecking ball. It is estimated that between 1945 and 1974 alone a minimum 250 houses of architectural and historic importance were demolished, bringing the total lost since the turn of the twentieth century to 1,200, and leaving fewer than 2,000 scattered across England, Scotland and Wales. Marcus Binney, who in 1975 founded SAVE Britain's Heritage, a charity that campaigns for endangered historic buildings, put the post-war figure rather higher, suggesting that as many as 600 (not all of them the homes of members of the aristocracy) might have been lost.[53]

Among those to succumb to the post-war wrecking ball was Panshanger Park, one of the homes of the legendary society hosts Willie and Ettie Grenfell, 1st Baron and Baroness Desborough, which was demolished by 1954.[54] Three years later, Lowther Castle, the 'Victorian half-castle half-cathedral, standing unlikely, alone and immense in the bareness of Cumberland', followed suit. For over six decades it had been the home of Hugh Lowther, 5th Earl of Lonsdale, the 'Yellow Earl' – famed for his yellow carriages and yellow cars, and his footmen dressed in canary yellow livery – who ruled over a kingdom in Cumberland and Westmorland that, in 1923, was said to comprise over 175,000 acres, and to include Windermere, Grasmere, the whole town of Whitehaven and coalfields stretching under the Irish Sea.[55] He owned yachts at Cowes, travelled from one family home to another accompanied by his private orchestra, ordered that each morning the Lowther coat of arms should be reproduced in coloured chalk on sand in the stable yard, described himself as the last of the Lowthers even though he had a younger brother, and was scathingly described by his brother-in-law Gilbert Heathcote-Drummond-Willoughby, 1st Earl of Ancaster, as 'almost an emperor, not quite a gentleman'.[56] For all his magnificence, though, he had not been able to sustain the lifestyle to which he aspired, and had been forced to abandon Lowther in 1936.

Thereafter the castle had followed a by now all too familiar spiral of decline: requisition by the army during the war; extensive sales of contents after Hugh's death in 1944 and the accession to the title of his 76-year-old brother, Lancelot; further financial pressure following the imposition of death duties after Lancelot died in March 1953 and was succeeded by his socialist grandson James, an engineer.[57] By the mid-1950s the estate was bust, and since the surrounding area was also impoverished ('Cumbria then was an extremely isolated place. The M6 hadn't been built,' James Lonsdale's third son the Hon. Jim Lowther explained in 2022), viable options for Lowther were virtually non-existent. James Lonsdale 'looked at what his friend the Duke of Devonshire was in the process of doing with Chatsworth, of opening it to the public, as a means of preserving the house and the collection, but thought that that type of solution wouldn't work here at Lowther'.[58] He offered the castle to local bodies, but all declined. With no takers, he decided that demolition was the only answer. Because locals in Penrith objected to the whole building going, the decision was taken in 1957 to leave the house a romantic ruin. The grounds were given over to a commercial timber business, and James Lonsdale used the concrete bases on the south lawns that the army had constructed to develop an intensive chicken farming enterprise. When he died in 2006, the title passed to his eldest son Hugh, who died childless in 2021. Thereafter it went to Hugh's half-brother William, and will, in due course, pass to *his* half-brother Jim, who, with his wife Vanessa, has restored the gardens and opened what remains of Lowther to the public. In 2016 Jim described how he didn't blame his father for the choices he made. 'His major objective was to save the estate, which he did achieve.'[59] This – at 102,000 acres – is the largest aristocratic estate in England.

Lowther succumbed in part because the architectural style in which it had been built was not at that time deemed worth saving.[60] Methley Hall near Leeds, on the other hand, the former home of the Savile family (created Earls of Mexborough in 1766), which was reduced to rubble six years later in 1963, was at its core a fine sixteenth-century building, even if it had been remodelled several times. Its great misfortune was, as the writer Oswald Barron described in a 1907 issue of *Country Life*, to stand in the midst of coal country: 'The drift of smoke comes down the air from far-distant chimneys, collieries throw up their dark mounds and the water of the Calder flows inkily foul from the washing of shoddy.'[61] It had largely been abandoned by the family during the First World War, had been requisitioned by the army during the Second, and had been considered for use as a police training college in 1958, until subsidence caused by nearby open-cast mining and an announcement that the plan was to extend mining operations to the whole of the park, put paid to any deal that might have been struck.

It took a while for the loss of houses such as Panshanger Park, Lowther and Methley to register with the general public. But as the destruction continued into the 1960s and 1970s with little sign of abating, people began to notice. Then they showed signs of disapproval. Then they started to express real concern at the cultural loss such demolitions involved.

Out of that concern emerged an exhibition staged at the Victoria and Albert Museum in London's South Kensington from October to December 1974 entitled *The Destruction of the Country House, 1875–1975*. Part reminder of what had been lost, part call to arms to save what still survived, it was masterminded by a roll call of experts and conservationists, among them the architectural historian John Harris who had kept a list of demolished houses; *Country Life*'s architectural correspondent Marcus Binney; the antiques dealer Christopher Gibbs; and the museum's director (now Sir) Roy Strong. Their timing was well chosen. 'One of the reasons for Roy commissioning the exhibition', remembers Binney, 'was that 1975 had been declared European architectural heritage year, so he wanted to fire the first trumpet blast.'

Looking back on it some years later, Strong described how the exhibition is 'now recognised as a landmark exhibition, changing people's perception ... the first time, as far as I know, that a museum exhibition [was] an exercise in polemic'.[62] Visitors were first confronted by a mock-up of the collapsing façade of a vast country house, each block of masonry actually a photograph of a house that had been lost. A recorded voice in the background read out the name of each one, delivering a message that was immediate and visceral. As Roy Heelas of the *Bristol Evening Post* observed upon viewing the exhibition: 'A sad sort of visitors' book has been started at the Victoria and Albert Museum. Instead of recording visitors' names, it serves to extend a list of country houses destroyed over the past century ... depressingly, the book has all of 244 pages, because it is felt that the toll is likely to be much greater than the organisers of a new exhibition at the museum imagined.' A series of 'menacing sound effects and a droning, endless recitation of the names of the vanished' added to the funereal atmosphere.[63] It was, in effect, a memorial to the country house.

Strong stood, on more than one occasion, '... watching the tears stream down the visitors' faces as they battled to come to terms with all that had gone'.[64] Reviewing the exhibition for *The Times*, Philip Howard described how 'an elegiac atmosphere of a vanished world, like the close of *Brideshead Revisited*', hung over it. 'It is a fitting tribute and possibly an epitaph to a great English institution.'[65]

When the V&A press office sent out a list of demolished houses to regional newspapers, 'a flood of cuttings came back,' remembers Binney. 'They all did a story about their local lost house.' At the time, Binney said, '[O]f course it is a good thing that people are no longer doomed to lifetimes of domestic service with no practical alternative.' 'But on the whole,' he went on, 'I think the destruction is regrettable. Many of the great country houses were communities in the best sense of the word. They provided a more secure way of life for everybody in them in those harsh times of hardship.'[66]

* * *

In the wake of the exhibition, at a local level, conservation groups lobbied for the preservation of individual examples of the country's heritage. There was a new and very real desire to conserve what remained of England's stately homes. Even so, the demolition of big houses carried on. Their contents, carefully accumulated over decades and centuries, continued to be dispersed. And in 1977, barely three years after the exhibition at the V&A closed its doors for the last time, one of the grandest of all went under the auctioneer's hammer.

Mentmore Towers, built by Mayer Amschel de Rothschild in the 1850s in a part of Buckinghamshire sometimes nicknamed 'Rothschildshire',[67] was one of the country's most masterful Victorian houses. Modelled on Wollaton Hall in Nottinghamshire, it was 'filled to overflowing with treasures, brought together with less regard to expense than to discrimination', its forty-foot central hall boasting a plate-glass ceiling, giant marble chimneypiece from Peter Paul Rubens' house in Antwerp and gilt lanterns from the Doge's

state barge in Venice.[68] In 1874, it had passed into the hands of the
Earls of Rosebery, an old Scottish Lowland family, when Archie
Primrose, 5th Earl of Rosebery, married Hannah de Rothschild,
the only child of its builder. Daunted by the expense of keeping it
going and by a death duties bill of £4.5 million[69] incurred when his
father Harry Primrose, 6th Earl of Rosebery, died in May 1974,
Neil Primrose, 7th Earl of Rosebery, opened negotiations with the
government, hoping he could sell them the house and most of its
contents so that it could either be opened to the public in its current
form or turned into a museum. The price tag he attached to it was
£3.6 million – a bargain in the view of his mother Eva, Countess
of Rosebery, who argued that the cost would swiftly be covered by
selling 'a few bits of furniture', since 'just one piece of the French
furniture is valued at £300,000.' Asked what was likely to happen
to Mentmore if the government would not take it, she replied: 'Oh,
sink it. It could become a lunatic asylum. It could become a health
resort, and then I could come and stay here.'[70]

   The government dragged its feet, so the Roseberys appointed the
Mayfair auction house Sotheby's to catalogue Mentmore's contents
and prepare them for sale. The valuation process proved a strange
and somewhat uncomfortable experience for those involved. Since
the Roseberys' main home was Dalmeny House near Edinburgh,
Mentmore had, for many years, been only partly lived in, and
was, consequently, both neglected and largely unheated.[71] James
Miller, one of the Sotheby's team on site, recalls that '. . . the electricity was only forty watts throughout, so during the winter months
it wasn't just very cold, but very dark, and we could only work
until about four o'clock in the afternoon.' 'Years of neglect were
visible everywhere, and such neglect in the long term was simply a
sentence of death,' wrote Sotheby's official historian Frank Herrmann.[72] 'The decorative detritus of several generations . . . had
accumulated in some of the larger downstairs rooms that were
kept permanently shuttered.'[73]

   With the government still baulking at the prospect of buying
Mentmore for the nation, Sotheby's sale of its contents began on

18 May 1977. Herrmann remembered this as a day '... as brilliantly sunny as an opening day at Wimbledon, and the atmosphere of mounting anticipation was not dissimilar'.[74] Cars streamed in early, the parking controlled by the estate staff. 'There were long queues of traffic crossing the south part of Buckinghamshire to get there,' Miller recalls. 'When you looked out from the house the field was completely full of parked cars.' The catalogues had sold out three weeks before and were reported to be changing hands on the opening day for £180. As the first lot – a Louis XV leather travelling trunk, which sold for £13,500 – was being prepared, a jacketless Neil Rosebery fiddled with a faulty microphone.[75] Eva Rosebery chatted with reporters, complaining that the police had taken her pistol away. For his part, a retired gardener on the estate proclaimed, 'I want to see his Lordship make a lot of money today.'[76]

The sale went on for ten days, during which a Louis XVI ormolu-mounted mahogany secrétaire, made for Marie Antoinette by the German cabinet maker Jean Henri Riesener, was bought by the Palace of Versailles for £51,000, and an eighteenth-century music box in the shape of an orange tree sold for £81,000. A Louis XV commode reached £59,000, and a pair of Louis XIV columnar silver-gilt table candlesticks went – possibly to a Greek shipping magnate – for £30,000. The government bought a few pieces in lieu of death duties – a rare sporting painting by Thomas Gainsborough, a nine-foot bureau and cabinet made for Augustus the Strong, King of Poland, and an ebony cabinet supposed to have been owned by Marie de' Medici. The painting of Madame de Pompadour by François-Hubert Drouais, which had hung over the stairs, was bought by the National Gallery.

The Mentmore sale might not have involved the wholesale physical destruction of a building witnessed elsewhere. Even so, the dispersal of the treasure it contained represents something of a post-war low point. Nor were its woes over. After service as the headquarters for the Maharishi Foundation for a couple of decades, it was purchased by a property developer who hoped to turn it into a luxury hotel. When his plans came to nothing, it started to decay. Today it's a sad shadow of its former self – a neglected shell prey to damp and vandalism, and now classified Category A on Historic England's 'Heritage At Risk' register.

But official attitudes were nevertheless gradually changing. Formerly, as Binney had said of the conservation page he contributed to in *Country Life* called 'Conservation in Action', '[I]t was as if the "in" and "action" were joined together, because it was mostly about historic buildings being neglected.' It had been relatively easy to destroy a listed building, he says. 'You wrote to the local authority saying, "I am planning to demolish this listed building," and if they didn't reply you could assume that you had permission.' *The Destruction of the Country House* exhibition, however, as John Harris put it, ultimately proved '[A] turning-point, not only for its theatrical revelation of the terrifying scale of a loss such as had never been sustained by any country in any period, except as a result of war, but because it offered alternatives to despair and destruction'.[77]

4

Brideshead Revisited

The Stately Home Today

Stately homes might have won popular sympathy in the wake of the V&A's 1974 exhibition, but official support for policies that might alleviate the financial burden on their owners proved to be rather harder to secure. In 1969 estate duty had peaked at 85 per cent on estates worth over £750,000. Under Harold Wilson's minority Labour government that took office in March 1974, a green paper proposing a wealth tax was circulated (if not acted upon) and a white paper on a new capital transfer tax appeared shortly afterwards. Wilson's chancellor Denis Healey, having issued a warning to those he regarded as property speculators, followed up with a Budget in which, among other things, he raised income tax levels. The same month, estate duty, which Healey viewed as a 'largely avoidable, indeed, a voluntary tax', was replaced by a new capital transfer tax that the chancellor hoped would put a stop to what he described as '. . . the unfair advantages enjoyed by generation after generation of the heirs and relatives of wealthy men'.[1]

The previous year a number of country house owners, feeling ever-more beleaguered, had got together to form the Historic Houses Association (HHA), their intention being to establish a lobby group that could campaign effectively on behalf of privately owned heritage. The Association's first committee was a roll call of the great and the good: the Dukes of Argyll and Marlborough; Charles March, the future Duke of Richmond; the Conservative MP and owner of Athelhampton House in Dorset, Robin Cooke;

and the Hon. David Lytton Cobbold, a banker and son of a governor of the Bank of England. George Howard, grandson of the 9th Earl of Carlisle and the future chair of the board of governors at the BBC, was the first vice-chairman, and the Association's patron was Hugh FitzRoy, 11th Duke of Grafton, owner of Euston Hall in Suffolk. Its first president was Edward Douglas-Scott-Montagu, 3rd Baron Montagu of Beaulieu, who had opened the National Motor Museum on his Beaulieu estate in 1952. Between them the committee presided over 100,000 acres scattered across the country.

In his 1959 preface to *Brideshead Revisited*, Evelyn Waugh wrote: 'It seemed then [in 1944] that the ancestral seats which were our chief national artistic achievement were doomed to decay and spoliation like the monasteries in the sixteenth century. So I piled it on rather, with passionate sincerity . . .'[2] Passionate sincerity was also the note struck at a seminar held the year after the Association was founded by Howard, owner of the troubled Whig palace Castle Howard in North Yorkshire,[3] when he offered a parody of the hymn 'All Things Bright and Beautiful':

> *The poor man in his castle*
> *the tourist at his gate*
> *the Chancellor and his wealth tax*
> *broke up the whole estate.*

Howard stressed the importance of collective action. He rang alarm bells about the challenges that he and his fellow stately home owners were experiencing. 'If we are not able to achieve anything,' he said, 'Henry VIII's dissolution of the monasteries will have nothing on Healey's disposal of country houses and their collections, and the actions of this Government will be remembered much as those of a previous Commonwealth, that of Cromwell. Does this Government really want to be remembered for its vandalism, its philistinism, and its destruction of so much of the history of Britain?'[4]

Whether or not the chancellor was aware of this direct challenge, he did take one step that over the ensuing decades was to prove hugely beneficial to those battling to preserve their family's – and the nation's – heritage: he introduced a tax loophole whereby, as former tax inspector and agricultural tax expert Oliver Stanley puts it, '[P]roperty could be passed down to the next generation without an immediate tax payment being required as an entry price.'[5] In immediate terms, though, the landed gentry continued to feel beleaguered. Nor did the advent of a Conservative government in 1979 provide much comfort. The early 1980s were tough times for Britain. Traditional industry was still in decline. Unemployment was high. In such an economically difficult environment it was hard to find a sympathetic ear in government for a group of people judged wealthy by most of society. Further protection would in time be afforded to listed buildings, thanks to the Planning (Listed Buildings and Conservation Areas) Act 1990, but that would be of little comfort to those struggling to maintain them.[6]

A chilly and unsupportive note was sounded by the secretary of state for the environment at the fifteenth annual general meeting of the Historic Houses Association at the Kensington Exhibition Centre on 22 November 1988. 'There have to be some opportunities for today's *nouveaux riches*,' he said, 'so I am not impressed by the case of the *anciens pauvres*.' He proceeded to offer a culinary metaphor. 'Aspic is all very well round quails. It is even bearable round salmon. But it will not do for a living heritage.'[7]

Not surprisingly, this brutal assessment did not go down well. 'I remember the look on people's faces,' says Charlie Lansdowne, then the association's president, who had invited the secretary of state to speak. 'I knew [him] and he was a very able man. He enjoyed ruffling feathers, that was part of his technique, and he was very successful, very clever. I don't think we knew he was going to be quite so blunt, but he had a reputation for being blunt.' A week later, a letter appeared in the *Telegraph* from the Lincolnshire squire the Reverend Henry Thorold, whose family had lived in the county since the fourteenth century. '[The secretary of state] does not seem to understand that the appeal of a historic house does not lie only in its bricks and mortar but in the history of the family who built it and, let us hope, still inhabit it,' he wrote. He gave the example of Staunton Hall in Nottinghamshire, the home of the Staunton family since 1041, where 'in the front door are the bullet holes, marked 1645, recalling the siege in the Civil War when the family defended the house against the Roundheads.' '[I]t is a horrifying thought', he said in sniffy conclusion, 'that any *nouveaux riches* should replace such families as these in their historic houses.'[8] Christopher Monckton, now 3rd Viscount Monckton of Brenchley, writing in the *Evening Standard*, described the minister's work as 'custard-pie politics', adding it was unfortunate that the 'British landed aristocracy' were his 'latest victims'.[9]

What must have been particularly galling for members of the HHA was that the man doling out the dose of hard-faced realism on that November day in 1988, far from being a member of the *nouveaux riches* he applauded, was a member of the very elite he was criticising. The Hon. Nicholas Ridley, MP, was the younger son of Matthew Ridley, 3rd Viscount Ridley, and had grown up at Blagdon Hall in Northumberland, a substantial mansion that had been the home of the Ridley family since 1698. But then, as Charlie Lansdowne says, perhaps he was doing no more than stating what needed to be stated. 'It was rather good for us,' he argues some thirty-five years after Ridley set the cat among the pigeons. 'He said the sensible thing which is if you can't afford these places then get the hell out before they break you. I think there was more inclination to hang on then. Remember that in 1988 quite a lot of the aristocracy, the people owning these properties, were left over from the war. They were hugely relieved that they were still alive, but they weren't qualified for very much. Nowadays, people look ahead much more, and say, "I must understand this and get the qualifications to do it."' Over the ensuing decades, this latter group would find ways to preserve their heritage, helped in part by the lifebelt a Labour chancellor of the exchequer had thrown them, and by an economic recovery that his Conservative successors oversaw.

* * *

The last quarter of the twentieth century proved to be one of varying fortunes for those aristocrats with big houses to maintain. Some continued to thrive much as they always had. Some fell by the wayside. Some compromised. Some adapted.

The owner of Charlton Park in Wiltshire falls into the last category. Saved once for the Earls of Suffolk by the 'dollar princess' Daisy Leiter (see Chapter 1), the house had by the 1970s become a millstone around the family's neck. The late Mickey Howard, 21st Earl of Suffolk and Berkshire, told me in 2018 how as a child he had played football in the hall: '[T]here's a pair of pillars at either end, and they were the goal posts.' But service as a wartime hospital and then a school had done little for the fabric, and the house had become a massive, rotten, inconvenient white elephant. In 1975, Mickey Suffolk did a deal with the property developer Christopher Buxton whereby Charlton was turned into eighteen apartments. He kept one for himself – carved out of a portion of the house that had once contained his parents' bedroom. 'I can't think of anything else that I'd do with the house. I wracked my brain for twenty, thirty years and couldn't find anything,' he said. In his view, converting the house to flats saved it – 'there's no question about it.'

Among those who fell by the wayside were the Lovats. Brigadier Simon 'Shimi' Fraser, 15th Lord Lovat, DSO, MC, was one of the real upper-class characters of the twentieth century. An officer in the Scots Guards, the Lovat Scouts – the regiment his father had raised for the Second Boer War – and then the Commandos, he had famously ordered his personal piper, 21-year-old Bill Millin, to pipe ahead of him as they jumped off the landing ramp at Sword Beach in Normandy on D-Day, and had then strolled through a storm of German bullets clad in a white jumper with 'Lovat' embroidered on the collar and bearing an ancient Winchester rifle. Millin later reckoned that he had survived only because the German snipers had thought him mad and so spared him out of pity. After the war Shimi's vast but unprofitable Scottish estates required constant cost cutting. At one point it even proved necessary to shut down the central-heating boilers at Beaufort Castle in Inverness-shire, the family resorting to wearing coats indoors to keep the cold at bay. As Shimi's sister Veronica, Lady Maclean put it, 'For us it was wartime, without much sign of victory ahead.'[10] But Shimi was determined to do what he could to preserve the status quo. Not for nothing did Veronica describe him as 'a traditionalist and a romantic Highlander'.[11]

His son Simon, by contrast, to whom Shimi had felt it necessary to start making over the Lovat estates when he suffered a heart attack in 1965 aged sixty-four, was a pragmatist who, according to Veronica, '. . . had not inherited my father's or my brother's affection for and dedication to their clansmen or their closeness to the people who lived on our estates'.[12] Simon was then twenty-five and working in a bank. He and his wife Virginia moved into Beaufort Castle, while Shimi and his wife Rosie moved into nearby Balblair House. Simon set to work to boost the family fortunes – '[A]nd to hell with tradition and out-of-date methods which impeded his efforts to do so,' as Veronica put it.[13]

As it turned out, he lacked both acumen and luck. A scheme to breed 1,000 head of cattle at Beaufort for the Shah of Iran left him out of pocket when revolution swept the Shah away. Equally dubious was the decision he took in the early 1960s to offer a personal guarantee on the lease of an upper-class London gambling club, the Clermont, operated by the questionable John Aspinall (for more on whom see Chapter 11). In an attempt to meet his rising debts, he took to selling off fishing rights on the Beauly that his family had held for hundreds of years, along with other tracts of estate land. He was acutely aware that Shimi disapproved of what he was doing. His response was to become ever-more secretive about his business ventures and the loans he was forced to take out.

In March 1994, Simon's youngest brother Andrew was killed by a buffalo while on safari in Tanzania. Eleven days later 54-year-old Simon himself dropped dead from a heart attack while out hunting. Only then did the full extent of his financial misjudgements emerge. His debts, it was calculated, amounted to £7.4 million, of which almost £1 million was due to Lloyd's of London, and £2.7 million to the Inland Revenue. When Shimi died the following summer at the age of eighty-three, it was in the knowledge that the estates he had been so desperate to preserve would have to be sold to meet Simon's debts. In May 1995, Beaufort Castle and about 19,500 acres of the by then much-reduced estate was put on the market for £6 million. Three months later, the castle, home farm and 800 acres were bought by the Scottish businesswoman Ann Gloag, co-founder of Stagecoach. Veronica Maclean was deeply upset, having been '. . . brought up to believe that the land was our family's heritage, to be cared for and held in trust by each generation for the next'. Eventually, though, she came to terms with the loss. The Lovat heritage she so valued was not dead, she decided; it had 'merely metamorphosed'.[14] After all, as the Lovats' estate manager, Giles Foster, pointed out, 'The Frasers have owned the land far longer than the current house so it is not quite such a wrench as one might think to sell the castle.'[15] Today, Shimi's grandson Simon Fraser, 16th Lord Lovat, and his wife Petra run what remains of the Lovat estates. Asked about his future as head of the family by reporters in August 1995, he said: 'The demands will be great, but I believe I can adapt.'[16]

Those aristocrats who decided to compromise ensured a boom time for the National Trust. In 1974 it assumed custodianship of the Angleseys' final bolthole, Plas Newydd on the Isle of Anglesey. The family decamped to the old nursery floor, and Henry Anglesey, son of the Charley Anglesey who earlier in the century had disposed of Beaudesert, retained his study by the front door. Visitors to the house could not infrequently detect the strong aroma of cigars as they stepped inside. For Henry living upstairs in his old family home was like 'living in the howdah on top of a white elephant which somebody else feeds'.[17] He never regretted his decision. 'My father was very proud of having got the National Trust to take Plas Newydd,' says his son Alex Anglesey. 'He was very pleased [with the outcome] and was very happy to be living in the family flat at the top of the house.' Four years later, newspaper publisher Langton Iliffe, 2nd Baron Iliffe's much-loved and freshly restored Basildon Park in Berkshire, came the Trust's way. And in 1984 Edward Cust, 7th Baron Brownlow's glorious but badly run-down Belton House in Lincolnshire, whose potential acquisition by the Trust had first been mooted a couple of decades earlier, was finally secured by them.[18] By the end of the century, the Trust had taken on forty-eight houses or estates directly from families within the hereditary peerage.[19]

The pace of acquisition slowed markedly as the millennium dawned, but a handful of impressive houses nevertheless continued to come the Trust's way. In 2002, Tyntesfield, Richard Gibbs, 2nd Baron Wraxall's Victorian Gothic Revival pile in Somerset, was brought under the Trust's care.[20] Seven years later, Seaton Delaval Hall in Northumberland followed suit. Commissioned by Vice-Admiral George Delaval in 1718, the work of the architect Sir John Vanbrugh, its history has been typical of so many country houses. A period of glory, during which it passed from the Delavals to the Norfolk landowner Sir Jacob Astley, who became 16th Baron Hastings in 1841 when the title was called out of abeyance. A period of sharp decline, culminating in the house's use as a prisoner-of-war camp during the Second World War. A rallying period, when Edward Astley, 22nd Baron Hastings, and his wife Catherine 'Nicki' Hinton did all they could to save the house as they undertook a punishing regime of repairing and restoring. A challenging period, following the death of 95-year-old Edward in April 2007, and Nicki Hastings eight months later, when their son Delaval, the new Lord Hastings, was faced with a significant inheritance tax bill. And, finally, the period when resolution came. The Trust reopened the house to the public in 2010 and has spent fifteen years restoring it.[21]

As for the Historic Houses Association (renamed Historic Houses in 2020), it now represents the custodians of some 1,450 properties scattered around the United Kingdom, including the vast majority of the country's best-known stately homes. Its annual general meeting is a bit like a trade show for the aristocracy, for although a relatively modest 15 per cent of member houses these days are owned by members of the hereditary peerage, directly or through trusts, at least a quarter of families who make up the country's hereditary peerage own properties within Historic Houses. Its senior echelons are a veritable *Burke's Peerage*. In 2023, its board of thirteen included a duchess, two earls, the wife of a baron, the grandson of an earl, the granddaughter of a marquess, the wife of a baronet, a viscount's son and heir, and a life peer. Four of its twelve presidents have been the proud possessors of hereditary titles. All but one have been men. The association's first female president, Martha Lytton-Cobbold, was elected in 2020. American by birth, she became Lady Cobbold two years into her tenure, when her father-in-law died and her husband Henry became the 3rd Baron Cobbold.[22]

* * *

Back in the early twentieth century aristocrats seeking to prop up their estates married new money. These days, aristocrats seeking to dispose of land or houses sell them to new money – 'not only investment bankers clutching record bonus cheques, but also artists, entrepreneurs and the second-generation wealthy' as well as 'foreign buyers', as an article in *The Times* put it in February 2006.[23] Alexander Fermor-Hesketh, 3rd Baron Hesketh, the former Formula 1 team owner, for example, who put his home of Easton Neston in Northamptonshire on the market in May 2004, found a buyer – for £15 million – in the shape of Russian–American fashion designer Leon Max.[24] By 2018, the Danish entrepreneur Anders Holch Povlsen – described to me by several Scottish landowners as 'that Danish man' – had become the biggest landowner in Britain, ahead even of Richard Montagu Douglas Scott, 10th Duke of Buccleuch.[25] His love of Scotland kindled as a child when he visited on a fishing trip with his father, he has made a number of purchases over the years, including the 42,000-acre Glenfeshie in the Cairngorms National Park, previously owned by another

Danish millionaire, Klaus Helmersen, and until the 1980s by Anthony Wills, 2nd Baron Dulverton.

Even so, while ancestral lands and homes are still being sold off on occasion, the flood of the post-war years has now become a trickle. A rare, recent example is Brechin Castle in Angus, put up for sale in 2019 by James Ramsay, 17th Earl of Dalhousie, the former Lord Steward, with a price tag of £3 million. The castle is built on land owned by his family since the twelfth century, but the costs of maintaining and running it were proving prohibitive. 'In a good year,' he said at the time, 'the estates run a deficit of about £250,000; in a bad year it's as much as £350,000. You can't go on spending that kind of money year after year.'[26] Brechin did not sell and was withdrawn from the market.

For the rest, owners of stately homes and estates continue to find ingenious ways to keep their heritage going. Some rent out their houses by the night on an 'exclusive-use' basis – while they take a mini-break elsewhere, or retreat to a private wing. Others hire them out for weddings, as Lady Cara and the Hon. James Willoughby started to do at Birdsall House near York in 2018.[27] Or they make money from film and television companies, as the Northumberlands did when Alnwick Castle was chosen as one of the principal locations for the first two films of the Harry Potter franchise ('Harry Potter has made a generous contribution to the upkeep of Alnwick Castle,' Ralph Percy, 12th Duke of Northumberland, says, pointing out that even twenty years after the films first appeared they are still inspiring fans to visit). Some stately home owners host music festivals, whether the psychedelic trance festival Noisily at the Hazleriggs' Noseley Hall in Leicestershire; the boutique music and arts festival Standon Calling at the Trenchards' Standon Lordship in Hertfordshire; or Latitude Festival at the Stradbrokes' Henham Park in Suffolk. Some have taken on opera, as the Ashburtons have done at The Grange, Alresford, after buying the house back from the estate of the industrialist Charles Wallach in 1964.[28] Some stage horse trials. The inaugural Badminton Horse Trials was held at Master Beaufort's Gloucestershire home in 1949. It was followed by Burghley Horse Trials in 1961, engineered by David Cecil, 6th Marquess of Exeter; and in 1999 by the reinstatement of horse trials, after a long hiatus, at Chatsworth.

In 2021, Luke and Julie Montagu, then Viscount and Viscountess Hinchingbrooke, the titles they used before February 2025 when Luke's father John Montagu, 11th Earl of Sandwich, died, launched a YouTube channel from Mapperton House in Dorset, making highly produced videos that chronicle their experience of making a life at Mapperton and keeping it going for the future. Their videos have shown them draining, cleaning and restoring the eighteenth-century swimming pool. They have taken viewers through hosting their first Christmas fair. Throughout, the couple have been refreshingly open about problems and mis-steps: 'The pool isn't working, the pumps aren't working, and the door is falling off the hinges,' Luke reports in one video. 'That is slightly the story of Mapperton, I'm afraid ... hanging by a hinge.'[29] It is overwhelmingly compelling, honest, addictive watching. The enthusiastic Illinois-born Julie, who has marketed herself as the 'American Viscountess' – and now the 'American Countess' – brings a refreshing perspective to things, having had no knowledge at all of the aristocracy when she met her future husband, co-founder of the Metropolitan Film School, at a party in 2003. 'When I took over Mapperton it was always my hope that I could combine these things in some way,' he says. 'I didn't realise it would be YouTube, but that's where we've got to and it's gone rather well.'

One factor that has helped many stately homes and their owners in recent years is the Downton (Abbey) factor. Just as Castle Howard became synonymous with *Brideshead Revisited* when it was used in the 1981 Granada adaptation of Evelyn Waugh's magnum opus, so the Earl of Carnarvon's Highclere Castle became world-famous as the setting for Julian Fellowes' aristocratic period drama, first aired in 2010. Up until then, Highclere was probably best known as the home of the family whose passion for Egyptology and deep pockets aided the discovery of the tomb of Tutankhamen in the Valley of the Kings in 1922. But, as Fiona Herbert, Countess of Carnarvon, says, the television series has been '. . . so enjoyed around the world, it's done so much good for people's view of tourism and stately homes and coming to see them. It's unwoven narratives of upstairs and downstairs without making either of them seem worse – it's given us a marketing platform.'

Her husband Geordie Herbert, 8th Earl of Carnarvon, describes Downton as, '[A] window on the world for Highclere. It's great to have a steady flow of visitors through the year because creating a stable income allows us to restore and repair as needed – that's what allows you to fix follies and difficult things that have no income, which is one of the big challenges here. People think it's just the big building, but in our case it's all of the eighteenth-century follies too. My ancestor Robert Herbert [uncle of the 1st Earl of Carnarvon] and later Herberts thought it would be great to build all of these buildings in the landscape – we love to look at them but there's absolutely no income attached to them and you've still got to be responsible for them.'

There has been an identifiable 'Downton effect' on houses beyond Highclere. As one landowner told me in 2018: 'I think [visitors] think the world here is like Downton, and that's been really good for us.' The Duke and Duchess of Argyll have also experienced something of the Downton effect, though not on the level of the Carnarvons, ever since their home, Inveraray Castle, in Argyll, was chosen as the main location of the 2012 Downton Christmas special. 'It was brilliant,' remembers Eleanor Campbell, Duchess of Argyll. 'They were delightful to work with, professional, lovely, didn't leave a scratch. The town loved it, being such a small town. It was great for us, and even now people come and say: "Is this where Lady Mary . . . where did Bates and Anna have their picnic?" etc. It's still being brilliant.'

* * *

Two houses – Hopetoun House near Edinburgh, and Wykeham Abbey near Scarborough – neatly represent the two ends of the stately homes scale today. One owes its upkeep to the visiting public. The other hides in plain sight.

Hopetoun House near Edinburgh has been home since 1699 to the Hope family, made Earls of Hopetoun in 1703, and Marquesses of Linlithgow in 1902. Conceived on a palatial scale, akin to that of Wentworth Woodhouse, it boasts a 657-foot-wide east front, a state dining room used by George IV when he visited the house in 1822 and had turtle soup for lunch, and a vast room built by William Adam that has served variously as a library, an indoor riding school and a ballroom. There's a walled garden – the biggest in Scotland[30] – where pineapples were once grown, and a surrounding estate covering 6,500 acres. One way and another it's a very large house for the family of six that call it home – Andrew Hope, Earl of Hopetoun, his wife Skye, and their four adult children.

Andrew Hopetoun has many of the attributes and enjoys many of the trappings associated with the aristocracy. Born in 1969, he was educated at Eton and Oxford, is a former deputy lieutenant of West Lothian, and is also a member of the Royal Company of Archers, the sovereign's bodyguard in Scotland. In September 2022 he was one of the retinue responsible for moving the body of Elizabeth II from the Palace of Holyroodhouse to St Giles' Cathedral. But he's also a particle physicist and self-confessed 'nerd'. 'I'm a computer gamer,' he says, 'I like science fiction and fantasy, and the fact that I was at the same Oxford college as J. R. R. Tolkien – Exeter.' In conversation, Middle Earth references roll off his tongue. When I say that I was named after Eleanor of Aquitaine, he says, 'Or Sam's daughter [Elanor Gardner] in *Lord of the Rings*.' He loves nothing more than to sit in the boudoir off his bedroom at Hopetoun playing World of Warcraft. Despite his upper-class heritage he was never a member of the exclusive Bullingdon Club while at Oxford: 'I'm not sure how many physicists were in the Bullingdon Club,' he says, grinning.

Andrew's grandfather, Charlie Hope, 3rd Marquess of Linlithgow, MC, who inherited Hopetoun from his father Victor Hope,

2nd Marquess of Linlithgow, in 1952, served with the 51st Highland Division during the Second World War, and was captured, escaped several times and ended up in the prison for incorrigible Allied officers, Colditz Castle, near Leipzig, where, as the son of a peer who was also the Viceroy of India, he was included among the 'Prominente', a label given to relatives of Allied VIPs. The post-war period was challenging for him, as it was for so many peers. In Andrew's view: 'My grandfather's generation had it tough. They came out of the other side of the war into a difficult economic climate and into all the taxation that led to the foundation of the HHA.' In September 1974, Charlie Linlithgow founded the Hopetoun House Preservation Trust, an early example of an independent charitable trust. 'He continued to live in it, as do we,' his grandson says, 'so it is not an irreversible move in the same way as giving it to the National Trust for Scotland might have been, but that was a big shift.' Andrew Hopetoun admires his grandfather and the choices he made in challenging circumstances. 'He had a tough time of it, and yet he put in place some decisions that are still absolutely right. He clearly saw a future for Hopetoun.'

Andrew always knew that he would ultimately inherit the house. 'I'm a scientist because I enjoyed it, but I knew that it wasn't likely to be forever. I knew this was on the horizon. I liked the fact that I had time to do something that I enjoyed doing and that gave me a different outlook on life, but I was always aware that I would end up running things at home.' In the event, though, things happened earlier than he had been expecting. When his father Adrian Linlithgow was approaching sixty, in the early 2000s, he surprised his son one day by mentioning that he was thinking of leaving Hopetoun, to move to a smaller house on the estate, and that he hoped Andrew would want to move in. 'I'm not sure I took it on board,' Andrew says. 'He rang me back three weeks later and said he was upset as he had been telling his friends that we were moving in, and he was moving out, but I hadn't mentioned it at all. I said I assumed he was joking.'

Today, Hopetoun is a busy house – not just a home for the

family, but a visitor attraction and, as Andrew puts it, 'a really viable business'. 'You've got the house, which is home, and also a tourist attraction to day visitors, and then we have the ability to do commercial and corporate events, some weddings, bigger events like fireworks and the Christmas fair, and we have an electric music festival in May.' Then there's the charitable, community side of the enterprise which, among other things, organises history workshops for around 4,000 schoolchildren a year. The ancillary buildings around the house, once home to the wheelwright, butcher, blacksmith and Hopetoun's own fire brigade, have been repurposed: the old carriage houses are now used for conservation work, the garage is an accountancy firm, the old stallion house that once contained the estate fire engines is home to the ranger and education services, who provide guided tours of the house and grounds, while the eighteenth-century stables built by Robert Adam have become a tearoom and function space.

The Hopetouns employ about a dozen staff at the house, the same again on the estate, and the same again in their farm shop five miles away, just off the M9. They also rely heavily on volunteers, in the house, the grounds and in the conservation studio. 'That's the other thing about having a charity – it makes it much easier to attract volunteers,' says Andrew. 'There's a slight psychological thing about working for a privately owned house rather than a charity.'

His set up, he says, is not uncommon. 'It's a good way of doing it – clearly there are tax benefits which are not unhelpful, but it's also a different way of thinking. It suits us. Effectively you are securing the future of the house by tying it up in a structure that associates it with either an income-generating capability or a pot of money. We have a terrific team of trustees here, which really helps.' He runs through the various approaches that fellow peers have adopted: 'You either run the house as a business or a company as others do, or you have it as a charity, or you can have it as a private home and you don't do much with it, or you have it as a private home that isn't open to visitors, like some still are.'

He accepts that his life is an unusual one and not for everybody: '[B]ut it is a hell of a privilege, and it has to have positives. It can't just be a case of: "Oh, my word, this is such a weighty responsibility, this is crushing me." It can be work as well – and you can even admit that it's work – but you must never pretend that it's grinding or shattering or ghastly or awful, because it isn't.' Is it a burden? He laughs. 'What would the alternative have been? I don't think it is a burden. It's hard work, and I think it should be hard work. These houses do need quite a lot of managing, and if you're not doing that then the risk is it's going undone.'

Hopetoun is not his whole personality, though naturally it looms large over anyone involved with it in any way. 'It is important not to be defined by a house, but it's also quite hard not to be,' he says. Though it is huge, it is very much home, and not just a family headquarters – or a wedding venue. 'It is a home, at times it is *the* home – we are in London a lot,' he says. 'In many ways, to be defined by Hopetoun as a home is a lot more positive than to be defined by it as a house.' Is it the best house in the world? 'It would be arrogant to say that it was, but it is certainly the one I love the most.'

If Hopetoun lives and flourishes in the public gaze, Wykeham Abbey, eight miles outside Scarborough, and close to the North York Moors National Park, is well hidden from it.[31] No visitor to the area particularly unversed in the characteristics of a country estate, and driving through the village of Wykeham would have an inkling that there is a very big house nearby. Past a gunsmith's, a row of estate cottages and a dead-end sign, and then, suddenly, rising up in front of you is a beautiful Georgian house, built on the site of a Cistercian nunnery. Wykeham manages to be both very large and extraordinarily charming. It almost gleams in the sun, thanks in part to the recent repaint that its drainpipes have had in the estate cream – a buttermilk colour.

Wykeham Abbey is home to Richard Dawnay, 12th Viscount Downe, and his mother Diana Dawnay, Viscountess Downe. The family have not always lived there, though they have long had a connection with Yorkshire. In around 1377, one Thomas Dawnay, the descendant of a Dawnay who had come over from Normandy to England in the eleventh century, married Elizabeth Newton of Snaith and settled in Escrick, south of York. Gradually the family acquired land around Cowick, between Hull and Leeds, and from 1660 the politician John Dawnay, created 1st Viscount Downe in 1681, began building Cowick Hall. As Richard Downe puts it, the family have a '. . . long history of mediocrity. They didn't rise, they didn't fall. There's no book that needs to be written about the Downes – at best, it's looking at the indexes of other books to see if you can find a reference.' 'We haven't had any foreign secretaries, or viceroys of India,' he goes on, 'almost no one of any note whatsoever.'

By the time Hugh Dawnay, 8th Viscount Downe, came of age in 1865, the Downes owned five country houses. As well as Cowick, there was Beningbrough Hall, north of York; Baldersby Park near Thirsk; West Heslerton Hall near Pickering; and Wykeham, which had come into the family in 1824. Even in that extravagant era, five houses seemed several too many, so Hugh Downe began to consolidate and reorganise. In 1869, he sold Cowick and moved its contents to Baldersby, and then in 1883 bought Dingley Hall in Northamptonshire. Baldersby was sold in 1900; Beningbrough, in 1916; and the Sessay estate near Thirsk, which the Dawnays had owned since 1484, was sold in 1918. After Hugh Downe's death in 1924, Dingley was sold and West Heslerton followed in 2010 upon the death of his unmarried great-niece Eve Dawnay. 'It's like musical chairs,' Richard Downe says, 'but I've got no idea why they moved. Sometimes you see them getting richer, sometimes you can see them getting poorer.' Wykeham was the one family constant, described by Richard Downe's father John Dawnay, 11th Viscount Downe, as a 'manor house', there being '. . . two types of slightly above average-sized house. One is a sort of house that an Italian would describe as a palace. The other type is what in England we'd call a manor house.' He regarded Wykeham as belonging to the second class, in that: '[T]here are not marble halls with ceilings that are so high in the air that you have to take a pair of binoculars to see whether you've got starlings nesting.'[32] On the spectrum between a genuine manor house and Blenheim Palace, says Richard Downe, 'We're clearly in a shade of grey. We had better put "manor house" in inverted commas.'

Richard, who inherited the house from his father in 2002, when he was thirty-four, is an Old Etonian and a banker. 'You can choose which least socially unacceptable label to use,' he says. Until he took the house over, he had had relatively little to do with its day-to-day running. 'The agent would send me minutes of meetings and I would get in from work at eleven p.m. and think, "Do I really want to sit down and read these?"' When the time came, he just got on with it. 'I didn't dread it, nor did I look forward to it. If I had worked full-time at HSBC for another ten years, I would have been happy.' He doesn't *look* much like a peer – if it can be said that peers have a look. True, when I meet him he's wearing a tell-tale checked shirt beneath his navy woolly jumper, but there's no sign of the usually obligatory pair of cords or the ubiquitous slip-on loafer. His father wore a tweed jacket and tie every day of his life, 'because that's what he felt comfortable in'. But Richard decided against that. 'Two or three people a year get a suit out of me.' That said, although the note I receive from him a few days before my visit advises that 'here we are very informal', he is careful not to pretend to an 'ordinariness' that does not exist. One of his Yorkshire neighbours, he tells me, conducts rent negotiations with tenants personally, and says 'please call me by my Christian name'. 'His tenantry aren't very happy about that, it makes them uncomfortable. I don't force informality, it's almost as rude as forcing formality.'

The Wykeham estate is beautiful and very well kept. It has a grouse moor, pheasant and partridge shooting – though its owner doesn't shoot – thriving shops, a Church of England primary school and a pub. Its economic good health owes much to John Downe, who took it firmly in hand when he inherited Wykeham in 1965 from his father Richard Dawnay, 10th Viscount Downe, a military man and something of a tyrant who, for a time, kept a pair of brown bear cubs as pets. Eleven years later, John Downe opened a caravan site on the estate, and then, in 1979, founded a nursery in the old walled garden at Wykeham. 'We had never done that sort of thing before,' says Richard Downe. 'My father changed the culture here. We will always owe an awful lot to him for that drive to change things ... I'm not at all sure if Wykeham would be solvent if we hadn't diversified, because it's not in a terribly rich area,' he goes on. 'What I get from rent compared to what you might get from rent in Gloucestershire is very different. My father was pretty forward-thinking on that. These things went in fashions: caravan sites were quite fashionable in the 1970s, then golf courses became fashionable, and we're lucky we didn't do that. Then, in the late 1990s, early 2000s, redeveloping old farm buildings became very fashionable, and we did do that, so some of the time we have done a couple of businesses that are genuinely original but some of the time we have frankly done what other people have done, but hopefully done it better.' This, he says, meant that, 'When I wanted to open the North Yorkshire Water Park [in 2017], everybody was totally comfortable with the idea – it was just something that Wykeham did.' Today, around 90 per cent of the estate's income comes from its various businesses. It's their health that allows Richard Downe the luxury of having the run of the house himself and not needing to open it to the public.

The day I visit, I am driven from Seamer railway station to the house in one of Wykeham's estate cars. It has a distinctive number plate, beginning 'VN', the old North Riding code. Richard explains that in the 1950s, his grandfather bought a car that happened to have a 'VN' plate, and so, at first unintentionally, started a tradition. The family now own VN1 to VN10, and VN12 (originally the numberplate on an old motorbike that John Downe purchased in the 1970s). VN11 no longer exists. When I arrive at the house, there's another 'VN' car parked outside. I assume it must be Richard Downe's, but later discover that although he is the son of an Aston Martin enthusiast, he himself doesn't drive.

The house seems to be remarkably free from the paraphernalia of modern life. You feel you have stepped back into the nineteenth century. The overall impression is one of both modesty and immodesty: unflashy, classic beauty but on an extraordinary scale, with utilitarian objects on display that could only grace an aristocratic home. In the corridor there is a stick rack that holds hunting whips and umbrellas with 'Viscount Downe, Wykeham Abbey, Scarborough' engraved on their silver collars. They have been here, unmoved, for as long as Richard Downe can remember, and he's lived at Wykeham for almost his whole life. There's a boot room that is so large it has space for a stuffed tiger in a glass cabinet, though it's now so bleached by sunlight that it looks like a Siberian tiger. Through a door and down a corridor is a cloakroom, complete with clothes brushes, bars of soap and old-style taps that stand so close to the sink that it's hard to get one's hands under them. Rugs cover the wooden floors, threatening to slide if anyone walks over them too quickly. But then it's hard to imagine that anyone ever would in such a peaceful house. Lunch has been placed on hot plates in an intimate dining room off the hall. Someone else has cooked it and laid the table with Downe crockery.

It is, as I have said, a big house. But it does not have wings to spare, or rooms that go unvisited. Nor is it the centre of Richard Downe's universe. 'If Wykeham was a Chatsworth, such a big responsibility, then almost everything else would be peripheral,' he says. 'To me, the responsibility is very much the estate, and the house is way down the list. It would be anathema to me to be defined by Wykeham. If the estate is working, it will produce the money needed for the house – if it doesn't, then we've got other problems anyway.' Most people in his position say the opposite, that the estate no longer pays for the house, and so the house must pay for itself. At Wykeham, the house is '. . . not top of the list. If a cottage has got a leak in the roof, that goes above Wykeham.'

Richard Downe is unmarried and has no children. He intimates that on his death the title and the estate might split. For most families this would be cause for sadness, but to my surprise he says, 'I don't think in reality there ought to be a connection between the two. I don't define myself by the viscountcy. I don't think any of our previous houses are now lived in by peers – the days of a peer having by right his estate have gone.' Anyway, one could lose it all at any time. 'Legislation could make an estate uneconomic almost overnight, and there wouldn't be much we could do. I can't think of anything more depressing than seeing a house fall down around your ears. One has got to accept that an estate might evaporate within a very short space of time, so trying to say, well, it's been with us since thirteen hundred and it will always be – it might not if the chancellor has a bad stomach ache one day. You can't look forward fifty years now.'

PART TWO

Decline and Fall?

Aristocratic Power and Influence

5

Work Suspended

The Peers and the House of Lords

On 29 September 1998, prime minister Tony Blair stood on a stage in Blackpool and addressed the crowd gathered for the annual Labour Party conference. 'There is no Tory opposition anymore,' he said. 'Well, there is. It is alive and well and unelected, in the House of Lords with a three to one majority over us.' The crowd applauded. 'Not a vote to their name, but able to vote down the plans that the people voted for in our manifesto. I call that arrogance.' More applause. 'And when we use the mandate the British people gave us at the ballot box to get rid of the power of those hereditary peers, I call that democracy.'[1]

Blair's speech may have gone down well with the party faithful, but reform of the House of Lords was not, in fact, a particular priority for the government. In the Labour manifesto it was tucked away in a section entitled 'We will clean up politics', and was both very clear and rather vague in its description. There was, on one hand, a stated intention to 'end the hereditary principle in the House of Lords', and as part of this 'the right of hereditary peers to sit and vote in the House of Lords will be ended by statute.' This statement, made in the manifesto, meant that any future legislation brought about would benefit from the Salisbury Convention (on which more later) that compelled the Lords not to vote down a government bill proposed in an election manifesto.[2] On the other hand, the nuts and bolts of reform were not explained in any detail.

'Any manifesto will have a section in it which says something like "constitutional change",' says Tony Blair's former private parliamentary secretary, the Labour life peer Bruce Grocott, Baron Grocott. 'All parties coming up to a general election have to have something on that, like you have to have a chunk on education, and on health. It was a given, not the kind of thing that you needed to debate. You don't inherit the right to legislate, it's pretty basic.' Indeed, reform of the Lords was so obvious a step, so banal, he says, so '... unimportant to us on the scale of things that we did when we came into government, that I am struggling to describe to you the mechanism that would have got it into the manifesto.'

Grocott had nailed his colours to the mast a few years earlier, in a speech he made in the House of Commons on 15 June 1994. 'The House of Lords has the most bizarre and indefensible composition of any parliamentary chamber in the world,' he had informed his fellow MPs. 'At the last count, there were 1,203 members of the Lords, 759 of whom inherited their title. Those 759 peers are there because they were born in the right bed at the right time.' Or indeed the wrong bed at the right time. 'Four of the dukes – of Buccleuch and Queensberry, of Grafton, of Richmond, Lennox and Gordon, and of St Albans – are', he went on to say, 'descendants of the various mistresses of Charles II.' He had nothing against Charles II's mistresses or their descendants, he hastened to add, '... but I cannot for the life of me see why they should inherit the right to legislate.'[3]

So far as Grocott was concerned, there was scarcely anything very radical in what he had to say. He himself was a moderate. Labour had long argued for constitutional reform. 'I don't think you would find at any level of the Labour spectrum anyone who thought that hereditary peers were a good idea,' he recalls. 'I don't think it, I know it! It really is not a dividing line. Maybe it's what they like to think. The idea that scrapping the House of Lords in its present form was something for swivel-eyed individuals at a particular point on the spectrum is just nonsense.'

Some of those sitting in the Lords reluctantly accepted the inevitability – or, at least, the likelihood – of reform. 'The mostly hereditary house was harmless, but very difficult to justify,' concedes Simon Arthur, 4th Baron Glenarthur, who took his seat in the Lords as a Conservative peer in 1977.

There were those, however, who were bitterly opposed.

*　*　*

On the last occasion on which the Commons and Lords had clashed over a proposal to reform the second chamber, the opposition of the landed aristocracy had proved so entrenched and vehement that it had provoked a constitutional crisis. Virtually from the moment it came to office in 1906, the Liberal government – first under Henry Campbell-Bannerman then under Herbert Asquith – had found its legislative efforts thwarted by a Conservative-dominated House of Lords that at that time had the power to veto bills passed by the Commons.[4] Matters came to a head in 1909 when chancellor of the exchequer David Lloyd George introduced a budget that had the wealthy and the privileged unashamedly in its sights. In order to raise the money required, in Lloyd George's words, 'to wage implacable warfare against poverty and squalidness', he proposed not only to raise income tax, and introduce a supertax on those who earned more than £5,000 a year, but to increase death duties and place a levy on profits made from the sale and ownership of property.[5] It was inevitable that the peers would object.

The battle lines were clearly and aggressively drawn from the start. Lloyd George, who relished the fight, taunted the Lords by telling a crowd assembled at the Palace Theatre in Newcastle upon Tyne on 9 October 1909 that the dukes had '. . . stepped off their perch, they have been scolding like omnibus-drivers, purely because the Budget cart has knocked a little of the gilt off their old stagecoach.' He declared that their stock was down, and that 'there has been a great slump in dukes. They used to stand rather high in the market, especially in the Tory market, but the Tory press has discovered that they are of no value.' 'A fully equipped duke', he continued, 'costs as much to keep up as two dreadnoughts; and dukes are just as great a terror and they last longer.'[6] Incidentally, the street in which Palace Theatre stood, Percy Street, shared its name with the family name of the Dukes of Northumberland.

For their part, the Lords were apoplectic. The keen huntsman Henry Somerset, 9th Duke of Beaufort, expressed his graphic desire to see Winston Churchill, then president of the board of trade, and Lloyd George put 'in the middle of 20 couple of dog hounds'.[7] Henry Manners, 8th Duke of Rutland, a man later described by the press baron Max Beaverbrook as one possessed of 'considerable stupidity',[8] told a crowd that the Liberals were a 'pirate crew of tatterdemalions'.[9] William Montagu Douglas Scott, 6th Duke of Buccleuch, the super-rich owner of over 460,000 acres, gave the Budget as his reason for refusing to give a guinea to a football club in Dumfriesshire. Algernon St Maur, 15th Duke of Somerset, declared that he would be forced to cut back on his donations to charity.

As the *Liverpool Daily Post* put it, the aristocracy were '. . . becoming very vocal [about] . . . what they are pleased to regard as a socialistic finance bill.' 'If the Duke of Rutland be an approved expounder of their views,' it went on, 'they must be becoming very angry. They have been rather roughly handled of late, and perhaps not unnaturally are beginning to resent it.' As for Henry Rutland, the *Post* continued, he was '. . . old enough to know better than to talk political Billingsgate [abuse], though his lapse into this style of oratory may draw upon him more popular attention than anything he has previously said or done during the twenty years or more that he has been in one or the other House of Parliament.'[10] The *Post*'s view that their lordships were perhaps rather overdoing their outrage was shared by some within their own party. The Tory MP William Joynson-Hicks concluded that 'it would have been a good deal better for the Conservative Party if, before the Budget was introduced, every duke had been locked up and kept locked up until the Budget was over.' Dukes or no dukes, he continued, '[T]hese men who are going about squealing and say they are going to reduce their subscriptions to charities and football clubs because they were being unduly taxed ought to be ashamed of themselves.'[11]

They were, evidently, not ashamed enough. In November 1909, the Lords exercised its historic right to reject a finance bill, something it had not done for two centuries. It was, Asquith argued, a breach of the unwritten constitution, and 'a usurpation of the rights of the Commons'.[12] The Lords' veto of the Budget, however, came with a potential lifeline for the government: if the Liberals could secure an electoral mandate for the bill, the Lords would – reluctantly – allow it to pass. Asquith duly called an election on the issue in January 1910. The result was a hung parliament, with Arthur Balfour's Conservatives securing only two fewer seats than Asquith's Liberals. Nevertheless, in April that year, the Budget was passed as promised.

For the Liberals that wasn't, and couldn't be, the end of the affair. Strong-arming the Lords into passing particular pieces of legislation wasn't enough. Their power needed to be curbed. A second election was therefore called in December 1910 on the issue of constitutional reform. Again, the result was a hung parliament, but this time Asquith threatened to push his reforms through the Lords by flooding it with an army of new Liberal peers. George V reluctantly went along with him. The Lords recognised that they had been checkmated.

The Parliament Act of August 1911 removed the right of the House of Lords to veto money bills, and reduced its power over other areas of policy from one of outright rejection to one of delay for two years.[13] It became a chamber that could scrutinise but not exercise control. Its membership, though, remained untouched and unchanged.

* * *

Over the next half-century, the role and nature of the Lords was periodically debated, but to no practical effect. The Bryce Commission, which reported in January 1918, proposed a remodelled second chamber with just 350 members, most of them elected by members of the Commons and the rest selected by a committee of both houses. It also argued in favour of giving the Lords back its power of veto, lost seven years earlier, and a disputes mechanism for settling any disagreements between the two houses. George Curzon, leader of the Lords, even got as far as drawing up a scheme for putting the recommendations into practice.

There was, it should be said, little general enthusiasm for reform, even if several peers, believing it might forestall something worse in the future, did express themselves in favour of it. William Palmer, 2nd Earl of Selborne, former first lord of the Admiralty, for example, put it this way to the former chancellor Austen Chamberlain in June 1918: 'I regard it as a very real danger that the Unionist Party will let this question stand over until a Labour Party comes into power – and then! Therefore, it seems to me, if I may say so quite frankly, that you will be missing a great opportunity which your position in Cabinet gives you if you allow the federal solution and the Second Chamber reform both to slide. If neither the one nor the other was accomplished I should regard the position of the country as very dangerous – I should regard revolution as very possible.'[14] Curzon completed his work on a Bryce-like scheme in July 1922. But four months later prime minister David Lloyd George lost the general election to the Conservative Andrew Bonar Law and Curzon's work was discarded.

Similar inaction followed Labour's landslide election victory in 1945. Again, reform was mooted; again, there were no practical legislative consequences. The one change that was introduced was more in the form of a gentlemen's agreement than a binding constitutional reform. The Salisbury Doctrine (or 'Convention' as it is sometimes known), named after Robert 'Bobbety' Gascoyne-Cecil, 5th Marquess of Salisbury, established that the Lords would not vote down a government bill proposed in an election manifesto. Dressed up as a concession, it was in reality more of a clever ploy to ensure that a government that could muster barely more than a dozen Labour peers would not feel compelled to take a constitutional axe to the Lords in the way that the Liberals had felt compelled to do in 1911.

If Labour felt that it was possible to live with the status quo – even that the status quo might be desirable in the short term if, in the long term, it showed that the Lords was 'indefensible' – the Conservative administration that followed, while aware of the risks of inaction, talked only in vague terms of tinkering with what was there.[15] Winston Churchill raised the prospect of possible reform in his election address of 1951, pledging that if a Conservative government were returned, it would summon an all-party group to consider the Lords anew. But when in January 1955 the former Liberal leader Herbert Samuel, 1st Viscount Samuel, pondered what that might mean in practice, it rapidly became apparent that the group Churchill had promised had never actually been convened. Samuel blamed the 'attitude' of the Labour Party for this. In response the Labour peer and former Lord Chancellor William Jowitt, 1st Earl Jowitt, admitted – one suspects with a sigh – that: '[W]e have been going rather round and round about it.'[16] When Samuel pressed his initial question, Lords leader Bobbety Salisbury responded: 'I seem to remember a great Liberal dictum: "Wait and see." '[17]

Bobbety's seeming imperturbability, however, belied his concern about the future prospects of an unreformed House of Lords. Unless something was done, he feared that – in the words of the constitutional historian Walter Bagehot almost a century earlier – the second chamber would die a death, not of '. . . assassination, but atrophy; not abolition, but decline'. '[T]he danger of the House of Commons', Bagehot had written in 1867, 'is, perhaps, that it will be reformed too rashly; the danger of the House of Lords certainly is, that it may never be reformed. Nobody asks that it should be so; it is quite safe against rough destruction, but it is not safe against inward decay.'[18] In immediate terms, as Bobbety told his grandson Robert Gascoyne-Cecil, 7th Marquess of Salisbury, his worry about the lords in the Lords was that 'the ones who are rich enough are too stupid, and the ones who are intelligent enough are too poor and have to work.' His solution was to pay the peers. 'A popular belief appears to persist in this country that all peers are rich men,' he told the Lords, 'but noble lords know that in these difficult days that is no longer true – if, indeed, it ever was, to the extent suggested by that popular belief. The vast majority of noble lords in this house can no longer afford to give their whole time to a job for which they receive no remuneration, not even payment of the many expenses incidental to the job itself.'[19] He feared that the chamber of his day was, on the whole, 'very feeble'.[20]

Robert Salisbury thinks his grandfather's instincts were the right ones. 'If the House of Lords is going to work then you've got to get new blood in, and [back then] the hereditary peers couldn't hack it any longer because they had lost power.' 'One of the things that the second chamber has got to have,' he continues, 'is a combination of power, status and respect.' Bobbety's campaign was successful. Proposals for the reimbursement of peers' expenses – as distinct from payment itself – were agreed in July 1957, and soon after a daily allowance of up to three guineas was instituted.[21]

That same year, the new Conservative prime minister, Harold Macmillan, became the first to seriously re-engage with the issue of further reform of the second chamber. Back in 1856 a proposal had been made to introduce life peers to the Lords to supplement the hereditary peers.[22] Nothing had come of it until 1876 when Benjamin Disraeli's Conservative government had introduced the Appellate Jurisdiction Act, which allowed senior judges to sit in the Lords as life barons, where they were known as Lords of Appeal in Ordinary – or the 'law lords'. Now Macmillan pushed through the Life Peerages Act, to allow the promotion of both men and women to non-hereditary peerages that would allow them to take a seat in the Lords.

These new peerages represented a new kind of 'nobility' – perhaps comparable to, in France, the *noblesse d'épée*, the original knightly class, and the *noblesse de robe*, those whose ranks were derived from holding judicial or administrative posts. Arguably, life peerages brought with them a spirit of greater professionalism in the Lords. They also offered retiring MPs a second, rather more cushy, career away from the firing line of the Commons, as well as ensuring that the politically ambitious offspring of those promoted to the Lords would not be burdened with a hereditary peerage that would keep them out of the Commons – a point of particular concern to Macmillan who was anxious to spare his son Maurice (an MP for almost thirty years) the curse of a hereditary peerage.[23]

Such middle-of-the-road reform was inevitably attacked both from the left and the right. On the left, there were, as Macmillan later recalled, '. . . those members of the Opposition who disliked a second chamber in principle and . . . feared in a reformed House of Lords a more effective barrier to their hopes'. On the right, there were those who '. . . believed that any infraction of the hereditary system was dangerous'.[24] Some disliked the prospect of life peerages being offered to women as well as men. It might have been forty years since Nancy Astor had become the first female member of parliament to take her seat in the Commons, but the relatively few female hereditary peers in existence in the middle part of the century were distinctly unwelcome in the Lords.[25] Christopher Roper-Curzon, 19th Baron Teynham, told the Lords in October 1957 that he was 'not much in favour' of the inclusion of women, arguing that 'it would alter the character of the House'. The future prime minister Alec Douglas-Home, 14th Earl of Home, speaking in the same debate, told the house that 'most of the troubles of the modern world date from the time when women were given the vote' – but did go on to say, 'I am willing to treat that as coincidence rather than consequence,' and concluded that 'taking women into a parliamentary embrace would seem to be only a modest extension of the normal functions and privileges of a peer.'[26]

The first new life peer to be created was the Conservative politician Ian Fraser, who became Baron Fraser of Lonsdale on 1 August 1958.[27] Fraser had been blinded by a German bullet during the Battle of the Somme in 1916, was a founding member of the Royal British Legion, and a governor of the BBC. Later that month, nine more new life peerages were created. Among them, on 8 August, was the first female life peer, the sociologist Barbara Wootton – though she was beaten to becoming the first to take her seat in the

Lords by Stella Isaacs, Marchioness of Reading, wife of the former Viceroy of India, who was made a life peer as Baroness Swanborough six weeks later. Wootton later recalled how her mother had taken her to see the Palace of Westminster in 1911 when the Parliament Act was being debated. As their carriage passed the House of Commons, her mother 'pointed up to the light in Big Ben and remarked: "That is where they are destroying the British Constitution." '[28] The incident made a big impression on Wootton.

She found the upper house 'a very agreeable community to which to belong'.[29] Perhaps a little surprisingly, she also recognised a case for maintaining the presence of hereditary peers there. 'No doubt the hereditary principle is now generally recognised as a ludicrous anachronism, though it seems to be an unconscionable time a-dying,' she recalled, echoing Charles II's description of his own death in 1685; but still, she felt that the hereditary peerage kept the Lords young. As she put it:

> Any chamber which was recruited on some supposed criterion of 'merit' would inevitably be heavily weighted with members well on in years, since few of the young would have time to make their mark. But in a predominantly hereditary house, thanks to the accident of premature death, a fair sprinkling of sons inherit their fathers' titles and take their seats quite early in life. Their presence in a community which might otherwise be unduly reminiscent of a geriatric institution is certainly refreshing. But this refreshment notwithstanding, even the sweets of victory are soured in the Lords, inasmuch as they can only be won by the votes of peers whose sole claim to legislative power is the fact that they (like other people) are the sons of their fathers.[30]

When Macmillan came to write his memoirs, he argued that the introduction of his 'modest constitutional reform' had changed the Lords for the better: '[U]ndoubtedly the powers and prestige of the House of Lords have been buttressed by the extension of its membership.'[31] But like many new initiatives it took time to kick in. Sir Michael Pownall, a former clerk of the parliaments, has pointed out that '. . . at the end of the 1959–60 session, only 25 life peers had been appointed under the 1958 Life Peerages Act and in 1960, more hereditary peerages (nine) were created than life peerages (three).'[32] Indeed, two hereditary peerages were created within three months of the giving of Royal Assent to the 1958 Peerage Act, one of which was given to a former public servant, Ellis Robins, who had only daughters and no son, and whose title, as a result, promptly became extinct four years later.[33] Judging from Macmillan's hostile reaction to the publication of the Queen's Birthday Honours list in June 1965, when six new life peers were created, this slow pace of change was precisely what he had had in mind. He described the list as 'absurd', and attacked the Labour prime minister Harold Wilson for pressing ahead with it. 'Is Wilson trying to swamp the House of Lords by these massive creations? No hereditary titles, peerages or baronetcies.'[34]

In the decade that followed the introduction of life peers, a total of 243 peerages were created, 172 of them for life, the balance – even though there was now no technical need for them – hereditary. Among the new hereditary entrants were politicians, lawyers, media owners, a governor of the Bank of England and a neurologist. Several were already holders of hereditary titles or related to those who possessed them. The Hon. Evelyn Baring, a former Governor of Kenya who incorporated the name of a valley in his beloved Cheviot Hills to create his new title, Baron Howick of Glendale, in 1960, was the younger son of the former consul general of Egypt Evelyn Baring, 1st Earl of Cromer. He was encouraged by Macmillan's son-in-law Julian Amery, MP, to use 'the House of Lords as a platform and not a sofa', but in the end spoke only five times during his thirteen-year tenure.[35] The Hon. John Wyndham, created 1st Baron Egremont[36] in November 1963, was already in line for a peerage as the son of Edward Wyndham, 5th Baron Leconfield. In 1952, he had inherited his uncle Charles Wyndham, 3rd Baron Leconfield's almost 70,000-acre estates, including Petworth in West Sussex, by his measure 'surely one of the most beautiful white elephants in Europe, an immense white elephant adorned by one of the most splendid collections of pictures to be found outside a public gallery'.[37]

Some of the new hereditary peerages went – inevitably – to politicians. The Conservative politician Sir Thomas Dugdale, 1st Baronet, for example, who had resigned from his job as minister of agriculture and fisheries in 1954 over the Crichel Down affair, was offered a peerage five years later.[38] At the time, hereditary peers could not renounce their titles in order to stand as MPs – a rule that prevailed until 1963 – so Dugdale consulted his son James, now 2nd Baron Crathorne, before he accepted. 'I've been offered the title,' he told him, 'but if you wanted to go into politics and become an MP then I would not accept it.' 'It was', James Crathorne reflects, 'an extraordinarily generous and thoughtful thing to do, bless him.' As it happened, James felt that he wouldn't be good at the 'cut and thrust of the Commons', and when his father died in 1977, joined the Lords.

If the old guard was forced to accept the inevitability of new life and hereditary peers – and even life peers who were women – some nevertheless drew the line at the prospect of female hereditary peers taking their place in the second chamber. Historically, there had never been more than a relatively small handful of potential candidates, since fewer than ninety peerages can be inherited by a female heir, but the thought of allowing any of them into the House of Lords was, apparently, a bridge too far. Speaking in a debate on 30 October 1957, Herbert Samuel described the notion as 'a surrender again to the hereditary principle' – slightly rich coming from a man whose own title had only been created twenty years earlier – though he generously conceded that 'there may be some who might well be brought in with advantage to the nation.'[39] During a further debate at the beginning of December, 28-year-old Robert 'Robin' Shirley, 13th Earl Ferrers – who, despite his views on this subject, later became a popular Conservative member of the Lords – proclaimed that he thought it would be 'an unmitigated disaster to have women in this House'. When Alec Home criticised this view, Ferrers, far from retreating, went further: 'I hate the idea of your Lordships' House becoming a repository for over-exuberant female politicians ... Frankly, I find women in politics highly distasteful. In general, they are organising, they are pushing and they are commanding ... I believe that there are certain duties and certain responsibilities which nature and custom have decreed men are more fitted to take on; and some responsibilities which nature and custom have decreed women should take on. It is generally accepted that the man should bear the major responsibility in life. It is generally accepted, for better or worse, that a man's judgement is generally more logical and less tempestuous than that of a woman. Why then should we encourage women to eat their way, like acid into metal, into positions of trust and responsibility which previously men have held? If we allow women into this House where will this emancipation end? Shall we in a few years' time be referring to "the noble and learned Lady, the Lady Chancellor"? I find that a horrifying thought.'[40]

Ferrers was immediately countered by retired naval captain Eric Fellowes, 3rd Baron Ailwyn, who lamented 'the somewhat ungallant remarks we have been hearing about the female sex' and added that he was 'not impressed by the arguments against admitting them.' 'I find them unconvincing,' he went on. 'Moreover, I should like to see peeresses in their own right admitted under this measure.' The writer and painter Rufus Buxton, 2nd Baron Noel-Buxton, concurred, arguing that 'the question of women in this House ... seems to be a perfectly obvious matter' – as did the Perthshire landowner Mungo Murray, 7th Earl of Mansfield: 'It is absolutely necessary, if women are to be allowed to sit in your Lordships' House, that their numbers should include the hereditary Peeresses in their own right,' he argued. 'It is an absolute insult to your Lordships to suggest that ladies who, but for the accident of sex, would sit among us should be excluded, while unknown female "whatnots", with Heaven knows what qualifications, are to be put among us.'[41]

Ferrers was not a lone voice. Quintin Hogg, 2nd Viscount Hailsham, the new chairman of the Conservative Party, was similarly opposed to women hereditary peers in the House of Lords, though his line of attack was spuriously legal rather than overtly sexist. 'The actual method of descent by which a peerage descends to a peeress in her own right is so difficult, so complicated and so anomalous,' he stated in a debate on Hallowe'en 1957, 'that I doubt whether many of your Lordships could accurately describe them; and certainly not one in a million of the public knows that they exist.' He proceeded to offer an opaque elaboration: 'The law of co-parceny and abeyance seems to me to be so anomalous that to extend the hereditary principle by including it in your Lordships' composition in 1957 would be a doubtful proposition.'[42]

Hailsham's ponderously expressed view was rejected by Alexander Fraser, 20th Lord Saltoun, who argued that in Scotland 'the method of descent is perfectly simple and clear,' and by Philip Cunliffe-Lister, 1st Earl of Swinton, who drew their lordships' attention to the contradictions that lay at its core. 'However their succession may come,' he pointed out, 'they are hereditary peeresses as much as noble lords are hereditary peers ... it seems to me a little illogical that if we are going to have women as life peeresses, we cannot have hereditary peeresses in your Lordships' House.' He pressed his argument further: '[S]uppose the prime minister of the day says that he thinks that it would be a good thing to appoint two or three ladies who are peeresses in their own right as life peeresses: is he entitled to do this, or are they barred? If they are barred, that means that the poor ladies are in a most unfortunate position; they are the only females outside a lunatic asylum who are not to be entitled to sit in this House.'[43]

On the afternoon of 21 January 1959, the matter was debated for the final time before being put to the vote. Bobbety Salisbury summarised the central issue. Historically, he said, women had been excluded 'purely and simply because of a sex disqualification'; now the Life Peerages Act enabled women who were not hereditary peers to sit in the second chamber: 'On what grounds, then, are we still to continue the disqualification of hereditary Peeresses in their own right who, but for their sex, would always have received the writ?

Why should we still penalise them alone?'[44] Gerald Isaacs, 2nd Marquess of Reading, then put forward a motion to end the discrimination against hereditary peeresses. It was passed by fifty-nine to fifty-one.[45] Even so, it was to be several years before Elizabeth Philipps, 14th Baroness Strange of Knokin, became the first female hereditary peer to take her seat in the Lords on 19 November 1963, following the passing of the Peerage Act, which made such an act possible. Three months later, she was joined by Mary Freeman-Grenville, 12th Lady Kinloss, who had previously lived the life of a 'very ordinary housewife' in Aden while accompanying her husband Greville Freeman-Grenville there while he was working for the protectorate in the 1960s.[46] She was, her daughter Teresa Freeman-Grenville, 13th Lady Kinloss explains, a shy woman, and it was brave of her to go into the Lords. 'My father encouraged her to – he thought it would help her get over her shyness.' Greville referred to his wife's commitment to the Lords as her 'queen's duty'.

If it took a long time for the Lords to make women feel welcome, it took even longer to make them feel comfortable. When Margaret of Mar, 31st Countess of Mar,[47] joined the Lords in 1975 following the death of her father James Clifton of Mar, 30th Earl of Mar, a former farmer in Kenya and a man, according to his daughter, who had 'kept the bar going' in the Lords, she found the facilities left a lot to be desired. There were no ladies' toilets on the principal floor, 'so you either had to go up to the peeresses' gallery, or downstairs to the cloakrooms.' And the chairs were all too tall – '... made for men with long legs. If you went to sit in the library, you were sort of sprawled out, you couldn't sit properly.' When in 1995 she was appointed deputy speaker and sat on the Woolsack[48] for the first session, 'Black Rod [then General Sir Edward Jones] came to meet me afterwards to ask how I'd got on, and I said it was fine except that my feet didn't touch the ground. The next day there was a lovely velvet footstool there, and that used to come out every time.'

* * *

If the debate over hereditary female peers suggests that the House of Lords of the 1950s and early 1960s was daily awash with their male equivalents, that was not the case. Indeed, as former clerk of the parliaments the late Sir John Sainty remembered, it wasn't a very aristocratic place at all.

John Sainty came to the Lords in 1959 via Winchester College, New College Oxford and a brief spell in his mother's native United States. Not sure what he wanted to do next, he visited the appointments bureau at Oxford, filled in various application forms, was asked 'What games do you still play?', and was then presented with a various uninspiring job options, all of which he declined. Finally, a bottom drawer was opened and a yellow file advertising a role for a clerk at the House of Lords was pulled out. 'It had never occurred to me that there were such people as clerks in the Lords, and I thought I'd give it a go, although I had no particular interest in parliamentary history at all.'

Himself the son of an engineer, he soon found that those who regularly attended the Lords were very much not those who possessed vast estates and who fitted the aristocratic stereotype. If we take 'aristocrat' to mean landowning and country-dwelling, the Lords 'wasn't a place of aristocrats', he said. 'It so happened that the leader of the House in 1959 was the Earl of Home, but [such figures] were few and far between. If you were interested in social advancement the House of Lords was not the place for you. It was extremely unusual for a still-landed nobleman to spend any time at the Lords.' True, some of the attendees possessed old titles, but few of those who attended still held their ancestral lands. Some thought those who had only the Lords left were a little pathetic.

A general lack of interest in politics – or, at least, a greater interest in other, more engaging activities – was not a recent phenomenon. Back in 1891, prime minister Robert Salisbury had complained to Arthur Balfour that Spencer Cavendish, Marquess of Hartington, soon to succeed as the 8th Duke of Devonshire, was '. . . at Newmarket and all political arrangements have to be hung up until some quadruped has run faster than some other quadruped.'[49] At various times in the nineteenth century, during one crisis or other, it was common for Parliament to sit well into August, much to the disgruntlement of those wanted to be away from London by the Glorious Twelfth on 12 August – the start of the grouse season. As late as the early 1990s, according to one peer, there was often no voting during Ascot and Cheltenham weeks. Now, Parliament is in recess during August. Robert Salisbury had long complained about the Lords being 'a paradise of bores', and suggested that 'a Quaker jollification, a French horse-race, a Presbyterian psalm, all are lively and exciting compared to an ordinary debate in the House of Lords,' which might have been better compared to 'a debate in one of Madame Tussaud's showrooms'. Perhaps, then, it wasn't such a surprise that peers were not so keen to attend. As Salisbury described, to treat the Lords as just 'a place for passing an idle hour or two before dinner' would soon persuade the public of this, which would lead to enemies of the lords and the Lords feeling justified in 'uttering that most frightful of all insults, "I told you so."'[50] As the current Robert Salisbury observes about the lords in the unreformed Lords, '[A]s survival became more important, in a curious way they made survival more difficult by not being interested in politics.' That remained the case decades later. As Benjamin Mancroft, 3rd Baron Mancroft, says of the Lords in the 1990s: '[T]he very grand ones never came – they weren't interested in politics and had other things to do.'

As a rule, if the grander lords did choose to attend on a particular occasion, it was only because what was being debated then directly affected them. During the furore over Lloyd George's 1909 Budget, for example, various aristocrats who had rarely if ever graced the Palace of Westminster previously, turned up to register their implacable opposition. A term was even devised to describe them: 'backwoodsmen', which has been defined as 'those noblemen who spent most of their time on their country estates, cared little for national politics and participated less, almost never appeared in the House of Lords, but could be relied upon to come to Westminster in vast numbers to veto seriously threatening Liberal legislation'.[51] Following the Budget defeat, the Lords commissioned William

Onslow – who we met earlier, pleading penury – to oversee a survey of the number of peers who did not attend, or attended fewer than ten times, during the sessions of 1902, 1906 and 1909. It revealed that 58 per cent of peers in 1902, 37 per cent in 1906 and 42 per cent in 1909 fell into one or other of those categories.

The 1950s and 1960s did not provide a similarly galvanising cause for the aristocratic backwoodsmen. But there was one acrimonious debate, in March 1961, that symbolised a barely perceptible shift in influence from the old upper-class aristocracy, few of whom visited the Lords other than rarely, to the newer middle-class peers, who were far keener. The two peers at the centre of it all were Bobbety Salisbury and Quintin Hailsham – and the row was over Africa.

The Salisburys had long had connections with Rhodesia (now Zimbabwe). The capital city, Salisbury, was named after their ancestor who had served as prime minister; the family owned land there; and when Bobbety Salisbury resigned as leader of the House of Lords in 1957, he went on to become a director of the British South Africa Company. He viewed Britain's post-war retreat from empire with concern, and the concessions that the British were starting to make in Kenya and Rhodesia with growing indignation. In the view of his grandson Robert Salisbury, he worried 'that we were giving independence [from the Empire] too soon. His opponents thought that this was a mask for saying "independence never", but I don't think that's what he thought . . . He was concerned by what he thought was too-rapid decolonisation. He realised that decolonisation would happen but he felt that if it happened too quickly, it would all collapse into a corrupt dictatorship.' For a while Bobbety kept his silence. But then, on 7 March 1961, he launched an attack on the colonial secretary, Iain Macleod, accusing him of being 'rather unscrupulous', of being 'too clever by half' and of having adopted 'a most unhappy and an entirely wrong approach' that had served to sow distrust between white settlers and Britain.[52]

The following day, Quintin Hailsham, looking, as one peer put it, 'like a vegetarian who had just had his first meal of meat',[53] stood up in the Lords to berate Bobbety in terms that left Arthur 'Boofy' Gore, 8th Earl of Arran, Bobbety's cousin, feeling compelled to leave the chamber, though not before asking whether Hailsham '. . . would cease his personal abuse [of Bobbety] and get on with his speech?'[54] Hailsham, hectoring on and on in his usual way, accused Bobbety of having taken away Macleod's 'personal honour': '[W]e can all be glad of our reputations as honest men. It was that which I thought the noble marquess was seeking to take away from my right honourable friend. If I had to choose between marquesses I prefer the Queensberry rules to the Cecil rules,' he went on, 'because the Queensberry rules at least prescribe that it is unfair to hit below the belt.'[55] If anything, this was a bare-knuckle fight in which upper-class Salisbury, grandson of the former prime minister, and a member of a family that had been active in politics since the time of Elizabeth I, was pitched against middle-class Hailsham, a second-generation peer, and the descendant of a director of the East India Company. As writer and journalist Anthony Sampson concluded, it was 'not only a conflict between classes, and between old and new Conservatives: it was a conflict between a generation strong enough to stand up to its enemies, and one preoccupied with solidarity and survival, and uncertain exactly who might be friend and who foe.'[56]

Later that week, Bobbety resigned from his local Conservative association. Another of his cousins, Roundell 'Top' Palmer, 3rd Earl of Selborne, resigned from the East Hampshire Conservatives, and Conservative peer and landowner Cecil Weld-Forester, 7th Baron Forester, stopped his subscription to the Ludlow and Wrekin Association, transferring his allegiance to the Rhodesian United Federal Party. '[T]he Cecils don't give a damn,' Clement Attlee said. 'That makes a lot of difference.'[57] Even so, it seemed at the time that the power of the Cecils at Westminster had finally come to an end.[58] When Bobbety died in 1972, he was, Robert Salisbury says, a 'sad man, mourning the passing of British power'.

* * *

Meanwhile the 'problem' of the backwoodsmen remained. When they didn't make an appearance at Westminster, their invisibility seemed to strengthen the case for further reform. When they did turn up, they invariably aroused feelings of irritation and resentment among their more diligent fellow peers. One of the Conservatives' best-respected hereditary members recalled 'one crucial vote – it might have been Maastricht [in 1993]' when 'a whole lot of Conservative peers arrived who we hadn't seen from one year to the next.' 'One of them', he went on, 'came up to me and said, "Which way is the government voting?" I said, "Well, it's this way," and he said, "Well, I'll have you know, I'm going in the other direction." There was a definite feeling amongst many of them that their independence was important.' It was not an attitude guaranteed to endear them to their colleagues.

More often than not, it was the invisibility of the backwoodsmen that was most apparent. Between 1955 and 1960, only eight of the twenty-seven non-royal dukes spoke at all in the Lords. No Duke of Rutland has made a speech in the Lords since 1946. When Sunny Marlborough made his maiden speech about badgers in February 1973, it had been forty-two years since a Duke of Marlborough had risen to say anything. No Duke of Westminster spoke in the Lords for the first ninety-one years of the twentieth century until Gerald Grosvenor, 6th Duke of Westminster, made his first and last speech, about the Territorial Army, four years after he took the oath. The Marquesses of Bath were slightly keener: a mere sixty years elapsed between Thomas Bath making a speech and his grandson Alexander following suit. Henry Bath, a member for forty-six years, never spoke at all. On 23 May 1988, the day of the vote on the unpopular poll tax, the former Labour MP and journalist Woodrow Wyatt, Baron Wyatt of Weeford, found the Lords '. . . utterly packed. Never seen so many people. When I saw Henry Bath I realised how intense the whipping has been.'[59]

'Maggie Thatcher could have sorted out the problem by saying "no backwoodsmen",' says Margaret Mar. 'In other words, you've got to attend the house so many times before you can vote. When there was a big vote on, a whole lot of people came into the house who simply didn't know their way around. I was absolutely livid. It's so wrong – you either take part, or you stay away altogether.'

Margaret Mar's arrival in the Lords in the mid-1970s followed closely on the heels of another abortive attempt at reform. In 1969, Dick Crossman, Harold Wilson's leader of the Commons, came up with a plan that would have split the peers in the Lords into two groups – those who would retain the right to vote, chosen by party whips, and those who did not. Under the proposed Parliament (No. 2) Bill, the Lords' ability to delay legislation would also be reduced.

But Crossman's idea barely left the starting blocks, in part thanks to an unlikely alliance between Labour MP Michael Foot and his Conservative colleague Enoch Powell. Foot's backbench rebellion, best remembered today for his description of the second chamber as 'a seraglio of eunuchs', was enough to persuade Harold Wilson to withdraw the bill.[60] Once that had occurred, Powell skewered the prospect of any revisiting of the subject by arguing that the '... traditional, prescriptive House of Lords posed no threat and injured no interests, but might yet, for all its illogicalities and anomalies, make itself felt on occasion to useful purpose.'[61] Merlin Hanbury-Tracy, 7th Baron Sudeley and a former president of the right-wing Monday Club, told me shortly before he died in September 2022, 'I started to attend the House of Lords only after the collapse of Harold Wilson's proposals. I didn't want to settle in the Lords if my position was going to be insecure.' But then, he added, as we sat shivering in his very cold flat in Marylebone, reform '... always foundered, because nobody could think of anything satisfactory to take its place.'

It would be nearly thirty years before another serious attempt was made.

* * *

In 1998, the year after Tony Blair secured his first general election victory, the Labour leader in the Lords, Ivor Richard, Baron

Richard, a former British ambassador to the United Nations, called a meeting between the leader of the opposition in the Lords, Robert Gascoyne-Cecil, Viscount Cranborne (now the afore-mentioned Robert Salisbury), and the Conservative whip Tom Galbraith, 2nd Baron Strathclyde, to discuss the possibility of launching a new initiative to reform the Lords. They met at Robert Cranborne's house in Chelsea for lunch. As he remembered, 'Ivor quite rightly thought that our initial contacts ought to be made rather discreetly. My house is reasonably discreet and it seemed to be a convenient venue which he was happy to come to.' Richard found the occasion 'very agreeable'; and if little immediate pro-gress was made – those assembled ended up talking more about farming than politics – Richard nevertheless felt that if sealing the deal had been left to that original grouping, '[W]e could probably have produced a package.'[62]

Richard believed the way forward was for two-thirds of the members of the Lords to be elected, and one-third to be appointed. As he later wrote, '[T]o carry out its functions effectively, and to be able convincingly to ask a government to think again, the second chamber needs to have at least a majority of its members dir-ectly elected.'[63] Blair didn't agree, favouring instead an appointed chamber, a solution Richard viewed as patronising to the elector-ate, and which was somewhat ironic given the Labour manifesto's commitment to making the Lords more democratic. Richard was sacked in July 1998: 'shafted', according to Cranborne, 'because he genuinely wanted an effective, reformed second chamber'. Reviewing events in a comment piece for *The Times* in August 1999, Richard argued that Blair had 'an historic opportunity to introduce major reform' to the Lords, but suggested 'it is not clear whether he will grasp it. Although the government's own pre-ferred blueprint for a reformed upper house remains opaque, the Labour Party's stance to date has, unfortunately, leaned towards a wholly nominated chamber. The canard at the heart of the debate is that a second chamber with a substantial elected element would threaten the legitimacy of the House of Commons. Nothing is further from the truth. It is this myth that undermines the expansion of democracy.'[64]

In Richard's place came Margaret Jay, Baroness Jay of Paddington, the sometime *Panorama* journalist and daughter of the former prime minister Jim Callaghan, Baron Callaghan of Cardiff. There was a certain irony here. Margaret Jay had been made a peer in 1993 and was the daughter of a life peer. Yet her job now was to evict a whole bunch of other peers, whose fathers had also been peers. 'I remember Margaret Jay being very rude about us, and to us,' says one former Conservative peer. 'Most people liked her father. It's not quite clear what she did to get here apart from being his daughter.' There was a symmetry too, in the fact that Margaret Jay and her father both sat in the Lords at the same time, and, through a complex scheme, so did Robert Cranborne (as Baron Cecil of Essendon) and his father, the 6th Marquess of Salisbury.

Rising to speak in the Lords in mid-October 1998 and quoting the Labour Party manifesto, Margaret Jay referred to the first step – 'an initial self-contained reform, not dependent on further reform in the future' – which would end the right of hereditary peers to sit and vote in the House of Lords. After that, she continued, further reform would follow to '. . . achieve an improved transitional chamber of appointed peers, and then develop an appropriate second chamber for the next century.' The imprecise nature of the language used struck Robert Cranborne as confirmation of his suspicion that Labour hadn't got as far as thinking what form further change might take: 'I have always thought,' he said, 'that the two-stage process the government are pursuing will guarantee that we shall never get beyond stage one . . . there will be no incentive whatsoever for the government of the day, whatever their political complexion, to implement stage two once stage one has been introduced and passed.'[65]

Whatever shape stage two might or might not have taken, Margaret Jay adopted a combative approach to launching stage one. Her first broadside was launched on 14 October 1998 when she rose in the Lords to announce that the 'most thoughtful' of the hereditary peers 'know that the time has come to say, "Thank you and goodbye."' The hereditaries, she said, were not representative of Britain in 1998: '[W]e know that 60 per cent of hereditary peers claim a background in landowning and farming and 42 per cent have had careers in the Armed Forces. Only 1.4 per cent describe themselves as workers – not exactly a cross-section of society that we recognise today. Today's Britain is multicultural and multi-ethnic but, for obvious reasons, that is nowhere reflected in the hereditary peerage.' Nor, with only sixteen female peers out of a total 750, were women properly represented in the Lords. Reform in her view was essential and long overdue. Cranborne responded. The government, he said, 'know that attacking the hereditary peers is the only political issue left that unites the upper classes of the Labour Party with their followers, the gentry of Islington with the helots of Old Labour'. He made his own position clear: 'As a hereditary peer, I assure the government front bench that I will go quietly if a properly independent chamber takes our place.'[66]

More than 100 peers followed Jay and Cranborne in this first debate, and many more in further debates over the following months. Robin Ferrers confessed that he worried about reforming the house in two stages. 'First, you get rid of the hereditary peers, and then you say, "What are we going to do?" That is rather like getting on a ship, going out into the middle of the ocean and then saying, "Where shall we go?" Not many people would think that that was a wise way of navigating.' For his part Martin Charteris, Baron Charteris of Amisfield, Queen Elizabeth II's former private secretary, pointed out that taking away the right of hereditary peers would endanger the monarchy: '[A]fter all, the monarchy is dependent on heredity. It will be rather difficult if our sovereign is the only person in the country who sits on the throne because of heredity.'[67]

The former Bletchley Park codebreaker Jean Barker, Baroness Trumpington, also came out in support of the hereditaries. 'Why should we be deprived . . . of the benefits we receive for free from noble Lords such as the noble Lords, Lord Gowrie, Lord Rothschild, Lord Shepherd and Lord Kilbracken, the noble Countess,

Lady Mar, and the noble Lord, Lord Selborne [*sic*], a Fellow of the Royal Society?[68] When I became a life peer eighteen years ago I found myself surrounded by my betters. That feeling has not changed today. But what of the future? Speaking personally, I can see no reason to differ between being the son of one's father as opposed to being a prime minister's favourite or a failed minister.'[69]

As the debates continued, Robert Cranborne worked furiously behind the scenes to salvage what he could for the hereditaries. By now he had resigned himself to the reality that most would have to go. But he hoped, as he embarked on a series of meetings with Derry Irvine, the Lord Chancellor, that some might be allowed to remain. His suggestion was that all the hereditaries should be allowed to vote for a given number who would then be retained. It was an idea based on two considerations: first, that it would ensure that some of the most useful members of the Lords would be kept on until further reform could be enacted; second, that his proposal was so obviously fudged that it would force the government to go ahead with a more considered further stage of reform. And if, for whatever reason, the government never pressed that additional stage, at least the hereditary principle would continue.

This is precisely what came about. Cranborne threatened Irvine that if he didn't agree to his scheme, the Conservative hereditary peers would wreak 'Somme and Passchendaele' on Labour, and the 'complete buggerisation' of their legislative programme.[70] Faced with such intransigence and with it the potential collapse of New Labour's wider plans, Irvine agreed.

Having established the principle of retaining some peers, the debate now moved on to haggling over precisely how many that might involve in practice. Eventually it was agreed that two places would be left for the Earl Marshal – then Miles Fitzalan Howard, 17th Duke of Norfolk, MC – and the Lord Great Chamberlain – then David Cholmondeley, 7th Marquess of Cholmondeley – and ninety hereditary peers would be voted on by the other hereditaries.[71] Irvine informed Tony Blair about the compromise that had been reached. Blair said he'd have to consult his official spokesman

Alastair Campbell. Cranborne duly met Campbell on 30 November 1998. 'I could tell the minute he walked in that he was enjoying the drama of it, the plotting, and the fact of consorting with an enemy, a subject he joked about frequently,' Campbell recorded in his diary.[72]

The Conservative leader William Hague was not quite as on board with the plan that had been concocted as Cranborne had hoped he would be. Indeed, the deal had been negotiated without his knowledge, and when all of the details emerged, Hague was furious. In a meeting with him, Tom Strathclyde and various other Conservative dignitaries Cranborne asked whether Hague would rather sack him or have him resign. Much to Cranborne and Strathclyde's barely concealed mirth, Hague chose to sack him. The Conservative leader then asked Strathclyde to take over Cranborne's job, a post he initially declined. Later, Robert Cranborne admitted he had behaved 'quite outrageously' in having gone behind Hague's back in his negotiations with New Labour, adding that he had run in 'like an ill-trained spaniel'.[73]

A quarter of a century later, Robert Salisbury looks back on the 1990s Lords reform discussions with a certain dry amusement. 'The reason why I went through the whole business – an extremely elaborate piece of politics, a sort of conspiracy with Blair and Alastair Campbell – was because it was clear that Blair was going to do stage one and abolish the hereditary peers, and that stage two was never going to happen,' he says. 'As I believe in a proper bicameral system, it was a constant reminder that this was unfinished business.' He maintains that we need 'proper constitutional reform', but 'this is going to be very difficult because, as Lenin said, everything is connected to everything else, and you can't reform the House of Lords without thinking about the relationship with the House of Commons. If you look to have a directly elected chamber – the sort of thing that [Tony Blair's successor] Gordon Brown and a lot of other people want – you will have resistance from the Commons. The Commons has spent centuries clawing power from their lordships, so why on earth should they give power back, which is what they would be doing if they permitted a directly elected house.'

Almost a year after Hague's night of the short, blunt knives, on 26 October 1999, the House of Lords Bill was read for the third time. Earlier that day, Charles Beauclerk, Earl of Burford, heir to Murray Beauclerk, 14th Duke of St Albans, had taken his seat on the steps of the throne in the Lords chamber, as eldest children of hereditary peers were permitted to do. Suddenly, he leaped up, and jumped onto the Woolsack, shouting, 'This bill, drafted in Brussels, is treason. What we are witnessing is the abolition of Britain . . . Before us lies the wasteland . . . No queen, no culture, no sovereignty, no freedom. Stand up for your queen and country and vote this bill down.'[74]

He remembers the day well. 'It's rather surreal looking back on it. I'm not sure how I physically managed to do it. Just as Lady Jay was sitting down, I seized my moment. It really felt as if some force picked me up and placed me on the Woolsack. I didn't realise it would be so wobbly, and I saw the Lord Chancellor bouncing up and down beneath me which was rather alarming.' Outside the chamber, the former foreign secretary Peter Carington, 6th Baron Carrington, was talking to the documentary maker Molly Dineen, who was making a film about the House of Lords. 'This is the great thing about the hereditary peerage, you never know what is going to happen next,' he said. 'He's dotty,' said Michael Onslow, 7th Earl of Onslow, 'he's been writing us all letters saying we're throwing away heritage'[75] – something that Charles Beauclerk, who has not used his title since 1999 feels strongly about: 'When these grants of titles were made historically, in our case by Charles II, they were made in perpetuity. Suddenly there was the presumption that that doesn't matter, it's just history, you can just dismiss it.'

Jumping on the Woolsack was, he admits, an extreme response, but he felt that no one had fought for the hereditary system. 'It was trashed without people discussing it and thinking it through. The Conservative Party was too busy cobbling together this deal which was a form of hoisting the white flag when they should have been taking it on. Speaking to a lot of the hereditary peers at the time, it struck me that they were lost – they didn't have a sense of nobility in the twenty-first century and what that could be. A lot of them were defeatist. There was so much pressure telling them to be ashamed of themselves and of what they have, that they just didn't believe in themselves anymore, and if they did they convinced themselves that the hereditary principle was not legitimate.'

The punishment meted out for Charles Beauclerk's protest was a lifetime ban not just from the Lords, but from the Palace of Westminster. He regards this as a huge over-reaction: 'I'm not planning on doing it again,' he says. 'The current Black Rod said that she would review it when my father dies.' In his view the hereditary peers are a valuable presence in the Lords: 'This isn't the chamber that generates the legislation, this is for checks and balances – being part of it involves work and dedication, and you had just the right number of people among the hereditary peers who were willing to step up. It was something very special in that regard. They were a tried and trusted element of our polity and brought something natural and unrehearsed to proceedings.'

In the event Charles Beauclerk's dramatic gesture proved to be just that – a gesture. The Lords passed the bill by 221 votes to eighty-one. A fortnight later, on 11 November 1999, it received Royal Assent. The House of Lords Act came into force that day.

The peers who wanted to be considered for election as one of the retained hereditaries were asked to submit an application with a seventy-five-word personal statement.[76] Some baulked at the prospect. The Conservative peer Angus Campbell-Gray, 22nd Lord Gray, a 'comparatively ordinary bloke' by his own account who ran a filling station in Argyll and who had, by then, been in the Lords for thirty-two years, was keen to put his name forward but ultimately concluded that 'I'm not going to write any advertisement in my favour'.[77] Robin Ferrers was similarly opposed to the writing of a personal statement, despite his wife urging him to do so, 'as it looked like each peer writing his own election manifesto. I said that I had been in the House of Lords for forty-four years and that people probably knew what they thought of me, and they would not take any notice of what I had written anyway.'[78]

The stockbroker and racing enthusiast John Denison-Pender, 3rd Baron Pender, noted his interest in standing for election on a piece of House of Lords headed paper, but in place of a carefully crafted personal statement offered just one word: 'Duty'.[79] 'I didn't want to show any degree of arrogance by not conforming to it at all, and I thought that to write seventy-five words about why I am a dunce was totally unacceptable and demeaning to one's self-esteem,' he said. Benjamin Mancroft complained that peers were being asked to 'stab our friends in the back. It's a pathetic pretence that this is democracy.'[80]

At ten-past one in the afternoon of 5 November 1999, the bewigged and begowned clerk of the parliaments, (now Sir) Michael Davies, rose in the chamber of the House of Lords to read out the list of elected hereditary peers. The atmosphere was 'pretty tense', he remembers. Afterwards, some of the peers who had stood but not been elected were in tears. Davies reckons that there had been 'some sort of Tory slate'; indeed, there were several. 'The people who got in were young men on the front benches, and all friends. They regarded themselves as those who worked the hardest.'

The Conservatives elected forty-two hereditary peers, Robin Ferrers securing the most with 190 votes, and Tom Strathclyde coming second with 174 votes.[81] Labour elected two peers,[82] and the Liberal Democrats three,[83] one of whom was Conrad Russell, 5th Earl Russell, son of the philosopher Bertrand Russell. Conrad Russell described the deal that had been struck as an 'acceptance that the hereditaries are people and entitled to be treated on equal terms without discrimination. After all, we're not as a caste superior to anyone else but we're not inferior either.'[84] Of the forty-two Tory peers elected in 1999, twenty-four of them remained in the Lords in September 2023.

Scarcely had Davies finished reading out the list than those peers who had failed to be elected were told to clear their lockers. The instruction did not go down well. 'Edward Jones, who was

Black Rod at the time, implemented what he believed was the consequences of the elections – that those who weren't elected should bugger off,' remembers Davies. 'He behaved as one from the military who had got an order and applied no common sense to it.' 'There were people who devoted their lives to this place and were summarily chucked out,' recalls another peer. 'It was no way to treat them. It was brutally done, and it didn't have to be. You could see that colleagues were bereaved by it.' Simon Glenarthur remembers how 'an awful lot of people were incredibly sad, and some died of a sort of heartbreak. It was ruthless. You were here, and then you were out.'

Charles Shrewsbury, who came twenty-fourth in the Conservative ballot, found himself experiencing something close to survivor's guilt. 'Although you felt privileged to be elected to stay on there, you felt: "I wonder what they think of me." ' Before he inherited his father's title in 1980, aged twenty-eight, he had had scant understanding of how the Lords worked. His godfather Michael Hicks Beach, 2nd Earl St Aldwyn, had been the Conservative chief whip, and the morning his father died, Michael rang him 'and said my father was hopeless and that he never made a maiden speech, or took part in anything, and that I was going to because it was my duty. He said I should come to the Lords as quickly as I possibly could, and make a maiden speech, so that's what I did.' Despite being the premier earl of England, descended from John Talbot, 'Old Talbot', 1st Earl of Shrewsbury, whose title was conferred on him in 1442, and apparently imbued with all of the grandeur that this brings, Charles Shrewsbury describes coming into the Lords as '[A] bit like going back to school. I didn't know anybody at all. I wasn't brought up in the atmosphere of a lot of fellow "hereds".' In February 1982, he made his maiden speech in the Shrewsbury and Atcham Borough Council Bill debate, on the history of the town of his title. He has been in the Lords ever since. Does this history weigh on him much? 'I am incredibly proud of it,' he says. 'From an accident of birth, I am so privileged, so lucky to have the handles that I've got and the history that goes with it.'

Could the hereditaries have hatched a scheme whereby they all remained in the Lords? 'Probably not,' says Tom Strathclyde, who inherited his grandfather's title in 1985. 'I would never have made a case for the continuation of a hereditary peerage. However, I recognise that it has served the interests of the nation and occasionally done a bit of good. It never did any harm to the fabric of the nation. It was part of that invisible thread that tied communities and institutions together. I never thought the hereditary peerage should be running the country, but to reserve a small part of your parliamentary process to a group of individuals chosen at random – by chance, by birth – actually provided a good deal of stability to the process of passing legislation.'

That random accident of birth, is, of course, deeply unfair. 'No part of me wants to defend [any of] that,' says Tom Strathclyde. 'People who try to go mad, after a bit. You can't and you shouldn't try – yet here we are in the third decade of the twenty-first century. If that was ever acceptable, it's long gone.' He ventures that the House of Lords has played only a small role in the life of the aristocracy. 'There were other things that shaped them which was much more to do with where they lived, who they represented, and the money they had.'

The procedure for new peers after the 1999 Act came into force was that, every six months or so, when a hereditary peer either retired from the Lords or died, a by-election notice should be issued. In the spring of 2022, for example, Ivon Moore-Brabazon, 3rd Baron Brabazon of Tara, retired, and Roger Swinfen Eady, 3rd Baron Swinfen, died, leaving the Conservatives with two places to fill. Twelve candidates stood for election, all but two of whom had thrown their hat into the ring on previous occasions. Nicholas Maitland-Biddulph, 5th Baron Biddulph, was on his eighteenth attempt. Not that he could boast that he was the peer to have stood the most times. That distinction went to John Cadman, 3rd Baron Cadman, who by 2024 had sought election twenty-two times since being excluded from the Lords in 1999. By August 2023, nearly a quarter of a century after the New Labour reform had been implemented, a total of 199 peers had stood for election to the Lords.

Barely a year later, a second stage of Lords reform that many had assumed would never come, finally hove into view, as the new prime minister Sir Keir Starmer announced his intention to remove 'the remaining connection between hereditary peerage and membership of the House of Lords', with the result that all of the remaining hereditary peers would be removed from the Lords.[85] Not surprisingly, the news did not go down well with the architects of the 1999 compromise, Tom Strathclyde and Robert Salisbury, who regarded it as less of a carefully thought-out conclusion to a long-contested debate and more of an opportunistic power grab. 'This is exactly what they promised in 1999 not to do,' Tom Strathclyde told me in July 2024. 'The whole premise of the ninety-two staying on was until there was a proper stage two reform. They're going back twenty-five years.' In 1999, he went on, '[T]here were several hundred anonymous aristos who were members of the House of Lords, most of whom never came. It was that anonymity that made it very easy for Labour to get rid of them.' But now, '[T]he Prime Minister, not satisfied with being able to control the House of Commons, is trying to get rid of forty Conservatives and thirty-odd crossbenchers [from the Lords] so that he can try and control the second chamber. In doing so, for the first time ever, he is creating a second chamber [for] which the only way in is by the Prime Minister ticking your name in a box. That is wrong, it is a highly partisan act. We used to complain to the United Nations about countries that did that.'

The century-long contention that surrounds the nature and composition of the second chamber shows little sign of going away. Perhaps a Lords vignette from May 2022 most neatly encapsulates the arguments made on either side. In the course of a debate on appointments to the House of Lords the former Lord Speaker Norman Fowler, Baron Fowler, asked whether it could be '. . . right that membership of this house can be by an exclusive back door marked "hereditary peers only"?' As he did so, the crossbench peer Charlie Courtenay, 19th Earl of Devon, glanced at his neighbour Charles Wellesley, 9th Duke of Wellington, descendant of the man who defeated Napoleon. 'I thought, what do you mean "the back door"? Waterloo is hardly the back door, and then he stood for election in an open way. The vast majority of the members of the Lords are there entirely by the back door – you have no idea what they did to get there: perhaps they paid for the wallpaper in Number 10, or they ran a newspaper that was favourable to Boris Johnson when he was Mayor of London.'

* * *

When I talked to those hereditary peers who sat in the House of Lords in the early 2020s, I was struck by what an interestingly varied bunch they were: landowners and farmers, of course, but also barristers, engineers and filmmakers, businessmen, submariners and Olympians. All, since Margaret Mar left the house in 2020, were male. Their average age in July 2023 was sixty-eight. Just under half of them attended Eton College, compared to roughly 40 per cent of the total hereditary peerage who are Old Etonians. Nineteen of them were only the third holder of their title; half were second to fifth in the family line; nineteen were tenth or more. The high proportion of those from relatively recently created peerages suggests that they came from more inherently 'political' families than those who sat in the Lords half a century ago – and, perhaps, were more committed to their role accordingly. They certainly weren't backwoodsmen.

Some would not have been out of place in the House of Lords of a century ago. Benjamin Mancroft, for one, ticks many of the boxes of a traditional Tory peer. He went to Eton. He became a master of foxhounds. And when I met him in the Lords, he sat languidly on a seat by the window dressed in a smart suit and braces, and wearing a shirt with an 'M' and baron's coronet monogrammed on it.

His father, the post-war politician Stormont Mancroft, 2nd

Baron Mancroft, was a distant figure during Benjamin's childhood. When he died in 1987, his heir, then aged thirty, contemplated a career in the Commons, but was persuaded to take up a seat in the Lords by the Conservative chief whip Bertie Bowyer, 2nd Baron Denham. 'I did my spiel about wanting to go into the Commons, and he said, "Well, you're swearing your oath on Tuesday, so don't be late."' Benjamin Mancroft made his maiden speech in May 1988 on the most contentious issue of the day: the poll tax. The chamber was packed. 'I sat next to John Margadale,[86] a friend of my parents',' he told me, 'and as I was about to speak he leaned over and said, "Have you got any nice young hounds this year?" My notes went everywhere.'

'Politics and hunting are very similar,' he argues. 'That's why lots of politicians are fox hunters and why lots of fox hunters go into politics. It's the long-term planning of it, it's complex with masses of facets to fit together. It's a great game, but it *is* a game. The difference between the House of Commons and the House of Lords is that they play politics on the national stage, and we play it in this building and nowhere else.' When I suggested that this sounded perhaps a little blasé, he qualified what he had just said: 'Maybe game isn't the right word. It's an activity, a way of life. I don't see the consequences of what I do very much but the process is fascinating. I'm not particularly interested in education policy, or whatever.' He is the ultimate conservative. 'I am of the view that on balance, "much better not". When people come up and say that they've got a great idea, I usually say, "Probably just drop it." Given my life again if I voted "not content" to everything coming up without looking at it, on balance that would be a good thing.'

In somewhat sharp contrast to Benjamin Mancroft was James Bethell, 5th Baron Bethell, another Conservative peer, who was elected to the House of Lords in 2018. 'My father was very clear that [the hereditaries' role in the House of Lords] was going to get taken away,' he said. 'He told me not to bank on it, and to get a proper job.' James Bethell accordingly pursued a busy career, first managing nightclubs and then in public relations before finally taking his seat in the Lords. He has never regarded himself as an aristocrat. 'Socially I was never one, I wasn't brought up to believe that. [My great-grandfather, the 1st Baron] John Bethell was a civil leader – he wasn't landed gentry, and there has never been any landed gentry in our lineage. I'm a Londoner through and through.' He might have been stretching things a little when he claimed – as a hereditary peer – to be upper-middle-class, but justified this by saying, 'Well, I didn't use the peer thing for the first forty-five years of my life.'

Representative of the more overtly political dynasties among those I spoke to was William Astor, 4th Viscount Astor. His American great-grandfather, William Waldorf Astor, son of the millionaire financier and philanthropist John Jacob Astor III, moved to the UK in the 1890s after a short career as an American politician, and was ennobled first as Baron Astor in 1916 and then promoted two years later. The current William Astor's grandmother, Nancy, was the first woman to take a seat in the Commons, and when he joined the Lords in 1973 at the age of twenty-one, he was taken to tea by Manny Shinwell, who told him that '. . . when he joined the House of Commons the only person who was more unpopular than him was Nancy Astor, and she bought him tea so he was returning the favour.' His father, Bill Astor, 3rd Viscount Astor, was briefly a Conservative MP before he joined the Lords, and notoriously became entangled in the biggest political scandal of the 1960s, following the revelation that the minister of war, John Profumo, who had had an affair with the model and showgirl Christine Keeler, had first met her at a party at the Astors' Buckinghamshire home, Cliveden.

There was never a question that William Astor wouldn't ultimately pursue the same political path as his father and grandmother had done. Bill Astor died aged fifty-eight in 1966, five years after the Profumo scandal broke. 'Profumo basically killed my father. He never really recovered,' William Astor told me. When William came of age seven years later, he phoned up the Lords for advice on what to do next, and, on their instruction, turned up with the legal document that had granted him his title: his letters patent.[87] He then took his seat in the Lords. His political affiliation was never really in doubt, even though he was deeply impressed by some of the Labour politicians he met who had fought in the Spanish Civil War. 'Someone came up to me on my first day and said, "Very nice to see you, delighted you're here, you'll join the ACP [the Association of Conservative Peers]." A bit nervous I said, "Yes, of course, sir." I was twenty-one and I had no idea that I had just joined the Conservative Party.' But then: 'Lots of things were odd in my life and that was one of them.'

* * *

When it comes to assessing the political power that hereditary peers have wielded over the past century or so, a distinction needs to be made between peers as members of the House of Lords and peers as individual politicians. As members of the House of Lords, their influence never recovered from the 1911 Parliament Act, was reduced further after the 1999 reforms, and declined further in 2009 when the chamber's role as the highest court in the land was stripped from it. By the time Sir Keir Starmer announced his intention to remove them altogether from the second chamber, they had long ceased to exercise real political power and had essentially become an advisory group.

As individuals in politics, on the other hand, upper-class men have played an outsize role – at least, until relatively recently. Anthony Eden, who became prime minister in 1955, was the third son of a baronet, his family had owned Windlestone Hall in County Durham since the seventeenth century, and in 1952 he married Clarissa Spencer-Churchill, officially great-granddaughter of John Spencer-Churchill, 7th Duke of Marlborough.[88] His successor, Harold Macmillan, may have been the great-grandson of an Arran crofter, but he married the daughter of a duke. And not just any duke's daughter, but the daughter of Victor Devonshire, sometime Governor General of Canada, and owner of a 200,000-acre estate. As Anthony Sampson put it, 'to marry a Cavendish was like marrying a princess,' and 'for a young Tory politician at that time there could have been no connection more advantageous.' Macmillan had a complicated relationship with the aristocracy, however, enjoying their company and their big houses, but professing himself bored by their philistinism and their obsession with horses and racing. For their part, the Devonshires, another of whose daughters married a brewer – 'Books is better than beer,' Victor Devonshire is supposed to have said when Macmillan came on the scene – were put off by Macmillan's bookish chat.[89] As Sampson observed, 'Macmillan did not feel entirely on top of the aristocracy until he had not only become prime minister, but had sacked his cousin Lord Salisbury.'[90]

Even so, Macmillan's 1962 administration and the institutions surrounding it were stuffed with the scions of aristocratic families. His foreign secretary was Alec Home. The governor of the Bank of England was Rowland Baring, 3rd Earl of Cromer. The chair of the defence committee, Sir Harry Legge-Bourke, was the great-grandson of William Legge, 5th Earl of Dartmouth, on one side and grandson of Charles Wynn-Carington, 1st and last Marquess of Lincolnshire, on the other. The ambassador to the United States, the Hon. David Ormsby-Gore, was the son and heir of William Ormsby-Gore, 4th Baron Harlech. And when a year later Macmillan was replaced by Home (a move made possible by Tony Benn's successful campaign to allow peers to disclaim their titles and so sit in the Commons, on which more in Chapter 12), there were those who were convinced that Home's elevation to the premiership was not in spite of his aristocratic credentials but because of them. In a particularly virulent attack, the *Daily Mirror* described him as 'a man without a face' and as a 'man existing solely in the imagination of the posher members of the Tory hierarchy and a handful of aristocratic, knicker-bockered, pheasant-shooting cronies', before going on to suggest that Emperor 'Caligula's appointment of his horse as a consul was an act of prudent statesmanship compared with this gesture of sickbed levity by Mr Macmillan.'[91] Curiously, Tony

Benn's father, William Benn, 1st Viscount Stansgate, defended Home, telling the journalist Robin Day at a cocktail party in 1960 that he wouldn't hear anything against him and urging those present: 'Don't underestimate Alec Home.'[92]

Home's defeat in the 1964 general election marks the moment when hereditary peers lost their hold on the major offices of government. But there was one late outlier. When Margaret Thatcher was elected prime minister for the first time in 1979, she appointed as her foreign secretary Peter Carrington – a descendant of the man who, as founder of Smith's Bank, had bailed out the finances of an earlier Tory prime minister, William Pitt the Younger. To a *New York Times* correspondent, writing in 1979, he was: '[O]ne of those members of the aristocracy to whom grace, consideration and self-mockery seem to come naturally'. To a contemporary Labour politician he was '. . . a charming anachronism . . . he actually believes in *noblesse oblige*, and he works hard at it.'[93] And when he died aged ninety-nine in 2018, one obituary suggested that he was '. . . a modest man with little to be modest about'.[94] He had a sly sense of humour, too. During the New Labour years, when John Sainsbury, Baron Sainsbury of Preston Candover, former chair of the family supermarket chain, was heard to complain that the chancellor of the exchequer was planning to raise income tax, Peter Carrington murmured – in, as another who was there remembers, 'a very Peter-esque' manner – 'Poor you.' The nature of his departure from frontline politics – he resigned following the Argentine invasion of the Falkland Islands in 1982 – was of a piece with his sense of *noblesse oblige*. As he later wrote: '[T]he nation feels that there has been a disgrace. Someone must have been to blame. The disgrace must be purged. The person to purge it should be the minister in charge. That was me.'[95]

The view of a number of hereditary peers these days is that there is an aristocratic 'glass ceiling' in politics that makes it extremely unlikely any of them will ever be offered high office – such a move would be deemed politically and socially unpalatable. Certainly, since Carrington's time, hereditary peers have played only backroom roles. In the 1990s John Major appointed twenty-seven hereditaries or their sons as MPs to his government, but they served only as junior ministers. After Major came Blair, who preferred life peers to hereditaries. In the fourteen years from 2010 that the Conservative Party was in power, fourteen hereditary peers served in government roles, paid and unpaid. The one peer to have achieved high cabinet rank recently – David Cameron, as foreign secretary for Rishi Sunak – was, appropriately enough for the times, ennobled as a life peer not a hereditary one.[96]

The hereditary peers operating within the confines of the House of Lords were still making a significant contribution to the work of the chamber even as the new prime minister was sharpening his axe. In November 2023, thirty-six of them, or just under 40 per cent, were serving as members of select committees, with eleven serving on more than one. Charles Hay, 16th Earl of Kinnoull, was then the hardest-working select committee member, with six under his belt, as well as his role as convenor of the crossbench peers.[97] Forty-six hereditary peers were members of all-party parliamentary groups or APPGs; twenty-one peers were members of both APPGs and select committees. Such power as they wielded was of a soft, somewhat abstract variety, deriving in part from their proximity to power, their being physically in the building – or in the other half of the building – where laws are made, in part from the very fact of their aristocratic lineage. As Benedict Westenra, 8th Baron Rossmore, put it to me: 'Money's a fiction that you don't have to believe in, but as long as other people believe in it then it has value. It's the same with the aristocracy, it's just a name. Some people are wowed by people with titles. So long as those people exist, then the aristocracy will have some power, because it's being bestowed on them by other people.'

6

By Special Request

Local Power, Local Influence

On 5 November 1955, Andrew Cavendish, 11th Duke of Devonshire, travelled from his home, Edensor House in Derbyshire, to Wetton Parish Church, just over the border in Staffordshire, to open the local fete. It was a red-letter day for the local community – 'the first time', the *Ashbourne Telegraph* reported excitedly, that 'a Duke [has] made an official visit to the village for a great number of years'.[1] Addressing the assembled crowd, Andrew Devonshire described how proud he was to continue a family association with Wetton that stretched back some four centuries. The Cavendish family, he said, '. . . had always valued their Wetton tenants, many of whom still bore the same name as those who tenanted the farms 400 years ago'.[2] A couple of years earlier, in January 1953, he had sent a £10 donation to a fund set up 'to defray the costs of repairing the perished stone mullions of the church windows'.[3]

It might have been the first time that Andrew Devonshire had made an official visit to Wetton, but there was nothing unusual about his presence at a local event. He was the pre-eminent dignitary of the region, the owner of some 120,000 acres and seven houses in England and Ireland, responsible for the livings and well-being of hundreds of tenants and estate workers. When Buxton needed a new mayor in the winter of 1951, it was to him they unsurprisingly turned. 'I was flattered and a little surprised,' he later recalled.[4] 'There was a time, in my father's day, when you half expected to be asked to be King of Albania,[5] but I'd always thought the Buxton mayoralty less haphazard, more the reward for application in the council chamber.'[6] He accepted the job.

His sense of paternalism went considerably beyond opening fetes and serving as a local mayor. According to Simon Seligman, a former long-term employee of the Devonshire estates, the duke and his wife Debo cared deeply about the people who lived on their estates and went out of their way to help them. 'There are repeated tales of gamekeepers getting cancer and anything the NHS couldn't do would immediately be funded by the duke,' says Seligman. 'Whether Andrew Devonshire would have, at the privacy of the dinner table, winked and said, "I'm not stupid, I know damn well that this is good PR," we'll never know. It doesn't matter either way but it had that effect.' He had, says Seligman, a 'very magnificent way of going about things'.

Andrew Devonshire's sense of *noblesse oblige* was scarcely unique. Even the far-from-admirable Hugh 'Bend'Or' Grosvenor, 2nd Duke of Westminster, found the time between his four marriages, multiple affairs and anti-Semitism to send presents to the children attending school Christmas parties on his Cheshire estate during the 'Christmas Blitz' on Manchester in 1940, as well as offering a week rent-free to each tenant (and the following year, 'with his customary generosity', extending the same courtesy to his Chester tenantry).[7] He also regularly supplied his tenants with free coal. Three decades or so after his death, his former agent George Ridley recalled encountering a tenant of one of the Westminsters' Chester properties who greeted him with the words: 'Our Duke was a gentleman, wasn't he, Mr Ridley? He looked after us – always shoved half a ton of coal under our door every Christmas.'[8] His nickname, incidentally, derived from the name of his grandfather's 1880 Derby-winning racehorse Bend Or, which in turn commemorated the Grosvenor family's coat of arms, 'Azure, a bend Or' (azure with a gold band).

Bend'Or's wider services to his country were of dubious quality. Andrew Devonshire, by contrast, had a genuine sense of duty to the nation.[9] He served as a minister of state in his uncle by marriage

Harold Macmillan's government from 1960 to 1964, and presided over charities that included the Cancer Research Campaign, the National Deaf Children's Society and the Royal National Institute for the Blind. On the sporting side of things, he became chairman of the Lawn Tennis Association in 1954 (though was slightly horrified to discover that he was expected to attend four days in each of the two weeks that Wimbledon was on) and a steward of the Jockey Club in 1966. These duties, though, never distracted him from his fundamental loyalty to his Derbyshire home. Among the many roles he took there was the presidency of Derbyshire Scouts, in which capacity he one day received a letter from an unworldly clergyman which began, rather unfortunately: 'Knowing as I do of your keen interest in Boy Scouts . . .'[10]

* * *

That aristocrats should have played a significant role in their local communities is scarcely surprising. After all, John Bateman's researches published in *The Great Landowners of Great Britain and Ireland* suggested that in the 1880s over 82 per cent – or 482 – of the total 585 peers owned between them over 16 million acres. David Cannadine identified 250 landowners active in the 1880s – whom he termed 'territorial magnates' – who each possessed more than 30,000 acres and had at least £30,000 a year to their name (or just over £3 million today). The majority of these, he wrote, '. . . owned at least two great mansions in the country, and boasted a grand London house, in Grosvenor or Belgrave Squares, in Park Lane or Piccadilly. Many were extensively involved in non-agricultural forms of estate exploitation, like mines and docks, markets and building estates, and some, like the Dukes of Sutherland, also maintained massive investments in the Funds and in railway shares.' Within this group was an inner elite of twenty-nine landowners, each of whom had an income in excess of £75,000 a year (or £7.6 million today). This premier league extended from dukes – of whom there were twelve – to the Marquesses of Anglesey, Londonderry,

Bute and Hertford, the Earls of Ancaster and Derby, and included Andrew Devonshire's great-great-grandfather. All '. . . owned lands in several counties . . . sometimes had more country houses than they knew what to do with, and [were] possessed [of] private art collections almost without rival in the world.'[11] They governed fiefdoms whose populations looked to them for everything from housing to employment to patronage to charitable works.

The twentieth century witnessed a considerable diminution in the estates and wealth – and the influence – of the territorial magnates. The Dukes of Sutherland, once owners of over one million acres, these days have 12,000. The Dukes of Buccleuch have halved their acreage to below 200,000. Some families, like the remaining Fitzwilliams, now have almost nothing – relatively speaking. Nearly six out of ten contemporary aristocrats are not significant landowners, and the total acreage owned by those who are has shrunk to 3.2 million.[12]

Even so, many remain powerful players. Richard Buccleuch, for example, may no longer own the 460,000 acres his predecessors possessed at the turn of the century, but his acreage in 2025 is nevertheless considerable. It is also better run and more diversified than it was a century ago, promising at least another century of prosperity for the Buccleuchs. The same can very reasonably be said of the Percys, the Dukes of Northumberland, whose holdings these days extend to 100,000 acres and two stately homes. While a total aristocratic holding of about 3.2 million acres today may be only a fifth of what it was 150 years ago, it's still the equivalent to three-quarters of the area of Wales.

In purely financial terms, the higher echelons of the peerage, especially, are still faring well. Seventeen of today's twenty-four dukes live in their ancestral homes or, at least, on their estates. In 2020, the richest eleven of them were estimated to be worth over £14 billion. My analysis shows that the wealth of the twenty-four peers who appeared on both the *Sunday Times* list of Britain's 400 richest people in 1990, and on its Rich List in 2020, increased by an average of over 314 per cent. The Westminsters, in particular, continue to be spectacularly wealthy, as owners of a vast Scottish estate – Reay Forest in Sutherland – which accounts for over 70 per cent of their total holding of 136,600 acres (an increase of 591 per cent on 150 years ago), of land in Liverpool, and of an estate in central London that was once marshland belonging to the heiress Mary Davies, where it was possible to shoot snipe as late as 1822. It was thanks to their Liverpool and London holdings in particular that in the years following the Second World War, Bend'Or Westminster was one of the richest men in the country – so wealthy, indeed, that when he died in 1953 the Inland Revenue had to set up a separate department to deal with the £20 million death duties that had accrued. His successors have proved equally canny. Among their various enterprises in recent years have been the open-air retail and entertainment centre Liverpool ONE that opened in 2008, and a new athletic facility at the British International School of Washington which was completed in 2023. According to the *Sunday Times* Rich List 2025, the current duke, Hugh Westminster, is worth £9.884 billion. When he married Olivia Henson in June 2024, he subsidised free ice cream for visitors to Chester city centre on his wedding day.

Given their continuing hold on land and money it's not surprising, therefore, that the landed aristocracy retained – and to an extent continue to hold – a degree of 'soft' power and influence both nationally and locally long after their power at Westminster had been largely broken. At a national level, for example, they kept a firm grip on the highest level of chivalry, the Most Noble Order of the Garter (founded by Edward III in 1348) right to the end of the last century, ninety-seven of them in all being appointed out of a total of 175 in the twentieth century.[13] At a local level, the role of lord-lieutenant – the sovereign's personal local representative, originally responsible for organising the county militia – tended to be disproportionately theirs, too. Between 1900 and 2023, 356 of the 994 lord-lieutenants appointed in England, Scotland, Wales and on the island of Ireland were hereditary peers, of whom forty-three were patriarchs of families of the old premier league.[14]

When it comes to the post of lord-lieutenant, the link with the sovereign who confirmed the role has historically required a due level of moral probity and decorum on the part of the officeholder. Sometimes such qualities have been clearly lacking, and the result has been a certain fluttering in the dovecotes. When, for example, it emerged in March 1944 that Geordie Sutherland, who had been appointed Lord-Lieutenant of Sutherland in 1913, was cited in Major Vincent Dunkerly, DSO, and his wife Clare's divorce case, consternation reigned and his continuation in a role that he had held for over thirty years was immediately brought into question. Technically, he was a single man at the time – his wife, Eileen, towards whom according to Chips Channon he had 'behaved abominably',[15] had died a few months previously, bestowing on the duke what he himself described as a 'grievous blow'.[16] But his liaison with Clare Dunkerly and the speed at which he married her – a month shy of the convention that the minimum period between the death of a spouse and remarriage should be a year – were deemed sufficiently egregious for Winston Churchill's principal private secretary Jock Colville to rule that Geordie's 'matrimonial delinquencies made it necessary for him to resign'.[17] He refused to comply, so a notice duly appeared in the *London Gazette* stating that the powers that be were 'determining the appointment of His Grace The Duke of Sutherland, K.T. as His Majesty's Lieutenant of the County of Sutherland' (a notice misinterpreted by Fleet Street to mean that the Duke had been *appointed* lord-lieutenant).[18] 'Fur flies,' Colville observed laconically.[19] Having resigned, Geordie found himself ostracised. In July 1948, dining with Channon and the socialite Margaret Sweeny, he complained that he and Clare were being 'treated like outcasts by the Court and that the foolish Queen refused to meet them'.[20]

These days, society is less censorious, and the role of lord-lieutenant has become considerably more meritocratic. Even so in December 2023, of the 106 lord-lieutenants in office, five were peers, three were wives of peers, another was the daughter of an earl, and another the daughter of a marquess.

Another local role that the aristocracy has traditionally fulfilled is that of justice of the peace – also known as a JP or a magistrate. At one time, the system for appointing them was very much rigged in favour of the upper classes, since a potential candidate had to be possessed of land to the value of £100 a year – or, after 1875, a house worth more than £100 a year[21] – to be considered. But by the turn of the twentieth century such a restrictive rule was causing practical problems, as the Liberal peer William Lygon, 7th Earl Beauchamp, pointed out in a Lords debate in 1906: 'Your Lordships will recognise how this qualification has restricted the appointment of Justices of the Peace in the past,' he said. 'In some places it has been impossible to discover gentlemen qualified in this particular way to become justices, and in some counties this has been a source of very real inconvenience in the administration of justice.' Beauchamp's view was that 'the best qualification for properly carrying out the duties of a Justice of the Peace is a thorough and sound education', and since, in his view, 'the happy diffusion of education and knowledge among all classes has qualified a large number of men for the office,' the property qualification should be dropped.[22] The law was changed accordingly.

Even so, for much of the twentieth century the aristocracy exerted something of a stranglehold, either in their role as lords-lieutenant nominating potential JPs to the Lord Chancellor, or as serving JPs themselves. (In the early 1920s just under 40 per cent of hereditary peers served as JPs or local magistrates.) George Herbert, 4th Earl of Powis, for example, who was Lord-Lieutenant of Shropshire between 1896 to 1951, was alleged by Liberal MP Charles Henry to ignore candidates who showed 'pronounced political activity'.[23] It was not until 1918 that Shropshire had a working-class JP, and not until 1940 that the number of working-class JPs in Shropshire reached double digits. Women had been permitted to become JPs in 1919; during the Second World War, George Powis considered one particular female candidate for a vacancy that had come up only because she was the wife of the local master of foxhounds. In the event, she wasn't appointed.

Even today, there's a close connection between the offices of lord-lieutenant and justice of the peace, with more than half of current peers who have served as a JP at some point in their lives having links with their local lord-lieutenancy – either because they have held the office themselves – as, for example, Richard Chaloner, 3rd Baron Gisborough, has done – or because they have been vice-lord-lieutenant (like Ailwyn Broughton, 3rd Baron Fairhaven), or a deputy lieutenant as more than 100 current peers have been, or are now. James Crathorne, who was Lord-Lieutenant of North Yorkshire from 1999 to 2012, worked behind the scenes and chaired the advisory committee of justices of the peace, although he never sat on the bench. 'My wife was a very active JP and was rather surprised when I became her boss,' he says. Even so, while the aristocracy has retained a toehold in lord-lieutenantships, they have largely vanished from the magistrates' bench. In 1921, 286 of the 771 hereditary peers were JPs. By 1985 that figure had dropped to seventy-eight. As of June 2024, twelve of the current hereditary peers had served as JPs at some point in the past, but none of them currently held the post.[24]

* * *

One other facet of local life over which the aristocracy traditionally had considerable control was the living of the local church. As they were often the owner of the land on which a church stood, many aristocrats had the right to select who should serve as vicar or rector. The successful candidate might be a clergyman they looked favourably on or whose religious attitudes were similar to their own. Alternatively, they might earmark a living for a younger son who was not in line to inherit and therefore in need of gainful employment.[25]

In the mid-nineteenth century, the aristocracy represented a minority of the total number of those exerting patronage over the church as a whole, but still had control of over one in five livings.[26] And some of those livings were very lucrative. William Lowther,

2nd Earl of Lonsdale, held thirty-two livings worth cumulatively £5,713 a year. Charles Fitzwilliam, 5th Earl Fitzwilliam, and William Cavendish, 6th Duke of Devonshire, were each patrons of twenty-eight livings, worth over £7,000 a year. Numbers and value fell sharply over the course of the twentieth century, but even so a perusal of the 1921 edition of *Debrett's* suggests that 232 hereditary peers were in possession of at least 229 livings between them, and that in 1985 there were seventy-seven peers with at least 326 livings under their control.[27] Today, while accurate figures are astonishingly difficult to come by, it would appear that the hereditary peerage is in possession of at least 250 livings, of which fourteen cannot be presented by their holders since they are Roman Catholics, and that at least fifty-eight peers are patrons of livings.

Part of the reason for this decline is, of course, that over the past century so much estate land – and the churches that sit on it – has been sold. Another part is that some peers have been more than happy to surrender their ancestral rights. Freddie Curzon, 7th Earl Howe, who controls four livings around his Penn estate in Buckinghamshire but whose great-uncle George Curzon, 4th Earl Howe, controlled eight, told me that the family had 'voluntarily relinquished' several livings in the Midlands, owing to their 'lapsed connection with that area of the country'. Henry Bath, whose family had twelve livings in 1921, opted to give them all away. 'No one's ever satisfied with the chap you've chosen for vicar,' he said in an interview he gave in the 1960s, 'and, anyway, it would be quite ridiculous for an out-and-out atheist like me to do the choosing, wouldn't it?'[28] A final factor has been the Church of England's ever-growing tendency to consolidate parishes when a member of the clergy retires or moves on. As the writer Max Wyndham, 7th Baron Leconfield, 2nd Baron Egremont, whose great-uncle Charles Leconfield, had at least twenty-five livings in 1921, explains: '[W]e did have a lot but because so many parishes have been joined on to other parishes we haven't got nearly so many now. It's difficult to count because of the constant mergers of the parishes. I had a letter the other day to say that another parish is going to be merged into a parish that already has two former parishes in it, and this happens the whole time.'

Perhaps, then, it is not surprising that so many of the peers I spoke to about church livings seemed rather vague about them. One ageing aristocrat I asked said he knew 'next to nothing' about whether he had any or not, while his son told me, 'My guess is that he's signed away whatever responsibility he may have to someone in the church and now just gets notices when things change.' Another peer said that, yes, he was the patron of one living, but then confessed: 'I don't know what "living" means!' Ned Lambton, 7th Earl of Durham, the patron of two livings, is aware of the responsibilities that he believes he ought to have, but says, a little regretfully, that

> [T]hey never consult me about anything, let alone ask me to choose the vicar, which I had imagined I was supposed to do. They do occasionally ask for money for a new roof and stuff like that, and I contribute if and when I can, and used to host an annual cheese and wine party for the tiny and ancient congregation, but that's it really. It's a bit of a mystery to me and in fact you are the first person to ever mention it.

There are some notable exceptions to this general rule. Both David Manners, 11th Duke of Rutland, and Freddie Howe actively involve themselves in the selecting of a new incumbent ('I have always done this in a collaborative way with the relevant parochial church council. My sense – so far! – is that the PCCs have been happy to have my input and involvement,' says Freddie Howe). In Norfolk, Tom Coke, 8th Earl of Leicester, who has five livings surrounding his home of Holkham Hall, says: 'I think the Church of England has surreptitiously tried to change the rules, as I recall my father saying every fourth vicar for the benefice of Holkham, Wells, Warham & Wighton, was his turn to appoint. When I took over from my father, we [representatives from the different villages] all sat in a consensual circle and chose together – very twenty-first

century!' But none of these men can compete with Guy Middleton, whom we met earlier, who by 1968 had presented fifty-two
vicars over a forty-year period, and had once gone to the unusual
extreme of advertising for candidates in *Horse & Hound*. 'The
archbishop found it a trifle unorthodox but I satisfied him it got
me the right man,' he said later.[29]

Teddy Stanley, 19th Earl of Derby, patron of seven livings,
explains the role the patron plays in selecting a new clergyman.

> Traditionally it was the patron who was responsible for doing the
> advertising, the interviewing, the recruiting, and so on. I tend to get
> involved in the conversations over whether there is going to be a parish
> reorganisation, and I occasionally attend parish profile-writing meet-
> ings, but I leave the Church [to find the person] – they know who is
> suitable, who is ready for promotion, who is moving on. I get involved
> with an interview when it's down to the last couple of people, or even
> the Church's preferred candidate.

The new clergyperson and holder of the living is presented at a
church service: '. . . a lower-scale version of a bishop's ordination.
The patron presenting the person comes in separately just after the
first hymn, and says, "Bishop, I present to you . . .' and then you
hand them over almost like a father handing his daughter over
at the beginning of a wedding.' It is, he recognises, all somewhat
anachronistic, but, he adds, '[T]here is much that is anachronistic.
Frankly, you could say at one level the entire peerage is anachronistic.' Then again, he says, there are occasions when the patron's
role as a dispassionate outsider can help smooth over differences
within a parish, or between a parish and their bishop. 'They can
see that I am totally apolitical. I am making no loss or gain out of
any of this stuff.'

* * *

The hereditary peerage, then, remains embedded in the life of the
regions, even if their role these days tends towards the symbolic

and their power to the circumscribed. But there are still a handful of families that wield considerable influence. And few wield more than two 'royal' aristocratic families – the 'kings' of, respectively, Lancashire and Northumberland.

The Kings of Lancashire are the Derbys, whose earldom was created in 1485 for the northern territorial magnate Thomas Stanley after the Battle of Bosworth. Unlike so many other senior peers, theirs was once an overtly political family. The current earl's great-great-great-grandfather, Edward Smith-Stanley, 14th Earl of Derby, was the longest-serving leader of the Conservative Party, who served twice as prime minister and also oversaw the abolition of slavery in the colonies. His grandson, and the current incumbent's great-grandfather Eddy Stanley, 17th Earl of Derby, was secretary of state for war during the First World War, and ambassador to France after it. Ten of the nineteen earls have been made Garter knights.[30]

The Derbys have long taken their local obligations seriously. A dozen have served as Lord-Lieutenant of Lancashire, while of Eddy Derby it could fairly be said that no Lancashire bazaar was too far away or too obscure for him to attend. He genuinely enjoyed local functions, according to his great-grandson Teddy Derby: they gave him an opportunity to get to know the people around him. 'I am now dealing with an awful lot of centenaries: "your great-grandfather opened our town hall in 1922," etc. It is extraordinary the scale of involvement that he had in the north-west at that time – he was local royalty.' Teddy Derby recalls how he was '. . . sitting next to the Queen Mother at lunch in Windsor one day before Ascot, and she said: "Your great-grandfather, he *was* the King of Lancashire." I could say only, "Well, ma'am, *you* can call him that . . ."'

If Eddy was a local monarch, he was also an immensely wealthy one, who nevertheless, in his great-grandson's words, 'lived massively beyond his means'. At Knowsley Hall, a few miles from Liverpool city centre, images of Eddy are everywhere – on the walls, display surfaces and mantelpieces. When he inherited the title and estates in 1908, the Derbys were possessed of nearly 70,000 acres, worth £163,000 in gross annual income, with a gross rent roll of almost £300,000. Needless to say, Eddy Derby lived in the manner to be expected of – and by – a rich Edwardian; in the years before the First World War, he kept fourteen indoor servants at Knowsley and his annual household expenditure amounted to almost £50,000.[31] 'He took an oversized stately home,' says Teddy Derby, 'and added on another floor on top to make it even bigger. He lived way beyond his means but enjoyed every moment of it.' He adopted an equally extravagant approach to his London bolthole. In 1910, he sold Derby House at 23 (now 33) St James's Square having decided '. . . that wasn't big enough, and he bought Stratford House – what is now the Oriental Club off Oxford Street,' says Teddy Derby. 'It seems to me that that would have been more than enough, but he had grand ideals and grand ideas.'

Teddy Derby, on the other hand, does not describe himself as a territorial magnate. 'No, my estates, although large, are only a quarter of what they were a century ago.' 'But,' he goes on, 'you can't have a title, the privilege of the estate and the stately home, and not put back into that community. You have to have something of a patrician view about it. It's weird, Liverpool is a very left-wing city but they don't mind the odd toff.' At the last count he was involved with over a hundred different organisations, of which over ninety are local. They include palliative care hospices, angling associations, golf clubs, cricket clubs and the Oxford Old English Game Fowl Club. He is also an honorary captain of the Royal Naval Reserves, life president of the Rugby Football League, and feoffee – or governor – of Chetham's School of Music in Manchester, an organisation with which his family has been connected since 1653, 'so you can't really say no to that.' On top of all this he has an estate to run, and serves as a trustee of ultra-high-net-worth advisers Stonehage Fleming, all the while overseeing a safari park that attracts over 500,000 visitors a year.

It's a busy life, and one that he relishes. 'I love it,' he says, 'it's fascinating. I do some extraordinary things.' He has a certain conspicuous grandness about him. Though we are friends on Facebook, I cannot help but always call him 'Lord Derby', a persona that is, one suspects, well curated and deliberate. But it is not unpleasant, nor oppressive: he just *is* Lord Derby. He talks of 'engagements' in his diary, as though he is a member of the royal family, a helpful reminder of what his family was and, to a large extent, still is.

The Kings of Northumberland are the Percys, who have dwelled in the magnificent Alnwick Castle since 1309. At their peak, in the nineteenth century, their landholdings extended to over 192,000 acres, 15 per cent of the whole of the county – their wealth vastly boosted by estates closer to London and by coal royalties. Their dukedom was created for the Yorkshire squire Hugh Percy (*né* Smithson) in 1766, who in 1740 had married Lady Elizabeth Seymour, *suo jure* 2nd Baroness Percy, and who had happily accepted the earldom of Northumberland when it became available in 1750. He had then brow-beaten George III into upping the offer of a marquessate to a fully-fledged dukedom. Flashy, ostentatious and vain, he was described by Dr Johnson as a man 'only being fit to succeed himself'.[32] The writer and Whig politician Horace Walpole described how 'the old nobility beheld his pride with envy and anger'.[33]

His namesake and great-great-great-great-grandson Hugh(ie) Percy, 10th Duke of Northumberland, reigned as de facto King of Northumberland for forty-eight years until 1988. Educated at Eton and Christ Church, like his father Alan Percy, 8th Duke of Northumberland – a right-wing political controversialist and letter writer of the kind 'that the wise often write, but only the unwise ever send off' – he inherited the title in May 1940 when his elder brother George, 9th Duke of Northumberland, was killed in Belgium while serving with the Grenadier Guards.[34] Chips Channon recalled in November 1940 how he had listened to George and Hughie's mother Helen Northumberland speak 'tenderly' of her late son, who, despite having been offered a job of comparative safety, had turned it down to go to the front. She then 'ranted against the Socialists and even recent govts [*sic*] who have pillaged and destroyed the great families by crushing taxation.'[35]

Hughie had a 'good' war with the Northumberland Hussars, serving in Crete and in the North African campaign.[36] A good war for him, though, was scarcely a typical war by the standard of most of his brother officers. While in Cairo in January 1941, he found time to attend a race meeting and then go shopping with Channon in the local souk, where he bought a French tortoise-shell box for his mother. Northumberland Hussars officer William Benson recalled an incident in April 1941, when the foreign secretary Anthony Eden turned up to visit the regiment's C Battery in Greece with a letter for Hughie from Alnwick which he forgot to hand over. Coming across it again months later, Eden arranged for a dispatch rider to take it 300 miles from Athens to C Battery's headquarters. Hughie duly opened it, to find that it was not a letter of vital military, political or even personal importance, but one from '. . . the kennel huntsman of the Percy Hounds on a small point concerning the pedigree of a bitch he was intending to breed from!'[37] Later that month, just south of Ptolomais, the brigade commander Harold 'Rollie' Charrington wandered over to Hughie, whose troops were under heavy fire, to remark, 'My dear fellow, how nice to see you. I've always wanted to tell you how marvellous your mother looked at the Coronation.'[38]

When news of George's death came through, there was immediate concern for Hughie's future safety. 'The Army did try to take care of their dukes,' Benson remembered, 'although they were sent into action and that always carried a risk . . . so when Hughie, as the new duke, got sandfly fever in the desert, he was sent home. They did not want a repetition.'[39] Returning to England in 1942, Hughie went to work in the War Office, lunched at the Ritz and Claridge's, and did the round of smart cocktail parties. In November 1944 he made his first speech in the House of Lords. When the doodlebugs, the V1 flying bombs, were heading towards Westminster during the Blitz, '[H]e was living at Syon [House, the Northumberlands' west London Tudor palace] and he used to go up onto the roof with a tin hat and watch them go by,' says his son Ralph North-umberland. 'One of them landed very close to the house at Syon and blew out all the windows.' Beyond such scattered reminis-cences, Hughie never talked about his war experiences – or about his brother George.

Hughie had a finger in every local pie during his forty-eight-year reign as the uncrowned and unchallenged King of Northumber-land. 'That generation were very involved in local politics – my father, the Allendales,[40] the Ridleys, they were all there, the great coal owners,' says Ralph Northumberland. Hughie served on Newcastle County Council for eleven years, was chancellor of Newcastle University for twenty-four years, Lord-Lieutenant of Northumberland for twenty-eight, and the president of numerous clubs and societies, from the Northumberland Boy Scouts' Asso-ciation to the Royal Agricultural Society of England. He was an honorary colonel of the Royal Northumberland Fusiliers, a lord-in-waiting – a government whip in the House of Lords – and, most importantly, master of the Percy foxhounds for almost half a century, thanks to which he knew every inch of the Percys' very many acres. In 1953, he bore the Sword of Mercy at Elizabeth II's coronation, just as his forebear Henry Percy, 4th Earl of Northum-berland, had done at Richard III's in 1483. A Garter knight, for the final fifteen years of his life he served as the late queen's Lord Steward of the Household – a role that involves overseeing the arrangements for state banquets and other ceremonial occasions and that comes with the accoutrements of silk stockings and a long white rod of office, '[O]ne which in the past would have been used to clobber any who pressed too close to a royal presence,' as Sir Roy Strong put it.[41] He was a good father, Ralph Northumberland says, who had a '. . . very quiet way of encouraging people to do things, rather than pushing hard. He would encourage me to go off fishing. He'd say, "What I'd really like for breakfast tomorrow is a little trout," and as a small child you'd do whatever you could to catch a trout, and you can apply that same thing to many walks of life.'

In June 1946 Hughie married Lady Elizabeth Montagu Douglas Scott, a former officer in the Women's Royal Naval Service, who was the eldest daughter of Walter Montagu Douglas Scott, 8th Duke of Buccleuch. Hughie had proposed to her a few months earlier at the Buccleuchs' Drumlanrig Castle in Dumfriesshire, having ridden there alone on his hunter for four long days from Alnwick. They had seven children. The eldest of these, Harry, became 11th Duke of Northumberland on his father's death in 1988, but died unmarried aged forty-two in 1995, having suffered with appalling depression for many years. And so his younger brother Lord Ralph Percy inherited the title, the estates and all the baggage that comes with being the Duke of Northumberland. Not that he likes to use that word. 'Because of my position, some people assume that one is different and on a different level and I try not to be that, but you can't help what people think,' he says. 'Everything in life is about compromise and there are many benefits from what we have here, but it's not always easy.'

Ralph Northumberland never expected to be the King of Northumberland, but history might have suggested to him that it was not unlikely. Of the twelve Percy dukes, only six have been eldest sons of the previous duke – before Harry, most recently Henry Percy, 7th Duke of Northumberland, who was born in 1846. Harry Northumberland, his brother says, was '. . . perfectly physically healthy, quite capable of getting married and having children. In one's worst nightmare one would think, "Oh, gosh, this might happen," but any younger son can think that – that their brother can be run over by a bus tomorrow.'

At the time Harry died, Ralph Northumberland, his wife Jane and their four children were living in Northumberland, having moved back up north two years earlier. Previously, Ralph, as a family trustee, had been a land agent working in the south of England. At the time he took over the estate, Alnwick was not in a great financial position. 'It was an old-fashioned agricultural estate, and in real terms the rural revenue was declining at an exponential rate. The challenge of my generation was to try and make it work, and preserve it.' In that ambition, the duke has been entirely successful. In 1990, his brother Harry Northumberland was said to be worth £125 million, with 80,000 acres in Northumberland, Middlesex and Surrey. Since then the family's acreage has increased to 100,000 acres in Northumberland itself, with, as the duke describes, 'additional land in Scotland, Surrey and Middlesex', and its estimated wealth by 300 per cent, a considerable increase given the economics of the period. In 2019, the Rich List quoted Ralph Northumberland's wealth at £419 million; in 2020 it was up £26 million to £445 million, and in 2025 he was said to be worth £517 million. These days, the family invest in commercial property, from retail parks to industrial estates, and from Britain to Germany, Switzerland and North America. Alnwick Castle averages about 200,000 visitors a year, while the Alnwick Garden, created by Jane Northumberland, has a footfall of up to 400,000; in 2022–3, admissions to the Alnwick Garden alone generated more than £2.6 million in revenue, though, according to its own balance sheet it barely broke even once costs were taken into consideration.

Despite all of this, the duke is broadly successful in his aim to retain a low profile. His wife Jane, rather than he, is Lord-Lieutenant of Northumberland – '[A]t the time my wife was the perfect candidate for the job, and she's done it really well. They did ask me years ago, after old Lord Ridley retired [in 2000], if I would be a candidate, and at that stage I had only just inherited and I thought it was one thing I could do without.' Together the Northumberlands are involved with over 200 charities, and in 2019 established the Northumberland Estates Community Fund to support community groups, charities and organisations in the county and on the estate in London.

To visit Ralph Northumberland at Alnwick Castle, with its battlements, herds of Land Rovers, gilet-wearing staff and robot lawnmowers – is an experience. Staff talk about 'the household' and 'the family', who may or may not be 'in residence'. When the duke is away from Alnwick, his flag is taken down; when he's in residence, it is put back up again.[42] In the duke's case, 'in residence' might also refer to Syon House, or Burncastle Lodge in the Scottish Borders where the Northumberlands decamp for that part of the year when Alnwick is open to the public, since it is challenging to spend any time there when so many tourists are around. His staff refer to the duke as 'His Grace'; he replies to my emails as 'RN' or 'Ralph'. This is pronounced 'Rafe'. In 2016 he said that he finds the whole 'Your Grace' thing rather awkward, but when I asked someone in his employ whether they would ever call him Ralph, they looked a bit uncomfortable. I took that as a no.

None of these trappings are an indicator of power as such, but they do give one the distinct impression that someone, somewhere still thinks that the Duke of Northumberland is the King of the North-East. It's not clear that that person is the duke himself, since all things considered he seems quite down to earth. As he stands in his kitchen at Alnwick, a painting of his black cocker spaniel Hector on the wall, he doesn't resemble someone who might be 'in residence' anywhere, but comes across more as a friend of the family who walks said dog and reads or writes books for much of the day. He's kindly and helpful, fielding my queries – both then and subsequently – efficiently and good-naturedly, hunting down press clippings that I might find useful, and helping me to gauge the views of the landowning class on news events, when asked. I'm not sure what a King of Northumberland ought to look like, but the slightly built Ralph Northumberland, in a suit, tieless and wearing leather loafers, certainly doesn't resemble one. (He has been described as having something of the actor Bill Nighy about him, but for me it's more the historian A. N. Wilson.) Nor does he regard himself as kinglike: 'Certainly, certainly not now! I think in past generations they would have considered themselves Kings of the North, and they were known as Kings of the North.' And he lacks the immodesty of a king. When I tell him, as he surely already knows, that he is considered one of the best game shots in the country, he immediately responds: 'That's really not true, there are so many good shots.'

The political role of the Dukes of Northumberland – which stretches back to the Percys' arrival in England at the Norman Conquest – is over. No duke has spoken in the Lords since 1957 – that time in a debate on the marketing of woodland produce. Though the current incumbent took his seat in parliament in June 1996, after Harry's death, being excluded in 1999 with the bulk of the hereditary peers, he made no spoken contributions in the Lords in his time there, nor has he chosen to stand for election subsequently. He can see that things changed midway through his father's forty-eight-year tenure as Duke and King of Northumberland, when it became '. . . much more a duty to look after the house, the heritage, the community, everything that goes with it'. That 'everything' comprises business parks, grouse moors, a popular garden reinvigorated by the duchess, forests and 20,000 acres of in-hand farming. It is one of those estates that now serves as a model to those looking to go on a similar journey. Has he ever had any desire to sit on Northumberland County Council? 'Um, no. No, I haven't. I don't think it would be an option now.'

As well as being indifferent to the responsibilities that were once considered necessary for a man in his position, he seems indifferent to his ducal status.

> It's just a title, and there are many titles that are now in the hands of people who don't have this sort of thing. Look back a hundred years ago and there would have been a hundred servants running around this castle – and you had to keep them, and look after them and their families. A century ago we still had some semblance of actual political power, despite there being a democracy.

No longer. Still, people ask him to do things because of who he is, of course: '[P]artly because it's traditional, partly because they just want a name on a letterhead. But it's good, it's all part of it. It comes back to duty and heritage. It is one's duty.' I wonder if he feels like it's a job. 'Well, you don't get paid for it – *you* pay for it.'

7
Labels

Fascists, Communists and Others

When they were little girls in the 1920s, the Hon. Jessica 'Decca' Freeman-Mitford and her sister the Hon. Unity Freeman-Mitford, two of the six daughters of David Freeman-Mitford, 2nd Baron Redesdale, and three years apart in age, shared a bedroom at Swinbrook House in Oxfordshire. In common with lots of little girls in a similar position, they divided their room in two. Decca's half was decorated with copies of the *Daily Worker* and a bust of Vladimir Lenin bought from a second-hand shop. Unity's was festooned with fascist insignia, a swastika, a collection of phonograph recordings of Nazi and Italian songs, photographs of Benito Mussolini – and a photograph of Sir Oswald 'Tom' Mosley, founder of the British Union of Fascists (BUF), trying to look like the Italian leader.

Decca went on to elope with her second cousin Esmond Romilly and live in the East End; later, with her second husband, she became an active member of the American Communist Party. Unity, meanwhile, travelled to Munich in the summer of 1934 to stalk Adolf Hitler and then to befriend him and members of his circle, not least Joseph Goebbels and his wife Magda. So close did Unity and Hitler become, indeed, that when he announced the German take-over of Austria (or Anschluss) in 1938, she was invited to appear alongside him on the balcony of the Hofburg in Vienna. Her subsequent flamboyantly pro-Nazi behaviour in Czechoslovakia – where she was spotted in the streets of Prague wearing a swastika badge in her lapel – led to her being 'booted' back to England, to the considerable relief of the staff of the British Embassy in Berlin who felt that she 'deserved what she got'.[1] Traumatised by the declaration of war the following year, she shot herself in the head in the English Garden in Munich. She survived but was severely brain-damaged and died in 1948, aged thirty-three.

Decca and Unity weren't the only politically active members of the family. While their sisters Pam (described by John Betjeman as 'Gentle Pamela / most rural of them all'), Debo (who married the future Andrew Devonshire and became a duchess) and Nancy (a successful writer and novelist) broadly steered clear of controversy, their other sister Diana married Unity's pin-up, Tom Mosley, at Joseph Goebbels' house in Berlin, having divorced her super-rich Guinness husband to do so.[2] She was sent to Holloway Prison in 1940 under Defence Regulation 18B, in part thanks to evidence given by her sister Nancy.

Diana never really repented of her fascist leanings. When interviewed by Sue Lawley on BBC Radio 4's *Desert Island Discs* in 1989, she said that she 'simply didn't believe' the reality of the Final Solution: 'I don't really, I'm afraid, believe that six million people were [murdered] . . . I think it's just not conceivable, it's too many.' Her concluding remark on the subject was equivocal: 'Whether it's six million or one million really makes no difference, morally, it's equally wrong.'[3] She then selected an excerpt from the end of the first act of *Die Walküre* by Hitler's favourite composer, Richard Wagner.

When she died in 2003, she was indeed described by the *Guardian* as 'unrepentant', a view with which her son Jonathan Guinness, 3rd Baron Moyne, agrees.[4] She was less virulent a Nazi than her sister Unity, he argues, '. . . but she had the same sort of feelings. She was aware, she knew what was going on, and she was quite bright about it.' Her anti-Semitism, he believes, was deep-rooted, a 'sort of disease'. And, like many diseases, it was infectious. If his mother hadn't been anti-Semitic, he says, 'I wouldn't have been; she made me like that.' His own views on anti-Semitism in particular and politics in general have moderated considerably over the years, but in the early 1960s he was rigidly right-wing, and like a number of other right-wing Conservatives a member of the Monday Club, a political pressure group founded in 1961 in reaction to Harold Macmillan's opposition to white majority rule in Southern Rhodesia. The club also featured such figures as the late Merlin Sudeley, a man once described to me as 'further right than Genghis Khan'. 'It supported apartheid South Africa and it was pro Ian Smith of Rhodesia,' says Jonathan Moyne. 'That seemed to me at the time right, but of course it wasn't.'

The Mitford girls – who, according to Jonathan Moyne, were 'brought up not just to be open-minded, but not to have fixed opinions' – were not the only members of a pre-war upper-class set to take extreme political positions.[5] The former Conservative secretary of state for air Charley Vane-Tempest-Stewart, 7th Marquess of Londonderry, was at best an enthusiastic supporter of Nazi Germany, as his unfortunate nickname the 'Londonderry Herr' suggests, and at worst Adolf Hitler's useful idiot. He kept a porcelain statuette of an SS man carrying a Nazi flag, given to him by then German ambassador to the UK Joachim von Ribbentrop in 1936, on the mantelpiece at Mount Stewart, his home in Northern Ireland. His biographer Sir Ian Kershaw viewed him as not a 'crypto-Nazi or Mosleyite fascist', but, in a way, something more dangerous: 'a serious-minded, if gullible, Conservative politician'.[6] Dorothy Dawnay, Viscountess Downe, a member of the British Union of Fascists, meanwhile, was described by Diana Mosley, in a letter to von Ribbentrop in August 1939, as a 'very good National Socialist'. 'The Führer would like her very much,' she wrote. 'She is an old friend of Queen Mary's and she does a great deal of good in a small way, trying to get people to see our point of view.'[7] Before the war, Dorothy was said to have written 'Heil Hitler!' in white paint on a road near her house, Hillington Hall, in Norfolk.

There were others, too. Gerard Wallop, 9th Earl of Portsmouth, was a member of the anti-democratic Conservative fringe group the English Mistery [*sic*], which expressed general opposition to social welfare, the United States of America and the London School of Economics. Later, he joined the 'more specifically pro-Nazi group' the English Array, and in 1943 the British People's Party (BPP), a far-right group founded by former BUF member John Beckett.[8] For his part, the utterly charmless Hastings Bedford, whom we last met back at Woburn Abbey alienating both his father and his son, provided some of the funding for the BPP. Not surprisingly, he was placed on MI5's 'Suspect List' as one who might serve in a Nazi puppet government if Germany ever invaded the UK. That he avoided internment under Defence Regulation 18B can only have been due to his social status. After the war, like Diana Mosley, he claimed that the figure of six million Jewish deaths during the Holocaust was exaggerated, and denied that there had been gas chambers in German concentration camps. His political fortunes had sunk long before. In July 1942, he was shouted down in the Lords by the then rather aged Liberal peer Jack Pease, 1st Baron Gainford, who begged 'to move that the noble Duke be no longer heard' after he rambled on, somewhat irrelevantly, in a debate about 'the Empire', making, as Gideon Oliphant-Murray, 2nd Viscount Elibank, told their lordships, '. . . a direct attack on the prime minister of the country without any regard to the Empire whatever'.[9] Nevertheless he attended Elizabeth II's coronation in 1953, one of the four non-royal dukes present who had either supported Germany immediately pre-war, or her appeasement.

Then there was Walter Buccleuch – not just one of the country's largest landowners, but from 1937 holder of the key royal appointment of Lord Steward to George VI.[10] Scarred by his experiences as an officer in the trenches of the First World War, when he served with the Grenadier Guards, he was understandably anxious to avoid war with Germany. Less understandably, he was an unflinching supporter of appeasement until the bitter end. On 2 October 1938, he wrote to Duff Cooper – who, the day after, denounced the Munich Agreement and resigned from his role as First Lord of the Admiralty in Chamberlain's cabinet – asking: 'Can any of us prove or judge in advance that it is impossible under any circumstances to trust Hitler or Germany?'[11] Six months later, shortly before Adolf Hitler's fiftieth birthday celebrations, he flew with the Nazi sympathiser Ronnie Nall-Cain, 2nd Baron Brocket, to Germany, where, as Chips Channon's diary records, he twice saw von Ribbentrop, '. . . who he was convinced did not want a war . . . [Walter] thinks we are on the wrong tack politically: that we are foolish to think war inevitable.'[12] Back home, officials were appalled. 'Ye Gods and little fishes! Is the world upside down?' was the response of the Foreign Office's permanent under-secretary Sir Alexander Cadogan upon learning of Walter's trip.[13] The British Embassy in Berlin intervened. Upon hearing that His Majesty wasn't so keen on the idea of his Lord Steward attending Hitler's birthday party, Walter suddenly discovered that he had another engagement that required his urgent attention and flew home.

Even as the war clouds gathered, Walter remained an unflinching appeaser. Channon described how, during a conversation with him in the House of Lords in May 1939, Walter told him that he was '. . . deeply concerned by our foreign policy, and rather committed to the pro-German view, or policy of appeasement'. 'Like me,' Channon went on, 'he sees the press, the Churchills, the [Duff] Coopers and others driving us to war.'[14] His amateur diplomacy, as Channon described it, earned him a ticking off by the king's private secretary Alec Hardinge at Buckingham Palace, shortly after which he was brought in front of the king, ostensibly for more ticking off. The king listened 'intently to all Walter said and was impressed thereby, so sucks to that shit Hardinge', as Channon inelegantly put it. 'Walter now hates him and proposes to say so to the Kents.'[15] By the end of that year, Walter had taken to writing to Channon '. . . almost every post urging peace. He is our defeatist duke, and perhaps he is right.'[16]

The following February, Walter tried to persuade the future prime minister Alec Dunglass (later Home), Neville Chamberlain's parliamentary private secretary, that peace was essential. As Channon relates, Walter could see that his time was coming to an end. The king, he believed, was avoiding him: '[He] often writes to him but fears that Alec Hardinge, that green-eyed monster of treachery, holds up the letters.'[17] Walter's last act of service for the king was in Lanarkshire, at Alfred Douglas-Hamilton, 13th Duke of Hamilton and Brandon's funeral, in March 1940, when he represented the king and queen. On 1 June, it was announced that Douglas Douglas-Hamilton, the new, 14th Duke of Hamilton and Brandon, had been appointed Walter's successor. He met the king to kiss hands and receive his Wand of Office a fortnight later. On 26 June, Walter and George VI parted ways, with an official audience. As the king told his diary: '[I]t was a rather painful interview as he has been "dubbed" as being pro-German in his attitude towards the war and has said stupid things, but we parted amicably.'[18] Channon was rather dismayed by the whole saga. '[Walter] tried to prevent the catastrophe of the war, the horrors and humiliations which we are now to endure: and his only reward is to be reviled by the unthinking.'[19]

Walter spent the rest of the war being ducal: opening parades, presiding over county council meetings, and speaking about hill farming and forestry in the House of Lords, while under a kind of house arrest – though, given his array of houses, this may not have been too onerous.[20] In September 1942, his name was put forward as prospective colonel of the newly formed Lowland Regiment, which wore the Buccleuch tartan. The king's assistant private secretary Sir Alan 'Tommy' Lascelles thought this a doubtful proposition: 'WB was at one time decidedly *lié* with Hess, if not with Hitler himself, and made no secret, before the war, of his pro-Nazi sympathies . . . But [Scottish landowner] Iain Colquhoun says that, in Scotland, the man-in-the-street knows nothing of these heresies, which Buccleuch has now recanted . . . In fact, Iain clearly thought that the lost sheep ought to be welcomed back into any convenient fold.'[21] Walter was made a Knight of the Thistle in 1949, and four years later, at Elizabeth II's coronation, he carried the Sword of Temporal Justice.

When he died twenty years later, his obituary in *The Times* made no mention of his pre-war political associations. Instead, it noted that 'forestry in all its aspects was his main preoccupation and all his estates are a model of timber husbandry.'[22] He was the arche-typal country duke, who 'planted more than a million trees every year on his own lands', but one who, not unlike his father, found it 'peculiarly distasteful to be treated according to rank', and was 'happiest entertaining people on any one of his huge estates, man-aging his farms, or hunting'.[23]

As his grandson Richard Buccleuch says, Walter's desperation to avoid war was to an extent forgivable. 'You cannot overestimate the influence of experiencing the First World War,' he cautions. '[Walter] survived, but he was in the trenches for three or four years. To have had that experience, and then the absolute disbelief that only twenty years later you would again be going to embark on it, that was such a huge thing. Grandpapa was wrong, and that's the reality of it, but you have to balance that with the experi-ence that they had. It must have marked them for life.'

For a fair sprinkling of aristocrats, though, appeasement went beyond a desire to avoid war. Many had long felt a violent dis-trust of those who might conceivably pose a threat to the status quo – 'radicals, Liberals, single-taxers, and socialists' among them, as F. M. L. Thompson described in 1989: anyone who might 'inflict vicious taxes and other anti-landowner measures'.[24] Socialism was viewed by the former Liberal prime minister Archie Rosebery, in 1908 as '. . . the end of all things. Empire, religious faith, freedom, property – Socialism is the death blow to all.'[25] In the 1920s and 1930s many such aristocrats were driven further rightwards by the spectre of Bolshevism towards that self-proclaimed bulwark against it, fascism. Then there were those who, by nature and inclination, were sympathetic to the trappings of Nazism – its militarism, its nationalism, its xenophobia. A seam of anti-Semitism had long run through upper-class circles, as Channon's diaries attest. In the years before the Second World War there were those, like Alan Northumberland, who believed that the world was in danger of falling to an international Jewish-Bolshevik conspiracy and who regarded Hitler as a potential saviour.

To that extent, aristocratic right-wingery in the middle decades of the twentieth century is not so surprising. What is rather more startling is that of the 60,000 or so members of the Communist Party of Great Britain in 1945, several could be found in *Debrett's Peerage*.

* * *

One of the better-known red toffs was Lady Noreen Branson, younger sister of Denis Browne, from 1952 10th Marquess of Sligo, the owner of an estate in County Mayo.[26] If Noreen's decision to join the Party in 1932 seems a little strange, given her social context, it must have come as a bombshell to her family.[27] Her upbringing had been deeply conventional, old-fashioned even – to the point where, when both of her parents died in 1918, she was pressed by her maternal grandparents into adopting full head to toe black mourning in a manner of which her Victorian great-grandparents would surely have approved. As Noreen's sister Sheelah remembered, '[W]e must have looked awful and very conspicuous as, though early-Victorian children may have worn such things, our generation certainly did not. How sad our parents would have been to have seen us.'[28] To make the girls' embarrassment more public, their grandmother Nettie Wormald insisted on driving them around town, not in the car that virtually all families such as theirs would have had by the 1920s, but in a horse-drawn carriage. 'We always longed to be "just ordinary" but I have very clear recollections of being dressed differently, and frequently doing things differently, to anyone else,' Sheelah remembered. 'This can be a great trial when one is young, but I don't think anything we did was more painful to us than having to go for a drive in the carriage.'[29] During the General Strike of 1926, her grandfather Edward Wormald thought he ought to do his 'bit' by '. . . giving a lift, just once, to a stranger. We buzzed round Berkeley Square in the Benz, but the stranger looked very worried and got out at the first opportunity.'[30]

In 1931 at the age of twenty, Noreen met and fell in love with a fellow member of the Bach Choir, the public school-educated painter and poet Clive Branson – and married him the same year. By this time Noreen's politics were already tending leftwards. Disappointed by the Labour leader Ramsay MacDonald, and his defection to lead the National Government in 1931, she and Clive joined the more avowedly left-wing Independent Labour Party (ILP) and campaigned it for in the poorer areas of Chelsea. The deprivation she witnessed convinced her that capitalism had failed and that even the ILP was insufficiently radical. With Clive, therefore, she joined the Communist Party in July 1932, moving to more uniformly working-class Battersea and becoming secretary of the local Communist Party branch. Their daughter Rosa, named after the Polish revolutionary 'Red Rosa' Luxemburg, was born the following year. During the Second World War, Noreen worked as a part-time air-raid warden, staying in Battersea until a bombing raid reduced virtually the whole of her street, bar her own house, to rubble; she recalled emerging from the destruction to find the local milkman cheerfully doing his rounds amid the devastation. She then moved to Highgate, to a flat adjacent to that of the Marxist writer Margot Heinemann, with whom, a few years earlier, she had written a history of Britain. After Clive was killed in Burma in 1944, Noreen devoted herself to writing full-time, becoming editor of *Labour Research*, to which she continued to contribute for the rest of her life.

A fellow aristocratic member of the Communist Party from 1937 was the charming, handsome, slightly dreamy Old Etonian Wogan Philipps, scion of a rich, peripatetic family that divided its time between the 'big house' – Llanstephan – in their native Wales, a townhouse in central London, an estate in Sutherland and a villa in the South of France. Though the wider Philipps family had long lived in Pembrokeshire, Wogan's father, Sir Laurence Philipps, was new money, having made his fortune in shipping and insurance before becoming 1st Baron Milford in 1939. There was a clear chasm between father and son in terms of attitude and outlook. Sir Laurence was, by all accounts, domineering and controlling.

'He was a very clever businessman, but a total philistine,' says his great-granddaughter Anna Woodhouse, Baroness Terrington. 'He wanted Wogan, his first-born son, to become a proper heir to him. He wanted to mould him.' Wogan, by contrast, 'was sensitive and artistic, and he wanted to be a painter – he tried very hard to be.'

By the spring of 1925, twenty-three-year-old Wogan, ignoring his father's insistence that he was too young to consider getting married, had become secretly engaged to the Hon. Daphne Vivian, later Marchioness of Bath. His hope was that such a fait accompli would ultimately persuade his father to change his mind. He was wrong. Returning from a gambling trip to Le Touquet 'depressed and introspective', as Daphne remembered, he was compelled by his father to write to her a couple of days before a scheduled visit to Glynn, her family home in Cornwall, to inform her that he no longer loved her. 'I opened the letter at breakfast, with a fried egg on a plate before me,' Daphne remembered. 'I have never been able to eat one since.'[31]

After the break-up of the relationship, Wogan was sent to South America for a year, returning in time to witness at first hand the General Strike, during which he volunteered to drive a bus. The national crisis came as an eye-opener for him. 'I remember very clearly him telling me, "I had no idea that people lived like this,"' says Anna Terrington. 'He just hadn't a clue – he had had a completely protected and privileged life, and it simply appalled him.' A couple of years later, Wogan married the first of his three wives, the writer Rosamond Lehmann, with whom he had two children. He was becoming ever-more politically engaged. When the Spanish Civil War broke out, he served as a volunteer with the republicans, driving supplies to Barcelona in February 1937, and later driving ambulances with the Franco-Belge International Battalion.

Laurence Milford died in 1962, by which time Wogan was married to his third wife, Tamara Kravetz, widow of William Rust, editor of the *Daily Worker*, and Wogan succeeded as 2nd Baron Milford. A year later, the Labour MP Tony Benn disclaimed his peerage, immediately followed by three other peers. Wogan was not one of them. Keeping his title was what Anna Terrington describes as a 'fuck you' to his father – '[T]wo fingers to his father who completely disinherited him, and had kept him on a very tight rein. It was the one thing that his father could not take from him. Perhaps it was his little joke,' Anna adds, recalling that Wogan had a wonderful sense of humour.

He took his seat in the House of Lords in May 1963, becoming the first (and only) hereditary peer to sit as a member of the Communist Party. In July of that year, he dedicated his maiden speech to an attack on the institution he had just joined. 'I wish to emphasise very strongly that I can never support any measure whatever which helps in any way to perpetuate this Chamber,' he told the assembled peers, during a debate on the Peerage Bill. He wasn't just unconvinced by the concept of the Lords itself, and the hereditary make-up of it, he went on, but the whole concept of the hereditary principle.

> My Lords, what, in fact, are we supposed to inherit? Is it some special ability or talent which enables us to function as legislators? No. What we inherit is wealth and privilege based on wealth – a principle which cuts right across every conception of democracy. Today this Chamber also consists of representatives of the more recently acquired wealth, such as bankers, steel magnates, newspaper proprietors and industrialists of all sorts. It represents, in fact, a more formidable concentration of wealth than that other place [the Commons] has ever done since the working people had a vote.

Next to speak was former Labour prime minister Clement Attlee, 1st Earl Attlee, who congratulated Wogan on his maiden speech, while pointing out that the debate was not dealing with major reforms of the House of Lords, but simply 'removing certain anomalies'. 'There are many anomalies in this country,' he went on. 'One curious one is that the voice of the Communist Party can be heard only in this House. That is the advantage of hereditary representation.'[32]

In fact, by the time Wogan arrived in the Lords – even by the time he married Tamara in 1954 – he had, as his granddaughter says, 'lost the bite of communism'. Tamara, 'a very strong, dyed-in-the-wool communist who had grown up in Georgia', was the more overtly political partner in their marriage. Even so, Anna remembers how, when she was growing up, her grandfather's politics were often remarked upon: '"Oh my goodness, your grandfather is a communist" – that sort of thing.' She remembers reading about Stalin and saying to Wogan, as he was always known to her – '[H]e was always Wogan, never Grandpapa – "How can you believe this?" And he would say, "It's gone wrong. If we could just start again it would work ... the greatest good for the greatest number of people."' He was something of a dreamer, she says. 'Tamara took him to Russia and in those days you were shown the sanitised version [of everything] so they'd be taken to a workers' commune with all the workers waving and smiling and having a delicious canteen lunch. I think he swallowed the propaganda, he was quite naive. He truly believed in the greatest good for the greatest number of people, and he was appalled at poverty, illness and misery, and he thought that working the soil and everybody having a slice of the cake was the answer, but I don't think he thought it through. He was very idealistic.'

Life at Butler's Farm, the house near Cheltenham that Wogan shared with his second wife Cristina Casati and then with Tamara, was extremely comfortable, with 'wonderful food, incredibly good wine, a beautiful home, such lovely company', remembers Anna Terrington. 'It was full of very interesting people – [the novelist] Laurie Lee was my godfather and he was there a lot, and [the poet] P. J. Kavanagh, who was married to my aunt [Sally] before she died. Wogan wanted to know what I thought, and what my friends thought, but not necessarily about politics. He wanted to know what made us tick. Going to stay with Wogan and Tamara was the biggest treat because he treated you like everybody else, and he was really interested in you and what you thought, and what you hoped, and what made you laugh. To be treated as a grown-up when you are a very callow teenager was such a treat.' He also took full advantage of the Lords, lunching there with Anna five or six times a year. 'He used it as a club,' she remembers. 'He said that he could actually do something there and people might hear – he said the House of Lords was much more comfortable than Speakers' Corner.'

In the early 1970s, Anna took her then boyfriend and now husband of fifty years the Hon. Christopher Woodhouse, from 2001 6th Baron Terrington, to meet Wogan and Tamara. 'His father was a Conservative MP, and Christopher was extremely worried about this,' she remembers. 'We went down to Butler's Farm and I could see that he was terrified, but they [Wogan and Christopher] became incredibly close friends, which was lovely. They were two people you would never have put together, but Wogan adored Christopher and Christopher adored Wogan.'

Anna remains 'enormously proud' of her grandfather for upholding what he believed in. 'He lost quite literally millions and millions [for the cause], so to stand up for what you believe, well, I really admire people who do that. If I had been one of his children, I think I would have cursed him to hell sometimes because they had to be brought up by their grandparents and money was a constant issue, but I admire him for sticking to what he believed.'

It's tempting to view Wogan's radical politics as personal rather than ideological: he disagreed with his father, and espousing communism was one way to rile him. There was, perhaps, an awkward tension between the vision of the world that Wogan championed and the comfortable life that he ultimately led. But his political stance was not a pose. His communism, like Noreen Branson's, was genuinely held and came about through exposure to the suffering of the poorest in society in the 1920s. Noreen saw it in the run-down streets of Chelsea; Wogan witnessed it during the General Strike. There are many elements that go to create a political outlook. Whatever else may have been going on in these well-privileged individuals' minds, a strong element of social idealism was certainly in the mix.

* * *

Before 1918 it was impossible for a peer to belong to the Labour Party. As the American historian Catherine Ann Cline pointed out, membership was predicated on belonging to an affiliated group, and '[S]ince non-workers were ineligible for trades-union membership, Labourites of the upper classes were to be found before the [First World] war only in the numerically weak Independent Labour Party.'[33] Even when that barrier was removed by a change to the Labour constitution that opened the party up to 'producers by hand or by brain', it must have been difficult for those aristocrats sympathetic to the cause to have felt particularly at home in the party.[34] Quite simply, they had virtually nothing in common with the vast majority of party members other than their political views. Even middle-class members, such as Clement Attlee, were, numerically, relatively scarce, though they tended to have a disproportionate grip on the leadership of the party. And even middle-class members didn't necessarily feel they were a natural 'fit'. It's telling in this respect that, as Attlee's grandson, John Attlee, 3rd Earl Attlee, reminds me, Attlee's wife Violet once told his biographer Kenneth Harris that: '"Most of our friends are Conservatives". "Clem was never really a socialist, were you, darling?" she went on. Attlee, sitting next to her reading *The Times*, pipe in mouth, made a mildly dissenting noise. "Well, not a rabid one," she said.'[35] His grandson, formerly a crossbencher, has sat as a Conservative in the Lords since 1997: 'I am a Tory but it doesn't mean I can't drive a truck or operate machine tools or weld two bits of metal together,' he says. As one would hope and expect of the grandson of the 1st Earl, he adds, 'I get on very well with the Labour peers.'

There are few dynastic Labour families in the hereditary peerage. John Wodehouse, 2nd Earl of Kimberley, can lay claim to being the first Labour peer (just beating Herbrand 'Buck' Sackville, 9th Earl De La Warr), in that he proudly supported the Labour candidate at a by-election in July 1920, though he himself was, as his grandson Johnny Wodehouse, 4th Earl of Kimberley, put it, 'content to be no more than a county councillor' and never achieved ministerial office.[36] Still, his son became a Liberal and his grandson a Conservative. Buck De La Warr – once described by Chips Channon as having 'an evil Bolshevik face'[37] – started out a Labour stalwart, but accepted the post of postmaster general in Churchill's Conservative administration in 1951. According to his grandson William De La Warr, Buck's son Billy – a true-blue Tory – once told him: '[I]t took me six months to realise that socialism was a load of rubbish; it seems to have taken you forty-five years.'

As for proud Labour man Pat Bingham, 6th Earl of Lucan, MC, appointed Labour chief whip in the Lords in 1954, his strongly Conservative parents professed themselves deeply distressed at the political choice that he and his wife Kaitlin made. When Pat died in 1964, the Labour peer A. V. Alexander, 1st Earl Alexander of Hillsborough, paid tribute to him, saying: 'He was always for the underdog. Wherever there seemed to him to be injustice he was against it. He was for the under-privileged. If there was a question of a minority being bullied by a majority he was there to speak for them.'[38] Perhaps, though, a degree of inter-generational conflict played its part; as Laura Thompson, writing about Pat's infamous son John Bingham, 7th Earl of Lucan's later disappearance, described: '[I]f one sought to write a concise history of the Lucan earldom, its thesis might be that each peer behaved, in some fundamental way, in reaction to his predecessor ... where the 5th Earl held, with a benign tenacity, to the values of the past, the 6th believed in stripping them away.'[39] When Pat's son John Lucan joined the Lords in 1968, it was as a Conservative peer.[40]

One of the most impressive Labour peers – in terms of what he was prepared to sacrifice in the furtherance of his political cause – was Billy Hare, 5th Earl of Listowel, who joined the Labour benches in 1931. His background and education were typical and traditional: he spent part of his childhood at his maternal grandparents' house, Hackness Hall, in North Yorkshire, where he learned to hunt and shoot with his father, the big game hunter Richard Hare, 4th Earl of Listowel; and he was educated at Eton. His politics, however, were such that they deeply offended his

Conservative father, who hoicked him away from Balliol College (where Billy had joined the Fabians) and sent him to Magdalene College, Cambridge, where he promptly joined Cambridge University Labour Club and insisted on being known around college as 'Mr Hare' rather than by his courtesy title of Viscount Ennismore.

Billy's interest in socialism had been sparked early in life by the sight of poor children playing barefoot in the street near the family's London home in Marylebone, and after university he worked at Toynbee Hall in East London, helping distribute the funds of the rich among the poor while he lived on £3 a week. He would never be wealthy himself. The Listowels' seat, Convamore in County Cork, had been burned down by Irish republicans in 1921 because of his grandfather William Hare, 3rd Earl of Listowel's 'aggressively anti-Irish' attitude.[41] And when his father died in 1931, Billy learned that both he and his unsporting, bookish younger brother Richard had been disinherited, and that most of the family fortune would pass to two other brothers: John Hare, later 1st Viscount Blakenham and chairman of the Conservative Party, and Alan Hare, sometime MI6 officer and chairman of the *Financial Times*. Undaunted, Billy the 'drawing-room Bolshie', as Chips Channon described him, stayed loyal to the Labour Party, becoming party whip, postmaster general in 1945, and then secretary of state for India and Burma.[42] Family frictions continued into the next generation, if less acrimoniously. Billy's son Francis Hare, 6th Earl of Listowel, has said that: 'I never knew my grandfather because my father had a very different political outlook to his forebears.'[43] Francis Listowel himself sat as a crossbencher in the House of Lords from 1998 to 2022.

In the years following the partial reform of the Lords in 1999, four Labour hereditary peers joined via the by-election system – each of them from a family that had been on a winding, if not avowedly complicated, political journey. Stephen Benn, 3rd Viscount Stansgate, who inherited his title in 2014 and took his seat in 2021, is the son of Labour firebrand Tony Benn, who spent much time and energy in his early career seeking to disclaim his title so that he could sit in House of Commons (see Chapter 12). David Pollock, 3rd Viscount Hanworth's father, was a crossbencher, as was the father of billionaire Littlewoods heir John Suenson-Taylor, 3rd Baron Grantchester. David Hacking, 3rd Baron Hacking, has ranged rather more widely. When in 1971 he inherited the title that his grandfather Douglas Hacking, a former Conservative Party chairman, had been given in 1945, he sat as a Conservative peer for twenty-seven years. He then crossed the floor to Labour following a disagreement over the Conservatives' policies on penal reform and European affairs in 1998. He was excluded from the Lords in 1999 following the reform of the chamber, returning to it again in 2021 – forty-seven years after he first entered the Lords – as a Labour peer.

* * *

Labour peers were and remain a minority, as is indicated by the fact that they made up only 3 per cent of 1,062 hereditary peers by succession who took their seats in the House of Lords between 18 May 1920 and 27 October 1999.[44] As one might expect, the largest group – 45 per cent – were Conservative peers for all or part of their political careers; 25 per cent were considered to be non-affiliated, for at least a portion of their political careers – that is, not members of any parliamentary group; 23 per cent were crossbenchers; and fewer than 3.5 per cent were Liberal or Liberal Democrat peers.

Today, it's safe to assume that a significant proportion – possibly the majority – of peers are Conservative-voting or, at least, conservatively minded. Of course, conservatism (and Conservatism) covers quite a range of views and beliefs. When deciding to stand for election to the House of Lords, Benedict Rossmore hesitated over which party to choose. He eventually opted for the Conservatives for the by-election in November 2023. He reflects that he is not a 'tribal Tory'.

I feel odd in very Conservative environments, but when I looked at the big issues of the last few years, I found I always sympathised with Tory backbenchers. I was very anti-lockdown, pro supporting the war in Ukraine, things like that – anti clamping down on freedom of speech and lots of quite extreme left positions . . . becoming pretty mainstream, which are things I strenuously object to, so that makes me a conservative, but it doesn't make me approve of everything they do.

Meanwhile the Gloucestershire and Staffordshire landowner Conroy Ryder, 8th Earl of Harrowby, the scion of a formerly very political family,[45] describes himself as 'conservative with a small "c"'; Jonathan Moyne, the former Monday Club member, views himself as a 'Tory remainer'; and Charles Richmond – who, having never stood for election to the Lords, has no publicly declared political stance – reckons that his father, who sat in the Lords for nine years as a crossbencher, never ever voted Conservative, despite the tweedy ducal image that a man of his position might possess. 'He was very liberal, very concerned about people. He didn't want things, wasn't interested in owning stuff. He just thought it was his job to look after it and pass it on.' By contrast, Charles Shrewsbury describes himself as: '[Q]uite roundly right-wing in my views. Since I was about thirty-five I have had a social conscience, but I also have sympathy for the right wing of the Conservative Party – the Conservative Party, not the wishy-washy type that we have at the current moment. I don't think they act like Conservatives. I'm an old-fashioned Conservative, a traditional Conservative. So yes, I am political.' Benjamin Mancroft says quite bluntly that his conservatism derives from the fact that: 'I don't like change.' 'Most changes are cock-ups,' he continues; 'they very rarely achieve what they're meant to.' He offers the European Union – which he voted to leave – as an example. 'I took the view that we'd be better out of it before it falls apart because it will drag us down with it. If you are part of a political system which is one of the oldest and most developed democracies in the world, and we've worked things out and developed it over several hundred years, and it sort of works, why would you throw that out of the window and take on a system which is untried, probably unworkable, and may well end in tears? Despite the trauma of the whole thing, I thought we were better off out of it.' Something of a parliamentary contrarian, between 2 December 1999 and 21 May 2024 he voted 'not content' two-thirds of the time and on a wide range of issues.

Arguably, the last hurrah of Conservative-leaning Lords was their opposition to the passing of the Hunting Act in 2004. So fierce was that opposition indeed that the Commons speaker Michael Martin had to invoke the Parliament Acts 1911 and 1949 to overrule the second chamber. In one of the many debates that were had on the subject, Robin Ferrers declared: '[I]t would be a monstrous use of the Parliament Act to use it for this Bill. It will split the countryside apart.'[46]

* * *

If the dyed-in-the-wool Tory tends to be the popular image of the average peer in Great Britain, in Ireland the stereotype has historically been of a slightly different shape and form. Peers in England, Scotland and Wales were usually Protestant, but they might well be Catholic – by late-Victorian times it really didn't matter much. Peers in Ireland were invariably associated with and defined by a religious creed that was unfamiliar to the majority of Irish men and women: Protestantism. Peers in Britain were establishment figures, rooted in the land they dominated. Peers in Ireland who were part of the Protestant Ascendancy were an alien ruling elite, who might well spend little or no time at all in the island over which they had such a stranglehold. In consequence, when calls for Home Rule and for independence gained real momentum in the early twentieth century, the Anglo-Irish peerage was viewed as symbolic of foreign – British – rule, and so became a very visible target for nationalist discontent.

During the Irish War of Independence that broke out in 1919, at least 275 houses belonging to members of the Anglo-Irish Ascendancy were burned by republican forces. Twenty-one of these were owned by members of the hereditary peerage. Derreen in County Kerry, for example, which belonged to Clan Lansdowne, former foreign secretary and Viceroy of India, was plundered and set ablaze in September 1922, devastating its owner who, though later compensated and so able to rebuild the house, felt that: '[A]fter all that had happened the place could never be quite the same.'[47] Bessborough House in County Kilkenny, which belonged to the Earls of Bessborough and in which they rarely lived for more than twelve weeks of the year, was burned by the IRA in February 1923. Fortunately, Vere Ponsonby, 9th Earl of Bessborough, had anticipated what might happen and had organised for most of the house's contents to be relocated to England before it was attacked. 'He removed quite a few of the family pictures, one by one, on the excuse that they had to come to London for cleaning or restoration, or whatever,' his great-nephew Myles Ponsonby, 12th Earl of Bessborough, said in 2020.[48] In 1924, having looked at more than sixty other houses, Vere Bessborough bought Stansted Park in West Sussex, which is now owned by a charitable trust. Bessborough was rebuilt in 1929, after which it was sold, along with the rest of the family's Kilkenny estate – which in 1883 had been almost 24,000 acres – and shortly after Vere Bessborough was appointed Governor General of Canada.

On occasion, not just the country house but its owner were targets. When Kilmorna House in County Kerry was burned down in April 1921, for instance, its owner Sir Arthur Vicars, former Ulster King of Arms, was dragged outside in his dressing gown, accused of being a British spy, and shot. A placard placed round his neck stated: 'Spy. Informers beware. IRA never forgets.'[49] But what is striking about a civil war that involved so much suffering and bloodshed is how relatively polite and courteous the republicans mostly were to their aristocratic victims and their households. The McDonnell family's ancestral home of Glenarm Castle in County Antrim and its inhabitants survived intact because the housekeeper also happened to be the sister of the leader of the local IRA brigade. 'He was more terrified of incurring the wrath of his sister than he was of his superiors, so aborted the plan,' says Randal McDonnell, 10th Earl of Antrim. The Fitzwilliams' Coollattin was similarly spared, even if Billy Fitzwilliam's agent in Ireland, Frank Brooke, was not. He was shot in 1920 in his Dublin office by IRA members – probably, according to his great-granddaughter Jane Pidcock, because: '[H]e had a foot in either camp – he was policing the locals and then telling London. My mum said that it served him right, you can't serve two masters.' When Billy Fitzwilliam died in 1943, he left Frank's widow £100 a year in his will, even though it had been twenty-three years since her husband's death.

Perhaps the supreme instance of gallantry in a time of war occurred at Moydrum Castle in County Westmeath, home of the pre-eminent peer of south Westmeath Albert Handcock, 5th Baron Castlemaine, and his wife Annie. The Handcock family had been granted over 5,000 acres in 1680 under the Act of Settlement and were raised to the peerage in 1812. By 1883 their estate had grown to over 12,000 acres, most of which they sold after the passing of the 1903 Land Act, which facilitated the transfer of land to Irish tenants. The family nevertheless continued to live at Moydrum with its 500-acre demesne. On 3 July 1921, a few days after a series of republican supporters' houses had been burned down by the Black and Tans – members of the Royal Irish Constabulary recruited from Britain – a revenge attack was mounted on Moydrum. Albert Castlemaine was selected, in part, remembered Athlone brigade officer Frank O'Connor, because he '. . . always opposed anything which was patriotic or Irish national and was really an enemy of Ireland. He had dismissed men from his employment because they would not join the British army. The destruction of his castle would hit in the spot where it would be most felt.'[50] Castlemaine was also a representative peer in the House of Lords, though before the First World War he had served on the Nationalist-dominated Westmeath County Council, being returned unopposed several times.

On the night of the burning of Moydrum, Albert Castlemaine

was away fishing in Scotland and the house was unprotected by soldiers. The IRA gang arrived carrying cans of petrol. They politely knocked at the front door, and when nobody answered – it was, after all, the middle of the night – they broke in. As O'Connor later recalled: 'When the [door] panels had been broken in, Lady Castlemaine and the butler opened the door. She was informed that the castle was going to be burned as a reprisal for the burning of houses by the Black and Tans.' Annie Castlemaine asked the gang for time to collect up some valuables, including silverware. They agreed, even though, as they pointed out, '[T]he Tans did not grant that privilege to the people whom they had burned out,'[51] and, as Tom 'Con' Costello, commanding officer of the Athlone brigade, remembered, '[T]he Black and Tans did not give the people they burned out time even to dress.'[52]

A party of ten IRA men went around the house helping Annie Castlemaine get some of her possessions out of the house, while another group rounded up the staff and guided them to safety. After that, as O'Connor recalled, 'Holes were made in the ceilings to give ventilation to fan the flames and the place was liberally sprinkled with petrol and paraffin which we found on the premises. Holes were also made in the roof by ripping off the slates.'[53] When Moydrum was ready for its ordeal by fire, the gang checked that everybody was accounted for. Then, as Annie Castlemaine and her 23-year-old daughter Evie sat on two armchairs that had been brought outside, the fire was set. Costello told Annie that 'we were not criminals', and that he viewed the burning as a justified reprisal for what had happened elsewhere. As he remembered, '[S]he was very dignified under the circumstances and never winced. She thanked me for my cooperation in saving her treasures and assured me that she quite understood.'[54] With Moydrum completely alight, the gang withdrew, saluting Annie on their way out.

Afterwards, when Annie Castlemaine was interviewed by the military about the incident, she refused to name members of the gang and said that she was in no position to identify any of them. According to Costello, she told the army that: '[T]he men who burned the Castle were gentlemen and behaved as such.'[55] In October 1921, Albert Castlemaine was awarded £101,000 in compensation. He elected to move to England with Annie and sold the Moydrum demesne to the Irish Land Commission in 1924.

* * *

In 1970, forty-eight years after the establishment of the Irish Free State, and two years after the outbreak of sectarian unrest in Northern Ireland in what came to be known as the Troubles, the Irish Conservative MP Sir William Teeling suggested that in order '... to keep things as they are in the North – I mean the *status quo* – may well mean that the UK will have to put in more troops and then the stately homes of the North which were untouched when those of the South belonging to "the Ascendancy" were burned to the ground in the early 1920s, may go the same way as those did in the South. We may yet be in for very worrying times.'[56] In other words, if the British government brought in their soldiers, it might mean bad news for the big house all over again.

There was, however, an important difference between the 1920s and the 1970s so far as attitudes to peers and country houses were concerned. In the 1920s, they were to the Nationalist community 'symbols of alien oppression', as Randal Antrim puts it. By the 1970s, they seemed less significant. The families that owned them '... had generally had their wings clipped quite materially'. 'They were not involved nearly so much in local Northern Ireland politics as their parents' generation, and they had seen their estates hugely diminished as a result of the Land Acts in the early twentieth century,' he adds. Of course, the Antrims are Roman Catholic, and as another, Protestant, Irish peer pointed out to me, that does make a difference.

But it doesn't mean that Irish peers didn't feel under threat. 'Things were really pretty heavy for people like me,' the late Henry Conyngham, 8th Marquess Conyngham, who inherited Slane Castle in County Meath in 1976, said of the 1970s and 1980s. 'At one stage I slept with a loaded shotgun beside my bed. If anyone had come through the bedroom door they would have got both barrels. Driving home at night you would be very wary of what cars were behind you.' His then father-in-law suggested that the children should be moved to England, but Henry insisted they stay in Ireland. 'I used to worry about the children, but this is my country – it is the country where I was born, and it is very close to my heart.'

In 1981, when Henry Conyngham organised for the Irish band Thin Lizzy to play at Slane, in what turned out to be the first of many rock concerts to be held on the estate, he received a threatening anonymous letter. 'Irishmen are tortured to death by your British friends your class have an easy ride in Ireland. Call off this vulgar Festival your [sic] promoting,' it read.[57] Roads around Slane were festooned with black flags, and mock funerals were held nearby. 'I remember being caught in the middle of one,' he said, 'and being unnerved by the possibility that somebody might recognise me.'

The Provisional IRA – successors to the IRA of the era of independence – certainly understood the importance of symbolism. Their assassination in August 1979 of Admiral of the Fleet Louis 'Dickie' Mountbatten, 1st Earl Mountbatten of Burma – the epitome of establishment power, who happened to have a holiday home in Ireland – is a case in point. In the same way, their murder of Sir Norman Stronge, 8th Baronet, MC, and his son James, on 21 January 1981, and the burning of their house, Tynan Abbey in County Armagh, was in part designed to send a message to those involved with the Royal Ulster Constabulary. But in neither case was the prime motivation to kill an aristocrat, even if on occasion it might have been a consideration. The Provisional IRA sometimes had the owners of country houses – slightly more often the houses themselves – in their sights. But their campaigns of the 1970s and 1980s were not focused on them.

Even so, a number of serious attacks took place. One of the earliest occurred on a Saturday afternoon in July 1972 at Stuart Hall in County Tyrone, the home since 1760 of the Earls Castle Stewart. First the staff received a warning call. Twenty minutes later, two fifty-pound bombs exploded, destroying most of the building. Stuart Hall's then owner Pat Stuart, 8th Earl Castle Stewart, was not in Northern Ireland at the time. Indeed, he had never felt close to it. The family had a house in East Sussex, and his American mother Eleanor Guggenheim, daughter of the American art collector Solomon Guggenheim, '... disliked going to Ireland – her heart was in Sussex,' says Pat's son Andrew Stuart, 9th Earl Castle Stewart. 'She didn't really encourage my grandfather to go to Stuart Hall particularly. The family looked after it, and were committed to it, but my father didn't really get the opportunity to spend much time there himself.'

From November 1941, with the Castle Stewarts in England, Stuart Hall had been let as a home for over 300 evacuees from Belfast. A year later, Pat's eldest brother David, Viscount Stuart, was killed in Egypt; just under two years on, his second brother Robert, the new Viscount Stuart, was also killed, in Italy, leaving sixteen-year-old Pat, then still at Eton, in line for his father Arthur Castle Stewart's title.[58] When the war was over, dry rot was discovered at Stuart Hall. Arthur Castle Stewart, who had won the Military Cross during the First World War, had worked as a public-school master and served for four years as an MP in England, opted to remedy it by removing the top floor – a 'rather radical and destructive decision that ruined the proportions of the Georgian mansion that was originally there and which was really quite beautiful', says his grandson. Of course, he adds, his grandfather experienced, like many others, the reality of a lack of building materials post-war, and the general shortages that came with that. But it was a decision that scuppered any hopes Arthur Castle Stewart had previously entertained of transferring Stuart Hall to the National Trust.

Suffering from depression, he ultimately took his own life, and Pat became Stuart Hall's custodian in November 1961. The following March, Pat declared he had 'no intention of disposing of Stuart Hall', and that his plans were 'to come over more often to County Tyrone'.[59] He took to forestry, and his industry shows, says Andrew Castle Stewart: 'Stuart Hall stands out as an oasis of trees in an area where they are otherwise quite lacking.'

Pat himself was never directly threatened by the IRA, but Andrew Castle Stewart says his father was aware of the potential danger: 'He liked to be involved in the cultural life of all the people of Northern Ireland and his natural inclination to meet people of all persuasions sometimes took him into potential danger. It was just as well that his housekeeper, who knew the area and the people of the area, could advise him on places to avoid – and he took her advice seriously.' The attack itself caused few ripples. Some newspapers mentioned it in passing. *The Times* appears not to have reported on it at all. To Andrew Castle Stewart's mind: 'It is hard to see what was achieved by the bombing. Stuart Hall was used for many purposes, and its social purpose was lost in the bombing, as was a beautiful house.' In the longer term, it left the Castle Stewarts without a proper base in Northern Ireland. The big house was never rebuilt: found to be structurally unsafe, after a contents sale in 1973 it was demolished the following year, and Pat was awarded £13,526 in damages. 'It had already been so badly damaged by my grandfather's removal of the top floor that it would have taken an extraordinary amount of money to put back together,' says Andrew Castle Stewart. The family had to make do with static caravans when they visited Northern Ireland until 1987, when Pat built a bungalow on the estate. Andrew has recently sold Stuart Hall. 'Part of my heart will always be there, I love it,' he says, 'and my wife has fallen for its charms. We both love the people and the way of life in Northern Ireland. I hope we never sever the link.' He reflects:

My father couldn't understand the hate. I don't understand the hate, I don't think anybody who isn't Irish understands the hate. Northern Ireland is a different country [to England], it really is, with a different culture. Strangely, my father being who he was, and me being who I am, does have meaning there. It's quite old-fashioned in that respect. For the IRA it made you a target, but for a lot of people it's a power for good. It gives you an intro and has a resonance there that it doesn't have in England. If you use your title here, you're more likely to get a 'Who does he think he is?' attitude, and it will count against you. The Irish have a deep connection with history that we've lost, or perhaps we never had.

After his father died aged ninety-five in November 2023, Andrew received many letters of condolence. One of them, from someone in Tyrone, described how he was 'iconic round here'. At Pat's funeral, Andrew described his father as: '[T]he kind of man that they don't make anymore. A common thread running through this extraordinary person was his desire to help people lead a better and more fulfilling life.'

Less than four months after the Stuart Hall bombing came an attack on another stately home, this time Caledon Castle, close to the border in County Tyrone, and home to the Alexander family since 1779. Denis Alexander, 6th Earl of Caledon, and his wife Elisabeth had seen someone walking around the grounds before they retired to bed, but a search had proved inconclusive. In the early hours of Friday 10 November 1972 a bomb placed next to the wall of the library exploded, blowing out three sets of columns, the balustrade, the library wall and every window in the house. Later that day, Denis Caledon was spotted on the ten o'clock news by his seventeen-year-old son, Nicholas, Viscount Alexander, now 7th Earl of Caledon, who was watching television in the sixth-form common room at Gordonstoun School in Moray. 'It was a shock, in those days they never told you anything,' he remembers. 'I suppose they were pretty busy and just hadn't thought of calling up the school.'

Denis Caledon, a former major in the Irish Guards, and in 1972 – the most deadly year of the Troubles – a colonel in the Ulster Defence Regiment, was the eldest nephew of the Second World War commander Field Marshal Harold 'Alex' Alexander, 1st Earl Alexander of Tunis. He had inherited the earldom, along with the house and its 3,000-acre estate, four years earlier from his unmarried uncle Erik Alexander, 5th Earl of Caledon, who seems to have lived a somewhat frustrated life – one dominated by his imperious mother Elizabeth, forty-one years a widow, who drank port as others might drink water, and who was too vain to wear spectacles in her later years, so opted for a reading glass instead. Her low opinion of Denis's father Herbrand, and of Alex, the unlikely field marshal, whom she 'fairly well ignored', led her to send them to Harrow.[60] Erik, whom she adored, was sent to Eton.

Caledon had borne early witness to the Troubles. In June 1968, just a month before Erik Caledon's death at the age of eighty-two, a Roman Catholic family had begun squatting in a house in Caledon village that had been allocated to a young, single Protestant woman, in protest at what they felt to be an anti-Catholic move. The Royal Ulster Constabulary had dragged them out onto the street, and the row that followed lit the touch paper for the Troubles – the sectarian conflict in his back garden that outlived Denis Caledon by eighteen years. Nor was the 1972 attack the final one. In March 1973 a second bomb destroyed the monument commemorating Du Pre Alexander, 2nd Earl of Caledon, sometime governor of the Cape of Good Hope.

As with the Stuart Hall attack, the first bomb at Caledon went curiously under-reported. Nicholas Caledon believes that his father wanted to keep it all low-profile. 'I think it is fair to say we were targets in those days,' he says. 'We were told by the authorities that we were targets. We had double trouble with the background of the field marshal, and my family, and me being in the UDR [Ulster Defence Regiment] too. The fact that we had a large block of land and a large house on the border was complicated. The IRA was murdering a lot of UDR people – and people like my father and myself. Our gamekeeper Thomas Armstrong was killed in 1979, and I was shot at by a heavy machine gun in 1991. I can't say that I ran around feeling terrified but it was pretty depressing in those days, as people were suffering and being killed.' In his view, being a peer didn't help. 'I don't think being an earl on the border was ideal,' he says. 'In their eyes we stood for everything that was British and wrong. I think that was the reason we became a target.'

Denis Caledon died in May 1980, aged fifty-nine, following

a heart attack. 'He suffered from very high blood pressure,' says Nicholas Caledon. 'He lived under enormous stress – people say even now how much stress he was under helping to run the UDR. It took its toll.' He had done his best, his son believes, in the circumstances. 'He was a very international man who had seen a lot of the world. He didn't have an axe to grind. He insisted on a policy whereby Roman Catholics and Protestants worked together and were employed together. He had cottages on the estate that staff lived in and if a Catholic family left for whatever reason, he would replace them with another Catholic family. He thought that what the IRA were doing was appalling, but we had the greatest number of Catholics in our company of the UDR than any other company in Northern Ireland.'

Life in the big house in those days was a challenge, he says. 'It was disrupting and unsettling to family life. It doesn't help your personal relationships. Life wasn't terribly happy for quite a long time.'[61] After the bombing, the government insisted on a wire fence being erected around Caledon, as well as floodlighting, and a night watchman armed with a rifle on the roof, 'like something out of a Second World War film'. Things have improved since the Good Friday Agreement of 1998, and after Elizabeth II came to Enniskillen in 2012, the Caledons felt sufficiently confident about their safety to install more low-key security equipment. 'I'm not saying I was miserable until 2012, but until the Good Friday Agreement, life was very different. I now love it, I genuinely do, and I've been here forty-five years, but it has had rather a history.'

Sectarian violence was beginning to escalate the first time Caledon was attacked. By the second occasion it was regularly occurring on both sides of the Irish Sea. A week before the bombing of the Caledon monument, a car bomb was set off outside London's Old Bailey; in June of that year, six Protestants were killed by an IRA bomb in Coleraine, County Londonderry; in September, there were bombings at King's Cross and Euston railway stations; the following February, twelve people were killed in a coach bombing on the M62. Two of the IRA volunteers involved in the Old Bailey bombing, sisters Dolours and Marian Price, were subsequently arrested, tried in Winchester in November 1973 and sentenced to life imprisonment. They immediately went on hunger strike, demanding to be moved to a prison in Northern Ireland.

On 2 June 1974, Michael Gaughan, an IRA member who had taken part in a bank robbery in north London to raise funds for the IRA, became the first Irish prisoner to die in an English prison since Terence MacSwiney, Sinn Féin Lord Mayor of Cork, starved himself in Brixton in 1920. That event, combined with anger over the Prices' hunger strike, which wasn't, seemingly, getting them moved to an Irish prison any quicker, prompted one IRA border unit to take action. The day after Gaughan's death, its members set out on a drive around the Irish countryside in search of a potential kidnap victim, in what Irish writer Paul Howard describes as 'an angry, confused gesture of retaliation'.[62] On 5 June 1974 the front page of the *Irish Independent* displayed the headline: 'Earl is kidnapped'.[63]

The kidnapped peer was John 'Ordy' Hely Hutchinson, 7th Earl of Donoughmore,[64] a former Conservative MP, albeit briefly, who had, by 1974, been out of politics for almost twenty years. He hadn't even been the original target. The gang's first choice had been John 'Tyrone' Beresford, 8th Marquess of Waterford, a polo-playing friend of Prince Philip, Duke of Edinburgh. But when they had arrived at the Waterfords' Curraghmore House in County Waterford, they had discovered he was in England for the Epsom Derby. Howard suggests that: '[T]his lack of basic intelligence on the target was symptomatic of a kidnapping plot that was more than just ad hoc; it was farcical.' An IRA man of the day expressed himself more forcefully: '[I]t was', he said, a 'complete fiasco. You had this unit driving around the Irish countryside with this fucking book, a hardback, *The Stately Homes of Ireland*, and they had it spread out on their laps. This is what they were working from. Pictures of rich people's homes. They decided first of all to go to Waterford to kidnap someone who was related somehow to the royal family. No planning, nothing. He was in England at the time. They abort the mission. They flick through the book again and they find another big house somewhere in Wicklow. They were going to take Sir Alfred Beit. No luck there either. Abort again. So they go back to the book and they find Knocklofty House in Tipperary, which was where the Earl of Donoughmore lived.'[65]

There was a certain irony to their final choice of victim. During the War of Independence, when Tipperary, Limerick, Cork and Kerry had been placed under martial law, Knocklofty had played host to IRA men, while during the Irish Civil War, Éamon de Valera, later first president of Ireland, had taken shelter within Knocklofty's walls. He had even left a note of thanks in the visitors' book upon his departure. The gang did not know this when they picked up the Donoughmores. As an IRA source recalled, '[I]f they were stupid enough to carry out a kidnapping in the Republic, then why did they have to target a family with their history of being friendly to republicans?'[66]

On the afternoon of 4 June, the gang was spotted by Joe Phelan, son of Ordy Donoughmore's chauffeur Tom, taking what seemed to be an unusual interest in the big house. That night, just before 11 p.m., there was a knock at Tom's door. When he answered it, he found himself confronted by three men brandishing revolvers. He was pushed backwards and hit in the face with a gun. He and his family were then tied up. The gang members demanded to know how best to get into Knocklofty. Tom suggested that they might consider going up to the front door and ringing the doorbell. Unamused, they kicked him in the face. On further reflection, they accepted that there was some wisdom to his advice. They set off for the big house and rang the bell. There was no answer. None of them thought to try the door, which was unlocked. Soon after, Ordy and his wife Jeanie, who had been having dinner with friends a few miles away, returned home.

Ordy Donoughmore's own reminiscences, shared with me by his younger son the Hon. Mark Hely Hutchinson, describe what happened next. Just as he was about to open the front door, he recalled, he heard Jeanie say: 'Who are you?' He looked up and saw a man: '[He was] carrying a long-barrelled revolver, wearing two stockings in the form of a mask, running towards me. He ran past me, between me and the house, and as he did so I saw three other rather small types, all waving guns, and yelling to us to lie down.' Ordy did not fancy sprawling on the ground, so instead rushed forward. That tactic, however, proved 'quite ineffective, as two or three of them began to clout me on the head with their guns'. By the time they had hit him five times on the head and once on the wrist – damaging his watch – he had sunk to his knees. Jeanie managed to bite Ordy's first assailant, whom he referred to as 'the Leader'. After that the couple were bundled into the gang's car and blindfolded. The car raced around the countryside for two hours, during which time Jeanie was sick. The gang then changed vehicles, before ultimately leading their hostages into a house where they were placed side by side on a sofa without cushions and their blindfolds removed. The two kidnappers in the room with them wore black masks over their faces, prompting Ordy to say, 'My God, you look like the Ku Klux Klan.'

The couple were warned that if they tried to escape the consequences would be severe (though escape would have been difficult given that, as Ordy pointed out, Jeanie had lost her shoes when they had swapped cars). Otherwise the two guards proved 'extremely polite and went out of their way to make us as little uncomfortable as possible'. They gave Donoughmores a large basin of water and some Dettol so that Ordy could clean up his injuries. They converted the sofa into a narrow bed and fed them well: an 'over-boiled' egg, bread and butter for breakfast; meat, peas and mashed potatoes for lunch; and 'an excellent fry for dinner (beautifully soft fried egg, sausages and back bacon)'. Jeanie asked one of the guards to congratulate the cook: '[T]he reply came back, thanking her and saying that he hoped that there might be a vacancy at Knocklofty.' The Donoughmores were provided with clothes and toothbrushes; the central heating was turned on; they were even able to have a bath and Ordy was allowed to shave. They played cards with their captors – the leader taught Jeanie Chinese Patience – and the gang gave them the racing section of the newspaper to read. 'They were very human,' remembered Jeanie after the event.[67]

Meanwhile, back in Clonmel, near Knocklofty, Catholics and Protestants alike gathered, filling the church and spilling out onto the streets in full view of the local IRA. More than 1,000 people from both sides of the sectarian divide prayed for the safe return of the Donoughmores. John Allen, Mayor of Clonmel, told those assembled: 'There are many images of Nationalism and sometimes crimes are committed in its name. But those who know Lord Donoughmore and his lady are only too well aware of their love of our aspirations and our way of life.' He described how Knocklofty had served as '[A] haven of sanctuary for those of our people who in our former history felt in need of succour and rest in times when many arms were raised against them', adding that, 'it is all the more sad, therefore, to discover that, in the winter of their years, [the Donoughmores] should fall victims to a situation of which they had no making.' Allen concluded by suggesting that the Donoughmores were 'more republican than many alleged republicans' – a remark, says Mark Hely Hutchinson, that was less a reflection of their real political views than a gesture of support.[68] 'My parents never got involved in any political issues, and neither publicly nor in the family expressed any political opinions. I think my father's position as grand master of the Irish freemasons may have had something to do with his reticence, but my parents were both supportive of any community activities and could thus be said to support everyone, whatever their political colour.'

On the fourth day of the Donoughmores' captivity, the Price sisters announced that they were abandoning their hunger strike after 208 days. The Donoughmores sensed that their ordeal was almost at an end. Ordy told his kidnappers, '. . . that for the first time in my life I was glad that Great Britain had a Labour government, because, I said, "The Conservatives would not have given in to you." The Leader of the IRA cell laughed and said: "Perhaps we would not have taken them on."' 'This was typical of his repartee,' Ordy went on, 'and of no political significance. I wonder, myself, whether the British government ever knew that we were hostages, until we published this fact.'

The kidnappers dropped the couple off at dawn, a hundred miles away from Knocklofty, in Dublin's Phoenix Park. Ordy and Jeanie made their way to a lodge on the perimeter and told the guard there who they were. 'I would rather have seen you than a hundred pounds,' he said. After a press conference outside the Garda barracks in Phoenix Park, still wearing a mixture of their own, bloodstained clothes and items their kidnappers had given them, they headed off to change, bathe and enjoy breakfast at the Hibernian Hotel with their sons Mark and Mick, the latter of whom succeeded his father as 8th Earl of Donoughmore in 1981.

Looking back on his ordeal, Ordy reckoned that 'the worst thing that we had to contend with was boredom'. He thought the leader of the cell was 'very well educated' and a 'great personality'. 'I suspect that he is a very eminent killer,' he ventured, 'as he was so careful about fingerprints.' He recounted one conversation they had when the Donoughmores had asked him if he found his terrorist calling tiring. 'He said that he did not feel tired, but did not usually sleep well on an operation. We asked him whether he could ever take a holiday. He said yes, he supposed that he could take one, whenever he liked, then added, "But, of course, there is nowhere in the world that I can now safely go to." We found that very sad.' On the first evening, when Ordy's head needed medical attention, the leader took over care of it from Jeanie, who was convinced that he had a surgeon's hands, a suggestion he denied. Both the Donoughmores ended up liking the leader. Ordy reckoned that 'he clearly fell heavily for Jeanie. He had probably never met anyone quite like her before.'

After the kidnapping, and the subsequent Garda debriefing, the Donoughmores were given police guards, principally to protect them from people who wanted to come and gawp at them. Being followed around everywhere – to the races, to church, to the local harvest festival – proved both a little exhausting and somewhat oppressive. Within a few months, the Donoughmores regarded the incident as closed. No one was ever charged with the kidnapping, but Paul Howard has suggested that the leader – whom he does not name – was a 'well-known IRA man from the Falls Road who later served as Belfast commander', a friend and ally of the future president of Sinn Féin Gerry Adams, and 'one of the organisation's most charismatic figures'.[69] Another member of the gang was later identified as Eddie Gallagher, who, with Rose Dugdale, the daughter of a millionaire underwriter and gentleman farmer from Devon – and a third cousin of a current hereditary peer – raided Russborough House in County Wicklow in April 1974.

Russborough had been the home since 1952 of Sir Alfred Beit, 2nd Baronet, a former Conservative MP and scion of a South African mining family, and his wife Clementine, first cousin of the Mitford girls. Gallagher and Dugdale's gang forced their way into Russborough and pistol-whipped the Beits, before tying them up and stealing nineteen Old Masters. Dugdale was later arrested and put on trial at the Special Criminal Court in Dublin where she pleaded guilty, telling the courtroom that Britain was 'a filthy enemy' and accusing the Irish government of being guilty of 'treacherous collaboration' with England.[70] She was sentenced to nine years in prison. Her biographer Sean O'Driscoll described her in the week of her death in 2024 as having 'an almost pathological hatred of upper-class society norms', which, he suggested, 'led her on a path towards radical socialism and Irish republicanism'.[71] Marian and Dolours Price were released from prison in 1980 and 1981 respectively; Dolours died in 2013.

Looking back on the kidnapping fifty years later, Mark Hely Hutchinson told me: 'I don't think the Northern Ireland Troubles as such had any real connection with my parents' kidnapping, except for the fact that the Price sisters were dragged into it as a rationale. As I understand it, these kidnappers were not controlled by the Provisional IRA or anyone else, but were a breakaway group, motivated by something else, and looking for a cause to espouse.' He described how differently his parents reacted to their ordeal. 'My father undoubtedly got it out of his system by talking

Days of pomp: the Fitzwilliams gather at Wentworth Woodhouse for Princess Mary, Duchess of Teck's visit in 1886. William Fitzwilliam, 6th Earl Fitzwilliam, is seated in the centre of the front row.

Henry Paget, 7th Marquess of Anglesey, at Plas Newydd cutting a dash, 1950.

The modern world encroaches as an open-cast mine is forced on the palatial splendour of Wentworth Woodhouse in 1946.

The wrecking ball comes to the Big House at Bowood, 1956. The post-war years saw the destruction of many aristocratic houses.

Woburn Abbey was a virtual wreck by 1945. Its fortunes were transformed by Ian Russell, 13th Duke of Bedford (shown here with his third wife Nicole in 1970), and his second wife Lydia.

Making the great house pay its way: Daphne Thynne, Marchioness of Bath, welcomes visitors to Longleat in 1949.

Sharing the challenges of keeping things going: YouTube star Luke Montagu, 12th Earl of Sandwich, at Mapperton, 2024.

Freddie Gordon Lennox, Earl of March and Kinrara, later 9th Duke of Richmond, poses with his latest car, 1931. Motor- and horse-racing have made the Goodwood estate immensely profitable.

Beneficiaries of the 'Downton effect': Geordie and Fiona Herbert, 8th Earl and Countess of Carnarvon, at Highclere Castle, 2021.

Relaxing at home: Edward Wood, 1st Earl of Halifax, stops to talk to his farm manager at Garrowby, 1946.

Messing about in boats: Peter and Obby Fitzwilliam, 8th Earl and Countess Fitzwilliam, early 1930s.

Harold Macmillan, along with Andrew and Debo Cavendish, 11th Duke and Duchess of Devonshire, out for a bracing walk around the Bolton Abbey estate, 1960.

Lavinia Fitzalan Howard, Duchess of Norfolk, and friend at Arundel, 1974.

Andrew Cavendish, 11th Duke of Devonshire, relaxes in the library at Chatsworth, 1995.

Caroline Somerset, Duchess of Beaufort, enjoys her garden at Badminton, 1981.

Power and politics: Alec Douglas-Home, 14th Earl of Home, Britain's last aristocratic prime minister, 1963.

Peter Carington, 6th Baron Carrington, a man with 'little to be modest about', as defence secretary in 1974. He would go on to become foreign secretary in Margaret Thatcher's government.

A towering figure in the House of Lords: Robert 'Bobbety' Gascoyne-Cecil, 5th Marquess of Salisbury, in 1953.

Salisbury's fellow peer and nemesis Quintin Hogg, Baron Hailsham of St Marylebone, formerly 2nd Viscount Hailsham, shows his human side, 1980.

Women peers were accepted, if not necessarily welcomed, in the House of Lords in 1958. By the time that Margaret of Mar, 31st Countess of Mar (shown here in her parliamentary robes in 1984), took her seat in 1975 there were forty-nine other sitting peeresses.

Tony Blair's government took the hatchet to hereditary peers in the House of Lords in 1999. Charles Beauclerk, the future Duke of St Albans, described the move as 'treason'.

Out of power, but not without influence: Robert Gascoyne-Cecil, 7th Marquess of Salisbury, at Hatfield, 2011.

A modern duke's daughter: Lady Violet Manners at Belvoir Castle, 2022.

Hons and rebels: the arch-appeaser Charley Vane-Tempest-Stewart, 7th Marquess of Londonderry (*middle*), poses with a dead stag in Germany in 1936. There was a reason why his nickname was 'the Londonderry Herr'.

The radical left: Tony Benn and two other generations of the family, 1958.

Diana, Lady Mosley, the Bright Young fascist, 1985.

Wogan Philipps, 2nd Baron Milford, the only Communist member of the House of Lords, 1962.

about it to anyone who would listen. My mother bottled it up and never spoke about it, but never really got over it, though she lived a lot longer than he did.' In the course of Ordy's various retellings, details tended to change – possibly out of a misplaced sense of gratitude to the gang for having treated them relatively well – and there was a slight sense that he came to view his ordeal almost as a *Famous Five* adventure. 'I always suspected that he knew a lot more than he let on,' says Mark.

Ordy Donoughmore died in August 1981, aged seventy-eight. His eldest son Mick Donoughmore said in 2019 that his death was 'entirely because of' the kidnapping, and 'in effect it was murder'. After the kidnap, Mick, then Viscount Suirdale, received threats against himself and his children. He took to visiting Ireland under an assumed name. As he said in 2019, 'I didn't want to go back and live in a country where my children were under threat of death, so we didn't move to Ireland when my father died.'[72] He put Knocklofty on the market soon afterwards.

* * *

Today, fewer than sixty out of 793 hereditary peers are peers by virtue of an Irish title alone and only eight of those live on the island of Ireland. That's not too surprising given that Irish peerages were so often given to non-Irishmen as a sop: they couldn't sit in the House of Lords but they got a title. As Simon Winchester put it in 1982, '[T]o have been given an Irish peerage – and an Irish peerage only – is the ennobling equivalent of having been damned with faint praise.' Or, in the words of one Irish peer, '[Y]ou are neither fish, flesh, nor good red herring, not noble enough to help make the laws of the land that ennobled you, not ignoble enough to be able to shake off the obligations of titledom.'[73] The title, in other words, had a certain social cachet but no political value. The 1801 Act of Union, which abolished the Irish parliament, also revoked the right of Irish peers to sit in the Lords, their number reduced to twenty-eight who would serve for life before a replacement was appointed – just as the Scottish peers met after each general election to elect a committee of sixteen to sit until the next one came around. As Randal Antrim puts it: 'I'm a hereditary peer in the Peerage of Ireland and that's all very interesting but people slightly forget that hereditary peers in the Peerage of Ireland have had nowhere to sit since 1801. It's a uniquely useless appendage, but it exists, it's a thing.' The election of twenty-eight peers went on until the creation of the Irish Free State in 1922. After this, the Irish representative peers were left to die off naturally, and when in January 1961 Francis Needham, 4th Earl of Kilmorey, died, the Lords was without a single Irish peer, except for those with other qualifying titles. The 1963 Peerages Act, which allows peers to disclaim their titles, does not apply to Irish peers.

Fifteen months after Francis Kilmorey's death, debates began over whether or not Irish representative peers should be allowed back into the Lords. Former Ulster Unionist MP Hugh O'Neill, 1st Baron Rathcavan, put the case for reform in a speech in April 1962: '[T]he Irish Peers have both a privilege and a disability,' he said. 'Their privilege is that they can stand as candidates for the British House of Commons, and can sit in the British House of Commons . . . their disability is that they cannot vote for a candidate in an election to the House of Commons.' Worse still, he went on, 'It has always seemed to me that the complete elimination of the Irish Peers from your Lordships' House has been most unfair and quite unjustifiable . . . a part of Ireland – that is to say, Northern Ireland – still remains an integral part of the United Kingdom and sends twelve members to the House of Commons at Westminster. Yet Northern Ireland is not allowed to send a single representative peer to this House.' He argued that it was 'obvious that a small number of Irish representative peers should be elected to represent Northern Ireland in this House. What the actual number should be I would not suggest – I really do not know; but obviously it should be something considerably less than the twenty-eight who came here when the whole of Ireland was in the United Kingdom.' John Whyte-Melville-Skeffington, 13th Viscount Massereene, agreed with Rathcavan, telling the Lords that he believed it to be 'quite extraordinary that Irish peers can stand for election to another place, for English constituencies, but cannot stand for election there for Northern Ireland constituencies'.[74] As William Teeling described, the Irish peers had woken up 'to their claims and rightful grievances'.[75]

A year after Hugh Rathcavan and John Massereene's pleas, the Irish Peers' Association (IPA) was founded by a group that included Paddy Butler, 28th Baron Dunboyne, the senior RAF officer Percy 'Paddy' Bernard, 5th Earl of Bandon, and Randal Antrim's grandfather Ran McDonnell, 8th Earl of Antrim. Its aim was to get justice for the Irish peers in the House of Lords, though it was an aim possibly not shared by all. (In 1981 one member described it as 'a very good dining club . . . rather irregular, of course . . . [but] it's only a couple of pounds a year, and the chaps are very good fun.')[76] Ran Antrim then petitioned the Lords in 1965: '. . . that your Lordships will declare that the peerage of Ireland has in accordance with the provisions of the Union with Ireland Act 1800 the right to be represented by twenty-eight lords temporal of Ireland elected by the peers of Ireland for life to sit and vote in your Lordships' House with privilege of Parliament.'[77] The law lord Richard Wilberforce ruled, however, that there was no mechanism by which Irish peers could be elected any longer, and that fresh legislation would be required. This was not sought, and in 1971 a clause was passed in the Statute Law Repeals Bill that revoked the sections of the Act of Union pertaining to the election of Irish representative peers.

In September 1975, by which time the chairman of the IPA was the former Irish Guards officer Richard Butler, 17th Viscount Mountgarret, the debate was rekindled. But Richard Mountgarret, writing to Ben McClintock-Bunbury, 5th Baron Rathdonnell, was rather cautious on the matter of the Irish peers and politics. 'I appreciate', he wrote, 'that there is/was a traditional responsibility of the peerage to govern, and indeed many of my ancestors were active in political life, but in changed times I have joined those who have abdicated this role. In my attempts to preserve my family property here and play some part in local affairs I have neither time nor money to devote to British politics.' Mountgarret went on: 'I have grave misgivings about peers normally resident in the Republic of Ireland becoming too involved with activities at Westminster at this very delicate period in Anglo-Irish relations . . . the unfortunate case last year of the Donoughmores illustrates this only too well.'[78] Later, in 1995, he told the Lords that: '[M]embers of the Irish peerage have rather adopted the role of the Flying Dutchman – they have nowhere to go.' He compared them to Sir Winston Churchill (whom he misquoted) saying: '. . . who at one time during his illustrious career, I think I am right in saying, found himself without a party, without a constituency and without a bottom.'[79]

As one member of the IPA said in the early 1980s, '[P]erhaps one day the House of Lords will be reformed in such a way as to admit elections from within the body of existing peers.'[80] This did happen, but no accommodations were made for Irish peers. Even in 2024, if peers with Irish titles wished to apply for election to the Lords, they could do so if they also had an English or British title that allowed them to take a seat there – but not otherwise.[81]

PART THREE

Officers and Gentlemen

The Aristocracy from Cradle to Grave

8

Vile Bodies

Love, Marriage and Adultery

On Wednesday 8 February 1984, a group of 550 mourners gathered at St Michael and All Angels, Badminton, Gloucestershire, for the funeral of Henry 'Master' Somerset, 10th Duke of Beaufort. They ranged from members of the royal family, including the duke's good friend Elizabeth II, whom he had served as Master of the Horse for twenty-five years, and various county worthies to those who had lived or worked on his estate. His mistresses were also there. There were quite a few of them.[1] Indeed, so many that the photographer Derry Moore, later 12th Earl of Drogheda, joked with the writer Lady Selina Hastings that they '. . . ought to have been parked, like nuns behind a grille, in the gallery of the church during the funeral.' 'How', he said, 'they would have hated each other.'[2]

Master's long-suffering widow, Lady Mary Cambridge, daughter of the German prince Dolly Cambridge, 1st Marquess of Cambridge, Queen Mary's brother, had long known that her husband was a philanderer. Some decades earlier she had even resorted to hiring private detectives to keep tabs on him at a time when he was pursuing an affair with Lavinia Fitzalan Howard, Duchess of Norfolk, wife of Bernard Fitzalan Howard, 16th Duke of Norfolk.[3] Lavinia had proved unashamed: much later, Master's successor-but-one, Harry Somerset, 12th Duke of Beaufort, suggested that the fact that she did not share the deep Catholic faith of her husband 'possibly made her less perturbed by any moral code her

241

marriage might impose'.[4] Master had been similarly unrepentant. He continued to invite his mistress to Badminton House, the family home, where she bossed the staff around and 'kept rearranging the menus, going into the kitchen and telling them what she wanted to eat and what the guests should have'.[5]

Eventually, Mary Beaufort banned Lavinia from Badminton, complained to her aunt, Queen Mary – who had lived at, and taken over, Badminton during the Second World War – and threatened divorce. An unsympathetic Queen Mary told her to 'return to Badminton and not be a fool'. Chips Channon noted in his diary in May 1950 that 'her [Queen Mary's] advice has been followed but the position whilst improving is not settled,'[6] and by December of that year, Peggy Petre, wife of the Essex landowner Joe Petre, 17th Baron Petre, was reporting from the Norfolks' Arundel Castle that 'the Norfolk ménage is going badly indeed' and that Mary Beaufort had indeed left Badminton. Channon, to whom she passed this gossip, concluded that 'the dark-ducal charmer is becoming public property'[7] and that – since he had recently heard that Charles Manners, 10th Duke of Rutland, wanted to divorce his first wife, Anne Cumming Bell[8] – 'the dukes are a "rum" lot.'[9]

Master's other mistresses included Margaret 'Peggy' Sidney, Viscountess De L'Isle, the widow of Wilfred 'Toby' Bailey, 3rd Baron Glanusk, the love of her life, who had died aged fifty-six in 1948, leaving her with a four-year-old daughter – heiress to Glanusk Park in south Wales.[10] Toby's grandfather had, according to Peggy, via Jim Lees-Milne, 'helped Master's father or grandfather by lending him money. I can't believe Master would be pleased to be reminded of this.'[11] Then there was the journalist Gloria Fremantle, Baroness Cottesloe, wife of John Fremantle, 4th Baron Cottesloe, who ghostwrote Master's memoirs in 1981. He later admitted that he had never read them or even 'so much as glanced at them'.[12] Both Peggy and Gloria were commoners married to aristocrats, Peggy being the daughter of an army general and Gloria an orphan born in a workhouse and adopted from the National Adoption Society in Ladbroke Grove at the age of two.

Another of Master's amours, Sally Grosvenor, Duchess of Westminster, had a troubled childhood of a different sort. Brought up in a family where there was 'no parental care, no family life, no friends', and where the food she and her sisters were given was prepared 'so frugally and injudiciously that they all developed rickets', her father was eventually revealed to be a fruit merchant, the self-styled 'Banana King of London' Roger Ackerley. The girls 'did not love or even like' their mother, the mysterious alcoholic fantasist Muriel Perry, their half-brother J. R. Ackerley wrote in his memoirs: 'she had less feeling for them than for her career and reputation.'[13] Sally married Gerald Grosvenor, the future if unlikely 4th Duke of Westminster, in 1945.[14] They never had any children. After Gerald's death in 1967, Sally and Master made little attempt to hide their relationship. In May 1973, following the annual Gloucestershire Society church service at Wickwar, Jim Lees-Milne and his wife Alvilde, who lived at Essex House,[15] a pretty Queen Anne house on the Badminton estate, watched on as the '... duke and wrong duchess – for Mary Beaufort conspicuously absented herself – walked arm in arm to their car and drove off.'[16] Sally Westminster was one of the 'nuns' at Master's funeral, along with Lavinia Norfolk, Peggy Glanusk, Cicely Hindlip and Gloria Cottesloe.[17]

Master's relationships with the cuckolded husbands of these women suggest that embarrassment was not a word that figured in his dictionary. John Cottesloe was among those invited to Badminton to shoot, and, on at least one occasion, given the best position in the line-up on every drive. And when Master was asked at dinner by the wife of his heir presumptive, his first cousin twice removed David Somerset, who he considered the greatest man of the twentieth century, he opted, not for such an obvious figure as Winston Churchill, but Bernard Norfolk, 'for his splendid work as chairman of the Marylebone Cricket Club'.[18] Master and Bernard Norfolk were both appointed Knights of the Garter in 1937, and thereafter they walked side by side, year after year, in the Garter procession.

But then Master was a very particular type of aristocrat. Pumped full of an extraordinarily exalted sense of self-worth and entitlement, he had little truck with conventional good manners or even basic politeness. He appeared to some a philistine, too. James Pope-Hennessy, visiting Badminton in November 1958 while researching his book on Queen Mary, Master's aunt-in-law, described how, when he remarked upon the loveliness of a pair of Canalettos in the Oak Room, Master had replied, saying, 'I don't know about their being lovely, but they're very like the house.'[19] As well as lacking an appreciation of anything much beyond fox hunting, he could display a fiery temper when thwarted by those whom he regarded as socially inferior – which was most of the population. On one occasion, when he was out riding with David Somerset, the pair reached a jammed gate, which couldn't be opened from horseback. 'Master', David's son Harry Beaufort recalled in his memoirs, 'noticed a man carrying out some maintenance work up a telegraph pole in the road beyond the troublesome gate, and respectfully asked if he would oblige. The man either did not hear this request or did not see why he should accede to it. His inaction prompted a total change of mood in Master, and he bellowed at full volume, "Open the bloody gate, damn you!"' The man shimmied down the pole like a fireman to open the gate, 'after which Master reluctantly thanked him and carried on with the ride, seeing nothing unusual in the exchange.'[20]

The Lees-Milnes also experienced the rough side of Master's tongue. As non-sporting types, the couple were regarded as suspect. 'What is the *point* of those Lees-Milnes?' Master said exasperatedly on one occasion. 'They don't hunt, they don't shoot, they don't fish.'[21] But they stepped right over the mark the day their whippets came across a vixen and her cubs that Master had been watching lovingly through his binoculars. As the dogs chased and worried at the foxes, Master was, as Jim later recalled, 'almost apoplectic'. 'Said he would not have our bloody dogs on his land. Bloody this and bloody that. He would get his gun and shoot them.' He called on Essex House in person to continue his ranting, and then sent his keeper round to warn that he would shoot the dogs 'if ever again they were seen loose'. Since, as Jim reflected, Master would be allowing his own hounds to tear these cubs to pieces before long, his outrage seemed more than a little strange. 'Ghastly values, ghastly people,' he concluded, and he and his wife avoided Master until the day in December 1979 when Sally Westminster managed to broker a truce.[22]

If hunting was one of Master's twin passions,[23] it was a passion he inherited from his father Henry Beaufort. Indeed, his father was out hunting the day that Master was born on 4 April 1900. Doffing his hunting cap, the duke told the assembled hunting party: '"Before we go off to draw, I thought you would like to know that early this morning my wife gave birth to a son." "May we give three cheers, Your Grace?" one of the huntsmen asked respectfully. "Certainly not! You might frighten the hounds." '[24] Hunting seems to have informed Master's comprehension of human psychology, too, in as much as he had any understanding of it. 'Poor Hughie Northumberland has terrible problems with his boy,' he said when he learned that the duke's eldest son Harry was suffering from depression. 'He's given up hunting,' he added, as if this alone was a sign of trouble ahead, showing a remarkable lack of understanding about the world he lived in.[25] For the rest, the man who was Master of the Horse for three monarchs for forty-two years, a Garter knight, a privy counsellor, and Lord-Lieutenant of both Gloucestershire and Bristol, was deeply conservative: no one was allowed into his employ if they were a Labour supporter, or, even worse, a Roman Catholic.

He was rarely bested. But there was certainly one occasion when he came off worse. On his way to the Great West Show with Gloria Cottesloe in tow, he asked his chauffeur to pull the Bentley over so that the pair could pop out of the car for a short 'walk'. The excursion completed, the car set off again but had to halt when it encountered a farmer's tractor. The chauffeur got out of the Bentley to ask the farmer to budge. The man's response surprised everyone: 'You can tell that dirty bugger that I know exactly what he's been doing and I ain't movin' until he gives me a fiver.'[26]

Master paid up.

* * *

If Master and Mary Beaufort were ever truly in love with one another it is impossible to tell. Whether or not their inability to have children was a factor in the breakdown of their marriage is similarly impossible to ascertain.[27] Beyond describing their early days together as a 'whirlwind romance', Master's memoirs express no particular fondness for his wife – but then, since they were written by Gloria Cottesloe, that is scarcely surprising.[28] Mary cared enough about what Master was up to hire private detectives to spy on him, but she never said much publicly about him during his lifetime beyond complaining to Queen Mary and, in 1950, taking the extreme measure for someone who loved horses as much as she did, of removing the ones she owned from Badminton.[29]

Only after his death, by then suffering from dementia, did she tell people how bitterly she had resented the way he had treated her.[30] The circumstances of his funeral, however, suggest that, even after his many betrayals, she retained, at the very least, a lingering fondness for him – though, in fairness, her training for such an event had been impeccable, and the queen was in attendance. In the days before, it had been arranged that she should be walking her dogs in the park at Badminton when Master's body was being moved to the church. On the day, sensing that something was up, she made for the church and went inside. Then, as Jim Lees-Milne described, '[She] went straight up to the coffin and demanded that the lid be opened. This was done. She bent over the face and gently kissed it. Turned away and walked straight out of the church without a word.' At the funeral two days later, accompanied by the new duke David Beaufort, she was looking 'tiny and bewildered in black,' as Jim put it.[31] 'Did she realise what was happening?' he wondered, as Mary glimpsed the coffin being lowered into the grave before David Beaufort piloted her away. Likely, not, since she had been unwell for some time by this point. The next hunt after Master's death had one the best runs in years, prompting the new duchess, Caroline Beaufort, to remark: 'Master has inhabited the fox!'[32]

Mary had once floated the possibility of divorce, and such a step would have been technically possible. But as Queen Mary's out-raged reaction to the suggestion illustrates, the Beauforts occupied an exalted stratum within English society where, until decades into the twentieth century, divorce wasn't the done thing. Just over a decade before Master inherited the Beaufort dukedom in 1924, Bend'Or Westminster, since 1907 Lord-Lieutenant of Cheshire had written to George V to say that he was contemplating the 'extreme measure'[33] of separating from his wife Shelagh (to whom he had been serially unfaithful[34]) – not only because she was having an affair with Jimmy Fitz-James Stuart, 17th Duke of Alba and 10th Duke of Berwick,[35] but because she had been absent when their only son Edward had been taken ill in 1909 and subsequently died – something for which Bend'Or could not forgive her. The king had returned his note, imploring him to '. . . remember your great pos-ition; not only that of your family but as my representative in the County of Cheshire & that in these days the example from those like yourself may do infinite good or harm in the country.'[36] When, six years later, the Westminsters did go ahead with a divorce on the grounds of Bend'Or's desertion and adultery (a legal necessity under the Matrimonial Causes Act of 1857), there was consternation at Court.[37] For months, officials and courtiers discussed Bend'Or's future role. Should he retain the Lord-Lieutenancy of Cheshire? Should he even be allowed to come to Court? In January 1920, the Lord Chamberlain William Mansfield, 1st Viscount Sandhurst, confirmed that '. . . no man or woman who has been divorced . . . should be allowed to come to Court' – and nor could Bend'Or rep-resent Cheshire.[38] The duke ultimately resigned his lord-lieutenancy, while the king declared that there would be no further royal visits to Bend'Or's home of Eaton Hall, from any member of the royal family, even from his aunt Meg Cambridge, Mary Beaufort's mother.[39] He remained ostracised from the royal presence until his death in 1953. By then he had divorced two more wives.[40]

If this suggests a certain double-standard among the peers of the realm, that's because there was one. Members of the aristoc-racy were seemingly free to indulge in any number of extra-marital affairs, and it was fine for their own set to be aware of these affairs, but anything that threatened to make their bad behaviour public – whether through the divorce courts, the newspapers or both – was considered extremely bad form. Reading Channon's diaries, it's sometimes difficult not to conclude that bed-hopping was almost *de rigueur* among the upper classes. The rule was not don't do it, but do be discreet about it.

Sir Oswald 'Tom' Mosley,[41] who crops up numerous times in Channon's diaries, reckoned that this upper-class world comprised no more than about 600 people, 'who all knew each other and knew much of what was going on between each other but who kept this secret from the outside world'. The 'rules-of-the-game', according to his son Nicholas, 'were like those which require honour amongst gangsters, that one should not talk'.[42] That was just as well in his case, because Tom was himself a serial adulterer. He had married Lady Cynthia 'Cimmie' Curzon in 1920 but had soon begun having affairs every which way – with her stepmother, her sister, with Georgia Sitwell, wife of the writer Sir Sacheverell Sitwell. He had a mistress in Paris; pursued Blanche Barrymore, wife of the actor John; and encouraged Cimmie to have her own affair, suggesting as a lover for her the painter Dick Wyndham. In his biography of his parents, Nicholas Mosley speculates what Cimmie thought of all this: 'It was a convention of the world in which she moved and had been brought up,' he suggests, 'that husbands were expected to take some interest in other people's wives: their own wives seemed to have evolved a state of mind by which they both did and did not notice what was going on. There were rules-of-the-game about what was acceptable; and so long as Tom kept to these – the purpose of which was to ensure that the whole business should remain somewhat childlike – then Cimmie could perhaps treat him as her naughty boy.'[43]

As it happens, there's a question as to how much Cimmie did know about what her husband was getting up to. When Tom's future second wife Diana Guinness (née Mitford) asked him why Cimmie should be so upset about their affair in particular, Tom replied that it was likely that she simply didn't know about the rest. The thought then struck him, Nicholas Mosley writes, that '[M]ight it not help Cimmie to know about the other women because then it would help to take her mind off Diana? So he went home and told Cimmie a list of his women: and Cimmie said, "But they are all my best friends!" '[44] Shortly afterwards he met the Conservative politician Bob Boothby at a dinner party and asked whether he would, as someone close to Cimmie, go and comfort her because she was clearly deeply upset at the revelation of what her husband had been up to.[45] When Bob asked whether Tom had told Cimmie about all the women he had been with, he replied, 'Well, all except her stepmother and her sister.'[46] (Incidentally, Boothby himself had form: he was the long-term Other Man in the life of Lady Dorothy Cavendish, wife of the future prime minister Harold Macmillan.)

The fear of public exposure, the dread of people outside one's circle observing the washing of dirty linen, is understandable in an era when fascination with the aristocracy and their comings, goings and doings were still prevalent. Readers of *The Times*, for example, could vicariously follow the lives of peers of the realm via the Court Circular, which recorded not just births, marriages and deaths but social schedules, even if it wasn't intended for that purpose.[47] On 26 July 1927, for example, one would learn that the Coventrys were relocating from 1 Balfour Place to Croome, the Harlechs were arriving at Glyn Hall, the Normanbys were departing 90 Eaton Square for Mulgrave Castle, and that 'the Duchess of Buccleuch, with Lady Angela and Lord George Scott, will leave London today for Drumlanrig Castle, where they will remain for about three months before going on to Bowhill.'[48] Given that many peers had several residences, there was a practical reason for imparting such information, as there was for Robert Devereux, 18th Viscount Hereford, and his sister the Hon. Bridget Devereux, who left for the south of France in July 1964, including in their note in the Court Circular that 'no correspondence will be forwarded';[49] for Margot, Countess of Buckinghamshire, in 1983, thanking 'all those who have sent letters of condolence on the death of her husband, Vere, Earl of Buckinghamshire';[50] or for Pansy Erskine, Countess of Mar and Kellie, announcing in January 1994 that she wished henceforth 'to be known as The Dowager Countess of Mar and Kellie'.[51] Victor Hervey, 6th Marquess of Bristol, appeared in *The Times* social column over sixty times in the course of thirty-three years to record, for example, his engagement to Juliet Fitzwilliam in 1960 and his 'regrets' at being absent from memorial services at which he was 'represented' by Juliet, as though he were some minor royal. (His first actual appearance in the newspaper as an adult was in April 1939 under the headline 'Alleged theft of jewels'[52] when it was revealed that he had been charged, with others, of having stolen jewellery and a mink coat to the value of £2,500 on one occasion, and jewellery to the value of £2,860 on another [see Chapter 11].) Such snippets of information were intended for other members of the aristocratic circle, of course, but they clearly also intrigued less exalted members of the public. To an extent, aristocrats and their lives fulfilled the place in popular culture now occupied by celebrities.

The fear, then, that wayward behaviour at the highest level of society might become a public sensation was well placed. Even in an era when society as a whole was infinitely more deferential than it is today, scandal not infrequently trumped respect. For the most part, newspapers had to observe quite tight restrictions on what they could and couldn't report. Bill and Sarah Astor's divorce in 1953, for example, received just two brief mentions a month apart under the distinctly untitillating headlines 'Viscount Astor seeks divorce'[53] and 'Decree for Lord Astor'.[54] The divorce of David and Mary Cecil, Lord and Lady Burghley, seven years earlier was given only marginally more attention, since David Burghley had been an Olympic athlete – but even then the headline 'Decree against athlete' can hardly have caused much of a stir.[55] But when there was more to go on, as there was with Henry and Daphne Bath's divorce in 1953, the press could have a field day. The couple had technically married one another twice, the first time in secret, away from their disapproving parents, in 1926; the second time officially in 1927. Consequently, when two years after their divorce in 1953, it emerged that a legal question remained as to whether the divorce court had actually dissolved both marriages, the headlines proved rather racier than usual. 'Former marchioness's secret wedding plea fails', read a headline in the *Leicester Evening Mail* in May 1955.[56] 'Four people in the dilemma of a peer's marriage' was the headline in the following day's *Daily Mirror*, which also featured front-page photographs of Henry, Daphne, Daphne's new husband Xan Fielding and Henry's new wife Virginia Bath, and asked the question that the country clearly needed to have answered: 'Is their marriage dissolved or not?'

One divorce above all in the couple of decades after the Second World War demonstrated the wisdom of aristocratic discretion – that between Ian Campbell, 11th Duke of Argyll, and his estranged wife, Margaret, which was played out in full public gaze in the first half of 1963.

* * *

Ian Argyll had not been born a duke, or even the son of a duke – but the great-grandson of the Liberal politician George Campbell, 8th Duke of Argyll, in Paris, in 1903. When he was four, his father Douglas Campbell left his American mother, Aimée, and ran off with his son's governess. Bolting ran in the family: Douglas's own father Lord Walter Campbell had abandoned his wife, Olivia, in Biarritz in the 1880s, taking their two children with him and informing her that he washed his hands of her. Ian grew up with his mother in America and when she died in January 1920 he moved to Europe, dividing his time between his grandmother's house in Paris and Scotland. He started a history degree at Oxford but was repeatedly sent down for failing to apply himself, and ultimately he abandoned his studies.

In January 1926, his father died at the early age of forty-eight, leaving him £15,000 – 'rather by oversight, I think. Like myself, he was not a man to leave money unspent,' Ian remembered.[57]

With Douglas dead, Ian was now heir presumptive to his eccentric unmarried first cousin once removed, Niall Campbell, 10th Duke of Argyll. He spent some time with Niall at Inveraray Castle in Argyll, learning about field sports, farming and forestry, but the pair found they had little in common and in 1927 Ian left Inveraray, not to return for twenty-two years. Instead, he headed for France, where that summer he met the Hon. Janet Aitken, daughter of the press baron Max Beaverbrook and his wife Gladys Drury. Ian swept her off her feet. His future in-laws, aware that while he might be 'long on charm' he was 'short on judgement at gaming tables', were less impressed.[58] The couple nevertheless announced their engagement on 15 November 1927. Among those who got in touch to offer their congratulations was Princess Louise, Duchess of Argyll, the fourth daughter of Queen Victoria who had in 1871 married Niall's uncle, John Campbell, the future 9th Duke of Argyll. Louise invited Janet to Kensington Palace, where, after lunch, served by a butler and two footmen, she presented Janet with a jewellery box containing a diamond and emerald tiara. A fortnight later, on 1 December 1927, Gladys Beaverbrook died, and eleven days later Janet and Ian were married at St Columba's on Pont Street.

Things quickly went downhill. On their honeymoon, Ian took Janet to a brothel in Paris. When they reached Jamaica she realised that the tiara Louise Argyll had given her was gone. Ian admitted that he had sold it but promised he would get it back. Janet now faced the bitter realisation that 'he was in debt up to his eyebrows and I was to bail him out . . . me and my money.' The problem was, she went on: 'I *had* no money.'[59] Ian's irresponsibility continued after the birth of their daughter Jeanne in December 1928. He pestered Janet for her jewellery, or for money to pay his debts. He even resorted to emotional blackmail of a high theatrical order. 'Then I must kill myself, Efelant,' he said on one occasion, using his tiresome nickname for her. 'There is no other way. Maybe it will be best for everybody,' he went on as he took a gun from a drawer, rushed from the room and let off two shots. When he returned, a shocked and tearful Janet told him to take the jewels.

'Still I didn't realise that his own sickness was far more serious than mine,' she said later. 'His was incurable.'[60] Shortly before their divorce in May 1934 she bumped into him in St James's Park and agreed to talk things through. He took her to a room at the Park Lane Hotel, where he beat her, breaking one of her ribs and a cheekbone and covering her in bruises. The following November, he married Louise 'Oui Oui' Clews, the daughter of a wealthy New York artist.

By this time, Ian was almost broke, having run through £200,000 in sixteen years. To kickstart his second marriage, he borrowed £30,000 against his rights of inheritance at Inveraray. Two years later, Louise gave birth to a son, whom they named Ian. The future Duke of Argyll now had his own heir. Ian spent most of the war years as a prisoner-of-war, having been captured while serving with the 51st Highland Division at St Valéry in June 1940. Reunited with Louise after hostilities had ceased, the couple moved to Biarritz, where, in May 1946, she gave birth to their second son, Colin.

Three years later, Niall Argyll died unmarried at Inveraray. 'So at last Ian has become a duke. He's been waiting for it for years,' said Clare Sutherland.[61] It was a dubious inheritance, though. Inveraray, built for Archibald Campbell, 3rd Duke of Argyll, in the 1740s, was a mess – a dry-rot-riddled shell of a house where as Ian remembered, 'twisted drainpipes hung down mildewed walls like lifeless snakes; washbasins were cracked and baths seeped.'[62] The armour in the hall had gone so long without being polished that it looked like lead. It didn't help that Niall Argyll had done no tax planning, and that Ian was burdened not only with putting Inveraray to rights but with death duties totalling £516,988.[63] And that was before his own debts were taken into account. In an attempt to make a start on tackling the vast problems he faced, he sold 28,000 acres in Kintyre.

Two years later, in March 1951, Louise divorced him on grounds of his adultery and took custody of their sons. Twelve days after the divorce was finalised, Ian married a woman with 'dark hair and green eyes' and a 'peach-like' complexion whom he had first met on the Golden Arrow train from Paris in 1947.[64] Margaret Sweeny was the daughter of a Scottish self-made millionaire, a former debutante of the year, and, according to Jim Lees-Milne, 'the great beauty of my generation'.[65] She was also a shameless self-promoter. According to the novelist Barbara Cartland, Margaret '... organised her own publicity, was charming to journalists and gave what we would now call press conferences. She had in consequence far better and more flattering press coverage than any film star.'[66] When, back in 1934, she had become ill with pneumonia, news of her illness had featured on the front page of the *News Chronicle*. Thousands of people had crowded around Brompton Oratory when she had married the American socialite Charlie Sweeny the previous year, just to catch a glimpse of her. During this marriage to Charlie, with whom she had two children, she had been immortalised as 'Mrs Sweeny' by the songwriter Cole Porter in his hit song 'You're the Top' from *Anything Goes*. Before her marriage to Charlie, she had been variously courted by Prince Aly Khan, son of Sir Sultan Mahomed Shah, Aga Khan III, 48th Imam of the Nizari Ismaili sect of Islam; the actor Fulke Greville, 7th Earl of Warwick; and Janet Campbell's own brother, the Hon. Max Aitken. In 1939, *Tatler* had described how '... no Ascot could possibly be convicted of being dowdy if Mrs Charles Sweeny were there.'[67]

Society hummed with gossip about the new couple. When she learned of Ian and Margaret's engagement, Nancy Mitford wrote to her mother Sydney Freeman-Mitford, Baroness Redesdale, who was staying on Inch Kenneth, an island just off Mull: 'Your local Duke has just eloped with old Margaret Sweeny, can you beat it?'[68] A week later, Chips Channon, then on a trip to the French capital, confided to his diary: 'Much chat in Paris about Margaret Sweeny's engagement – if one can become engaged to a married duke – to Ian Argyll. I hope for her sake that she will wriggle out of it. He is a fraud, a liar, and a cad.'[69] Channon was right. Long before their wedding day, Ian had called her two children spoiled brats, and had vilified her father, friends, and Margaret herself. She was bewildered. He had been capable of such kindness – to her, and to the children – and now he was behaving like this. She unwisely put it down to pre-marital nerves. On the day itself, wearing a grey and black checked dress, she walked down the aisle as Mrs Sweeny, and back up it as the Duchess of Argyll. The day after the wedding, the newlyweds repaired to Inveraray where they were piped in to the strains of 'The Campbells Are Coming'. Ian, wearing a kilt, carried his new wife across the threshold.

Margaret – and her money – provided much-needed support at Inveraray. Wearing her oldest clothes, she would direct teams of estate workers as they cleared out the junk-filled rooms and put the rickety structure to rights. Out of earshot, they called her 'Maggie'. A few weeks before Elizabeth II's coronation in 1953, the Argylls opened Inveraray to the public. After that, they divided their time between the castle and Margaret's house in Mayfair, at 48 Upper Grosvenor Street. Ian, a keen gardener and birdwatcher, preferred the country, and Margaret, a socialite, the town. The arrangement didn't work. 'In exchange for my spending time in London I thought she should spend a reasonable amount of time at Inveraray,' Ian remembered.[70] Tensions mounted. In the autumn of 1954, Ian discovered that Margaret had a young man staying in a mews cottage in the grounds of the Upper Grosvenor Street house. When he challenged her about it, she retorted that surely she was allowed to have friends – 'I've got to have somebody to take me to parties. You can't, can you, when you're stuck up at that dreary hole in Scotland for most of the year?' Irritation rose to anger when she asked Sigismund von Braun, brother of Wernher von Braun, inventor of the V-2 rocket, and his wife Hildegarde to Inveraray; 'I detested the very name,' he remembered. According to Ian, Margaret kept on seeing von Braun, for the same reason, he supposed, as 'she sought the society of famous public figures – because they were the "right" people.'[71]

When the Conservative politician Sir Henry d'Avigdor Goldsmid visited Inveraray with his wife Rosie over the Whitsun weekend of 1957, Rosie found Ian 'a perfectly charming host to us' but noted that this was 'rather in contradiction to his general attitude to his wife'. 'During the weekend we were there,' she remembered, 'he was constantly needling her.'[72]

The final implosion of their marriage began while they were away on a trip to Australia in 1959 when Ian came across love letters that Margaret had written to an unknown man. He then sneaked a look at her diary, to discover 'interspaced between notes of trains caught and cheques cashed ... the times and dates of appointments with half a dozen different men'. 'From a brief perusal,' he continued, 'I deduced that she had had "affairs" with one or two of them, certainly Sigismund von Braun.' A furious Margaret caught him going through her things. Ian accused her of adultery. She did not deny it: 'Why, you've hardly taken me out in four years! All you think about is poking around your garden. You don't like parties. You dislike my friends. You loathe to entertain. What was I supposed to do?'[73] For the first time, '[T]he possibility of divorcing Margaret crossed my mind. She had proved her worthlessness as a wife.'[74] He returned home earlier than planned and headed to the Upper Grosvenor Street house to search for further evidence of his wife's affairs. After pulling open cupboards and drawers and peering into 'any dark corner which Margaret could have used as a hiding place', he found in a bookcase in the study an envelope containing photographs of his wife with a naked man whose head was – conveniently or inconveniently – cropped out of the print. He took everything he had discovered and gave the photographs to his bank manager for safekeeping. After Margaret's return to London, he went back with his daughter Jeanne to steal her current diary. Jeanne, he wrote later, 'thought it a great joke'. 'I looked quickly round the room and found what I wanted, the current diary on a bedside table. I put it in my pocket and called Jeanne to leave – just as Margaret picked up the phone to dial 999.'[75]

The following month, Ian banned her from Inveraray, allowing her just one visit to identify the various heirlooms that she believed he had handed over to her possession, in a deed of gift. He greeted her curtly. She grinned at him and then proceeded to tour the state rooms saying, 'That, that, and that is mine,' picking out the pieces that she thought belonged to her.[76] It turned out that the heirlooms had not been Ian's to give away – he had already mortgaged them, and it was this mortgage that provided him with the £1,000 a year he was living on when Margaret met him.

Four years later, in 1963, the longest and most expensive divorce in Scottish legal history took place. The press had a field day. 'Duchess and the four men', cried the *Daily Herald*; 'Judge says Duchess was promiscuous', declared the *Peterborough Evening Telegraph*; 'Duchess of Argyll's lovers', read the headline in the *Daily Mirror*. In an interview a decade later Margaret would say that she felt the press were 'bewitched' by the scandal.[77] Two years hence, she would claim, 'I've had the most ghastly publicity in the world,' contrasting what she felt was the more gentle (and deferential) coverage of earlier years with the 'unkind' nature of more recent journalism.[78] Given the salacious details of her marriage revealed during the divorce proceedings, not least the photograph of the mysterious 'headless' lover, it's not surprising that there should have been such hunger for the story. Nor, given the judge Lord Wheatley's censorious remarks about Margaret, that she should have emerged with her reputation shredded. He described her as a 'highly sexed woman who had ceased to be satisfied with normal relations and had started to indulge in what I can only describe as disgusting sexual activities to gratify a basic sexual appetite', and '[A] completely promiscuous woman whose sexual appetite could only be satisfied by a number of men, and whose attitude to the sanctity of marriage was what moderns would call enlightened, but in plain language could only be described as wholly immoral'.[79] She was ordered to pay seven-eighths of the divorce costs. Her son Brian Sweeny sent a cable to his mother: 'Desperately sorry verdict and humiliation. Disbelieve evidence completely. All possible moral support.'[80]

A year later, Ian sold his memoirs to the *People*, reflecting in the final paragraph how: '*[M]y* family motto is "Forget Not"[81] – and truly I cannot forget those unhappy years I spent with Margaret.'[82]

Such public airing of his memories and grievances did not go down well at his club, White's. Faced with expulsion, he opted to resign his membership in January 1965. He had, unforgivably, broken the code of aristocratic silence. It's hard to disagree with Margaret's view that 'clearly the sole purpose of these articles was to attack me, and to revive details of the divorce action.'[83]

Margaret herself wondered years later, 'Why exactly did we fail, Ian and I? What poisoned our life together?' Her conclusion was that it was the money side of things that had proved so corrosive. Ian, she said, '. . . needed to marry money – but he resented that need. It undermined him as a man.'[84] Sarah Phelps, who wrote the 2021 BBC One three-part drama, *A Very British Scandal*, about Ian and Margaret's marriage, believes that Margaret 'loved to be adored, she loved conquests and she loved attention'. In her opinion, Ian '. . . was a hole, an abyss – there was nothing, not women, gambling, amphetamines, horses, alcohol, that could fill up the void of need in him. It was [a case of] here you are, you're a duke now, and he thought, what does that mean? He was not of that land. That sense of entitlement is a noose around the neck – it marches you up the front to lead men, and it mows you down.' 'There's damage and trauma right from the earliest days,' she suggests, but ultimately, 'he was an absolute brute, an alcoholic, a drug addict. He had a monstrous life, but he was also a monster in life.'

Ian remarried five weeks after his divorce from Margaret, and died in 1973, aged sixty-nine, having suffered a stroke in Paris two months earlier. His ashes were buried, where his father had been interred, on the island of Inishail, Loch Awe, on Friday 13 April. As for Margaret, she remained active on London's social scene – 'she loved going out and being seen . . . she would go to the opening of an envelope' – but ran through her money at a rate of knots and ended up in St George's Nursing Home in Pimlico.[85] There, the writer Charles Castle remembered seeing '. . . this huge picture of her father on the wall and two pictures of her children. There were no pictures of the grandchildren, only these two of [her daughter] Frances aged about six months old and Brian when he was about two years old. No modern pictures.'[86] 'Never had so much fortune been used to achieve so little,' he concluded.[87] Margaret died in the nursing home in July 1993, aged eighty. She would doubtless have been pleased to see how much press coverage her death received. Her aristocratic friends would doubtless have reflected that her life demonstrated the wisdom of keeping sordid personal details private.

* * *

The relaxed attitude the twentieth-century aristocracy took towards extra-marital affairs (as long as they did not become public) extended to gay and bisexual relationships too. The diaries of Chips Channon – who married a Guinness heiress but also conducted affairs with the likes of the playwright Terence Rattigan – are peppered with accounts of men in his set who, married or not, had affairs with other men, or who were, at the very least, in a poorly concealed closet. Meeting Sir George Arthur, 3rd Baronet, in March 1928, Chips experienced what he described as 'the usual homosexual handshake' from Arthur, former personal private secretary and biographer to Herbert Kitchener, 1st Earl Kitchener, following it up in his diary with the comment: 'I'm sure everything points to the fact that Lord Kitchener was homosexual; his whole life indicates that.'[88]

Then there was the former Lord Steward, Governor of New South Wales and Lord Warden of the Cinque Ports William Lygon, 7th Earl Beauchamp. When he died aged sixty-six in November 1938, Channon recorded that he had, 'rank, riches, arrogance, intelligence, achievement, high office, seven children, the god's gifts at his feet, and he gaspillé-ed [wasted] them all for the most sterile of all vices – footmen!! There has never been such a scandal in England, and yet people, on the whole, minded very little. The whole story very Roman, classic.'[89] According to one account, at dinner at Madresfield, the Beauchamps' moated country house in

Worcestershire,[90] a guest asked Harold Nicolson if he really had just heard Beauchamp whisper 'Je t'adore' to the butler. Nicolson, covering for him, said no, the guest was mistaken; in fact, Beauchamp had said 'shut the door'. Beauchamp's indiscretions were, however, widely known about in the circles in which he moved. When in June 1927 he was asked to present the prizes at Cheltenham College's speech day, old boy and former Conservative MP Arthur Lee, 1st Viscount Lee of Fareham, 'painfully cognisant of [Beauchamp's] unsavoury moral reputation', berated the headmaster for extending the invitation.[91] Nor did Beauchamp make much attempt to be discreet:[92] one of his servants once came across him and his doctor *in flagrante* on the sofa in the drawing room of the Beauchamps' Belgrave Square house.[93]

It was his lack of caution that led directly to the 'scandal' alluded to by Chips: someone told George V. Who that someone was is not known, though some have pointed the finger at his own brother-in-law, Bend'Or Westminster, who, according to one theory, was jealous that Beauchamp had three healthy sons[94] when his only legitimate son had died young; or according to another, was acting to protect the sensibilities of his pious sister Lettice Beauchamp; or according to yet another, rather more convincing one, was furious that his brother-in-law should be allowed to cavort promiscuously and yet remain a Knight of the Garter and Lord-Lieutenant of Gloucestershire, when he himself had had to resign from the Cheshire lord-lieutenancy because of a petty divorce case. However the revelation came about, what is certain is that one evening in June 1931, Beauchamp found himself admitting a deputation of two Garter knights and a peer, Jack Hamilton-Gordon, 2nd Baron Stanmore, to Madresfield, who proceeded to inform him that the king was aware of what he had been up to and was not happy.[95] If the popular story is to believed, George V's actual remark on hearing of Beauchamp's activities was: 'I thought men like that shot themselves.'[96]

Was George V being slightly disingenuous on this occasion? Perhaps. He might have expressed shock but as his biographer

Kenneth Rose pointed out, the king was: '[Q]uite fond of a bit of smut – gossip and scandal. He liked British ambassadors abroad to write to him about the private habits of kings and prime ministers – for example, one prime minister who was addicted to sodomy.' But perhaps the point with the Beauchamp case was that the king felt, along with other members of the ruling class, that Beauchamp had broken the discretion rule. In 1922, Christabel Russell and her husband the Hon. John 'Stilts' Russell, heir of Oliver Russell, 2nd Baron Ampthill, went to court after John claimed that he could not be the father of their child, Geoffrey, since they had never had sexual intercourse, and so the baby must be someone else's. When the case didn't go Christabel's way, and the Court of Appeal proved unsympathetic, she appealed to the House of Lords, who ruled that no child born after a marriage, as Geoffrey had been, could be declared illegitimate merely on someone's say-so. It was this case that prompted the king to complain, via his private secretary Arthur Bigge, 1st Baron Stamfordham, about the 'repulsive' details of divorce cases, and the exposure of matters which an 'unwritten code of decency' had once considered 'sacred and out of range of public eye or ear'. The king wondered whether it would be possible to '... try such cases *in camera*'. In the end, his protest led to restrictions on reporting details of divorce cases, and the Judicial Proceedings (Regulation of Reports) Act 1926.[97] His love of gossip, however, remained undimmed.

The king might have expected Beauchamp to shoot himself. He did not, but the very public humiliation he then had to endure perhaps justifies the writer Beverley Nichols' judgement that 'maybe it would have been better if he had':

> He resigned honour after honour – each resignation was gloatingly recorded in the popular press – and finally he left the country, never to return. No, that is wrong, he *did* return ... once, for a single hour. He had a last ambition to see again the home of his ancestors ... how, I do not know. Some say that the authorities

relented or turned a blind eye ... a few months later he died. He
was a fairly young man and still had foreign honour of which even
the King could not deprive him; but the newspapers, which had
found plenty of space to chronicle his misfortune, spared hardly an
inch for his decease. Yes, it might indeed have been better if he had
shot himself.[98]

Diana Mosley observed that while her generation was on Beauchamp's side, his own was not. 'He was awfully off-putting. Lord
Beauchamp would have evoked much more sympathy if he hadn't
been so absurd in his pomposity. If someone poses as a hero of
rectitude and then something like that happens, people are not as
sympathetic as with someone more modest.'[99] His family paid a
high social price for their father's indiscretions. His third daughter
Maimie who had been tipped as the future wife of Prince George,
later Duke of Kent, lost him when the scandal broke about her
father – ironic given that George Kent, known to his friends as
'Babe', was bisexual, and was alleged to have had a nineteen-year
affair with Noël Coward. Towards the end of her life, Maimie's
sister Sibell '... passed the time reading the memoirs, diaries and
biographies of her peer group in an attempt to keep up with the
families that, by birth, she would – had her father not fallen from
grace – have counted among her circle.'[100]

In one regard, Beauchamp was lucky. He had broken the aristocratic code and for that he was socially punished. But, unlike
errant heterosexual peers, he had also broken the law, and for that
he could have gone to prison. Until 1967 in England and Wales –
in Scotland 1981, and Northern Ireland 1982 – homosexuality
was punishable by a two-year jail sentence with hard labour, and
until 1861 a convicted man faced being hanged. Theoretically,
Beauchamp could have been subjected to the same punishment as
Oscar Wilde had received in the 1890s. As it was, he was spared
that humiliation, though, like Wilde, he felt he had no choice
but to spend the rest of his life beyond the shores of his country
of birth.

Edward Douglas-Scott-Montagu, 3rd Baron Montagu of Beau-lieu, was less fortunate. He had known that he was, at the very least, bisexual since his time at Eton in the 1940s when he fell in love with another boy – an experience he found 'disquieting'.[101] The attraction he felt to other men persisted, and he pursued various gay liaisons in his adult life, though he married two women.[102]

Unlike Beauchamp, Montagu took great pains to be careful. And perhaps at another time that might have been sufficient to save him. But it was his misfortune to be caught out when Britain was going through one of its periodic bouts of censoriousness. The 1950s was a peculiarly contradictory era. On the one hand, the country viewed itself as entering an exciting 'new Elizabethan Age', embracing a progressive future (given physical form at the Festival of Britain in 1951), and moving away from the economic restrictions of the immediate post-war years and the social restrictions of the pre-war years. On the other hand, in a world made uncertain by the Cold War and the fear of communism, Britain was capable of being highly reactionary. 'Not only did they [the establishment] see reds under every bed; they saw them *in* every bed as well' as Montagu later put it. And it was in this spirit of reaction and, indeed, paranoia that home secretary David Maxwell Fyfe, later 1st Earl of Kilmuir, ordered a police crackdown on men engaged in homosexual activities, supported in his endeavours by the Lord Chief Justice Rayner Goddard, who, from his seat in the Lords, later opposed the legalisation of homosexual acts, and the commissioner of the Metropolitan Police Sir John Nott-Bower, '. . . who was convinced that the British way of life was threatened by a homosexual conspiracy.'[103] 'Traditional' standards needed to be upheld at all costs.

During August Bank Holiday 1953, a group of Boy Scouts had camped on Montagu's Beaulieu estate in Hampshire, helping out as guides in Palace House. That weekend, Montagu had some friends to stay, including the film director Kenneth Hume.[104] Since the weather was fine, Montagu invited the group down to the beach for a swim. Later, he discovered that his camera was missing and reported its loss to the police. When they came to talk to him, they informed him that one of the scouts had alleged that Montagu had sexually assaulted him, and that another had accused Hume of the same crime. Montagu denied the accusations and briefly left England for Paris, to avoid the British press. On his return, he was charged with a serious offence against a boy scout. Arriving at Lymington Magistrates' Court, he found a crowd of 250 people had turned out to see him. His lawyer tried to challenge the evidence against his client, but the magistrates were unconvinced, and a trial was booked at Winchester assizes. Prosecuting counsel at Winchester was Geoffrey 'Khaki' Roberts, who, along with David Maxwell Fyfe, had been on the prosecuting team at the Nuremberg trials. Montagu didn't like the look of Khaki: he was 'a formidable opponent with a reactionary distaste for what he considered "unnatural practices"'.[105] Khaki began his remarks by describing the case as 'very serious and sordid' with 'nothing pleasant about it from beginning to end'.[106]

Despite this, at the end of the trial the original charges were dismissed, and the jury failed to reach a verdict on an additional charge of inciting 'certain male persons ... to commit serious offences with male persons' introduced by the Crown during court proceedings. But Montagu wasn't off the hook. On the morning of 9 January 1954, police arrived at Palace House, where they detained Montagu without giving him the opportunity to have breakfast, shave or contact his lawyer. Simultaneously, two other groups of officers arrested two associates of Montagu's: his third cousin once removed, the landowner Michael Pitt-Rivers, at home in Dorset, and his friend the *Daily Mail*'s diplomatic correspondent Peter Wildeblood, at home in London. The trio were charged with the offence of conspiring to 'incite certain male persons ... to commit serious offences with male persons'.[107] The incidents were supposed to have happened on a variety of dates between April and October 1952, a year before that involving the scouts.

Montagu protested his innocence. 'It was', he wrote many years later, 'entirely wrong that such charges should have been levelled against anyone at all. The allegations were that grown adult men had indulged in homosexual relations with each other. In no circumstances could I bring myself to agree that this constituted an offence.'[108] The language used in the trial, however, showed what a mountain he had to climb if he were to be acquitted: there was, he recalled, a 'constant repetition of "conspiracy", "gross indecency" and "buggery"'.[109] Montagu was referred to as 'that wretched man', Khaki Roberts informing him that 'you are subjected to temptations and desires to which the normal man is not subjected.'[110] The judge, Mr Justice [Sir Benjamin] Ormerod, seems to have been particularly shocked at the class gulf between Montagu, Wildeblood and Pitt-Rivers, and the lower-class men with whom they were accused of consorting. One letter between Montagu and a man named Reynolds received particular attention. Montagu had begun it 'Dear Johnny' and signed it 'Edward', but came to the conclusion as the trial wore on that the judge would have 'preferred me to begin "Dear Reynolds" and sign it "Montagu of Beaulieu". I was not so pompous,' he said.[111] As Harry Hylton-Foster, QC, a future speaker of the House of Commons, defending Pitt-Rivers, put it to the court: 'Foreigners think we are a nation of snobs. I daresay we are, but you must have got to some pretty basic snobbery in this case. It is now said that because on a sunshiney holiday with chaps in bathing clothes in a beach hut, because they were calling one another by their Christian names, therefore that is the badge of some indecent association. Did ever snobbery put forward a more greasy exterior than that by the prosecution in this case?'[112] And as William Fearnley-Whittingstall, QC, acting for Montagu, said: '[N]ot everyone keeps himself aloof because he is wealthy or a peer.'[113]

At 4.30 p.m. on 24 March 1954, Montagu, Wildeblood and Pitt-Rivers stood in the place, in Winchester Great Hall, where Sir Walter Raleigh had been tried for treason in 1603. They were pronounced guilty on almost every charge. Sentencing the three, the judge described how he was dealing with them '. . . in the most lenient manner possible, but it is quite impossible for these offences to be passed over.'[114] Wildeblood and Pitt-Rivers received eighteen-month jail terms; Montagu was sentenced to a year in prison.

The Sexual Offences Act 1967 legalised sex between men over the age of twenty-one. It owed its inception to recommendations made by the Wolfenden Report a decade earlier, who called on Peter Wildeblood as a witness. As for Montagu, he was released from prison in November 1954, after eight months. He married Belinda Crossley in 1958, with whom he had two children, the eldest of whom, Ralph Douglas-Scott-Montagu, 4th Baron Montagu of Beaulieu, now runs the Beaulieu estate as a popular tourist attraction. David Maxwell Fyfe did not mention the case at all in his 1964 memoirs, nor once did he use the word 'homosexual'.

* * *

All the evidence suggests that the aristocracy have not traditionally viewed themselves as bound by 'middle-class' notions of morality – that they have tended to believe that provided sexual indiscretions do not become a matter of public knowledge, they are perfectly acceptable. Whether or not that means peers as a whole have been – or are – more promiscuous than other groups in society, is rather more difficult to ascertain. Not surprisingly, official statistics in this area simply don't exist. The nearest thing we have to impartial evidence about relationships is divorce numbers, and, of course, divorce can be sought for any one of a number of reasons, even if traditionally and legally, infidelity was the one most often offered. To seek a divorce also suggests that one party to the marriage does not believe that sexual incontinence is acceptable, and, as we've seen, while aristocratic double-standards not infrequently operated here, with one unfaithful partner furious at the unfaithfulness of the other, there is also evidence of marriages surviving and even thriving amid a flood of extra-marital affairs. Infidelity and divorce, in other words, do not automatically go hand in hand. For every Ian and Margaret Argyll and their messy public separation, there was a Walter and Mollie Buccleuch who remained married for fifty-two years until his death in 1973, even though Mollie had liaisons with a succession of men. Indeed, her escapades were such that they won her the nickname 'Midnight Moll' – a nickname that followed her into her dotage when the diplomat Sir Charles Johnston overheard a wife saying to her husband at a dance at Windsor Castle for the Queen Mother's eightieth birthday in 1980: 'Now you're *not* to dance with Midnight Moll – otherwise we shall never get away.'[115]

There's an added complication with historical divorce figures. Up until 1969 divorce was a difficult and expensive process, requiring among other things in the era when 'adultery' had to be proved, the employment of a professional co-respondent who could be witnessed meeting the would-be divorcé in a hotel room for assumed improper purposes. For the most part responsibility for the assignation was taken by the husband, whether or not he was the guilty party, but there were exceptions. Mark Pepys, 6th Earl of Cottenham's decree *nisi*, granted in January 1939, contained two unusual features. First, it named the actual person with whom one partner in the marriage had committed adultery. And the person named was the lover, not of the earl himself (as tradition generally demanded, whatever the reality of the situation) but of his wife Venetia, who, according to the official document, had committed adultery with Christopher Courtenay, 17th Earl of Devon, 'at an hotel in Brighton in August 1938'.[116] They went on to marry the following summer. According to Venetia and Christopher Devon's grandson Charlie Devon: 'Typically if a lady wanted to divorce her husband he would do the decent thing and go and get photographed in a hotel in Brighton, but Venetia insisted that "I am the one who is leaving you," and that effectively cast them out of society.'

Such a tortuous and costly process was not one the average citizen would embark upon without first giving the ramifications of it very careful consideration. To that extent, therefore, the relatively high proportion of legal separations that aristocratic divorces do

undoubtedly represent for much of the twentieth century is ultimately a reflection of the ability of the better-off in society to meet
the expense of achieving them. Johnny Kimberley, who married
six women and was divorced five times between 1945 and 1982,
reflected late in his life that, 'paying off five countesses didn't come
cheap. Nor did years of intensive womanising.'[117] His family, incidentally, had form here: his grandfather's last words – to the nurse
who was tending to him – were, apparently, 'take off your clothes'.[118]

Insofar as divorce figures and infidelity *are* connected, it's only
with the easier access to divorce that the 1969 legislation allowed
(not least through the establishment of the principle of 'no fault'
divorce) that tentative comparisons can really be made. In that
year twelve peers were divorced, representing just over 1 per cent
of their total number. In the same year in England and Wales as
a whole, there were 51,310 divorces in total, representing 0.2 per
cent of the total population.[119] Five years later, in 1974, by which
time the number of divorces had had risen to 113,500 (0.45 per
cent of the population), there were eleven divorces of hereditary
peers, roughly 1.25 per cent of the peerage as a whole.

If such figures suggest a disproportionate level of 'badly behaved'
aristocrats in British society, there is certainly plenty of anecdotal
evidence to support the contention. Master Beaufort's successor, David
Beaufort, was so promiscuous in the course of his forty-five-year
marriage to his first wife Caroline, that his friend Woodrow Wyatt
referred to him in 1992 as 'the great woman slayer'.[120] Caroline
faced down his affairs stoically, later telling her son: 'You either
marry a man or a mouse.'[121] James Stuart, 1st Viscount Stuart of
Findhorn, one of Mollie Buccleuch's long-time beaux, who according to his daughter the Hon. Davina Ritchie's assessment was
'drop-down-dead handsome', was a life-long philanderer. 'He had
a take-it-or-leave-it attitude and they couldn't resist it. All he had
to do was raise an eyebrow or give them a half smile and they were
captivated.'[122] His wife Lady Rachel Cavendish was later described
by a contemporary as, '[T]he most marvellously loyal and tolerant
kind of wife that any philanderer could have hoped to have'.[123]

Rachel's brother Eddy Devonshire, a modest man who wore paper collars and did not possess an overcoat, married Lady Mary 'Moucher' Gascoyne-Cecil – who was wont to keep some of the Devonshire family jewels in an old Elastoplast tin kept together with a rubber band – in 1917 and proved serially unfaithful to her.[124] For several years from 1938 onwards, he was said to have been having a 'hot affair'[125] with Maureen Hamilton-Temple-Blackwood, Marchioness of Dufferin and Ava (whose husband Basil was in love with the journalist Virginia Cowles), and, according to Chips Channon, had by June 1943 become the American socialite Laura Corrigan's 'latest ducal conquest'.[126]

In more recent times, Anthony Ashley-Cooper, 10th Earl of Shaftesbury, pursued affairs with various women in the course of his three marriages, his penchant being for those who were foreign-born, since English girls, he is said to have declared in the *Eton Chronicle*,[127] were nothing more than 'round-shouldered, unsophisticated garglers of pink champagne'.[128] In 2004 he travelled to Nice to meet up with his estranged third wife, and then vanished without trace. It was not until the following year that it emerged that he had been strangled by his wife's brother, after he had revealed that he was seeking a divorce in order to marry his latest girlfriend.[129] His body was discovered in a valley near Cannes.

Aristocratic bed-hopping might have been an 'accepted' feature of upper-class social culture, it might have been practised on a wide scale and tolerated by some of the spouses who had been wronged, but it still had the capacity to make a lot of people very unhappy. And it also had the capacity to bring out the very worst in some. Ian Argyll is a case in point. So, in terms of sheer pettiness, is Bobo Roxburghe whose divorce from Lady Mary Crewe-Milnes, daughter of the ambassador to France Robert Crewe-Milnes, 1st Marquess of Crewe, and Lady Peggy Primrose, is a textbook case of small-minded cruelty. Bobo and Mary had married in 1935 but by the late 1940s, with no children,[130] they were effectively living separate lives, and Bobo had taken up with another woman, Elisabeth Church, whose own marriage was in trouble. 'Apart from anything else he greatly admired her riding skill,' Bobo's cousin Major Sir Arthur Collins remembered, rather loyally.[131] Mary initially seemed willing to consent to a divorce, but then changed her mind. In January 1953, while the couple sat at one of their silent breakfasts at Floors Castle, a member of staff presented a silver salver to Mary on which lay a letter from Bobo's lawyers instructing her to leave the castle immediately – a husband's right under Scottish law. When she refused, Bobo tried to force her out, dismissing the staff, and then successively removing the telephones, the electric lights, and cutting off the gas while he went to live elsewhere. He tried to deprive her of water too; when she filled a bath for use as a reservoir, Bobo's agent, a man described by the historian Hugh Trevor-Roper as one 'of feudal obedience and heart of stone', pulled out the plug.[132] It was only when Mary's trustee and Borders neighbour Alec Home intervened, pointing out that without water, Floors wasn't insured, that Bobo reluctantly called a halt.[133]

Local society friends took sides in the first siege in the area since James II was killed at nearby Roxburgh Castle by an exploding cannon in 1460. Walter Buccleuch and his wife Mollie were split: Mollie sympathised with Mary, and Walter with Bobo. George 'Dawyck' Haig, 2nd Earl Haig, and his sister Lady Xandra Howard-Johnston, who lived nearby, sneaked food into Floors for Mary, while John Ellesmere from Mertoun House, six miles away, smuggled in a small paraffin stove to stave off the winter cold in what was, after all, a very big house in Scotland. Bobo's response was to get his lawyers to inform John Ellesmere that if the stove caused a fire at Floors, he would be liable. The McEwen family from nearby Marchmont House, meanwhile, fed the only maid that Mary had kept with her. Finally, reason prevailed, and then, as Arthur Collins put it, '. . . after the then necessary circus performance, Bobo and Elisabeth stayed the night together at a Scarborough hotel and a Scottish divorce followed.'[134]

When it was all over, Mary was, as Hugh Trevor-Roper – who married Xandra Howard-Johnston in 1954[135] – described,

'. . . refreshed in spirit, as in pocket, by the victory, while the otherwise unemployed aristocracy of the Borders [were] busily arranging a new and . . . less turbulent marriage for her.'[136] The Roxburghes' divorce was granted on 15 December that year. Three weeks later, Bobo and Elisabeth married. Bobo set Mary up in a flat in Hyde Park Gardens with a substantial allowance; later, she moved to West Horsley Place, the house in Surrey that she inherited from her mother Peggy Crewe after her death in 1967. Mary died in 2014, aged ninety-nine, never having remarried but beloved by her friends. Bobo's grandson Ted Innes Ker says of his grandfather that: '[H]is reputation was one of at times a rude, unemotional man determined to have an heir at all costs, and at the expense of his first marriage. According to several accounts, he treated Mary poorly, and then found a male-producer in my grandmother.'[137]

* * *

Whether or not the sexual etiquette of the peerage in the 2020s is as relaxed as it was for their forebears is impossible to say. The bare statistics reveal that of today's 793 hereditary peers, born between 1924 and 2004, 193 have been divorced at least once, and between them have had 948 wives (an average of an uncomfortable 1.19 each). What is beyond question is that there has been a significant shift in attitudes, even in that traditionally hidebound, vaguely defined entity known as the establishment. In George V's time, as we have seen, divorced peers were not admitted at Court. Early in the Second World War, when a group of Coldstream Guards officers were invited to attend a shoot with George VI, Christopher Devon was excluded, along with a couple of his colleagues, because of their personal circumstances. The ban was only lifted when the king expressed the view that it seemed odd that they '. . . were good enough to shoot His Majesty's enemies, but not his pheasants'.[138]

When Elizabeth II was crowned in 1953, Bernard Norfolk as Earl Marshal is said to have told an unnamed divorced peer that divorced peers would be welcome at the ceremony, since 'this is the Coronation, not Ascot.'[139] The following June, pressure was being brought to bear on the duke, who was also the queen's representative at Ascot, to end the rigid rules that governed who was and who was not permitted to enter the exclusive, invitation-only Royal Enclosure. The restrictions were relaxed for the 1955 season to permit admission to the divorced, though Bernard Nor-folk made it clear that 'the queen is in no way relaxing the Court rules concerning divorce.'[140] No one seems to be quite sure when those Court rules were finally changed.[141] Robin Janvrin, Baron Janvrin, who joined the Royal Household in 1987 and rose to become Elizabeth II's private secretary, cannot remember there being any issue during his tenure about divorce in the context of invitations to royal events. Nor does he recall there being a docu-ment marked 'Court rules' governing such an issue, or any other, and indeed was told that: 'There is no such thing as protocol, there is only common sense.'

Society as a whole has become less judgemental about – and also less interested in – what the upper classes get up to than they once were, unless, of course, a member of the royal family is involved. There was no defined moment when this happened, but perhaps a more relaxed attitude started to take root as the minority per-missive views of the 1960s became more mainstream in the early 1970s. By the 1980s and 1990s, not only was the bulk of the popu-lation much less judgemental about the state of other people's marriages than it had formerly been, but its focus had turned to other types of celebrity.

In this respect, the 1973 sex scandal surrounding Conservative MP Antony 'Tony' Lambton, Viscount Lambton (who had disclaimed his promotion as 6th Earl of Durham in 1970), is instructive. Tony clearly had a certain magnetic attraction. When Lady Annabel Vane-Tempest-Stewart, now Goldsmith, first met him at Wynyard Hall in County Durham in the late 1940s, she was immediately struck by the 'tall, slim, strikingly Byronic' peer-not-quite-to-be; '... he wore a bottle-green velvet coat, a decades-early Sergeant Pepper look ...

he was a figure of glamour and difference.'[142] The thirteen-year-old Annabel and her sister Jane would vie for his attention: '[A] flattering comment from him would be mulled over for days,' she remembered, well into her seventies; 'even now I recall him telling me that I had beautiful hands, and the intensity I read into this could occupy me for hours.'[143] Years later, Tony admitted to Annabel that '[H]e would watch Jane and me and wonder which of us he would pursue when we had reached a suitable age' – and indeed he and Jane did ultimately have an affair.[144] For women of a certain generation, Annabel thought, Tony in his heyday was 'the arch-lover, the Casanova of his time'; he could charm anyone.[145] And though he had a family, no one could accuse him of being a family man. When Annabel was young and he was a frequent visitor to Wynyard, she remembers him bringing his family – his wife Belinda 'Bindy' Blew-Jones, with whom by 1961 he had six children – with him 'only once'.[146]

The 1973 sex scandal arose when the *News of the World*, who had been offered compromising photographs of Tony by the boyfriend of a prostitute, Norma Levy, ran a series of stories about his liaisons with call girls. Few details were omitted. Readers learned of the games he and Norma had played, and of the drugs that he took, some of which were found by police in his house in St John's Wood. He was unrepentant. Drugs, so far as he was concerned, were something of '. . . a fetish with me. It was my fetish to talk about drugs when I go to bed.'[147] As for his liaison with call girls: in his view they were 'part of the life of all manly men', as he later told the writer Chapman Pincher: 'I can't think what all the fuss is about . . . surely all men patronise whores.'[148]

Such a story would have made the headlines in any earlier decade of the twentieth century. The striking feature about the Lambton affair, though, as it unfolded day after day in 1973, was that journalists and commentators showed far less interest in the fact that Tony Lambton was Viscount Lambton who might have become 6th Earl of Durham than in the fact that he was Antony Lambton, MP, parliamentary under-secretary for defence. The *Daily Mirror* nailed its colours to the mast in a leader on 24 May. 'If a private citizen becomes involved with a call girl and one or two of her friends – as Lord Lambton did – that is not an offence in the eyes of the law,' it argued. 'Nor is it a matter for public concern. The sexual behaviour of private citizens is their affair.' However, Lord Lambton 'was not a private citizen'; he was a government minister, in '. . . a department where security is crucial. By his stupidity, he put himself in a position where he MIGHT [*sic*] have been the victim of a blackmail attempt.'[149] After the scandal, Tony Lambton moved to Cetinale, his seventeenth-century villa near Siena with his long-term girlfriend Claire Ward. He and Bindy, who remained at home in England, never divorced, Tony unable to afford to do so.

By the turn of the twenty-first century, upper-class shenanigans scarcely raised any disapproving eyebrows. The late Alexander Thynn, 7th Marquess of Bath, probably now best known for the sometimes erotic and always unusual murals that he painted on the walls at Longleat – the house his father had saved post-war – won more curiosity than notoriety for the collection of mistresses or, as he termed them, 'wifelets' he maintained.[150] He also had an actual wife, Anna, whom he had married in 1969, and two legitimate children. In 2002, he described himself as a '. . . polygynist . . . I like to think I have got very good relationships going with several lovely ladies.' Asked whether his wifelets got jealous of one another, he said, '[T]here has been that problem . . . But hopefully, if the relationship is of value to them, they won't want to throw one another out of the window.'[151] Such media coverage as he received focused as much on his perceived eccentricity as his standards of personal morality. Among the obituaries that ran after he died in 2020, at the beginning of the Covid-19 pandemic, was one from the BBC that described him as the '. . . eccentric owner of Longleat famous for his collection of erotic murals and his numerous affairs'; the *Telegraph*, meanwhile, celebrated the life of '. . . Britain's most flamboyant and eccentric aristocrat', while the *Guardian* talked of the '. . . eccentric aristocrat and chatelain of the Longleat safari park who was a favourite of newspaper gossip columns'. *The Times* referred to him as the 'colourful' aristocrat known as the 'loins of Longleat'.[152]

One of the more recent aristocratic separations is that involving the Rutlands, which occurred in 2012. David Manners, Marquess of Granby, later 11th Duke of Rutland, met Welsh farmer's daughter Emma Watkins at a dinner party in 1990. He gave her his card, which read: 'Marquis of Granby, Registered Firearms Dealer, David Granby'. She wasn't sure how to interpret this; perhaps he owned a pub. They were married in 1992 and had five children. Emma has described how in August 1999, weeks after the birth of their son Charles, she discovered that her husband was having an affair. She confronted him, he moved out, and they went to counselling, vowing to give it another go. In 2009, when Emma organised a party for her husband's fiftieth birthday at Belvoir Castle, she suspected that he was again having an affair. Three years later, the Rutlands separated, moving into different parts of the castle. They remained married, but they are legally separated and live their own lives. 'David and I are best friends,' she says. 'We share five children – there's nothing that we don't discuss and don't know about what's happening in each other's lives.'

Compare that relatively low-key separation with the headline that greeted readers of *The Times* half a century or so earlier on 11 April 1963 – 'Premier Earl of England Divorced' – and the level of detail about John and Nadine Chetwynd-Talbot, 21st Earl and Countess of Shrewsbury and Waterford, that contemporary readers would have been able to glean from that and other newspapers.[153] They would have learned that John Shrewsbury had married the opera singer Nadine Crofton in 1936, that they had six children, but that he had sought a divorce in 1959, on the grounds that his wife was having an affair with 27-year-old Anthony 'Tonykins' Lowther, his former secretary and tutor to the Shrewsburys' daughters. Since John Shrewsbury had had an on–off relationship with the former actress Doris 'Nina' Mortlock since 1941, his own reputation wasn't exactly spotless. After eighteen days in court, during which it was revealed that a member of staff had seen Nadine and Lowther kissing 'in a rather passionate way' on the Blue Landing at Ingestre Hall, the Shrewsburys' home in Staffordshire, and that the butler, Dan De Plaats, entering Lowther's room one Sunday morning, had spotted a pair of women's shoes peeking, *Wizard of Oz*-style, from behind a door, the judge threw out John Shrewsbury's petition, agreeing that, yes, Nadine had committed adultery, but that, after all, John had committed adultery with Nina Mortlock.[154] The case cost a small fortune; his son Charles Shrewsbury explains that his father's trustees sold the ground rents of Pimlico to pay his legal bill.

As 1960 dawned the contents of Ingestre proved fair game too: paintings plus fine English and foreign silver were sold initially, and then in November there was a two-day contents sale at the house followed a little later by the disposal of the estate itself. Nadine was devastated. 'Just because I live in a stately home, don't think my feelings about home are different from those of other women,' she said. 'They are not. Ingestre Hall is my home. I have lived here since I was married in 1936 and I love it with all my heart.'[155] John Shrewsbury denied that the sale of Ingestre had anything to do with the divorce, telling the local newspaper that the problem was that the house had become uneconomical; he planned to keep the estate, he said, 'including the farms, and I am going to continue to farm two of the farms myself.'[156]

The war of the Shrewsburys was not yet over. Although after the first court case John had declared that 'I am definitely not going back to my wife, but I'm afraid she will never divorce me'; in June 1962, Nadine did just that.[157] She obtained her decree *nisi* the following April, on the grounds of his – fresh, since the last case – adultery with Nina Mortlock. The judge, Mr Justice [Sir Roger] Ormrod, declared that for the couple's children to carry on living in the knowledge that their father was conducting an affair with Nina, '. . . would be an embarrassment to [them] and possibly an obstacle to the future development of their relations with their father'.[158]

It was a painful time for everyone, remembers Charles Shrewsbury, who was twelve at the time. 'It was a grossly unpleasant divorce – one of the biggest of the century – with both sides per-juring themselves.' His father took him to one side and told him that while he didn't want custody of Charles' four sisters, he did want Charles himself. Would he like to come and live with him? 'I said yes,' he remembers, 'and there was a court case about that too. Thereafter I was looked after by the Official Solicitor, and for about two years I wasn't allowed to see either parent.' In October 1963, John Shrewsbury and Nina Mortlock were married quietly at Cheadle register office. They later moved to Switzerland. A month after their wedding, Nadine Shrewsbury placed a note in the Court Circular requesting that she should in future be known as Nadine, Countess of Shrewsbury and Waterford.

9

The Loved One

In Search of the Male Heir

Most families think in decades. The aristocracy think in generations. Inheritance, succession, the preservation of the family name, the passing of titles and assets from one to another – these necessarily concern the nobility.

Over the centuries, Europe's aristocracy have tried various approaches to the question of inheritance, but the one that has come to dominate in Britain is male-line primogeniture. At a practical level it makes some sense. By ensuring that one (male) heir inherits everything, estates are kept together and so – in theory, at least – remain going concerns. In France, by contrast, where the Napoleonic Code holds sway and estates are divided equally between heirs, it can be very difficult to preserve the integrity of ancestral homes: '[Y]ou get these wonderful, huge houses,' Debo Devonshire once wrote, 'but they are practically empty, as every child has had a go at the furniture and pictures.'[1]

Practical, though, is not the same as equitable – or, on occasion, even sensible.

* * *

Although some aristocratic families have traditionally allowed succession through the female line, they have always been in a minority. Of the 793 hereditary peers today, only about ninety could, in theory, be female, either because the title they hold is so old that it predates male primogeniture or because it's a Scottish title and so not bound by Salic law – the originally Frankish law that, as adopted in England, generally precluded women from aristocratic succession. It's not surprising therefore that the birth of a son has long tended to be welcomed rather more effusively than the arrival of a daughter. The son is the heir. The daughter just needs to make a good marriage.

Such has traditionally been the pressure to produce a male heir that the women of many families have been expected to produce offspring until they get the right result. Between 1962 and 1984, for example, Robin Neville, later 10th Baron Braybrooke, fathered daughter after daughter in the hope of ultimately coming up with a male heir. When his great-great-uncle, Henry Neville, 7th Baron Braybrooke, died in 1941, he entailed his estate at Audley End in Essex for two generations so that if his son Richard, an officer in the Grenadier Guards, died in the Second World War – which he did, in 1943 – and his successor Henry's son Robin did not have a son, the estate would revert to the descendants of his own daughter Catherine. Ultimately, after eight daughters by two wives, Robin Braybrooke had to concede defeat: his obituary in *The Times* shortly after he died in 2017 described him as an '. . . aristocrat who loved women and trains and doted on the eight daughters unable to inherit his land'.[2] According to the second of these, Caroline 'Cazzy' Stanley, Countess of Derby, '[B]y the end of his life he was at peace with what had happened. However much or little you have it's still just things, and when you die they don't go with you, unless you're Egyptian.' On Robin Braybrooke's death, the estate passed to his second cousin Louise Newman, and the title went to his fourth cousin once removed, Richard Neville.

As for the – often many – daughters of aristocratic families, they were generally dealt a pretty raw deal and all too often treated as something of a disappointment. 'Poor Mildred Chelsea,' wrote the American philanthropist Mary Harcourt to her stepmother-in-law Elizabeth Harcourt in 1901, following the birth of a daughter, Victoria, to Mildred Cadogan, Viscountess Chelsea, and her husband

Henry Cadogan, Viscount Chelsea: 'isn't it cruel luck. 5 Girls!!! What an infliction [*sic*] she will now say "not only have I got 5 girls (instead of 4) but I have got to find 5 fools to marry them." '³ Mildred's luck appeared to change a couple of years later when a son, Edward, was finally welcomed into the world. But it soon swung back again when he died aged seven in 1910, two years after his father's death from cancer at the early age of forty, and the title passed to Henry's younger brother Gerald.

When Harry Percy, later 11th Duke of Northumberland, was born half a century later in July 1953, Chips Channon declared 'what a relief' it was that 'he' was 'not another girl', since Hughie and Elizabeth Northumberland had had three girls already.⁴ The following March, Channon sat in the Smoking Room of the House of Commons with Tony Lambton who told him that his wife Bindy was having another baby. '"Probably a girl again," he said.'⁵ And so it transpired: Tony and Bindy's fourth daughter Anne was born in July 1954. The Lambtons would wait another seven years, and another daughter would be born, before their son Ned arrived in October 1961.

In some aristocratic families, similar attitudes were being expressed as late as the 1980s and 1990s. 'When my sister-in-law was born in the 1980s,' says the daughter-in-law of one peer who asked not to be named, 'her grandfather instructed the estate to light a series of pyres and beacons to herald the arrival of the next heir. But then my mother-in-law trotted out a girl, and they just took them all down. From day dot, she has been unimportant.' In 1997, following the birth of her third daughter Lady Eliza Manners, Emma Manners, then Marchioness of Granby, suffered a similar indignity when a local dowager approached her at a hunt ball, not to congratulate but to commiserate: 'Sorry to hear the news ... that the new baby is another girl!' Emma excused herself, '... managing to hold it together until I found a bed I could lie down on, and then I cried and cried.'⁶ Two years later, when the Granbys' – who had, in the intervening years, been advanced to the Rutlands – son and heir Charles was born, seven cannons were fired from Belvoir Castle, and the family flag was run up the pole.

Lady Liza Campbell recognises such sentiments only too well. The second daughter of Hugh and Cath Campbell, 6th Earl and Countess Cawdor, she was born in 1959, the last child of an Earl Cawdor to be born at Cawdor Castle in Nairnshire, the family seat since 1510. As a daughter, she was never in line to inherit the title or the estate. Even if the rules had been changed so that the first-born child inherited, it would have gone to her older sister Emma, who, she says, would have been perfectly capable of rising to the challenge. 'The heir gets all the spoken and unspoken messages as the chosen one, but who knows what they are because none of them will be aimed at the daughters.'

Somehow being a younger sister cast her even further into outer darkness. Emma had been acceptable because when Hugh Cawdor was born in 1932, he too had an older sister, Carey. One girl, and then a boy – that was fine. But two girls? When Liza was born, and bucked the trend, her arrival was greeted 'with undisguised consternation', as she recalled in her 2006 memoir.[7] Her shy, awkward grandfather Jack Campbell, 5th Earl Cawdor, was up a ladder in the garden when he heard the news. 'While digesting the bulletin he lost his balance and fell into a flowerbed, breaking an ankle.'[8] From his hospital bed, he issued his only missive on the topic: that the baby should be called Elizabeth or Carolyn. After this, Cath, then Viscountess Emlyn, set about trying to work out how to conceive a boy, buying self-help books and following 'salt-free, low-potassium diets, followed by high-potassium, salt-filled diets'.[9] In 1962, pregnant again, she gave birth to Colin, the longed-for heir, in Carmarthen Hospital. She went on to have two more children, Fred in 1965 and Laura in 1966.

When Jack Cawdor died in 1970, Hugh, Cath and the five Campbell children moved from the family's estate in Wales to Cawdor. Suddenly, Hugh was boss, 6th Earl Cawdor, 25th Thane of Cawdor. Much later, Liza wondered what impact this experience of inheriting must have had on him: '[T]his gain that came with the death of a loved parent and the greatest sense of loss any of us can experience. What must it be like to have one's life predestined in this way?'[10] It soon became clear that Hugh's inheritance overwhelmed him. To cope with it he became an autocrat, making it clear to his daughters that the path of aristocratic succession would never be theirs, that they must be 'subordinate to the institute of primogeniture'.[11] He groomed them to accept that the men were special and that the women should expect nothing. When Hugh and Colin flew anywhere, they would – to be on the safe side – fly separately. No such caution was deemed necessary with the girls.

Liza understood that in order to keep Cawdor together one person had to inherit it, and so it was going to be unfair either way, but she thought age discrimination preferable to sexism. As it was, had Colin and Fred not made an appearance, on Hugh's death everything would have passed to the next-nearest male, however far-flung, whether or not he had any interest in Cawdor at all. 'It seemed to me completely absurd that male blood differed from female,' Liza wrote in her memoirs.[12] 'I was told it was because the title could not be passed down the female line – no medals for guessing who had made all these rules up. All privileges were reserved for men because that was just how it was.'[13]

Once, she tried to talk to her father about it. 'Big mistake. As sole beneficiary of an antiquated hierarchy, Pa was the least likely person to enter into a reasoned debate. "What do you think would happen if we three girls took you to the Equal Opportunities Commission?" I said. "What's it like being a half-wit?" he retorted.'[14] His vision for his daughters was to marry well; before the wearing of car seat belts became mandatory he told Liza to strap up saying, 'Your face is your fortune, so you'd better not smash it up.'[15]

In time, she realised that her mother was enmeshed in this patriarchal structure too. On one occasion, she recalled, when she was about twelve, she and Cath were sitting in the car waiting for the rain to stop when Liza asked Cath what she had been like as a baby. 'She laughed about how oddly I had crawled – straight legs, bum in the air – and then, as an afterthought, added that she had despaired at having given birth to a second girl. She laughed at the memory, but the hairs on the back of my neck stood up. My mother was an intelligent woman brought up in a family less tied to its past, but she saw no contradiction in championing the opposite sex over her own to fit the customs of her husband's family.' Liza didn't know what to do with this information. 'Until that moment I had had no proper inkling that girls were a disappointment. It was as if Emma's birth had been the equivalent of a toothless couple entering a draw hoping for the first prize of false teeth but winning only dental floss. On entering it again, they had won a toothbrush.'[16]

Looking back now, says Liza, as we sit opposite one another in a central London bookshop, she realises she hadn't appreciated how deeply rooted her mother's belief was that she *must* have a son. 'I remember being really taken aback. My mum didn't even see the oddness of what it was. The repression is complete when you get the repressed to enforce it. The depth of the message gets inside the women, in their bones.' It was so internalised that it didn't occur to Cath that she was expressing sexism against her own sex. 'I was a child coming into thoughtfulness in the 1970s, the era of bra burning and equal pay, and we seemed to be in this bubble of utter separateness. It was normal that these women, like my mother, were commiserating about the fact that they haven't had a son, and they go on and on and on having daughters.'

Not only have aristocratic girls been less enthusiastically received into the world than boys, they have often been treated less than preferentially as they grow up. Dr Joanna Martin, the eldest child of Christopher and Oona Methuen-Campbell, who was born in 1951, describes how 'I was put down for Eton before I was born' but '. . . when my parents discovered that I was a girl, they lost interest in my education.' Since no plans were put in place, she had to make do with a school where there was no waiting list. 'My mother's main criterion was that I should not go to a school where I would be forced to play hockey,' she recalls. Also rejected were 'more academic schools', such as Cheltenham Ladies' College, '[B]ecause they were full of the daughters of professional families. I ended up at Cobham Hall in Kent, largely because it only opened in 1962, the year before I went.' Her parents' decision was also influenced by the fact that her younger brother James was at prep school nearby: they thought they would be able to get their visits to their children over in one go.

The parental discrimination that saw her sent to Cobham Hall continued while she was there. She recalls complaining to her father, 'because he barely looked at my reports, and spent a long time reading James's', and being informed that '. . . my education didn't really matter, because I would only leave school and get married, while James would have to earn a living'. 'I saw the logical flaw in that immediately,' she says, 'and pointed out that James would eventually inherit one estate, if not two.' She went on to became the first female member of the Methuen family to go to university.

It wasn't just her parents who made her feel like a second-class citizen. Her 'deeply unpleasant' grandfather, the Hon. Laurence Methuen, favoured her brother – 'he liked to think that James might become Lord Methuen one day' – while largely ignoring her and her two sisters. On the rare occasions that the family saw him, she says, '[H]e would give James an expensive present, while I would be fobbed off with something that he had made his second wife get for me.' 'On one occasion, when I was about eight,' she goes on, 'I was given a cheap puzzle book – the sort that I could buy with my pocket money – in which half the puzzles had already been done (wrongly) by my father's half-sister, Caroline, who was a year younger than me!'

Joanna's family are titled on both sides – and each practises the ancient art of primogeniture. Her father Christopher was the grandson of the Boer War commander Field Marshal Paul Methuen, 3rd Baron Methuen, whose family have lived at Corsham Court in Wiltshire since 1745. His mother Olive was the daughter of Archibald Campbell, 4th Baron Blythswood, on whose estate Penrice on the Gower Peninsula in South Wales

Joanna and her siblings spent much of their childhood.[17] But the Methuen-Campbell children learned more about the peerage from their maternal grandmother Lady Sheelah Treherne, older sister of the communist Noreen Branson, whom we met earlier, and the twin sister of Denis Browne, 10th Marquess of Sligo. 'Uncle Denis used to sit in the House of Lords quite regularly, and my grandmother had tea with him there from time to time,' says Joanna. Meanwhile, Corsham Court and the Methuen title hardly figured, but were there in the background. 'We knew that James might eventually inherit Corsham,' says Joanna, 'but it was a very distant prospect when we were young.'

In the event, James did inherit – the Methuen estate in 1994, and then the Methuen title in 2014. But as it turned out, he did not inherit Penrice, which went instead to Christopher Methuen-Campbell's son by his second marriage, Thomas. To make that happen, Christopher had to break the entail – which was to his eldest son James. 'Nobody seems to have thought that my sisters and I had any right to be consulted, nor did they consider the impact that it might eventually have on us and our children,' Joanna reflects. James, nevertheless, did well. With Corsham Court, which he inherited from his first cousin once removed John Methuen, 6th Baron Methuen, came '. . . an exceptional art collection, and a large chunk of the town of Corsham, with property in the surrounding parishes. It must all be worth hundreds of millions now.' His three sisters had to make do with £5,000 each, reduced from £10,000, when their father died in 1998. Joanna points out that had the estate been handed on according to seniority rather than gender, eleven women (herself included) would have been in line to inherit ahead of James.

* * *

Those expecting and waiting to inherit have a clear destiny and clear expectations laid out for them. Alexander 'Mungo' Murray, 9th Earl of Mansfield, who was born in 1956, knew from an early age that, as the eldest son, he was going to inherit the Mansfields' Scottish estates, and that was that. His father William Murray, 8th Earl of Mansfield, was unequivocal about what he expected from his son and heir: he would dedicate his life to running Scone Palace – the crowning place of Scottish kings, a sandstone pile at the top of a hill above the Tay, near Perth – and its estate. That was the lighted pathway, no arguments. He was, says Mungo Mansfield, a man of great determination and the best of intentions, '[A]lthough Dante Alighieri would point out that the road to hell is paved with good intentions. He was determined to do his best by our family, and that governed his attitude to me. He had a much clearer idea of my path than I did myself.' And when his son didn't meet the required standard, he was subjected to ferocious, wounding tongue-lashings.

William Mansfield's strictness was in part a reaction to his own father's rather more lackadaisical attitude to succession. Mungo Murray, 7th Earl of Mansfield, was a giant of Perthshire, for eleven years its lord-lieutenant, and president, chairman or committee member of practically every local organisation going. 'My grandfather assumed that my father would pick it up as he went along, and because he was interested in farming, that gave my grandfather a feeling that he didn't have to push and shove very much,' says his namesake who, by contrast, did a stint working for Air France, then, following what he characterises as an early midlife crisis in his twenties, moved to Sotheby's and afterwards Christie's as a valuer. These auction houses, however prestigious, were not on the list of William Mansfield-approved establishments. 'He regarded a lot of people in the auction world with extreme suspicion, as an obstacle to life proceeding in an orderly fashion towards a pre-decided end.' Ultimately, Mungo accepted the destiny his father had in mind for him, and on his father's death he inherited the Mansfield title in 2015. 'It seemed to be the most natural thing that my life was laid out for me. I realised that for a large number of my friends that wasn't so, but my attitude was: "Well, they are them, and I am me, and things for me are different."'

His son William Murray, Viscount Stormont, has also been on the lighted pathway since he was a teenager, when Mungo started to take him around the estate's farms and introduce him to the families who had lived there for, in some cases, hundreds of years. 'When you meet Mr X and the cows, it begins to imbue you with this sense of responsibility,' William says. He is glad that his parents took the approach they did. 'You don't want to crush the innocence of the child, but it is important to introduce children to their future as early as possible, so that they're not afraid of it.' 'When I got older,' he goes on, 'the messaging was there that at some point it would be expected that I would take over. It was encouraged, but it wasn't prescriptive.' He hasn't felt conscripted into it. 'I had a much more open remit than my father had. It was clear where I was going, but how I got there and how I managed it was much more open.'

He inherited Scone on paper in 2023, a few months before his own son and heir Helier, Master of Stormont, was born. When I ask if he feels that his inheritance might be a burden as well as a blessing, he talks of 'the golden handcuffs, the golden cage'. 'I flip and flop from feeling the burden, to seeing opportunities, to feeling the burden again. The duty and responsibility can weigh heavy, but at the same time it is an incredibly privileged position to be in. One should feel very lucky.' Though his parents have allowed him the space to find his own path, he admits that '[E]verything I have done has been guided by my future duty and responsibility, but I don't resent that.' The weight of Scone and all that comes with it isn't a spectre, but '. . . an ever-present feeling of something that always needs to be considered. Whether that means that I have made decisions that I will come to regret, time will tell.'

* * *

While succession conventions dictate that titles and estates generally pass from father to eldest son, life's many uncertainties often make things rather more complex and involved. Of the current batch of hereditary peers, forty were not the direct heirs but were younger sons who inherited either when their older brothers died, or – where the older sibling died young – instead of them. One, Charles Hay, 14th Marquess of Tweeddale, inherited his title from his twin brother in 2005, and upon his death the title will pass to their third brother Lord Alistair Hay, a botanist. Successive twin peers are, not surprisingly, few and far between but include the 3rd and 4th Earls of Durham (younger twin Freddy following the racing fanatic John 'Determined Jack' Lambton in 1928) and the 2nd and 3rd Viscounts Knutsford (Sydney followed by Arthur Knutsford in 1931).

David Kennedy, 9th Marquess of Ailsa, who grew up at Cassillis House in Ayrshire, home of the Kennedys since 1373, is one such peer to inherit from an elder brother. 'My brother Charles knew from the get-go that he was going to inherit, and my mother was always telling him how wonderful he would be,' he says. David therefore set out to forge his own path, attending agricultural college and embarking on life as a farmer before in 1979 returning home to Ayrshire to run the Ailsa estate that his brother, an alcoholic, 'wasn't fit to run' and had little interest in. Their father recognised his eldest son's problems and accordingly adjusted his will so that Charles would inherit only the marquessate and Ailsa Craig – the 240-acre island off the Scottish mainland owned by the Kennedy family since 1548 – which, he optimistically believed, his heir would never presume to dispose of. In fact, Charles, who inherited in 1994, ended up putting Ailsa Craig on the market in 2011. To save it for the family, David bought it. Charles Ailsa died in 2015 at the age of fifty-eight. He had two daughters, but no sons, and so David inherited the family title. 'I didn't wish my brother dead, it's just the way things go. He died and by virtue of the system I inherited the marquessate. The way I live my life hasn't changed. I still farm, I still get up and drive a tractor or a crop sprayer, that's the same. That's life.' There is little 'Lord Ailsa-ing' at home in Ayrshire. His tenants call him 'Lord David', David or just 'LD'. One day he was shooting with another peer who, when he heard one of the beaters calling David by his name, was quick to make the correction – 'It's Lord Ailsa' – much to the beater's bemusement. 'I know them all,' he says of his tenants. 'It's important that they can come to me. I farm alongside them and with them.'

The Hon. Philip Howard's experience has not been dissimilar. The younger son of Charlie Howard, 12th Earl of Carlisle, he was brought up at Naworth Castle in Cumbria, and always knew where he stood in the family pecking order. 'For as long as I could listen, I was told, "Do not even think this will ever be yours, it's going to your brother,"' he says. 'That was the deal.' But the deal fell apart when his brother George, now 13th Earl of Carlisle, made it clear that he didn't want Naworth, and so in 1992, Charlie Carlisle sold the castle to his younger son, who has run it ever since.[18] His father, he says, was an expert on trees and wildfowl, and was a font of advice, but 'you would never ask him to implement anything because it would be disastrous: he would try to do it on the cheap.' When Philip took over Naworth the estate was a shadow of its former self, having shrunk from 10,000 acres in the early 1960s to just 2,500 by the 1980s as Charlie struggled to keep financially afloat, not helped by the Lloyd's insurance crisis and near collapse. Fixtures and fittings were being sold off, too. 'My father would say, I'm going to sell these bookcases, or this Burne-Jones relief, and I'd say, "It's a fixture, you can't."'

Philip's determination to keep Naworth intact has, he admits, caused trouble with his three siblings. 'I think they thought all I was interested in was cash and material objects. What I really loved, and love, is Naworth.' His older brother George, he says, 'was very helpful to me' initially, but their father's funeral on 28 November 1994 – two years after Philip had bought Naworth – was the last time the two men spoke to one another. They are very different characters. Philip describes his brother as 'a proper Whig – both he and my father were born a couple of hundred years later than they should have been. He would consider it horrific that I was interested in money, and that I was an admirer of Margaret Thatcher.'

He doesn't attribute the status of their relationship to the Carlisles being aristocratic, but agrees that this has exacerbated the situation: 'if you have more things and money and assets to fight about . . .'

As for George Carlisle, a former officer in the 9th/12th Royal Lancers, he is unmarried and has no children. In due course the family title will likely pass to Philip, who suspects that his brother would rather outlive him than let this happen.

> Sibling rivalry is as potent a rivalry as any other, even if there isn't something to fight over. He got the title and I got the castle, and I'm quite happy about that. He probably would like to have had all of it – by which I mean the concept of the house, title and land, in a sort of ephemeral way on the basis that that is what Earls of Carlisle would have, as he is one of the most unmaterialistic people I have ever come across . . . I can't talk for him. Do I want to be Earl of Carlisle? No. To be the Earl of Carlisle is not my great aim in life. I'd love to see Carlisle United win the European Cup. There's more chance of that happening than me being Earl of Carlisle.

* * *

It was not uncommon in the twentieth century for those not immediately in line to succeed to take up residence abroad – not infrequently in one of Britain's colonies. In Kenya in the 1930s, for example, younger sons swelled the ranks of the titled and moneyed expatriates who came to be associated with the hedonism of 'Happy Valley' and rose to unwelcome prominence following the much-publicised murder of the notorious womaniser Josslyn Hay, 22nd Earl of Erroll, in 1941, possibly at the hands of the Cheshire landowner Sir Jock Delves Broughton, 11th Baronet.

Lieutenant-Commander Hon. John Stuart, the second son of Morton Stuart, 17th Earl of Moray, owner of the powerful Moray empire, was one such expat. Having left the Royal Navy in 1920 he set off for Africa in a car with a canvas roof, married a woman he met in Bulawayo, and embarked on a safari lifestyle in the middle of bush country in the Bechuanaland Protectorate, modern-day Botswana, fifty miles from the nearest railway station (where, according to his younger son James, the station master's wife 'spent her life trying to hatch ostrich eggs between her legs'). Here his daughter, Hermione, and three sons – James and his twin brother Charles, and their older brother Douglas – were born, and there they might well have stayed had his older brother Francis, from 1930 18th Earl of Moray, not died unexpectedly in 1943 with three daughters and no son, while John was back in the navy directing convoy protection. The new Morays promptly moved back to Scotland, and to Darnaway Castle in Moray, with its medieval banqueting hall and castellated facade. 'We went from having a life of absolute adventure, where the river was open to any type of activity, to moving here to Scotland where the river was sacrosanct,' says James Stuart. 'You had to fish in a certain way, you couldn't do what we did in Africa and tie chunks of meat on a hook. Here you had these little things called flies, and you had to have a keeper. It was an amazing change – we were so distressed living in this bloody great castle.' The new John Moray never made a fuss about his change in circumstances. 'He never made any point of it, he just got on with his life,' says James Stuart. He reflects that his father must have known what would likely happen. 'Francis was getting older, and the chance of him having a boy was getting more distant, and then it all came to a dramatic end.' He took to being Lord Moray well. 'He recognised that he had a responsibility, and he sacrificed a life of independence in Africa for it. He was ready for it. He must have known that someday he would have to come back, but it was never a threat hanging over us.'

At about the same time, the heir to the Exeter marquessate, Lord Martin Cecil, was happily ensconced in British Columbia. His brother David, born in 1905 and from 1956 6th Marquess of Exeter, had seemed to have it all: the extraordinary Burghley House outside Stamford, built for William Cecil, 1st Baron Burghley, chief adviser to Elizabeth I; a substantial, if not enormous estate of 30,000 acres; a gold medal from the 400-metre hurdles at the 1928 Amsterdam Olympics; and – crucially – a son, John. This little boy was 'the most adorable child, with very fair hair and blue eyes', as his younger sister Lady Angela Oswald put it. But John died aged thirteen months on 1 June 1934. Angela believes that her mother, Mary, wasn't particularly maternal before John's birth. She remembers her aunt Lady Romayne Brassey telling her how 'your father had been very proud of his son, but your mother absolutely adored him'. Mary, says Angela, 'gave him all her love, and was utterly devastated by his death'.[19] David and Mary went on to have two more healthy children before the couple divorced in 1946. Neither was a boy.

Martin Cecil meanwhile had moved to British Columbia in 1931 to manage his father's 12,000-acre ranch and three years later married a young Hungarian woman called Edith Csanády de Telegd, whom he had met at a dance in France in 1929 while ashore with the navy. 'My grandparents didn't think very highly of my father marrying an infidel Hungarian, but my Hungarian family goes back to the 1300s and to a Hungarian Catholic bishop,' says their son Michael Cecil, 8th Marquess of Exeter, who was born in 1935.

Martin elected to stay in Canada when his father William Cecil, 5th Marquess of Exeter, died in 1956, but it was already clear that his side of the family was likely to succeed when David died, a situation that caused a certain tension between the two brothers. As Michael Exeter says of his uncle: 'I think the death of his son and the disruption that caused had some effect on how he looked at the future of the family. He had quite an open, friendly relationship with my father when they were younger, and when my parents got married, my uncle was best man. Later, their relationship became more distant.'

And there was still the issue of Burghley to sort out. If Martin stayed in Canada, 4,500 miles from Burghley, who would run it in the event of David's death? As Michael Exeter explains: '[M]y understanding is that Uncle David wisely saw a need for change in the way the Burghley estate, including the house, had been operated over the centuries. With legal advice, he formed the Burghley House Preservation Trust in 1968, to take charge of the overall operation.' This meant, and still means today, that 'the titleholders of the day would be a step removed – starting with him, as he lived for another thirteen years or so – when this went into effect.' It was always the case that Martin was, as his son describes, 'unlikely to be involved with day-to-day operations, as his life in North America was very full'. When David Exeter died in October 1981, aged seventy-six, Martin became 7th Marquess of Exeter, and the following year David Exeter's youngest daughter Lady Victoria Leatham took over the running of Burghley. Six years later, Martin Exeter died, aged seventy-eight, and Michael succeeded him. When we first spoke in spring 2022, he smiled as he said, 'I've been around for thirty-four years. I am the oldest titleholder ever in my family.'[20]

* * *

As Robin Braybrooke's eight daughters and the complicated line of inheritance in the Methuen family demonstrate, male primogeniture often involves dead ends and complex lurches across family trees. Not all inheritances are straightforward. While 655 of the current batch of 793 peers inherited their titles from their fathers, twenty-six were in a direct line of succession from their grandfathers. Just one, Nicholas Lowther, 2nd Viscount Ullswater, can point to a straight line from his great-grandfather, since both his father and grandfather died young.[21] Fifteen peers inherited their title from their first cousin or their first cousin once removed, and twenty-one from cousins more distantly related. When Rod Balfour became 5th Earl of Balfour in 2003, it came as a surprise to many – not least him: 'Most people when I was at school, and even until I was about fifty-five, had absolutely no idea' that he stood to inherit the title originally given to his great-great-uncle, the former prime minister Arthur Balfour, he told me in 2019. 'Then they woke up one day to read my cousin's obituary: "The heir to the earldom is his second cousin once removed, Roderick Balfour."' One slav-ish follower of aristocratic developments passed his table at lunch the following day and said, '"I hear you've changed your name." I replied, "No, I haven't, I'm still Roderick Balfour." "Strange," he replied, "the person who told me usually knows about these things!"' In the case of David Carnegie, 14th Earl of Northesk, who died in 2010, it proved necessary to search the family tree back to the seventeenth century in order to find a suitable heir – his eighth cousin once removed, the writer Patrick Carnegy.

A quick journey through the recent history of the Earls of Buck-inghamshire shows just how complicated inheritance can be. The title had originally been granted to the brother of one of George II's mistresses, the MP John Hobart, 1st Baron Hobart of Blickling, in 1746. When John Mercer-Henderson, 8th Earl of Buckingham-shire, who was known as 'Bertie Bucks', died unmarried in 1963, the title passed to his second cousin Vere, who had temporarily emigrated to Australia with £50 in 1919, worked as a sheep farmer, a railway worker and on Royal Australian Air Force cargo planes deployed to transport Japanese prisoners-of-war, before returning to Britain in 1949, where, as an employee of Southend Corpor-ation, he was sweeping the town's snowy streets when news of his elevation to the peerage came through. 'I shall probably take up the title, but it will not make any difference to me,' he said. 'I am happy as I am and do not want any changes.'[22] He took the next day off work and resigned soon afterwards. Six months later, bored by unemployment, he rejoined the council as a playground attendant.

When Vere Buckinghamshire died in 1983, the title wound its way back to the children of Augustus Hobart-Hampden, 6th Earl of Buckinghamshire, and down through his fifth son's family (bypassing an older daughter on the way) to the pensions consult-ant Miles Hobart-Hampden, Vere's second cousin once removed, who duly became the 10th Earl. 'It was never a big issue in my life until Vere's death,' he says. 'I knew that I was descended from John Hampden,[23] whose daughter Mary married Sir John Hobart of Blickling, but it was only after I inherited the title that I became more aware of the Hobart history and in particular with the Hobart connections around the world. I met the 8th Earl on one occasion, when he gave my parents and myself a tour around Hampden House [in Buckinghamshire], and I attended his funeral, taking the day off from my labourer's job on a building site. I am sure that my grandfather would be really surprised that I'm the earl – he was one of seven with a lot of males ahead of him.' Proving Miles' claim to the title was a long and involved business. When he submitted supporting evidence via the Lord Chamberlain's office, he was told, 'you've missed one'. 'My lawyers had to find that missed possible claimant and prove that he left no male heirs in line to inherit the title before me. It was exhausting. I also had to prove that the 9th Earl didn't marry while he was in Australia, and if he had married that he had no male children. That last affidavit came from his sister who we discovered in a nursing home in British Columbia.'

Though not particularly enthused by his inheritance, which didn't come with a house, land or a fortune, Miles Buckinghamshire never seriously thought of not taking the title. 'Why would I not take it?' he asks. 'If you're not taking it, you're denying something. It wasn't as though I was so politically driven to stand for election as an MP and I was not inclined to deny my heritage, so there was no reason for me not to take it. I enjoyed my fifteen years in the House of Lords and regarded it as an honour and a privilege.' He goes by Miles Buckinghamshire now, rather than Miles Hobart-Hampden, but doesn't particularly identify as a member of the aristocracy. 'Apart from the title I'm solidly middle class,' he says, 'certainly financially, and I was fortunate enough to work in a profession which I enjoyed for nearly fifty years before finally retiring in 2019. I'm not sure I am a good representative. I would hope that I'm not, I'm just an example of somebody who has acquired something. I had a choice not to take the title, but I've never felt that was appropriate. On the other hand, I very rarely make use of it. You take the cards that you're handed and you make the best of it that you can. I'm proud of the people who went before me – it's a fine title. In any shape or form, being able to trace your ancestry back to John Hampden, and then back to 1065, is worth something.' He adds that none of his endeavours – being made a goodwill ambassador for the city of Hobart, Tasmania, in 2009, and his connections to liberal arts colleges in the United States that are connected to the Hampdens – would have been possible without the support of his wife of nearly fifty years, Alison.

Miles Buckinghamshire is now in the same situation as Bertie Bucks was: he has no biological children, and so on his death the title will go on another long journey, to his fourth cousin once removed, Isle of Wight parish counsellor Sir John Hobart, 4th Baronet, who has two sons.

* * *

While male primogeniture dominates the peerage, there are about ninety titles[24] that can in theory be inherited by a female heir and may pass in the female line. In practice, since the beginning of the twentieth century, fifty-one women have succeeded to thirty-nine hereditary titles, of which thirty-four are extant, although, as of March 2024, only ten peers are women.[25]

One of these ten is Margaret Mar, who entered the line of succession for her family's title following her younger brother David, Lord Garioch's premature death in 1967, eight years before their father James Mar's. 'I didn't know about [the title] at all until I was about twelve when my father told me that I would have the title of Lady one day, and I thought, "OK, so what?"' she says. 'We were living in Kenya at the time and it meant absolutely nothing. My brother died when he was twenty-two and that's when I came into the line, because he would have inherited it otherwise.' She became 31st Countess of Mar in 1975, aged thirty-four. Her husband, John Jenkin, is the only man in the country who is married to a countess but who is not an earl; as she explains, 'We're Countess and Mr.' Another of the female peers is Teresa Freeman-Grenville, 13th Lady Kinloss. It very nearly didn't happen. When in August 1944, her grandfather Reverend Luis Morgan-Grenville, Master of Kinloss died, and then his mother Mary, 11th Lady Kinloss, two months later, Luis's eldest daughter Mary Morgan-Grenville was first in line for the title, since the Kinloss title can pass to a woman.[26] But Mary's uncle Tom Morgan-Grenville tried to claim the title. 'My mother's solicitor stepped in and said that it was my mother's because she was my grandfather's eldest child, and my grandfather had been the heir, even though he hadn't become Lord Kinloss. Titles do funny things to people.'

Not surprisingly, quite a few aristocratic women reckon they could do the job better than the men of the family. Rosemary Muir whom we met in the Introduction believes that her elder sister Lady Sarah Spencer-Churchill would have made a more suitable head of the family than her brother Sunny, who inherited the Marlborough dukedom in 1972.[27] 'The females in my family are much more impressive, more organised, more hands on,' she says. 'She would have made a much better duke than my brother who wasn't a very good duke. I don't believe in primogeniture at all. There ought to be a choice – it ought to go to the person who is most suitable. We would have been much better off with Sarah, who was full of energy. He was perfectly *compos mentis*. He didn't do a bad job, but he didn't do a good job either. He was spoiled.'

Women may only occasionally be able to inherit, but many are now closely involved in ensuring that aristocratic estates remain viable, though 'close involvement' is about as far as it goes, and usually their influence comes through marriage rather than blood. The day that a major landowning family allows a daughter to inherit the estate over the son will be a watershed. A millennial woman from one such peerage family snorts when I suggest that this might ever happen. In the family company, she says, 'They go on about diversity and inclusion. I always think, how can you talk about diversity and inclusion in a company whose founding principle is one of primogeniture?'

At Burghley, the Exeters have got around primogeniture by establishing the Burghley House Preservation Trust. Today, David Exeter's granddaughter Miranda Rock is in charge as the executive chair. She lives there with her husband Orlando Rock, UK chairman of Christie's, and their four children, while her first cousin once removed Michael Exeter lives in Canada and has only a limited role at Burghley. He doesn't feel burdened by his title, nor by the relationship that it has with Burghley, but feels '. . . called to keep connection with what's going on with the Burghley House Preservation Trust. If I have anything to add to what I see, I do that, and they pay attention to it.' But in day-to-day life in North America, his title 'means nothing. As far as I'm concerned, I'm Michael Cecil.'

The influence of the women who have married in is often profound, as Lady Violet Manners, the eldest daughter of David and Emma Rutland, can attest, having observed her mother run Belvoir Castle near Grantham since 1999. 'It takes an enormous amount of work to reimagine the wheel with a 200-year-old building. How do you reinvent the wheel again? I've watched Mum do it for twenty-five years and it's a massive job.' In 2021, the two of them started a podcast during the course of which they interviewed chatelaines of stately homes, many of whom take the lead day-to-day. 'Whether you're a man or a woman you've got to have the determination and the grit [to run a big house], and I don't know that that's determined by sex – I think that's determined by character,' Violet says. Though she is the eldest of her parents' five children, she feels fortunate to have grown up at Belvoir with the ability to then be free to 'do my own thing'. It's a relief, she says. 'I can go off and become whatever it is I can imagine, and I can do my best to make sure I can get it done. That freedom is very lucky. There is no greater sense of pride than you can get from making your own money and buying your own rug, or house, being successful in your own right.' Still, she says, 'There needs to be a conversation around primogeniture.'

Other millennial women, however, are less happy with the status quo. One told me how much she would love to inherit her father's title. 'I'm desperate to,' she says. 'I used to have so much energy for it before the Princess of Wales had Prince George – if she had had a girl first, it was all going to change, and it was going to be really exciting. The government doesn't have the capacity for it now. No one cares, it's not an election winner.' As a result, she says, 'I don't know where I stand on it anymore, but the title means a huge amount to me – I'm the eighteenth generation of my family and my dad has done nothing but push the history on me. Everywhere I go there's some old relic. It makes me feel rather sad talking about it.'

Even when women do inherit in one generation, titles have a tendency to revert to the male side in the next. Indeed, of the thirty-nine titles that came to women in the course of the twentieth century, nineteen have now passed to men – either as their main or subsidiary title. The Mountbattens offer a case in point. In 1946 when Dickie Mountbatten was made 1st Viscount Mountbatten of Burma, the title was created with – at Dickie's insistence – what is known technically as special remainder to his eldest daughter Patricia Mountbatten (then Baroness Brabourne on account of her 1946 marriage to John Knatchbull, 7th Baron Brabourne). After Patricia died in 2017, the Mountbatten title, which was upgraded to an earldom in 1947, passed to her eldest son Norton, who had inherited his father's barony in 2005. Similarly, when Geordie Sutherland died in 1963, his ducal title passed to his third cousin once removed John Ellesmere (who we last saw at Floors, giving a paraffin stove to Mary Roxburghe), while the Sutherlands' separate, but identically named earldom was inherited by Geordie's 41-year-old niece Elizabeth.[28] With the earldom, the oldest in Scotland, came Dunrobin Castle and its 120,000-acre estate that had been held by Geordie Sutherland since 1913.[29] When Elizabeth Sutherland died in 2019, the earldom passed to her son Alistair. Because his only son Alexander, Lord Strathnaver, died three years later, his eldest sister Lady Rachel Sutherland, Mistress of Sutherland, is now her father's heir. In the event that neither she nor her younger sister Lady Rosemary Sutherland has children, the title will pass to their youngest sister Doctor Lady Elizabeth Costin's son, Isaac.

The same pattern can be observed with Diana 'Dinan' or 'Puffin' Hay, 23rd Countess of Erroll, daughter of the murdered philanderer Joss Erroll and his ultimately five-times married and divorced first wife Lady Idina Sackville.[30] At the time of her father's murder in January 1941, fifteen-year-old Puffin was living in England with her aunt and uncle, Lady 'Avie' and Frank Spicer, her mother having dropped her off with them some seven years earlier. They never told her what had happened to her father: she found out about it by accident when she was browsing through the newspapers on the counter at the village shop. Thereafter she would slip downstairs before breakfast each day and read every inch of newsprint she could find about her parents, about the man accused of her father's murder, Jock Delves Broughton, and about his ultimate acquittal for lack of evidence.[31] Needless to say, by the time she made her official appearance at the breakfast table the relevant articles had been snipped out.

If her uncle and aunt were unforthcoming about the circumstances of her father's death, they were equally uncommunicative about the fact that Puffin was now chief of Clan Hay, hereditary Lord High Constable of Scotland, and Countess of Erroll – a title '. . . so ridiculously grand', according to her great-niece Frances Osborne, 'that, like very, very few other British titles, it could be inherited by a woman.'[32] By the time she saw her mother again, Puffin was engaged to the genealogist Sir Iain Moncreiffe of that Ilk, 11th Baronet, and, understandably, wanted little to do with her. Idina had, after all, been largely absent from her daughter's childhood and had dragged the family name through the mud. Some doubts were even expressed as to whether Puffin was actually Joss Erroll's daughter, though these were dispelled when her son Merlin, now 24th Earl of Erroll, grew up to look exactly like his grandfather. Puffin was Countess of Erroll for thirty-seven years but the title has now become firmly wedged within the male side of the family, since Merlin Erroll has at least six male heirs.

Other titles created for women now appear only as the titles of the wives of peers. Anne Scott, daughter of Francis Scott, 2nd Earl of Buccleuch, was made Duchess of Buccleuch in her own right in 1663. Today, that title will only ever belong to a duchess by marriage. The same is true of the Countess of Cromartie, a title created in 1861 for Anne Sutherland-Leveson-Gower, Duchess of Sutherland.[33]

How different things would be in so many families if the principle of male primogeniture did not hold sway. Had it been done away with before February 1988, for example, when John Strutt, 5th Baron Rayleigh, died, the new Lady Rayleigh would have been the Conservative politician Anne Jenkin, since 2011 Baroness Jenkin of Kennington. Ironically, the Rayleigh title was created, in 1821, for a woman, Lady Charlotte Strutt, after her husband Joseph Strutt declined the honour and proposed that she took it instead. In the same way, had the rules changed by 2001, when Frank Pakenham, 7th Earl of Longford – himself a younger son – died, his eldest child, the historian Lady Antonia Fraser, would have succeeded him as 8th Countess of Longford. Instead, her brother Thomas inherited not just the title which, ironically, he does not use, since he regards it as anachronistic, but the family estate in County Westmeath. As he has said, the 'cruel rule' of primogeniture enforces the idea of 'winner takes all'.[34] And had the rules been changed before June 2016, when the pig farmer John Harding, 2nd Baron Harding of Petherton, died, his eldest daughter the Hon. Diana 'Dido' Harding, since 2014, like Anne Jenkin, a life peer as Baroness Harding of Winscombe, would have become 3rd Baroness Harding of Petherton – and possibly, therefore, not the head of NHS Test and Trace during the Covid-19 pandemic.

Since 1837, there have been eight debates at Westminster that feature the word 'primogeniture' in the title. During the first, which came shortly before Queen Victoria succeeded William IV, the Liberal MP William Ewart declared that '... much of what was monstrous in the social and political condition of this country would be traced to the prevalence of the law and custom of primogeniture.'[35] At a debate in 2020, two days after International Women's Day, Charles Shrewsbury first stated his qualifications to speak on the subject: 'I have four older sisters. My eldest child is my daughter, Victoria. My eldest son, James, has three daughters and a son – my grandson, George, who is the youngest. My father had three elder sisters, so male primogeniture and older sisters is a subject with which I am somewhat familiar.' Then he made it clear that, in his view, '[M]ale primogeniture is one of the remaining bastions of the hereditary system which should and must be changed.'[36] Thirteen months later in April 2021, during a debate entitled Gender-balanced Parliament and Male Primogeniture, when the Conservative peer Ralph Palmer, 12th Baron Lucas, asked the government 'what plans they have to amend male primogeniture', the life peer Pola Uddin, Baroness Uddin, stated that 'male primogeniture is indefensible and damages our striving for equality and justice,' adding that '[I]t may well be that some people in the country have other priorities.'[37]

The voices of those in parliament opposed to male primogeniture have been amplified by campaigning groups beyond Westminster. In 2013 Liza Campbell and the journalist Victoria Lambert, Countess of Clancarty (whose only child, Lady Rowena Trench, cannot inherit her father, a Liberal Democrat peer's earldom), established The Hares, a campaign group so-named after Conservative peer David Trefgarne, 2nd Baron Trefgarne declared that changing the rules on succession to the Crown would 'set the hare running' on primogeniture.[38] Five years later, another group, Daughters' Rights was founded by Charlotte Carew Pole, who married Tremayne Carew Pole, son and heir of Sir Richard Carew Pole, 13th Baronet in 2010.[39] 'We lady aristocrats demand equality too!' was how a *Daily Mail* headline marked its launch.[40] One of those involved with Daughters' Rights is Lady Tanya Field, the eldest daughter of Richard Parker, 9th Earl of Macclesfield, and a community worker in Barton, a suburb of Oxford. It never particularly worried her, she says, that she was not a favoured male or that she got the 'definite sense' that her grandfather preferred her cousin Timothy to the girls of the family. Nor did she particularly want the material trappings that went with the title: 'I have no interest in old buildings, in antiques, in super-expensive paintings, nothing could bore me more. I can live on a shoestring.' However, she says, 'I love the thought of having been able to stand for election for the House of Lords to advocate on various things. That's the only bit that I care about. Whatever you think of the aristocracy,' she goes on to say, 'it's fundamentally wrong that there is this gender imbalance.'

Changing the rules would involve certain practical difficulties, but these are not insurmountable. During a debate in 1997 Ian Balfour, 2nd Baron Balfour of Inchrye (whose title became extinct when he died without a male heir in 2003), suggested that given the 'material disarray that would be caused by the dispossession of eldest sons who have lived their entire adult lives in the service of an assured inheritance', perhaps a compromise might be to '. . . confirm all peers in their titles on a given date, the 1st January, 2000, for example, and from that date to deduce their successor according to the rights of heirs general'.[41] Yet there seems to be little institutional desire to grasp the nettle. During the 2021 debate the minister of state for the Cabinet Office Nick True, Baron True, stated that '[A] review is not currently under way.'[42] Perhaps there's a level of social and family embarrassment involved, too: it's a debate that those involved with know is far removed from most people's experience, and one that, whatever solution might be arrived at, could cause some family friction.

As it is, the current convention is not only, in many people's view, grossly unfair but can lead to titles and the estates to which they belong being split apart from one another. The Norfolks offer a case in point. Bernard Norfolk, who died in 1975, had four daughters, all of whom could have taken on his Arundel estate, but instead his second cousin once removed Major-General Miles Fitzalan Howard, MC, succeeded him as duke.[43] At the time of his ducal succession, Miles Norfolk was styled 12th Baron Beaumont and 4th Baron Howard of Glossop, the former element having come from his mother, Mona, 11th Baroness Beaumont, a title she had inherited as an infant. This is now subsumed into the Norfolks' pile of eight titles. As Miles' younger son Lord Gerald Fitzalan Howard, who lives at Carlton Towers in North Yorkshire, the original Beaumont house, told me in 2018, 'The sad thing is that my brother is now Duke of Norfolk and Lord Beaumont, the title from this house, but now the title is split off from the house and we'll never get it back. It will only split out again. My brother has got three sons – if there's no male heir two generations down, then the eldest daughter will become Lady Beaumont and it'll split out again but of course by then they'll have no idea about Carlton, it'll be two or three generations ago.' In theory, his brother Edward Norfolk could transfer it to him, but it would require a deed of parliament. 'It's a great shame,' he says, 'Carlton is a Beaumont house – it would be quite cool to be Baron Beaumont.'

Meanwhile, Lady Kinvara Balfour, the second of Rod Balfour and Edward Norfolk's older sister Lady Tessa Fitzalan Howard's four daughters, looks at the Norfolk set-up from the vantage point of gender equality.

My grandpa [Miles] Norfolk inherited the title because Bernard Norfolk had daughters. We can't erase the past. The dukedom came to my uncle indirectly, I'm not questioning that – I'm not trying to claim pure line bloodline to the 1st Duke of Norfolk, but it bothers me that females are simply bypassed in this realm. [She is proud of her family history on both sides.] I see the role of the Duke of Norfolk in *Henry V*, and I think, wow, that's my ancestor, how fascinating. I am extremely proud of my heritage, of my family, that Arthur Balfour was a British prime minister who made great reforms for the Jews – I have come from a family that has dared to make big change.[44]

Everywhere on Instagram it's like, 'Be the change you want to see in the world!' You think, OK, I'll join in, but because it's to do with aristocracy people think, 'Poor little rich girl, you're so out of touch.' If I wasn't Lady Kinvara Balfour and I was fighting for women to have equal rights and primogeniture then maybe I wouldn't be so derided. But few speak out about this particular human rights injustice because they're not experiencing it, whereas I am, on both sides of the family.

* * *

The point here, as Kinvara Balfour says, is that it's the principle of the thing. Some would certainly like the trappings that go with a title and an estate. But many know that these are not unalloyed pleasures: with privilege comes hard work and the pressures of keeping ancient buildings watertight and their surroundings in good order. Francis Fitzherbert, 15th Baron Stafford, doubtless speaks for many when he describes the worries he felt when he inherited Swynnerton Hall in Staffordshire, following his father's death in 1986. He had, he says, never felt more isolated. 'The greatest threat to the business was my death, so at the first estate meeting after Dad died, I was already being written off,' he remembers. 'Inheriting estates is incredibly lonely. Everybody thinks you are fine, but it's very emotional. Your siblings no longer have their bedrooms at the big house, because it's no longer their home, and suddenly your wife's family come in as a right, and your siblings have to be invited as guests.' He has managed his son Ben's succession to Swynnerton with a ten-year plan to avoid the difficult handover. People keep assuming that he is the new Lord Stafford, he says, laughing. 'Someone came here recently and said that they had just met the new Lord Stafford. I said, "I don't think you have!" I used to be in control – I even introduced myself the other day as "Ben's father".'

Quite a few second sons I have spoken to have expressed their relief at *not* being the heir to a title and all that goes with it. James and Charles Stuart, the younger twin sons of John Stuart, 19th Earl of Moray, for example, have never regretted that when their father died in 1974, it was their older brother Douglas who inherited, or that it was Douglas's son John who took over as the 21st Earl of Moray when Douglas died in 2011. 'We were off the hook, free agents,' says James Stuart, chuckling. 'We rejoiced in being the vagrant twins. Being the second and third sons was a benefit, otherwise we would have been stuck with the aches and pains of running an estate. Douglas adapted to what had happened to him, but his life was tied to the millstone of landownership in Scotland. We had the best deal out of life.'

There is such a thing as 'second son syndrome', a number of younger sons confirm – and as others have demonstrated in public in recent years. Ted Innes Ker, younger son of Guy Innes Ker, 10th Duke of Roxburghe, and Lady Jane Dawnay (née Grosvenor), and younger brother of the current incumbent, Charlie Roxburghe, has 'always known' his position in the family, and, as he explains, 'I got my head around it at a pretty early age.' Obviously, much comes down to how well – or badly – siblings get on. 'If you're good mates with the person who is going to inherit the house or the estate or whatever it is, and you get on, then it's absolutely fine. It's a personality thing . . . I've always got on extremely well with my brother and been delighted that Charlie is going to be doing that [running Floors] rather than me, because it means that not only do I not have that responsibility, but I have the choice of where my life goes.' As he points out, that choice extends to where he opts to live. 'I bought my house in the Borders in 2020 and committed to Scotland – I had the ability to make that decision, whereas Charlie doesn't have that luxury. If Scottish Independence comes along then I can sell my house whereas Charlie can't sell Floors.'

The Hon. David Herbert, younger son of Reggie Herbert, 15th Earl of Pembroke, expressed a similar view in his 1972 memoirs, which, rather pertinently, he called *Second Son*. On the one hand, he said, when his older brother Sidney inherited the Pembroke earldom in 1960, he took on a title dating from 1551, a 'tradition of personal service to the Crown', and Wilton, 'one of the most beautiful and romantic of English country houses'. On the other hand, that very inheritance had to be 'closely guarded and carefully tended'.[45] 'It is', he wrote, 'a task that entails heavy responsibilities.' Had David been in his brother's place, or had he succeeded him, he would have '. . . taken on the responsibilities with zest. But I should never have liked becoming a public figure. I should have hated to mount a platform as Mayor of Wilton, or even lord-lieutenant, make speeches and have my picture in the paper cutting ribbons at the county show. I am interested in public affairs – up to a point – but do not wish to take part in them.'[46]

Sidney Pembroke, meanwhile, had to accept that with the title and the estate came obligations and restrictions. 'From birth [he] would have loved to have gone out towards wider horizons,' his brother reckoned. Instead, he was 'faced with a ready-made job' and the knowledge that 'he had to follow his destiny.'[47] 'It is a great honour to be the head of a family whose name goes deep into the roots of history, but it is – or can be – a millstone.'[48] Like David Herbert, the former provost of Eton and Conservative minister William Waldegrave, Baron Waldegrave of North Hill, younger son of Geoffrey Waldegrave, 12th Earl Waldegrave, knew from his earliest days that 'everything would go one day to my brother.' And like David Herbert, he never resented it: '[T]hat was how the world was, and he was a hero fit to be worshipped. If I was not going to have the family name, I had better make my own . . . I would have to make my own way.'[49] Colin Clark, younger son of the art historian Kenneth Clark, later Baron Clark, similarly concluded that being a younger son was the better option. 'The joy of not being expected to succeed makes any success seem doubly sweet . . . More than anything else, a younger brother, younger son can be free.'[50]

If any life story demonstrates the truth that lies in that sentiment, it is that of Jack Osborne, 11th Duke of Leeds. In theory, he enjoyed just about every advantage that life could offer. His family owned Hornby Castle in North Yorkshire, which as the only son among five children, he was always destined to take over. His parents doted on him. He was educated at Eton and then went on to Cambridge. And yet, once he inherited the family estate in 1927, his life went into a precipitous decline.

His early years were comfortable, privileged ones. One story, related by his daughter Lady Camilla Osborne in a 2015 BBC Two documentary, *The Last Dukes*, tells how as a small boy the Marquess of Carmarthen, as he then was, was on board a bus with his nanny when it became snarled up in traffic. 'Nanny, why aren't we moving?' he asked. She explained the situation. 'Well, they wouldn't do this if they knew the little marquess was on board!' he responded.[51]

Jack had been much wanted by his mother Katherine Osborne, Duchess of Leeds, who had had a succession of four daughters in the seven years from 1885. Finally she had success when Jack arrived, in March 1901. Shortly before his birth Katherine had been to a casino in Monte Carlo, where according to Camilla, '. . . because she was pregnant she had second sight, and all the numbers came up.' With the money she won she bought a house, the Villa Selva Dolce, just over the Italian border in Bordighera, and it was here that Jack spent much of his early childhood. When the time came for him to go to Eton, he begged to be spared. 'Yes, I know, horrid, horrid,' his mother said. When he continued to protest, '[S]he replied that if he was very good and didn't fuss then she'd give him anything he wanted. He said he wanted "a pair of shoes, like Giovanni". He told her that Giovanni was the gardener's son who had a pair of yellow leather shoes, and how he wanted a pair just like that. He arrived at Eton in a pair of yellow leather winklepickers.'

Following an undistinguished time at Cambridge, Jack went to work for the private bank Child & Co. In 1925 he was rumoured to be engaged to American heiress Mary Landon Baker – a brave, possibly foolhardy move given that she had only comparatively recently left her previous fiancé, the American millionaire Allister McCormick, at the altar, not once but three times, and would ultimately notch up sixty-five proposals of marriage. Then in May 1927, his father George Osborne, 10th Duke of Leeds died and Jack succeeded him. After that, his life started its downwards trajectory.

He began his ducal reign by offloading those parts of the estate in which he had no interest. Hornby Castle itself was disposed of by auction in April 1930, possibly because Jack disliked the house, but also possibly – according to what Camilla was told by a North Yorkshire neighbour – to pay off his father's gambling debts. Shortly after that, Jack met a Serbian ballet dancer named Irma de Malkhozouny, who went, as Camilla explains, by the name 'Marianne', and they were married in Nice in March 1933. A photograph of Marianne, Jack and his mother Katherine Leeds taken after the nuptials shows a delighted Marianne, a somewhat concerned Jack, and his mother, sporting a cloche hat and looking, as Camilla puts it, 'like only a duchess would look if your only son is marrying a Serbian ballet dancer'. Jack and Marianne spent their honeymoon in Egypt, then moved to Paris. Marianne, in Camilla's view, '. . . was incredibly charming and seductive – she liked the high life. There were stories of them having their own carriage on the train, and pictures of them on the *Queen Mary*, with him looking miserable.' Still, Jack preferred this life to the one prescribed for him back home in England. 'I don't think he had a single friend in the English establishment,' says Camilla. 'He didn't subscribe to any of the ducal activities except drink.'

When the Second World War broke out, Jack put Marianne on a ship to America, where she promptly fell in love with an American millionaire called Frank Howard, whom she later married. Jack then met and married Camilla's mother, Audrey Young, in December 1948. He was a friend of her father's, and her senior by almost a quarter of a century. 'They were very happy for a bit in London after the war, before I was born,' says Camilla. 'They lived in a flat, and she did the cooking, and carried his breakfast up on a tray. They had a normal domestic life.'

Not long after Camilla was born in 1950, the couple became tax exiles in Jersey, on the advice of Jack's trustees. It was not a good move. 'They couldn't have gone anywhere that he would have hated more,' says Camilla. 'There wasn't anywhere he could get his suits made. There was one cinema, one theatre that did pantomime, and no bars – just a round of cliquey expat cocktail parties, night after night. He was just desperate, he hated it.' Soon Audrey had abandoned Jack for a Coldstream Guards officer, Captain Sir David Lawrence, 3rd Baronet. 'My stepfather had to leave the army,' Camilla recalled, 'and apparently his commanding officer said, "Well, Lawrence, this is jolly sad, isn't it – chorus girls are one thing but I'm afraid duchesses are quite another."'[52] For his part Jack was marooned in Jersey with his daughter and a young woman, Caroline Vatcher, who had taken a shine to him.

According to Camilla, '[H]e took her out to dinner on New Year's Eve, and she made a scene and said, "You've got to marry me." I can hear him saying it, "Why, God, why?" She said that everybody was talking about them, and I'm sure they were. He said, "Oh, God, alright then." The next morning, there was a scene like from an operetta, with him flying around the house in his silk dressing gown, saying, "What shall I do, what shall I do?" Then there was a ring on the doorbell, and it was Caroline and her father.' They married in February 1955. 'One of my cousins said, "Jack's wives get younger and younger – he doesn't seem to realise that he is getting older and older."'

Jack's final years were sad ones. 'He had absolutely no purpose in his life, except getting through the day, by going to the cinema, going to the tailor or having a third Pernod. That was his life.' A heavy smoker as well as drinker, he found his circulation starting to give way. Ultimately, he had to have both legs amputated and was confined to a wheelchair. When he died in 1963, the dukedom passed to his second cousin once removed Sir D'Arcy Osborne, a former British minister to the Holy See and a close friend of Queen Elizabeth the Queen Mother. When D'Arcy Leeds died eight months later, the dukedom became extinct.

Jack Leeds had inherited a title, but he was never able to inhabit it. 'He really was without any purpose,' says Camilla. 'He drank a lot. His life was so formed by living in Italy when he was little – gardeners, cooks and waiters loved him, and it wasn't because of the tipping. He had this extraordinary charm and empathy and was at his happiest in a restaurant – not that he ever ate anything.' She repeats a story that one of her cousins told her about her father. 'One day somebody had bumped into him in St James's and asked him what he was doing. He said that he was having his suit measured or something – he was passionate about his clothes, a tailor's dream because he had such a good figure – and that the next day he was going to have his shoes fitted or something. They said, "But, Jack, they're next door, why don't you do it at the same time?" He said, "Well, if I did that, I'd have nothing to do tomorrow."' The exchange was, his daughter thought, '[A] little bit tongue in cheek, but not that much'.

Camilla inherited a sizeable fortune but seemed also to inherit her father's deep-rooted sense of purposelessness. To that extent the family title and all that went with it perhaps proved something of a curse. In 2015 she said that 'I think maybe, like my father, if I hadn't had it, I would have had a happier life, or a more fulfilled one. When you read death announcements they say "After a life well lived" or "After a fulfilled life", and sometimes in my more gloomy moments, I think I wouldn't say that. [It's] not that I've been unhappy but I've had sort of the same aimless life as my father did.'[53] I ask if she still thinks this. 'I do sort of believe it,' she says. 'I've never had a career, I got into university but I didn't finish. My marriage didn't last.[54] I should have been forced to knuckle down to do something.' Was her father in any way to blame? 'Perhaps. There really was no example to follow.'

10

A Little Learning

Childhood and School

What are the best-known, perpetually pushed stereotypes of the British aristocracy? First, there is their reputation for eccentricity. One thinks, for example, of the reclusive Victorian peer John Cavendish-Scott-Bentinck, 5th Duke of Portland, who built a series of tunnels and rooms underneath his Nottinghamshire home of Welbeck Abbey, so that he could avoid being seen by members of the public or his own staff; and of cross-dressing Toppy Anglesey, referred to by subsequent generations of his family as 'Mad Ux', who became known as 'the dancing marquess' thanks to his favoured solo performance, the Butterfly Dance. He possessed the world's largest collection of walking sticks and a huge wardrobe containing 260 pairs of white kid gloves and 200 gold scarf pins, and died in 1905 in considerable debt.

In more recent times the bespectacled Frank Longford initially turned down Clement Attlee's suggestion that he could become First Lord of the Admiralty in May 1951 with the words, 'I feel I am too eccentric,' changing his mind only when the prime minister pointed out that: 'The Navy has survived Winston [Churchill] and Brendan Bracken. It will probably survive you.'[1] Frank's demand that his book on humility should be more prominently displayed in bookshops can be interpreted as displaying either eccentric other-worldliness or a strange lack of self-knowledge. And then there was Brinsley Le Poer Trench, 8th Earl of Clancarty, a noted ufologist and sometime editor of the *Flying Saucer Review*, whose rare interventions in the House of Lords were almost invariably to do with extra-terrestrial activity. By the time he died in 1995, he was the author of eleven books on the subject, and had installed a UFO detector on a wall in the bedroom of his flat in Belgravia. The opening line of his fifth book, *Operation Earth*, published in 1969, reads: 'All of us on the planet Earth are Space People.'[2]

Eccentricity is, it would seem, one of the perks of privilege. You can do or be what you like because, quite simply, others can't stop you. Often it's the manifestation of a sense of entitlement. On occasion, paradoxically, it's a manifestation of the precise opposite. William 'Paddy' Westenra, 7th Baron Rossmore, who was, according to his son Benedict Rossmore, 'unassertive to an almost dangerous level', exhibited a 'lack of confidence' that on occasion caused him to behave in a manner that by anyone else's standard would be regarded as too eccentric to cope with the world. In later life he bought a cottage in County Cork that initially lacked a washing machine. His best friend Sally Phipps, daughter of the writer Molly Keane, who lived nearby, offered him the use of hers. Such, however, was his desire not to 'inconvenience his best friend by washing his bed sheets in a house that is ten minutes down the road', that he flew his washing to his house in London and then brought it back to Ireland.[3] 'He dressed unbelievably badly,' his son says, 'and I don't mean he had bad taste in clothes – all of his clothes had holes in them. He looked like a tramp.' When he died in 2021, his obituaries focused on the period of his life in the 1970s when he had a relationship with the rock singer Marianne Faithfull. 'I thought, that's quite cool,' says Benedict Rossmore, 'but that's so uncharacteristic of what I knew of him. I can't square that with dating Marianne Faithfull. He seemed to be quite successful on the dating scene and I cannot understand this.'

The other popular stereotype about the aristocracy, however, involves the very opposite of eccentricity. It's the notion that peers are all emotionless automatons who have become that way because they were brought up by nannies and sent away to school away from their cruel, unfeeling families. As with the reputation for unorthodox behaviour, this latter stereotype has a certain foundation in reality.

Back in Edwardian times, as Lady Alice Montagu Douglas Scott (later Princess Alice, Duchess of Gloucester) recalled in her memoirs, aristocratic parents were viewed as occasional visitors only. Her father John Montagu Douglas Scott, Earl of Dalkeith, later 7th Duke of Buccleuch, was an MP, 'and rarely got home before our bedtime', while her mother Margaret was shy and retiring, and visited the nursery only on the odd occasion, always seeming 'busy in her own little sitting-room or lying on a sofa with a headache'. Her children were occasionally allowed in to sit with her, 'But one always had to be quiet and do a jigsaw puzzle or something equally boring.' To be fair to Margaret Dalkeith, she had eight babies in eighteen years, and during Alice's childhood was often either pregnant or recently postpartum. When the Montagu Douglas Scott children graduated from the nursery to the schoolroom, they were allowed to have lunch in the dining room – albeit at their own table, in a corner. As Alice remembered, 'If there were treats, like strawberries and cream, we would suffer agonies in case they were finished before reaching us. The butlers and footmen always tried to make sure there was something left over for us.'[4]

If this sounds especially antiquated, it is worth remembering that all this was happening in an era when it was not unusual for the Buccleuchs to take the family's state coach when attending Court functions. On one such occasion, Alice was woken at night to watch her grandparents set off: '[T]he harness was shining silver,' she recalled, 'and there were a wigged coachman and footman in font and two postilions behind – all in livery, with red breeches and white stockings. The family coat-of-arms, picked out in fairy-lights, had been mounted for the occasion over the front door.'[5] At that time Montagu House, the Buccleuch house on Whitehall, was staffed with liveried footmen who would sit on mahogany benches ready and waiting to answer the door.

In many aristocratic families, it was deemed unimportant

Aristocratic dynasties: the Dukes of Northumberland – or the Kings of the North: (*left to right*) Hughie (*c.*1967), Harry (1980) and Ralph Northumberland (2018).

Three generations of Bedford dukes: Ian, Robin and Andrew, at a surprise party thrown for Robin's fiftieth birthday, 1990.

The 'Byronic' Tony Lambton, not quite the 6th Earl of Durham, in the halcyon days before he was caught in a sex scandal, 1961.

Edward Douglas-Scott-Montagu, 3rd Baron Montagu of Beaulieu, outside Lymington Magistrates' Court, after he was charged with a serious offence against a boy scout, 1954. He was subsequently tried at Winchester for the supposed crime of committing offences with a male person, and spent eight months in prison.

'Marg of Arg': Margaret Campbell, Duchess of Argyll, with Lady Edith Foxwell, 1959. Her divorce from Ian Campbell, 11th Duke of Argyll, in 1963 caused a very public scandal.

The aristocratic penchant for gambling was well served by John Aspinall, seen here (*on the left*) arriving at court with his financial director John Burke and mother Lady (Mary) Osborne in 1958, after police raided one of their gambling parties. He would go on to establish the Clermont Club, home from home for, among others, the 11th Duke of Marlborough and Lord Lucan.

Henry 'Master' Somerset, 10th Duke of Beaufort, who hunted both women and foxes in equal measure, being painted by Terence Cuneo, 1976.

The premier earl of England John Chetwynd-Talbot, 21st Earl of Shrewsbury, whose very public war with his wife Nadine ended in a messy divorce in 1963. Portrait by Cuthbert Julian Orde, 1937.

The flamboyant and eccentric Alexander Thynn, 7th Marquess of Bath, in front of one of the erotic murals that he painted at Longleat House, 1998.

A question of upbringing: Sebastian Browne, 12th Marquess of Sligo's christening, 1964. The future marquess is flanked by his parents Lord and Lady Ulick Browne.

An old-fashioned childhood in Scotland's largest inhabited house: Lord Ted Innes Ker and a nanny at Floors Castle in the early 1990s.

Mungo Mansfield squared: the 7th and 9th Earls taking tea, c.1958.

The 'Limpopo Twinkles': the
Hons. James and Charles Stuart
in the Bechuanaland Protectorate, where
they grew up before moving to Scotland
after their uncle's death, c.1943.

Lady Jane Grosvenor,
future Duchess of
Roxburghe, and the Hon.
Sarah Astor, preparing to
ride their horses from Land's
End to John o' Groats, 1972.

School days: the Eton
College Jazz Quartet,
featuring the future
2nd Baron Crathorne on
drums, 1958.

Moments in the season: Louis 'Dickie' Mountbatten, 1st Earl Mountbatten of Burma, at Cowes, 1965.

Harry Smith, 4th Viscount Hambleden, and Lady Annabel Birley (now Goldsmith) preparing for a Russian-themed night at Annabel's, the club her husband founded and named after her, 1966.

Maureen, Marchioness of Dufferin and Ava, one of the 'Golden Guinness Girls', with her daughters Ladies Caroline and Perdita Hamilton-Temple-Blackwood at a Hurlingham Club ball, 1952.

Guy and Virginia Innes Ker, 10th Duke and Duchess of Roxburghe, with their winning racehorse, Attraction, Newmarket, 2004.

Peers and monarchs: Bernard Fitzalan Howard, 16th Duke of Norfolk (*right*), one of the twentieth century's foremost dukes, with George VI, the future Elizabeth II and Queen Elizabeth at Epsom Racecourse, 1948.

Richard Montagu Douglas Scott, 10th Duke of Buccleuch, as Captain-General of the Royal Company of Archers with Elizabeth II at the Palace of Holyroodhouse, 2022.

Nicholas Alexander, 7th Earl of Caledon, with the future Charles III in Northern Ireland, 2021.

Working peers: Robin Russell, Marquess of Tavistock, the future 14th Duke of Bedford, at de Zoete & Bevan, the London-based stockbroker, 1974.

Tim Bentinck, 12th Earl of Portland, was born on a sheep station in Tasmania, and is now best known as David Archer in Radio 4's long-running series, *The Archers*, shown here on the set of the television drama *By the Sword Divided*, 1983.

Harry Primrose, 8th Earl of Rosebery, then Lord Dalmeny, chairman of Sotheby's taking bids, 2017.

An earl in hi-vis: John Stuart, 21st Earl of Moray, is following in his ancestors' footsteps and building a new town – Tornagrain, near Inverness, 2017.

whether or not the parents were around all the time, sometimes, or virtually never. After all, there were plenty of members of staff on hand to fulfil parental duties – notably, nannies. Growing up at Bowood in the 1930s, baby of the house Elizabeth Lambton (née Petty-Fitzmaurice) soon found that there were strict demarcations in the way the household operated: 'Girls stayed at home with nannies and governesses and the boys went off to school,' while 'our parents' lives were another "compartment".'[6] Only at certain times of the year did the constituent parts of the family actually come together.

The Hon. Fiona Campbell, who was born in 1932, the youngest daughter of Alastair Campbell, 4th Baron Stratheden and Campbell, a Coldstream Guards officer, similarly recalls a household at Hunthill House, in the Scottish Borders where the father was a distant figure, the mother only slightly less so, and the governess and nanny the centre of the children's world. 'One was looked after by a nanny, and then our governess. We came down after tea in our tidy clothes, and either were read to or played games.' Fiona's mother Jean 'always came to say goodnight to one when one had been put to bed', but spent much of her time working for the Girl Guides, ultimately becoming Girl Guide chief commissioner for the Commonwealth. 'I remember being rather disappointed that she was always going for meetings. She wasn't very present, but she was when she was there.' The Campbell girls' governess taught not only Fiona and her sister Clayre, but the children of family friends too. 'It was almost like a little school,' Fiona remembers. 'I was well read compared to some of my contemporaries who were at school.' Her father wasn't very grand, but she remembers how his rank affected the behaviour of those around him. 'The gamekeeper, who was old-fashioned, addressed him in the third person, and I think that would have been quite usual a generation back. If they were going shooting it would be, "Would His Lordship like to take the car?"' Such respect on the part of a servant to their master was not always matched by the children of the house. The late Mickey Suffolk recalled life at Charlton Park in the late 1930s and

1940s being something of a riot. 'The reason we were so badly educated,' he told me in 2018, 'was that when Nanny used to teach us,
we just used to disappear. With 123 rooms she would never find us.'

Alongside the nanny, as an ever-declining number of members
of the hereditary peerage recall, was a domestic world peopled
with butlers and maids, chauffeurs, French chefs and footmen.
Even relatively poorer aristocratic families during the middle decades of the twentieth century felt it necessary to maintain – and
present to the outside world – a certain lifestyle and the retinue of
servants that made that lifestyle possible. Gerald Fitzalan Howard
describes how in the 1920s and 1930s at Carlton Towers, home
of his grandfather Bernard Fitzalan Howard, 3rd Baron Howard
of Glossop, and his wife Mona Beaumont, all the niceties were
observed, despite tight family budgets. 'There was never much
money so there weren't endless servants,' he says. But they did
have a cook, 'who managed to poison the bull by giving it the
scraps', as well as two gardeners and a butler. Peaches were culti-
vated by the gardeners in the estate's walled garden, and Bernard
Howard would ship them down to London in the family's Rolls-
Royce. As Gerald's wife Emma puts it, '[T]hey weren't wealthy
per se but they had the lifestyle that aristocrats were supposed
to lead, with a Rolls-Royce and a five-storey house in Knightsbridge.' Her husband adds that, to be fair, '[T]he only reason they
had a Rolls-Royce is because it saved money on train fares – they
had eight children to get up and down to London.' Even after
the outbreak of the Second World War, some families managed
to preserve a semblance of the *ancien régime*. On the Arley estate
in Cheshire, home of the Warburton family since the twelfth century, Michael Ashbrook recalls there being 'gardeners still here,
and even a butler, though admittedly he was called up halfway
through. There were housemaids, a nanny and a cook all through
the war. My mother never cooked, and there were people that
came in to clean, and a chauffeur.'

For many aristocrats, the staff who looked after them were
more than servants. Alice Gloucester spoke for many when she

wrote 'what real family friends' those who worked for her family became. 'Some of them were part of the family as far as we were concerned, having been connected with us for generations.'[7] Children often formed strong relationships with those who had been with the family for a long time. When I visited Knepp Castle in West Sussex in 2018, Sir Charlie Burrell, 10th Baronet, told me all about those who looked after his grandparents in the 1960s: 'Mr Pink, for me, or Pink, for them, was the butler, Mrs Tewk was the cook and Mr Crook was the under-butler.' A woman named Edith Pugh had been his father Raymond's nursemaid, and she left Knepp after eighty-two years of service.' At Wentworth Woodhouse, house steward Samuel Garton worked for the Fitzwilliams for nearly forty-five years before his retirement in 1929. At Peter Fitzwilliam's coming-of-age party in 1932, another milestone was celebrated – the eightieth birthday of William Oates, accountant in the Wentworth estate office, who had been in service to the family for nearly sixty-five years. Peter's sisters had a governess called Kathleen 'Moffy' Moffat who had been their mother Maud's own much-loved governess at Aske Hall.

Even today, it's possible to catch an occasional glimpse of this otherwise largely vanished world. In 2015 I interviewed James Marlborough's then head butler at Blenheim Palace, Stephen Duckett, who now works as a calligrapher. A butler's role is a varied one, he told me. 'During the shooting season it's a very busy day, primarily involving care of the duke and duchess, their family and their guests. A lot of people expect [a butler to be] setting tables, serving at tables, serving from the bar, which is all true, but you're doing absolutely anything that is thrown at you, and caring for the restoration and conservation of the house.' The silver requires special attention: 'There's always a tug of war with how often do you polish it. If you polish it quite a lot then it's not good for conservation, but if you don't and it's being used then you have to bridge the gap.' It's no small task, either: there's so much silver at Blenheim that it can take two days to clean it. And, of course, everything else requires cleaning and tidying as well. 'What I think a lot of people don't understand in a house like this is that things have to be done regardless of whether there's somebody in residence or not. Everything has to be cleaned, everything has to be perfect so that when someone turns up, it's done. They can turn up at any time.'

In 2015, Duckett worked alongside a traditional team of indoor staff, with two trainee butlers, a housekeeper, a lady's maid, an 'understairs maid', a chef, the chef's assistant, a chauffeur, the duke's private secretary, a laundry lady and, at busy times, additional staff to help out with cleaning boots and other tasks.

> People think it's like Downton Abbey. They think of Carson, and a lot of people think of [P. G. Wodehouse's] Jeeves but he was never a butler – he was a valet, a general factotum, and he would follow his employer around. It's difficult to distinguish exactly what a butler is because it's such a subjective job, and a supremely relational job. You have to know your employer inside out or strive to do so. If you don't, there's no point.

The role is not without its fundamental challenges and contradictions.

> The greatest joy and one of the great difficulties in butlering is that [you work] for someone who, at the end of the day, goes home and can kick their shoes off, put their slippers by the fire and be themselves, whereas that's the forum that the butler works in – you're working in someone's home.

The Stephen Ducketts of this world are relatively rare beasts these days. More typical are the couple of 'dailies' employed by the nonagenarians Neil and Deirdre Rosebery, who lived, until July 2024 when Neil Rosebery died aged ninety-five, at Dalmeny House near Edinburgh in a reasonably low-key way for people of their position and generation. 'My mother hates having anybody fiddling so she won't have a cook,' her son Harry Primrose, 8th Earl of Rosebery, told me in 2019. 'We used to have a butler, years ago, but he retired and was never replaced. My grandparents lived in quite a formal way, but my parents have never really lived like that, they're not terribly grand.'

* * *

About 40 per cent of today's hereditary peers were born between the end of the Second World War and 1960, and a fair proportion of those had childhoods that weren't far removed from those of their parents and grandparents. The former Lord Chamberlain Willie Peel, 3rd Earl Peel, was born in 1947 and grew up at Hyning Hall in Lancashire, in an environment which 'by most people's standards would have been regarded as rather grand'. Holiday time was divided between Hyning and the 32,000-acre Gunnerside estate in North Yorkshire which his father Arthur Peel, 2nd Earl Peel, had bought in 1946. The Peels would decamp en masse to Gunnerside a couple of times a year, everyone travelling in an old American wood-panelled estate car that had once belonged to George Formby – except Arthur Peel, who took the Rolls-Royce.

Of course, grandness is relative, and the Peels were not so grand 'by many country house standards', says Willie Peel.

> I wouldn't describe either of my parents as being particularly grand, they were very down to earth actually. My father was very shy, he did a tremendous amount of good works in addition to running the family business which he inherited from his mother. I never got to know him as well as I would have liked. He was brought up in a Victorian environment and I was just beginning to get to know him when he died. There was an element of being seen and not heard, certainly. We had nannies, varying in quality. My mother ruled the domestic roost – we saw both of our parents quite a lot, but there was a discipline to the day.

Arthur Peel, great-grandson of the former prime minister Sir Robert Peel, lived as befitted a man of his rank, with a butler, housekeeper and maid, as well as a team of gardeners. From January 1962, the garden team was led by Edgar Kettlewell, whose son

David was a year older than Willie Peel. 'Lady Peel wasn't too bad, she had been a nurse during the war, and she had nursed Lord Peel who had had a leg injury,' David Kettlewell remembered. 'But if you saw Lord Peel [in the gardens] you would go and hide in the bushes and turn your back on him. He didn't speak to staff, he was the old school. You were there to do the work but you weren't to be spoken to, or to speak to him, you weren't allowed.' He spoke to Edgar '. . . by appointment. My dad used to be "Yes, m'lord, no, m'lord", that kind of thing.'[8]

Benjamin Mancroft remembers his 1960s childhood as being 'very nice', though the relationship with his father was at arm's length.

> My father was quite distant. Like a lot of his generation they were pushed away by mothers and nannies, and my father spent most of his life in his library, and we children spent most of our lives upstairs in the nursery. It was a very old-fashioned, Edwardian sort of upbringing, but it wasn't bad. My mother was gentle, affection-ate and very strong, and I was brought up by the most wonderful nanny. People always say, 'how awful to be brought up by a nanny', but I think, thank God I was brought up by a caring professional. If I'd been raised by two blithering idiots like my parents, I'd be a complete psychological wreck. They were kept as far away from us as possible. My father was a wonderful man, but not an easy father and had no idea what to say to us at all.

And he never learned.

> We hardly ever had a proper conversation, and then I left home, and then he died. He's been dead nearly forty years, and still now, driving along the motorway, I rehearse conversations that I'd like to have had with him, which we never had. I still meet people, bear-ing in mind how long he's been dead, who come up and say: 'I heard your father speaking about such and such a thing and he had such an impact on my life.' My sisters and I often go, 'Oh, yeah, lucky you, he had no effect on ours.' He was marvellous with other

people, but hopeless with us. He used to communicate through my mother. She'd say, 'Your father thinks, your father says, your father would like you to . . .', and we'd think, why can't he tell us himself? But he just couldn't. Extraordinary.

Crispin Money-Coutts, 9th Baron Latymer, born in 1955, had a similar 'classic English upbringing' in a large house in Hampshire where the nanny and the three children lived on the top floor. 'We each had our own bedroom, Nanny had a bedroom, and there was a kitchen and bathroom,' he remembers. His father Hugo Latymer went up to London on Sunday nights, and '. . . reappeared after we had gone to bed on Friday evening, so we didn't see a lot of him. My mother used to go up to London on Tuesday afternoon to be with Dad, and she came back on Thursday evening, so we saw a bit more of her. We thought that was normal – we had staff, and we had a small farm, so we were either up at the farm playing in the haystacks, or else we were being taken to school by Nanny.' This was the Money-Coutts children's comfortable rhythm until 1963 when Hugo and his wife Ann separated, and Hugo went off with Jinty Calvert, a cousin of Ann's – and, as his son puts it, 'one of the most beautiful women in the world'. He was thirty-seven and she was nineteen. With this, Hugo Latymer disappeared from his children's life for three years, sailing across the Atlantic and the Pacific, and eventually settling in Majorca. 'I suppose my friends will think I'm crazy,' he said at the time, 'but I'm tired of fighting my way across London's traffic and tussling with people in the Underground. Everything has come easy to me in life so far, now I want to try it the hard way.'[9]

The children, plus nanny, moved up to London, where Ann bought a house next door to her mother Evelyn Emmet, later Baroness Emmet of Amberley, in a mews off Eaton Terrace, and 'rented a house on the other side for Nanny and us'. This all seemed perfectly normal at the time, he says. 'I remember sitting on the end of my bed with my brother Giles when Mum had a drinks party or a dinner party. We'd pull back the curtains and play Spot Mum. If you look at it through the lens of the modern day it was not only enormously privileged but something that very few families did or still do.' Subsequently, he would see his father for a fortnight a year. 'We were never particularly close,' he says. 'Mum never married again and was incredibly discreet about having any male friends. It was quite a relief going on to boarding school because you got surrounded by friends. In those days parents couldn't come down at the weekend. In the Easter term you might have had a Sunday where you saw them.'

Lady Silvy McQuiston was born in 1958, the youngest of her father Henry Bath's five children and the only one from her father's second marriage to her mother Virginia Tennant. Henry Bath did not always have a good relationship with his three sons. His eldest son Alexander Weymouth, later Alexander Bath, knew that he was much wanted by his parents, 'in the sense that I was in some way the fulfilment of a parental ambition', but his relationship with his father was always quite reserved.[10] His 'general approach towards me was often to adopt a teasing tone, which I frequently misread,' he remembered. On one occasion, Henry asked him which of his parents he liked best. '"Come on," he said, "you can tell us. We won't be angry."'[11] Alexander told him it was his mother Daphne, and Henry left the room. Daphne then 'went to great pains to explain to me that what I ought to have answered was that I loved the two of them equally, which was such an evident falsehood that I couldn't understand why she wanted me to say such things.'[12]

By the time Silvy came along, Henry was fifty-three and had mellowed. Being a girl, Silvy never had a shot at inheriting Longleat, but she got the best of her father. Today, she still lives in his old house, a former mill near Longleat. Scarcely touched since the 1950s, it's cosily decorated. Silvy uses Henry's office, just as it was, with an estate map of Longleat on a pulley against the wall. Reminders of Henry and Virginia are all over the house: their photographs and illustrations everywhere; their gardening tools hanging on the wall in the hall, where they were originally lined up by a fastidious Henry who was, says Silvy, '. . . beautifully tidy.

If you didn't put the screwdriver back on the wall, he would go around asking who had taken it.' He was also a stickler for good manners. 'He couldn't bear it if my fork was showing out of the side of my hand while I was eating and would shout "Fork!"' He was a lovely father to Silvy, though perhaps a little less so to her brothers. 'He beat Alexander for washing the dog once, and Alexander understandably held that against him.' Alexander remembered that the beating that followed this incident '. . . was the softest that I'd ever received . . . it was the humiliation and the destruction of our relationship that truly hurt . . . I was outraged that he should judge that I had done anything that deserved a beating.'[13] He took himself off to his room and cried. 'Dad felt that Alexander shouldn't be too pleased with himself, being the future marquess,' says Silvy. 'They had a difficult relationship. Dad told a story about a time when a band was playing outside Longleat and he and Alexander went to watch. Alexander was about five, and while the band were playing he played a whistle and Dad really told him off. He felt he was bigging himself up, but this poor little boy was just playing his whistle. Alexander himself said that his respect for Henry never recovered from the beating over the wet dog.' 'On the whole,' says Silvy, 'we can be a bit cold, the Thynnes.'

Strict fathers emerge as something of a recurring motif in any study of the aristocracy. Mungo Mansfield had to endure a stern father who had a rather unpleasant way with words.

It's difficult to get the idea across because of the idiotic counter-psychological view that sticks and stones may break my bones but words may never hurt me. A lot of people don't understand how wounding words can be, and at times my father was very wounding. I don't think perhaps he intended to be. He was looking for an improvement. He wasn't like Tatton Sykes [4th Baronet] – not the present one, an eighteenth-century one, who thrashed his son because he discovered that the son owned a toothbrush. [His father] . . . could be really jolly tough indeed. It was mostly my brother James and me who were regarded as being below the required level. There was a time when he said my brother should be more enterprising and show more initiative, whereupon my brother then set himself up as the Loretto School[14] wine merchant. The school authorities didn't like that. My father had to explain to James that this wasn't quite actually what he meant.

Benjamin Mancroft reckons that his was the last generation to experience that kind of Victorian childhood. Ted Innes Ker, born in 1984, begs to differ. The Roxburghe children, he says, had an old-fashioned life at Floors on the nursery corridor at the top of the house. 'I just about remember the rigidity of formal childhood – we were dressed for tea and presented for a cuddle and a slice of cake,' says Ted. 'If our parents wanted to come and see us then they would, but we were a long way up.' The house, with hot and cold running staff, enabled this old-world structure. 'It's pretty big,' says Ted of Floors, which is often described as Scotland's largest inhabited castle. 'If one of the children is crying and you want to run upstairs to check, it's not exactly a quick journey. These really big houses lend themselves to Nanny staying on the top corridor where the kids are.'

After the Roxburghes divorced in 1990, Jane Roxburghe moved to a smaller house seven miles away, where if her children called from the top of the stairs she would be able to hear them. 'If I called from the top of the stairs at Floors, you would struggle to hear me. I wouldn't be able to get to the stairs anyway, there was a closed door in between,' says Ted. Before he went to boarding school, Ted would visit his father at Floors during the week. 'I remember the sound of the wind,' he says. 'My brother and sister weren't there, my mum wasn't there, and my dad was miles away. I felt quite lonely up there at night. I asked if I could come down and sleep in Dad's dressing room, so I would do that instead of being up in my bedroom.' Now himself a father of two, he runs around with his children non-stop. 'It's so important to have a massive role in your children's upbringings, which is not to say that my parents weren't involved with our upbringing as they were, but we were brought up in a different time to the extremely hands-on way we tend to parent these days.'

William Seymour, Earl of Yarmouth, eldest son of Harry and Beatriz Seymour, 9th Marquess and Marchioness of Hertford, similarly experienced the aristocratic life of a former era at Ragley Hall in Warwickshire in the 1990s. Memories of childhood create a reflective mood in William. 'Hindsight is everything,' he says when we meet at his farmhouse near Ragley. 'I recognise that it was definitely a privileged childhood. People would come round the house and go: "This is amazing." I knew surely this is not usual.' 'I recognise the fact that not everyone has their house open to the public with people walking around seeing photos of you in nappies,' he goes on. 'It's not comfortable but it's kind of accepted that that's what brought the business in. I also recognise the fact that we had this amazing landscape, this amazing heritage, this amazing house, and it needs to be looked after.' An unsaid 'but' lingers in the air and emerges after he describes the appreciation of art, history, mythology, classical literature and music he developed as he grew up, and when he begins to talk about his relationship with his parents. Harry Hertford has talked of how, as a dyslexic, he struggled at school, and left Harrow as soon as he could; his first job was as a shepherd for Johnny Montagu Douglas Scott, 9th Duke of Buccleuch, at Boughton House in Northamptonshire. William, though, knows little about his father's own childhood but says: 'I think my grandfather cast a pretty big shadow that is still felt to this day, and that for anyone is a really hard act to follow, almost impossible.' After his father died in 1997, though he had already been running Ragley for seven years, Harry Hertford admitted that sometimes he felt like 'a prisoner marking off crosses on the wall'.[15]

When I visited the Hertfords in 2016 to interview the two of them together, Beatriz Hertford said: 'What my parents-in-law went through [in rescuing Ragley from demolition and making it a going concern] was unspeakable. I cannot imagine what a life they had, and my husband has been very proud to be part of it.' William, she said then, was '... very close to his father, [always] going to things together . . . [it] is very useful to know that the next generation is pre-pared to take it on so lightly, it's a relief.' She spoke of how Ragley takes two. 'A big house like Ragley needs a degree of partnership, and we girls tend to notice different things. It's a partnership and it would not exist if we both didn't want the same things.' Their aim, she said, was '. . . for our son to inherit in the best possible way in the best possible state, and so it will never be a white elephant in his life.'

This contrasts with what William says about his father now. 'When I was a child, my father wasn't a talkative man. If you opened the door to his study, he would be working at the computer, and you would have to do or say something quite outstanding for him to look away. You realised [later] that he may not have been working but perhaps playing spider solitaire.' In 1987, Harry Hertford had an accident in which he broke his neck. He was later diagnosed with ataxia, a condition similar to multiple scler-osis in some of its effects. 'For a long while it wasn't clear to us what he was ailing from,' says William, 'but he was in discomfort. I kept hearing, "Your father is being tough on you . . . we're being hard on you because we don't know the future, so you need to be prepared."' He accepts that he didn't know his father before his accident, when he was active on the hunting field, and long before when he was a cowboy in Texas. He also knows now that his father is fond of poetry, and of Russia, where he went with his wife on their honeymoon. However, he only found this out because his father 'kept telling other people about it'.

After a three-year stint living in Brazil, William was sent to boarding school. The reality of his position as heir was brought home to him when as a young teenager he was told to join the trustees' meetings, and had to be taken out of school from time to time to attend them. 'I never had the voice to say no,' he says. 'I was meant to listen, agree and be quiet, and focus on how it's meant to be done.' His position as heir became integral to his whole exist-ence. 'I was always informed that I needed to be a part of Ragley, and that I['d] need to know this and that because I would inherit it like my father had done when he was in his thirties. I was told very clearly that I would be expected to take over the reins from my father when I turned thirty.' He was sent on a course to learn about what to do in a kidnapping scenario, for example, while his siblings were not, and saw the difference in their childhoods in sharp relief when he turned twenty-one. 'My siblings were given the choice for their twenty-first birthdays of would you like a party or a car? While there's no hardship either way, I was told that I was having a party because "the estate" needed to invite the tenants, and have the trustees over – it was a formal coming-of-age.' William Yarmouth married Kelsey Wells in 2018, with whom he has two sons – Clement, the future 11th Marquess of Hertford, who was born in 2019, and Jocelyn, who was born in 2021 – neither of whom, the Yarmouths say, have been welcomed by their paternal grandparents, as the relationship between the generations has broken down.

Like William Yarmouth and Ted Innes Ker, almost all of the twenty-seven millennial peers went away to board at school, some many hundreds of miles from home. This practice still goes on: as one Scottish landowner once told me of his Generation Z children: 'They're at boarding school down south – they get deposited at Glasgow and get on a Flybe.' Of the twenty-four of the twenty-seven millennial peers whose schooling I could confirm, five went to Eton College – a relatively high proportion, though considerably lower than that for the current peerage as a whole – while all the others, bar one, attended independent, fee-paying schools, and all but two boarded at school. For the wider peerage, the homogeny is even more stark. Less than 3 per cent of the 793 current hereditary peers were educated at state schools. The overwhelming majority attended about 130 fee-paying schools scattered around the world, and over half were educated at the seven English schools termed 'public schools' by the Public Schools Act 1868: Charterhouse, Eton, Harrow, Rugby, Shrewsbury, Westminster and Winchester. Almost 90 per cent of them attended boarding schools for at least a part of their education, and in many cases from the age of eight.

* * *

Being sent away to school at a young age proved traumatic for some. James Crathorne describes how during the Second World War he was initially educated at the village school in Crathorne in North Yorkshire, where he felt 'completely immune from the world', even though he could hear the noise of aerial bombardments on Teesside. He had, he says, no idea what was causing the racket, and told his mother how he wished 'the bangs would come closer'. He can still vividly remember the look of absolute horror on her face. That early school experience was almost always a joy, even though he recalls once '. . . being beaten on the hand by the headmistress. She was a great friend of my mother's and rang up to say that she'd had to cane me for persistent talking to my neighbour, who was an attractive girl who also lived in the village.' But then, aged eight, he was ripped from his home on the estate that his great-grandfather had bought a century earlier, and sent 230 miles away to board at preparatory school at Cothill House in Oxfordshire. 'The day I was taken down to prep school in the south was one of the most traumatic days of my life, being left suddenly by my parents,' he says. 'I still have memories of that really terrible moment.' He learned later it was difficult for his mother, Nancy, too. 'She really hated the idea of my brother David and me going away to school.'

After five years at Cothill, he went to Eton in the Lent term of 1953. This, he remembers, was simply a given, '. . . because my father and grandfather went there. There wasn't ever a discussion about where I went on to school – I was going.' An arty, musical boy, who enjoyed his time in the pottery at Eton and playing drums in a jazz group, he went through the public school system 'hoping not to be noticed very much, which is more or less what happened'. Other peers seem to have had a similarly neutral experience. Richard Buccleuch, for example, says that school – prep school in Berkshire and then Eton – was '[A] sort of non-event that passed me by. On the whole I got through school, I got by. It didn't really matter. You were there, and then you went on.' Even being the son of a peer didn't necessarily attract much attention. John Attlee remembers that when he was at prep school in the 1960s he was teased for being a socialist, on the grounds that his grandfather Clem had served as Labour prime minister from 1945 to 1951. 'I didn't know what a socialist was. I didn't know what I had done wrong,' he remembers. Once he went to Stowe School in Buckinghamshire aged thirteen, he was largely left alone: 'Nobody cared at all, they weren't interested in politics.'

For some, though, the title proved something of a millstone. Piers North, 10th Earl of Guilford, was relentlessly bullied at prep school over the courtesy title he then held – Lord North. 'The idea of the title and specifically the word "lord" had a bigger effect on me in a negative way than it ever did in a positive way,' he says. 'My parents hadn't brought me up to be the Big I Am. I was so unhappy, such a skinny, weak kid. By the time I was sixteen I had become a martial arts instructor, thinking, no one's ever going to beat me up again.'

Rod Balfour, who attended Eton in the 1960s, similarly came under attack for his name, though in his case the barbs were slightly better-natured. 'I was teased mercilessly at Eton about Arthur Balfour,' he remembers. 'In the 1960s he came across as this sort of foppish, wimpy character who had overseen the biggest loss by the Tory Party ever in history.' He recalls that a member of the Churchill family, who happened to be in his house, 'always mobbed me up about it', and bemoans the fact that because he hadn't learned about the early setbacks in Winston Churchill's career – notably the fiasco of the Gallipoli campaign in the First World War – he wasn't armed to retaliate. One peer remembers how one of the masters whipped the back of his legs as he lagged behind during a cross-country run, shouting, '"Hurry up, m'lord." The title seemed to mean more to them [the teachers] than the boys.' Another was told that, because he was a lord, he would be given the task of cleaning the blackboard every day.

Even in the supposedly progressive 1960s many public schools remained resolutely old-fashioned. Senior boys still ruled the roost, much as they had done back in the days of the fictional

Tom Brown. Junior boys, known as fags, had to run errands, and corporal punishment, administered both by senior pupils and masters, was the common order of the day. It was finally made illegal in 1998. The headmaster at Eton during James Crathorne's time there was the Old Rugbeian and former headmaster of Charterhouse Robert Birley, who was one of the authors of the 1944 Fleming Report, which considered the relationship between Britain's leading independent boarding schools and the state, and a former adviser to the Control Commission in the British Zone in post-war Germany, where he had a role in rewriting Nazi history textbooks. Some of the boys, remembers James Crathorne, called him '"Red Robert", because of his left-wing views'.[16] 'Of course,' he adds, 'none of us had anything to do with him. The only time I met him was when I was leaving school and he gave us all our leaving book.' Yet he presided over an institution where beatings were still permitted.

James Crathorne himself wasn't often beaten, but does vividly recall one particular occasion when he was given 'six of the best' by an older pupil. His crime had been to miss 'boy call' – an Eton custom that involved one of the senior boys (or a member of the 'library'[17] as they were known) standing outside his room and shouting 'boyyyyy-up' in a very loud voice to summon the junior boys to carry out some task for him. The last one to arrive had to fulfil the commission. On this occasion, the task involved taking a letter to a boy in another house, but 'all the boys who should have run were in the same room, and they decided to sit tight'. 'The problem was', remembers James Crathorne, 'that I was sitting on the window ledge, and a member of the library walking across The Field[18] spotted that I was there, and knew I should have run, but I was the only one that they could see. He had no idea that we were all in the same room.' The senior boy beat him very hard for this minor infraction. 'It was a pretty severe beating, for failing to run. I think a slightly more assured boy would not have felt it necessary to beat with such vehemence.' Boys came to see if the older boy had done a good job, judged by the distance between each stroke – a good job having very little space between one stroke and the next. 'The marks were still visible the next half.[19] Being beaten was just part of school life and we never really thought much about it – looking back it now seems somewhat barbaric.' It was such a part of school life for many that they bragged to their fathers back home about having done a good job in one beating or other.

Eton finally did away with corporal punishment in the early 1980s. Former Eton geography master and future headmaster of Harrow Barnaby Lenon was there when the decision was made. 'One day in "chambers", the mid-morning staff meeting, the then headmaster Eric Anderson called all the house list-makers – the people who were going to be housemasters but weren't yet housemasters – into a back room and said, "We need to decide what we're going to do about caning. Though I don't cane boys, there are one or two housemasters that do and I'd be interested to know your views." So we had a vote, and we voted to end caning. I think it ended on that very day, even though none of us had ever used a cane or seen anyone being caned. It hadn't formally been abolished in the school but we abolished it on that day.'

Fagging also took a long time to die. It had not been a feature of the earliest public schools – those founded in the Middle Ages – but it had become common during the seventeenth and eighteenth centuries when boys from the upper classes attended in ever greater numbers. And once established, it proved remarkably resilient. As historian Malcolm Falkus puts it, '[B]eing drawn from an aristocratic elite the boys . . . were prone, even more than other boys, to be intensely jealous of tradition and established patterns of behaviour.'[20] Over the years, various headmasters tried to reform it – notably the Charterhouse headmaster John Russell in 1811 – but they were rebuffed, and by Victorian times it had come to be seen as such a fundamental feature of public school education that it was deemed by some heads even to be essential. 'I hardly know which is most useful,' wrote George Moberly, headmaster of Winchester College from 1835 to 1866, 'the habit of obedience which it requires from the lower boys or the exercise of authority on the part of the higher ones. It appears to me to be admirable on both sides.'[21] Giving evidence to the Clarendon Commission in 1864, Henry Butler, headmaster of Harrow, was emphatic about the power of boy governance: '[N]o great school could long live in a healthy state without it,' he argued; 'the only true way to govern boys is to train them to govern themselves.'[22]

When James Crathorne went to Eton in 1953, he fagged for Ben Guinness, Viscount Elveden, the future 3rd Earl of Iveagh, 'a nice man', he remembers. 'One had to cook eggs and tidy the rooms. You were like an orderly. You made beds, polished shoes, all very important.' In time he, too, had a boy to fag for him, and if he can't now remember his name, he believes that just as 'Ben Elveden was particularly nice to me', so 'certainly I would have been nice to my fag'. Fagging at Eton was finally done away with twenty-two years after he left, the headmaster responsible for its demise, Michael McCrum, describing it as 'outdated' and suggesting that '[O]utsiders are inclined to look at it in terms of *Tom Brown's Schooldays*.'[23] The news was not well received by all Old Etonians. 'With the utmost disgust we hear that fagging has been abolished at Eton,' wrote the explorers Sir Ranulph Fiennes, 3rd Baronet, and Oliver Shepard from Ryvingen Camp, Antarctica on 30 April 1980. 'As the two most southerly OEs in the world, over-wintering in cardboard huts prior to an attempt on the South Pole, we daily empty lavatories, clean and cook. Having spent two or three years of our formative years doing menial tasks for others, this comes easily. Many who go to Eton need their self-esteem lowered and fagging was an excellent way of achieving this.'[24]

The practice receives mixed reviews from Old Etonian peers. Some, like the actor Charlie Shaughnessy, 5th Baron Shaughnessy, who went to Eton in 1968, remember it quite fondly. It was, Charlie says, an '... incredibly clever system. You would arrive as a young kid from your prep school where you were the captain of the eleven, head boy, you think you're the bee's knees. Then suddenly, you're in this big pond, you're a junior, you don't know where you are. It's good for you to recognise that it's all relative. Just because you were a big cheese in the last place, it doesn't mean that you're a big cheese there. You're the same as everyone.' His memory is that fagging was never really very taxing.

> You'd wake them up with a cup of tea, polish their shoes, do their errands. When you were a junior you didn't have much going on. You had this huge school and nothing to do, and this gave you a job. You would meet your fellow fags as you were running around school, figuring out where everything was. You learned how the world worked around you so you could be a worker bee in it. You had a purpose, and you had a senior guy who was your personal mentor. He was a big cheese, and he knows *you*, and he is looking after *you*. And then you grow up and get to that point yourself, and you get someone to work for you, and you learn how to be responsible for giving orders to someone and looking after their welfare. [T]here were cases when it crashed and burned because of the personalities involved [but] where it worked, and in my case it did, it was a brilliant system.

Some are more ambivalent, if not downright critical. Charles Beauclerk, who arrived at Eton as Lord Vere of Hanworth a decade after Charlie Shaughnessy, feels that it could be unfair. 'It gave boys a lot of power over others at a young age. I had only been there a few days when I was punished for missing chapel. I missed it because my fag-master, the head of house, had told me to make his bed, and I hadn't made it satisfactorily, so he asked me to make it again.' He reflects that the idea was that: '[Y]ou put up with it so that one day you could exercise that same power. For it to work, you had to want to exercise that kind of power. But I wasn't thinking, if I'm obedient now I'll get to lord it over someone else.' He contrived to leave Eton as soon as he could.

* * *

There's a common assumption – not least among some Old Etonians – that Eton is the best school in the world. Whether or not it is true today, it certainly wasn't the case in the immediate post-Second World War period. Benjamin Mancroft says that it '... deteriorated after the war. I suspect it wasn't a very good school. Nobody had got a grip on it, and all the beaks were too old.' He largely blames the leadership. 'The post-war headmaster Anthony Chenevix-Trench became a drunk, and it wasn't until he had beaten about half the school that they realised that it wasn't working. Then they brought in Michael McCrum, who was a rather cold academic who didn't seem to like boys at all, to sort out the educational side of it, which he did.'

Today, a teacher at Eton needs a '... a degree (2:1 or above) and/or a further degree in a directly related subject ... strong inter-personal skills ... a positive attitude, an optimistic approach to change and development, a balanced sense of perspective and a good sense of humour'.[25] In the past, a modicum of eccentricity seems to have been a not uncommon trait – as it was in many English public schools (and indeed in many novels about public schools: Captain Grimes, the one-legged war veteran turned beak in Evelyn Waugh's debut novel *Decline and Fall*, who says that he 'thinks' he lost a leg in the war but who was 'actually run over by a tram in Stoke-on-Trent' when he was 'one-over-the-eight', is an old Harrovian[26]). One who fitted the eccentric profile was the bachelor housemaster and classics beak Charlie Rowlatt, an Old Etonian himself, who had been gassed during the First World War while serving with the Rifle Brigade and who returned to his old school permanently in 1920, supposedly with a 'tin stomach and a head entirely held together by wire'.[27] George Lascelles, the future 7th Earl of Harewood, was placed in Rowlatt's house in 1936, and remembered him as 'a disciplinarian, good at not interfering but also skilful at knowing what was going on. He was on that account a good housemaster, but an odd, remote, rather uncultivated kind of person, very much a bachelor and, my mother used to think, thoroughly scared of women. He thought of the arts as peripheral, and he wouldn't let anyone in the house act in school plays.'[28] Rowlatt would, the writer Quentin Crewe remembered, '... cover his mouth with a vast, expensive handkerchief and announce thickly: "I am a passionate man." He would then sit silent, shivering with rage, for half an hour. We sat, trembling too, with nothing to do.'[29] He worked as an assistant master for thirty-two years, before becoming vice-provost in 1952, and dying in post seven years later.

The artist Wilfrid Blunt went to work in the drawing school at Eton in 1938, where he stayed for twenty-one years. In his department was a second drawing master, Llewelyn Menzies-Jones, universally known as 'Mones', but not, he insisted, 'Moans'. He existed in '. . . a kind of dream-world,' remembered Blunt, 'in a different era or stratum from the rest of us. Had he said "Prithee" one would hardly have been aware of it.'[30] Aged almost fifty he once raced a group of boys around the parade ground at 7.30 a.m. and was beaten by Johnnie Spencer, the future 8th Earl Spencer.

Claude Beasley-Robinson also ticked the eccentric box for the mid-century Eton master. An 'eager-faced man' with a 'measure of religious mania', he was prone to raising his hands in geometry class to pronounce, 'Chaps, chaps, God is in this room.'[31] A wealthy man, he loved hunting, God, and cars, and drove a Vauxhall 30-98 Wensum called the Yellow Peril. Such a devotee of religion was he that he had a room in his house converted into an oratory. When he left Eton in 1946, he swapped hunting for the church and became Father Claude SSJE. The oratory was subsequently deconsecrated. Another rich beak, who returned to Eton as a master in 1947, was the Hon. Giles St Aubyn, son of Francis 'Sam' St Aubyn, 3rd Baron St Levan, the owner of St Michael's Mount in Cornwall. One day, when accused by a colleague of extravagance, he replied, 'I'm not extravagant, I'm just *rich*.'[32] The newly appointed provost Sir Nicholas Coleridge, who went to Eton in 1970, recalled St Aubyn's displays of wealth. To fill time, he would jangle coins in his pocket, and say, 'I have a quantity of money in my pocket. If any boy can guess what it is to the nearest half pence, they can have it. But before you guess, you must bear two things in mind. One, I am very well dressed, so I would not have very much change in my pocket. On the other hand, it is well known that I am immensely rich, so for all you know I could have many, many thousands of pounds, without it causing me the slightest of problems.'[33]

In 1955, over a third of Eton beaks were old boys themselves, and almost half had been to Oxford or Cambridge. Unsurprisingly for the mid-1950s, a fair number had served during the Second World War – classics beak David Macindoe, later vice-provost, was awarded the Military Cross; Sappers officer Cyril Chamier was injured at Dunkirk, spent two years in and out of hospital and then joined Eton as general manager of the school stores and as a maths beak where he remained for the next thirty-two years; John Bolton contracted polio in Palestine and was almost totally paralysed, before returning home to England where he got a degree in natural sciences from Cambridge and moved into teaching, joining Eton as a biology beak in 1953, where he was, despite his disability, an enthusiastic junior rugger coach, and part of the Combined Cadet Force. He died in 1968, having written a note to his wife saying that he '. . . felt he had become, like Captain Oates in Scott's Antarctic Expedition, a burden to his companions'.[34] Still working at Eton in 1955 were a number of First World War veterans too. Leslie Jaques managed to get his Military Cross despite only having left school in 1917; Julian Lambart did four years on the Western Front and promptly returned to Eton in 1919, seven years and a whole world war after he'd left it, while his colleague Charles Mayes was injured at the Somme and declared unfit for any future service abroad. Many of them could be considered part of a group of masters who '. . . radically affected the character of the school. They were the least school-masterly of schoolmasters, combining sound scholarship with the keenest appreciation of the absurd. All pedantry, stuffiness and pretentiousness were blown out of the window on a genial gale of mirth,' as Eton housemaster Matthew Nicholson put it in his 1983 obituary of the classics beak Francis Cruso, who was '[P]erhaps the most genial of them all. One could not go near him without finding him surrounded by folk in fits of laughter.' Of course, Nicholson went on, it wasn't that Cruso lacked '. . . seriousness in his approach to life or learning. No one could be fiercer when a rebuke was deserved, and no one was more dismissive of the vulgar, both in style and language. When a self-admiring preacher enquired rhetorically: "But am I being fanciful?" "No, only boring", was the response overheard by Francis' neighbour in the pew.'[35]

Some went on to teach at other schools, but many devoted their lives to the school: both Julian Lambart and Charles Mayes gave fifty years of service to Eton. Some inspired their charges. Some terrified them. Some were victims of their practical jokes.[36] 'It was the commitment of the boys to break our housemaster Watkin "Fishy" Williams,' remembers Michael Exeter, who went to Eton in 1949, and had not initially enjoyed it before deciding one day, while standing in a bookshop in town looking out at the rain, that he should change his attitude 'from struggling to survive to taking hold of my life'. Taking hold of his life included joining a group of boys from his house who one night went up onto the roof of the house when Williams, who had a very short temper, was having a dinner party downstairs. 'He had a white tablecloth on the table, and we dropped a firecracker down the chimney that went to the dining room, and they were sitting there having dinner when it exploded in the fireplace and blew ashes all over the room. He came rushing up to find out who had done this, furious, but we were all back in our rooms, the picture of innocence!'

This eccentric note in school life survived the immediate post-war period. The history beak Michael Kidson, who retired from Eton after almost thirty years in 1994, became something of a legend as far as the boys were concerned. He was prone to walking his dog along Eton High Street off the lead, barking – he, rather than the dog – at lorry drivers when his dog got in their way. Mungo Mansfield once had the temerity to stroke one of Kidson's dogs and was told, 'Don't touch my dog! You'll give it fleas.'[37] Kidson was beloved by the boys, who looked forward to his lessons and wanted to impress him, even if he deliberately got their names wrong. The former banker Charlie Egerton-Warburton was known as Forbes-Cockell, '. . . because someone of that name had sat in my seat in div [lesson] three or four years earlier and also had a double-barrelled name.'[38] When two German exchange students called Bommel and Hoffman came to Eton, they became, as former prime minister David Cameron remembered, Rommel and Hofmeister. One boy whose name Kidson did get right was Charles Spencer, 9th Earl Spencer, then Viscount Althorp, who was told that he must be a 'fearful ignoramus' if he couldn't pronounce his own name properly – 'Alltrup', rather than 'Allthorpe'.[39]

* * *

Eton was founded in 1440 by Henry VI to provide free education to poor boys. Later, it developed a reputation for being a school of, and for, the rich. As former master and vice-provost Tim Card puts it, by 1860 the school's main draw wasn't academic success, but social climbing: 'the desire of parents to have their sons in a school that enjoyed royal favour, and where they would meet the right company'.[40] 'Examinations did not play a large part in the lives of any but the most gifted scholars,' remembered the former foreign secretary Peter Carrington, who went to Eton in 1932. 'If one aspired to go to Oxford or Cambridge it was taken for granted one would get there. Few boys worried greatly about future employment or the gaining, one day, of qualifications.'[41] The same was true in James Crathorne's time, twenty years later. 'Being brainy at Eton was not a particularly admired attribute; skill playing games was considered much more important,' he remembers. An exception was made for the scholars, the colleger, nicknamed 'tugs' after the Latin *gens togata*, 'togaed people', since they wore robes. But then these colleger were 'much despised', remembered Quentin Crewe of his wartime Eton experience.[42] One Old Etonian peer quipped to me, '[A]s Marcus Kimball said about [former Conservative foreign secretary] Douglas Hurd, "The thing about tugs is that they're just not sound."' The same peer pointed to Quintin Hailsham, and his son Douglas Hogg, 3rd Viscount Hailsham, both Eton scholars: 'too clever by half'. Quintin Hailsham accepted that he was 'too clever', but 'not "by half" '.[43] What Eton was looking for, says John Claughton, who joined the Eton's classics department in 1984, was not academic excellence but 'breadth'.

For well-heeled, well-connected parents, admission to Eton was – until about the turn of the millennium – a relatively painless task. You put your son down for the school at birth by asking one of the housemasters (whom you knew personally or by repute) to add them to the house list. With any luck, he would agree, and thirteen years later, provided your son passed the common entrance exam, he would be offered a place at the school. In other words, provided you had the contacts and the money, your son was virtually guaranteed an Eton education. Nor was Eton alone in soft-pedalling the academic factor. Harrow had a similar ethos. When Barnaby Lenon arrived there as headmaster in 1999 – having spent twelve years at Eton teaching geography – he found that there was no official admissions team, and that boys would turn up for a new year at school without anyone really knowing they were coming.

The house list system puzzled many incoming middle-class, non-Etonian housemasters and masters. Lenon began making a house list in 1983. 'Parents would ring me up and say, "Can we come and see you, Mr Lenon?" They would turn up, a young, probably Old Etonian and his wife and their tiny baby, born maybe a month ago. I would interview them – the boy with some difficulty – and then I would offer them a place, and that was it.' When in 1986 he had an appraisal with Eton's headmaster Eric Anderson, he was asked if there was anything he wished to say about the school. He told Anderson that he thought the admissions system was 'absolutely bonkers', given that he was having to assess children under the age of one. In time, an admissions review committee was set up, with Lenon on it, which began the process of reform that led to the wholesale scrapping of the house list system, and a new system whereby you cannot apply to a house until you have passed the entrance tests aged eleven.

While on the admissions review committee, Lenon asked why the system had been set up that way. 'Nobody was sure,' he says, but many felt it suited the school. 'Having a certain proportion of Old Etonians as parents meant that they knew what to expect. There is something to be said for any school having a proportion of alumni's children, because then there is no misunderstanding about how the school works.' He left Eton in 1990, before succeeding to the house for which he had been building his list, to become deputy head of Highgate School. 'I decided that I would rather be a deputy head than a housemaster,' he says. After Highgate, he took the headship of Trinity School in Croydon, before that of Harrow in 1999.

Given the family connection element of the traditional public school, it's scarcely surprising that of the 40 per cent of current hereditary peers who were educated at Eton, almost 60 per cent have fathers who also attended Eton, and at least 43 per cent also have paternal grandfathers who went to the school. The 'old school tie' has a resonance with and hold over certain families, regardless of whether or not the latest graduate enjoyed their experience. Take James Crathorne. Despite having only 'got through' Eton, he put his own son, Thomas, down for the school when he was born, and off he duly went in 1991. For Nicholas Monson, 12th Baron Monson, Eton was the only option – not just for him but for his son Alexander. 'My family have been going to Eton, every male member, since 1745, the time of the Jacobite rebellion, so we have all had our characters shaped by it, my father and my father's father, and so on and so forth. I did actually feel genetically that this was correct, that I was right being here.'[44] With three weeks of Alexander's birth in 1984, Nicholas had put him down for Eton. It was, to him, a natural reflex. The 'force of history' was at work.[45]

The peerage family with probably the longest relationship with Eton are the Earls of Carnarvon, with Geordie Herbert, 8th Earl of Carnarvon, the eighth in his line to have attended the school since the 1st Earl was admitted in the 1750s, and his son and heir, George Herbert, Lord Porchester, following suit in 2006. The Carnarvons are rivalled by the Earls of Romney (eight consecutive generations of Etonians) and the Marquesses of Salisbury (seven;

the pattern was broken by Robert and Hannah Salisbury who sent their eldest son to the King's School, Canterbury in the 1980s). The Dukes of Roxburghe, the Viscounts Downe, the Earls of Jersey and the Earls of Dudley have each clocked up six generations of Etonians, and the Dukes of Richmond five. In this loyalty battle, the Earls of Derby might have proved the ultimate victors, since the current generation is the ninth to have attended Eton, had there not been a lapse in the late nineteenth century when Eddy Derby was sent to Wellington. The Derbys' relationship with Eton ultimately goes back to the current earl's great-great-great-great-great-grandfather, the 12th Earl, in 1764.

After Eton – the clear market leader in educating peers and future peers – the second most popular school among today's hereditary peers is Harrow, which, in September 2024, had educated fifty-nine, or 7 per cent, of the current crop of peers. Of those, twenty-two have fathers and thirteen have grandfathers who are or were Old Harrovians. In third place, with 3.5 per cent of the peers, is Winchester College. Overall, across all the schools that the hereditary peerage patronises, 146 of their number have attended the same – almost always fee-paying – school as their father, and 176 the same school as both their father *and* grandfather. Even those who didn't follow directly in their father's footsteps didn't stray far from the paternal path. Ned Durham was sent to Eton by his father Tony Lambton who had been at Harrow and hated it. Previously, '... his father had hated Eton, so ... sent him to Harrow.'[46] Others have broken different patterns. Charlie Devon is the first Etonian in his ancient family – before him were three Wykehamists, old boys of that school for preternaturally bright boys, Winchester College, and a gaggle of Old Westminsters; James Marlborough is the first Harrovian in his family after eight Etonian dukes dating back to his seven times great-grandfather the 3rd Duke in the 1720s, with just one Wykehamist in the 1880s.

There has always been a Roman Catholic tinge to the aristocracy, so it is not wholly surprising that 3 per cent of hereditary peers attended Ampleforth College in North Yorkshire – the school 'for left-footers', as an Old Etonian Anglican peer described it to me. Not that Catholic peers any longer attend only Catholic schools. Both William Stonor, 8th Baron Camoys, and his late father Tom, who in 1998 became the first Roman Catholic Lord Chamberlain since the Reformation, attended Eton. Simon Lovat is the first Fraser in at least three generations not to go to a Catholic school: his parents chose Harrow instead. The Peels split the difference, explains Willie Peel, whose mother was Catholic and whose father was Anglican. 'My brother is much cleverer than I am so he went to Eton, and as my mother wanted the Catholic side to be represented, I went to Ampleforth and loved it. I had Basil Hume as my housemaster for a short while. We were always told that he was runner up to be Pope – whether it's true or not, I don't know. I was terribly disappointed that he didn't become Pope because I'd have loved to have said I'd been beaten by the Pope.'[47]

* * *

That peers tend to be attracted to a small group of public schools is not the same as saying that a small group of public schools is dominated by peers. In 1921, about 56 per cent of the 771 hereditary peers then living had been educated at Eton, yet six years later, the number of peers or sons of peers at Eton was only sixty-eight – three earls, one viscount, two lords, forty-three honourables and seventeen with courtesy titles, comprising only 6 per cent of the school's nominal roll.[48] The same pattern can be found throughout the rest of the twentieth century. In 1967, just over 5.5 per cent of Etonians had titles or courtesy titles. If one adds to that the forty sons of honourables, sixteen of whom became peers themselves (and another one who will do in future), that may be a lot of upper-class pupils, but it is nevertheless a small proportion of the overall school population of 1,200. In 1990, there were thirty-three peers or sons of peers among the total 1,278 boys – comprising just 2.5 per cent.

It's understandable, therefore, why many of today's Old Etonians bristle slightly when people say that it is a school for toffs. Of course, even a handful of aristocrats is a handful more than the vast majority of schools in the country can claim to have educated. Roger Royle, who started work as Conduct – the senior chaplain – at Eton in 1974, described how in one class he had two earls and a viscount. 'I often thought that all I needed was an ace and a jack and I'd have had a poker hand,' he remembered. Privilege more generally was also well represented. 'Another class made me drunk just to look at them. There was a Guinness, a Charrington, a Whitbread and a Worthington all sitting within a few feet of each other.'[49] Yet many Etonians have said they found the school refreshingly unstuffy and unstuck-up. Crispin Latymer, who started there in 1968, told me: 'I am no great academic but the thing about Eton is that it provides such a wide range of things for the boys to do, and every single child has one thing at which they are a little bit better than their peers.' The school was 'very good at helping me find what it was that was for me, which was rowing'. Aged fifty, he sailed across the Atlantic. He pooh-poohs the notion put forward by a slightly younger contemporary that Eton is a 'comprehensive for the landed gentry'. This, he says, is '. . . so far from the truth, but it reflects the public view of Eton which is somewhat outdated.'

Whether or not a public school education creates a certain type of outlook or personality is a subject on which people have strongly differing views. Crispin Latymer reckons that plenty of 'shockers' emerge from Eton at the age of eighteen, and concedes, 'I was probably one.' He goes on to explain why:

Eton gives you an inflated sense of self-confidence and it needs the next two or three years of work, where you slide down the snakes having moved up on the ladders, to kick you into shape and make you understand what real life is like instead of school life. Maybe Eton isn't very good at – or perhaps it wasn't when I was there – teaching those who are really successful that actually life is not all about being a member of Pop [the Eton Society, a group of prefects].

The real world actually values you for the most part on what you can contribute rather than what your name might be.

Charles Beauclerk felt there was a distasteful element of snobbery.

People were there largely to satisfy their parents' vanity, so it was a strange atmosphere. Over the years it has gained a certain prestige, partly because it has retained all of the old traditions and therefore respects the divisions of class and has that sense of itself. It's almost ritualistic, with the special vocabulary they use for things.

Charles Hay, 16th Earl of Kinnoull, who went to Eton in 1976 as Viscount Dupplin, felt that the aristocratic seam that ran through the school militated against any individual assuming themselves to be a cut above everyone else.

Sometimes in life you turn up in a room and you're the only aristocrat, and that immediately affects the way the room operates. It's deeply dispiriting, because you don't feel any different from anyone else. At Eton there were quite a few people [like me] around, and so it didn't matter. I was often in forms with other aristocrats and no one felt like we were any different. It meant that the whole thing was not relevant, and the school in no way pandered to it.

By ignoring people's so-called rank, the school avoided the over-inflation of ego. 'One of the troubles', says an Old Etonian peer, 'is that people can end up thinking that the world owes them something. If you reach the end of Eton and there's been none of that, that's pretty helpful.'

* * *

Even today, Eton continues to divide opinion. Its defenders point to the efforts it has made in recent years to include children from less privileged backgrounds, and the outreach work it does with other schools. Its critics regard it as a 'four-letter word', a byword for elitism and establishment cronyism (twenty Old Etonians have gone on to be prime minister), and an anachronism that is too fond of its traditions and archaic vocabulary. It is surely the only school about which many people who did not attend it, and have never visited it, think they know a lot. It is the A-list celebrity of the independent school sector. Images of it are used to illustrate newspaper articles that have nothing to do with it, or any schools like it.

More generally, the small circle of private schools favoured by the aristocracy are felt by their detractors to form a kind of private club which others are not able to join or are discouraged from joining – the kind of club that has its own codes and in-jokes: 'What are truisms at Rugby are paradoxes at Harrow, and an Eton custom would prove a Marlborough revelation'; 'A lady wants a chair: the Wykehamist fetches, the Etonian offers it, the Harrovian sits in it.' (James Priory, the headmaster of Tonbridge School, suggested to me in 2020 that had a Tonbridge boy been involved in the latter scenario he would have 'gone off to make the tea'.) Like all generalisations such critical views can be simultaneously fair and unfair, just as the stereotype of the privileged pupil of a public school – entitled, arrogant, overly confident in limited abilities – seems grossly unfair when applied to many and understated when attached to a notorious handful. This handful certainly includes scions of the peerage. But then it includes some non-aristocrats, too.

I I

When the Going Was Good

Leisure and Vice

Until a couple of generations or so ago, it was not the norm for peers to work – or, at least, it was not usual for them to take up what most people would regard as a conventional 'job'. They had their estates to look after, of course – though many devolved the day-to-day grind to a land agent. Many were busy in the local community, whether as magistrates or lord-lieutenants. They opened fetes, sat on the boards of charities or were patrons of worthy causes. Some attended the House of Lords. But 'work' as such was not generally on the cards. In the 1921 edition of *Debrett's Peerage*, just 110 of the 771 hereditary peers were listed as having a job, as opposed to occupying an honorary role in, say, the diplomatic, military or political spheres. And those who were managing directors or bankers or engineers – in other words, those who could boast that they had a 'profession' – tended to come from recently ennobled families, not from the old aristocracy. Indeed, seventy-seven of those 110 had had their titles created within the last couple of decades.

Not only was work not the norm, it wasn't really the done thing. The American heiress Eleanor Castle Stewart (née Guggenheim) recalled how she once asked a young aristocrat to whom she had been introduced what he did in life. 'I don't do anything. I'm a peer of the realm,' came the lofty reply. 'In America we call that a bum,' she responded.[1] As Henry Bath observed of his parents' generation, in an era when the wealthy were still largely unaffected by taxes and death duties, the important thing was to be 'considered a gentleman', and just as that didn't involve a vulgar pursuit of wealth – 'plenty of people had made fortunes out of the war, but they were regarded as profiteers and beyond the pale' – nor did it involve holding down the sort of job that middle-class people might aspire to.[2] In any case, those who had a job title beyond 'peer' didn't necessarily work very hard. When the Conservative MP William Montagu Douglas Scott, 6th Duke of Buccleuch, stood again for his Midlothian seat in 1880 as Earl of Dalkeith, against the Liberal leader William Gladstone, a neatly produced pamphlet entitled 'The Political Achievements of the Earl of Dalkeith' was circulated. It was blank. William Dalkeith lost to William Gladstone by 211 votes.

Even after the Second World War, when many aristocrats were feeling the pinch and stately homes were being demolished, sold off or transferred to the National Trust, there remained a hard core of wealthy peers who did not work and did not expect to have to do so. Paradoxically, in an era when a fair proportion of their brethren were struggling, they were actually doing rather well. Those burdened with expensive estates had managed to shift the responsibility for running them to others or were benefitting from the sharp rise in value of houses and estates in the more affluent areas of the country. Despite the burden of taxation, some families of the premier league, particularly those with London estates, were enjoying a boom time, and for those prepared to strip their ancestral homes of their trappings there was a thriving art market to fill. Such people did not feel it necessary to stoop to working for a living.

For those who did want to work, the title occasionally proved a barrier. The Hon. Bryan Guinness, who qualified for the bar in 1930, found that because it was assumed he was immensely wealthy (which as great-great-grandson of the founder of the family brewery, and co-heir to his father's significant share in it, he in fact was), it was felt unnecessary to find briefs for him in the way that it was for his colleagues. In the 1960s, Jack Hastings, 16th Earl of Huntingdon, complained that 'people take you for a dilettante whatever your skill, unless maybe you're in one of the recognised professions.' He argued that the peers had become overly associated with what he termed 'the Amateur Tradition' because 'up to recent times there were so many things and jobs a lord wasn't allowed to do.'[3] Henry 'Pelham' Pelham-Clinton-Hope, 9th Duke of Newcastle, went further, declaring in 1968 that 'people find it hard to accept that you have any skills at all.'[4]

All of which begs a question. Given that so many of the landed aristocracy didn't work at all or didn't have to work hard, what did they do to fill the time?

* * *

Until well after the Second World War – and still, to an extent today – each aristocratic year followed a set pattern, centred on 'the season' – those spring and summer months when families with homes in both the country and the capital spent more of their time in their London houses, hosting parties, attending receptions and finding suitable husbands for their daughters, many of whom – until the custom was abolished in 1958 – would be officially presented at Court to demonstrate publicly that they were now of marriageable age. Former debutante Celestria Hales, who came of age in the 1970s, describes the rhythm of these months: 'It was tea parties, lunch parties, the Berkeley Dress Show at the beginning of April,' she says, 'followed by Queen Charlotte's Ball in May and then the Caledonian Ball, followed by the private dances which were during weekdays and weekends. It finished with Goodwood week, followed by Cowes for those who went.'

As Celestria Hales' calendar shows there was and is a strong sports motif to the aristocratic year: racing at Cheltenham, Epsom, Aintree, Ascot and Goodwood; Badminton Horse Trials; sailing at Cowes; and then the Glorious Twelfth on 12 August, which marks the start of the grouse season. Irish families might attend the Dublin Horse Show in August, along with race meetings at Punchestown,

Leopardstown and the Curragh. Ted Innes Ker describes how his grandfather Bobo Roxburghe started fishing in April:

> [He] would be on the river until 12 August, on the Tweed, or the Alta, in Norway, and then from 12 August he would be up shooting at Millden in Angus. In September he went to the Lammermuirs where he would shoot until 1 October, then he'd go fishing for a couple of weeks on the Tweed, before spending until 31 January shooting pheasants, partridges, hares, rabbits, anything. God knows what he did in February and March.

It was – and for some, still is – a peripatetic existence. Families with multiple houses divided their time between each of these, depending on the month (today, Richard Buccleuch, almost uniquely, still alternates between Boughton in Northamptonshire, Drumlanrig Castle in Dumfriesshire and Bowhill in the Borders each week). Back in the 1930s the Fitzwilliams travelled regularly between Wentworth, Coollattin and their London home, while also accepting seemingly endless invitations to hunt and shoot at other people's houses. Billy and Maud Fitzwilliam's highlights of 1933 included a trip to the 11th annual military ball of the 5th Battalion the King's Own Yorkshire Light Infantry at the Mansion House in Doncaster, a spell in Madeira, a party at Buckingham Palace, the Derby, the annual regimental dinner of the Royal Army Service Corps at the Hotel Metropole on London's Northumberland Avenue, several days at Ascot and a ball at the Dorchester attended by the Duke and Duchess of York. Billy then went to Cowes, while in late August Maud headed to her childhood home Aske Hall to stay with her mother. A few race meetings followed. Just before Christmas, Billy attended the Eton College Beagles dance at the Savoy.

There were more louche pastimes, too, involving private members' clubs, cocktail parties and nights out at venues such as the 400 Club – an establishment in a basement in Leicester Square that attracted numerous members of the upper classes in the 1940s and 1950s, not least Princess Margaret. In mid-June 1951, a now-ageing

Chips Channon was still keeping up a hectic social pace. Over the course of just a few days he rolled from Ascot – where Winston Churchill received a standing ovation – to the House of Commons, before going on to dinner at the Orleans Club in St James's. The following day, he returned to Ascot for lunch at Buck's tent, where he '. . . lost money, talked to the wrong people and sexually was unlucky, although I looked extremely handsome.'[5] After that, he returned home to London for '[A] long lovely evening at first – I am so "spent" – and then a wild night of delights, delirious, unbelievably – my sexual prowess increases, keeps pace with my growing appetite.'[6]

* * *

One particularly popular aristocratic pastime was gambling, a perhaps inevitable indulgence for those who had both wealth and time to waste. A vice with a long aristocratic pedigree that stretched back certainly to the eighteenth century, it proved the ruin of many aristocratic men over the years and caught a few aristocratic women in its meshes, too. Georgiana, Duchess of Devonshire, for one, ran up huge gambling debts in the latter decades of the eighteenth century. Her reputation for never winning was matched by that of her supposed lover, the Whig politician Charles James Fox, who bankrupted himself twice at the gaming table. The exclusive gentlemen's club White's – one in which women are not even allowed to set foot, let alone be members – was founded in 1693 as a Mayfair shop selling drinking chocolate, and was soon transformed by betting peers and their associates into an exclusive gambling joint, being described by the Irish writer Jonathan Swift as 'the common rendezvous of infamous [card] Sharpers, and noble Cullies [dupes]'.[7] In the early 1760s, two clubs were formed following the establishment of a private society that itself began when the founders were blackballed from White's. The first of these, Boodle's, was founded in January 1762 by William Petty, later prime minister and 1st Marquess of Lansdowne. The second, Brooks's, came along two years later, a club founded by a group of twenty-seven Whig peers as a place to bet on whist and hazard – and to place rather more outrageous wagers. In the 1780s, George Cholmondeley, 1st Marquess of Cholmondeley, bet Edward Smith-Stanley, 12th Earl of Derby, 'To receive 500 gs. [guineas] whenever his lordship fucks a woman in a balloon one thousand yards from the earth'.[8]

In the twentieth century, gambling devotees could make their way from race meeting to race meeting during the season. Those who enjoyed travelling abroad could spend time at the casinos in Monte Carlo or Baden-Baden. In the 1930s Peter Brougham, who we last met almost but not quite marrying Obby Plunket, whose great-great-uncle, Henry Brougham, 1st Baron Brougham and Vaux, had helped to popularise Cannes among the upper classes, was said to have broken the bank at Monte Carlo not just once, but twice. At home he became, as he put it, 'a great gambler on the turf', soon dispelling any reputation for invincibility that his success in Monte Carlo might have given him by running through his inheritance in double-quick time, and, consequently, being forced to sell off parts of his Brougham Hall estate and the Bentley tourer that he had only recently purchased, in order to cover his debts.[9] Finally, in 1933, he was left with no option but to sell Brougham Hall to a local landowner, thus bringing to an end a family connection with Cumberland and Westmorland that stretched back to the Norman Conquest.[10] By 1953 he was thrice married and destitute, reduced – as he told reporters after leaving bankruptcy court – to doing the football pools. 'Now they are my only hope,' he said.[11] He died in June 1967, the latest casualty in a long aristocratic tradition.

The foundation in 1962 of a new gambling joint at 44 Berkeley Square, in the heart of Mayfair, was very much a continuation of this tradition. And true to the tradition, the new and sumptuously decorated Clermont Club proved a magnet for peers with money to lose.

The man who established the Clermont – John 'Aspers' Aspinall – was not himself an aristocrat. He was the son of an army doctor, who had become hooked on gambling while at Oxford University. He had a genius for cultivating the friendship of the upper class. While at Oxford, he met the hedonistic Balliol law undergraduate Ian Maxwell-Scott, second cousin of Bernard Norfolk, and great-great-great-grandson of the poet Sir Walter Scott, and immediately saw in him someone with whom he could have a lot of fun. Ian wasn't, in the words of the biographer of Aspers' set, John Pearson, 'remotely tainted with tedious concerns of middle-class morality'. He was like 'a gun dog [that] knows instinctively how to work the field from centuries of careful breeding', a man whose 'entire way of life seemed ruled by an instinctive sense of how a gentleman behaved'.[12] As an undergraduate he was prone to running up large bills for food, wine and champagne, 'showing his effortless disdain for vulgar wealth', despite being unable to pay unless he was fortunate enough to secure a gambling windfall.[13] That was enough to impress Aspers, and, after graduating, the two men took a room at the Ritz where they hosted poker parties for the wealthy. The manager didn't question their credentials, nor those of their smart friends, and the parties went on for several months. Champagne was on the house.

Gradually, Aspers branched out from the Ritz to gambling parties held in private houses in Mayfair and Belgravia. Back in the 1930s, roulette and baccarat had been the games of choice for rich gamblers betting their surplus wealth in the comfort of plush European casinos. Aspers, however, opted for *chemin de fer*, a form of baccarat probably more open to pure chance than any other card game in existence. The Greek writer and gossip columnist Taki Theodoracopulos once compared its addictive qualities to those of heroin. He also recorded how regularly losing his allowance at Aspers' establishments 'was almost a pleasure as I lost it to friends and to gentlemen'.[14]

Key to the success of Aspers' 'chemmy' parties was the roll call of the great and the good, the rich and the even grander, who attended them. They included men such as Porchy Carnarvon, the Hampshire landowner and son of the discoverer of Tutankhamen's tomb; Andrew Devonshire; and Bill Cadogan, 7th Earl Cadogan, the owner of Chelsea in west London. Mowbray Howard, 6th Earl of Effingham, was a habitué even if he did not count as either a particularly rich man or a shining example of an honourable peer: he was, variously, a director and front man of the Knightsbridge gambling club Esmeralda's Barn owned by the East End gangster Kray twins, found guilty of a drink-driving charge, separately charged with manslaughter for running over a labourer and killing him, and, ultimately, a bankrupt. Then there was Bill Stirling, a Scottish landowner and elder brother of David, co-founder of the SAS. At one all-night chemmy party during Ascot week in 1959, he lost £174,500 (equivalent to almost £4.4 million today). Writing an IOU in Aspers' financial director John Burke's account book, he then waved down a waiter to order a plate of scrambled eggs before turning up in the Royal Enclosure at Ascot later that day, apparently unbothered by the events of the previous evening. His gambling habits would ultimately cost him the Keir estate near Stirling, which had been in his family since 1448. His wife, whom he failed to inform of his decision to sell, loyally defended him: 'The estate has been sold,' she said, 'because my husband needed the money but gambling debts simply did not come into it. My husband is, by nature, a gambler but not in the sense that he could lose gigantic sums at the tables.'[15]

Arguably the grandest and most lavish of Aspinall's circle was John Stanley, 18th Earl of Derby, grandson and from 1938 heir of Eddy Derby, the 'King of Lancashire'. John had served with the Grenadier Guards during the Second World War and won the Military Cross in Italy. He might well have continued with his military career had his grandpapa Eddy not died just three years after the war ended. Now his life took a different course, as he took over not only Eddy's assets, but his local responsibilities too; at various times he was Lord-Lieutenant and Custos Rotulorum of Lancashire, honorary captain of the district Royal Naval Reserves, and among other local roles, president of the Liverpool chamber of commerce. In the same year that he succeeded to the title, he married Lady Isobel Milles-Lade[16] in a lavish wedding that was attended not only by members of the royal family (disparagingly referred to as 'those Germans' by Isobel on one occasion) but by over 400 tenants brought down from the Derbys' Lancashire estates by a special train.[17] Channon declared Isobel a lucky girl: '[P]eople smilingly remark that "London's fastest filly has won the Derby."'[18] Five years later, her husband carried the Royal Standard of England at Elizabeth II's coronation.

One of John's great passions was racing. It seems an appropriate enough pursuit for a man whose four-times great-grandfather had given his name to England's most famous turf race, though his successor Teddy Derby has no evidence to suggest that John himself bet on the horses.[19] But although inheriting the family link with the Derby and fulfilling his various other duties should have been sufficient to keep him busy, the author John Pearson argues that there was something in John Derby that rendered him '... congenitally restless ... bored, lonely and king of nowhere in particular'.[20] It was true that he had experienced more than his fair share of loss, both at home – having lost his father[21] in 1938, when he was twenty – and during the course of his military service during the Second World War. It's possible that his friend Andrew Devonshire's family losses – since his brother Billy and his 55-year-old father Eddy Devonshire had died within six years of one another – and his experiences as a combatant during the war were factors in his alcoholism. That wasn't the case with John Derby, who, Teddy Derby says, preserved a disciplined relationship with alcohol.[22] But perhaps the family tragedies he suffered were factors in turning him into an enthusiastic gambler.

When he inherited, a certain retrenchment proved necessary. Eddy Derby had left estates valued at just under £4 million, but with estate duty at 75 per cent, expenses had to be cut and land sold to meet tax obligations. At the end of the war, Eddy himself had sold off part of Knowsley village to Liverpool Corporation for housing, and had also disposed of Derby House on Stratford Place, off Oxford Street.[23] In 1950, John announced that he would be selling the rest of Knowsley village, not least because he felt unable to fund the installation of modern sanitation that the sixty or seventy tenanted cottages he owned required. Three years later, he sold around 900 acres near Ormskirk, along with half of his 9,000-acre Crag estate near Macclesfield, and the following September, he parted with the 9,000-acre Fylde estate. The same year, a selection of books from Knowsley Hall were sold at Christie's and the house itself, which had been opened to the paying public in 1949, was subjected to a drastic programme of remodelling that involved the demolition of some acre and a quarter of floor space. Teddy Derby points out that the house had been 'ludicrously large', but the new version, reduced in size by architect the Hon. Claude Phillimore, was still a grand conception: there were rooms for a valet, housekeeper, comptroller, agent, butler, footmen, housemaids, and even an old-style servants' hall, a canteen for dailies and a social club for estate staff.

In 1963, John and Isobel commissioned a new, ten-bedroomed house in the park. It was once more designed by Phillimore and, again, on a scale that to anyone else would seem needlessly lavish. There were bedrooms for maids, lady's maids and manservants, a china room, pantry, larder, utility room, brushing room, scullery, staff sitting and dining rooms – all to service a couple who occupied one bedroom apiece. The move was prompted in part by a desire to live a slightly more scaled-back life: Knowsley, even in its recent, reduced incarnation, seemed very large for a childless couple. It was also a reaction to an incident that had occurred there in 1952 when a mentally unbalanced footman, Harold Winstanley, had shot Isobel while she was dining alone at home and had then gone on to shoot and kill the Derbys' butler and under-butler. The incident had caused a considerable stir at the time, not just because of its extraordinary nature or because Isobel (who had feigned death when she was shot) made a remarkably swift recovery, but because it was evidence of the battalions of staff still employed by the Derbys. As Mark Girouard described, the event '. . . drew coveys of servants out of the corridors and backstairs of Knowsley, on a scale which was thought to have gone for ever'.[24] Society was generally somewhat bemused by this; as Winston Churchill's assistant private secretary Jock Colville later recalled to Churchill's biographer Sir Martin Gilbert, there was 'general surprise that in the 1950s anybody, even Lord Derby, still had an *under*-butler'.[25] In 1968 Lancashire Police moved into the big house, paying, as Teddy Derby discloses, 'a little under 10p per square foot', and taking a long lease that in 1974 became Merseyside Police's, who did not vacate until 1997. Not surprisingly, in the words of Teddy Derby's wife Cazzy, Isobel 'didn't want to come back here – she didn't feel safe in her home.'

John Derby nevertheless remained a wealthy man. His nephew points out that: '[H]e had a chauffeur driving him in a Rolls-Royce until the day he died [in 1994], and a valet. He was living on a very grand scale.'[26] As a result, his compulsion to gamble on the sort of scale that would have bankrupted a less affluent man never proved ruinous to him. That much became evident in June 1960 when he played his most infamous hand of chemmy, at Aspers' house at 93 Eaton Place, against European playboy Gianni Agnelli, head of Fiat and one of the richest men in the world. Initially, Agnelli kept losing. When he was down £200,000[27] he announced that his game was over. John Derby had no idea who Agnelli was, asking John Burke, 'Tell me, Burkie, who is that foreign chap? He won't have a decent punt,' and daring Agnelli to play on.[28] But his challenge proved to be a mistake. Agnelli's luck changed. John began losing. Soon Agnelli had recovered almost all the money he had lost. By the end of the evening, he left with a cheque for £22,400.[29] Nine years later, Agnelli and Fiat bought Ferrari.[30] John Derby retained his new house at Knowsley and his extravagant lifestyle.

Unlicensed betting of the sort in which John Derby was involved on that evening in 1960 was illegal at the time, and Aspers had some narrow escapes. A tip-off to the press during Derby week 1959 had, for example, led to a scrum of reporters gathering outside John Burke's flat at 60 Eaton Square, forcing the gamblers – one of whom was John Derby – to escape via the basement, a courtyard

and a low flat roof into a side street. Prior to that, on 10 January
1958, the police raided a gambling party being held at the home
of Aspers' mother Lady (Mary) Osborne, 1 Hyde Park Street,
and hauled those present off to Paddington police station. Mary
Osborne protested that: '[I]t is a poor thing if you can't have a private party in a private flat without the police coming.'[31] She, Aspers,
his wife Jane, and John Burke, accordingly pleaded not guilty at
their trial at the Old Bailey that March. They won the case.

Their acquittal had two inter-related consequences. First, in 1960
it prompted a liberalisation of the law on gambling. And second, it
encouraged Aspers to take a twenty-one-year lease on a run-down
Georgian property in London's Berkeley Square, where, with financial help from his rich acquaintances, he could give his gambling
friends a more permanent home. The new club was appropriately
named after one of the house's former owners, William Fortescue,
1st and last Earl of Clermont, a keen racing man who had won the
Derby in 1785.

Initially, Aspers' club was limited to 600 members, each of
whom paid an annual membership fee of 20 guineas. Among their
ranks were: '[F]ive dukes and five marquesses, nearly twenty earls,
one actor (Peter Sellers), one member of the royal family (Prince
William of Gloucester), one writer (Françoise Sagan), two Cabinet Ministers, two Gettys, two Packers, two Goldsmiths, two
Arab princes, two American ambassadors, and the producer of the
James Bond films, Albert Broccoli'.[32] As Aspers' biographer Brian
Masters describes, Aspers managed to '. . . resurrect the elegant surroundings which made gambling such a pleasure in the eighteenth
century, and rescue the activity from the trough of shameful-
ness and squalor to which it had sunk as a result of Victorian
prudery'.[33] At the launch party, Oliver Brett, 3rd Viscount Esher,
remarked that the Clermont 'takes me back to my boyhood when
a town house was a town house'.[34] Given that the club opened in
the same year as the Cuban Missile Crisis took place, it's tempting to think that, just as the Second World War appears to have
created a new generation of gamblers seeking release in a world

dominated by conflict, so the spectre of nuclear war contributed to the Clermont's early success.

The following June, Aspers' friend Mark Birley, son of the society portrait painter Sir Oswald, and his wife Lady Annabel Vane-Tempest-Stewart, daughter of Robin Vane-Tempest-Stewart, 8th Marquess of Londonderry, opened a club in the Clermont's basement. Birley called it Annabel's, after his wife. (She never much liked the name but reflected that having a nightclub named after you is much better than being immortalised as a rose, as so many aristocratic women have been.) Linked to the Clermont by a cast-iron circular staircase, Annabel's was, like the club above it, very exclusive indeed. Annabel – who later divorced Birley and married fellow Clermont member, the businessman Sir James Goldsmith – described the building as a whole as 'the most fashionable if hedonistic address in London'. She recalled one occasion when she was 'running a winning bank while sitting beside Ian Fleming, as Frank Sinatra hovered behind my shoulder'.[35] Other regulars included Bill Stirling and his son Archie, and Sunny Blandford, the future 11th Duke of Marlborough.

Aspers encouraged his generation of over-resourced, underworked toffs to enjoy themselves, offering admiration and flattery while simultaneously fleecing them. To Jonathan Moyne, '[H]e was a very naughty man [but] I liked him. He was like an honest smuggler.' A peeress whose husband spent a lot of time both at Annabel's and the Clermont describes how Aspinall would '... take these young men's fortunes off them, when they had just inherited their estates. They would come to the club and lose, and their family would have to fund that. He was a huge influence on the gambling world, on those young people.' But, she adds, both she and her husband were close to Aspers, and she doesn't mean this critically: 'It was just a risk for enthusiastic young men back in the glamorous gambling world in those days.' The peers couldn't resist, 'delighted to be able to indulge in what he never stopped telling them had always been the traditional red-blooded pastime of the aristocracy'.[36] At the Clermont, '[T]he descendants of Regency gamblers could once more gamble to their hearts' content in these grandiose surroundings to remind them of a world that they had lost.'[37]

Among the many inevitable losers was Henry Vyner, who, following the death of his brother Charles in the latter stages of the Second World War, inherited Studley Royal, a 17,000-acre estate in North Yorkshire that included the ruins of Fountains Abbey. His stepdaughter Anna Terrington remembers him as 'a very sensitive man with a wonderful eye for detail, an incredible gardener', who battled to make the stable block at Studley habitable as a home after a fire in 1946 had gutted most of the main house. He had, she says, fallen in love with her mother, Margaret, while he was at Cambridge and had married her against the wishes of his 'appalled' parents Commander Clare and Lady Doris Vyner, close friends of Queen Elizabeth the Queen Mother, since 'she was a divorcee with a child'. It was not, however, a reciprocal relationship: Margaret once admitted to Anna that she had never loved Henry, but had agreed to marry him because she believed that he could offer her the security she craved.

It must have come as a particularly cruel irony to Margaret, therefore, that this wealthy man was also an inveterate gambler. Anna recalls how, 'if he was bored', he would go to the Clermont or to White's where 'he played backgammon very well – alas, not well enough.' On one night alone at Aspinall's establishment he lost over £33,000. Margaret was distinctly unimpressed, later telling John Pearson that: '[T]he truth was that, being rather middle-class myself, I regarded losing large amounts of money at anything as infantile as *chemin de fer* as quite ridiculous.'[38] Over the next few years, Henry's fortunes waxed and waned, and, sadly, waned more than they waxed. 'I can't remember which sister [was about to be born] but the telephone was cut off because Henry hadn't paid the bill and [my mother] was about to go into labour. I remember her being furious about that,' says Anna. Finally, in 1965, Henry felt compelled to put the family home up for sale. Anna vividly recalls the moment when the letter arrived at her prep school informing her that there would be 'no more Studley': 'It was possibly the worst moment of my life.' Quite what precipitated the final disaster is not clear. It's possible that Henry got involved, via a friend of Aspers, in a Ponzi scheme. But there's no doubt that the Clermont played a role in the loss of Studley.

It was a mark of what 'a really lovely man' Henry was, says Anna, that his friends stood by him when Studley had to be sold. 'They didn't point and say "you hopeless loser".' She regards him as a 'a very loyal, kind, generous man' and regrets that 'he didn't have the support of his wife.' Margaret and Henry Vyner divorced in 1981, and he remarried the following year. But by this time he had turned to drink, 'feeling that he had failed', and by the time he died in 1996, aged sixty-three, he was a functioning alcoholic. 'He was a really heavenly man and I miss him to the bottom of my heart every day,' says Anna.

Arguably the most well-known member of the Clermont circle – certainly the most notorious – was an aristocrat who, on paper certainly, could least afford to lose money there: the Hon. John Bingham, from 1964 7th Earl of Lucan. His family had once owned over 60,000 acres in County Mayo, as well as 2,000 acres in England. But by the time John Lucan was born in 1934, the family's holdings had been much reduced, and at the point when he inherited his father's title – with £250,000 cash, equivalent to over £4 million today, and a private income from family trusts – all that was left were the ground rents due from 600 Irish tenants, proceeds from 100 acres in Staines, and modest properties in both London and Rhodesia. By the standards of those with whom John Lucan rubbed shoulders at the Clermont it wasn't much. As his son George Bingham, 8th Earl of Lucan, explains, '[C]ontrary to popular belief, my father did not inherit a large fortune and even following the death of his father in 1964, there was little by way of cash as the family trusts were still realising assets to pay death duties for many years. The family trust was run by Coutts & Co. and I recall them mentioning that he rarely, if ever, drew on his trust income. His parents were each dedicated socialists, his mother being chair of the Marylebone Labour Party for a decade and his father being Labour chief whip, and so they were not willing to subsidise his lifestyle to any great extent.'

Even so, John never felt the need or the desire to stoop to regular employment. After Eton and National Service in Germany with the Coldstream Guards, he worked, fleetingly, for the merchant bank William Brandt's – 'to make my "pile"' as he wrote to his uncle in 1956.[39] In the same letter he described how: '[T]here is no financial reward for hard work today as our system of taxation is designed to prevent people from accumulating large or small capital sums. Anyone in England who lives on a decent scale is either evading taxation or spending his capital . . . if I had wanted to be a play-boy and could have afforded it I should have stayed on in the army which is the only place one can be a play-boy without being labelled one.'[40]

His gambling habit, which had begun at Eton, had taken firmer root during his time in the army, where he took up poker, and had blossomed during his stint in the City where, his son says, he 'found that he had a very good mathematical ability, excellent memory and a consequent talent at cards and games of chance'. He put in the odd evening at the House of Lords after his father died, but never spoke. And he called a halt to his career in banking, which paid £500 a year, when, in 1960, he won £26,000 at chemmy over two nights, a feat that won him the nickname 'Lucky'. His friend Charlie Sweeny[41] remembered him saying, 'Here I am working for so much a year less tax and I can win £26,000 in two nights! I'm going to quit and gamble.' When Sweeny tried to dissuade his friend, the response was: 'Oh, no, no, it's just a waste of time. I'm going to quit.'[42] He became, in Annabel Goldsmith's words, 'part of the furniture' at 44 Berkeley Square: 'rarely did I walk into the Clermont and not see Lucan sitting at a table playing backgammon.'[43]

Perhaps, for John, gambling bore a fleeting resemblance to banking, since it involved money and the hours were long. A colleague from the bank told the journalist James Fox that John's '. . . intelligence may not have been too bad but as far as education was concerned he was a very limited fellow. He had no economic training whatsoever.'[44] Even so, his son's understanding is that he made his living from gambling for about twelve years. 'I have never known the details but some of the sums going in and out of the bank account were very, very large when translated into current prices,' he says. 'In any event I do not suppose that anyone survives that long at the tables unless that person has some skill and technique.'

All that came to an end on a November night in 1974 when the Lucans' nanny Sandra Rivett was murdered and John Lucan vanished. He has not been seen since.

Two years earlier, Aspinall had sold the Clermont to Victor Lowndes, owner of the Playboy Club. In 1978, he opened another club in Knightsbridge, Aspinall's. But by now the aristocratic lustre had worn off. Aspers' old money pals had been replaced by a more international set. In 1975, he opened Howletts Zoo, on his property in Kent, to the public, and the following year, Port Lympne Zoo near Hythe, both of which are now run by his family's Aspinall Foundation. He died aged seventy-four in 2000.

* * *

Whether or not the aristocracy have been particularly prone to gambling is questionable. It's probably more accurate to say that it's a pastime that – certainly since the nineteenth century – has appealed unequally across society, drawing in the upper and working classes while being largely avoided by the middle class. Racing, for example, had always been an aristocratic pursuit. It then attracted a working-class following in Victorian and Edwardian times, as factory workers and others discovered the appeal of 'taking a flutter', either at the racetrack or in the local pub where bookies' runners operated. The middle class, meanwhile, were largely responsible for the passing of the Street Betting Act of 1906, which sought to curb aspects of working-class gambling. It was the 1906 legislation that Aspers was successfully to campaign against half a century later.

WHEN THE GOING WAS GOOD

The strangely U-shaped nature of a pursuit such as gambling is one that psychiatrist Scott Alexander Siskind explained in his 2014 essay, 'Right is the New Left', in these terms:

> Everyone wants to look like they are a member of a higher class than they actually are. But everyone also wants to avoid getting mistaken for a member of a poorer class. So for example, the middle class wants to look upper-class, but also wants to make sure no one accidentally mistakes them for lower-class. But there is a limit both to people's ambition and to their fear. No one has any hopes of getting mistaken for a class two levels higher than their own: a lower-class person may hope to appear middle-class, but their mannerisms, accent, appearance, peer group, and whatever make it permanently impossible for them to appear upper-class. Likewise, a member of the upper class may worry about being mistaken for middle-class, but there is no way they will ever get mistaken for lower-class, let alone underclass.[45]

Comedian Billy Connolly put things more bluntly: 'The serious upper class, ignore that suburban fucking mob, the proper big shots, they're all nuts and they are a great laugh. The working class are all fucking nuts as well and they are a great laugh. It's just the middle that sucks.'[46]

As to why the upper classes should have proved to be so keen on gambling, various reasons can be suggested. They had the time for it, of course. They also had – or, at least, started out with – the wealth that made it practically possible. But, as with working-class gambling, there was a strongly cultural aspect to it as well. Working-class punters enjoyed the conviviality of venues where they could swap tips, enjoy winnings and commiserate on losses. Aristocratic punters attending Brooks's in the eighteenth century or the Clermont in the twentieth could mix with similarly privileged members of society, swap gossip and relax. It's more than conceivable that aristocrats gambled not just for the enjoyment of the activity or out of boredom but because they felt it was the thing to do. The fact that so many events on the social calendar – the Derby, Cheltenham, the Grand National – provided suitable opportunities for different types of betting inevitably helped.

Other vices that have a link with club life – notably heavy drinking and drug use – have also blighted the lives of many of the great and good. Cocaine achieved a certain popularity in Victorian times. In the 1930s and 1940s, if the diaries of Chips Channon are to be believed, the amphetamine Benzedrine was rife among the smart set. Channon would lace his and his friends' cocktails with the drug, noting how, on the whole, 'nobody noticed'.[47] He managed to keep his own drug use largely under control, although it was likely a contributing factor to his death at the age of sixty-one in 1958. Others struggled. John Derby's mother Portia Stanley, Channon reported in July 1939, was 'half mad with herbs, drugs, sleeping draughts, money and misery' nine months after the death of her husband Edward.[48] The shipping heiress Nancy Cunard, a confirmed alcoholic and drug user since the 1920s, eventually had to be committed to an asylum. She died soon after she was discharged.

There are, obviously, many reasons why people drink or take drugs, and it would certainly be simplistic to suggest that peers did so because, as peers, they didn't have enough else to do to fill their days. Perhaps it is more accurate to say that – certainly so far as alcohol was concerned – because it was generally ready to hand in aristocratic households, because it formed part of the aristocratic way of life, it became part and parcel of aristocratic culture – just as gambling was. The line between heavy social drinking and alcoholism is a difficult one to draw. There's no doubt, though, that the peerage had its share of heavy drinkers and that some of those heavy drinkers could be termed alcoholics.

One of the saddest figures in this regard was Robin Londonderry, son and heir of the aforementioned 'Londonderry Herr', Charley Londonderry. In their time, the Londonderrys had land and wealth in abundance, their fortune largely stemming from the coal mines that littered their Durham landholdings. They owned several serious houses, too: Mount Stewart in County Down, Wynyard Hall, north of Stockton-on-Tees, and Londonderry House on Park Lane. But by Charley Londonderry's time their glory days were behind them, and although Charley could still afford to employ forty-four members of staff at Londonderry House in the years before the Second World War, he and his wife Edith 'Circe' Londonderry, aware that they needed to make some economies, spent most of their time at Mount Stewart.[49] Charley had political ambition, but poor judgement. His views on Nazi appeasement and his clumsy attempts at amateur diplomacy in the years leading up to the Second World War consigned him to the wilderness, and he died a disappointed man in 1949. Robin, from whom he had been estranged for some time, had long had what his daughter Annabel described as a 'temptation to drink'.[50] While his wife Romaine was alive he had been able to keep that temptation at bay, not least because Romaine, who had reacted to the alcoholism of her own father by becoming a strict teetotaller, had made it clear to him that she would not tolerate drunkenness on his part.[51] Her death from mouth cancer in 1951, aged forty-seven, however, destroyed his hard-won sobriety. Their daughter Annabel records: '[A]s he began quickly to sink into a state of terrible drunken despair, we children were in effect orphaned.'[52] For a while, Robin was able to function and to entertain guests at Wynyard Hall, where he had set up home, helped by his eldest daughter Jane, who as Annabel put it, had assumed 'a demanding future role as a surrogate wife to Daddy'.[53] But he was lonely and frequently depressed. Before long he was routinely drunk by breakfast and took to shuffling around the house in his pyjamas. When Jane asked him 'why he was drinking so much and putting us through such hell', he said, quite simply, 'Because I want to die.'[54] He did so in October 1955, of liver failure, aged fifty-two.

Among some other aristocrats, a dynastic tendency to drink has not infrequently been apparent. 'Alcoholism is quite a fault in my family,' says Silvy McQuiston of the Baths. 'My mother drank to keep Dad company. We used to go on lovely holidays and they always wanted to find the drink of the country – so if we went to Mexico they would drink tequila. They drank a lot. It wasn't so much of a problem with Mum, but Dad's drink of choice was whisky, always whisky. We used to have a big drinks table at home which I got rid of because it was just a temptation for people.' A contemporary of Silvy's who grew up in the Longleat environs remembers how Henry Bath 'went through a period of his life where he was drinking the better part of a crate of Pils lager and a bottle of vodka a day', with a tendency to serve large glasses of vodka to his administrators in meetings. The Osbornes had an issue with drink too, says Camilla Osborne, whose father, Jack Leeds, was an alcoholic. Her aunt Lady Dorothy Osborne married Pat Bowes-Lyon, 15th Earl of Strathmore; their son Timothy Strathmore was also a known alcoholic.[55]

Andrew Devonshire once suggested that alcoholism had run in his family for generations – certainly back to William Cavendish, 6th Duke of Devonshire, who was born in 1790 – and described how both his father Eddy Devonshire and his uncle Lord Charlie Cavendish suffered from 'what is generally acknowledged as the family weakness'. Indeed, Charlie ultimately died from his addiction in 1944.[56] 'Whisky killed him,' Chips Channon wrote at the time. 'He became a confirmed, constant drunkard and it is a miracle that he survived so long. For many years, he had been bed-ridden, hopeless, helpless, sodden with alcohol.'[57] Eddy Devonshire died prematurely, too, suffering a fatal heart attack – not helped by his alcohol consumption – in November 1950 while chopping wood at his East Sussex home of Compton Place aged fifty-five. Andrew, meanwhile, started drinking as an Eton schoolboy. By the time he was a junior minister in his uncle by marriage Harold Macmillan's government, his drinking had progressed to 'over-indulgence rather than incapacitation'. Later, as the 1980s dawned, he slid into full-blown alcoholism, having his first tipple each day at midday, wine at lunch and, '[A]s the problem got worse, an alarmingly early drink about 4 p.m. and a steady intake until I finally went to bed.'[58]

Finally, his long-suffering wife Debo decided that enough was enough. In September 1983, when the Devonshires had guests staying at Chatsworth for the racing at Doncaster and 'Andrew's behaviour was out of control and frightening to watch,' she phoned a counsellor who had been helping her manage her husband's condition, to ask for advice. He suggested that she should send the guests home, cover the furniture with dust sheets and then move somewhere else for a time. Only by doing that, he felt, could she shock Andrew into believing that his behaviour had driven her to leave him for good. 'And for all I knew I had,' she remembered.[59] She stayed away for a few days before Andrew phoned asking her to come home. That's when, as he recalled, 'the miracle occurred'. 'I realised that apart from all the suffering I had caused, I was not my own master. I decided the slavery must stop once and for all.' After that, he never had another drink, despite the lure of the laden drinks tray in his study. Reflecting on his life in 2004, Andrew could only be 'horrified' by his time as an alcoholic. 'It is, of course, a common failing, some would say an illness.'[60]

* * *

If there is one modern aristocratic family that exemplifies the extreme forms addiction can take, it is the Marquesses of Bristol, owners of Ickworth House in Suffolk. Their tragedies were played out over two generations, culminating in the premature death of John Hervey, 7th Marquess of Bristol in 1999.

John's alcoholic mother Pauline Bolton, the daughter of a businessman, left her first husband Victor Hervey when John was five. For his part, Victor was a fantasist, a liar and a crook. Born in 1915, he was unfortunate enough to have a father, Lord Herbert Hervey, later 5th Marquess of Bristol, who was largely absent from his childhood, and a mother, Lady Jean Cochrane, a daughter of Douglas Cochrane, 12th Earl of Dundonald, who vanished from the scene when Victor was still a baby. Herbert, known by the family as 'Poor Old Herbert' – or 'P.O.H.' – worked for the consular service and spent a lot of time in South America.[61] Jean, variously described as 'not a maternal woman', 'flighty', 'possessor of the best Scotch medicine cabinet in London', and – not surprisingly – 'a bolter', was ultimately divorced from Herbert in 1933.[62] It was largely left to Victor's uncle Frederick Hervey, 4th Marquess of Bristol, and his wife Dora, to bring him up at Ickworth – where as a child he once tried to wring the necks of ducks belonging to the postmistress[63] – and to provide him with a handsome allowance while he was at Eton.[64] When the school authorities found that he had taken up bookmaking, they asked him to leave – though in the embellished version of his life that he relayed to his son, he claimed that the reason for his expulsion had actually been that 'when he was there, he almost killed someone.'[65] He then spent brief spells at two crammers. He was kicked out of both.

A flirtation with the idea of becoming an army officer survived only a ten-month stint at Sandhurst, after which Victor briefly tried to become a City broker. When the Spanish Civil War broke out, he abandoned the City to become an arms trader, not least because, having run up debts of almost £124,000, he had recently been declared bankrupt and was desperate for some ready money. Not surprisingly, his activities soon attracted the attention of the government: in May 1937 the Conservative MP Victor Cazalet, MC, asked foreign secretary Anthony Eden in the House of Commons whether on a recent visit to Finland that Victor had undertaken, 'any attempt was made by him to purchase arms or munitions on behalf of General Franco.'[66] Victor (Hervey) claimed that following an encounter with a drunken Spaniard in a bar in Cannes, he had agreed, in July 1936, to supply five planes to the republicans, and that while he had offered them at £5,000 each, the Spaniard had, for some reason, insisted on paying £10,000 per plane.[67] One of several problems with this story is that, as the historian Gerald Howson pointed out, 'No group of five French civil aircraft crossed to Spain at this period.'[68]

The lies continued, alienating his aunt Dora Bristol, though not his uncle who retained a touching faith in Victor, believing him, according to Victor's first cousin once removed, the Hon. David Erskine, to be a fundamentally 'nice chap'.[69] It was almost as though Victor couldn't help himself. In July 1939 he claimed in an article he wrote for the *Weekly Dispatch* that Sandhurst had not been for him but that, as the headline read, 'At 21 I was dealing in millions'. In the same newspaper feature, he congratulated himself on having got to know '. . . any number of the "boys", and become persona grata with the racing "spivs" and the "con" men, the small timers and the big timers in the twilight world of Soho.' 'I do know my West End better than almost anybody,' he went on. 'I ought to – it took me five years of hard playing, and even harder money spending, to learn how to get around in the right circles.'[70] Later he would claim to John that he had been awarded the Sword of Honour while at Sandhurst.

The occasion for what became a series of articles in the *Dispatch* was Victor's arrest and subsequent conviction for stealing jewellery and a mink coat to the value of £2,500, and for having stolen more jewellery on another occasion to the value of £2,860. When the case was reported, it inspired headlines about the 'Mayfair men', a group who had, in December 1937, robbed Cartier employee Etienne Bellenger at the Hyde Park Hotel. Some people became convinced that Victor had been one of the perpetrators, but, as the journalist Marcus Scriven pointed out, '[T]hat detail is as mythical as his [Victor's] claims to have flown with Morato [the nationalist fighter pilot in the Spanish Civil War] or to have led an infantry assault with pipers and buglers.'[71] Nevertheless, when Victor *was* actually involved in a jewellery theft, in July 1939, reports of the case inspired headlines about the 'Mayfair men' all over again. Two of his co-conspirators were sentenced to fifteen-to-twenty strokes of the cat-o'-nine-tails and a spell in prison. Victor himself was sentenced to three years' penal servitude. His father wept in court. Even then, and despite the social disgrace that his crimes brought him, Victor couldn't avoid embellishing the story of his conviction, claiming that he, like his criminal associates, had been publicly flogged. Years later, his son would excitedly tell his friends about the scars Victor still bore on his back. If they seemed invisible, that is because they were.

Victor was released from prison after two years in 1941. His hope was that he could join the RAF. When that was denied to him, he began making things up again. Claiming to speak four languages, he declared that he worked for the French Deuxième Bureau in Germany (France's former equivalent of MI6) and Czechoslovakia, and that he had been named in 'a secret Nazi document, drawn up by Himmler, as one of the enemies of the Third Reich'.[72] In fact, he seems to have spent most of the war years as a somewhat negligent fire watcher.

In 1949, Victor married Pauline Bolton. Their child, John, was born five years later, by which time the marriage was failing. Given Victor's record and reputation it seems remarkable that he should then have managed to persuade one of England's richest heiresses, Juliet Fitzwilliam, to marry him. Their wedding took place in April 1960, just eighteen days after his father's death and Victor's advancement to Marquess of Bristol. Juliet's family was, not surprisingly, horrified. As her nephew Charles Plunket, whose father Benjamin was sent by his sister Obby to dissuade Juliet from the union, says, '[N]one of us could understand why she married Bristol.' She was after all, extremely dignified, sensible and clever – an Oxford graduate with a degree in fine arts (and so perhaps the wrong person for Victor to inform that all the pictures at Ickworth were Old Masters when they so clearly weren't).

Victor never managed to fool his aunt Dora. Faced with the prospect of Ickworth ultimately falling into her nephew's hands she opted instead, in 1956, five years after her husband's death, to offer it to the National Trust, along with a cheque for £180,000, in lieu of death duties. Nor did Victor ever erase the social stigma his misdemeanours and notoriety had brought on him. It was a stigma that was passed on to the next generation, as one of John's school friends, Robin Cayzer, 3rd Baron Rotherwick, recalls when describing the consternation of a guest of his parents. 'In those days,' he says, 'peer pressure regulated things. For example, if you were rude to somebody or if you were divorced it was unlikely that you would be asked to stay. If you were rude about somebody's religion or sex or something, you got ostracised.' It wasn't surprising, therefore, that the lady in question '. . . was outraged and considered whether she would stay with us when she knew that John was there because, as they put it, there was bad blood in the family and that was never going to change.' 'Sadly,' he concludes, 'she was right.'

Victor may have continued to arouse suspicion and dislike among some, and his aunt might have clipped his wings somewhat by handing over Ickworth to the National Trust, but he was still able to pursue a life of luxury and pleasure in the sixty-room east wing of the house, which the family retained on a ninety-nine-year lease. Visitors were greeted by an army of servants who would whisk away and unpack their suitcases and valet their cars; white-gloved footmen stood behind their chairs at dinner; each guest bathroom was kitted out with hotel-style toiletries (a novelty at a time when most country houses didn't even have separate bathrooms for visitors); breakfast was brought up to female guests on trays. Victor himself drove a black Rolls-Royce embellished with the Hervey mascot, a gold snow leopard, on the bonnet, and hand-painted coats-of-arms on the doors.

As for John at the time, he was described to me by Robin Rotherwick as 'studious, hardworking' and a 'charming, kind, decent person'. 'Like me he had a very narrow band of friends, both of us were quite introvert, private people.' On his visits to Ickworth, Robin noted how relatively little contact John had with the adult members of his family, spending much of his time in an austere lino-floored nursery that contrasted starkly with the extravagance of Victor's downstairs rooms.

I had a similar upbringing but not so bad as John's. I wasn't allowed to have a meal with my parents until I was about seven, and we only got brought down to say goodnight to our parents. John's upbringing was very similar, so I have good knowledge of what this does. It doesn't leave people very grounded. It leaves them with a huge protective shell around them where they feel like it doesn't matter what happens to you, you always feel that you can cope, which is the classic upbringing of my generation in those circumstances. It was the complete opposite to being a snowflake. John was very much like that. If someone upset you, you swallowed hard, put your chin up, and got on with it.

John was fascinated by Victor's tall tales, but Robin could see that a gulf existed between father and son. 'There was always a distance between them, and I think John was mixed in his emotions towards his father. He was in awe of some of the things he'd done, but at the same time he disapproved, was horrified by what his father was and how he conducted his life.' John sought Victor's love but never gained it. The art dealer Guy Sainty believed that Victor did love John in his own way, but he 'had no idea how to show it'.[73] When John was ten, Victor had joked, in front of his friends, that one of them might adopt him and take him off his father's hands. Later, Robin says, the distance between John and Victor increased, '[S]o that they arranged that neither was in the same house as the other. When John was at Ickworth, his father wasn't – when his father was at Chapel Street, John wasn't.'

It didn't augur well for the future.

In 1973, when he was not yet nineteen, while out shooting with his childhood friend the Hon. Henry Wodehouse, a paralytically drunk John accidentally fired into his friend's leg just below the knee. 'Four pieces of shot, like four hornet stings,' Henry remembered. When Henry remonstrated with him, John replied, 'Oh, sorry, old boy, better luck next time.'[74] By 1977, he was taking his first drink by eleven in the morning. He was also experimenting with drugs. As his friend Imogen von Halle put it, '[E]verybody else was doing it – everybody in the circle we mixed in. It was the 1970s and some of us had a little bit too much money, and not enough to do.'[75] Initially, John wasn't a heavy user – but he was easily influenced by others, and before long he was an addict. After a stint living in Paris, in 1982 he moved to New York, where the following year he was arrested for his alleged part in a conspiracy to import both heroin and cocaine. He might have served fifteen years in prison had the charges not lapsed.

Victor, who had for some years been a tax exile in Monaco and who, after his divorce from Juliet in 1972, had remarried again and had three more children, died in 1985. John now inherited the title that went with the 8,000 acres he had inherited on his twenty-first birthday. It was all that was left of the Bristol estate. Robin Rotherwick believes that at one level he desperately wanted to 'do the traditional thing' – in other words, marry (which he did in 1984, even though he was gay; Victor declined to attend the wedding), have children, and an heir. In an interview with a local journalist in Suffolk in 1987, John described how he loved Ickworth 'more than anything else in the world', and how important he felt it was as head of the family to 'contribute to the running of the country, i.e. take up a seat in the House of Lords and play a part in the day-to-day administration of the country' when he felt that 'the moment is right'.[76] But his inner demons rendered a happy ending impossible. He was extravagant, spending a fortune on his flat in Brompton Square (described by one visitor as 'a kind of James Bond sort of flat'); on gadgets which had to be, as von Halle remembered, 'always the latest'; and on displays of reckless generosity.[77] A taxi driver local to Ickworth recalled in 2006 that while the fare from Ickworth to Bury was generally in the region of £10–12, John '... would hand over £50 and say "keep the change"'.[78] And he remained a drug addict, despite occasional attempts to kick the habit. In an interview in 1984 he said, '[T]he truth is I hate drugs and they are not any part of my life. If anyone came to my house with drugs I'd throw them out.'[79] But drugs had a way of insinuating their way back into his life, whatever the penalties. It's no surprise that by the end of his life he had run through an estimated £20 million of the family fortune.

His final years had a Rake's Progress air to them. In late 1989, he told the journalist Jessica Berens[80] he had a 'depressive illness'. 'My father had manic depressions and my mother had them. I feel I am in a sort of grey rainy late afternoon and nothing in the house has any features at all. There are no objects that are beautiful. Trouble is I've gone too far down the road now. If you take coke for ten years your metabolism alters. But it is very difficult to justify because, to the public, cocaine is simply a Class A drug and bad.'[81] That November, John was back in court charged with driving under the influence of drugs. In April 1990 he was deported from Australia. In November 1991 he was charged with possession of drugs and again in March 1992, by which time he was almost totally broke, his American Express card good only for cutting up drugs. That October, the estate company was liquidated with over £650,000 of debt. In June 1993 John was sent to a drugs rehabilitation clinic but left after a month to take more drugs in the south of France, before being jailed again in December 1993 for failing to stay in rehab. When asked whether prison had changed him, he replied, 'Christ, no! What's it supposed to do anyway? Sure, it might work for stupid people but it's designed for the lower classes really, isn't it?'[82]

In February 1994, the National Trust indicated its intention to terminate John's lease on Ickworth, so as to safeguard visitors. The remaining 2,200 acres were sold for £3 million. Soon afterwards, in early 1995, John fell seriously ill and was admitted to hospital. He had AIDS.[83] In June 1996, Sotheby's sold what remained of the Bristols' contents of Ickworth over two days – pictures, porcelain, silver and several cars – making £2.3 million, more than expected. John moved to Little Horringer Hall, on the Ickworth estate that he no longer owned. Ickworth's East Wing went to the National Trust in 1998. John died at Little Horringer on 10 July 1999. He was forty-four.

It's hard to feel sympathy for a man who had everything and chose to waste it. But it's also hard to resist the suspicion that a strong and damaging sense of entitlement ran through his life, as it had coursed through his father's. Robin Rotherwick says: 'Victor was arrogant and tried to massage his ego by [hosting] things like the Monarchist League,[84] which was ridiculous.' For his part, John never learned to accept that the Bristols no longer commanded the whole of Ickworth – that, as Robin puts it, 'all their family silver [was] locked up by the National Trust.' John constantly skirmished with the new caretakers of his ancestral home. On one occasion, when horse trials were taking place there that he felt impinged on the family area of the estate, he drove his car into one of the fences – a course of action, which, as Robin says, 'did neither the car nor the fence any good'. Another time, high on cocaine, he circled Ickworth's rotunda in his helicopter, bellowing through a loud-speaker at a National Trust employee as he did so. Victor believed that, as Marcus Scriven, the closest thing either John or Victor has to a biographer, puts it, 'hereditary status was the primary determinant of a person's worth.' John arguably inherited that belief. Certainly, one boy in his house at Harrow recalled later that he 'very, very aware of who he was'.[85] The writer Anthony Haden-Guest regarded him as, '[A] throwback to a time before aristocrats had taken to disguising themselves as middle class, and [he] could be as flashy, overbearing and whimsical as any oligarch today'.[86]

Robin Rotherwick, though, takes a more sympathetic view:

> He could have gone either way. He tried hard to be an upstand-ing, good person but the support package wasn't there. His friends didn't help him at that time, they led him on, and there wasn't any family support. If you are nurtured by a lovely family you tend to go on well. Occasionally, you used to hear, "Well, he's the black sheep in the family," but if you have a dysfunctional family, the chances are you are going to be dysfunctional. If you go to a therap-ist they will tell you that, however hard you try, if your father was a domestic bully, you will be a domestic bully. Is that in their DNA or is it nature–nurture?

In 1987, John had told the journalist who visited him at Ickworth: 'I was a spoiled brat – but at twenty-two with a million quid in your pocket you tend to think you are Jack the Lad.'[87] He'd simply had too much, too young. Victor hadn't helped, of course. 'Victor was the cause of a lot of John's problems, but ultimately John knew and had the strength and grace to acknowledge that we are responsible for our own actions,' says Scriven, when we talk on the phone about the Bristols. John admitted as much in the interview he gave to Jessica Berens, saying: '[Y]ou can buy something that is self-gratifying, but self-gratification does not last long enough and it does not turn into happiness.'[88] 'That's fundamental,' says Scriven. 'That showed his intelligence and his awareness.' In his obituary, John and his life was described thus by Berens:

Periwigged lordly decadence, the shadow of aristocracy in the Jungian sense, darkened the life of a man who wore his crest on his chest but was not protected by it. His was the profligacy that exiled Rochester, the privileged hedonism that, in the history of England's landed families, has always caused shame, bankruptcy and death.[89]

When she'd visited him at Ickworth, a decade earlier, Berens found John:

... faced not only with serving a kind of sentence for his father's crimes, but also with the confusion that arose when he appreciated that the world had damned the one person he was naturally inclined to respect and admire. There seemed little point in being anything but what people assumed he was. Whatever one may think of the Lord Bristol, it would have taken a uniquely divine personality to shake off what everybody saw as a genetic curse.[90]

Ultimately, John struggled to bridge the gulf between what he thought he was born to be and what he thought he in fact was. As Scriven says: 'John was brought up by Victor to define himself by his starting point in life, that he was top of the heap.' But:

Put yourself in his skin. How well would you do if both your parents were alcoholics, you were told you are defined by your starting point in life, you're told that you're at the top and you don't need to work, you need to rip people off to show you're cleverer, as Victor inculcated in him, you're gay and you can't express it – 90 per cent gay, and you're growing up in a time when drugs are freely available, and then you've got [John's drug dealer], who, every time you're trying to get off the drugs, says, 'Come on, come on . . .' See how well you do.

12

Excursion in Reality

Work and Careers

John's half-brother Fred Hervey, 8th Marquess of Bristol, suggests that John's coterie was the last group from the last generation, or half-generation, to have unlimited access to often significant wealth at a very young age, often in their early twenties. 'A lot of his peer group', he says, 'were given a lot of money, very young, with few restrictions on how they spent it. Now, the majority of those with big estates and lots of money do not give their children the same financial access. Because of this the heirs now are often low key, not particularly extravagant, they don't spend a lot. It's gone back to Victorian times in a sense.' Celestria Hales, who was born the same year as John Bristol, describes how it was in her generation that, for the first time, '[S]ons and heirs who were going to inherit what my uncle used to call "some draughty old barracks, poor them", got jobs.' She cites Johnny Grimston, 7th Earl of Verulam, 'who went into banking', becoming a director of both Barings and Kleinwort Benson. 'He's about two or three years older than me, and that was unusual [for his generation]. Most of them didn't have that about them. David [Douglas-Home, 15th Earl of] Home and Tom Camoys also got jobs in banks.[1] They were clever enough to realise that they needed paid jobs outside the home, so they flocked to the City. It went from this old-fashioned thing of "let's have a lord on the board because that will look good" to them having to have real jobs.'

If one focuses on the 'premier league' of the peerage – the top twenty-nine families in the nineteenth century, of which twenty-six are still extant – it would appear that even among these major landowners there has been a gradual widening of roles and careers. Just over a quarter between 1900 and the present had or have had a professional job outside landownership, the military and their associated county obligations.[2] But nearly half of the current generation of premier-league peers have at some point in their lives been employed by companies independent of their family estates, and five have never had anything to do with landowning at all.[3] They include an actor – Tim Bentinck, 12th Earl of Portland (to whom I will henceforth refer by the name he is best known in public, Tim Bentinck), who plays David Archer in BBC Radio 4's long-running drama *The Archers* – and a historian, Max Egremont. Among their working-age heirs William Cavendish, Earl of Burlington, the future 13th Duke of Devonshire, is a photographer; the future 20th Earl of Derby, Oxford graduate Ed Stanley, works, like his father, in finance; Henry Russell, Marquess of Tavistock, has followed his father Andrew Bedford to Harvard; while Henry Fitzalan Howard, Earl of Arundel, the future Duke of Norfolk, formerly competed as a Formula 3 driver and now works in insurance.

Among the wider aristocracy, the range of careers pursued is astonishingly broad. George Milne, 3rd Baron Milne, is a self-employed chair caner. 'I don't make a fortune, but I always have clients, if that makes sense,' he said in 2011. 'It is peaceable and keeps me occupied. I work all day and at five p.m. meet my pals in the pub for a few pints.'[4] Adrian Pease, 5th Baron Gainford, has been restoring Citroën DS cars at his Norfolk workshop since 2001, while Francis Newall, 2nd Baron Newall, was for twelve years chair of the Greyhound Board of Great Britain. Several peers are horticulturalists – Randle Siddeley, 4th Baron Kenilworth, for example, has been a landscape gardener for over forty years; Nicholas Lysaght, 9th Baron Lisle, specialises in exotic climbers. Maurice FitzGerald, 9th Duke of Leinster, has described how he was given three choices by his father Gerald when he left school, 'the army, the church or the horses'. He 'didn't have the O-levels' to apply to the army, the church 'didn't really appeal', so he opted for the horse route but decided after three years or so that it wasn't for him. He turned to his mother for advice, and she suggested he try gardening. 'I said, "Oh, am I allowed to?" And she said, "You've got no bloody choice."' Not that he found the peerage and gardening altogether natural bedfellows: 'You're dealing with the building fraternity and having a title doesn't necessarily go [down] well.'[5]

Charlie Kerr, 2nd Baron Teviot, meanwhile, who died in 2023, worked for a time as a bus driver and as a bacon hand, behind the butcher's counter at Sainsbury's, while Gerard Collier, 5th Baron Monkswell, worked for five years as a customer services adviser in B&Q. The future 17th Earl of Westmorland, Sam Fane, has a You-Tube channel where he makes videos about cars; Nick Ashley-Cooper, 12th Earl of Shaftesbury, was a DJ in New York before he inherited the title and the Shaftesbury estates in Dorset; Jamie Sempill, 21st Lord Sempill, chief of Clan Sempill, runs the tour company Clan Chief Tours; and Adam Drummond, 17th Baron Strange, a former Grenadier Guards officer, who was disinherited in his mother's will in 2005, has worked at a Perthshire housing association. Two hereditary peers are Olympians: Colin Moynihan, 4th Baron Moynihan, was a coxswain, and Clifton Wrottesley, 6th Baron Wrottesley, a skeleton racer. The latter is now a director of a natural burial company on his family's former estate in Staffordshire. James Lindsay, 3rd Baron Lindsay of Birker, has worked as an Australian diplomat and as a geophysicist. His winding career path befits someone whose own family history has not exactly moved in a predictably straight line. His father Michael Lindsay, 2nd Baron Lindsay of Birker, until 1941 an economics lecturer at Yenching University, spent the war years smuggling radio and medical supplies to communists in China resisting the Japanese occupation. After the attack on Pearl Harbor, he escaped from Japanese-controlled Beijing with his student Hsiao Li, whom he had married in June 1941, and trekked 500 miles to Yenan, where he took up work in the communists' radio department and then at the New China News Agency. James was born in a cave en route.

Some peers, inevitably, have joined the family business, or at least felt an obligation to follow in the career steps of their illustrious ancestors. One peer, whose family were industrialists, relates that he was required to enter the army, before the family firm, before being sent to agricultural college to learn about farming in preparation for coming home to his family estate to work. He laments the ironic lack of opportunities his privilege has offered him. Hugh Trenchard, 3rd Viscount Trenchard, whose grandfather was Marshal of the Royal Air Force Hugh Trenchard, 1st Viscount Trenchard, founder of the Royal Air Force, grew up acutely aware of the cult of 'the great man' that hung over the household. 'My father grew up in his shadow, and so did I. The house was full of photographs of him, trophies, books. I was told lots of things about what he had achieved in his life and I felt a huge burden of expectation. I often wished that I could escape. Why was I an Honourable? Why couldn't I be like my friends and not have anything and any expectations of what I was going to do?' In the end Hugh served for eight years in the Royal Green Jackets, and then went into banking. In 2006 he became Honorary Air Commodore of 600 (City of London) Squadron. As for Jonathan Moyne, scion of the Guinness brewing dynasty, he says he would very much like to have worked full-time for the company, 'But my father didn't want me to. I didn't have the right qualifications, which would have meant being a chemist which I never was.' At least he enjoyed the drink, which is more than can be said for former chief executive Ernest Saunders: 'Apparently, if he used to have to have a glass, afterwards he would pour it into a flowerpot.' Indeed, Jonathan Moyne became a director of Guinness in 1961, and remained so until 1988.

* * *

While today's peers pursue a wide range of jobs, certain careers are particularly favoured. Of the 673 whose professions are a matter of public record, 300 can be described as 'landowners' – though some of these fulfil other roles, too. Over 100 peers work in finance – the career of choice for a similar proportion of the next generation, too. Landowning and finance are intricately connected: thirty-one of those 100 peers are also landowners, controlling between them over 181,000 acres and thirty-five houses. Randal Antrim, owner of Glenarm Castle estate in County Antrim and also a wealth manager working in London, explains why: 'I knew that if I was going to be able to hang on to it [the estate] then I was going to have to get a reasonably well-remunerated career.' Some families have long finance pedigrees. Eighteen fathers of peers in finance also worked in the sector.[6] Matt Ridley, now 5th Viscount Ridley, was the third generation of his family to sit on the board of Northern Rock and was in place when it imploded in 2007. ('A fantastically painful memory,' he said in an interview in 2010. 'There's not a week I don't think about it.'[7])

After financiers come lawyers, of whom there are currently thirty-two.[8] Here an aristocratic title can cause some confusion in court. The late Conservative MP and Scottish barrister Michael Kerr, 13th Marquess of Lothian, ceased using his formal title at work when it became apparent that it was rather unhelpful. He would, he explained to me, six days before he died in October 2024, give his submission to the judge, ending this with 'my lord', as per protocol, but then the judge would reply thanking him, Lord Ancram – the title he held until 2004 – for his submission, and then burst into laughter. Lord Ancram felt this hardly helped with the serious image that he was trying to cultivate, and so a less formal mode of address was agreed. As Earl of Ancram, which he was for fifty-nine years before succeeding as the Marquess of Lothian, he became known to his friends as 'Crumb', following an incident at a party in the 1960s when he introduced himself as 'Lord Ancram' and was announced by the butler as 'Mr Norman Crumb', with one or two very close friends even still, in his later years, opting for 'Norman'.

Those peers closely involved with their estates tend to oversee rather than farm them themselves – on a tractor, in a field, day by day. Back in 1968 the writer Roy Perrott found that '[I]n the course of personally visiting about fifty landed lords and gentry, I met only one who could simply be described as a farmer.'[9] The same is largely true today, a comparatively rare exception being David Ailsa, who spends a fair amount of his time with his tenants, and who describes how, 'I farm alongside them and I farm with them. I do all the crop spraying, cultivating, though I have an estate office and office manager.' He enjoys the role he has assigned himself. 'There's peace and there's podcasts. You're seeing and speaking to nobody – in serious crop-spraying time I live in a crop sprayer, I leave the house early in the morning, and don't come home until late at night, and I am just crop-spraying all day; same with cultivations. It's great thinking time.'

For others, it's a question of estate management rather than hands-on work. The charming and down-to-earth Pete Czernin, 11th Baron Howard de Walden, was, at the time we met in 2022, plain the Hon. Pete Czernin,[10] son and heir of the billionaire central London landowner Hazel Czernin (pronounced Chairneen), 10th Baroness Howard de Walden; she died in July 2024. He described then how the family estate (which includes the village of Marylebone) was 'a massive part of the family's life', and how it operated as 'a commercially successful property business with a family focussed culture. The estate was very close to my heart and part of all of the family's DNA.' He emphasised, too, the very different path his life had taken to those of his grandparents and ancestors: co-founder of Blueprint Pictures, an Oscar and Bafta-award-winning film and television company, he worked in a sector where aristocratic connections count for nothing – which may have been part of its appeal. 'I couldn't have found an industry harder to break into . . . it wasn't a case of my mum or dad, or godfather pulling strings saying "slip him into the Bank because he's a good egg", especially in a world where some families think that "Job" is a book in the Old Testament.'

One throwback to the grand landowners of the past is Richard

Buccleuch, one of the double dukes,[11] who has had a role in stewarding the fortunes of his family lands for the past fifty years. Back in the 1880s the Buccleuchs owned over 460,000 acres.[12] Today the figure stands at 196,000 acres, but that still makes them the UK's largest aristocratic landowner by about 60,000 acres (the difference roughly the combined size of the French islands of Saint Pierre and Miquelon).[13] The Buccleuchs are still very much magnates: '[I]f you're measuring your landholdings in terms of six figures,' Richard Buccleuch gamely accepts, 'you can't say you're not a territorial magnate.' There are only a handful of others left who can make the same claim.[14]

At one level, Richard Buccleuch seems the archetypal peer of the old school. Born in 1954 to Johnny Montagu Douglas Scott, Earl of Dalkeith, and his wife Jane McNeill, he, like his father and grandfather before him, went to Eton and then on to Christ Church, Oxford, where he was a member of the Bullingdon Club. He is chief of Clan Scott; Captain-General of the Royal Company of Archers, the monarch's bodyguard in Scotland; a trustee of the Royal Collection Trust; High Steward of Westminster Abbey; former Lord High Commissioner of the General Assembly of the Church of Scotland; Lord-Lieutenant of Roxburgh, Ettrick and Lauderdale; Knight of the Order of the Thistle, and from 2023 its chancellor; and at the coronation of Charles III in May 2023, he bore the Sceptre with Cross. In other ways, he is the opposite of what people assume that a man in his position must be like. Exceptionally low-key and endlessly polite and generous, he gives you the impression that he'd rather not have any land at all. School offered little to shout about, and as for the Bullingdon, '[Y]ou couldn't not be [a member], if you see what I mean, because everyone was.' 'I'm not a particularly clubby person,' he reflects. 'Probably not so good in all-male company.' He takes a relaxed view of the fact that the family holdings have become, in his words 'significantly smaller'. 'I am very happy that in the hills between Langholm and Newcastle, significant amounts of land have been transferred into community ownership . . . [15] From my perspective, disposal to the right people for good reasons should be welcomed. I have surprised myself in that. It's taken a long time for that territorial possessiveness to have worn off, but it definitely has worn off.' He's proud, though, of the four principal houses in his care and their collections – which are so extraordinary that his father once said that if you laid beneath the chandelier on the staircase at Drumlanrig you would be in 'the only place in the world where you can see simultaneously a Rembrandt, a Holbein and a Leonardo da Vinci'.[16]

As a young man, Richard Buccleuch knew what he was destined for – a life running the estates – and didn't think to challenge it.

> I wasn't troubled by it. I probably should have been more troubled than I was, but I was incredibly old-fashioned. I loved the art context that we live in from an early age. I look back and think how anoraky it was. How could I have been interested at the age of twenty-one in looking at French furniture with my grandmother? But I was. The prospect of having an engagement with it all for the rest of my life was actually a plus rather than a worry.

He has taken rather a different tack from his father and grandfather before him in managing his family's empire, looking beyond the estate for sustenance, rather than being focused totally on that, on the ground, all the time. 'I've been hugely lucky to participate in a succession of public appointments – as a trustee of the National Heritage Memorial Fund, a member of the Millennium Commission, a trustee of the Royal Collection Trust, president of the National Trust for Scotland, all of which I threw myself into,' he says. 'I did those things rather than being the person who went around and visited every tenant farmer. I regret not having been closer to them, I would admit that. In my twenties and thirties I spent a lot of time walking around the estates, but I haven't done it for the last two decades. You can't be everywhere.' In 2019, he informally retired from Buccleuch, and his son Walter, Earl of Dalkeith, took over as vice-chairman of Buccleuch.

Estate management also involves estate development, and over the last 250 years, various aristocratic families have played significant roles in the building of the country's towns and cities. Cardiff, for instance, was largely the creation of the Marquesses of Bute: John Crichton-Stuart, 2nd Marquess of Bute, 'in a manner of speaking the ruling monarch of the town', built the docks in 1839; his son John Crichton-Stuart, 3rd Marquess of Bute, rebuilt Cardiff Castle in the 1860s; when, in 1938, the 4th Marquess elected to sell the family's landholdings in the city, they included 20,000 houses, 1,000 shops and 250 pubs.[17]

The Butes have their twenty-first-century equivalents. Among the foremost of these is John Stuart, 21st Earl of Moray, whose ancestor was made Earl of Moray in 1562 by his half-sister Mary, Queen of Scots, and whose four-times great-grandfather Francis Stuart, 9th Earl of Moray, bought the land on which his son would later develop the Moray estate in Edinburgh New Town.[18] John Moray, the son of Douglas Moray, whom we met in Chapter 9, was himself brought up on the family's vast Doune estate in Perthshire, where he can remember watching the filming of *Monty Python and the Holy Grail* at Doune Castle in 1974 – which was leased to the Scottish Ministry of Works (now Historic Environment Scotland) in the 1980s.

These days the Morays' principal seat is Darnaway Castle near Forres, and the estate's nearly 30,000 acres comprise farms, forests, properties, wind and hydro-electric generators sufficient to power up to 4,000 houses, and salmon fishing on the Findhorn and the Teith. And it is near Darnaway that a major scheme of house building has been underway since the early 2000s. This isn't just some small housing development, though, but a whole new town called Tornagrain.

John Moray is proud of the family name – '[T]he Morays have never done anything particularly wrong, as far as I know,' he says – but he downplays his title: '[I]n this day and age it's important not to try and leverage it, because I don't think anyone would be impressed by that.' That said, the long association of the family with the area has gone a long way to calm any local qualms that might have been felt at the prospect of development taking place. In the early days of the scheme, '[P]eople said that the fact that it was Moray Estates gave the process credibility – we have been around for a long time and have a vested interest in doing something that would be of enduring quality. That was gratifying, as we weren't sure how we would be perceived, being a traditional estate.'

Inverness underwent major expansion in the 1980s and 1990s, and soon a disconnect was beginning to appear between its outer suburbs and the centre. In 2002 local planners approached the Moray estate to see whether it might be possible to build three communities, each of 2,000 people. The estate brought in consultants, who recommended that those three small communities should in fact be one larger one; that way, as John Moray explains, '[Y]ou get sufficient economies of scale to be able to have a health centre and schools. Around 10,000 people is the minimum to have a self-sufficient standalone town.' In 2006, the estate held a charrette – a series of public interactive design meetings – bringing in the architect and urban planner Andrés Duany from Miami to help.[19] Planning permission for Tornagrain followed six years later, by which time John, formerly Lord Doune, had become John Moray, following his father Douglas's death in 2011. When we were introduced in 2016, the first house was being built. By May 2023, 800 people were living in 300 houses at Tornagrain and six businesses were operational. There is a waiting list for houses, which are being sold freehold, so that in due course the estate will hand over its administrative function to community bodies. When this happens is down to the people of Tornagrain. 'We certainly won't stand in the way of them taking on the responsibilities,' says John Moray. 'That is a sign of a community maturing and finding its feet.' It is probable that the estate will retain some of the commercial buildings at Tornagrain and have a stake in the social housing; in the next phase of houses to be built, over 50 per cent will be social housing. 'There will always be affordable housing at Tornagrain,' he says. 'It will always be a Highland community with local people.'

John Moray's tenth cousin once removed David Carnegie, 4th

Duke of Fife, an accountant by trade who read law at Cambridge, is also in the business of building a town – and has been since 2007. Like John Moray, in the time that it has taken to build so far, he has changed titles. When his father Jamie Carnegie, 3rd Duke of Fife, died in 2015, he was promoted from Earl of Southesk to Duke of Fife, the youngest dukedom, created for his great-grandfather Alexander Duff, 6th Earl Fife, on the day of his marriage to the 'highly-strung but . . . apathetic' Princess Louise,[20] eldest daughter of the future Edward VII, in 1889.[21]

The original idea for some kind of development on or near the Fifes' 2,000-acre Elsick estate eleven miles from Aberdeen came about when they heard that the local council was devising a twenty-five-year strategic plan. This identified various 'corridors' where development should be focused, and Jamie Fife's Elsick estate was on one of them. Back then, David and his wife Caroline weren't very involved in the area; with their sons Charlie, George and Hugh, their focus was on Kinnaird Castle in Angus.[22] Jamie Fife was living happily at Elsick House, thirty-six miles away, where after his 1966 divorce he had brought up David and his sister Alexandra.[23] 'Elsick was my home with a capital "H",' says David Fife. 'It's not an enormous house, and it's not particularly grand, but it has a nice feel to it. It sits in its own landscape so it feels like a very private place. As a child it was great, you got on your bicycle and off you went into the woods to muck around.'

When it looked as though development was going to take place, either on or around Elsick, David Fife adopted the view that if change was coming, he might as well be part of it. And he wanted to make sure that if he was part of it, there should be none of the poor planning, isolated housing estates and botched infrastructure that have dogged British towns and cities since the Second World War. He told the council: ' "[W]e'll take all of the problems away from you for forty years, have everything in one place, have the scale to do it, and plan it out properly forever." ' 'One thing I've learned about the planning system,' he says, 'is that if you want to succeed then be the least-worst option, because everybody else supports you.'

In March 2009, he went to a meeting with the planning officials with a proposal to build a settlement of 4,000 houses. 'It was clear early on that it was going to be a big development or nothing at all. Once you're in for a big development, you're in for a town. Ten places with 400 houses is a lot more work, and would create something that is a lot less sustaining. The thought was to make a proper job of it so it could grow over time.' Initially, his idea wasn't accepted – '[T]hey were looking to divide the allocation of housing up, and put one half somewhere, and another half somewhere else.' But luck smiled on them when '. . . the councillors rejected that advice and supported us, which was very satisfying.' Since then, '[W]e've never had anything other than full support.'

As it has been for John Moray, the fact that the proposal was being put forward by a family who had been in situ for several hundred years helped rather than hindered. 'There was pretty low confidence from most people in the usual suspects, people who had done development in the area previously, and the ability of the council to hold them to that. It was felt that the family's involvement was an added level of quality control.' Still, he was nervous. 'I've never been a particularly public person, and the idea of having to stand up and justify a very large-scale development in front of people who might not be receptive didn't appeal particularly.' Nor, he is prepared to admit, had he any experience in construction. 'One of the first things I asked was: how do you build a town? Does anyone know how to build a town?' Still, he says, as a man who is not a town planner by profession but has become one by default, '[T]he whole thing has been much more pleasant and far easier than I imagined. It's been ten years of my life that I wasn't expecting to spend in quite this way. When you walk around it and see what's built, on a sunny day it's a very pleasing experience.' It certainly keeps him occupied. 'I used to think I was quite busy and then I got involved with this.'

Planning permission was granted in October 2013, and infrastructure works began immediately. Construction of the first houses started in May 2014, with a young married couple becoming Chapelton's first residents on Valentine's Day 2015. By May 2023, Chapelton had 340 houses occupied, and about seventy at various stages of construction. Events have slowed progress: the oil price crash in 2014, Covid-19, and then 'Liz Truss and Kwasi Kwarteng making a mess of the mortgage market' in autumn 2022. Like the Morays, the Fifes have reached the point of needing a primary school, and when they get to 500 houses, they will be able to support a supermarket. When complete, Chapelton will cover the whole of the Elsick estate, bar three fields.

Chapelton will be for David Fife's eldest son Charlie, Earl of Southesk, who works in asset management, to finish. It was never going to be a one-generation project but represents a nest egg for future generations of Fifes.

> That's the hope. I suspected that my lifetime would be the difficult stages financially, and if it works then Charlie's generation would do well out of it. People seem to think that property development is a shoo-in and you just make money out of it, but when you're leading development like this you're putting an awful lot of money in in the first place. [The cost of infrastructure alone has been in the region of £10 million.] We accepted that would be the case, but we want to get our money back and make some money out of it. Given time that's where we'll get to. Overall, the creation of something better has both a public and private benefit.

* * *

One profession that the aristocracy has largely parted company with is the military. Of the fathers of today's 793 hereditary peers born between 1880 and 1967 (the vast majority of whom were also peers), some 556 served in one of the three branches of the military – not in itself a surprising figure given two world wars and post-war National Service, but it's worth noting that in 1914, at the outbreak of the First World War, seven out of ten Life Guards officers alone had titles. Of the current batch of peers, born between 1924 and 2004, 112 have served in the armed forces. Only one of those peers – Air Vice-Marshal Richard Broadbridge, 5th Baron Broadbridge, CB – was still in the military as of April 2024 and only two future peers were then serving. Almost all were or are officers.[24] The majority served in the army, and more than half of those in one of the seven 'smart' regiments that make up the Household Division – the Coldstream, Grenadier, Scots, Welsh and Irish Guards, and the two regiments of the Household Cavalry, the Life Guards and the Blues and Royals.

Accounts of peers in action suggest that many displayed a suitably aristocratic disdain for the enemy, along with a certain sang-froid. Charlie Hopetoun (later Linlithgow), son of the Viceroy of India, for example, who was captured at St Valéry in 1940, escaped, was recaptured and finally ended up in Oflag IV-C, situated at Colditz Castle in Saxony, in 1943. One day, en route to Colditz at Eichstätt, along with John Elphinstone, later 17th Lord Elphinstone, Elizabeth II's first cousin, and John Egerton, Viscount Brackley, the future 5th Earl of Ellesmere and later still 6th Duke of Sutherland, he was summoned to have his photograph taken. He refused, exclaiming loftily to the commandant, 'It's extraordinary that you should have picked out a relation of the royal family and a couple of lords!'[25] There's no doubt, though, that alongside aristocratic disdain, bravery and sacrifice were very much in evidence, too. Ten peers' fathers were killed in action between 1939 and 1945, and the wider group of fathers – almost all peers themselves – won seventy-nine gallantry medals between 1915 and 1950. As of 2025 only two aristocratic winners of gallantry medals were still living: John de Grey, 9th Baron Walsingham, born in 1925, who was awarded his Military Cross in Malaya in 1952, and the much younger former Irish Guards officer Tom Orde-Powlett, 9th Baron Bolton, who won his Military Cross in Iraq in 2003.

Not all have been happy to serve. Count Henry Bentinck, later

11th Earl of Portland, disliked his time in the army so much that he ran away from officer training, inspiring the local newspaper headline: 'Boy Count Missing from Sandhurst'.[26] He then headed to California to work as a cowboy, before returning to England in 1939, getting married and registering as a conscientious objector. The death of a friend in action, however, prompted him to join the Coldstream Guards – initially as a private soldier – in service with whom he was wounded twice. On the second occasion, he was found by German troops lying in a bomb crater. He had learned a little German at school, and so was able to work out that they were debating whether to shoot him first and ask questions later. Forewarned, he called out *'Freund, Freund, nein, nein, nein!'* ('Friend, friend, no, no, no'), according to his grandson Will Bentinck, Viscount Woodstock (to whom I will henceforth refer as Will Bentinck since he does not use his title), 'and they took him prisoner.' Family lore has it that the incident inspired the headline 'Count missing again' and caused a relative, who assumed that Henry had absconded for a second time, to disinherit him. 'It's one of those things that Pa used to talk about, but it seems we have no proof,' says Tim Bentinck who, like me, was unable to track down the clinching 'Count missing again' evidence.

Part of the reason why the appeal of the military has declined is that it has become a much more unstable career, less guaranteed to offer a long-term future than was once the case. Maurice Roche, 6th Baron Fermoy, a second-generation Household Cavalryman who joined the Blues and Royals in 1987, points out that most young members of aristocratic families these days want to go to university, and so must calculate whether they really want to join up at twenty-one or -two when so many others are joining at nineteen. They also worry whether there will be a job for them in the outside world once they decide to leave: 'Nowadays you can't just ring up someone from Savills and say, "Will you see my son?"' That situation is unlikely to change. It is more than a little symbolic in this respect that the latest member of a long family line of soldiers, Charles Wellington, never considered a career in the armed forces, but instead chose the world of business.[27] Since 1993, he has been chairman of luxury goods group Richemont Holdings, owners of Cartier and the gunmakers Purdey among many other companies. 'I'm afraid I was of a generation where [it was] just after National Service had ended and a lot of people felt it was no longer a requirement,' he said in 2015.[28]

Younger sons have also moved away from the military service they once flocked to, just as they have also largely abandoned the church as a profession. There are a few exceptions on the clerical front. Until autumn 2024, the Reverend and Hon. Mike Erskine, younger brother of James Erskine, 14th Earl of Mar and Kellie, Hereditary Keeper of Stirling Castle, was minister of Alyth Parish Church in Perthshire; while the Reverend and Hon. Sydney Maitland, younger son of the politician Patrick Maitland, 17th Earl of Lauderdale, who was ordained in 1987, worked for thirty-five years in local government and now serves as priest-in-charge at All Saints, Glasgow. Stretching the point a little, the Hon. Jonathan Monckton, third son of Gilbert Monckton, 2nd Viscount Monckton of Brenchley, is, rather fittingly, a former monk.[29]

The army and the church, along with the law and the civil service, were formerly favoured by the aristocracy because, as David Cannadine describes, they were traditionally regarded as high-status institutions, involvement in which confirmed younger sons' 'patrician position'. Their appeal was also that they were comfortingly familiar – other members of the family would have served as officers or clergymen – and that they were 'reinforced by purchase and by property', since church livings were in the gift of the local landowner, who might well have been a relative, while military commissions could be, and were, once upon a time purchased, some for alarmingly large sums. Such socially respectable roles had something else in common, too: their ethos was '. . . leisured and amateur . . . rurally based and hierarchically organised'.[30] And they were necessary: younger sons were always expected to work, since in most cases they had no estate income available to them. As Davina Ritchie, James Stuart's daughter, remembered, '[M]y father as the third son would stand to inherit nothing. He was by no means well off and needed to earn money, otherwise he wouldn't have had a bean.'[31]

In today's very different world, the jobs taken by younger brothers follow not dissimilar patterns to those of heirs and peers. Forty-five of the 390 younger brothers whose jobs I was able to trace work in finance. Then comes the law with twenty-two, while fifteen younger brothers have served in the armed forces. Beyond that, the range is astonishingly wide. Some are actors – the bluegrass country singer the Hon. Thomas Bewicke-Copley, whose stage name is Percy Copley, has starred in UK arena tours of *Thomas the Tank Engine Live* as the Fat Controller. The Hon. Dr Peter Blackwood specialises in Aboriginal cultural heritage; Tom Leicester's brother the Hon. Rupert Coke is an architectural gilder who has done work at the family's Holkham Hall in Norfolk; while the Hon. George Plumptre was, until, summer 2025, chief executive of the National Gardens Scheme, his brother Henry is a blood-stock manager, and their elder brother Julian Plumptre, 22nd Lord FitzWalter, a former surveyor, runs the family seat of Goodnestone Park in Kent. Meanwhile the Hon. Christopher Rowley-Conwy, younger brother of Owain Rowley-Conwy, 10th Baron Langford, who runs Bodrhyddan Hall in Denbighshire, and younger son of Geoffrey Rowley-Conwy, 9th Baron Langford, the longest-lived peer on record, has worked as an aviation firefighter. Others have taken a role in the family business: so, for example, Richard Buccleuch's younger brother Lord Damian Montagu Douglas Scott, owner of Heming, the jewellers founded in 1745, sits on the board of Buccleuch, while the Hon. Rory Guinness, younger son of Ben Iveagh, who is the owner of Rory Guinness Experiences which offers 'VVIPS unique tours of Dublin, Ireland and the UK, building on the unique heritage of the Guinness family', is also chair of the family's Iveagh Trust, a social housing provider in Dublin. No member of an aristocratic family needs to worry too much these days about what employment is deemed 'respectable', although when Jasper Duncombe, the future 7th Baron Feversham, decided to become a maker of pornographic films in the early 2000s he was promptly disinherited. The family's Duncombe Park estate is now looked after by his younger brother Jake.

In the past, estates invariably passed to a single heir. Nowadays, some younger brothers are also given a share. In the mid-1980s, Peter Kerr, 12th Marquess of Lothian, gave one each of the family's various houses to his eldest son Michael (until his death in October 2024 13th Marquess of Lothian) and his younger son Lord Ralph Kerr (now 14th Marquess of Lothian), endowing them with Monteviot in the Borders and Melbourne Hall in Derbyshire respectively.[32] The Manners family have established a similar setup, in that David Rutland and his younger brother Lord Edward Manners both have an estate to manage: the duke at Belvoir Castle, and his brother at Haddon Hall in Derbyshire. The Hon. John Rous, younger half-brother of Robert Rous, 6th Earl of Stradbroke, inherited the Clovelly estate in north Devon from his mother Mary Asquith in 1983, while his brother, who lives in Australia and has worked as a sheep farmer, has nominal control of the Henham estate in Suffolk, which is run by his third son the Hon. Hektor Rous. The Percys have made landownership and custodianship all-consuming for older and younger brother alike: Ralph Northumberland's game shooting-mad younger brother Lord James Percy, who has designed wax jackets for Barbour, made a name for himself as a writer on field sports and often graces lists of 'best shots', farms the 14,000-acre Linhope estate he inherited from his father Hughie Northumberland. Meanwhile, in North Yorkshire, Gerald Fitzalan Howard, younger brother of Edward Norfolk, runs Carlton Towers. 'He does his thing, and I do my thing,' he told me in 2022 when I asked him about his appearance on ITV's *Keeping up with the Aristocrats*.

* * *

Much, then, has changed over the decades. But there's something slightly comforting in the fact that certain aristocratic roles persist:

that there are still hereditary sheriffs, constables, high stewards and falconers, just as there were a century ago. Such offices are largely ceremonial these days, and so even to the most ardent of modernisers must seem harmless and unproblematic. Then there are the truly arcane ones. The Dorset farmer Richard Arundell, 11th Baron Talbot of Malahide, for example, is Lord Admiral of Malahide and Adjacent Seas, a hereditary role created in 1475 to require the Talbot family to oversee the exercise of maritime law and the levying of customs charges just north of Dublin. Chef Jack Crichton-Stuart, 8th Marquess of Bute, is the Hereditary Sheriff and Coroner of the county of Bute. Torquhil Campbell, 13th Duke of Argyll, isn't just chief of Clan Campbell[33] but also Hereditary Master of HM's Household in Scotland, Keeper of the Great Seal of Scotland, Keeper of Dunoon, Carrick, Dunstaffnage and Tarbert Castles, Admiral of the Western Isles, and Hereditary Sheriff of Argyll. Harry FitzRoy, 12th Duke of Grafton, is the Ranger of Whittlebury Forest. Quentin Wallop, 10th Earl of Portsmouth, is the Hereditary Bailiff of Burley, New Forest. Ian Maitland, 18th Earl of Lauderdale, is the hereditary bearer of the national flag of Scotland, while Alexander 'Croc' Scrymgeour, 12th Earl of Dundee, is the hereditary standard bearer for Scotland, which is somehow a different thing altogether. Meanwhile Charles Shrewsbury is Hereditary Lord High Steward of Ireland, and the rules dictate that the hereditary office of Lord Great Chamberlain, which is currently held by Rupert Carington, 7th Baron Carrington, and will be until Charles III dies, will then be passed to whoever is the head of the Cholmondeley family at that time – either David Cholmondeley, who served for thirty-two years in the same role under Elizabeth II, or his son, Alexander, Earl of Rocksavage, born in 2009 – since the role is divided between three families and is transferred, not on the death of the current bearer but on the death of the monarch. Assuming that the current king's grandson one day assumes the throne as George VII, the role is likely to be fulfilled by Merlin Miller, the probable future 30th Baron Willoughby de Eresby, whose father Sebastian St Maur Miller is co-heir of Jane

Heathcote-Drummond-Willoughby, 28th Baroness Willoughby de Eresby, whose father James Heathcote-Drummond-Willoughby, 3rd Earl of Ancaster, held the role of Lord Great Chamberlain under George VI.

As for David Brudenell-Bruce, 9th Marquess of Ailesbury, he is the 31st Hereditary Warden of Savernake Forest, a role that he inherited in 1987 when his father Michael Ailesbury passed it over to him, and that since 1939, when the family signed a lease with the Forestry Commission, giving them timber rights over the bulk of the forest, has been largely symbolic. His father (who died in 2024) was, he says, more interested in the outcome of the 2.30 at Kempton than in family heritage, his fascination with gambling having begun very early in life. 'His peers [at Eton] would say that he would offer you odds on which of two raindrops would reach the bottom of the window first.' Traditionally the Warden of Savernake Forest would blow a twelfth-century ivory horn, carved in Italy, each time the sovereign passed through the forest. That came to an end when Michael Ailesbury sold it half a century ago. His son is still aggrieved by what he did. 'I am the first warden in nearly a thousand years not to be able to blow the horn. I'm not sure I'll ever be able to forgive my father for that – or for pocketing the proceeds.'

Unlike his father, David takes his role seriously. Savernake Forest is open to the public 364 days a year. But on the 365th – usually the first working day of the new year – the forest is closed to passersby and you will find David Ailesbury, 'shivering with cold at his road barrier with a picnic and the day's newspaper', camped out among the trees over which he and his family have exercised guardianship for so many centuries to mark and maintain the forest's private status. 'It seems appropriate,' he says, 'that the warden should be on the station guarding the private space.'

13

Remote People

The Aura of a Title

Inheriting a hereditary title is, for those whom it concerns, a fact of life – an inexorable, unavoidable given. It is not something that can be undone. You cannot become the Earl of Somewhere and then suddenly unbecome it. You are it. You just are. The inheritance comes with no coronation, but also no mechanism to abdicate. Though a title (or titles) can now be legally disclaimed for a generation, and put on ice, it remains technically attached to the person who disclaims it, whether that individual likes it or not. He or she remains a peer – or, at least, they remain the person who, according to the reference books, occupies the inheritable title belonging to their family at that point in history. For some, that is all a title comes down to – an accident of birth, an unshakable but benign marker that means very little, certainly to any notion of identity. Others lean into it and take it more seriously.

Since 1963, when the Peerages Act made it possible for peers to disclaim their titles, only eighteen have chosen to do so. Today, the relevant reference books include the words 'does not use' before the titles of only seven. In four cases it doesn't make much practical difference, since they involve surnames that are the same as title names. The retired firefighter Charles Keyes, 3rd Baron Keyes, for example, would be referred to as Charles Keyes regardless of whether he used his title or not. Just occasionally, peers who wish to untitle themselves have made their desire public. The Conservative politician Richard Needham, 6th Earl of Kilmorey, was, from

1961 to 1977 by courtesy Viscount Newry and Mourne, but, taking the view that 'being without land or inherited money [this] invited ridicule rather than reward', he chose not to use the title, placing a notice in *The Times* on 1 January 1969 stating that: 'Viscount and Viscountess Newry now wish to be known as Mr and Mrs Richard Needham.'[1] More often, though, an informal decision is made not to use a title. 'I feel happy to downplay it, and not really use it on a day-to-day basis,' John Moray says of his ancient title. 'It's fine as long as it is in its context – something of historic interest rather than something that allows you in any way to capitalise on it. It's special but in a particular, quite circumscribed respect.'

When I first approached Benedict Rossmore, and addressed him – correctly – as Lord Rossmore, he replied: 'How did you find me?' as if he were a fugitive and I a private detective. He doesn't much use the title; indeed, when we spoke again in November 2024, after the announcement that the remaining hereditary peers would be excluded from the House of Lords, he added that he had stopped using it altogether. It had a habit of getting in the way.

> Someone I know likes the fact that I have a title – not a friend of mine, a contact – and I can't stand the fact that he brings it up. I was at a lunch once with twelve people who I was meeting for the first time and he brought it up in front of them. It annoys me because I've worked hard to have an independent life and a successful career, and this is something I haven't earned. I don't see it as being a large part of my identity. You get some people who get hung up on that stuff.

David Ailsa describes his title is 'an inescapable fact'. Does he feel he is 'the Marquess of Ailsa'? 'I inherited quite late in my life,' he says. 'I left my passport and everything else as Lord David Kennedy, as that is who I have been for most of my life.' I point out that when we were first in touch, he signed off as 'David Ailsa'. 'You were writing to me as Lord Ailsa. In some situations if I think it will help I'll use it, but I don't really use it, and still see myself as

Kennedy.' After we have had tea at my house, he signs my visitors' book 'David Ailsa'; it is, after all, his name.

Will Bentinck, the future Earl of Portland, has long shied away from telling people about the Portland connection, to the extent that he doesn't use his courtesy title Viscount Woodstock at all. In his case, the rationale is a historical one. His branch of the Bentinck family, which came over from Holland with William III during the Glorious Revolution, had nothing to do with the Portland titles until the death, without surviving male heirs, of 93-year-old Bill Cavendish-Bentinck, 9th Duke of Portland, in 1990. At that point, the dukedom became extinct, but the Portland earldom created in 1689 for William of Orange's favourite Hans Willem Bentinck had surviving male-line descendants from his second marriage to Jane Temple in 1700. 'All three of us – me, my father, my grandfather,' he says, 'are considerably prouder of being Bentincks than we are of being titled. For me, Bentinck is so much more of a heritage – but it is literally more of a heritage because my Portland heritage only extends as far as my grandfather.' Will's grandfather, the aforementioned Henry Bentinck, incidentally, described the Bentincks as 'socking great Dutch snobs', who had once had their own army, their own currency, and had ruled the principality of Aldenberg. They invented the word 'per' which originally meant 'poor', he suggested, '. . . to distinguish the poor people from those who were not, but it had nothing to do with riches, it simply had to do with being or not being what is commonly now known as "U" except that the Bentincks reckoned that nearly all the people in Nancy Mitford's class of "U" were complete social write-offs. For example, anybody who played golf was per, so were those who fished. This was because the Bentincks didn't do it themselves and had never enquired as to whether or not it was pleasant or good fun.'[2]

A mile away from Will Bentinck's office, across the City of London, another heir to another peerage, investment banker Tom Taylour, Earl of Bective, heir to Christopher Taylour, 7th Marquess of Headfort, also keeps his head down. 'I'm proud of my history, though I haven't tried to educate myself on it, but equally I don't know a single example in my life where being part of the aristocracy has helped me in any way at all,' he says. He goes by 'Mr Thomas Bective' at work, feeling that his title would hinder rather than help his career: 'People would make judgements as to your wealth, your entitlement. There are no benefits to me of having the title now – no family estate, no significant monies that can be expected – and I still have to work.'

Nor, in any case, does he have much interest in it all. He has never visited his family's former seat, Headfort House in County Meath, sold by his grandfather in 1981, and looks blank when I ask about his great-great-grandmother, the former chorus girl Rosie Boote, probably the most famous of all his ancestors, who scandalously married Geoffrey Taylour, 4th Marquess of Headfort, in 1901. Were he to inherit paintings of his ancestors, he doesn't think he'd want them in his house. 'What happened two hundred and fifty years ago in my family doesn't have any impact on my life. I'm just not interested. I'm proud of who I am and of my family, but that only extends to my grandparents.' In due course, he will most likely become the 8th Marquess of Headfort – 'if I outlive my father'. He wonders how he will manage the next name change, from Bective to Headfort, having negotiated becoming Earl of Bective while on his gap year between school and university. 'My friends would know, but people in the work environment and those less familiar with my family history would be asking questions. I don't know if I would be comfortable answering them, because in doing so you change people's perception of you.'

By contrast, William Yarmouth was consistently told that there was something special about him, and this has conditioned his view of his title. He has been Earl of Yarmouth since 1997 – the chosen one, with the shining Hertford marquessate and a country estate to look forward to. His title has been stamped into every aspect of his life, its purpose reiterated over and over again. He is wedded to it – not through a sense of entitlement, but more what I would describe as a kind of Stockholm Syndrome: he's lived with the prospect for so long that the thought of an alternative path has never entered his mind.[3] The illusion of choice briefly flickered in his life when he was asked what he would like to study at university. When he chose ancient history and art, he was directed instead to study rural estate land management at what is now the Royal Agricultural University in Cirencester. In recent years the Hertfords and the Yarmouths have not got along well, but William still feels a strong sentiment for his title. 'I've been brought up with it, I'm comfortable holding a title,' he says. 'I can't just willy-nilly say "You know what, I don't fancy being the Earl of Yarmouth", and choose not to be.' Of course, plenty of others do just that.[4]

* * *

The man who made it possible for peers to disclaim their titles, Anthony Wedgwood Benn – who preferred to be known as Tony Benn – came from a family that had only very recently been ennobled. His father, William Wedgwood Benn, the younger son of a first-generation baronet and a distant relation of the famous potter Josiah Wedgwood, was a Liberal turned Labour member of parliament when he agreed to prime minister Winston Churchill's offer of a peerage.[5] He did so with some reluctance, stating that he'd take the title only: '[I]f you make it plain it's not an honour. I'm going up for a duty.'[6] Churchill agreed. Accordingly, when just before Christmas 1941 William Benn's peerage, along with that of three other MPs, was announced, it was made clear that '. . . these creations are not made as political honours or rewards, but as a special measure of State policy.' 'They are designed', the official statement went on, 'to strengthen the Labour Party in the Upper House, where its representation is disproportionate, at a time when a coalition government of three parties is charged with the direction of affairs.'[7]

Before William Benn formally agreed to become 1st Viscount Stansgate, he consulted his eldest son Michael – who, of course, stood to inherit the title – and asked him if he had strong views on the subject. Michael had not: his intention, once the war was over and he had left the RAF, was to pursue a career in the church rather than in politics, and so for him a title was neither a help nor a hindrance. Tony, on the other hand, who learned about his father's peerage only when he came across a mention of it in the press in December 1941, was, as he later wrote, '... very angry. Father later said I "roundly abused" him. He hadn't told me because, he said, I was a chatterbox and there was a convention that you don't tell anyone if you are offered a peerage. They don't give it to you if it leaks out before the official announcement. We didn't have a row – I didn't have rows with him – but I was upset that at the age of sixteen I hadn't been told.'[8] A month later, William Benn's peerage was created, and he entered the Lords. 'I am meeting tremendous opposition to Dad's peerage,' Tony wrote to Michael in January 1942.[9] Asked at his Oxford admission interview what his father did, he replied that he was an RAF officer – a technically correct response, since William Stansgate, a First World War veteran, had joined up again at the age of sixty-three, much to everyone's surprise. '"Nonsense," said the interviewer, mouthing "Peer of the Realm" slowly as he wrote it down.'[10]

At 11 p.m. on 22 June 1944, Michael Benn took off in his Mosquito from RAF Tangmere in West Sussex. Shortly afterwards, he radioed to say that his air-speed indicator was faulty. Instructed to return to base, he overshot the runway and in the ensuing crash broke his neck. His mother Margaret was with him at St Richard's Hospital, Chichester when he died. He was twenty-two. Five days later, Tony, then based in Southern Rhodesia (now Zimbabwe) with the RAF, received a telegram informing him of the news. 'When I saw the words at first, I was stunned and felt as if something inside me had stopped,' he recorded in his diary. 'The realisation of the desolation came to me in waves.' Returning to his hut, he sobbed for ten minutes. 'It was good to give vent to my feelings – it eased things a lot. I was sick at heart.'[11] Tony never fully got over his brother's death.

After the war he decided to follow in his father's political footsteps, and duly became MP for Bristol South East in November 1950. Almost exactly ten years later, on 16 November 1960, while waiting to speak in a Lords debate on the constitution of Rhodesia, 83-year-old William Stansgate suffered a heart attack and was taken to hospital. The following evening, on his fortieth wedding anniversary and with his family gathered around him, he died. After just a decade in the House of Commons, his son was automatically elevated to the Lords as 2nd Viscount Stansgate. It was not an elevation he sought or desired.

The challenge which he now faced was one that another MP, Quintin Hogg, the Conservative member for Oxford, had experienced just a few years before when, in 1950, he had inherited his father's 21-year-old viscountcy and become 2nd Viscount Hailsham, and so had ceased 'to be entitled to sit in the House of Commons'.[12] Unlike Tony Benn, Hogg had favoured his father's ennoblement, even advising him on what title name to take ('Might I suggest Lord Hurstmonceux with a U as being slightly the most attractive? . . . Hailsham is possible . . . what about Marylebone?'[13]). Like Benn, though, he wasn't keen to assume the title himself. He therefore wrote to prime minister Clement Attlee to ask for 'a change in the law relating to the succession of a hereditary peerage'. He wasn't hopeful of a sympathetic response 'from that rather mean-minded, waspish man', and events proved his pessimism to be well founded.[14] Attlee turned down his request. As Hailsham later reflected: '[P]erhaps there is something paradoxical in the fact that the unsuccessful plea was made by a Conservative to a Labour prime minister whose party was pledged to the abolition of the hereditary peerage on principle, while the successful plea was made by a left-wing Labour member of parliament to a Conservative prime minister who, though committed to the continuance of a hereditary House of Lords, was at least prepared to admit the injustice of one who was admittedly unwilling to join its numbers.'[15]

Less than a year later, Quintin Hailsham's Conservative colleague Alec Douglas-Home, Lord Dunglass, MP for Lanark, and sometime right-hand man to Neville Chamberlain, joined him in the Lords as 14th Earl of Home, on the sudden death of his father Charles Douglas-Home, 13th Earl of Home. The new Lord Home was at dinner in the Commons when he received the news of his promotion. 'I had left some notes in the Chamber, and unthinkingly went in to fetch them,' Home recalled.[16] 'I learned later that someone had reported me to the authorities for breaking a rule, which of course I had done, for I was already a peer.' He assumed, understandably, that he would never return to the Commons: 'I was resigned to the ending of my political career.'[17]

Tony Benn was not resigned to future obscurity in the Lords. He was also concerned that as members of the second chamber were not paid for their work, he faced a future of surviving on reimbursements of just three guineas a day. His would be an uphill battle. On 21 November, four days after his father's death, he went to see the speaker of the House of Commons, Sir Harry Hylton-Foster, who told him that he had 'made an order, my Lord, that you are to be kept out of the chamber'.[18] The Labour leader Hugh Gaitskell was no more sympathetic. 'You can't expect the party to make a fuss over you,' he said, suggesting that, from Labour's point of view, his elevation was all to the good, since the party needed some new young peers.[19] Tony found the Conservative home secretary Rab Butler more sympathetic; Butler described Tony's plan as 'very interesting'.

Benn launched a media charm offensive, personally calling on the editors of *The Times*, the *Daily Telegraph* and the *Guardian*, and producing press releases that outlined his cause, though he waited until his father's obituaries had run before he distributed them. He even signed an instrument of renunciation of his peerage, an ancient mechanism that the Commons hadn't acknowledged since the seventeenth century, and petitioned the Commons to set up a select committee to consider the issue. The press called him the reluctant peer. He preferred 'the persistent commoner'.[20] Gradually, support started to build. The former journalist and future life peer Barbara Castle for Labour, the future Liberal leader Jeremy Thorpe, and the moustachioed backbencher Gerald Nabarro for the Tories, each sent round private entreaties to their colleagues calling on them to support Benn. The solicitor general Sir Lynn Ungoed-Thomas circulated a draft of the Peerage (Renunciation) Bill, that would enable any peer to renounce their peerage.

Even so, ultimate success seemed unlikely. The Committee of Privileges met eleven times to consider the issue, and though Benn was allowed to represent himself, the scope of his testimony was severely limited to purely factual matters. The attorney general, Sir Reginald Manningham-Buller, himself later ennobled as Baron and then Viscount Dilhorne, '. . . bullied and hacked at me as if I was a man who had been caught red-handed in the act of rape and was then pleading mistaken identity,' Tony Benn remembered.[21] When the committee's report was published in March 1961, it didn't find for the man who would not be a peer. His instrument of renunciation was ruled invalid. The existing House of Commons Disqualification Act was deemed insufficient for the purpose for which Benn wanted it used.

Benn was not deterred, declaring that '[F]ar from being the end of the matter, [this] marks the beginning of a campaign in favour of common sense, personal freedom and democracy.'[22] He began a charm offensive with the clerks in the Lords, hoping to overcome their natural opposition to what must have seemed contrary to all they stood for. To begin with, they were suspicious of him, 'insulted that anybody didn't want to be a peer'. 'If', he later wrote, 'I had arrived with a stain around my trousers and a choker scarf and said I was a dustman but thought I had a strong claim to be the Earl of Dundee I think they would have treated me with more respect.' In the end, they acknowledged that they shared a common interest, and softened towards him, 'much as someone who collects toy soldiers is delighted if you go along and offer to rearrange them in a new way.'[23]

He next wrote to the Hon. Sir George Bellew, the Garter Principal King at Arms, commonly known as 'Garter'. His response was bluntly unhelpful. The mere notion of renouncing a title was, he said, 'unthinkable'. Imagine, he went on, if a duke chose to renounce his peerage. What would the consequences be for his son, or his duchess, 'both of whom would presumably suffer social demolition by his action'.[24] Benn had little sympathy for such trivial matters. He felt, not for the first time, that he was facing an uphill battle. Just before New Year's Eve 1960, he and Garter took part in a television programme about the honours list. Afterwards, Garter asked him whether he would like his support in the matter of his peerage. As Benn remembered: 'After the programme he asked me, "Would you like me to come over on your side?" So I said, "Of course. It would be wonderful if you'd come out." "How much is it worth to you?" he asked with a laugh. "You know we live on the fees of the College of Arms and for one hundred and fifty guineas we get you a coat of arms. Perhaps for three hundred we might take it away." '[25]

Benn's impending removal to the Lords necessitated a by-election in his Bristol seat. In the lead up to polling day on Thursday 4 May 1961, he campaigned furiously, addressing bus queues at 6 a.m., work canteens at 8 a.m. and press conferences at 11 a.m.; and then dedicating whole afternoons to pleading his cause to anyone who would listen. It rained on polling day. Undeterred, he went out first thing with his megaphone and then knocked on doors until well into the evening. The count was held at St George's Grammar School. A crowd gathered, chanting, 'We want Benn!'[26] When the returning officer appeared it was to announce that Tony Benn had received 23,275 votes to his Tory rival Malcolm St Clair's 10,231.

It was a theoretical victory only. On 8 May, the day when the Bristol MP would, in principle, take his seat in the Commons, Conservative Party Central Office put down a petition in St Clair's name to unseat Benn. Benn approached the speaker, asking to be allowed into the chamber, but his request was declined. When he tried again to gain entry to the Commons, this time accompanied by Bill Wilkins, MP for Bristol South, and the Labour chief whip Herbert Bowden, waving his election certificate, the doorkeeper barred his access. In the end, Benn, his wife Caroline and their nine-year-old son Stephen heard the petition debated as members of the public, from the Strangers' Gallery. After seven hours, the

Commons determined that Benn could not be heard at the bar, despite having won a considerable majority, and no, said the Commons, he could not take his seat.

That July, the election court sat for ten days. Benn, representing himself, batted away 650 interventions from the ponderous Sir Andrew Clark, 3rd Baronet, QC, who was acting for Conservative Party Central Office, and rehearsed yet again the case for disclaiming a title. He pointed out that '. . . an heir to a peerage could not enter the Lords without personally applying for a writ of summons; he could not have one foisted upon him.'[27] Benn had not applied for a writ of summons, he said, and yet he was being disqualified from the Commons as though he had in fact done so. This, he suggested, was '. . . contrary to the basic equitable principle that you cannot punish a man for something until he has actually done it'.[28]

The judges were impressed. They suggested that Benn might want to consider a new career as a lawyer. But, ultimately, they ruled against him, on the grounds that the hereditary system could not be modified by the courts. He was disqualified from the seat for which he had won 70 per cent of the vote. In June 1961 he suffered a further blow when his application to sit on the National Executive Committee of the Labour Party was rejected. Later that year he wrote to *The Times*, which had taken to referring to him as Lord Stansgate, to ask whether they would revert to calling him Anthony Wedgwood Benn. *The Times*' editor, Sir William Haley, responded unsympathetically: '[A]n election court has declared quite unequivocally that you are Lord Stansgate and it is for that reason that you cannot sit in the House of Commons. It seems to me that if *The Times* were to go on referring to you as Mr Wedgwood Benn it would perpetuate a fiction.'[29]

It seemed Benn had run out of road. But then, in June 1962, George Montagu, 9th Earl of Sandwich, died, and his son, Victor 'Hinch' Montagu, Viscount Hinchingbrooke, Conservative MP for South Dorset, found himself in the same position as Benn. What just a few months ago had been dismissed as a minor constitutional issue, affecting one disgruntled peer, now became an important issue of political principle that affected both the main parties. Less than a year later, on 30 May 1963, the Peerage Bill was passed by the House of Commons, allowing Tony Benn and any other peers who wished to do so to disclaim their titles.[30]

The morning of the day the bill was due to receive Royal Assent – 31 July 1963 – the phone rang at the Benns' house so incessantly that Benn found it impossible to shave. Outside, an army of reporters and photographers gathered. Nine-year-old Hilary Benn informed one journalist that: '[T]he hereditary system is ridiculous and Britain ought to have a president who was elected instead of a Queen who was not.'[31] That evening, Benn, Caroline and his mother Margaret Stansgate went to the Lords to observe as Royal Assent was given to the Peerage Act. As soon as the clerk had spoken the words of enactment, 'La Reyne le veult' – 'The Queen wishes it' – the Benns left the gallery of the chamber. They were escorted to the office of the Clerk of the Crown Sir George Coldstream. Benn handed over his instrument of renunciation, and in the presence of the bewigged Coldstream placed his thumb on a green seal, saying as he did so, 'This is my deed and my act.'[32] And so '[T]he peerage disappeared from me and became dormant, in which case it will remain until my death, when it will be wholly and fully revived in the person who is my heir at that time.'[33] Coldstream beamed, and told the former peer in front of him that he was glad that he had been the first to disclaim.

The Act did not bar members of Benn's family from assuming the title in due course, as indeed his oldest son Stephen would do in 2014, when his father died. The viscountcy wasn't dead, it was just having a rest. Meanwhile, on 20 August 1963, Benn was elected – for the second time – as the MP for Bristol South East, with a majority of 15,000. He believed that he had won the greater prize. On the evening he renounced his title, he attended a party at which Colonel Paul Freyberg, 2nd Baron Freyberg, MC, was present. Paul had recently inherited his father's title. Benn, as he later confided to his diary, '... felt so "one up" on him. If status symbols mean anything, far and away the best is to have had it and given it up.'[34]

Alec Home and Quintin Hailsham swiftly followed Benn in October 1963. The following July, just within the window for peers who had succeeded before the Peerage Act passed to do so, Hinch Montagu disclaimed his promotion too. 'I don't think he cared very much about titles,' his son, the late John Sandwich, told me in 2022. 'He was wedded to Westminster, and had become very actively anti-Common Market.' In 1964, he was sent up to Accrington to stand as the Conservative candidate and lost by 5,500 votes. 'I remember going knowing it was going to be a failure,' John Sandwich recalled. 'It was very unfair to have to succeed to a title if it wrecks your career, and that's what happened.' Hinch never got back into the Commons again. His grandson Luke Montagu, 12th Earl of Sandwich, who regards him as 'a grand man, a natural aristocrat', confesses himself puzzled that 'that he was willing to take that risk'. In the same year, at the other end of the political spectrum, the sometime communist and Spanish Civil War fighter Dr William Collier, for three months 4th Baron Monkswell, disclaimed his peerage, writing to Harold Wilson to say that: '[A]s a socialist and member of the Labour Party, it seems to me wrong that anyone should inherit a seat in parliament, with all the influence that goes with it.'[35]

In total, seventeen peerages have been disclaimed since 1963, two of which have since become extinct. One, the Silkin barony, created in 1950 for the Labour politician Lewis Silkin, has been disclaimed by two consecutive holders. Seven holders of previously disclaimed titles have returned to the Lords, of whom in September 2023, six were still members. Before Alec Home's son David died in 2022, successors of all four of the original 1963 disclaimers – Stansgate, Altrincham, Home and Hailsham – were back in the House of Lords.

Political ambition marks most disclaimers, whether official or unofficial, but not all. Charles Beauclerk stopped using his courtesy title Earl of Burford after his protest against Lords reform in 1999, not because he hated it, but, rather, because he respected it – and felt that its value was being tarnished by the legislation that was being proposed. 'If you do something like that it usually does mean a lot to you,' he says. 'I have a romantic, slightly poetic attitude to it all. I came at it through the history, and that's where it resides in my soul.' He had proved an avid listener when his grandfather Charles Beauclerk, 13th Duke of St Albans, had regaled him with stories of his ancestors and explained the various family portraits hanging on the walls. But his father Murray St Albans, who was not close to his own father, has been less comfortable with the title, and has always seemed to keep both the history of the family and any thought of the significance of the title firmly under lock and key. Beauclerk cautions against some peers' suggestion that they are somehow not members of the aristocracy. 'One shouldn't be fooled by that – it doesn't mean that the title and their family history doesn't mean an awful lot to them. It's often a front that they put on, a mask to wear, but underneath there are deep, instinctual, ancestral feelings that don't go away.' He suspects that his father is the bearer of one such mask: 'I sense that it is a lot more important to him than he makes out.' Perhaps, he says, one day, when he assumes the dukedom, he will be prepared to use the ducal title, but only if it can be used for the public good, and a new relevance can be found for it. As for the Earl of Burford's costume, it never comes out these days. 'It's at the back of the wardrobe, probably very moth-eaten now.'

* * *

For those taking on a title, inheritance can be a complex affair, both legally and emotionally. On the legal side, there are forms to be filled in – proof offered that you are indeed the child of the former holder of the title or that you have the strongest claim to it. Sebastian Browne, 12th Marquess of Sligo, who in 2014 inherited his title from his first cousin Jeremy (who preferred to be called Jeremy Altamont, and who changed his name by deed poll to reflect this), recalls a process that was 'so involved that even I can't remember all the steps'. 'My mother', he says, 'was unable to lay her hands on her marriage certificate – that might not have been such a problem, but my parents were married in Switzerland and I didn't know the province in which they were married.' Ultimately, Sebastian had to obtain his father's death certificate, that of his former wife, their marriage certificate and their wills. He then had to go through the same process with Jeremy's family.[36]

For the father of the retired teacher Paul Capell, 11th Earl of Essex, the process was even more involved. Bob Capell had spent part of his 1920s childhood in a railway orphanage in Woking, after his father Arthur de Vere Capell – who had squandered his allowance from his Essex cousins – died, and his mother Alice found she couldn't cope. All he had to suggest that aristocratic blood coursed through his veins was a page his mother had given him from *Burke's Peerage*. 'I don't think it proved anything but it was reassuring because the name "de Vere Capell" was there,' says Paul Essex. 'My father knew that his father, the black sheep of the family, had been married twice and that he was the son of the second marriage.' What he didn't appreciate was how close he was to the earldom.

It was actually Reginald de Vere Capell, 9th Earl of Essex, who in 1966 embarked on the genealogical journey that would lead to Bob. An article in the *Saffron Walden Weekly News*, with the headline 'In Search of an Heir', in May of that year, described how 'since the 9th Earl of Essex succeeded to the title last year' he had puzzled over who his heir presumptive might be. There was a suggestion that the strongest claim was that of a Californian man named Bladen Horace Capell, of Yuba City, who was the 'forty-six-year-old great-grandson of another nephew of the 6th Earl'.[37] But Bob, who was sent the newspaper cutting by a friend, reckoned he had the stronger claim. 'It's shaken me rather to discover that I might be the heir,' he said a few months later. 'My mother used to kid me a bit that I would be the earl one day – but I never believed her . . . I gather that it is almost certain that I am next in line for the title.'[38] He enlisted the help of the editor of *Debrett's Peerage*, Patrick Montague-Smith, and together they pored over the records. It took three years, during which several key witnesses died and every conceivable piece of relevant information had to be submitted. Bob finally took his seat in the Lords in June 1989. Television cameras were invited in for the occasion, but the news was overshadowed by that of Ayatollah Ruhollah Khomeini's first funeral, during which the body of Iran's religious leader fell out of the coffin. Ironically, after all that, Bob's son, who became the 11th Earl in 2005, told me, 'I usually call myself Paul Capell,' and confessed that he rarely puts his Earl of Essex hat on.[39]

The emotional complexity of changing names arises predominantly from the fact that someone has to die before it can occur. 'Most ladies will come across it in their lives but for happy reasons,' says Charles Kinnoull, who for over fifty years was styled Viscount Dupplin. 'For me it was for a sad reason, so the name-changing bit was pretty tough. I only got my Kinnoull driving licence nine years on. My passport had to say Kinnoull immediately for legal reasons, and there are still utility bills and things that come in in the name of Dupplin more than a decade later. It's quite odd changing a name like that.' For Francis Stafford it was a particularly painful transition because his father was only fifty-nine when he died in 1986, and Francis himself thirty-one. People, he said, had constantly reminded him that one day he would be Lord Stafford, but, 'I would say no – no, because in order for me to be Lord Stafford, my father has to die, and please tell me, anybody, who wants their father to die?' Forty years on, he considers 'Lord Stafford' and 'Francis' to be two different people. 'I've always viewed the name "Lord Stafford" as a trade name.' Like Lord Stafford Inc.? 'Yes! I was Francis Fitzherbert for thirty-one years, and then I became Lord Stafford.' When his father died he had to decide whether to be Francis or 'm'lord'. He thought times had moved on and that he'd be Francis. One day, an old retainer, who had worked for the Staffords for seventy-three years, came to talk to him at home at Swynnerton. 'He turned to me and said, "M'lord?" That cut me to the quick, because there was only one person who was "m'lord" and that was my father.' His voice cracks. 'I get really emotional even now, because he was saying, "You're on."' And once 'on', there's no turning it off again. He finds that people want him to be 'Lord Stafford' rather than Francis. 'I sign all my emails Francis, and they all come back "Dear Lord Stafford".'

Then there are the names that arouse emotion because they bear a particular historical resonance. For most people, 'Lord Byron' immediately brings to mind the 'mad, bad, and dangerous to know' poet whose many conquests included the woman who came up with this epithet, Lady Caroline Lamb.[40] The current Lord Byron – Robin Byron, 13th Baron Byron – admits to having had a poster of his illustrious forebear up in his room when he was an undergraduate at Trinity College, Cambridge – 'I thought it might help in attracting girls' – but admits that otherwise the two have little in common. Though he has written a novel, he has never attempted poetry and whereas George Gordon Byron was an itinerant hedonist, Robin Byron is a retired lawyer and married father of four who lives in the New Forest. For the bicentenary of the poet's birth in 1988, Robin was asked to lay a wreath for the Byron Society on Holles Street in London, where the poet was born. On arrival, he found a television crew there. He was somewhat surprised – he remembers thinking, 'don't tell me the BBC is taking an interest' – but then discovered that it was a Russian TV crew who were keen to ask him: 'Have you got a message for the Russian people?' Byron, he says, is well known in Russia because of his influence on the national poet Alexander Pushkin.[41] Meanwhile in Greece, Byron is 'huge', thanks to his involvement in the Greek War of Independence, and 19 April – the day he died at Missolonghi – is celebrated as Byron Day. 'They are slightly wary,' says Robin Byron. 'As far as they are concerned there was only one Lord Byron, so who is this guy wandering around Athens calling himself Lord Byron?' At home, few make the connection. 'The other day my daughter was trying to spell her name on the telephone, and eventually they cottoned on: "Oh, like the hamburger chain!" People often think that "Lord" must be your first name because they are not terribly familiar with meeting lords, and Byron is nearly always misspelt "Bryon", so usually it's "Mr Lord Bryon", which is not particularly flattering.' Still, he finds that he can '. . . pass without note really, not that I need to be noticed or want to be noticed.' Of Byron, he says, 'if you're going to have a title, it's quite a good one to have.'

For Benedict Baldwin, 5th Earl Baldwin of Bewdley, and great-grandson of prime minister Stanley Baldwin, the title is a source of ambivalence. When we spoke in early 2023, almost two years after his father Edward Baldwin, 4th Earl Baldwin of Bewdley's death, he began by saying, 'I have been slightly wrestling with how I feel about the whole thing. I'm trying to process all of it. Years have gone by without me even thinking about it.' After his grandfather died in 1976, when he was two and a half, he became officially known as Viscount Corvedale, but he has never used the title in everyday life, and has never had much interest in his illustrious background. 'We had family heirlooms around the house when I was growing up, but beyond that I never really had anything much to do with the Baldwins. I never thought of "lord stuff". I kind of forgot about the title.' At one point in his twenties he asked his father – a teacher and later a schools inspector – whether it was possible to remove the title from his passport, 'because I always booked my tickets in the name of "Ben Baldwin" and passport officers in foreign countries would sometimes get confused that I was using different names,' he said. 'I didn't want to make too much of a big thing of it. I had been bullied for it at school – someone had heard that my father was a lord. I learned then that it was something to be ashamed of.' Today he lives in Sweden and soft-pedals his pedigree. 'My wife didn't even know until quite a way into our relationship. We got our bathroom fixed the other day, and the plumber was a bit embarrassed asking me about it, as he had Googled me.' Whether future generations of Baldwins will find themselves in the same situation remains to be seen: Ben has two daughters, but neither he nor his brothers have sons.

When I spoke to David Brudenell-Bruce in 2022, he was Earl of Cardigan; since then his father Michael Brudenell-Bruce, 8th Marquess of Ailesbury, has died, and David has become 9th Marquess of Ailesbury. He has therefore been able to leave behind his connection with the member of his family who ordered the disastrous charge of the Light Brigade at the Battle of Balaclava in 1854, a name, he told me, that was 'tied around my neck wherever possible'. That said, Ailesbury – not Aylesbury, as one might reasonably assume – carries its own historical baggage. The result of a clerical error at the time of the title's creation in 1821, it requires the bearer of it constantly to spell it out. 'For some reason no one was quite brave enough to go back to the Court, to the king and say "Your Majesty, thank you so much, but it's spelled wrong."'

And then there are the titles that are a matter of relative indifference to those who bear them, either because they feel instinctively uncomfortable about using them or because the title itself carries no particular resonance so far as they are concerned. In the former camp come such figures as Robert Sackville-West, who asked to be named thus in this book rather than as 'Robert Sackville', as would be conventional, and who says he has 'no views whatsoever' about his title, beyond that 'the whole title thing is slightly anachronistic'; Ralph Northumberland – 'It's just a title'; and Benjamin Mancroft: 'I don't take it seriously or unseriously, it's just there.' In the latter camp you find the late Jacob Rothschild, 4th Baron Rothschild, who told me in 2023 that he didn't regard himself as an aristocrat '. . . because you think of old English families and we're not an old English family'. 'I don't think it's about being Jewish or not being English,' he went on, 'it's to do with not having been around for more than a hundred years. We just haven't been in England, we started as German Jews. Aristocracy, I think, has been around for hundreds of years.' Henry Ashton, 4th Baron Ashton of Hyde, similarly feels that because '. . . my title is only a hundred years old – I didn't grow up surrounded by coronets on every drainpipe', it's not an integral part of who he is. Nor, he adds, has he ever found it particularly helpful. 'People say it's useful for restaurant reservations, but it isn't. It doesn't make any difference.' Sometimes, indeed, it is merely a cause of embarrassed confusion. On a trip to America, he found that the reception desk at the hotel he was hoping to stay at didn't have his reservation under Ashton, or Hyde, or Lord. Eventually, 'I dug in my case and got the reservation and they said, "Oh, Mr Of!"' It sounded, he says, 'Like a Russian baddie in James Bond.'

That sense of slight detachment is also inevitably felt by those peers who grew up wholly separated from the title they ultimately inherited. John Pelham, 9th Earl of Chichester, is a case in point. The son of John Pelham, 8th Earl of Chichester, and his German wife Ursula von Pannwitz, he was born after the death of his father, in April 1944. John Chichester Senior had met his wife while working as a press attaché at The Hague with Nicholas Elliott, the future MI6 officer, 'an earl and a bachelor, albeit impoverished'.[42] When Germany invaded the Netherlands in 1940, the Chichesters left for England, where John joined the Scots Guards. Four years later, he was in an army vehicle on the A1 north of Doncaster during a blackout when it collided with a lorry. Aged thirty-one, he died of a broken neck. Ursula was seven months pregnant, with a toddler already in tow. Seven weeks later, her second baby was born. It was a boy, and Ursula called him John. He was the Earl of Chichester from his first breath, but that fact was never made particularly apparent to him.

After the Second World War, John Chichester Senior's executors sold Stanmer House, the Chichesters' disused seat near Brighton, and Ursula packed up her family and moved to Argentina, where her mother, Catalina Roth, had spent part of her childhood. Catalina, Käthe to her intimates, had married Walter von Pannwitz, a successful lawyer and art collector, in 1908, and together they built a villa, the Palais Pannwitz, in the Wilmersdorf district of Berlin to house their collection of European paintings, bronzes and ceramics.[43] After the First World War, the von Pannwitzes moved to Holland, where they bought the Hartekamp estate in Heemstede, not far from where Kaiser Wilhelm II was exiled. Rumours swept

Berlin society that Catalina was having an affair with the kaiser, but John Chichester doesn't believe them. 'He and my grandmother were friends – he used to go to the Hartekamp for lunch, and we have photographs of what my mother called "the kaiser's male voice choir", the exiled snobs who came with him.' Still, Catalina and the emperor were close; in all, he visited her at home 103 times, every twenty-fifth visit marked by the construction of a floral triumphal arch. They did not always agree, however. John Chichester recalls how his grandmother criticised Adolf Hitler's 19 million Reichsmark spend on the 1936 Olympic Stadium, and took the kaiser to task over his support for this. 'It took her a long time to forgive him for his outburst when he was defending Hitler,' he says. Later, when we speak a subsequent time, he qualifies this: 'although the kaiser was intensely patriotic, always hoped to be recalled to Germany, and initially supported the idea of one-party rule rather than democracy, he was quite disgusted by Hitler and what he called his gang of thugs.'

After the Second World War, Catalina joined Ursula, John and his sister Georgiana in Argentina, where they set up home in a colonial-style bungalow half an hour outside Buenos Aires. Theirs was a simple existence, one of earth roads to the Roths' farm in the Pampas – as John remembers, 'If it rained a lot you tended to get stuck and get stuck for many hours until someone appeared with a tractor' – and a house where the one link with the outside world, the telephone, was an old-fashioned wind-up model: 'You talked through a local exchange in the village if you wanted to put a call through to Buenos Aires, and they would say "tomorrow at two o'clock we can make a connection".' 'It was a wonderful way of life,' he recalls. He can remember when traffic lights were introduced in Buenos Aires. 'My mother was driving us to the dentist – I think he must have been an ex-concentration camp dentist, because he always found a tooth to drill; we had more cavities than teeth. She stopped at a red light and was abused by a policeman who said she was impeding the flow of traffic.'[44]

John Chichester, in other words, grew up a world away from

that of the English upper class to which he theoretically belonged: '[I]t was irrelevant really, out of context. I didn't go to Eton, Harrow or Winchester, I didn't grow up with any sort of English family. I played with my friends on the farm, and knew Argentines of my age,' he says. He is a fluent Spanish and German speaker. 'My English is much better than it used to be, and my Spanish isn't as fluent as it used to be.' He doesn't sound anything but English, and he now feels English and divorced from the Argentine – but it has taken a long time. During the Falklands War, he was for the British and his sister Georgiana was for the Argentine. He bought his handsome Wiltshire home, Little Durnford Manor, in 1966. 'People used to ask me where I was from, with my accent. There was a hostility to anyone from the outside.' He remembers how 'one choleric old colonel accused me of wanting to build a Tesco supermarket and filling station on my farm. The view that British was best in every sphere and anything foreign was innately suspect and certainly inferior was firmly held and to challenge this was not advisable.'

On earlier visits to England with his sister he had spent time with his grandmother in East Sussex and they would visit Stanmer, but the Chichester link remained a distant one. There were photographs of his father in the house, but John still knows little about him. His mother, who died in 1989, didn't talk about her husband, nor did he ask. 'This is one of the sadnesses – one doesn't ask the right questions because they don't seem relevant or important at the time.' He has none of his father's personal effects either. This may partly be due to the Chichesters' rapid evacuation from Holland in 1940. 'I'm trying to think if I ever saw anything of his. You'd think that you would inherit your father's watch. I don't know what happened to his stuff, I have absolutely nothing personal of his.' His father is buried at Stanmer, alongside his parents and siblings. Nearby are houses with the Pelham crest on. John Chichester won't be joining them. 'I don't want to be buried there, I don't want to be in a place where I've never lived. I am very conscious of my English family's history and my forebears, it's just that because of circumstances, I never had the chance to "connect" with Sussex.' He loves the county, and is pleased when he sees Pelham cottages around, but 'the title, it doesn't mean much to me. It doesn't bring any advantages, and those it did bring were trivial and ignoble.'

* * *

Of course, for every John Chichester who is indifferent to their title – or who might have gone so far as to renounce it – there's at least one who is proud of the family inheritance and sees no issue with others being aware of it, too. One future peer in his forties is addressed by his title at home where he has taken over his family estate. 'Plenty of people who work here choose to do it,' he says. 'Others don't want to do it, but everyone who works here is working for a family business, and there's an element of formality and hierarchy. Those things may not be fashionable but they have served us well. I don't want forelock tugging but it is part of the enterprise – we're not trying to run Google here.' Indeed, he is not alone. Numerous peers adopt a similar formula for the employer–employee address, some using the title as a kind of job title that is relaxed at home. The Carnarvons at Highclere Castle are, for example, known as 'Lord C' and 'Lady C'. As one duchess explains, she is known at home by the formal address for a duchess, 'Your Grace': 'It's the appropriate thing to call me,' she says. 'They would call me Mrs X if that was my name. I don't think they are calling me "Your Grace" because it is really grand and they are rolling their eyes.'

Mungo Mansfield argues that: '[I]n the same way as Mr Jones should be politely addressed as Mr Jones, until he says "call me Evan"', so people should address him as Lord Mansfield, although he concedes that 'a lot of people call me Mr Mansfield' and that, ultimately, 'As long as people call me something that is polite and shows a minimum of human decency, I'm happy. The days of throwing my weight around because people have failed to bow low and call me "your lordship" are over.' Visiting the House of

Lords when a portrait of William Murray, 1st Earl of Mansfield, was unveiled, he was addressed in the formal manner of 'your lordship' or 'my lord'. 'I found it slightly disconcerting at first, but then it became quite natural – it was obvious that it was the natural thing for the civil servants and attendants in the house to do. [But] I think that anybody who has a title who throws their weight around over its use is a man who is riding fast for a fall, and a very severe fall too.' The future Duke of Buccleuch, Walter Montagu Douglas Scott, Earl of Dalkeith, believes that 'the title bears a weight of responsibility that requires a great deal of hard work, but can help you have a platform and give you that voice to be able to speak to the right people.' 'My father', he adds, 'has been the sort of duke who has used that incredibly well – being able to promote charities, to promote his causes – and that is a good thing.' Though, as he points out, 'It has to be done with a degree of thought, careful consideration and responsibility.'

'I never quite understand this idea of using or not using it,' says Benjamin Mancroft. 'It's on the front, like "Doctor". It's just there. To deny it would be odd.' Having said that, he adds, 'You quite often go places and people will say "Are you a real lord or one of those funny new ones?"[45] There's an idea that people dislike peers, but they don't actually – no one has ever been rude to me about it. I've never heard of anyone being rude to a peer because they're a peer.' Randal Antrim has opted for a middle ground, hanging onto his old name 'Randal Dunluce' – after his courtesy title, Viscount Dunluce – for his job in investment management. 'I would think at least 50 per cent of my firm doesn't know that Dunluce is a title, which is how I want it to be,' he says. Sometimes, he has the opportunity to put on his Antrim hat. In October 2022, a century after his great-grandmother Peg Antrim laid the foundation stone at the County Antrim war memorial, he was asked to lay a wreath as a deputy lieutenant for County Antrim. 'On that occasion, I briefly stepped into being the Earl of Antrim, which was a nice thing, and a great honour.' The title is 'an adornment', something that 'needs to be handled with a lightness of touch, and then it's fine,' he says.

'There's the part of the world where you can be the Earl of Antrim and there's 95 per cent of your life when you're not.'

* * *

Charles Beauclerk, heir to the dukedom of St Albans, described to me how a title often evokes the kind of feelings that cannot be overridden. And that is true of so many of the aristocrats I have spoken to. Some may be slightly embarrassed about their titles – to the outside world at least. Some are indifferent. Many are openly or quietly proud. And somehow it seems only appropriate to close with one family that has no qualms about its status: the Salisburys. For this titanic political family, self-assurance comes as part of the deal. Lord David Cecil, grandson of prime minister Robert Salisbury, recalled an exchange that his mother, Alice, once had with the former premier. She '. . . spoke to him agitatedly about the failure of some philanthropic scheme which she believed in. He answered her soothingly. "But, Lord Salisbury," she urged, "surely this failure matters very much." My grandfather smiled gently. "My dear," he said, "nothing matters *very* much." '[46]

Such confidence and balance have been inherited by the former premier's great-great-grandson, the current Salisbury incumbent, Robert Gascoyne-Cecil, 7th Marquess of Salisbury, a Knight of the Garter, and a descendant of Elizabeth I's chief adviser, Lord Burghley. To sit and talk to him is rather like attending a tutorial at an Oxford or Cambridge college. You have brought your notes and essay, and he comes prepared with thought-provoking questions, prompts and challenges, his speech peppered with unselfconscious signs of a high-powered intellect: an 'as Lenin said' here, a 'do you know what Gladstone's wife said about him?' there. The sitting room of his Chelsea townhouse is appropriately eclectic for a man who can effortlessly talk about two such political opposites in the same conversation – loose covers on the furniture, piles of books that range in subject matter from pigs to the Tudors, an array of lamps, and a portrait of his family by the Spanish artist Andrés

Nagel on the wall opposite his desk. Tea is brought to us and we have a biscuit each. He treats me kindly but firmly, asking questions that he expects to hear considered answers to, even though I'm supposed to be interviewing him. He nods and commiserates, laughs and gossips in an entirely relaxed manner. On second thoughts, it's not confidence that he projects. It's beyond that. It is an ease so well refined as to be extraordinary.

His conversation is serious and challenging, political and artful. The first time we meet, we swiftly get on to the subject of China ('why anyone thinks that Huawei is independent from the Chinese government is quite beyond me'); the second time he ruminates on the Austro-Hungarian empire (and in a later phone conversation makes an effortless comparison between the workings of that empire and the 'speed of decision and bureaucracy in Whitehall'. Indeed, it gets to the point where his repeated mention of the former Habsburg empire in each of our conversations, on a variety of topics, becomes a bit of a running joke). None of this is for show or done to impress. It's how one feels his family have talked for generations. Our various conversations put me in mind of a story he told me about his grandfather Bobbety Salisbury's uncle Hugh 'Linky' Gascoyne-Cecil, 1st Baron Quickswood, whom as a child he used to visit in Bournemouth, and who would often write to him. 'I remember one letter that said: "[A]fter your agreeable visit, I reflected on the remarkable fact that I am exactly twelve times as old as you are . . . nor can we quite forget the mystical importance of the number twelve – Lord Jesus Christ Himself had twelve apostles . . . " He talked to you as if you were a complete adult. You were very flattered. He would say, "What you are you reading? I could recommend perhaps Boswell's *Life of Johnson*. If I were you, I would omit the conversational parts because you may find them a little tedious."' Robert Salisbury has that same effortless professorial air.

It's this sense of ease that makes him the consummate aristocrat. True, he does shoot. Yes, he has two country houses and estates. Yes, there is a Salisbury art collection, even if he is swift to tell me that it's not the finest in the country: as his daughter reminds him, 'we're not Chatsworth, you know' – though Robert Salisbury and Peregrine 'Stoker' Cavendish, 12th Duke of Devonshire, are second cousins. Yes, there is an extraordinarily rich family archive that stretches back to the sixteenth century. And, yes, he has been a (well-known and genuinely influential) politician, if not a working one since 2017. But it's his overall manner that strikes one most, rather than these other trappings of the peerage.

He was born in 1946, the son of Robert Gascoyne-Cecil, 6th Marquess of Salisbury, and his wife Mollie Wyndham-Quin, and educated at Eton and then Christ Church, Oxford. His father had a 'difficult' war – he was nearly killed when a Hurricane accidentally opened fire on the group of soldiers he was with on Salisbury Plain, and then again when he 'drove his tank over a cliff'. After hostilities had ended, he recuperated on the Salisbury estate in Rhodesia, while his children spent much of their time with their grandparents, Bobbety and Betty Salisbury, at the Salisburys' ancestral home, Hatfield House, in Hertfordshire, listening intently as Bobbety and Betty read them Lang's *Book of Saints and Heroes* and the works of Rudyard Kipling and Harrison Ainsworth.[47] Young Robert was closer to Bobbety than to his father, describing him as 'a great chum, possessed of very strong opinions, quite nervy, funny'. He also thought him a man of good political judgement: 'he got on extraordinarily well with Americans. If he had been foreign secretary in the early 1950s some of the misunderstandings about Suez wouldn't have happened.'

Politics was never far away from life at Hatfield. One year, Winston Churchill came for Christmas lunch and sat next to Robert. Influential Americans – Allen Dulles and Lewis Strauss among them – visited. Other members of the Salisbury family called in, in particular Linky Quickswood and his brother, the stone-deaf Robert 'Uncle Bob' Gascoyne-Cecil, 1st Viscount Cecil of Chelwood, who had been awarded the Nobel Peace Prize in 1937 for, as Robert Salisbury puts it, 'inventing the League of Nations' and who, with his wife Nelly, regularly spent New Year at Hatfield. Uncle Bob also possessed that other trait common to so many aristocrats: a certain eccentricity. Robert Salisbury describes how, on one New Year's Eve, with the family assembled in the north gallery, 'Uncle Bob opened a window, and, waiting because the house clock was always five minutes behind the church clock, with his watch in his hand, said, "Gentlemen, the church clock." We waited in agonising silence for five minutes, and then he said, "Gentlemen, the house clock. May I wish you all a very happy new year."' Robert Salisbury also recalls witnessing Bobbety showing a group of American senators around Hatfield. 'They came across a half-finished picture of Uncle Bob by Augustus John, and said, "Oh, Lord Salisbury, it must be wonderful for you having a Nobel Prize winner in the family." My grandfather couldn't pronounce his Rs, and said, "Well, actually, when you come to think of it, it is weally wather embawassing as most Nobel Pwize winners have done more to pwomote war than peace."'

Since Uncle Bob and Linky were the sons of the great Victorian prime minister Salisbury, '[I]t made the link with the great man seem a short one,' says Robert Salisbury. His presence was keenly felt at Hatfield. 'He was a scientist, with an enquiring mind, and he fitted the house with electricity but without insulation, which must have been incredibly dangerous. He also installed telephones around the house, some of which were still working when I was a child.' I ask if he feels he has much in common with people like Uncle Bob and Linky. 'The rhetoric and the jokes were very much continuity from the early part of the century. You felt you were a part of that, and equally you did feel something for these rather mysterious sixteenth-century new men whose pictures were surrounding you all the time.'

When Robert Salisbury's father returned from Africa in 1955, the family moved to Cranborne Manor in Dorset and lived what sounds to have been an idyllic life. While his father farmed and managed the estates – 'with mixed success, but the big decisions he got right which is what mattered, and we survived' – his mother set herself up as a landscape gardener. The then director of the

Victoria and Albert Museum, (now Sir) Roy Strong, visited the Cranbornes in 1976 and found Mollie's garden '. . . a paradise. Perhaps the most perfect small-scale country-house garden I have ever seen, delicate, sensitive, English, wholly resistant of conifers and quick-growing effects. The setting of the house is idyllic, in a valley, with a pretty walled courtyard and red-brick gatehouse.'[48]

In January 1970, Robert Salisbury married Bill Stirling's daughter, Hannah. Their son Ned, now Viscount Cranborne, was born later that year. Despite it all, Robert Salisbury didn't ever particularly consider that he would one day become the Marquess of Salisbury. 'My father was a relatively young man and my grandfather was alive,' he says. (Bobbety died in 1972, when his grandson was twenty-five.) 'If one did think about it, it was in some distant part of the future. It would have been a mistake to become obsessed by it.' When he stood for parliament in 1979, in the South Dorset constituency – the seat previously held by Bobbety and then by Hinch Hinchingbrooke – it was as Viscount Cranborne, his courtesy title. To use any other name would have been insulting to the electorate. 'In my experience the electorate are not the fools that everybody takes them for. Why should I be ashamed of it, anyway?'

He told Hannah that he would sit as an MP for one term only. She said she thought it would be 'a bit wet to just do one', so they compromised on two. He stood down in 1987. He hadn't, he says, planned to become an MP. 'I didn't know what I wanted to be. My grandfather said why didn't I become a lawyer, but I thought that was barking because I'd be a hopeless lawyer. I would have liked to have been some sort of a writer.' But politics, he found, '. . . is a disease which is very contagious, and I caught it sometime in the 1980s even if I didn't have it before.' He thinks he was 'probably a bit immature' early on and 'hadn't worked out what I really thought', but while he doesn't judge himself to have been a particularly successful MP, 'I enjoyed being there.'

In 1992, the new prime minister John Major asked if he would join the government in the House of Lords. 'I said to my wife,

"You'll never guess what's happened, but don't worry, I'll say no," and she said, "Don't be ridiculous, of course you have to take it." So I rang Major back and said I'll do it for a couple of years and then I'll retire again. This is what is described as backing into the limelight.' By a writ of acceleration, he entered the Lords as Baron Cecil of Essendon and became a junior minister at the Ministry of Defence. Two years later, Major asked if he would be leader of the Lords. 'I couldn't say no,' he remembers, 'and that was extremely entertaining, although a bit depressing with the wheels coming off the government. I enjoyed it a lot, and I'm very fond of John Major.'

He survived Blair's reform of the Lords in 1999, remaining there for a further eighteen years, after which he took a leave of absence. In 2003 he inherited the Salisbury title. It is, he says, 'something you get used to'. He ruminates for a moment. 'What does it mean? I don't know what it means. People who haven't met someone like me before don't know what to expect. You can't generalise about nobs, they're all different. Is it important? I am proud of my ancestors but I'm not the only one that is descended from them so it doesn't make me unique, but it does make me a sort of flag waver for them.' Being Lord Salisbury, bearing the name of someone so famous, seems not to bother him at all. 'My primary responsibilities are to keep the show on the road,' he says, when I ask whether he has had oversized shoes to fill. 'I'm not particularly interested in business – my son is much better at it than I am. If Hatfield is to survive, the only way to make it work is for it to be supported by a business which is big enough to ensure its continued survival. You have got to plan for a business which is resilient and profitable for the long term.'

It is when he mentions the Hatfield estate that one remembers that he is a landowning aristocrat with the usual worries borne by custodians.

I'm incredibly lucky to have this wonderful house and all that goes with it. Thinking about how to survive and prosper in the modern age, everybody who has one of these places has a different answer to that question. You know there is absolutely no guarantee that you'll survive. Much of what kept these places together is going, but they can be a great force for good locally, and they can make a contribution to national life. An awful lot of how they do that and what they decide to do within the general rubric is down to the aspirations and personality of the incumbent.

The title, he says, '. . . probably is rather important to me, it is inevitably part of what I am.' But if it vanished, he wouldn't mind. Or so he says. 'If I were not allowed to use it tomorrow, I don't think I'd lose any sleep.'

Epilogue

Are We All Middle-Class Now?

Rosemary Muir's reminiscences of the Spencer-Churchill family of the 1930s, which opened this book, evoke a world in which the aristocracy stood apart from the rest of society and made no secret of the fact. Lady Emma Paulet's description of the Winchester family at the end of the century suggests a very different world today. She grew up in Pretoria, South Africa in the 1990s, in a branch of an ancient English family that had relatively little money and lived a relatively ordinary life. Her grandfather Nigel Paulet, 18th Marquess of Winchester, might have been the premier marquess of England and a direct descendant of the Tudor courtier (and judge at the trial of Sir Thomas More) William Paulet, but he preferred a quiet life in the background.[1] 'In my first year at university,' Emma recalls, 'one of our assignments was to interview a family member, so I interviewed him about the family lineage and what it meant to him, and he said that it didn't really mean much – that it was academic to him, and it wasn't something that he really used.' The death of Rosemary Muir's father, Bert Marlborough, in 1972 was covered deferentially and comprehensively in the national press. Nigel Winchester's death in 2016 went broadly unnoticed until 2023, even to *Debrett's*, whose last print edition in 2019 listed him as still living. His successor, Emma's father Christopher Paulet, for nearly half a century styled Earl of Wiltshire, a former member of a heavy metal band, is similarly reticent about his heritage.[2] 'It's become more meaningful to him since his parents have died, and

I think he finds some kind of connection there, but he never refers to himself as the Marquess of Winchester,' says Emma. 'Sometimes it'll come up, but very seldom.'

Day-to-day aristocratic life, too, has changed almost beyond recognition from the ostentation and privilege on display in Rosemary Muir's youth. Even those contemporary peers who continue to live in stately homes tend not to have the run of them but are restricted to relatively modest apartments within their walls – either for practical reasons or, if the house is open to the public, to ensure a degree of privacy. At one big house, the resident couple have dispensed with using the main kitchen, since it is on too much of a rat run for the house guides, handymen and other members of staff, and have instead built in a kitchenette upstairs in their sitting room in order that they can create a little space between them and the myriad other people with whom they now share their house. The rule is that if the door to the sitting room is closed, no one is allowed in, no one is allowed to come and ask questions. The family kitchen at Inveraray Castle in Argyll is similarly down to earth. 'Generations change,' says Eleanor Argyll, the no-nonsense, jolly-hockey-sticks duchess, of her home life with Torquhil Argyll. 'Our generation want to get homework done and listen to bagpipe practice and sit down and watch the latest *Line of Duty* or whatever – we don't have staff cooking. I can knock up a scrambled egg, but he's the cook and I do the washing up, and the Tesco shop online.' At Belvoir Castle, Emma Rutland's late mother-in-law Frances Rutland always had breakfast in bed and never used the kitchen. Now, the private wing at Belvoir has a family kitchen, and when they're all there the family live in two rooms – the kitchen and the sitting room – just as most beyond the castle walls do.

It's tempting to assume that the peerage has or is in the process of merging with the rest of society, that it's becoming indistinguishable from the well-to-do, professional middle class. Ask the average person today who they think of as a 'toff' and they're more likely to name those who affect upper-class personas – the Jacob Rees-Moggs and Boris Johnsons of this world – than suggest that only a duke, marquess or earl could be defined by that word.

But even today, in my view, peers remain something of a class apart. Not every single one, it is true, but a significant proportion. Taken as a whole, the hereditary peerage remains a landowning entity, and those at the top of the tree still own vast swathes of the country. They are very rich, too. Hugh Grosvenor, 7th Duke of Westminster, is the fourteenth-richest man in the country – worth almost £10 billion according to 2025's *Sunday Times* Rich List. Between them, Hugh Westminster, Edward Cadogan, 9th Earl Cadogan, Christopher Portman, 10th Viscount Portman, Pete Howard de Walden, Jonathan Rothermere and John Grantchester control over £23.6 billion. And that's just the billionaires. Meanwhile, Richard Buccleuch divides his time between three stately homes, all of which he considers home. He describes himself as 'a nomad with some very substantial tents'.

Many aristocrats do, of course, have expensive estates to run, but as I toured the country visiting those estates, I didn't get the sense that their owners were cash-strapped, even if several assured me that they were. I still recall a conversation with one peer who assured me that all his wealth was tied up in his property and that he had no cash to spare while we drove around his lands in his astonishingly expensive brand-new car. Benjamin Mancroft, who believes that the aristocracy 'isn't really declining, it's staying the same but fading from public view and has no influence anymore,' argues that, '[T]he landed gentry in the last twenty-five years have done incredibly well.' It is hard to contradict that. It has never been a better time to own and run a stately home. Or at least, it hadn't been until October 2024 and the arrival of Rachel Reeves' Budget, with its inheritance tax revolution.

With their estates comes a strong sense of local loyalties and bonds. David Fife recognises that, for historical reasons, his family doesn't have deep roots in the dukedom of Fife. But it does in the earldom of Southesk, his previous title, created for his ancestor in 1633. 'The Southesk title has a purpose here, at Kinnaird, insofar it has any purpose at all,' he says. 'There's nothing that goes with a title now, no position in the House of Lords or any of that sort of stuff, but it does have a meaning, I suppose, in connection with the estate, because that is where the Earl of Southesk and his family have lived for a very long time.' Local loyalties come with local positions – often honorary – and involvement in local traditions. Since he succeeded his father in 1986, Francis Stafford has launched sponsored walks, cut the tape on nature trails, unveiled drinking fountains, judged gardening plots for the disabled, posed for photographs trying out gym equipment and so much more. In July 1989, he was the star attraction of a Staffordshire county show when he volunteered to milk a cow. He sends me a list of over sixty roles that he has held or still does: 'You get announced first, or if the lord-lieutenant is there then it's "the lord-lieutenant, Lord Stafford, ladies and gentlemen". It's there in that physical sense, and inevitably you're at table number one. You're never on table ten.' The title enters the room before he does. 'As Francis, I'm way down on the list. Locally, it is a big deal. If I was to grow my hair and go off the ball, I would be a constant source of conversation. It is a responsibility.' Others, as we have seen, retain a say in the selection of the local vicar. The only reason Francis Stafford cannot add this obligation to his list is because he is a Roman Catholic.

And then there are the other group-defining features of the aristocracy. The narrow range of careers they tend to pursue. Their continuing bond not just with fee-paying education but with particular schools. The continuing belief in the importance of a male heir. A sense of lineage and a sense of responsibility for that lineage. Charles Beauclerk has described how 'underneath there are ancestral feelings that don't go away.' 'I don't lie awake at night thinking: I've got a title,' says Willie Peel. 'The significance clearly is fading and probably quite rightly so. But with titles go certain responsibilities and I think you have got to try and take them seriously.' Will Bentinck similarly talks of the sense of 'duty and obligation' felt by many peers. 'Ask the average person when the last time was that they heard the word "duty" . . . it just doesn't exist in the same way as it did. To me it is doing good, having a responsibility to improve things, to make people's lives better.' Knowing that you are in line to inherit a particular role, and that you will then pass that role on to the next generation, shapes your whole life and your attitude to it. Charles Richmond described for me his feelings when he went from being Earl of March to Duke of Richmond on the death of his father in 2017 in these terms:

> I guess it's the same experience for everybody, when a parent dies, but like it or not, a lot goes in a name. There's a lot of responsibility there. Even though I was running Goodwood long before my father died, he was there, and somehow you're still the child. Now, you're the next to go, and you're responsible. It's not: 'Let's do this together'; it's suddenly you, and you're it.

Few of the peers I have met demand the deference their ancestors would have expected by right. Some clearly feel slightly embarrassed to talk about their titles. 'My father spent his entire life trying to normalise himself,' says Charles Kinnoull. 'He was very happy booking a hotel room as "Mr Kinnoull", as am I.' But what has often struck me is how differently people behave towards them when they find out that John X is actually the Earl of Y.[3] They become slightly flustered. They worry that they may say the wrong thing or act in an inappropriate way. In my years of writing about the hereditary peerage, I have often been asked whether I felt intimidated when I met so-and-so, or if Lord X is 'very grand', as though the aristocracy is a species apart. The peers notice this too. John Attlee says: 'When I go into a new group of people, I try to delay as long as possible letting them know I am a peer because I want to know what their real colours are.' Freddie Howe understands this inclination. 'If I meet somebody for the first time, I certainly do not introduce myself as a member of the House of Lords, or somebody with a title. It is a social barrier, and most of us want to engage with other people in a natural, normal way, and not be inhibited.'

'There are some people who think one is more important than

one is,' agrees Philip Sidney, 2nd Viscount De L'Isle. 'I don't think one goes on about it unless one needs to. Just don't mention anything, and then occasionally when people start talking about the nobility then one has to own up, but in a low-key way.' Among those who work with or for them, I have noticed time and time again that even when his lordship asks to be referred to by his first name, his staff feel more comfortable calling him by his title.

Indeed, I can't help wondering sometimes whether the self-deprecating nature of so many aristocrats that I have met isn't in fact a rather clever smoke screen. True, they are aware that society is far less deferential than it was even thirty or forty years ago ('Who gives a toss nowadays about whether you're an earl?' says Piers Guilford. 'People don't care, and why should they?'). But by avoiding the glare of public attention, they do what the British aristocracy have always been good at: adapt to changing times without having to concede everything they formerly had.

There was, of course, a time when the aristocracy really did own most of the country, and manage it, too. As prime minister (for the third time) in 1900, Robert Salisbury, presided over a government that contained seven members of his own family, prompting the writer and politician Henry Du Pré Labouchère to give the administration the nickname 'the Hotel Cecil', after the luxury hotel built on Cecil land south of the Strand. In that era, an aristocrat of the standing of a Salisbury could simply brush off such implied criticism, just as he could dismiss the understandable charge of nepotism levelled by the Conservative MP (later Sir) George Bartley, with the remark to his nephew Arthur Balfour that there were '. . . exactly the same number of "relations" . . . in the government in July 1895 as there are now. The arrangement has therefore been before the country during two general elections without provoking any adverse comment.'[4]

No peer has wielded such power for decades now. The short-lived Liberal prime minister Archie Rosebery was said to have three aims in life: to win the Derby, to marry an heiress and to become prime minister. He achieved all three. When in 2017 I asked his great-grandson, Harry Rosebery, UK chairman of Sotheby's, what his goals were, he came up with a rather more modest list. 'You know,' he said, 'I want to be extraordinarily good at something that I have not had on a plate. I want to make my family secure, but not in a hedge of thorns way.' For his five children, he said, 'I want them to feel that what you go out and make for yourself in life is much more important than what you get given. It doesn't allow you to abdicate your responsibilities.' And, he added, 'The other thing I would really like to do is ride the Cresta Run from top to bottom in under fifty seconds.'

For some, the eroding – or, rather, slow metamorphosis – of the old aristocracy is something that has proved difficult to accommodate. Several current aristocratic families contain, and have contained, members who struggled to find a role in a changing world. Brian Masters observed of the grandson of the 'Londonderry Herr', Alastair Vane-Tempest-Stewart, 9th Marquess of Londonderry, that as a young adult in the mid-1960s he was '. . . wracked by a sense of non-achievement. All that he possessed had come to him by right of birth, not through desert, and though he had been educated well at Eton (he claimed not to have enjoyed it), he had never been to university because he had not needed to.' He wanted to accomplish 'something through his own efforts . . . he wanted to be somebody,' but somehow that never happened even though he was an accomplished pianist and musician and something of an expert on the composer Franz Liszt. Masters felt that he was 'a mass of contradictions'. He had 'that natural confidence which comes through centuries of position', but '. . . the confidence was paper-thin . . . it was as if the Marquess was the role, and Alastair the actor striving to fill it.'[5] He was proud of his family and their past, but he was not, Masters thought, 'proud of himself', and he had 'a mighty contempt for the affairs of men'. He never took up his seat in the Lords, viewing 'political and social posturing as Lilliputian'. He was, Masters concluded, 'a misanthrope, beset with an ineradicable melancholia which came with his father's genes and had tormented generations of Stewarts . . . when he felt the onset of an attack of melancholia, Alastair knew himself well enough to protect those around him from the sight of disintegration – he locked himself in his study and would not emerge, neither for meals nor repose, for two or three days at a time.'[6]

But for every Alastair Londonderry or John Bristol (see Chapter 11) there's a Christopher Woodhouse, 6th Baron Terrington, the urologist; a Gathorne Gathorne-Hardy, 5th Earl of Cranbrook, for almost seventy years a zoologist, and in whose honour a species of white-toothed shrew has been named; and a Raymond Asquith, 3rd Earl of Oxford and Asquith, who, in his role as MI6 station commander in Moscow was responsible for smuggling the KGB–MI6 double agent Oleg Gordievsky out of Russia to the Finnish border in the boot of his car. For some, the aristocratic title and its accoutrements can prove crushing. For others it is a boon. As Tom Leicester says of his mighty Holkham inheritance: 'It hasn't been a burden to me. I dare say if one was cut from a different cloth some folk might say, I don't want to do this. Sometimes I am asked if I have sleepless nights – no, I don't.' In their quiet way, those who are comfortable with their aristocratic lineage are continuing to thrive.

When at the age of ten Emma Paulet first heard about her family history and about the significance of her name, she thought it was 'really cool'. 'My grandmother was quite proud of the title and used it where she could – like registering my dad for school, she put him down as "Lord Christopher John Hilton Paulet".' By the time she was at university, Emma found herself surrounded by people who were more sceptical about the peerage and what it stands for. She joined Liza Campbell's Facebook group for The Hares (the primogeniture campaign group, see Chapter 9), and in 2013, just ahead of the birth of the then Duchess of Cambridge's first child, added her signature to a letter in the *Telegraph* calling for parliament to seize the opportunity to grant gender equality to the families that possess Britain's hereditary titles. 'As the person I am today, I think that it would be fairer [if the system wasn't] based on gender,' she says. 'But as it stands, I'm not invested in fighting for it.' It would be a shame, she argues, if hereditary titles 'just stopped altogether'. 'I know it's a very privileged position I am in to be able to trace back my family tree so far. So many people have documented it over the years because of the title. I have a fondness for history and heritage and I wouldn't want something like that to be abolished.'

On a day-to-day basis, Emma gives no hint of her Winchester heritage. She blends in. But the more attentive will notice that she has a signet ring with the family crest on it. Her brother Michael Paulet, currently Earl of Wiltshire, the future 20th Marquess of Winchester, has one too. In the summer of 2023, Emma visited England for the first time with her partner. While they were there, they looked around Powderham Castle, the Devons' home near Exeter, where the Paulet coat of arms is on display, and where she discovered how in 1545 Lady Elizabeth Paulet, daughter of John Paulet, 2nd Marquess of Winchester, married Sir William Courtenay, *de jure* 2nd Earl of Devon. Sometimes her partner calls her 'Princess Paulet'. She corrects him. 'Actually, it's Lady.'

Acknowledgements

A huge number of people have helped with this book in various ways, from editors who supported my journalism by commissioning tangential interviews and features, to friends, relations and colleagues who I no doubt bored for hours in pubs, restaurants, coffee shops and over the phone, going on about people they didn't know. Above all I must acknowledge those who kindly, and usually with little evidence that I wasn't going to embarrass them publicly, entrusted me with their stories. The very many interviewees, most of whom are named but others who are not, are integral to this book. I am truly grateful to all of those who talked to me candidly, so many of whom had never spoken in detail about their lives on the record. For most of those I interviewed there were few press cuttings or published memoirs to consult since they had never done anything like this before.

First, enormous thanks and gratitude to Sheila Thompson, this book's fairy godmother, who in a garden in Kensington insisted that I contact Sophie Scard, my agent at United. To Ian Thomson and Alison Brown, my clever, dogged English teachers, who gave me so much and from whom I took so many hours; to Professor Clair Wills, my final-year supervisor at Queen Mary University of London, who memorably and mortifyingly (for me) corrected my pronunciation of Anthony Powell's surname, and in doing so steered me closer towards this topic. To Simon Heffer, who introduced me to Nigel Wilcockson, my publisher at Penguin Random House, to whom I also owe unlimited thanks, and who from our first conversation I knew was the right editor for whatever this book was to become. Together with my many interviewees, Nigel has made writing this book a pure joy.

To Sir David Beamish, KCB, Merlin Waterson, CBE, Professor John Beckett, Dr Robin Eagles and Hugo Vickers for reading early versions of the book, as well as to Lynn Curtis, my superb copyeditor, and from Penguin Random House to Hannah White-Steele for her tireless efforts organising images for the book, and to Laurie Ip Fung Chun for guiding me through to publication.

To my dear friend and colleague Patrick Kidd, late of *The Times*, for listening, for always offering useful advice, and for tolerating my unbridled ambition; to Helen Davies, from the *Sunday Times*, for her constant support, even when every idea sounded impossibly mad; to Andrew Baker from the *Daily Telegraph*, and to Liz Hunt, late of the *Telegraph*, for teaching me how to be a journalist and unknowingly opening so many doors. To Andrew Knight, for good counsel, and for great wisdom and inspiration in remembering that reporting is the greatest privilege available to any writer; and to his wife Marita Crawley, for her hospitality and to whom I will always be grateful. To Matthew Paton, not just for his guidance in my study of aristocratic families building towns (of which his is one), but for being with me from a distance with useful thoughts, answering very specific questions and making introductions, and to my great friend Robbie Kerr, for listening to me and making helpful suggestions. To Angus and Zara Gordon Lennox for introducing me to the Duke and Duchess of Fife, all those years ago; and to Isabelle Fraser, Anna White, Lauren Davidson and Sam Brodbeck for allowing me the space to commit some of those introductions to newspaper print.

To everyone else who made an entrée for me and who gave references, particularly the Earl of Derby, Thomas van Straubenzee, Sir Christopher Ghika, KCVO, CBE, and Hugh Petter; and to those to whom I fielded endless queries on an incredibly wide range of subjects – especially the Earl of Derby, again, and the Duke of Northumberland.

ACKNOWLEDGEMENTS

Unlimited thanks and gratitude are owed to Lady Juliet Tadgell, to whom this book is dedicated, for her generosity in allowing me access to her mother Obby's papers. My thanks also go to every member of the wider Fitzwilliam, Plunket and Doyne families to whom I spoke: Ian Bond, Michael Bond, Sara Cumani, Philip Doyne, Robin Fitzwilliam, Willie Gething, Sir Philip and Lady Isabella Naylor-Leyland, Jane Pidcock and Charles Plunket. Huge thanks also to Jackie Dale from Bourne Park for her patience and kindness, and to David Allott from the Wentworth Woodhouse Preservation Trust, not only for his hospitality, but for listening, reading and searching with me for two years about the Fitzwilliam family.

My thanks also to Orlando and Miranda Rock, for their support of my work over the years, and especially to Orlando for pointing me in the direction of James Stourton. They say it takes a village to raise a child – and, well, it took half of St James's to research this book.

I am indebted to Lady Silvy McQuiston, who lent me not just videos of her father the Marquess of Bath, but his unpublished memoirs.

The nature of writing a book like this is that people have tended to die halfway through its progress, and a recurring feature of the research has been writing letters of condolence. Some peers were simply too ill or old or forgetful – or deaf – to talk to me, but with only very few exceptions everyone was polite. A peer who will go unnamed gave me the biggest laugh of all, declining my request on the grounds that I must be working for the 'deep state'.

I kicked myself for not having written to architectural historian and curator John Harris earlier, and too many times wished I was twenty years older so that I could have written to many others, seeking their wisdom. Often I stumbled upon someone I thought would surely have all the answers, only to find that they had died just a few years before. It was more frustrating to find that people had died un-interviewed within the timespan I had been writing about this subject than it was to receive a refusal from someone still living. The passage of time robbed me of so many conversations, but such is the reality of studying history – and I am lucky that so many people had survived long enough to contribute to this volume.

In writing this book I have been privileged to be invited to ask questions of many people who do not usually answer them, and for this I will be forever grateful. To all the interviewees all over the world to whom I said 'I do hope this wasn't a torture for you', I sincerely mean it, and I thank you for your patience. By name, I would like to thank the following – and hope to goodness I have not missed anyone out:

The Dukes of Abercorn, Bedford, Buccleuch and Queensberry, Fife, Northumberland, Richmond and Gordon and Rutland; the Duchesses of Argyll, Fife and Rutland. The Marquesses of Ailesbury, Ailsa, Anglesey, Bristol, Exeter, Hertford, Lansdowne, Salisbury, Sligo and the late Marquess Conyngham. The Earls of Antrim, Attlee, Baldwin of Bewdley, Balfour, Bective, Bradford, Buckinghamshire, Burford, Caledon, Carnarvon, Cassillis, Chichester, Dalkeith, De La Warr, Derby, Devon, Dunmore, Durham, Dysart, Essex, Guilford, Harrowby, Home, Hopetoun, Howe, Kerry, Kinnoull, Leicester, Lucan, Mansfield, Moray, Onslow, Orkney, Peel, Portland, Rosebery, Sandwich, Shrewsbury, Stair, Yarmouth and the late Earls of Airlie and Sandwich. The Countesses of Carnarvon, Derby, Harrowby, Mansfield, Mar and Yarmouth. Viscounts Addison, Ashbrook, Astor, De L'Isle, Downe, Lymington, Stormont, Trenchard, Woodstock, the late Viscount Tenby, Viscountesses De L'Isle and Downe, Elizabeth, Baroness Ashcombe, and the Baroness Terrington.

Ladies Kinvara Balfour, Liza Campbell, Daisy Fane, Tanya Field, Celestria Hales, Jane Kaplan, Alice Manners, Violet Manners, Silvy McQuiston, Rosemary Muir, Camilla Osborne, Angela Oswald, Emma Paulet, Arabella Stuart, Cara Willoughby; Lords Gerald Fitzalan Howard, Robin Innes Ker, Ted Innes Ker, Robert Mercer-Nairne, Charlie Scott and the Master of Falkland.

Lords Ashton of Hyde, Ashtown, Berkeley, Bethell, Byron, Crathorne, Fisher, Glenarthur, Howard de Walden, Howard of Penrith, Joicey, Kindersley, Kingsale, Latymer, Lucas, Mancroft, Monson, Moyne, Penrhyn, Rossmore, Rotherwick, Sackville, Shaughnessy, Shuttleworth, Stafford, Strathclyde, Walsingham, Willoughby de Broke and the late Lords Rothschild and Sudeley.

The Hons. Adam Bruce, Turtle Bunbury, Clare Beresford, Fiona Campbell, Charlie Fitzroy, Nick Howard, Philip Howard, Jim Lowther, Jamie Savile, Dr Philip Sidney, James Stourton, Charles Stuart, James Stuart and Grace Walpole.

Nicola Allen, Helen Beard, Philip Beresford, Clementine de la Poer Beresford, Marcus Binney, CBE, Andrew Boggis, Clare Brittain, John Claughton, Ben Cowell, OBE, Dr Oliver Cox, Professor Emma Crewe, Michael Crick, Jon Culverhouse, Sir Michael Davies, KCB, Charles Dawnay, William Diggle, Charlotte Doherty, Kerry Ellis, William Fergusson-Cuninghame, 18th of Caprington, Shana Fleming, Matthew Floris, Gilly Goldsmid, Hannah Gutteridge, Martin Hammond, Dr Tim Hands, Andrew Harle, Robert Harris, Wensley Haydon-Baillie, Victoria Howard, OBE, Harriet Hunt, Dafydd Jones, Antonia Kearney, Stephen Kershaw, CBE, Melica Khansari, Mark Kildea, Julian Lambton, Barnaby Lenon, CBE, Paula Lester, The Reverend Patrick Mansel Lewis, Magnus Linklater, CBE, Dr Stephen Lloyd, Catherine Macmillan, Laurence of Mar, Dr Joanna Martin, Jonathan Meades, James Miller, Mitzi Mina, Tim O'Donovan, Sarah Phelps, Sir Michael Pownall, KCB, James Priory, Jane Procter, Matt Purvis, Kate Reardon, Dr Lizzie Rogers, Sarah Roller, Graham Rust, Flora Scott, Simon Seligman, Alexandra Shulman, CBE, Richard Simpkin, David Skrine, Etan Smallman, Josie Armand Smith, Rachel Sperring, David Steel, Tom Sutcliffe, Dr Christopher Tadgell, D. J. Taylor, Mark Thistlethwayte, Michael Thornton, Robert Totty, Guy Walters, Merlin Waterson, Dr Andrew Wells, Patrick Wheare, Michael Zander, KC, the late Sir David Butler, CBE, the late Sir John Sainty, KCB, and the late Philip Ziegler, CVO.

Jojo Bowman, Sophie Cade, Rachel Conway-Doel, Annabel Miller, Rosie Sobieraj, Barbara Speed, Olivia Żeber, and to all my other friends whom I have neglected during the writing of this book.

And the biggest thanks and all my love, as always, to Tom, Meg and to my parents, who have supported me unflinchingly, and listened to me bore on about the aristocracy for longer than anyone would like to admit.

Bibliography

BOOKS

Ackerley, J. R., *My Father and Myself*, Poseidon Press, 1968

Adams, Jad, *Tony Benn*, Macmillan, 1992

Adonis, Andrew, *A Class Act*, Penguin, 1998

Argyll, Margaret, Duchess of, *Forget Not*, W. H. Allen, 1975

Austen-Cartmell, James, *The Finance Act, 1893 so far as it relates to the new estate duty and other death duties in England*, Wildy & Sons, 1894

Bagehot, Walter, *The English Constitution*, Chapman & Hall, 1867

Bailey, Catherine, *Black Diamonds*, Penguin, 2007

Bailey, Catherine, *The Secret Rooms*, Penguin Books, 2013

Baird, Rosemary, *Goodwood: Art and Architecture, Sport and Family*, Frances Lincoln, 2007

Balsan, Consuelo Vanderbilt, *The Glitter and the Gold*, Harper & Brothers, 1952

Barber, Lynn, *Mostly Men*, Viking, 1991

Bard, Robert, *Watford Past*, Historical Publications, 2005

Barrow, Andrew, *Gossip: Fifty Years of High Society*, Pan Books, 1980

Bateman, John, *The Great Landowners of Great Britain and Ireland*, intr. Spring, David, Leicester University Press, 1971

Beaufort, Duke of, *Memoirs*, Littlehampton Book Services Ltd, 1981

Beaufort, Harry, *The Unlikely Duke*, Hodder & Stoughton, 2023

Beaulieu, Lord Montagu of, *Wheels Within Wheels*, Weidenfeld & Nicolson, 2000

Beckett, J. V., *The Aristocracy in England, 1660–1914*, Blackwell Publishers, 1988

Beckett, John, *The Rise and Fall of the Grenvilles*, Manchester University Press, 1994

Beckwith, Muriel, *When I Remember*, Nicholson & Watson, 1936

Bedford, John, Duke of, *A Silver-Plated Spoon*, Sphere, 1967

Beeson, Trevor, *The Bishops*, SCM Press, 2002

Beevor, Antony, *Crete*, Penguin, 1992

Behan, Paddy, *Part of this Place*, privately printed, 2017

Bell, Anne Olivier, ed., *The Diary of Virginia Woolf, Volume V: 1936–41*, Penguin, 1984

Bence-Jones, Mark, *The British Aristocracy*, Constable, 1979

Benn, Tony, *Out of the Wilderness: Diaries, 1963–1967*, Hutchinson, 1987

Benn, Tony, *Years of Hope: Diaries, Letters and Papers, 1940–1962*, Ruth Winstone, ed., Hutchinson, 1994

Bentine, Michael, *The Reluctant Jester*, F. A. Thorpe, 1993

Beresford, Philip and Rubinstein, William D., *The Richest of the Rich: The Wealthiest 250 People in Britain since 1066*, Harriman House Publishing, 2007

Blackett, Jamie, *The Enigma of Kidson*, Quiller, 2017

Bloch, Michael, *James Lees-Milne*, John Murray, 2009

Blunt, Wilfrid, *Slow on the Feather*, Michael Russell, 1986

Bond, Michael Shaw, *Way Out West*, McClelland & Stewart, 2001

Boswell, James, *The Life of Samuel Johnson, Volume I*, Sir Isaac Pitman & Sons, 1907

Bouverie, Tim, *Appeasing Hitler*, The Bodley Head, 2019

Boyce, D. George, ed., *The Crisis of British Unionism: The Domestic Political Papers of the Second Earl of Selborne, 1885–1922*, The Historians' Press, 1987

Bradford, Earl of, *Stately Secrets*, Robson Books, 1994

Bradford, Sarah, *Disraeli*, Stein & Day, 1983

Brown, Tina, *Life as a Party*, Andre Deutsch, 1983

Brown, Tina, *Vanity Fair Diaries*, Weidenfeld & Nicolson, 2017

Bryant, Chris, *Entitled*, Doubleday, 2017

Buchan, William, *The Rags of Time*, Ashford, Buchan & Enright, 1990

Byrne, Paula, *Mad World*, HarperPress, 2011

Cadbury, Deborah, *Princes at War*, Bloomsbury, 2016

Campbell, Alastair, *Power & The People: The Alastair Campbell Diaries, Volume II: 1997–1999*, Arrow Books, 2001

Campbell, Liza, *Title Deeds*, Doubleday, 2006

Camplin, Jamie, *The Rise of the Plutocrats: Wealth and Power in Edwardian England*, Constable, 1978

Cannadine, David, *Aspects of Aristocracy*, Penguin, 1998

Cannadine, David, *The Decline and Fall of the British Aristocracy*, Yale University Press, 1990

Cannadine, David, *G. M. Trevelyan*, W. W. Norton, 1993

Cannadine, David, *Lords and Landlords: The Aristocracy and the Towns, 1774–1967*, Leicester University Press, 1980

Card, Tim, *Eton Renewed*, John Murray, 1994

Carpenter, Edward, *Archbishop Fisher: His Life and Times*, The Canterbury Press Norwich, 1991

Carpenter, Louise, *An Unlikely Countess*, HarperPerennial, 2005

Carrington, Peter, *Reflect on Things Past: The Memoirs of Lord Carrington*, Fontana, 1988

Cartland, Barbara, *We Danced all Night*, Robson Books, 1994

Castle, Charles, *The Duchess Who Dared*, Swift, 2001

Catterall, Peter, ed., *The Macmillan Diaries, Volume II*, Macmillan, 2011

Cecil, David, *The Cecils of Hatfield House*, Constable, 1973

Chambers, Anne, *At Arm's Length: Aristocrats in the Republic of Ireland*, New Island Books, 2004

Chancellor, Henry, *Colditz*, William Morrow & Co., 2001

Channon, 'Chips', see Heffer, Simon, ed.; and Rhodes James, Robert, ed.

Chipperfield, Jimmy, *My Wild Life*, Macmillan, 1975

Churchill, Randolph S., *Lord Derby 'King of Lancashire'*, Heinemann, 1959

Churchill, Viscount, *Be All My Sins Remembered*, Coward-McCann, 1965

Churchill, Winston S., *His Father's Son*, Weidenfeld & Nicolson, 1996

Churchill, Winston S., *Triumph and Tragedy*, Houghton Mifflin Company, 1953

Clark, Colin, *Younger Brother, Younger Son*, HarperCollins, 1998

Clark, William, *From Three Worlds*, Sidgwick & Jackson, 1986

Clayton, Michael, *Endangered Species*, Swan Hill Press, 2004

Cline, Catherine Ann, *Recruits to Labour*, Syracuse University Press, 1963

Cokayne, G. E., *Complete Peerage of England, Scotland, Ireland, Great Britain and the United Kingdom, Volume IV*, George Bell & Sons, 1892

Cokayne, G. E., *Complete Peerage of England, Scotland, Ireland, Great Britain and the United Kingdom, Volume VIII*, George Bell & Sons, 1898

Coleridge, Nicholas, *The Glossy Years*, Fig Tree, 2019

Coleridge, Nicholas, *Paper Tigers*, Mandarin, 1993

Collier, Peter and Horowitz, David, *The Kennedys: An American Drama*, Summit Books, 1984

Colville, Sir John, *Those Lambtons!*, Hodder & Stoughton, 1988

Colville, Sir John, *The Fringes of Power*, W. W. Norton & Company, 1985

Cooper, Artemis, *Cairo in the War*, John Murray, 2013

Cooper, Artemis, ed., *Mr Wu and Mrs Stitch: The Letters of Evelyn Waugh and Diana Cooper*, Hodder & Stoughton, 1991

Cooper, Diana, *Autobiography*, Faber & Faber, 2008

Cooper, Diana, *The Rainbow Comes and Goes*, Century, 1984

Cowles, Virginia, *The Phantom Major*, Ballantine Books, 1966

Crewe, Emma, *Lords of Parliament: Manners, Rituals and Politics*, Manchester University Press, 2005

Crewe, Quentin, *Well, I Forget the Rest*, Hutchinson, 1991

Curtis, Sarah, ed., *The Journals of Woodrow Wyatt, Volume I*, Macmillan, 1998

Curtis, Sarah, ed., *The Journals of Woodrow Wyatt, Volume II*, Pan Books, 1999

Curtis, Sarah, ed., *The Journals of Woodrow Wyatt, Volume III*, Macmillan, 2000

D'Abo, Lady Ursula, *The Girl with the Widow's Peak*, D'Abo Publications, 2015

Danziger, Danny, *Eton Voices*, Viking, 1998

Davenport-Hines, Richard, ed., *Letters from Oxford, Hugh Trevor-Roper to Bernard Berenson*, Weidenfeld & Nicolson, 2006

David, Saul, *Churchill's Sacrifice of the Highland Division*, Brassey, 1994

Davis, John H., *The Guggenheims: An American Epic*, William Morrow & Co., 1978

De Courcy, Anne, *Circe*, Sinclair-Stevenson, 1992

De Courcy, Anne, *The Viceroy's Daughters: The Lives of the Curzon Sisters*, Weidenfeld & Nicolson, 2000

Dempster, Nigel, *Nigel Dempster's Address Book*, Weidenfeld & Nicolson, 1990

Devonshire, Deborah, *All in One Basket*, John Murray, 2011

Devonshire, Deborah, *Wait for Me!*, John Murray, 2011

Devonshire, Duke of, *Accidents of Fortune*, Michael Russell, 2004

Dickie, John, *The Uncommon Commoner*, Pall Mall Press, 1964

Dinesen, Isak, *Letters from Africa, 1914–1931*, University of Chicago, 1981

Dobree, Bonany, ed., *The Letters of Philip Dormer Stanhope, 4th Earl of Chesterfield, Volume I*, AMS Press, 1932

Dooley, Terence, *Burning the Big House*, Yale University Press, 2022

Dorril, Stephen, *Blackshirt*, Penguin, 2007

Douglas-Home, Charles, *Evelyn Baring, the Last Proconsul*, Collins, 1978

Duff, Charles, *Charley's Woods*, Zuleika, 2017

Eden, Clarissa, *A Memoir*, Phoenix, 2008

Egremont, Lord, *Wyndham and Children First*, Macmillan, 1969

Elliott, Nicholas, *Never Judge a Man by his Umbrella*, Michael Russell, 1991

Elrington, C. R., ed., *The Victoria History of Shropshire, Volume III*, University of London Institute of Historical Research, 1979

Evans, Howard, *Our Old Nobility*, E. J. Kibblewhite, 1879

Falkus, Malcolm, 'Fagging and Boy Government' in *The World of the Public School*, St Martin's Press, 1977

Fareham, Viscount Lee of, *A Good Innings*, John Murray, 1974

Ferrers, Earl, *Whatever Next?*, Biteback Publishing, 2012

Field, Frank, ed., *Attlee's Great Contemporaries*, Continuum, 2009

Fielden, Kate, *Bowood Revisited*, ELSP, 2015

Fielding, Daphne, *The Duchess of Jermyn Street*, Little, Brown, 1964

Fielding, Daphne, *The Face on the Sphinx*, Hamish Hamilton, 1978

Fielding, Daphne, *Mercury Presides*, Eyre & Spottiswoode, 1954

Fitzalan Howard, Alathea, *The Windsor Diaries: A Childhood with the Young Princesses Elizabeth and Margaret*, Hodder & Stoughton, 2020

Forbes, Grania, *My Darling Buffy*, Charnwood, 1997

Fort, Adrian, *Nancy*, St Martin's Press, 2012

Freeman, Kerin, *The Civilian Bomb Disposing Earl: Jack Howard and Bomb Disposal in WW2*, Pen and Sword, 2015

Gaze, John, *Figures in a Landscape*, Barrie & Jenkins, 1988

Gilbert, Martin, *Winston S. Churchill, Volume VIII: Never Despair, 1945–1965*, Houghton Mifflin, 1988

Gill, Robin, *The Myth of the Empty Church*, Society for Promoting Christian Knowledge, 1993

Girouard, Mark, *A Country House Companion*, Yale University Press, 1987

Glenconner, Anne, *Whatever Next? Lessons from an Unexpected Life*, Hodder & Stoughton, 2022

Glendinning, Victoria, *Vita*, Phoenix, 1983

Gloucester, Princess Alice, Duchess of, *Memories of Ninety Years*, Collins & Brown, 1991

Goldsmith, Annabel, *Annabel: An Unconventional Life*, Weidenfeld & Nicolson, 2004

Goldsmith, Annabel, *No Invitation Required*, Weidenfeld & Nicolson, 2009

Gorst, Frederick John with Andrews, Beth, *Of Carriages and Kings*, Thomas Y. Crowell Company, 1956

Green, David, *The Churchills of Blenheim*, Constable, 1984

Green, Martin, *The Delavals: A Family History*, Powdene Publicity Limited, 2014

Greville, Charles C. F., *The Greville Memoirs*, Henry Reeve, ed., Volume III, Longmans, Green & Co., 1875

Griffiths, Richard, *Patriotism Perverted*, Constable, 1998

Hailsham, Lord, *The Door Wherein I Went*, Collins, 1975

Hailsham, Lord, *A Sparrow's Flight*, Fontana, 1990

Halifax, Lord, *Fullness of Days*, Dodd, Mead & Company, 1957

Hamilton, Lord Ernest, *Forty Years On*, Hodder & Stoughton, 1922

Harewood, Lord, *The Tongs and the Bones: The Memoirs of Lord Harewood*, Weidenfeld & Nicolson, 1981

Harling, Robert, *The Great Houses and Finest Rooms of England*, Viking Press, 1969

Harris, John, *No Voice from the Hall*, John Murray, 2000

Harris, Kenneth, *Attlee*, Weidenfeld & Nicolson, 1982

Harry, Prince, *Spare*, Bantam, 2023

Hart-Davis, Duff, ed., *King's Counsellor: The Diaries of Sir Alan Lascelles*, Orion, 2006

Hartley, L. P., ed., *Lady Cynthia Asquith's Diaries, 1915–18*, Hutchinson, 1968

Hattersley, Roy, *The Devonshires*, Chatto & Windus, 2013

Heffer, Simon, ed., *Henry 'Chips' Channon: The Diaries, Volume 1: 1918–38*, Hutchinson, 2021

Heffer, Simon, ed., *Henry 'Chips' Channon: The Diaries, Volume 2: 1938–43*, Hutchinson, 2021

Heffer, Simon, ed., *Henry 'Chips' Channon: The Diaries, Volume 3: 1943–57*, Hutchinson, 2022

Heffer, Simon, *The Life of Enoch Powell*, Phoenix Giant, 1999

Herbert, David, *Second Son*, Peter Owen, 1972

Herrmann, Frank, *Sotheby's: Portrait of an Auction House*, Chatto & Windus, 1980

Hillier, Bevis, *The Virgin's Baby*, Hopcyn Press, 2013

Hillier, Bevis, *Young Betjeman*, John Murray, 1988

Hindlip, Charles, *An Auctioneer's Lot*, Third Millennium Publishing, 2016

Hoare, Philip, *Serious Pleasures: The Life of Stephen Tennant*, Hamish Hamilton, 1990

Home, Lord, *The Way the Wind Blows*, Collins, 1976

Howard, Paul, *Hostage: Notorious Irish Kidnappings*, The O'Brien Press, 2004

Howard de Walden, Lord, *Earls Have Peacocks*, The Haggerston Press, 1992

Howson, Gerald, *Arms for Spain*, St Martin's Press, 1999

Jackson, Anne, ed., *Art at Auction: The Year at Sotheby Parke Bernet, 1976–77*, Sotheby Parke Bernet, 1977

Jackson, Patrick, *The Last of the Whigs: A Political Biography of Lord Hartington*, Fairleigh Dickinson University Press, 1994

James, Robert Rhodes, ed., *Chips: The Diaries of Sir Henry Channon*, Weidenfeld & Nicolson, 1967

James, Robert Rhodes, *Bob Boothby*, Hodder & Stoughton, 1991

'Janitor', *The Feet of the Young Men*, Duckworth, 1929

Jekyll, Gertrude, *Some English Gardens*, Longmans, Green & Co., 1904

Jenkins, Jennifer and James, Patrick, *From Acorn to Oak Tree*, Macmillan, 1994

Jolliffe, John, ed., *Sir Iain Moncreiffe of that Ilk*, The Stourton Press, 1986

Jones, Clyve, ed., *Institutional Practice and Memory: Parliamentary People, Records and Histories – Essays in Honour of Sir John Sainty*, Wiley Blackwell, 2013

Joyce, Joe, *The Guinnesses*, Poolbeg, 2009

Junor, Penny, *Diana*, Simon & Schuster, 1984

Kennedy, Michael, *Portrait of Walton*, Oxford University Press, 1989

Kenward, Betty, *Jennifer's Memoirs*, HarperCollins, 1992

Kerry, Simon, *Lansdowne: The Last Great Whig*, Unicorn, 2017

Kershaw, Ian, *Making Friends with Hitler*, Penguin, 2005

Kidd, Janet, *The Beaverbrook Girl*, Collins, 1987

Kimberley, The Earl of, *The Whim of the Wheel*, Merton Priory Press, 2001

King, Greg, *The Last Empress*, Birch Lane Press, 1994

Kipling, Rudyard, *Just So Stories*, Doubleday Page & Company, 1922

Knight Bruce, Rory, *Timothy the Tortoise*, Orion, 2004

Knightley, Phillip, *The Rise and Fall of the House of Vestey*, Warner Books, 1993

Lacey, Robert, *Aristocrats*, BBC, 1983

Le Poer Trench, Brinsley, *Operation Earth*, Neville Spearman, 1969

Lees-Milne, James, *Ancestral Voices*, Charles Scribner's Sons, 1975

Lees-Milne, James, *Ancient as the Hills*, John Murray, 1997

Lees-Milne, James, *Caves of Ice*, Faber & Faber, 1984

Lees-Milne, James, *Deep Romantic Chasm*, John Murray, 2000

Lees-Milne, James, *Diaries, 1984–1997*, John Murray, 2009

Lees-Milne, James, *Harold Nicolson: A Biography, Volume I: 1886–1929*, Archon Books, 1982

Lees-Milne, James, *Holy Dread*, John Murray, 2001

Lees-Milne, James, *Midway on the Waves*, Faber & Faber, 1985

Lees-Milne, James, *People and Places: Country House Donors and the National Trust*, John Murray, 2001

Lees-Milne, James, *Prophesying Peace*, Charles Scribner's Sons, 1977

Lees-Milne, James, *Through Wood and Dale*, John Murray, 1998

Levine, Naomi B., *Politics, Religion and Love*, New York University Press, 1991

Litchfield, Michael, *The Murder of Lord Shaftesbury*, John Blake, 2016

Lloyd George, David, *The People's Budget*, Hodder & Stoughton, 1909

Longford, Elizabeth, ed., *Louisa, Lady in Waiting: The Personal Diaries and Albums of Louisa, Lady in Waiting to Queen Victoria and Queen Alexandra*, Mayflower Books, 1979

Longford, Elizabeth, *The Royal House of Windsor*, Alfred A. Knopf, 1974

Longford, Lord, *Avowed Intent*, Little, Brown, 2004

Macdonald Fraser, George, intr., *The World of the Public School*, St Martin's Press, 1977

Maclean, Veronica, *Past Forgetting*, Review, 2002

Macmillan, Harold, *The Blast of War*, Macmillan, 1967

Macmillan, Harold, *Riding the Storm*, Macmillan, 1971

Magnus, Philip, *Edward VII*, Penguin Books, 1979

Mandler, Peter, *The Fall and Rise of the Stately Home*, Yale University Press, 1997

Marnham, Patrick, *Trail of Havoc*, Penguin, 1989

Masters, Brian, *The Dukes*, Frederick Muller, 1988

Masters, Brian, *Getting Personal*, Constable, 2002

Masters, Brian, *The Passion of John Aspinall*, Jonathan Cape, 1988

Mather, Carol, *When the Grass Stops Growing*, Leo Cooper, 1997

May, Jonathan, *D-Day, Minute by Minute*, Marble Arch Press, 2014

McConnell, J. D. R., *Eton: How it Works*, Faber & Faber, 1967

McTaggart, Lynne, *Kathleen Kennedy*, The Dial Press, 1984

Mee, Graham, *Aristocratic Enterprise*, Blackie, 1975

Mitchell, L. G., *Charles James Fox*, Oxford University Press, 1992

Mitford, Jessica, *Hons and Rebels*, Indigo, 1996

Mitford, Nancy, *Noblesse Oblige*, Hamish Hamilton, 1956

Mitford, Nancy, *The Pursuit of Love*, Penguin, 2010

Montgomery, Maureen E., *Gilded Prostitution: Status, Money, and Transatlantic Marriages, 1870–1914*, Routledge, 1989

Montgomery-Massingberd, Hugh, *Blenheim Revisited*, Beaufort Books, 1985

Montgomery-Massingberd, Hugh, ed., *Fifth Book of Obituaries*, Pan Books, 1999

Montgomery-Massingberd, Hugh and Sykes, Christopher Simon, *Great Houses of Scotland*, Laurence King Publishing Ltd, 1997

Moore, Sally, *Lucan*, Sidgwick & Jackson, 1987

Morgan, Lady, *Lady Morgan's Memoirs: Autobiography, Diaries and Correspondence, Volume I*, Bernhard Tauchnitz, 1863

Morrell, Lady Ottoline, *Ottoline*, Faber & Faber, 1963

Mosley, Charlotte, ed., *The Letters of Nancy Mitford*, Hodder & Stoughton, 1993

Mosley, Charlotte, ed., *The Letters of Nancy Mitford and Evelyn Waugh*, Sceptre, 1997

Mosley, Nicholas, *Rules of the Game*, Secker & Warburg, 1982

Mount Charles, Henry, *Public Space, Private Life: A Decade at Slane Castle*, Faber & Faber, 1989

Mullally, Frederic, *The Silver Salver*, Granada, 1981

Mulvagh, Jane, *Madresfield, The Real Brideshead*, Transworld, 2009

Murphy, Rosaleen, *The Mayflower and the Thistle*, Kindle Scribe, 2018

Musson, Jeremy, *Up and Down Stairs*, John Murray, 2009

Neil, Andrew, *Full Disclosure*, Macmillan, 1996

Newark, Tim, *Highlander*, Constable, 2009

Nichols, Beverley, *The Sweet and Twenties*, Weidenfeld & Nicolson, 1958

Nicolson, Adam, *Gentry*, HarperCollins, 2012

Nicolson, Harold, *Diaries and Letters, 1930–1964*, Stanley Olson, ed., Atheneum, 1996

Nicolson, Nigel, *Alex: The Life of Field Marshal Earl Alexander of Tunis*, Atheneum, 1973

Norwich, John Julius, ed., *The Duff Cooper Diaries*, Weidenfeld & Nicolson, 2005

O'Hea O'Keefe, Jane, *Voices from the Great Houses*, Mercier Press, 2013

Osborne, Frances, *The Bolter*, Virago, 2009

Paul, Leslie, *The Deployment and Payment of the Clergy*, Church Information Office, 1964

Pearson, John, *Edward the Rake*, Weidenfeld & Nicolson, 1975

Pearson, John, *The Gamblers*, Arrow, 2007

Peel, Mark, *The Patriotic Duke*, Thistle Publishing, 2013

Peill, James, *Glorious Goodwood: A Biography of England's Greatest Sporting Estate*, Constable, 2019

Perrott, Roy, *The Aristocrats*, Weidenfeld & Nicolson, 1968

Pincher, Chapman, *Inside Story*, Sidgwick & Jackson, 1978

Pine, L. G., *Tales of the British Aristocracy*, Burke, 1956

Pless, Daisy, Princess of, *Better Left Unsaid*, E. P. Dutton & Co., 1931

Pope-Hennessy, James, *Queen Mary, 1867–1953*, George Allen & Unwin, 1959

Pope-Hennessy, James, *The Quest for Queen Mary*, Hugo Vickers, ed., Zuleika and Hodder & Stoughton, 2019

Pryce-Jones, Alan, *The Bonus of Laughter*, Hamish Hamilton, 1987

Pryce-Jones, David, *Unity Mitford: A Quest*, Weidenfeld & Nicolson, 1976

Rawnsley, Andrew, *Servants of the People*, Hamish Hamilton, 2000

Reginato, James, *Great Houses, Modern Aristocrats*, Rizzoli, 2016

Reoch, Ernest, *The St Valéry Story*, privately published, 1965

Riddington, Max and Naden, Gavan, *Frances*, Michael O'Mara Books, 2003

Ridley, George, *Bend'Or, Duke of Westminster*, Robin Clark, 1985

Roberts, Andrew, *Salisbury*, Weidenfeld & Nicolson, 1999

Roberts, Ann, *We'll Never be Young Again*, Ann Roberts, 2008

Robinson, John Martin, *The Latest Country Houses*, The Bodley Head, 1984

Romilly, Giles and Alexander, Michael, *Hostages of Colditz*, Praeger, 1973

Rose, Kenneth, *The Later Cecils*, Harper & Row, 1975

Rose, Kenneth, *Superior Person*, Weidenfeld & Nicolson, 1969

Rosen, Greg, ed., *Dictionary of Labour Biography*, Politico's Publishing, 2001

Rossmore, Lord, *Things I Can Tell*, Eveleigh Nash, 1912

Roth, Cecil, *The Magnificent Rothschilds*, Pyramid Books, 1962

Rothschild, Lord, *Meditations of a Broomstick*, Collins, 1977

Rowse, A. L., *The Churchills*, Harper & Brothers, 1958

Royle, Roger, *A Few Blocks from Broadway*, Hodder & Stoughton, 1987

Rutland, The Duchess of, *The Accidental Duchess: From Farmer's Daughter to Belvoir Castle*, Macmillan, 2022

Sackville-West, Robert, *Inheritance: The Story of Knole and the Sackvilles*, Bloomsbury, 2011

Sackville-West, Vita, *Knole and the Sackvilles*, Ernest Benn, 1969

Sampson, Anthony, *Anatomy of Britain,* Hodder & Stoughton, 1962

Sanderson, Sir T. H. and Roscoe, E. S., eds, *Speeches and Addresses of Edward Henry 15th Earl of Derby, KG*, Longmans, Green & Co., 1894

Saunders, Frances Stonor, *The Woman Who Shot Mussolini*, Faber & Faber, 2010

Scriven, Marcus, *Splendour and Squalor*, Atlantic Books, 2011

Shaughnessy, Alfred, *Both Ends of the Candle,* Peter Owen Publishers, 1976

Sheepshanks, Mary, *Wild Writing Granny: A Memoir*, Stone Trough Books, 2012

Shinwell, Emanuel, *The Britain I Want*, Macdonald & Co., 1943

Shinwell, Emanuel, *Conflict Without Malice*, Odhams Press, 1995

Shinwell, Emanuel, *When the Men Come Home*, Victor Gollancz, 1944

Sinclair, Catherine, *Shetland and the Shetlanders*, D. Appleton & Co., 1840

Sisman, Adam, ed., *Dashing for the Post: The Letters of Patrick Leigh Fermor*, John Murray, 2016

Sisman, Adam, *Hugh Trevor-Roper*, Weidenfeld & Nicolson, 2010

Spence, Lyndsy, *The Grit in the Pearl*, The History Press, 2019

Spencer-Churchill, Henrietta, *Blenheim and the Churchill Family*, CICO Books, 2013

Spencer-Churchill, John, *A Churchill Canvas*, Little, Brown, 1961

Spicer, Paul, *The Temptress*, Simon & Schuster, 2011

Stanley of Alderney, Thomas Lord, *The Stanleys of Alderney, 1927–2001, A Politically Incorrect Story,* AMCD (Publishers) Limited, 2004

Stanley, Oliver, *Taxation of Farmers & Landowners*, Lexis Law Publishing, 1987

Stone, Lawrence, *An Open Elite? England 1540–1880*, Clarendon Press, 1984

Strong, Roy, *The Destruction of the Country House, 1875–1975*, Thames & Hudson, 1974

Strong, Roy, *The Roy Strong Diaries, 1967–1987*, Weidenfeld & Nicolson, 1997

Stuart, Denis, *Dear Duchess*, Victor Gollancz, 1982

Stuart, James, *Within the Fringe*, The Bodley Head, 1967

Summerson, John, *The Classical Language of Architecture*, Thames & Hudson, 1980

Sutherland, Douglas, *The Landowners*, David & Charles, 1988

Sutherland, Douglas, *The Yellow Earl*, Merlin Unwin, 2015

Sutherland, The Duke of, *Looking Back*, Odhams Press, 1957

Swift, Jonathan, *Irish Tracts, 1728–1733*, Basil Blackwell, 1964

Sykes, Christopher Simon, *The Big House*, HarperPerennial, 2005

Tanner, Michael, *The Suffragette Derby*, Robson Press, 2013

Tavistock, Henrietta and Levin, Angela, *A Chance to Live*, Headline, 1991

Taylor, D. J., *Bright Young People*, Chatto & Windus, 2007

Teeling, William, *Corridors of Frustration*, Johnson, 1970

Thompson, Douglas, *The Hustlers*, Pan Books, 2008

Thompson, F. M. L., *English Landed Society in the Nineteenth Century*, Routledge & Kegan Paul, 1963

Thompson, Laura, *A Different Class of Murder*, Head of Zeus, 2014

Thornton, Michael, *Royal Feud*, Ballantine Books, 1985

Thorpe, D. R., *Eden*, Pimlico, 2004

Thorpe, D. R., *Supermac, The Life of Harold Macmillan*, Chatto & Windus, 2010

Thynn, Alexander, *A Degree of Instability*, Top Spot Publishing, 2005

Thynn, Alexander, *The Early Years*, Artnik, 2002

Thynn, Alexander, *Top Hat & Tails*, Artnik, 2003

Thynn, Alexander, *Two Bites of the Apple*, Artnik Books, 2003

Tinniswood, Adrian, *Noble Ambitions*, Jonathan Cape, 2021

Tolstoy, Leo, *Anna Karenina*, Heinemann, 1972

Torday, Jane, *Wish Me Luck As You Wave Me Goodbye*, The Spredden Press, 1989

Tuckwell, William, *Reminiscences of Oxford*, Cassell & Co., 1900

Turner, E. S., *Amazing Grace*, Michael Joseph, 1975

Unger, Irwin and Unger, Debi, *The Guggenheims*, HarperPerennial, 2006

Vickers, Hugo, *Behind Closed Doors*, Hutchinson, 2011

Vickers, Hugo, *Clarissa: Muse to Power, The Untold Story of Clarissa Eden, Countess of Avon*, Hodder & Stoughton, 2024

Vickers, Hugo, *Elizabeth, the Queen Mother*, Hutchinson, 2005

Vickers, Hugo, *Gladys, Duchess of Marlborough*, Holt, Rinehart & Winston, 1979

Vickers, Hugo, intr., *The Unexpurgated Beaton Diaries*, Phoenix, 2002

Waldegrave, William, *A Different Kind of Weather*, Little, Brown, 2016

Waley, S. D., *Edwin Montagu*, Asia Publishing House, 1964

Walpole, Horace, *Memoirs and Portraits*, Matthew Hodgart, ed., B. T. Batsford, 1963

Walsingham, Lord, *One More Onion Peeled*, New Generation Publishing, 2021

Waterson, Merlin, ed., *The Country House Remembered*, Routledge & Kegan Paul, 1985

Waterson, Merlin, *A Noble Thing: The National Trust and its Benefactors*, Scala, 2011

Waugh, Evelyn, *Brideshead Revisited*, Penguin Books, 2000

Waugh, Evelyn, *Decline and Fall*, Chapman & Hall, 1928

Waugh, Evelyn, *The Diaries of Evelyn Waugh*, Michael Davies, ed., Penguin, 1979

Waugh, Evelyn, *The Letters of Evelyn Waugh*, Mark Amory, ed., Penguin, 1982

Waugh, Evelyn, *The Sword of Honour Trilogy*, Penguin Books, 1999

Waugh, Evelyn, *Vile Bodies*, Chapman & Hall, 1965

Westminster, Loelia, Duchess of, *Grace and Favour*, Weidenfeld & Nicolson, 1961

Williamson, Philip and Baldwin, Edward, eds., *Baldwin Papers*, Cambridge University Press, 2004

Willis, Tim, *Nigel Dempster and the Death of Discretion*, Short Books, 2010

Winchester, Simon, *Their Noble Lordships*, Random House, 1982

Winterton, Earl, *Pre-War*, Macmillan, 1932

Wiseman, Karen and Waterhouse, Michael, *The Churchill Who Saved Blenheim*, Unicorn, 2019

Wootton, Barbara, *In a World I Never Made*, George Allen & Unwin, 1967

Worsley, Giles, *England's Lost Houses*, Aurum Press, 2002

Wyatt, Woodrow, *Journals* – see Curtis, Sarah, ed.

Wyndham, Ursula, *Astride the Wall*, Lennard Publishing, 1988

Ziegler, Philip, *Diana Cooper*, Alfred A. Knopf, 1982

Ziegler, Philip, *King Edward VIII*, Alfred A. Knopf, 1990

Ziegler, Philip, *Osbert Sitwell*, Chatto & Windus, 1998

ACADEMIC WORKS

Anderson, Olive, 'The Wensleydale Peerage Case and the Position of the House of Lords in the Mid-Nineteenth Century', *English Historical Review*, vol. 82, no. 324, 1967, pp. 486–502

Beckett, John and Turner, Michael, 'End of the Old Order? F. M. L. Thompson, the Land Question, and the burden of ownership in England, c.1880–c.1925', *Agricultural History Review*, vol. 55, no. 2, December 2007

Crick, Bernard, 'The Life Peerages Act', *Parliamentary Affairs*, vol. 11, no. 4, 1957

Dykes, Christina, 'Hugh Richard Arthur Grosvenor, 2nd Duke of West-minster (1879–1953), known as Bend'Or: A Reappraisal', PhD thesis, February 2021

Phillips, Gregory D., 'The "Diehards" and the Myth of the "Backwoods-men",' *Journal of British Studies*, vol. 16, no. 2, 1977

Thompson, F. M. L., Presidential Address: 'English Landed Society in the Twentieth Century, I Property: Collapse and Survival', *Transactions of the Royal Historical Society*, vol. 40, 1990, pp. 1–24

ORGANISATIONAL PUBLICATIONS

Eton College Chronicle
The Guards Magazine
London Gazette

NEWS MEDIA

The Times and *Sunday Times*, via paper archives and thetimes.co.uk
Guardian and *Observer*, via paper archives and theguardian.com
Independent, via independent.co.uk
Daily and Sunday Telegraph, via paper archives, telegraph.co.uk and newspapers.com
Irish Times, via paper archives and irishtimes.com
BBC, via bbc.co.uk
Financial Times via ft.com
New York Times, via nytimes.com
Daily Mail, via dailymail.co.uk
Vanity Fair, via vanityfair.com
Gstaad Life, via gstaadlife.com
Time, via time.com
STV, via news.stv.tv
All other publications via the British Newspaper Archive, newspapers.com, other private family clippings collections, as well as my own.

UNPUBLISHED MEMOIRS

Bath, The Marquess of, *Longleat Preserved*, undated
Bentinck, Count Henry, *Clogs to Clogs in Six Hundred Years*, undated

Collins, Sir Arthur, *My Recollections of Floors and the Family*, undated
Lambton, Lady Elizabeth, *Memories*, 2006
Treherne, Sheelah, *Looking Back*, 1975
Wharncliffe, Elfreda, *Reminisces about Wentworth Woodhouse*, undated

AUDIO AND VIDEO MATERIAL

Various interviews conducted by Maurice O'Keeffe and hosted on irishlifeandlore.com
Recording Morecambe Bay; recordingmorecambebay.org.uk
Desert Island Discs Archive, BBC Radio 4
It Runs in the Family podcast
Duchess podcast
Mapperton Live: This (un)Aristocratic Manor Life; youtube.com/@ MappertonLive
The Aristocracy Business, Alan Whicker, Yorkshire Television, 1968
The Lady and the Lords, Michael Cockerell, BBC Two, 2000
The Last Dukes, Michael Waldman, BBC Two, 26 October 2015
The Lords' Tale, Molly Dineen, Channel 4, 2002
Two Night Stand, Billy Connolly, 1997; as seen here: youtube.com/watch?v=pRZeYHM1GzQ .

OTHER ARCHIVE MATERIALS

Bureau of Military History Witness Statements, 1916–1921

CURRENCY CONVERSIONS

All currency conversions are rudimentary and only intended to give an impression. They are all calculated using the Bank of England's inflation calculator.

PARLIAMENTARY MATERIAL

All debate materials from the House of Commons and the House of Lords are taken from the official Hansard online archives; hansard.parliament.uk and api.parliament.uk/historic-hansard

BIBLIOGRAPHY

PRIVATE INFORMATION

Some families have been kind enough to give me access to private papers
and information in addition to the many interviews I have conducted,
and I have been judicious in my use of these throughout the book.

INSTITUTIONAL ARCHIVES

The Churchill Archive, via Churchill Archives Centre, Cambridge;
churchillarchive.com. Any material from this is marked 'CHAR'.
The Wentworth Woodhouse Preservation Trust was particularly generous
in allowing me access to its archives. Any material from these is marked
'WWPT'.

GOVERNMENT REPORTS

Houses of Outstanding Historic or Architectural Interest, report of a committee appointed by the Chancellor of the Exchequer, His Majesty's
Stationery Office, 1950
Reports of Her Majesty's Commissioners appointed to inquire into the revenues and management of certain colleges and schools and the studies
pursued and instruction given therein, Volume II, Eyre & Spottiswoode,
1864

Appendix: The Hereditary Peerage

DUKES

Abercorn (1868)
Argyll (1701)
Atholl (1703)
Beaufort (1682)
Bedford (1694)
Buccleuch and Queensberry (1663 and 1684)
Devonshire (1694)
Fife (1900)
Grafton (1675)
Hamilton and Brandon (1643)
Leinster (1766)
Manchester (1719)
Marlborough (1702)
Montrose (1707)
Norfolk (1483)
Northumberland (1766)
Richmond, Gordon and Lennox (1675 and 1876)
Roxburghe (1707)
Rutland (1703)
St Albans (1684)
Somerset (1547)
Sutherland (1833)
Wellington (1814)
Westminster (1874)

MARQUESSES

Aberdeen and Temair (1915)
Abergavenny (1876)
Ailesbury (1821)
Ailsa (1831)
Anglesey (1815)
Bath (1789)
Bristol (1826)
Bute (1796)
Camden (1812)
Cholmondeley (1815)
Conyngham (1816)
Donegall (1791)
Downshire (1789)
Ely (1801)
Exeter (1801)
Headfort (1800)
Hertford (1793)
Huntly (1599)
Lansdowne (1784)
Linlithgow (1902)
Londonderry (1816)
Lothian (1701)
Milford Haven (1917)
Normanby (1838)
Northampton (1812)
Queensberry (1682)

Reading (1926)
Salisbury (1789)
Sligo (1800)
Townshend (1787)
Tweeddale (1694)
Waterford (1789)
Winchester (1551)
Zetland (1892)

EARLS

Airlie (1639)
Albemarle (1697)
Alexander of Tunis (1952)
Annandale and Hartfell (1662)
Annesley (1789)
Antrim (1785)
Arran (1762)
Attlee (1955)
Aylesford (1714)
Baldwin of Bewdley (1937)
Balfour (1922)
Bathurst (1772)
Beatty (1919)
Belmore (1797)
Bessborough (1739)
Bradford (1815)
Buchan (1469)
Buckinghamshire (1746)
Cadogan (1800)
Cairns (1878)
Caithness (1455)
Caledon (1800)
Carlisle (1661)
Carnarvon (1793)
Carrick (1748)
Castle Stewart (1800)
Cathcart (1814)

Cawdor (1827)
Chichester (1801)
Clancarty (1803)
Clanwilliam (1776)
Clarendon (1776)
Cork and Orrery (1620 and 1660)
Cottenham (1850)
Courtown (1762)
Coventry (1697)
Cowley (1857)
Cranbrook (1892)
Craven (1801)
Crawford and Balcarres (1398 and 1651)
Cromartie (1861)
Cromer (1901)
Dalhousie (1633)
Darnley (1725)
Dartmouth (1711)
De La Warr (1761)
Denbigh and Desmond (1622)
Derby (1485)
Devon (1553)
Donoughmore (1800)
Drogheda (1661)
Ducie (1837)
Dudley (1860)
Dundee (1660)
Dundonald (1669)
Dunmore (1686)
Durham (1833)
Dysart (1643)
Effingham (1837)
Eglinton and Winton (1507 and 1859)
Eldon (1821)

Elgin and Kincardine (1633 and 1647)
Enniskillen (1789)
Erne (1789)
Erroll (1453)
Essex (1661)
Ferrers (1711)
Fortescue (1789)
Gainsborough (1841)
Galloway (1623)
Glasgow (1703)
Gosford (1806)
Gowrie (1945)
Granard (1684)
Granville (1833)
Grey (1806)
Guilford (1752)
Haddington (1619)
Haig (1919)
Halifax (1944)
Hardwicke (1754)
Harewood (1812)
Harrington (1742)
Harrowby (1809)
Home (1605)
Howe (1821)
Huntingdon (1529)
Iddesleigh (1885)
Ilchester (1756)
Inchcape (1929)
Iveagh (1919)
Jellicoe (1925)
Jersey (1697)
Kilmorey (1822)
Kimberley (1866)
Kingston (1768)
Kinnoull (1633)
Kintore (1677)

Lauderdale (1624)
Leicester (1837)
Leven and Melville (1641 and 1690)
Lichfield (1831)
Limerick (1803)
Lincoln (1572)
Lindsay (1633)
Lindsey and Abingdon (1626 and 1682)
Lisburne (1776)
Listowel (1822)
Liverpool (1905)
Lloyd-George of Dwyfor (1945)
Longford (1785)
Lonsdale (1807)
Loudoun (1633)
Lucan (1795)
Lytton (1880)
Macclesfield (1721)
Malmesbury (1800)
Mansfield (1776)
Mar (1404)
Mar and Kellie (1565 and 1619)
Mayo (1785)
Meath (1627)
Mexborough (1766)
Minto (1813)
Moray (1562)
Morley (1815)
Morton (1458)
Mount Edgcumbe (1789)
Mountbatten of Burma (1947)
Nelson (1805)
Newburgh (1660)
Norbury (1827)
Normanton (1806)
Northesk (1647)

Onslow (1801)
Orkney (1696)
Oxford and Asquith (1925)
Peel (1929)
Pembroke and Montgomery (1551 and 1605)
Perth (1605)
Plymouth (1905)
Portarlington (1785)
Portland (1689)
Portsmouth (1743)
Powis (1804)
Radnor (1765)
Ranfurly (1831)
Roden (1771)
Romney (1801)
Rosebery (1703)
Rosse (1806)
Rosslyn (1801)
Rothes (1457)
Russell (1861)
St Aldwyn (1915)
St Germans (1815)
Sandwich (1660)
Scarbrough (1690)
Seafield (1701)
Selborne (1882)
Selkirk (1646)
Shaftesbury (1672)
Shannon (1756)
Shrewsbury and Waterford (1442 and 1446)
Snowdon (1961)
Spencer (1765)
Stair (1703)
Stockton (1984)
Stradbroke (1821)
Strafford (1847)

Strathmore and Kinghorne (1606)
Suffolk and Berkshire (1603 and 1626)
Sutherland (c. 1235)
Swinton (1955)
Tankerville (1714)
Temple of Stowe (1822)
Verulam (1815)
Waldegrave (1729)
Warwick (1759)
Wemyss and March (1633 and 1697)
Westmeath (1621)
Westmorland (1624)
Wharncliffe (1876)
Wilton (1801)
Winchilsea and Nottingham (1628 and 1681)
Winterton (1766)
Woolton (1956)
Yarborough (1837)

VISCOUNTS

Addison (1945)
Allenby (1919)
Allendale (1911)
Arbuthnott (1641)
Ashbrook (1751)
Astor (1917)
Bangor (1781)
Bearsted (1925)
Blakenham (1963)
Bledisloe (1935)
Bolingbroke and St John (1712 and 1716)
Boyd of Merton (1962)
Boyne (1717)

Brentford (1929)
Bridgeman (1929)
Bridport (1868)
Brookeborough (1952)
Buckmaster (1933)
Caldecote (1939)
Camrose (1941)
Chandos (1954)
Charlemont (1665)
Chelmsford (1921)
Chetwynd (1717)
Chilston (1911)
Cobham (1718)
Colville of Culross (1902)
Combermere (1826)
Cowdray (1917)
Daventry (1943)
Davidson (1937)
De L'Isle (1956)
de Vesci (1776)
Devonport (1917)
Dilhorne (1964)
Dillon (1622)
Doneraile (1785)
Downe (1680)
Dunrossil (1959)
Eccles (1964)
Esher (1897)
Exmouth (1816)
Falkland (1620)
Falmouth (1720)
Gage (1720)
Galway (1727)
Gormanston (1478)
Gort (1816)
Goschen (1900)
Hailsham (1929)
Hambleden (1891)

Hampden (1884)
Hanworth (1936)
Harberton (1791)
Hardinge (1846)
Hawarden (1793)
Head (1960)
Hereford (1550)
Hill (1842)
Hood (1796)
Kemsley (1945)
Knollys (1911)
Knutsford (1895)
Leathers (1954)
Lifford (1781)
Long (1921)
Mackintosh of Halifax (1957)
Marchwood (1945)
Margesson (1942)
Massereene and Ferrard (1660 and 1797)
Melville (1802)
Mersey (1916)
Midleton (1717)
Mills (1962)
Molesworth (1716)
Monck (1801)
Monckton of Brenchley (1957)
Montgomery of Alamein (1946)
Mountgarret (1550)
Norwich (1952)
Oxfuird (1651)
Portman (1873)
Powerscourt (1744)
Ridley (1900)
Rochdale (1960)
Rothermere (1919)
Runciman of Doxford (1937)
St Davids (1918)

St Vincent (1801)

Samuel (1937)

Scarsdale (1911)

Selby (1905)

Sidmouth (1805)

Slim (1960)

Soulbury (1954)

Southwell (1776)

Stansgate (1942)

Stuart of Findhorn (1959)

Tenby (1957)

Thurso (1952)

Torrington (1721)

Trenchard (1936)

Ullswater (1921)

Valentia (1642)

Waverley (1952)

Weir (1938)

Wimborne (1918)

Younger of Leckie (1923)

BARONS AND LORDS OF PARLIAMENT

Aberconway (1911)

Aberdare (1873)

Abinger (1835)

Acton (1869)

Addington (1887)

Aldenham and Hunsdon (1896)

Aldington (1962)

Altrincham (1945)

Alvingham (1929)

Amherst of Hackney (1892)

Ampthill (1881)

Amwell (1947)

Annaly (1863)

Arlington (1664)

Ashbourne (1885)

Ashburton (1835)

Ashcombe (1892)

Ashton of Hyde (1911)

Ashtown (1800)

Astor of Hever (1956)

Auckland (1789)

Avebury (1900)

Aylmer (1718)

Baden-Powell (1929)

Bagot (1780)

Baillieu (1953)

Balfour of Burleigh (1607)

Banbury of Southam (1924)

Barnard (1698)

Basing (1887)

Beaverbrook (1917)

Belhaven and Stenton (1647)

Bellew (1848)

Belper (1856)

Berkeley (1421)

Berners (1455)

Bethell (1922)

Bicester (1938)

Biddulph (1903)

Birkett (1958)

Blyth (1907)

Bolton (1797)

Borthwick (1452)

Borwick (1922)

Boston (1761)

Brabazon of Tara (1942)

Bradbury (1925)

Brain (1962)

Brassey of Apethorpe (1938)

Braybrooke (1788)

Braye (1529)

Bridges (1957)

Broadbridge (1945)

Brocket (1933)

Brougham and Vaux (1860)

Brownlow (1776)

Bruntisfield (1942)

Burden (1950)

Burgh (1529)

Burnham (1903)

Burton (1897)

Byron (1643)

Cadman (1937)

Calverley (1945)

Camoys (1383)

Carbery (1715)

Carew (1834)

Carnock (1916)

Carrington (1796)

Castlemaine (1812)

Catto (1936)

Cawley (1918)

Chesham (1858)

Chetwode (1945)

Chorley (1945)

Churchill (1815)

Churston (1858)

Clanmorris (1800)

Clifford of Chudleigh (1672)

Clinton (1299)

Clitheroe (1955)

Clwyd (1919)

Clydesmuir (1948)

Cobbold (1960)

Cochrane of Cults (1919)

Coleraine (1954)

Coleridge (1874)

Colgrain (1946)

Colwyn (1917)

Colyton (1956)

Congleton (1841)

Cornwallis (1927)

Cottesloe (1874)

Craigmyle (1929)

Cranworth (1899)

Crathorne (1959)

Crawshaw (1892)

Croft (1940)

Crofton (1797)

Cromwell (1375)

Crook (1947)

Cullen of Ashbourne (1920)

Cunliffe (1914)

Dacre (1321)

Darcy de Knayth (1332)

Daresbury (1927)

Darling (1924)

Darwen (1946)

Davies (1932)

de Clifford (1299)

de Freyne (1851)

de Mauley (1838)

de Ramsey (1887)

de Ros (1264)

de Saumarez (1831)

de Villiers (1910)

Decies (1812)

Delamere (1821)

Denham (1937)

Denman (1834)

Derwent (1881)

Dickinson (1930)

Digby (1620)

Dormer (1615)

Dowding (1943)

Dudley (1439)

Dufferin and Clandeboye (1800)

Dulverton (1929)

Dunalley (1800)

Dunboyne (1324)

Dunleath (1892)

Dunsany (1439)

Dynevor (1780)

Elibank (1643)

Ellenborough (1802)

Elphinstone (1509)

Elton (1934)

Fairfax of Cameron (1627)

Fairhaven (1961)

Faringdon (1916)

Farnham (1756)

Fermoy (1856)

Feversham (1826)

ffrench (1798)

Fisher (1909)

FitzWalter (1295)

Foley (1776)

Forbes (1445)

Forester (1821)

Forres (1922)

Forteviot (1917)

Freyberg (1951)

Gainford (1917)

Garvagh (1818)

Geddes (1942)

Gerard (1876)

Gifford (1824)

Gisborough (1917)

Glanusk (1899)

Glenarthur (1918)

Glenconner (1911)

Glendevon (1964)

Glendyne (1922)

Glentoran (1939)

Gorell (1909)

Grantchester (1953)

Grantley (1782)

Graves (1794)

Gray (1445)

Greenway (1927)

Grenfell (1902)

Gretton (1944)

Grey of Codnor (1397)

Gridley (1955)

Grimston of Westbury (1964)

Grimthorpe (1886)

Hacking (1945)

Haden-Guest (1950)

Hamilton of Dalzell (1886)

Hampton (1874)

Hankey (1939)

Harding of Petherton (1958)

Hardinge of Penshurst (1910)

Harlech (1876)

Harmsworth (1939)

Harris (1815)

Harvey of Tasburgh (1954)

Hastings (1295)

Hatherton (1835)

Hawke (1776)

Hayter (1927)

Hazlerigg (1945)

Hemingford (1943)

Hemphill (1906)

Henley (1799)

Henniker (1800)

Herbert (1461)

Herries of Terregles (1490)

Hesketh (1935)

Heytesbury (1828)

Hindlip (1886)

Hives (1950)

Hollenden (1912)

HolmPatrick (1897)

Hotham (1797)
Hothfield (1881)
Howard de Walden (1597)
Howard of Penrith (1930)
Howick of Glendale (1960)
Huntingfield (1796)
Hylton (1866)
Iliffe (1933)
Inchiquin (1543)
Inchyra (1962)
Inglewood (1964)
Inverforth (1919)
Ironside (1941)
Jeffreys (1952)
Joicey (1906)
Kenilworth (1937)
Kennet (1935)
Kensington (1776)
Kenswood (1951)
Kenyon (1788)
Kershaw (1947)
Keyes (1943)
Kilbracken (1909)
Killanin (1900)
Killearn (1943)
Kilmaine (1789)
Kilmarnock (1831)
Kindersley (1941)
Kingsale (c. 1340)
Kinloss (1602)
Kinross (1902)
Kirkwood (1951)
Langford (1800)
Latham (1942)
Latymer (1432)
Layton (1947)
Leconfield and Egremont (1859
and 1963)

Leigh (1839)
Leighton of St Mellons (1962)
Lilford (1797)
Lindsay of Birker (1945)
Lisle (1758)
Londesborough (1850)
Louth (1541)
Lovat (1458)
Lucas of Chilworth (1946)
Lucas of Crudwell and Dingwall
    (1663 and 1609)
Luke (1929)
Lyveden (1859)
MacAndrew (1959)
Macdonald (1776)
Maclay (1922)
Macpherson of Drumochter (1951)
Mancroft (1937)
Manners (1807)
Manton (1922)
Marchamley (1908)
Margadale (1965)
Marks of Broughton (1961)
Martonmere (1964)
Massy (1776)
May (1935)
McGowan (1937)
McNair (1955)
Merrivale (1925)
Merthyr (1911)
Meston (1919)
Methuen (1838)
Middleton (1711)
Milford (1939)
Milne (1933)
Milner of Leeds (1951)
Milverton (1947)
Moncreiff (1873)

Monk Bretton (1884)

Monkswell (1885)

Monson (1728)

Montagu of Beaulieu (1885)

Monteagle of Brandon (1839)

Moran (1943)

Morris (1918)

Morris of Kenwood (1950)

Mostyn (1831)

Mottistone (1933)

Mountevans (1945)

Mowbray, Segrave and Stourton
  (1283, 1295 and 1448)

Moyne (1932)

Moynihan (1929)

Muskerry (1781)

Napier and Ettrick (1627 and
  1872)

Napier of Magdala (1868)

Nathan (1940)

Nelson of Stafford (1960)

Netherthorpe (1959)

Newall (1946)

Newborough (1776)

Newton (1892)

Noel-Buxton (1930)

Norrie (1957)

Northbourne (1884)

Northbrook (1866)

Norton (1878)

Nunburnholme (1906)

Ogmore (1950)

O'Hagan (1870)

O'Neill (1868)

Oranmore and Browne (1836 and
  1926)

Palmer (1933)

Parmoor (1914)

Pender (1937)

Penrhyn (1866)

Petre (1603)

Phillimore (1918)

Piercy (1945)

Plunket (1827)

Poltimore (1831)

Polwarth (1690)

Ponsonby of Shulbrede (1930)

Poole (1958)

Raglan (1852)

Rankeillour (1932)

Rathcavan (1953)

Rathcreedan (1916)

Rathdonnell (1868)

Ravensdale (1911)

Ravensworth (1821)

Rayleigh (1821)

Rea (1937)

Reay (1628)

Redesdale (1902)

Reith (1940)

Remnant (1928)

Rendlesham (1806)

Rennell (1933)

Renwick (1964)

Revelstoke (1885)

Ritchie of Dundee (1905)

Riverdale (1935)

Robertson of Oakridge (1961)

Roborough (1938)

Rochester (1931)

Rockley (1934)

Rodney (1782)

Rollo (1651)

Rootes (1959)

Rossmore (1796)

Rotherwick (1939)

Rothschild (1885)
Rowallan (1911)
Rugby (1947)
Russell of Liverpool (1919)
Sackville (1876)
St Helens (1964)
St John of Bletso (1559)
St Levan (1887)
St Oswald (1885)
Saltoun (1445)
Sanderson of Ayot (1960)
Sandford (1945)
Sandhurst (1871)
Savile (1888)
Saye and Sele (1447)
Seaford (1826)
Selsdon (1932)
Sempill (1489)
Shaughnessy (1916)
Shepherd (1946)
Sherfield (1964)
Shuttleworth (1902)
Silkin (1950)
Silsoe (1963)
Simon of Wythenshawe (1947)
Sinclair (1449)
Sinclair of Cleeve (1957)
Sinha (1919)
Skelmersdale (1828)
Somerleyton (1916)
Somers (1784)
Southampton (1780)
Spens (1959)
Stafford (1640)
Stamp (1938)
Stanley of Alderley (1839)
Strabolgi (1318)
Strange (1628)

Strathalmond (1955)
Strathcarron (1936)
Strathclyde (1955)
Strathcona and Mount Royal (1900)
Stratheden and Campbell (1836)
Strathspey (1884)
Sudeley (1838)
Suffield (1786)
Swansea (1893)
Swaythling (1907)
Swinfen (1919)
Talbot of Malahide (1831)
Tedder (1946)
Tennyson (1884)
Terrington (1918)
Teviot (1940)
Teynham (1616)
Thomson of Fleet (1964)
Thurlow (1792)
Tollemache (1876)
Torphichen (1564)
Trefgarne (1947)
Trevethin and Oaksey (1921 and 1947)
Trevor (1880)
Tryon (1940)
Tweedsmuir (1935)
Vaux of Harrowden (1523)
Ventry (1800)
Vernon (1762)
Vestey (1922)
Vivian (1941)
Wakehurst (1934)
Walpole (1723)
Walsingham (1780)
Waterpark (1792)
Wedgwood (1942)

Westbury (1861)

Westwood (1944)

Wharton (1544)

Wigram (1935)

Willoughby de Broke (1491)

Willoughby de Eresby (1313)

Windlesham (1937)

Wise (1951)

Wolverton (1869)

Wraxall (1928)

Wrenbury (1915)

Wrottesley (1838)

Wynford (1829)

Zouche (1308)

Notes

INTRODUCTION

1. Her three elder sisters, Edith, Portia, Cynthia, similarly married men of means, and the four of them were caricatured in *Tatler* in 1927, arms linked, as 'Cadogan Square'. Her sisters' husbands were Arthur Mills, 3rd Baron Hillingdon (1891–1952), Sir Edward Stanley, Lord Stanley (1894–1938), and Captain Humphrey de Trafford (1891–1971).
2. Daphne Fielding, *The Face on the Sphinx*, Hamish Hamilton, 1978, p. 66
3. His nickname derived not from his particularly cheery disposition but from his courtesy title, Earl of Sunderland.
4. Sunny had married Consuelo in 1895 for her money. In 1883 the Marlboroughs had a small estate, for a ducal family, of 23,511 acres, with a gross income of only £36,557 a year (roughly equivalent to £3.7 million in May 2024).
5. His parents had divorced in 1883 in the wake of the Aylesford Scandal. His father had an affair with the Countess of Aylesford, a former interest of the Prince of Wales, who declared George 'the greatest blackguard alive'. (John Pearson, *Edward the Rake*, Weidenfeld & Nicolson, 1975, p. 85) After Sunny's death in 1934, Charley Vane-Tempest-Stewart, 7th Marquess of Londonderry, wrote to Winston Churchill describing how: 'I think Sunny's childhood was badly mismanaged somehow: his pessimism always seemed to reflect an early grievance and I think he always imagined the world was against him.' (Karen Wiseman and Michael Waterhouse, *The Churchill Who Saved Blenheim*, Unicorn, 2019, p. 16) Many years later, Sunny's second wife Gladys Deacon described how 'he was wounded as a

child'. His aunt Maud Lansdowne told Gladys in January 1922 how 'up to ten years old he was one of the most charming boys I ever met & most joyous; after that his spirits seemed to have vanished & he quite changed'. (Hugo Vickers, *Gladys, Duchess of Marlborough*, Holt, Rinehart & Winston, 1979, p. 67)

6. David Green, *The Churchills of Blenheim*, Constable, 1984, p. 148

7. *The Times*, 15 March 1972

8. Major Charles Loraine Carlos Clarke (1892–1970) was not, as Rosemary's description might make him sound, only a chap who ran a farm. Born in 1892, the son of Charles Carlos Clarke, a stockbroker and Surrey cricketer who was, in 1896, caricatured by Leslie Ward – the artist known as 'Spy' – for *Vanity Fair*, he was educated at Eton College. During the First World War he served with the Royal Buckinghamshire Hussars, being wounded at the Dardanelles, and afterwards went on to work at Lowesby. Charlie married three times and had two children by his first wife Lady Eileen Knox, daughter of Uchter Knox, 5th Earl of Ranfurly, and two more by his third wife Myra Lynn. His sister Jessie married Arthur Butler, 6th Marquess of Ormonde, in 1924.

9. After Bert succeeded, Lowesby was let to Eloise Heathcote-Drummond-Willoughby, Countess of Ancaster, by then separated from her husband Gilbert Ancaster, and described in March 1935 by Chips Channon as a 'mad unhappy maniac . . . Surfeit has ruined her: position; jewels; millions; palaces and castles, and latterly lovers by the dozens – now nothing, for in shedding her husband and severing herself from all family contact, she has lost everything except three strings of pearls and about £12,000 per annum.' (Henry 'Chips' Channon, *The Diaries, Volume 1: 1918–38*, edited by Simon Heffer, Hutchinson, 2021, p. 398). In January 1935, Lowesby was sold to Sir Keith Nuttall, 2nd Baronet, who died six years later in the Second World War.

10. Hugh Montgomery-Massingberd, *Blenheim Revisited*, Beaufort Books, 1985, p. 171

11. Despite this, in early 1945, Bert and his first cousin once removed Winston Churchill discussed the prospect of selling Blenheim. In February, Bert wrote to Churchill about the £60,000 he owed the Inland Revenue for death duties following his father's death eleven years prior, positing how a sale of Blenheim to the War Office might be

prudent. A couple of weeks later, shortly before British and American troops crossed the Rhine, the prime minister told Bert that he felt he was right to contemplate selling Blenheim, since 'the trends of modern life will make it increasingly difficult for any private person to live in so splendid a setting.' He added that he thought it doubtful that the state would buy it, and if they did, not for very much. (Churchill to Bert, 1 March 1945; CHAR 1/386/58-59; churchillarchive.com)

12. There are 1,227 baronetcies in total, but 237 of these are held by peers.

13. E. S. Turner, *Amazing Grace*, Michael Joseph, 1975, pp. 15–16

14. Ibid., p. 76

15. Elizabeth Longford, *The Royal House of Windsor*, Alfred A. Knopf, 1974, p. 25

16. Lord Harewood, *The Tongs and the Bones: The Memoirs of Lord Harewood*, Weidenfeld & Nicolson, 1981, p. 2. Counting the number of marquessates created since the first is a slightly tricky task, since some of those that seem to qualify were created only as courtesy titles to dukedoms – including those of Blandford (Marlborough), Granby (Rutland) and Tavistock (Bedford). But, as an illustrative example, of the twenty-eight marquessates created in the Peerage of the United Kingdom between 1801 and the present day as standalone titles, rather than as courtesy titles or those that were immediate precursors to a duke-dom (like Wellington), there have been an average of 4.39 holders per title. By comparison, seventy-one earldoms that are held in their own right, i.e. not used as courtesy titles (like Burlington and the Duke of Devonshire), have been created in the same period, and these average 5.85 holders. George Harewood's father chose the right promotion. Marquess is the usual spelling though some peers prefer the French spelling, 'marquis'. Incidentally, the surname of the Earls of Woolton is 'Marquis', making them both earls and marquises in different ways.

17. Roy Perrott, *The Aristocrats*, Weidenfeld & Nicolson, 1968, p. 74

18. A further note about names. Sometimes, information listed about the spelling or hyphenation of names and surnames in the official refer-ence books, such as *Debrett's Peerage* and *Who's Who*, has proved to be contrary to the reality of day-to-day life. Indeed, some individuals appear to have spelled their own names 'wrongly' or used hyphens in their surnames when this was not the family 'rule'. Hyphenation can vary between branches of families and is often not standardised. To the best of my ability, what appears here is correct: I have checked

with every family about whose names I had queries and have made reference in the footnotes to this in a few cases.

1. UNCONDITIONAL SURRENDER

1. Equivalent to £304 million in May 2024, per the Bank of England.
2. Equivalent to £418 million in May 2024, per the Bank of England.
3. Philip Beresford and William D. Rubinstein, *The Richest of the Rich: The Wealthiest 250 People in Britain since 1066*, Harriman House Publishing, 2007, p. 261
4. In 2022, Andrew Fane, chairman of the Stowe House Preservation Trust, told me that Stowe is bigger than Wentworth. 'We have got more rooms, and our south front is longer by six metres,' he said. Not that it's a competition: 'I just wanted you to know.'
5. *Peterborough Standard*, 22 July 1905
6. *Jarrow Express*, 23 September 1910
7. There was some dispute about Billy's parentage. He was born in Canada in July 1872 to William Fitzwilliam, Viscount Milton, the epileptic eldest son of the 6th Earl Fitzwilliam, and his wife Laura Beauclerk. Not least because he was born away from Wentworth, rumours began to develop that Billy might be a changeling. Could the Miltons have swapped their newborn daughter for a local baby boy? This seems far-fetched. No one from the Fitzwilliam family with whom I spoke for this book understood Billy to be a changeling. 'Nonsense,' said one. 'Total fantasy,' said another, 'he was definitely a Fitzwilliam.' As Billy's great-great-nephew Michael Bond puts it, 'Billy had all the attributes expected of a Fitzwilliam – including the goatish instincts of his father and grandfather.' (Michael Shaw Bond, *Way Out West*, McClelland & Stewart, 2001, p. 233)
8. Billy and Maud's enormous society wedding of 1896 was a meeting of two great Yorkshire families, but not for the first time. They were third cousins once removed: in 1764, Lady Charlotte Fitzwilliam, daughter of the 3rd Earl Fitzwilliam, had married Thomas Dundas, 1st Baron Dundas of Aske, and in 1806 their daughter Mary Dundas married Charles Fitzwilliam, 5th Earl Fitzwilliam.
9. Helena was not the only one in the extended family to receive these two middle names. On 11 June 1930, Elfin gave birth to her fourth daughter, Mary, who, like Helena, was given Marie Gabrielle as two

of her middle names. Just under five years later, Elfin gave birth to a little boy she named Alan James.

10. Catherine Bailey, *Black Diamonds*, Penguin, 2007, p. 207

11. His grandfather William Fitzwilliam, Viscount Milton, was born in 1839, but predeceased his father, the 6th Earl, and so never succeeded to the title. When the 6th Earl died in 1902, Billy Fitzwilliam inherited the title from his grandfather.

12. *South Yorkshire Times and Mexborough & Swinton Times*, 15 November 1913. As a young man, Billy qualified as a 'muck engineer', having been trained at his own establishments to dig and mine. As the *Sheffield Independent* put it in January 1910: Billy could 'wield a pick with the best of them, and there isn't a mining manager, engineer, or expert in all Yorkshire that can teach him anything about mining. Indeed, it is commonly said round Sheffield that Lord Fitzwilliam saves the services of at least one mining engineer a year by doing the work himself.' (*Sheffield Independent*, 27 January 1910)

13. *Penistone, Stocksbridge and Hoyland Express*, 11 September 1915

14. Hugh Howson, founder of Eton's Alpine Society, joined the school's staff in 1918. He and three other Eton beaks were killed in a climbing accident in the Swiss Alps in 1933.

15. *Eton College Chronicle*, 25 March 1926

16. *Irish Times*, 13 September 1930

17. *Dundee Evening Telegraph*, 19 April 1933

18. WWPT/RY/3.00562

19. *Sunday Sun*, 25 March 1934

20. *Yorkshire Post and Leeds Intelligencer*, 12 October 1934

21. Emanuel Shinwell, *Conflict Without Malice*, Odhams Press, 1995, p. 16

22. Ibid., p. 17

23. Harold Macmillan, *The Blast of War*, Macmillan, 1967, p. 121

24. Emanuel Shinwell, *The Britain I Want*, Macdonald & Co., 1943, p. 38

25. *The Guards Magazine*, Winter 1942

26. Emanuel Shinwell, *When the Men Come Home*, Victor Gollancz, 1944, p. 26

27. Evelyn Waugh, *Sword of Honour*, Penguin Books, 1999, p. 318

28. Evelyn Waugh, *The Diaries of Evelyn Waugh*, edited by Michael Davies, Penguin, 1979, p. 487

29. Evelyn Waugh, *Letters of Evelyn Waugh*, edited by Mark Amory, Penguin, 1982, p. 149

NOTES TO PAGES 29–41

30. Winston S. Churchill, *His Father's Son*, Weidenfeld & Nicolson, 1996, p. 184
31. Waugh, *Diaries*, p. 491
32. Later, briefly, Sir Toby Milbanke, 12th Baronet, before he took his own life in 1949, two years after succeeding his brother Sir John 'Buffles' Milbanke, 11th Baronet, the so-called Boxing Baronet. Their father Sir John Milbanke, 10th Baronet, VC, was killed at Gallipoli in 1915.
33. Carol Mather, *When the Grass Stops Growing*, Leo Cooper, 1997, p. 50
34. *London Gazette*, 14 July 1944
35. *Truth*, 12 October 1945
36. *Daily Mail*, 9 April 1946
37. Ibid., 15 April 1946
38. *Yorkshire Post and Leeds Intelligencer*, 6 March 1946
39. *Rotherham Advertiser*, 13 April 1946
40. *Daily Mail*, 15 April 1946
41. *Rotherham Advertiser*, 13 April 1946
42. *Sunday Times*, 5 May 1946
43. *Daily Mail*, 15 April 1946
44. *Sheffield Telegraph*, 15 April 1946
45. *Yorkshire Post*, 16 April 1946
46. James Lees-Milne, *Caves of Ice*, Faber & Faber, 1984, p. 53
47. Paddy Behan, *Part of this Place*, privately printed, 2017, p. 35
48. Ibid., pp. 36–7
49. Peerage law is a funny old beast. If a child is born of unmarried parents who later marry, they become legitimate. Except in Scots law, under peerage law they still cannot inherit titles. A modern example is found in the Harewood earldom's line of succession. David Lascelles, 8th Earl of Harewood, was not married to his first wife, Margaret, at the time of their daughter Emily's birth in 1975, nor at the time of their eldest son Benjamin's birth in 1978. Accordingly, it is their younger son Alexander who will become 9th Earl of Harewood in due course, since his parents married in February 1979, fifteen months before his birth.
50. John Bateman, *The Great Landowners of Great Britain and Ireland*, intr. David Spring, Leicester University Press, 1971, p. 8
51. *Speeches and Addresses of Edward Henry 15th Earl of Derby KG*, edited by Sir T. H. Sanderson, KCB, and E. S. Roscoe, Longmans, Green & Co, 1894, p. 141

52. Number of Land and House Owners, debated 19 February 1872, House of Lords
53. *Spectator*, 4 March 1876
54. Tea, debated 3 May 1909, House of Commons
55. David Cannadine, *The Decline and Fall of the British Aristocracy*, Yale University Press, 1990, p. 90
56. James Austen-Cartmell, *The Finance Act, 1893 so far as it relates to the new estate duty and other death duties in England*, Wildy & Sons, 1894, pp. 95–6
57. Duke of Devonshire, *Accidents of Fortune*, Michael Russell, 2004, p. 45
58. Deborah Devonshire, *Wait for Me!*, John Murray, 2011, p. 149
59. Another, less sympathetic interpretation of what transpired for Guy Middleton is that he made the best of things, having seen this coming over the horizon. Disposing of Wollaton, a dirty coal estate on the periphery of Nottingham, meant that he could retreat to the rural comfort of Birdsall. Perhaps.
60. From '*The Masque of B-ll--l*' [Balliol], 1880: 'My name is George Nathaniel Curzon, / I am a most superior person. / My face is pink, my hair is sleek, / I dine at Blenheim once a week.' (William Tuckwell, *Reminiscences of Oxford*, Cassell & Co., 1900, p. 280)
61. Kerin Freeman, *The Civilian Bomb Disposing Earl: Jack Howard and Bomb Disposal in WW2*, Pen and Sword, 2015, p. 15
62. Green, p. 102
63. Ibid., p. 101
64. A. L. Rowse, *The Churchills*, Harper & Brothers, 1958, p. 178
65. Ibid., p. 177
66. Ivor Wimborne was well known to believe that his money – of which, as the grandson of the owner of the world's largest iron foundry, he had plenty – entitled him to anything and everything, even that which 'the *droit du seigneur* would not anyway secure him'. (Philip Ziegler, *Diana Cooper*, Alfred A. Knopf, 1982, p. 83) This included Lady Diana Manners (from 1919, Cooper), on whom he lavished presents and meals out. One evening together cost him almost £10, which included £1 on a four-shilling taxi fare because, as he told her, '"you're in it".' (Diana Cooper, *The Rainbow Comes and Goes*, Century, 1984, p. 256) He relentlessly and somewhat aggressively pursued her, his advances verging on sexual harassment. As Diana's

biographer Philip Ziegler put it, 'Lord Wimborne had sufficient energy for a wife and a multitude of paramours; his death-bed was to be the only resting place in which he did not hope Diana could be induced to join him.' (Ziegler, *Diana Cooper*, p. 86)

67. Karen Wiseman and Michael Waterhouse, *The Churchill Who Saved Blenheim*, Unicorn, 2019, pp. 31–2
68. Ibid., p. 33
69. Ibid., p. 34
70. Consuelo Vanderbilt Balsan, *The Glitter and the Gold*, Harper & Brothers, 1952, p. 53
71. Ibid., p. 54
72. Ibid., p. 83
73. Ibid., pp. 71–2
74. Ibid., p. 72
75. Ivor was recognised as Sunny's but he was in fact the son of Consuelo and the American socialite Winthrop Rutherfurd, whom Consuelo had wished to marry instead of Sunny, but was convinced otherwise by her demanding mother.
76. The only biography of Sunny so far published is called *The Churchill Who Saved Blenheim*, though, really, the person who saved Blenheim was Consuelo.
77. Montgomery-Massingberd, *Blenheim Revisited*, p. 127
78. Green, p. 125
79. Women were not permitted in the Lords until the introduction of life peers during Harold Macmillan's premiership in 1958.
80. Charles C. F. Greville, *The Greville Memoirs*, edited by Henry Reeve, Volume III, Longmans, Green & Co., 1875, p. 19
81. In fairness, James Ullswater was hardly from poor stock. His family had ruled supreme over the Lake District since the 13th century, and in 1807 his great-grandfather had been created 1st Earl of Lonsdale.
82. Bill 145 Second Reading, debated 19 April 1883, House of Commons
83. William Buchan, *The Rags of Time*, Ashford, Buchan & Enright, 1990, p. 125
84. Frederic Mullally, *The Silver Salver*, Granada, 1981, p. 38
85. *Vanity Fair*, August 2006
86. *The Times*, 21 December 1918
87. *Country Life*, 17 September 1910

88. Adrian Fort, *Nancy*, St Martin's Press, 2012, p. 336
89. He went on to co-found car manufacturer Clement-Talbot in 1902.
90. Charles Duff, *Charley's Woods*, Zuleika, 2017, p. 11. Charles Duff, Charley Anglesey's grandson, went further with this description, describing him as 'perhaps not the sharpest card in the pack'. (Duff, p. 11)
91. And not, as some accounts have it, in the House of Commons.
92. *The Times*, 10 December 1924
93. *Estates Gazette*, 3 January 1920
94. Ibid., 31 December 1921
95. F. M. L. Thompson, *English Landed Society in the Nineteenth Century*, Routledge & Kegan Paul, 1963, pp. 332–3
96. John Beckett and Michael Turner, 'End of the Old Order? F. M. L. Thompson, the Land Question, and the burden of ownership in England c.1880–c.1925', *Agricultural History Review*, vol. 55, no. 2, December 2007, p. 279
97. F. M. L. Thompson, Presidential Address: 'English Landed Society in the Twentieth Century, I Property: Collapse and Survival', *Transactions of the Royal Historical Society*, vol. 40, 1990, pp. 1–24
98. Beckett & Turner, p. 285
99. He had inherited his great-great-uncle the 'Canal Duke' Francis Egerton, 3rd Duke of Bridgewater's enormous wealth in 1903.
100. There were two similarly named buildings relevant to the Ellesmeres. Francis Egerton, 3rd Duke of Bridgewater, inherited the seventeenth-century Worsley Old Hall in 1748, and quickly commissioned a new house on the estate, Brick Hall. Later, in the 1840s, his great-nephew Francis Egerton, 1st Earl of Ellesmere, replaced Brick Hall with a new house, Worsley New Hall, and this was completed in 1846. Researching the Ellesmeres' departure from Worsley, it became clear to me that the house was known as 'Worsley Hall', at least in official publications and indeed in the Court Circular.
101. Rationalisation of the great estates continued right to the end of the twentieth century. In 1969, for example, Hugh(ie) Percy, 10th Duke of Northumberland, sold Albury Park in Surrey, where his mother Helen, Duchess of Northumberland, had lived as a widow until her death in June 1965, because, according to his son Ralph Percy, 12th Duke of Northumberland, 'As he and his family lived at Syon [House, opposite Kew Gardens] during the summer, there was no need for another huge house.' Albury was duly converted into flats.

102. The received wisdom is that Mabel didn't get on with Billy. '"He had so much and everyone else had so little" – that was her line,' remembered Joyce Smith, whose father Godfrey Smith, Mabel's brother-in-law, had been a vicar at Wentworth. (Bailey, *Black Diamonds*, p. 399) But when in April 1897 Maud opened her visitors' book for the first time to welcome guests to Carnew Castle, her home as a newlywed in Ireland with Billy, the very first signature was Mabel's. Subsequently, she visited several times, both alone and with her husband Billy McKenzie Smith, and stayed with Billy and Maud at Coollattin too. Billy certainly did not bar his sister from his house.
103. A two-part sale took place in March and April 1948, before Peter's death. In July 1949, a six-day sale dispersed the wider collection. This sale was arranged by Peter but overseen after his death by members and employees of the family.

2. A HANDFUL OF DUST

1. Lady Dorothy Onslow married Edward Wood, from 1944 1st Earl of Halifax, sometime foreign secretary, wartime ambassador to the United States, and Viceroy of India in 1909. She had first met him in the refreshment room at Berwick-upon-Tweed railway station when they were both changing trains en route to two different balls in the Borders. Theirs was a happy marriage, despite his affair with Lady Alexandra 'Baba' Metcalfe, on whom more later. Her sister Lady Gwendolen married Rupert Guinness, 2nd Earl of Iveagh, of the eponymous brewery, once the richest man in Ireland, in 1903.
2. *The Times*, 16 June 1909
3. *Boston Guardian*, 26 June 1909
4. *Daily News*, 24 June 1909
5. *Norfolk News*, 19 June 1909
6. *Northern Daily Telegraph*, 28 July 1909
7. *The Times*, 10 April 1911
8. Lord Halifax, *Fullness of Days*, Dodd, Mead & Company, 1957, p. 56
9. Channon, *Diaries: 1918–38*, p. 467
10. Henry 'Chips' Channon, *The Diaries, Volume 3: 1943–57*, edited by Simon Heffer, Hutchinson, 2022, p. 292
11. John Gaze, *Figures in a Landscape*, Barrie & Jenkins, 1988, p. 88. Gaze himself was the Trust's former director of historic properties

and, as Merlin Waterson, who held the same role, points out, a land agent 'through and through, so thought buildings, and the historic buildings staff who looked after them, were a mistake'. It is not quite true, he says, that the Trust from its inception was not so concerned about buildings: '[T]hat is simply not borne out by the early acquisition of properties, including, as you say, Barrington Court.' Indeed, he adds, the Trust's shifting position on many issues, 'including the fate of country houses, was greatly influenced by its chronic shortage of money. The wave of property acquisitions in the 1970s and 80s were made possible by the National Heritage Memorial Fund and the Heritage Lottery Fund, and by the rapid increase in the number of members, paying increasing subscriptions.'

12. Gaze also points out that 'the preservation of buildings seems to have been almost a last-minute inclusion in the self-prescribed role of the Trust.' (Ibid., p. 87)

13. Ibid., p. 121

14. James Lees-Milne, *People and Places: Country House Donors and the National Trust*, John Murray, 2001, p. 170

15. James Lees-Milne, *Ancestral Voices*, Charles Scribner's Sons, 1975, p. 3

16. Lees-Milne, *People and Places*, p. 170

17. Ibid., p. 173

18. Ibid., pp. 181–2

19. Channon, 1943–57, p. 594

20. *The Times*, 16 October 1950

21. Lees-Milne, *Caves of Ice*, pp. 15–16

22. First, Captain Hon. Lawrence Kay-Shuttleworth had been killed at Vimy Ridge in March 1917. Then his brother Ted perished in a motorcycle accident that July. When Ughtred Kay-Shuttleworth, 1st Baron Shuttleworth, died aged ninety-five in December 1939, proud of having been the last survivor of Gladstone's final government, he was succeeded by his eldest grandson Richard, a Battle of Britain pilot. Nine months later, he was killed while flying a Hurricane. His brother Ronnie succeeded him, but in November 1942 he was killed in North Africa.

23. James Lees-Milne, *Midway on the Waves*, Faber & Faber, 1985, p. 217

24. Thompson, Presidential Address

25. *The Times*, 26 March 1963

26. Ibid., 1 January 1936

27. Ibid., 4 January 1956

NOTES TO PAGES 80–85

29. Jeremy Musson, *Up and Down Stairs*, John Murray, 2009, p. 265
30. James Lees-Milne, *Prophesying Peace*, Charles Scribner's Sons, 1977, pp. 63–64
31. Lees-Milne, *Ancestral Voices*, p. 174
32. Ibid., p. 193
33. James Lees-Milne, *Ancient as the Hills*, John Murray, 1997, p. 85
34. Lees-Milne, *Prophesying Peace*, p. 231
35. *Houses of Outstanding Historic or Architectural Interest*, report of a committee appointed by the Chancellor of the Exchequer, 1950, p. 3
36. Simon Kerry, *Lansdowne: The Last Great Whig*, Unicorn, 2017, p. 14
37. In terms of acreage, he lagged behind Henry Conyngham, 4th Marquess Conyngham, who owned 166,710 acres. In terms of the gross annual value of his estates, Clan was the sixth-richest marquess, at £62,025, but the fifth-poorest per acre. None of the marquesses could claim to be the richest by acreage, gross annual value and pound per acre. Henry Conyngham had the largest acreage, but his was worth the third-least per acre. John Crichton Stuart, 3rd Marquess of Bute, enjoyed the highest value, at £151,135, for his estates in England, Scotland and Wales, spread over 116,668 acres, the fourth-largest estate of all the marquesses, but the average per acre was £1.29. Henry Paget, 4th Marquess of Anglesey's acreage was most valuable, averaging £3.71 per acre, over his 29,737 acres in England and Wales.
38. Kerry, p. 14
39. Ibid., p. 15
40. Henry Petty-Fitzmaurice, 3rd Marquess of Lansdowne, 'the sage on whose counsel' the Whigs relied, served as a nineteenth-century home secretary and chancellor of the exchequer. A moderate Whig, he was trusted by Queen Victoria, who considered him a friend and who in 1857 offered him a dukedom, which he refused. 'He was not without ambition, but his ambition was completely under the control of his judgement,' *The Times* said after his death (*The Times*, 2 February 1863). As *Punch* put it: 'Lord Lansdowne won't be Duke of Kerry. / Lord Lansdowne is a wise man, very. / Punch drinks his health in port and sherry.' (*Punch*, 3 October 1857)
41. Clarissa Eden, *A Memoir*, Phoenix, 2008, p. 19
42. Marquess of Bath, *Longleat Preserved*, unpublished, p. 183
43. *The Guards Magazine*, Autumn 2015

44. *The Times*, 4 January 1945
45. Lady Elizabeth Lambton, Memories, 2006, unpublished
46. *The Duff Cooper Diaries*, edited by John Julius Norwich, Weidenfeld & Nicolson, 2005, p. 345
47. Jane O'Hea O'Keefe, *Voices from the Great Houses*, Mercier Press, 2013, p. 166
48. *The Times*, 6 June 1955
49. Ibid., 24 June 1955
50. Ibid., 28 June 1955
51. Ibid., 29 June 1955

3. PUT OUT MORE FLAGS

1. *The Times*, 15 April 1950
2. In 1963, the architectural historian Sir John Summerson declared 'the great towered and turreted houses of Elizabethan and Jacobean times' the 'most daring of all English buildings' (*The Classical Language of Architecture*, Thames & Hudson, 1980, p. 86)
3. Bath, pp. 12–13
4. Ibid., p. 197
5. The Baths were in the upper third of the thirty-three marquesses who occupied the peerage in the 1880s. They were tenth out of thirty-three for the most acres, and fifth for the relative value of their land.
6. Bath, p. 232
7. Peter Mandler, *The Fall and Rise of the Stately Home*, Yale University Press, 1997, p. 79
8. Ibid., p. 71
9. David Green, p. 172
10. Ibid., p. 173
11. John, Duke of Bedford, *A Silver-Plated Spoon*, Sphere, 1967, p. 25
12. Ibid., p. 10
13. Ibid., p. 64
14. Ibid., p. 38
15. Ibid., p. 160
16. Ibid., p. 191
17. Ibid., p. 192
18. Ibid., p. 167
19. Ibid.

20. Ibid., p. 194
21. Ibid., p. 196
22. Ibid., pp. 196–7
23. Ibid., p. 197
24. Ibid., p. 170
25. Ibid., p. 199
26. Ibid., p. 170
27. *Daily Telegraph*, 18 August 2006
28. Bedford, p. 215
29. Ibid., pp. 218–19
30. Jimmy Chipperfield, *My Wild Life*, Macmillan, 1975, p. 159
31. Ibid., p. 160
32. Equivalent to £168,618.20 in May 2024, per the Bank of England.
33. Equivalent to £561,808.84 in May 2024, per the Bank of England.
34. *The Times*, 2 September 1965
35. Channon, *1943–57*, p. 872
36. James Peill, *Glorious Goodwood: A Biography of England's Greatest Sporting Estate*, Constable, 2019, p. 236
37. Equivalent to £8,121,315.55 in May 2024, per the Bank of England.
38. *The Country House Remembered*, edited by Merlin Waterson, Routledge & Kegan Paul, 1985, p. 15
39. Ibid., p. 232
40. Catherine Sinclair, *Shetland and the Shetlanders*, D. Appleton & Co., 1840, p. 202
41. Freddie's cousin George 'Geordie' Gordon Lennox, who watched as the sale of Gordon Castle went through, was rather more fond of the house than Freddie; his father Lord Bernard Gordon Lennox, third son of the 7th Duke, had been killed in October 1914, and Geordie had spent happy summers at Gordon Castle with his grandfather. After the Second World War, during which the castle had been taken over by the army, it was in a bad way, riddled with both wet and dry rot. In 1952, helped by his half-aunt Helen, Duchess of Northumberland, Geordie bought back the castle, and two years later knocked most of it down, leaving only the medieval six-storey tower and the two-storey east wing. It remains in his branch of the Gordon Lennox family, run and owned by his grandson Angus, the current duke's second cousin, and his wife Zara, who have diversified the estate and restored the eight-acre walled garden.

42. Roy Strong, *The Destruction of the Country House, 1875–1975*, Thames & Hudson, 1974, p. 169

43. Ibid., p. 170

44. *Staffordshire Advertiser*, 29 April 1950

45. Gerald and Mary had met at a party near Weston after the Second World War and had married on Hallowe'en 1946. A colonel's daughter, she was born in Northern Ireland, and, like Gerald Newport, was a linguist, who had lived in Holland before the war, during which time she attended a Nazi rally in Nuremberg. When war came, she went to work at Bletchley Park in the German naval section, and then joined the BBC as the second head of the Austrian department. 'She never went back to Holland,' says Richard Bradford. 'All her friends had died in camps.' When Richard went to Cambridge in the 1970s, he became a good friend of a man called Hywel Jones. One day, after university, the pair had lunch, and discussing the Bradfords, Jones said, ' "Well, of course, your parents were both spies." I think that probably was the case,' says Richard Bradford.

46. This was an eighteenth-century Gothic house near Wolverhampton which had passed to the Bradfords in 1854. George Bridgeman, 2nd Earl of Bradford, had had no desire to live at Tong, and let the house to the Hartley family, from Wolverhampton, who stayed until 1909. Two years later, it was badly damaged in a fire. The Bradfords offered it for sale in 1913, but there were no takers; it was then offered to the War Office to house German prisoners-of-war but was deemed lacking in sanitary arrangements; after which the copper and lead were removed from the roof and the contents sold.

47. Earl of Bradford, *Stately Secrets*, Robson Books, 1994, p. 23

48. *Birmingham Weekly Mercury*, 10 May 1964

49. Robert Harling, *The Great Houses and Finest Rooms of England*, Viking Press, 1969, p. 141

50. *Birmingham Daily Post*, 6 January 1977

51. *The Times*, 29 September 1987

52. Ibid.

53. Sir Michael Culme-Seymour, 5th Baronet, owner of Rockingham Castle in Leicestershire, argued that the total number of houses 'demolished, gutted, or gravely reduced' in the thirty years after the end of the Second World War was 780, in *Country Life* in October 1974.

54. Ettie Desborough had died heirless in 1952, having lost two sons in the First World War. The house had then failed to attract a buyer.
55. Viscount Churchill, *Be All My Sins Remembered*, Coward-McCann, 1965, pp. 34–5
56. Douglas Sutherland, *The Yellow Earl*, Merlin Unwin, 2015, p. 4
57. A twenty-one-day sale of the contents of Lowther that began in April 1947 was said to be the largest country house contents sale of the twentieth century. Only £144,000 was raised for the almost 8,000 lots, which included the oak table at which Napoleon signed his abdication at Fontainebleau in 1814. Further sales took place in in 1950 and 1952.
58. *The Lost Castle of Lowther: The Power of Play*, Blooloop, 21 September 2016; blooloop.com
59. Ibid.
60. Writing in the *Coventry Evening Telegraph* in November 1956, Andrew Everard asked: 'Can nothing be done in Britain to prevent the 20th century obliterating the 19th century? . . . Lowther Castle was built in 1806, so it escapes the stigma of being dubbed Victorian, although with its uncompromising grey stone mass it resembles many mansions but years later. If it had been built in the now fashionable 18th century, it may well have stood a chance of survival . . . People have in Britain have been educated during the past few decades in the need for preserving the nation's architectural heritage – but that seems to exclude the 19th century except for the favoured Regency period.' (*Coventry Evening Telegraph*, 29 November 1956)
61. *Country Life*, 23 June 1994
62. Roy Strong, *The Roy Strong Diaries, 1967–1987*, Weidenfeld & Nicolson, 1997, p. 139
63. *Bristol Evening Post*, 23 October 1974
64. Strong, *Diaries*, p. 140
65. *The Times*, 30 September 1974
66. Ibid.
67. The term 'Rothschildshire' was coined in recognition of the large number of Rothschild-owned houses that there were locally. This is now rather in the past tense, but they had been: Mentmore, built between 1852 and 1855 by Mayer Amschel de Rothschild; Aston Clinton, bought by Sir Anthony Rothschild in 1851; Halton, bought by Lionel de Rothschild in 1853; Tring, also bought by Lionel de Rothschild in 1852, and given as a wedding present to his son

Nathaniel Mayer Rothschild, 1st Baron Rothschild; Ascott, bought in 1873 and expanded by Leopold de Rothschild; and Waddesdon, built by Baron Ferdinand, Meyer's cousin, between 1875 and 1880.

68. Cecil Roth, *The Magnificent Rothschilds*, Pyramid Books, 1962, p. 141. As Roth continued, the hall was 'hung with priceless tapestries, and floored with parquet (then an unusual luxury) and Persian carpets. An open arcade ran round above, and the visitor looked down through arches into the hall, which was filled with gorgeous masses of flowers and every sumptuous object that wealth could command. From the great central hall hung with tapestries branched off lobbies filled with white marble: then three drawing-rooms, two (why two?) libraries, and a billiard-room – all crammed with precious articles in enamel, lime, bronze, gold, silver, amber, jewels, and all manner of other things of beauty and especially of price.' (Roth, pp. 141–2)

69. Equivalent to £41 million in May 2024, per the Bank of England.

70. *The Times*, 28 January 1977

71. Until 1929, the family had another house, The Durdans in Epsom, where the former prime minister Archie Primrose, 5th Earl of Rosebery, bred racehorses.

72. Frank Herrmann, *Sotheby's: Portrait of an Auction House*, Chatto & Windus, 1980, p. 431

73. Ibid., p. 430

74. *Art at Auction: The Year at Sotheby Parke Bernet*, 1976–77, edited by Anne Jackson, Sotheby Parke Bernet, 1977, p. 10

75. He had met his wife Deirdre in Oxford in the theatre while he was working as a sound engineer.

76. *Art at Auction*, p. 10

77. John Harris, *No Voice from the Hall*, John Murray, 2000, p. 31

4. BRIDESHEAD REVISITED

1. Estate Duty, debated 26 March 1974, House of Commons

2. Evelyn Waugh, *Brideshead Revisited*, Penguin Books, 2000, p. 8

3. The Howards suffered appallingly during the first half of the twentieth century. In 1921 Liberal MP the Hon. Geoffrey Howard inherited Castle Howard in awkward circumstances (see Chapter 9), but by June 1935, both he and his wife Kitty were dead within three years of one another, leaving five children, the youngest of whom was only four.

Geoffrey's close friend the Hon. Oliver Stanley became guardian to the three boys, his second cousins, and the great house was left in trust to the eldest of these, Mark, but he was killed in France in July 1944, followed by his younger brother Kit in October the same year when his plane was shot down over Germany. Their middle brother, George, returned home from his war service with the Green Howards, with whom he had served in India and Burma and been severely injured, to discover that he was the sole inheritor of the Howards' great North Yorkshire palace. Neither Castle Howard nor George Howard were in good condition. In November 1940, a large part of the house was destroyed in a fire that ripped through the east wing, collapsing the famous dome in the process. In the years following George Howard's inheritance of Castle Howard, he and his wife Lady Cecilia FitzRoy began to put it back together, and in the early 1960s the dome was rebuilt. George Howard's son the Hon. Nick Howard explains that when his father left hospital after the war, '[H]e discovered that his trustees had unilaterally decided that nobody would ever live in the house again, and were negotiating a very long lease with the school that had been evacuated there, and beginning to sell off contents. I've always believed that sheer anger at the lack of consultation was one of the main driving forces behind his decision to re-occupy the house.'

4. Lord Montagu of Beaulieu, *Wheels Within Wheels*, Weidenfeld & Nicolson, 2000, p. 159

5. Oliver Stanley, *Taxation of Farmers & Landowners*, Lexis Law Publishing, 1987, p. 217

6. A rare example of a 1990s demolition is Minto House in the Scottish Borders, then owned by Gilbert Elliot-Murray-Kynynmound, 6th Earl of Minto. The Mintos had, however, been granted permission to demolish the house some twenty years earlier.

7. *The Times*, 23 November 1988

8. *Daily Telegraph*, 29 November 1988

9. *Evening Standard*, 28 November 1988

10. Veronica Maclean, *Past Forgetting*, Review, 2002, p. 70

11. Ibid., p. 355

12. Ibid.

13. Ibid., p. 356

14. Ibid., p. 357

15. *The Times*, 31 May 1995

16. Ibid., 25 August 1995
17. Merlin Waterson, *A Noble Thing: The National Trust and its Benefactors*, Scala, 2011, p. 180
18. By the time I moved to the old Brownlow estate village of Manthorpe, next to Belton, in 2022, none of the forty old Brownlow-built cottages remained in the family.
19. Shortly after Belton's acquisition, Charles Sherborne's successor Ralph Sherborne died, and bequeathed his house, Hinton Ampner, to the Trust too. Further houses taken on by the Trust in the last quarter of the century included the reclusive Christian socialist Roger Grey, 10th and last Earl of Stamford's Dunham Massey Hall in Cheshire, bequeathed upon his death in 1976 with its estate, contents and an endowment; and the Sherborne estate near Cheltenham, bequeathed to the Trust on the death of the childless Charles Dutton, 7th Baron Sherborne, in 1982. The Robert Adam masterpiece Kedleston Hall in Derbyshire, home of the Curzons, came to the Trust in 1987 thanks in part to a significant grant from the National Heritage Memorial Fund. It's still home to one branch of the latest generation of Curzons: the Hon. Richard Curzon and his family.
20. When the reclusive Richard Wraxall died unmarried, his brother inherited the family title. The house passed to a group of trustees who then put Tyntesfield and its 1,000-acre estate on the market. The National Trust's then director general Fiona Reynolds launched an appeal for £35 million to save Tyntesfield. The purchase was completed in June 2002.
21. Today, the National Trust is not the country house-rescuing organisation that it once was, but cares for the properties it already tends. 'We haven't been particularly active [in acquiring new properties],' the Trust's director general Hilary McGrady told me in 2019, 'largely because people have stopped giving us stuff.' She added: 'A lot of the big house owners have been able to support themselves, and for us that's a result.'
22. In November 2024, Jason Lindsay, grandson of David Lindsay, 28th Earl of Crawford and a former Sotheby's Old Masters specialist, succeeded as president with as his deputy Andrew Hope, Earl of Hopetoun, the future 5th Marquess of Linlithgow, who we are about to meet.
23. *The Times*, 23 February 2006. Two months later, the property-buying agency Property Vision reported a 50 per cent rise in the number of clients looking to spend at least £20 million on a house in London or in the country.

24. 'The rough number I use is that in a good year it loses £500,000, and in a bad year it could lose £1.5 million,' he said at the time. *(The Times*, 19 May 2004)
25. Povlsen's landholdings in Britain in 2018 reached 221,000 acres.
26. *STV News*, 20 June 2019
27. In 2022, having hosted successful weddings and other events, it struck the Willoughbys that below stairs offered possibilities too, and in April 2024 they opened a nightclub in the nineteenth-century basement kitchen complex, which had been deserted since the 1950s. Now, where once stood a large country house kitchen supported by endless pantries, ice houses and meat larders, is a party room with a bar and dancefloor.
28. The late John Baring, 7th Baron Ashburton, told me in 2018 that when as a young banker, he visited Wallach at home at The Grange in the early 1960s to ask if he could buy it back, Wallach responded: 'You are far too young to have a house of this quality – you don't realise that this is the finest country house in England outside Windsor Castle.' 'I was so gobsmacked at him thinking about Windsor Castle being the finest country house,' John Ashburton said, 'I could hardly speak.' Incidentally, John Ashburton picked up the nickname 'Basher Baring' for his propensity to knock down buildings: the Barings' Stratton Park in 1963, and a large portion of The Grange, shortly after.
29. 'Our HUGE 18th Century Swimming Pool DEMOLITION – Start to Finish!', Mapperton Live: This (un)Aristocratic Manor Life, 8 June 2024; youtube.com/watch?v=s4RxBnKrZMk
30. This, says Andrew Hopetoun, is nothing to brag about: 'You don't want things to be that big.'
31. The 'Wyke' in Wykeham rhymes with 'bike', rather than 'wick'.
32. Alan Whicker, *The Aristocracy Business*, Yorkshire Television, 1968

5. WORK SUSPENDED

1. Leader's speech, Blackpool 1998, Tony Blair; britishpoliticalspeech.org
2. Labour Party manifesto, 1997
3. Hereditary Peers (Democratic Rights), debated 15 June 1994, House of Commons. In fairness to the Buccleuchs, the Buccleuch earldom predates Charles II, from whom they are usually (correctly) said to be primarily descended. James Scott, Duke of Monmouth, son of the king and Lucy Walter, married Anne Scott, Countess of Buccleuch, the

daughter of Francis Scott, 2nd Earl of Buccleuch. Francis Buccleuch was himself the son of Walter Scott, 1st Earl of Buccleuch, whose father was created 1st Lord Scott of Buccleuch in 1606. Without Charles II's help, they would not, however, have been able to sit in the Lords until 1707, when the Act of Union made it possible for Scottish peers to elect representatives from their number to sit in the Lords.

4. Two recent prime ministers had been peers and members of the Lords. Archie Rosebery succeeded to his grandfather's title in 1868 but since titleholders from the Peerage of Scotland were not all members of the Lords, only those sixteen representative peers, he succeeded to the Lords as 2nd Baron Rosebery, the title from the Peerage of the United Kingdom that his grandfather had been given in 1828. Archie Rosebery served as prime minister 1894–5, and was succeeded by Robert Gascoyne-Cecil, 3rd Marquess of Salisbury, in the third of his three terms.

5. David Lloyd George, *The People's Budget*, Hodder & Stoughton, 1909, p. 57

6. *The Times*, 11 October 1909

7. *Gloucestershire Echo*, 7 August 1909

8. Ziegler, *Diana Cooper*, p. 4

9. *Liverpool Daily Post*, 20 September 1909

10. Ibid.

11. Finance Bill, debated 29 November 1909, House of Lords

12. House of Lords (Refusal to pass finance bill), debated 2 December 1909, House of Commons

13. Reduced to one year by the 1949 Parliament Act. The 1911 legislation also reduced the maximum term of a parliament from seven years, as stipulated in the Septennial Act of 1716, to five.

14. *The Crisis of British Unionism: The Domestic Political Papers of the Second Earl of Selborne, 1885–1922*, edited by D. George Boyce, The Historians' Press, 1987, p. 221

15. Bernard Crick, 'The Life Peerages Act', *Parliamentary Affairs*, vol. 11, no. 4, 1957

16. House of Lords Reform, debated 25 January 1955, House of Lords

17. Ibid.

18. Walter Bagehot, *The English Constitution*, Chapman & Hall, 1867, p. 162

19. House of Lords Reform, debated 25 January 1955, House of Lords

20. Lord Salisbury memorandum, March 1956. FO 1109/350, National Archives, Kew

21. Incidentally, from May 1946 reimbursements had been paid to regularly attending peers for rail fares. The rule, former clerk of the parliaments Sir David Beamish explains, 'applied to members attending one-third of sittings or, in respect of peers resident in Scotland, one-third of sittings at which Scottish business was taken'. As Philip Cunliffe-Lister, 1st Viscount (later Earl of) Swinton, put it, speaking in the Lords in May 1946, '[T]hose who come from furthest afield . . . find that it is a really tremendous burden . . . we are not all rich men. Riches are something to which the doctrine of relativity certainly applies today.' (Peers' Travelling Expenses, debated 21 May 1946, House of Lords)

22. This became known as the Wensleydale peerage case. In 1856, the chancery lawyer Sir James Parke was created Baron Wensleydale for the term of his natural life. When the new session began in the Lords, however, the validity of his patent was submitted to the privileges committee, who ruled that as a new-fangled 'life peer', he could not sit and vote as a peer of Parliament. Shortly after, he was created a hereditary peer and the matter of life peers was dropped again until 1887. As George Cokayne explains in *The Complete Peerage*, '[T]he object of this life peerage . . . was to create a precedent whereby the House of Lords might be strengthened by men whose means were insufficient to enable them to support an hereditary peerage.' (*Complete Peerage of England, Scotland, Ireland, Great Britain and the United Kingdom, Volume VIII*, edited by G. E. C. [George Edward Cokayne], George Bell & Sons, 1898, p. 94) The case 'has become familiar as a demonstration of the Indian summer enjoyed by the British landed aristocracy after 1846, in whose mild climate the House of Lords remained not only unreformed, but formidable enough to be unreformable and to retain its role in the political life of a persistently deferential society'. (Olive Anderson, 'The Wensleydale Peerage Case and the Position of the House of Lords in the Mid-Nineteenth Century', *English Historical Review*, vol. 82, no. 324, 1967, pp. 486–502)

23. Harold Macmillan died on 29 December 1986. He was predeceased by his son Maurice, who died on 10 March 1984 and was thus styled Viscount Macmillan of Ovenden for only thirty days. As a result, he never inherited the unexpected earldom that his father had accepted in 1984, though by then, in fairness, the curse of the hereditary

peerage had been removed by the ability for peers to disclaim their peerages in 1963 (see Chapter 13). Winston Churchill said in 1945, '[I]t is a terrible thing for a father to doom his son to political extinction, which must happen to many if they have not had time to make their way in the House of Commons.' (Winston S. Churchill, *Triumph and Tragedy*, Houghton Mifflin Company, 1953, p. 742)

24. Harold Macmillan, *Riding the Storm*, Macmillan, 1971, p. 731

25. The first woman to be elected to the Commons was Constance Markievicz, in 1918, but as a member of Sinn Féin she did not take her seat.

26. Constitution of the House of Lords, debated 30 October 1957, House of Lords

27. David Beamish points out that Fraser's being the first life peer created was likely 'due to his speed in meeting Garter [the Garter Principal King at Arms, the senior king of arms and officer of arms of the College of Arms] to settle his title'. He adds: 'The norm used to be that after that meeting a month was allowed for the letters patent to be prepared by the calligrapher. The fact that after 22 August the next set were dated 22 September may well mean that Garter went on holiday!'

28. Barbara Wootton, *In a World I Never Made*, George Allen & Unwin, 1967, p. 267

29. Ibid.

30. Ibid., p. 271

31. Macmillan, *Riding the Storm*, p. 732

32. 'Sir John Sainty and the House of Lords, 1959–90', Michael Pownall, *Institutional Practice and Memory: Parliamentary People, Records and Histories – Essays in Honour of Sir John Sainty*, edited by Clyve Jones, Wiley Backwell for The Parliamentary History Yearbook Trust, 2013, p. 8

33. It is likely that Sir Ellis Robins, as he then was, was made the offer of his peerage prior to 30 April 1958, the day on which the Life Peerages Act received Royal Assent; therefore at that point there was no such thing as a life peerage, despite it being obvious that his hereditary title would soon become extinct. Moreover, it was certainly thought by some – as remains the case today – that a life peerage was inferior, as shown by the case of Gavin Simonds who was made a life peer, Baron Simonds, as a law lord, in 1944, and succeeded as Lord

Chancellor in 1951. The following summer, in the Birthday Honours List, he was created Baron Simonds again, this time as a hereditary peer, and was promoted to Viscount Simonds in 1954. When he died in 1971, his title went extinct, owing to the fact that all three of his sons had predeceased him, and all before the point at which he had been offered a hereditary peerage.

34. *The Macmillan Diaries, Volume II*, edited by Peter Catterall, Macmillan, 2011, p. 663

35. Charles Douglas-Home, *Evelyn Baring, the Last Proconsul*, Collins, 1978, p. 309. The younger Evelyn Baring was appointed a Knight of the Garter in 1972.

36. This was not the first time that 'Egremont' had been used as a title for the Wyndham family. In 1748 Algernon Seymour, 7th Duke of Somerset, was created Earl of Egremont, and upon his death in 1750 this title passed to his nephew Sir Charles Wyndham, 4th Baronet. The earldom became extinct in 1845, before its name was used again as John Wyndham's new barony over a century later.

37. Lord Egremont, *Wyndham and Children First*, Macmillan, 1969, p. 197

38. The 1954 scandal involved the Crichel House estate in Devon, owned until 1940 by Napier Sturt, 3rd Baron Alington. Part of the estate was compulsorily purchased by the Air Ministry in 1938. Three years later prime minister Winston Churchill promised the Sturt family that the land would be returned to them after the Second World War, but the promise was reneged on, with the land claimed for use by the Ministry of Agriculture. Mary Marten (née Sturt) began a campaign for the government's promise to be kept and a public inquiry was launched. In July 1954, agriculture and fisheries minister Sir Thomas Dugdale told the Martens that they could buy the land back, and resigned from his post, as well as his seat in the House of Commons.

39. Constitution of the House of Lords, debated 30 October 1957, House of Lords

40. Life Peerages Bill Hl, debated 3 December 1957, House of Lords

41. Ibid.

42. Constitution of the House of Lords, debated 31 October 1957, House of Lords

43. Ibid.

44. Rights of Women Hereditary Peers, debated 21 January 1959, House of Lords

45. The vote was close, but it is striking how few peers voted on it at all. This in turn reflects the attendance levels in the House of Lords. In the 1959–60 session, the net total number of peers (i.e. including members who had not taken the oath, but excluding members without writ of summons, on leave of absence or disqualified) was 639, and in 1959–60 the average number of peers attending the Lords on a daily basis was 136, only 21 per cent of the total. Today, we might be surprised by this low level of attendance, but it was not the lowest point reached: House of Lords records show that in April 1956, there was a day on which only twenty-two peers were present in the House.

46. Aden, Perim and Kuria Muria Islands Bill, debated 17 July 1967, House of Lords

47. This is the correct surname. Margaret Mar was born Margaret Lane, but when her father James Lane succeeded as 30th Earl of Mar in 1959, he was recognised by the Lord Lyon in the style of Mar, and his children were styled the same way, with the surname Lane dropped.

48. The Woolsack is where the Lord Speaker sits in the House of Lords. Thought to have been introduced in the fourteenth century in recognition of the important role that the wool trade then played in the country's fortunes, it is a large square cushion covered in red cloth.

49. Patrick Jackson, *The Last of the Whigs: A Political Biography of Lord Hartington*, Fairleigh Dickinson University Press, 1994, p. 262

50. Andrew Roberts, *Salisbury*, Weidenfeld & Nicolson, 1999, p. 494

51. Gregory D. Phillips, 'The "Diehards' " and the Myth of the "Backwoodsmen"', *Journal of British Studies*, vol. 16, no. 2, 1977, pp. 105–20

52. Central Africa, debated 7 March 1961, House of Lords

53. Anthony Sampson, *Anatomy of Britain*, Hodder & Stoughton, 1962, p. 81

54. Central Africa, debated 8 March 1961, House of Lords

55. Ibid.

56. Sampson, pp. 81–2

57. *Attlee's Great Contemporaries*, edited by Frank Field, Continuum, 2009, p. 104

58. It was ironic, really. In 1955, when Princess Margaret wished to marry her late father's former equerry, the divorced Group Captain Peter

Townsend, negotiations took place to establish whether this would be possible. In the end, it was deemed not to be. William Clark, then prime minister Anthony Eden's press secretary, described it as 'the event that for the last time simultaneously and automatically brought into play all the pieces on the traditional English chessboard – Crown, Prime Minister, Archbishop, *The Times*, Lord Salisbury.' (William Clark, *From Three Worlds*, Sidgwick & Jackson, 1986, p. 159)

59. Woodrow Wyatt, *The Journals of Woodrow Wyatt, Volume 1*, edited by Sarah Curtis, Macmillan, 1998, p. 563

60. Parliament (No. 2) Bill, debated 3 February 1969, House of Lords. Another factor in this, it was believed at the time, was Wilson's wish to avoid complicating and frustrating progress concerning Barbara Castle's employment relations proposals and her white paper *In Place of Strife*. In the end, ironically, this was never passed either.

61. Simon Heffer, *The Life of Enoch Powell*, Phoenix Giant, 1999, p. 521

62. *The Lady and the Lords*, Michael Cockerell, BBC, 2000

63. *The Times*, 6 November 1999

64. Ibid., 18 August 1999

65. House of Lords Reform, debated 14 October 1998, House of Lords

66. Ibid.

67. Ibid.

68. Indeed, Lord Selborne was in fact Earl of Selborne, and the Hansard record should read, 'the noble Earl, Lord Selborne'. This error is Hansard's own.

69. House of Lords Reform, debated 14 October 1998, House of Lords

70. Andrew Rawnsley, *Servants of the People*, Hamish Hamilton, 2000, p. 202

71. The Dukes of Norfolk have held the hereditary office of Earl Marshal since 1672. This makes the duke one of the Great Officers of State, and gives him responsibility for organising ceremonial events, such as coronations and state funerals, as well as having oversight of the College of Arms. The Lord Great Chamberlain is entrusted with the parts of the Palace of Westminster not given to either the Commons or the Lords – principally the Robing Room and the Royal Gallery. He oversees the arrangement of the State Opening of Parliament and has the right to dress the monarch on Coronation Day. The officeholder is another of the Great Officers of State, and traditionally the role has taken charge of the Palace of Westminster. It

has been divided between several families (see Chapter 12), with the Marquesses of Cholmondeley taking a half-share. The officeholder changes not on his death, but on the monarch's.

72. Alastair Campbell, *Power & The People: The Alastair Campbell Diaries, Volume Two: 1997–1999*, Arrow Books, 2001, p. 578

73. *The Times*, 3 December 1998. Nevertheless, Cranborne believed that the deal he had struck was the right one. Following his sacking, he told of how he accepted that politics was a '... rough old game. If you have a thin skin you should not be in it ... every morning you should get up and say you could be sacked today. It's a very good exercise in humility.' (*The Times*, 3 December 1998)

74. *Guardian*, 27 October 1999

75. *The Lords' Tale*, Molly Dineen, Channel 4, 2002

76. About 240 peers stood for election in the end, among them fewer than half of the total Conservative hereditary peers.

77. *The Lords' Tale*

78. Earl Ferrers, *Whatever Next?*, Biteback Publishing, 2012, p. 255

79. The peers were not compelled to meet the seventy-five-word limit for their personal statement. One successful candidate, Euan Geddes, 3rd Baron Geddes, used only three words to make his case, remembered by David Beamish as, 'Brains, brevity, breadth!'

80. *The Lords' Tale*

81. After this followed David Trefgarne, 2nd Baron Trefgarne, and then the former chief whip Bertie Bowyer, 2nd Baron Denham, Benjamin Mancroft, Freddie Curzon, 7th Earl Howe, Ivon Moore-Brabazon, 3rd Baron Brabazon of Tara, Malcolm Sinclair, 20th Earl of Caithness, Simon Arthur, 4th Baron Glenarthur, and a pair of Astor cousins, Johnny Astor, 3rd Baron Astor of Hever, and William Astor, 4th Viscount Astor.

82. David Kenworthy, 11th Baron Strabolgi, and Jan Simon, 3rd Viscount Simon.

83. Robert Methuen, 7th Baron Methuen, Dominic Hubbard, 6th Baron Addington, and Conrad Russell, 5th Earl Russell.

84. *The Lords' Tale*

85. House of Lords (Hereditary Peers) Bill, 5 September 2024, House of Commons

86. John Morrison, 1st Baron Margadale (1906–96), former Conservative MP, raised to the peerage in 1965. More pertinently, he was

MFH, South and West Wilts Foxhounds 1932–65. At the time he gave his maiden speech, Benjamin Mancroft was MFH, Vale of White Horse Hunt.

87. David Beamish explains that, as the heir, William Astor would have needed 'not only the letters patent but proof that [he was] the eldest legitimate son of the previous peer. Having proved that to the satisfaction of the Crown Office, you get a writ of summons, and that is the key document.'

88. Clarissa was legally the daughter of Major John 'Jack' Spencer-Churchill, Winston Churchill's younger brother, and Lady Gwendoline 'Goonie' Bertie, but later she became sure that her biological father was the Liberal politician Harold 'Bluey' Baker, not least as after he died in 1960, she saw his will and discovered that he had left her all of his books. Indeed, Clarissa's brother Johnny wrote in his own memoirs of how Bluey was 'a lifelong friend' of Goonie's, and how he regarded Clarissa, with whom he was close, 'as one of the few women in this world with a first-class brain'. (John Spencer-Churchill, *A Churchill Canvas*, Little, Brown, 1961, p. 43) Incidentally, Jack Spencer-Churchill was thought not to be a Churchill, either – not the son of Lord Randolph Spencer-Churchill with his American wife Jennie Jerome, but of Jennie and another man. Many were suggested, the best of these being Evelyn 'Star' Boscawen, 7th Viscount Falmouth, and Johnny told Chips Channon that he believed as much.

89. Sampson, pp. 324–5

90. Ibid., p. 325

91. *Daily Mirror*, 19 October 1963

92. Sampson, p. 324

93. *New York Times*, 22 May 1979

94. *The Times*, 11 July 2018

95. Peter Carrington, *Reflect on Things Past: The Memoirs of Lord Carrington*, Fontana, 1989, p. 370

96. And, of course, Gordon Brown appointed two life peers as secretaries of state: Andrew Adonis as transport secretary, and Peter Mandelson as business secretary.

97. Charles Kinnoull was appointed to this role in April 2023, the first hereditary peer by succession in the office. As Tom Strathclyde describes, 'He is a very clever, decent man who would never have become convenor of the crossbenchers if he wasn't capable of doing it.'

6. BY SPECIAL REQUEST

1. *Ashbourne Telegraph*, 14 October 1955
2. Ibid., 11 November 1955
3. Ibid., 2 January 1953
4. Duke of Devonshire, p. 52
5. This was not far off. Colonel Hon. Aubrey Herbert, younger son of Henry Herbert, 4th Earl of Carnarvon, an intelligence officer who was a supporter of Albanian independence, was offered the throne to that country in 1914 and again in 1920.
6. Duke of Devonshire, p. 52
7. *Cheshire Observer*, 27 December 1941
8. George Ridley, *Bend'Or, Duke of Westminster*, Robin Clark, 1985, p. 155. Weekly tenants regularly received a hundredweight of coal at Christmas – equivalent to a half-year's rent rebate.
9. Within the family, he was known as 'Ivan' (the Terrible) or 'Peter' (the Great) according to his mood.
10. Duke of Devonshire, p. 56
11. Cannadine, *Decline*, p. 10
12. Some 280 out of 793 peers own in the region of 3.2 million acres. Today, the twenty-two families of the original twenty-nine premier leaguers who remain landowners are in possession of at least 1 million acres, and are worth in the region of £16 billion. Almost half of all this is in the hands of three families. Four dukes, along with a fifth ducal estate now owned by a charitable trust, control around 430,000 acres in northern England and Scotland. Of the five titles of the premier league that have become extinct in the last century, wealth, art, property and land have passed to other extant titled and untitled branches of their families to the tune of over £483,000,000.
13. Though for Eddy Devonshire, appointed Knight of the Garter in 1942, it was a close-run thing. As Winston Churchill's principal private secretary Jock Colville remembered, there was plenty of discussion as to whether he was to be given it or not. In the end, Churchill, in whose gift the Garter was, argued that Eddy was 'not bad as dukes go'. (Sir John Colville, *The Fringes of Power*, W. W. Norton & Company, 1985, p. 311) Fifty-one of the ninety-seven knights came from families to whom the dignity had been offered before, including seven pairs of father and son. The Dukes of Wellington and the Marquesses of

Salisbury had three individual titleholders appointed after 1900, while the Dukes of Devonshire boasted a grandfather, son and grandson in the Order. Jim Lees-Milne remarked in 1996 that he was surprised by Andrew Devonshire, who had been miserable for years at not being appointed, finally having been given the Garter: 'I would not have thought he was considered respectable enough. Debo would have been a worthier recipient.' (James Lees-Milne, *Diaries, 1984–1997*, John Murray, 2009, p. 452) Between 1956 when her husband the former prime minister Anthony Eden was installed as a Garter knight, and his death in 1977, Clarissa Eden used to attend Garter services. She recalled how in the late 1950s, Gerald Wellesley, 7th Duke of Wellington was rather down on the Order. The trouble was, he complained, that it was 'full of Field Marshals and people who do their own washing up.' (Hugo Vickers, *Clarissa: Muse to Power, The Untold Story of Clarissa Eden, Countess of Avon*, Hodder & Stoughton, 2024, p. 165)

14. Twenty out of the twenty-nine families of the premier league were represented in national lord-lieutenancies between 1900 and 2023, most more than once.

15. Channon, *1943–57*, p. 8

16. The Duke of Sutherland, *Looking Back*, Odhams Press, 1957, p. 208

17. Colville, *Fringes of Power*, p. 530

18. *London Gazette*, 1 December 1944

19. Ibid., p. 532

20. Channon, *1943–57*, p. 481. Geordie Sutherland devoted no space whatever to the circumstances of his marriage to Clare in his memoirs.

21. This change came about as part of an amendment to the Qualification of the Justices of the Peace Bill, passed in 1875. A proposal in 1875 by George Keppel, 6th Earl of Albemarle, had been to enact that an income of £300 a year from a personal estate should be equal to an income of £100 a year. Despite there having been strong feeling from peers in the Lords chamber, afterwards the proposals were watered down, resulting in, as Francis Cowper, 7th Earl Cowper, described in the Lords in 1891, '... nothing but the addition of the Inhabited House Duty Clause which included anybody ... who possessed or occupied a house worth £100 a year in the place for which he was to be appointed to act as Magistrate'. (Justice of the Peace Qualification Amendment Bill Hl – [No. 39], debated 3 March 1891, House of Lords) Inhabited House Duty was, itself, a tax assessed on inhabited

property, according to annual value, and a tax of its type had first been imposed in 1696. It was finally abolished in all forms in 1924, having been described by Lord Henry Bruce, MP for Chippenham, in 1889 as 'a tax on the working man'. (The Inhabited House Duty, debated 12 April 1889, House of Commons)

22. Justices of the Peace (No. 2) Bill, debated 14 June 1906, House of Lords

23. *The Victoria History of Shropshire, Volume III*, edited by C. R. Elrington, University of London Institute of Historical Research, 1979, p. 225

24. Those twelve peers were born between 1924 and 1944, making them part of a particular generation. This is surely no surprise. The most recent of the twelve to have served as a JP is Rear-Admiral Michael Harris, 9th Baron Harris, who served as JP for North West Hampshire from 2002 to 2011, though he did not, admittedly, serve as a JP while a peer, succeeding only in 2023.

25. In 1964, a report titled 'The deployment and payment of the clergy', by the clergyman Leslie Paul, led to reform of the church patronage system, including changes to the way payments were made to clergymen. Paul noted that in 1906 the average clerical income was £150, though some were in receipt of £1,500 or more, with the Dean of Durham earning £3,000, and the Archbishop of Canterbury £15,000. The result of the Paul Report was that, explains Max Wyndham, 7th Baron Leconfield and 2nd Baron Egremont, '[T]he Church of England seized all of the endowments, so a clergyman here [at Petworth] is now paid exactly the same as he would be paid in any living of a similar size.'

26. A list of 6,509 livings and their patrons was published in 1855 as '. . . a guide to all ecclesiastical patronage in the hands of the nobility and gentry, corporations, hospitals, and trusts'. It records there being 3,772 patrons in total, of which, alongside the East India Company, Dulwich College and Benjamin Disraeli, almost 300 were peers, who had, between them, almost 1,500 livings worth £445,330 a year. That makes the proportion of peers within the total patrons about 8 per cent, while the peers were in possession of about 23 per cent of all livings. This data analysis does not quite match with the assertion made by David Cannadine that in the late 1870s, 'over one-half of the 13,000 livings were in the gift of individuals, by definition, most

of them landowners,' since my qualifying individual for analysis was solely limited to members of the hereditary peerage, and not to the generic 'landowner', a label which could mean a world of different things. (Cannadine, *Decline*, p. 255)

27. In 1921, as in 1855, the peers with the greatest number of livings were Hugh Lowther, 5th Earl of Lonsdale, with forty, Victor Cavendish, 9th Duke of Devonshire, with thirty-eight, and Charles Wyndham, 3rd Baron Leconfield, with twenty-five. The figures I have calculated for 1921 and 1985 are not beyond reproach, since they rely on information given to the editors of *Debrett's*, and, as I have discovered when I have spoken to peers, that information can be partial.

28. Perrott, p. 64

29. Ibid., p. 191

30. And nine of them have been called Edward.

31. Equivalent to £4.8 million in May 2024, per the Bank of England and choosing 1912 as the representative year.

32. James Boswell, *The Life of Samuel Johnson, Volume I*, Sir Isaac Pitman & Sons, 1907, p. 378

33. Horace Walpole, *Memoirs and Portraits*, edited by Matthew Hodgart, B. T. Batsford, 1963, p. 152

34. 'Janitor', *The Feet of the Young Men*, Duckworth, 1929, p. 128

35. Henry 'Chips' Channon, *The Diaries, Volume 2: 1938–43*, edited by Simon Heffer, Hutchinson, 2021, p. 454

36. The Northumberland Hussars were made part of the Royal Artillery for the war's duration.

37. Jane Torday, *Wish Me Luck As You Wave Me Goodbye*, The Spredden Press, 1989, p. 20

38. Antony Beevor, *Crete*, Penguin, 1992, p. 37

39. Torday, p. 23

40. The Beaumont family, created first Barons Allendale in 1906 and Viscounts Allendale in 1911, live at Bywell Hall in Northumberland, forty-five miles from Alnwick, and became wealthy from coal-mining activity in the West Riding of Yorkshire.

41. Strong, *Diaries*, p. 171

42. In fairness, he isn't the only peer – or even the only duke – to fly his flag at home: the Duke of Wellington flies his flag at both Apsley House in London and at Stratfield Saye, Hampshire.

7. LABELS

1. David Pryce-Jones, *Unity Mitford: A Quest*, Weidenfeld & Nicolson, 1976, p. 187
2. Bevis Hillier, *Young Betjeman*, John Murray, 1988, p. 302
3. *Desert Island Discs*, BBC Radio 4, 26 November 1989
4. *Guardian*, 13 August 2003
5. None of them took it as far as the Hon. Violet Gibson, daughter of Edward Gibson, from 1885 1st Baron Ashbourne, however. As her biographer Frances Stonor Saunders describes, Violet's early life was 'safely entrenched in a caste outfitted with privilege, topped with picture hats, and a title that signals her significance in the Anglo-Irish ruling elite.' (Frances Stonor Saunders, *The Woman Who Shot Mussolini*, Faber & Faber, 2010, pp. 20–21) Little was expected of her within her '. . . genteel, sequestered existence, far removed from the blood and mire of Irish politics and the subsistence conditions in which most of the population lived'. (Saunders, p. 23) In 1902, she converted to Catholicism and began to develop a social conscience, visiting derelict parts of London and giving alms to the poor. After her brother Victor died in 1922 she had a breakdown and spent some time in a west London nursing home. Following her release, she attacked her housekeeper's daughter with a knife, leading to her being certified insane and spending six months in Holloway Sanatorium in Surrey. Following a series of mental health crises, she procured a revolver and attempted the assassination of the Italian Fascist leader, Benito Mussolini. In the end, her motive was not proved to be political. She died in 1956 aged seventy-nine, unmourned by her family and buried with a plain headstone in a cemetery in Northampton.
6. Ian Kershaw, *Making Friends with Hitler*, Penguin, 2005, p. 340
7. Stephen Dorril, *Blackshirt*, Penguin, 2007, p. 463
8. Richard Griffiths, *Patriotism Perverted*, Constable, 1998, p. 53
9. The Empire, debated 21 July 1942, House of Lords
10. A friend of Edward VIII, Geordie Sutherland was appointed Lord Steward by the new king in 1936, but since tradition dictates that with a new monarch comes a new Lord Steward, he lasted only seven and a half months in the job. 'I thought I ought to accept the king by accepting this invitation,' he remembered. 'Thus, for the first time, I now served in an official capacity a royal master whom I had known for a great many years as a friend.' He admitted that he did not find the

post terribly exciting: 'I cannot pretend that it involved me in any very great or exceptionally interesting work. My duties were essentially of a routine matter. I was given my own room at Buckingham Palace, and my main purpose was to ensure that the high standards, from a social point of view, that had been expected by King George V and Queen Mary were maintained, and to see that any special requirements of the new King were fulfilled.' (Duke of Sutherland, pp. 189–90)

11. Duff Cooper Papers, Duke of Buccleuch to Cooper, 2 October 1938, DUFC, 2/19, as seen in Tim Bouverie, *Appeasing Hitler*, The Bodley Head, 2019, p. 332

12. Channon, *1938–43*, p. 107

13. Bouverie, p. 332

14. Channon, *1938–43*, p. 115

15. Ibid., p. 118

16. Ibid., p. 227

17. Ibid., p. 253

18. George VI's War Diary, Volume II, 26 June 1940, as seen in Deborah Cadbury, *Princes at War*, Bloomsbury, 2016, p. 165

19. Channon, *1938–43*, p. 328

20. In the 1880s, Walter's great-grandfather and namesake Walter Montagu Douglas Scott, 5th Duke of Buccleuch, had twelve principal homes in England and Scotland and 460,000 acres. His enormous landholdings were described by his son's brother-in-law Lord Ernest Hamilton as an 'embarrassing accumulation', 'not only greater by far than those of any other subject, but . . . probably greater than those of any crowned head in Europe'. (Lord Ernest Hamilton, *Forty Years On*, Hodder & Stoughton, 1922, pp. 132–3).

21. *King's Counsellor: The Diaries of Sir Alan Lascelles*, edited by Duff Hart-Davis, Orion, 2006, p. 58

22. *The Times*, 5 October 1973

23. Brian Masters, *The Dukes*, Frederick Muller, 1988, p. 110

24. Thompson, Presidential Address

25. *The Times*, 13 March 1908

26. The Sligo marquessate was created for the Anglo-Irish peer John Browne, 3rd Earl of Altamont, in 1800. Given its relative youth, it was incredible that Denis should become the 10th Marquess – especially since his grandfather Henry Browne succeeded as the 5th Marquess in 1903. Denis's father Lord Alfred Browne was the youngest of

Henry Sligo's ten children. Of these, five were sons, and one after the other – with a brief diversion for George Browne, 6th Marquess of Sligo's son Ulick, who held the title for almost six years – became Marquess of Sligo until Terence Browne, 9th Marquess of Sligo, died in 1952, having held the title for only fourteen months.

27. Noreen tended to be somewhat economical with the truth as far as her background was concerned, telling people that her grandfather Edward Wormald was 'quite well off', her great-niece Dr Joanna Martin explains, 'but it's clear that he was a multi-millionaire in present-day terms.' Indeed, when their grandparents died in the 1920s, Noreen, her sister Sheelah and her two brothers Denis and Ulick each inherited in the region of £55,000, somewhere in the region of £3 million today. 'I was always told that Aunt Noreen and her husband had given all their money to the Communists,' says Joanna, 'but she must have had some left, as she lived in a house in Highgate during the latter part of her life.'

28. Sheelah Treherne, *Looking Back*, unpublished memoirs, 1975, p. 16

29. Ibid., p. 19

30. Ibid., p. 21

31. Daphne Fielding, *Mercury Presides*, Eyre & Spottiswoode, 1954, p. 100

32. Peerage Bill, debated 4 July 1963, House of Lords

33. Catherine Ann Cline, *Recruits to Labour*, Syracuse University Press, 1963, p. 6

34. Ibid., p. 7

35. Kenneth Harris, *Attlee*, Weidenfeld & Nicolson, 1982, p. 56

36. The Earl of Kimberley, *The Whim of the Wheel*, Merton Priory Press, 2001, p. 2

37. Channon, *1918–38*, p. 446

38. *The Times*, 22 January 1964

39. Laura Thompson, *A Different Class of Murder*, Head of Zeus, 2014, p. 70

40. Jack Hastings, 16th Earl of Huntingdon, the son of a hunting-mad countryman, is another example of a 1930s Labour peer. In 1925 he married Cristina Stampa di Soncino, the daughter of the Marquis Camillo Il Casati Stampa di Soncino. While in Spain in 1937, during the civil war, and by then unhappily married, she met the equally unhappily married Wogan Milford and shortly after embarked on an affair with him. In 1943, the Hastingses – by then the Huntingdons – were divorced, and Cristina and Wogan married the following year. She died in 1953.

41. *Irish Times*, 21 October 1921
42. Channon, *1918–38*, p. 513
43. Interview with Francis Hare, 6th Earl of Listowel, Irish Life and Lore archive. Indeed, Richard Listowel died thirty-three years before his grandson was born.
44. Owing to incomplete parliamentary records and, incredibly, no central list of hereditary peers by party either in the Lords itself, or independently, it is a challenging task to calculate the party status of every single peer who took his or her seat from 1920 to the partial reform of the Lords in 1999. The total is in the region of 1,500. For greater clarity, I have chosen a neutral sample of 1,062 – the peers whose parties could be easily identified using immediately available public records. These are also not entirely reliable, given the ability of peers to change political allegiances.
45. The Harrowbys have a more political pedigree than many of their fellow peers. The 1st Earl was foreign secretary under William Pitt the Younger and several more recent Earls of Harrowby have served in both the Commons and the Lords in ministerial positions. Dudley Ryder, 6th Earl of Harrowby, was, Conroy explains, '[A] historian by nature, though he was of the generation which didn't have to go out and do a job. His job was politics and he was PPS to secretary of state for air Sir Samuel Hoare.' In 1968, his son, also called Dudley and sometime deputy chairman of Coutts and of NatWest, resigned from his role as president of the Wolverhampton South West Conservative Association following the local MP Enoch Powell's 'rivers of blood' speech.
46. Hunting Bill, debated 15 November 2004, House of Lords
47. MacDonnell of Swinford papers, MS. MacDonnell D 238, f. 48, 13 June 1925, cited in Kerry, p. 322
48. Interview with Myles Ponsonby, 12th Earl of Bessborough, Irish Life and Lore archive
49. *The Times*, 15 April 1921
50. Frank O'Connor, Bureau of Military History Witness Statements, 1916–1921 (BMH), WS 1309, p. 21
51. Ibid., p. 22
52. Thomas Costello, BMH, WS 1296, p. 21
53. Frank O'Connor, BMH, WS 1309, p. 22
54. Thomas Costello, BMH, WS 1296, p. 21
55. Ibid.

56. William Teeling, *Corridors of Frustration*, Johnson, 1970, p. 89
57. Ibid., p. 57
58. Worse still, this wasn't even the first time in recent Castle Stewart history that this had happened. Arthur Castle Stewart, also a third son, had only become the 7th Earl in 1921 following the deaths of both his elder brothers in the First World War.
59. *Belfast Telegraph*, 12 March 1962
60. Nigel Nicolson, *Alex: The Life of Field Marshal Earl Alexander of Tunis*, Atheneum, 1973, p. 10
61. He has been thrice married and has two children.
62. Paul Howard, *Hostage: Notorious Irish Kidnappings*, The O'Brien Press, 2004, p. 85
63. *Irish Independent*, 5 June 1974
64. A note on hyphens. Within the family, as Ordy's son the Hon. Mark Hely Hutchinson explained to me, there is a difference of opinion on the use of hyphens in their surname. Though other branches do use a hyphen between 'Hely' and 'Hutchinson', his part of the family, himself included, do not – apart from, he says, 'for the phonebook, to ensure the "Hely" comes first, but I am relaxed if people choose to use one for other reasons.' He adds: 'My grandmother [Elena Donoughmore] used to say that "Hely and Hutchinson were joined by love and not by hyphens," but that doesn't prove anything.'
65. Howard, p. 89
66. Ibid., p. 115
67. *Belfast Telegraph*, 10 June 1974
68. Ibid., 7 June 1974
69. Howard, p. 100
70. *The Times*, 26 June 1974
71. *Sunday Times*, 24 March 2024
72. Interview with Michael Hely Hutchinson, 8th Earl of Donoughmore, Irish Life and Lore archive
73. Simon Winchester, *Their Noble Lordships*, Random House, 1982, pp. 200–1
74. House of Lords Reform, debated 10 April 1962, House of Lords
75. Teeling, p. 90
76. Winchester, p. 209
77. Irish Peers, debated 24 November 1966, House of Lords
78. Rathdonnell family information.

79. Barony of Fareham, debated 5 July 1995, House of Lords
80. Winchester, p. 209
81. An example of this is John Boyle, 15th Earl of Cork and Orrery, who also holds the title Baron Boyle of Marston in the Peerage of Great Britain. This enabled him to stand for election to the Lords, though as is convention, he is known by his senior, Irish title.

8. VILE BODIES

1. As far as I know, Master's mistresses didn't have their own collective noun, unlike those belonging to Duff Cooper, whose womanising was such that his coterie of mistresses were said to be known by his wife Diana as 'the dairy' because their names sounded like cows' names: Mollie (Buccleuch), Poppy (Baring), Daisy (Fellowes) and Biddy (Carlisle); she would tell him, 'please keep out of the dairy.' (*Dashing for the Post: The Letters of Patrick Leigh Fermor*, edited by Adam Sisman, John Murray, 2016, p. 346)
2. James Lees-Milne, *Diaries, 1984–1997*, John Murray, 2009, p. 9
3. Bernard Norfolk was described by Channon as rather resembling a Holbein portrait. He was a man who, when managing the England cricket team in the 1960s, while on a tour of Australia, told reporters that he wished it to be an informal tour and that they should address him merely as 'Sir' rather than 'Your Grace'. He took his wife's extra-marital relations graciously, playing 'the *mari complaisant*' – a cuckolded man who accepts his wife's infidelity – and flirting with Ann de Trafford, future mother-in-law of Camilla Parker-Bowles, later Queen Camilla. 'This is indeed a scandal of high society,' summed up the diarist. (Channon, *1943–57*, p. 616)
4. Harry Beaufort, *The Unlikely Duke*, Hodder & Stoughton, 2023, p. 200
5. Woodrow Wyatt, *The Journals of Woodrow Wyatt, Volume 3*, edited by Sarah Curtis, Macmillan, 2000, p. 490
6. Channon, *1943–57*, p. 616
7. Ibid., p. 670
8. This divorce eventually took place in 1956, Anne having been 'abandoned', according to Channon, four years previously, ready to be 'replaced by yet another mannequin'. In 1958, Charles Rutland married Frances Sweeny, daughter of the American socialite Charlie

Sweeny and his wife Margaret, whom we shall meet in a few pages' time. (Channon, *1943–57*, p. 833)

9. Ibid., p. 670
10. Peggy was not only Toby Glanusk's widow but also actually married to Bill Sidney, 1st Viscount De L'Isle, to date one of only two men to have held both the highest order of chivalry – the Garter – and the highest order of gallantry – the Victoria Cross. (The other was Field Marshal Frederick Roberts, VC, 1st Earl Roberts (1832–1914).)
11. Lees-Milne, *Ancient as the Hills*, p. 160
12. James Lees-Milne, *Deep Romantic Chasm*, John Murray, 2000, p. 157
13. J. R. Ackerley, *My Father and Myself*, Poseidon Press, 1968, p. 161
14. He was unlikely since his father Lord Hugh Grosvenor was *his* father Hugh Lupus Grosvenor, 1st Duke of Westminster's sixth son, and in theory, there ought to have been plenty of men ahead of him in the Westminster line of succession. As it was, several of Gerald's uncles and cousins were unmarried and without issue, and the others did not have surviving sons.
15. Known to some of the Lees-Milnes' friends as 'Bi sex' house.
16. Lees-Milne, *Ancient as the Hills*, p. 38
17. The Lady Hindlip named by Derry Moore was Cicely Allsopp, wife of Henry Allsopp, from 1966 5th Baron Hindlip and the daughter of Malcolm 'Peach' Borwick, a popular master of foxhounds.
18. Beaufort, p. 209
19. James Pope-Hennessy, *The Quest for Queen Mary*, ed., Hugo Vickers, Zuleika and Hodder & Stoughton, 2019, p. 327
20. Beaufort, p. 28
21. Michael Bloch, *James Lees-Milne*, John Murray, 2009, p. 297
22. Lees-Milne, *Deep Romantic Chasm*, p. 24
23. As one familiar with him remarks: 'He liked running after things. If it had four legs, he hunted it, if it had two legs, he seduced it.'
24. Duke of Beaufort, *Memoirs*, Littlehampton Book Services Ltd, 1981, p. 2
25. Beaufort, p. 30
26. Ibid., p. 208
27. According to Channon, Mary wasn't able to have any, owing to the fact that '. . . neither she nor her sister Lady Helena Gibbs have ever menstruated.' (Channon, *1943–57*, p. 617) This was not just hearsay, and, appallingly, Mary Beaufort's family knew it too, though, as the

story goes, Master did not. There is a suggestion that Mary Beaufort's aunt Queen Mary may have arranged the union.

28. Duke of Beaufort, p. 55
29. When Master and Mary had married in 1923, Channon had described their union as a '... *liaison hippique* [an equine marriage, since both were passionate riders] and most suitable'. (Channon, *1918–38*, p. 69)
30. Though she couldn't have predicted the decline in her mental condition, Mary Beaufort did, in earlier life, take a view on some of the conditions that affected her wider family. 'Tell me,' she asked James Pope-Hennessy in 1958, 'why we are all so mad? ... My grandfather was raving, then there's the Duke of Windsor, Prince John, the Duke of Gloucester, and then I'm mad too.' (Pope-Hennessy, *The Quest for Queen Mary*, p. 331)
31. James Lees-Milne, *Holy Dread*, John Murray, 2001, p. 147
32. *Independent*, 30 April 1995
33. Windsor, The Royal Archives (RA), PS/PSO/GV/C/D/1491/1, 21 March 1913, as cited in *Christina Dykes, 'Hugh Richard Arthur Grosvenor, 2nd Duke of Westminster (1879–1953), known as Bend'Or: A Reappraisal'*, PhD, February 2021.
34. Bend'Or had numerous mistresses during his eighteen-year marriage to Shelagh. One of these was rumoured to be Pamela Bulwer-Lytton, Countess of Lytton, whose younger son John, Viscount Knebworth, was believed to be Bend'Or's son. Another of his mistresses was the Gaiety Girl Gertie Millar who left Bend'Or after she discovered that he was also keeping the ballerina Anna Pavlova, having wrongly 'believed herself to be the "only woman"'. (*Lady Cynthia Asquith's Diaries, 1915–18*, ed. by L. P. Hartley, Hutchinson, 1968, p. 414)
35. Later, Francisco Franco's man in London.
36. RA/PS/PSO/GV/C/D/1491/2, March 1913, as cited in Dykes.
37. Shelagh had proof in plenty. On 18 June 1919, *The Times* carried a full report of the case, detailing Bend'Or's working routine – 'he would go to his study in the morning and there he would remain at work for some time. He would then go to luncheon without telling his wife where he was going ...' – and transcripts of their letters: 'I beg you to return to me,' Shelagh wrote to Bend'Or. 'If you will do so I am willing to allow all bygones to be bygones, and do what I can to make you happy.' By June 1917, the paper reported, Shelagh had had reason to believe that Bend'Or had been unfaithful to her; that

month, she discovered that he had gone to Brighton and hired a suite of rooms at the Grand Hotel, where he had met a woman.

38. RA/PS/PSO/GV/C/D/1491/12, Sandhurst to Stamfordham, 7 January 1920, as cited in Dykes. Bend'Or wasn't alone in being a man with a complex marital situation who was banned from Court events. When Sunny and Consuelo Marlborough legally separated in 1907, Edward VII instructed his private secretary Francis Knollys, 1st Viscount Knollys, to write to Winston Churchill, asking him to tell the Marlboroughs that they 'should not come to any dinner, or evening party, or private entertainment at which either of Their Majesties are expected to be present'. (Philip Magnus, *Edward VII*, Penguin Books, 1979, p. 497) Sunny was also a Knight of the Garter and though he did, on occasion, attend meetings of the Order at Windsor, his carriage would be called before the others sat down to eat with the king. He attended the Accession Council in May 1910, following Edward VII's death, but nevertheless continued to be ostracised by George V, who sent James 'Jem' Gascoyne-Cecil, 4th Marquess of Salisbury in his place to attend his funeral in July 1934.

39. Seven years later, in November 1927, an inconsistency as regarded dukes, scandal and Court roles was revealed by Bend'Or, almost by accident. He instructed his private secretary Detmar Blow to write to the former chief whip Edmund FitzAlan Howard, 1st Viscount FitzAlan of Derwent, to ask why it was that Sunny Marlborough, who had divorced his first wife Consuelo in 1921 after a long separation, had been allowed to stay on as Lord-Lieutenant of Oxfordshire, to which role he had been appointed in 1915. After some back and forth, it was admitted that Sunny, supported by his friend F. E. Smith, 1st Earl of Birkenhead, and his cousin Winston Churchill, had refused to resign. George V's private secretary, Arthur Bigge, 1st Baron Stamfordham, had complained about David Lloyd George's inaction over the affair, since though he had agreed to ask for Sunny's resignation, no further action had been taken and he had been allowed to stay on. As Christina Dykes describes in her 2021 PhD reappraising Bend'Or, 'Marlborough, and the politicians, had called the King's bluff. Bend'Or had been a pawn in a contest between the King and modernity. The King might have used his discretion, as Stamfordham suggested. But the King was too rule-bound and concerned about lapses in the upper class's behaviour to alter his view.' (Dykes, February 2021)

40. Of the 126 dukes since 1900 to the present day, over a quarter have been divorced, including eight of today's twenty-four dukes. Of those thirty-three divorced dukes, nine were or have been divorced more than once.

41. A note re Sir Oswald's name. His stepson Jonathan Guinness, 3rd Baron Moyne, explained to me that his mother Diana, Oswald's second wife, always called him 'Kit'. This, he explains, had also been her nickname for her first husband, Jonathan's father, the Hon. Bryan Guinness, later 2nd Baron Moyne, 'which then got transferred to Mosley. He became known as Kit to everybody in my generation and afterwards, but all the older people called him Tom.' Since Diana's brother was also called Tom, 'that would have been confusing to her, and so I have a feeling that's why that didn't happen. But did my mother ever call Bryan "Kit"? I'm not sure.'

42. Nicholas Mosley, *Rules of the Game*, Secker & Warburg, 1982, p. 93

43. Ibid., p. 96

44. Ibid., p. 248

45. Bob was himself no hero in this arena. When in August 1930 Dorothy and Harold Macmillan's fourth child, Sarah, was born, Dorothy informed her husband that the baby wasn't his but Bob's. Later, Boothby denied to Macmillan that this was the case; an experienced Casanova, he knew how to avoid getting women pregnant. Macmillan – and the rest of Society – had long known about the affair, which his wife had initiated, and which had begun in either late 1929 or early 1930. But divorce would not do; as Macmillan's biographer D. R. Thorpe describes, the abdication crisis had shown in 1936 that it was 'the ultimate social solecism'. (D. R. Thorpe, *Supermac, The Life of Harold Macmillan*, Chatto & Windus, 2010, p. 94) Macmillan was advised not to grant Dorothy a divorce, but instead to adopt the upper-class tradition of living in separate wings, one still favoured by a few aristocratic couples today. Dorothy remained the loyal political wife in public, but nevertheless carried on her liaison with Bob. In November 1933, he wrote to John Strachey that: 'Dorothy remains a permanent menace to my peace of mind, and to any marriage I may make.' (Robert Rhodes James, *Bob Boothby*, Hodder & Stoughton, 1991, p. 118) This fear proved to be justified. Two years later, Bob married Dorothy's cousin Diana Cavendish but they were divorced within two years. Somehow, Bob managed not to mention his affair with Dorothy in his 1978 memoirs, nor her name at all – not even once.

46. Mosley, p. 248. Cimmie had two sisters, Lady Irene 'Nina' Curzon, from 1925 Baroness Ravensdale, who never married; and Lady Alexandra 'Baba' Curzon, who married Major Edward Dudley 'Fruity' Metcalfe, a close friend of and equerry to Edward VIII. Baba, it's fair to say, was not very faithful to Fruity. She was engaged in a long-running affair with the foreign secretary Edward Halifax, and owing to her flirtation with a number of fascists in the 1930s, including her brother-in-law Tom Mosley, she was nicknamed 'Baba Blackshirt'. Fruity and Baba divorced in 1955, an event that escaped much press attention since it was concluded during a newspaper strike. As Anne de Courcy describes in her biography of the Curzon sisters, it was somewhat ironic that Baba should be 'the favourite female companion of both the British foreign secretary and the representative of Mussolini's fascist regime [Dino Grandi]'. Later, Baba had an affair with Halifax's son-in-law Charles 'Sim' Duncombe, 3rd Earl of Feversham. (Anne de Courcy, *The Viceroy's Daughters: The Lives of the Curzon Sisters*, Weidenfeld & Nicolson, 2000, p. 319)

47. I will use the shorthand of 'the Court Circular', though this today specifically refers to the record of royal engagements that is still published in *The Times* and the *Telegraph*, rather than a roll call of aristocratic weekends away.

48. *The Times*, 26 July 1927

49. Ibid., 30 July 1964

50. Ibid., 11 May 1983

51. Ibid., 7 January 1994

52. Ibid., 18 April 1939

53. *Bradford Observer*, 29 January 1953

54. *Dundee Courier*, 28 February 1953

55. *Yorkshire Evening Post*, 18 October 1946

56. *Leicester Evening Mail*, 5 May 1955

57. *People*, 15 November 1964

58. Janet Kidd, *The Beaverbrook Girl*, Collins, 1987, p. 91

59. Ibid., p. 103

60. Ibid., pp. 107–8

61. Margaret, Duchess of Argyll, *Forget Not*, W. H. Allen, 1975, p. 117

62. *People*, 22 November 1964

63. Equivalent to £15,313,488.66 in May 2024, per the Bank of England.

64. *People*, 15 November 1964

65. Lees-Milne, *Midway on the Waves*, p. 132
66. Barbara Cartland, *We Danced all Night*, Robson Books, 1994, p. 49
67. *Tatler*, 21 June 1939
68. *Letters of Nancy Mitford*, edited by Charlotte Mosley, Hodder & Stoughton, 1993, p. 259
69. Channon, *1943–57*, p. 623
70. *People*, 13 December 1964
71. *People*, 29 November 1964
72. Argyll, p. 157
73. *People*, 13 December 1964
74. Ibid., 6 December 1964
75. Ibid., 13 December 1964
76. Argyll, p. 178
77. Interview with Margaret Argyll, 5 November 1975, Thames TV; youtube.com/watch?v=4qodF0C_8sw
78. Compilation of interviews with Margaret Argyll; youtube.com/watch?v=q23J67YvmX8
79. *The Times*, 9 May 1963
80. Argyll, p. 199
81. When Margaret's own, rather bland memoir was published in 1975, she called it *Forget Not*.
82. *People*, 13 December 1964
83. Argyll, p. 202
84. Ibid., p. 239
85. Charles Castle, *The Duchess Who Dared*, Swift, 2001, p. 273
86. Ibid., p. 284
87. Ibid., p. 287
88. Channon, *1918–38*, p. 317. In 1928, Channon was told by Gladys Spencer-Churchill, Duchess of Marlborough, how '... there are only three great fraternities', those of Catholics, Jews and 'La Pédérastie': '[I]f one does not belong to one, one is left out in the cold of life.' Ibid., p. 310
89. Channon, *1938–43*, p. 28
90. Madresfield is widely believed to be the model for Brideshead Castle, in Evelyn Waugh's 1945 magnum opus, *Brideshead Revisited*. Waugh denied there being a connection between the two families, and the book's epigraph is clear: 'I am not I; thou art not he or she; they are not they.' But he told Diana Mosley that the real-life Lady Marchmain was 'the sister of a prominent Duke' – just as Lady Beauchamp was the older

sister of Bend'Or Westminster. Waugh's friend and Diana's sister Nancy Mitford spotted the Lygons immediately in the fictional Flyte family: '[S]o true to life being in love with a whole family,' she wrote to him. (*The Letters of Nancy Mitford and Evelyn Waugh*, edited by Charlotte Mosley, Sceptre, 1997, p. 12) Meanwhile, up in North Yorkshire, the Howard family of Castle Howard – where the 1981 Granada adaptation of the book was filmed – fervently believe Brideshead to belong to them. As Vicky Howard told me in 2019, 'Maybe I'm biased, but Brideshead *is* Castle Howard! It's baroque, it has a dome, and a fountain.'

91. Viscount Lee of Fareham, *A Good Innings*, John Murray, 1974, p. 282
92. The only person, seemingly, who was not wise to his predilections – since his own children knew and warned their friends accordingly when they came to stay at Madresfield – was his wife, Lettice Beauchamp, Bend'Or Westminster's elder sister. Sources are slightly confused on this point. An undated letter written by Lettice to her children gives the strong suggestion that she did have at least some notion of her husband's exploits, and that she wasn't quite the innocent: '[F]or many years,' she wrote, 'I had strongly suspected that (with Daddy) all was not as it should be – and that one side of his life and desires went contrary to everything that is right, normal and natural.' (Paula Byrne, *Mad World*, HarperPress, 2011, p. 148) After Lettice's mother Sibell died in February 1929, and Lettice and Bend'Or's childhood home of Saighton Grange (somewhat appropriately, this is pronounced 'Satan') near Chester became empty, Lettice had somewhere to hide. She did so, taking her youngest son Dickie with her. From Saighton she drew up divorce papers as a likely nudge for her husband to sort himself out and, ideally, leave England.
93. It has been widely reported, including in the *Dictionary of National Biography*, that the novelist Hugh Walpole told Virginia Woolf, as reported in her diary in March 1939, how when at the baths at the Elephant and Castle he had seen not only 'Ld C' – named by the *Dictionary of National Biography* as Alexander Mountbatten, 1st Marquess of Carisbrooke – naked but also Lord B – given by the dictionary as Beauchamp – 'in the act with a boy'. (*The Diary of Virginia Woolf, Volume 5: 1936–41*, edited by Anne Olivier Bell, Penguin, 1984, p. 211) But since Beauchamp had been dead for five months by then, unless Walpole and Woolf were referring to an early occasion when this occurred, Beauchamp can be excused.

94. In the end, though, Beauchamp's three sons were no use in helping to continue the Beauchamp title or the family line. Two died without issue, and the youngest, Dickie, only had daughters. In 1979 the Beauchamp earldom became extinct – not that Bend'Or lived to see this happen.

95. Jack Stanmore is alleged, by the historian Michael Bloch, to have been homosexual himself. Irony lives.

96. Beverley Nichols, *The Sweet and Twenties*, Weidenfeld & Nicolson, 1958, p. 101

97. Bevis Hillier, *The Virgin's Baby*, Hopcyn Press, 2013, p. 70

98. Nichols, p. 101

99. Jane Mulvagh, *Madresfield, The Real Brideshead*, Transworld, 2009, p. 384

100. Ibid., p. 417

101. Montagu of Beaulieu, p. 80

102. Much later, he reflected that his '. . . sentence was supposed to act as a deterrent. I doubt if it deterred a single person's desires or actions and it certainly did not change mine. My sexuality has not altered, although as with us all the desire for companionship becomes more important as one's sex drive fades away.' (Ibid., p. 287)

103. Ibid., p. 98

104. In 1961, he married the singer Shirley Bassey.

105. Montagu of Beaulieu, p. 104

106. Ibid.

107. Ibid., p. 106

108. Ibid., p. 107

109. Ibid., p. 109

110. *Birmingham Daily Post*, 19 March 1954

111. Montagu of Beaulieu, p. 114

112. *Cambridge Daily News*, 23 March 1954

113. *Daily Mirror*, 24 March 1954

114. Ibid., 25 March 1954

115. Hugo Vickers, *Elizabeth, the Queen Mother*, Hutchinson, 2005, p. 419

116. *The Times*, 14 January 1939

117. Kimberley, p. 9

118. Ibid., p. 5

119. The total population of England and Wales in 1969 was 48,738,000.

120. *The Journals of Woodrow Wyatt, Volume II,* Sarah Curtis, ed., Pan Books, 1999, p. 645
121. Beaufort, p. 210
122. Grania Forbes, *My Darling Buffy*, Charnwood, 1997, p. 188
123. Ibid., p. 200
124. His daughter-in-law Debo Devonshire said that he 'would stand, oblivious of the weather, in the freezing wind on Chesterfield Station in a threadbare London suit'. (Deborah Devonshire, *Wait for Me*, p. 118)
125. Channon, *1938–43*, p. 50
126. Ibid., p. 1027
127. Though I couldn't for the life of me find this reference. It goes uncited in both his obituaries and in the only book about him, and does not seem to appear in the *Chronicle*.
128. Michael Litchfield, *The Murder of Lord Shaftesbury*, John Blake, 2016, p. 30
129. On the death of Anthony Shaftesbury, the title passed to his eldest son, also called Anthony. He died from a heart attack in May 2005, while visiting his younger brother Nick, a DJ, in New York, and so Nick inherited the title and the family estate of St Giles in Dorset. The house was a wreck when he took it over, but he and his German-born wife Dinah Streifeneder set to work, and in 2015 their work on the house won them the Historic Houses Association and Sotheby's restoration award.
130. This at least partly owed to the fact that both Bobo and Mary were produced, in one way or another, by a Harley Street gynaecologist called Dr Jervois Aarons, who was popular with women struggling to conceive a baby. As Diana Cooper described in 1980, the joke went that 'they were all his . . . he may have had a stud of handsome footmen lined up outside, but he claimed that they were a genuine case of artificial insemination.' (Vickers, *Elizabeth*, p. 97) The Roxburghes, who were said to have been unable to have children of their own owing to the way they themselves had been conceived, were not the only so-called Aarons' babies in society: the eccentric socialite the Hon. Stephen Tennant was also said to be one. 'There were quite a lot of us,' observed Tennant's second cousin the Hon. Ursula Wyndham, eldest daughter of Edward Wyndham, 5th Baron Leconfield, whose mother Gladys had also been to see Aarons. (Ursula Wyndham, *Astride the Wall*, Lennard Publishing, 1988, p. 16)

131. Sir Arthur Collins, *My Recollections of Floors and the Family,* unpublished, undated, p. 16

132. *Letters from Oxford, Hugh Trevor-Roper to Bernard Berenson,* edited by Richard Davenport-Hines, Weidenfeld & Nicolson, 2006, p. 127

133. Bobo wasn't the only twentieth-century duke to have gone to extreme lengths to remove his wife from the family home. When Sunny Marlborough and his second wife Gladys Deacon were separated in 1933, the duke employed a variety of unpleasant tactics to encourage her departure from Blenheim, variously leaving the house and taking with him critical members of staff, refusing to dismiss those who remained whom she disliked, banning her from the family's London residence on Carlton House Terrace, and making her effectively homeless. She responded by sitting vigil in Carlton House Terrace for ten days, during which time copies of the *Telegraph* were brought to her and friends joined her on the balcony overlooking the Mall. One day a group of men came to the house and locked the larder. Over the course of the following few days, the telephone, gas and lift ceased to operate, and Gladys had to resort to living by candlelight, eating food smuggled in by a neighbour, and boiling water for coffee over a coal fire.

134. Collins, p. 17

135. Ironically, Xandra and Hugh had long been having an affair. They had met in April 1953 at Bemersyde, Xandra's ancestral home in the Scottish Borders, and the following January Xandra's husband Rear-Admiral Clarence 'Johnny' Howard-Johnston petitioned Xandra for divorce in the High Court on the grounds of her adultery. The decree *nisi* was pronounced on 23 July, and Xandra and Hugh married in October that year.

136. *Letters from Oxford,* p. 128

137. As Ted adds, Elisabeth managed to produce plenty of male heirs. 'She was married to Church and had four boys with him, and then two boys with my grandfather, so she had six boys in her life. After my grandfather died she married [the merchant banker] Jocelyn Hambro who already had three boys, so she ended up with nine sons and stepsons, which I think is quite a good effort.'

138. Rory Knight Bruce, *Timothy the Tortoise,* Orion, 2004, p. 61

139. *Chips: The Diaries of Sir Henry Channon,* edited by Robert Rhodes James, Weidenfeld & Nicolson, 1967, p. 471. It was nevertheless the case, though, that Ian and Margaret Argyll, while welcome at

Westminster Abbey for the coronation were not, as a doubly divorced duo, invited to the reception at Buckingham Palace afterwards.

140. *Daily News*, 9 October 1954

141. I asked several former private secretaries to Elizabeth II, members of her circle, and the royal historian Hugo Vickers about this, and no one knew the answer, though Vickers points out that George Harewood, Elizabeth II's cousin, was banned from Court for years following his divorce in 1967.

142. Annabel Goldsmith, *No Invitation Required*, Weidenfeld & Nicolson, 2009, p. 133

143. Ibid., p. 135

144. Ibid., p. 138

145. Ibid., p. 143

146. Ibid., p. 137

147. *Daily Mirror*, 14 June 1973

148. Chapman Pincher, *Inside Story*, Sidgwick & Jackson, 1978, p. 272

149. *Daily Mirror*, 24 May 1973

150. Thynn, rather than Thynne, as per the rest of the family, is the correct spelling. Alexander Bath adopted the former spelling of his family's surname in 1976.

151. *Observer*, 10 March 2002

152. BBC, 5 April 2020; *Telegraph*, 5 April 2020; *Guardian*, 5 April; *The Times*, 6 April 2020

153. *The Times*, 11 April 1963

154. *Liverpool Echo*, 21 December 1959

155. *Weekly Dispatch*, 17 January 1960

156. *Staffordshire Sentinel*, 19 January 1960

157. *Time*, 4 January 1960

158. *The Times*, 11 April 1963

9. THE LOVED ONE

1. James Reginato, *Great Houses, Modern Aristocrats*, Rizzoli, 2016, p. 168

2. *The Times*, 10 June 2017

3. Mary Harcourt to Lady (Elizabeth) Harcourt, 30 October 1901, Harcourt Papers, dep. 647; fold 78-78v, Bodleian Library, Oxford; as seen in Maureen E. Montgomery, *Gilded Prostitution: Status, Money, and Transatlantic Marriages, 1870-1914*, Routledge, 1989, p. 100

4. Channon, *1943–57*, p. 901
5. Ibid., p. 960
6. The Duchess of Rutland, *The Accidental Duchess: From Farmer's Daughter to Belvoir Castle*, Macmillan, 2022, p. 199
7. Liza Campbell, *Title Deeds*, Doubleday, 2006, p. 58
8. Ibid.
9. Ibid., p. 59
10. Ibid., p. 138
11. Ibid., p. 321
12. Ibid., pp. 193–4
13. Ibid.
14. Ibid., p. 195
15. Ibid., p. 194
16. Ibid., p. 192
17. Christopher's eventual inheritance of Penrice proved complicated. His grandmother Evelyn, Lady Blythswood, had inherited it from her spinster aunt Emily Talbot, but to avoid death duties had made it over to her daughter Olive. When Olive died first, in 1949, the plan went awry, but when Evelyn Blythswood died in 1958, Christopher and Oona picked up the baton, doing up the neglected house, demolishing parts of it and restoring the gardens.
18. Naworth is part of a complicated family inheritance that is ultimately tied up with the powerful Howard family who are descended from Thomas Howard, 4th Duke of Norfolk, second cousin of Elizabeth I. Until 1921 the family occupied one of England's greatest houses, Castle Howard, near York. That year the resolute teetotaller and Howard family tyrant Rosalind Howard, Countess of Carlisle, died, having specified that the Carlisle property that she had been left by her husband George Howard, 9th Earl of Carlisle, should be split between her four daughters. Her eldest son Charley Howard, 10th Earl of Carlisle, had died in 1912, and instead of leaving Castle Howard to his son George Howard, 11th Earl of Carlisle, Rosalind left it to her eldest daughter Lady Mary Murray, who passed it to her younger brother the Hon. Geoffrey Howard, in whose branch of the family it remains. George Carlisle got Naworth instead, and the Carlisle estates, which in 1883 had been 78,540 acres, were split. 'It galls me that Castle Howard is not mine,' his son Charlie Carlisle said in 1980, 'I would not be human otherwise.' (*Sunday Sun*, 24 February 1980)

19. Mary Burghley herself had not had the most maternal of mothers. Indeed, both her parents, John and Margaret Buccleuch, adopted the distinctly hands-off approach to childrearing that was so characteristic of their class (see Chapter 10). There is a story told of Mary, who was the sixth of their eight children, being out in the grounds of one of the Buccleuchs' family houses with her nanny, when she happened upon her parents out walking. John Buccleuch stopped and said, 'Which one of my daughters are you?' 'Mary,' she replied. 'I'm four years old and it's my birthday.' The duke exclaimed his delight, and gave her half a crown.

20. Michael Exeter's cousin Lady Angela Oswald adds: 'It was always expected in the family that on my father's death, when my uncle Martin became 7th Marquess, that his son Michael, as Lord Burghley, would move into Burghley House. To this end, Michael was brought over to England at the end of the war, lived at Burghley with our grandparents, and was educated at Scaitcliffe and Eton to prepare him for his future inheritance. While circumstances changed, I have always had huge admiration that Michael should have accepted the situation without rancour, and over the years has enjoyed many happy visits to Burghley as head of the family, while leading his own valuable life in North America. While Victoria, succeeded by her daughter Miranda, have been – and are – doing a super job as House Director at Burghley, nevertheless, it is my fervent hope that one day the titleholder, whoever he may be, will be reunited and living back at Burghley House, thus restoring over 400 years of history.'

21. His grandfather Major the Hon. Christopher Lowther, MP, died in January 1935 aged forty-seven, and his father John Lowther, secretary to Prince George, Duke of Kent, died with the duke in an air crash in 1942, aged thirty-one.

22. *The Times*, 3 January 1963

23. The parliamentary leader famed for his opposition to Charles I.

24. 'About' ninety since some are in abeyance.

25. The intricacies of each of these titles requires more room than there is here for a full explanation of the whys and wherefores of their respective succession, but suffice to say, each has its own set of circumstances that allow women to inherit – be it a special remainder, the creation by writ which allows peerages to pass to heirs general, by charter, or where a title has spent some time in abeyance and has at some point been called out of abeyance for a woman. Each of

the ten titles currently (in March 2024) held by women was created before 1665, the earliest in 1313; half are titles in the Peerage of England, and half in the Peerage of Scotland.

26. The Kinloss title was the last remaining of the family's titles. Mary's father, Luis Morgan-Grenville, was the son of another Mary Kinloss – Mary Temple-Nugent-Brydges-Chandos-Grenville, 11th Lady Kinloss, the eldest daughter of Richard Temple-Nugent-Brydges-Chandos-Grenville, 3rd Duke of Buckingham and Chandos. When her father died in 1889 the dukedom became extinct but the Kinloss title, created in 1602, could pass through the female line, and so did. Mary Kinloss the younger was born in 1922, a year after her family's ancestral home, Stowe, in Buckinghamshire, was sold following the total decline of the Grenvilles, thanks to the excesses of the 2nd Duke.

27. What's more, had there not been any boys in the family, she could in theory have inherited, since the Marlborough dukedom can pass in and through the female line, though it is highly unlikely ever to do so.

28. His brother Lord Alastair Sutherland-Leveson-Gower's daughter, who had been orphaned in 1931, at the age of nine.

29. Some say the name of the castle is ironic if pronounced 'Done-Robbin' since the Sutherlands were responsible for the nineteenth-century Highland Clearances in which people were forced to leave agricultural land given over to sheep.

30. Idina was the model for the much-married mother of the narrator of Nancy Mitford's 1945 and 1949 novels *The Pursuit of Love* and *Love in a Cold Climate* – a woman who '. . . ran away so often, and with so many different people, that she became known to her family and friends as the Bolter.' (Nancy Mitford, *The Pursuit of Love*, Penguin, 2010, p. 2)

31. The following year, he died from a morphine overdose at the Adelphi Hotel in Liverpool.

32. Frances Osborne, *The Bolter*, Virago, 2009, p. 162

33. Of the nine female hereditary peers today, three have a son who will inherit, and six a daughter, one of whom is Lady Clare Hurd, wife of the Conservative politician Nick. Of those four with male heirs – either sons or, in the case of Lady Jane Heathcote-Drummond-Willoughby, 28th Baroness Willoughby de Eresby, her first cousin once removed – two of those male heirs have older sisters. As of September 2024, fifteen peers had inherited their titles from their mothers; of these, three had living sisters, who, logic suggests, ought

to have inherited first. So far as Jane Willoughby de Eresby is concerned, she inherited this ancient title in 1983 when her father James Heathcote-Drummond-Willoughby, 3rd Earl of Ancaster, died, her brother Timothy, Lord Willoughby de Eresby, having gone missing at sea in 1963. The Ancaster earldom cannot pass down the female line and so went extinct, but the barony could.

34. Interview with Thomas Pakenham, Irish Life and Lore archive
35. Primogeniture, debated on 4 April 1837, House of Commons
36. International Women's Day, debated on 10 March 2020, House of Lords
37. Gender-balanced Parliament and Male Primogeniture, debated on 20 April 2021, House of Lords
38. *Independent*, 19 October 2013
39. Sir Richard died in December 2024, at which point his son became Sir Tremayne Carew Pole, 14th Baronet, and Charlotte Lady Carew Pole.
40. *Scottish Daily Mail*, 21 July 2018
41. Address in reply to Her Majesty's most gracious speech, debated on 19 May 1997, House of Lords
42. Gender-balanced Parliament and Male Primogeniture, debated on 20 April 2021, House of Lords
43. Bernard Norfolk's daughters were not left with nothing: three out of four of them successively inherited their grandmother Gwendolen Norfolk's Scottish lordship, Herries of Terregles. In due course, the youngest and last surviving of Bernard and Lavinia Norfolk's daughters, Jane, 16th Lady Herries of Terregles, who in 1975 married Michael Kerr, Earl of Ancram, from 2004 13th Marquess of Lothian, will pass her title to her daughter Lady Clare Hurd. The Lothian title cannot pass to a woman, and when Michael Lothian died in October 2024, it passed to his younger brother Lord Ralph Kerr.
44. In 1917, the British government issued the Balfour Declaration announcing its support for the establishment of a 'national home for the Jewish people' in Palestine.
45. David Herbert, *Second Son*, Peter Owen, 1972, p. 14
46. Ibid., pp. 14–15
47. Ibid., p. 14
48. Ibid., p. 13
49. William Waldegrave, *A Different Kind of Weather*, Little, Brown, 2016, pp. 41–2. Ironically, both William Waldegrave and his brother

Jamie Waldegrave, 13th Earl Waldegrave, can now both be addressed as 'Lord Waldegrave'.

50. Colin Clark, *Younger Brother, Younger Son*, HarperCollins, 1998, p. 231

51. *The Last Dukes*, BBC Two, 26 October 2015

52. Ibid.

53. Ibid.

54. In 1971, Camilla married Robert Harris, who worked in advertising, and after having one daughter they were divorced in 1976. The following year she married the *Daily Mail*'s gossip columnist Nigel Dempster, with whom she had a daughter. 'I think he saw me as a challenge,' Camilla said of Dempster in 2010. He died in 2007, aged sixty-five, five years after he and Camilla divorced. (Tim Willis, *Nigel Dempster and the Death of Discretion*, Short Books, 2010, p. 98)

10. A LITTLE LEARNING

1. Lord Longford, *Avowed Intent*, Little, Brown, 2004, p. 110

2. Brinsley Le Poer Trench, *Operation Earth*, Neville Spearman, 1969, p. 15

3. The Rossmores' ancestral home, Rossmore Castle in County Monaghan, was demolished by the state in 1975. Paddy then sold the park to Coillte, the Irish Forestry Division, and moved to a cottage in the south end of the park called Lady Rossmore's Cottage, which was destroyed by the IRA in 1981. In 2020, he donated 2,300 acres of the remaining Rossmore landholdings to An Taisce, the National Trust for Ireland. Benedict Rossmore remembers going to visit the castle ruins with his father. 'He was surprised that they weren't there – it's almost as if they hadn't notified him.' The loss of the Rossmore land makes Benedict Rossmore sad, not because he doesn't own a castle – 'it's a hassle owning one' – but because his father was entrusted with the responsibility of looking after heritage which was handed down to him over generations, and he lost it. 'It's not the fact that it fell out of family hands, so much as it doesn't exist at all anywhere. Rossmore Park is worse off because he sold it to Coillte – he could have sold it to anyone else and it would be better looked after. It's just irresponsible.'

4. Princess Alice, Duchess of Gloucester, *Memories of Ninety Years*, Collins & Brown, 1991, p. 12

5. Ibid., p. 13
6. Lambton, *Memories*
7. Gloucester, p. 26
8. Oral history interview with David Kettlewell and Josephine Kettlewell: Life at Hyning Hall, Warton, Recording Morecambe Bay, 3 April 2017 (H2H.0587)
9. *Telegraph*, 15 November 2003
10. Alexander Thynn, *The Early Years*, Artnik, 2002, p. 66
11. Ibid.
12. Ibid., pp. 66–7
13. Alexander Thynn, *Top Hat & Tails*, Artnik, 2003, p. 71
14. Scotland's oldest boarding school, near Edinburgh.
15. *Birmingham Weekly Mercury*, 29 March 1998
16. This is disputed. The artist Wilfrid Blunt, who went to teach art at Eton in 1938, dismissed the notion that Birley was called 'Red Robert' because of his left-wing views. As far as he was concerned the name was derived from a portrait of 'the aged Brahms, hanging outside his office when he was in Germany, being mistaken for that of Karl Marx. He was never more than palest pink.' (Wilfrid Blunt, *Slow on the Feather*, Michael Russell, 1986, pp. 171–2)
17. The Eton phrase for boys in the top year of the house; the word derives from the room used by the oldest boys and has little to do with books. As the publisher Anthony Blond remembered, '[I]t would have been considered insolent and presumptuous to actually borrow a book from the Library. It would have been like going behind the altar to drink the wine, that wasn't what it was for.' (Danny Danziger, *Eton Voices*, Viking, 1998, p. 45)
18. The prime sports pitch at Eton, where, as another Old Etonian describes, the 'first XV play in Michaelmas'.
19. 'Half' is the Etonian word for term.
20. 'Fagging and Boy Government', Malcolm Falkus in *The World of the Public School*, St Martin's Press, 1977, p. 57
21. Ibid., p. 62
22. Reports of Her Majesty's Commissioners appointed to inquire into the revenues and management of certain colleges and schools and the studies pursed and instruction given therein, Volume II, Eyre & Spottiswoode, 1864, p. 281
23. *The Times*, 25 April 1980

24. Ibid., 2 May 1980
25. Advert seen on etoncollege.com
26. Evelyn Waugh, *Decline and Fall*, Chapman & Hall, 1928, p. 36. Indeed in *Decline and Fall*, Evelyn Waugh gives a now-famous description of different school ratings. ' "We class schools, you see, into four grades: Leading School, First-rate School, Good School, and School. Frankly," said Mr Levy, "School is pretty bad." ' (Ibid., p. 28)
27. Mary Sheepshanks, *Wild Writing Granny: A Memoir*, Stone Trough Books, 2012, p. 50
28. Harewood, p. 22
29. Quentin Crewe, *Well, I Forget the Rest*, Hutchinson, 1991, p. 30
30. Blunt, p. 10
31. Crewe, p. 30
32. Blunt, p. 191
33. Danziger, p. 77
34. *Eton College Chronicle*, 6 December 1968
35. Ibid., 1 July 1982
36. As was the housemaster Le Bas in the opening chapter of Anthony Powell's *A Question of Upbringing*, when his charges, Charles Stringham, the narrator Nick Jenkins and Peter Templer, notice how he faintly resembles a con man wanted locally named 'Braddock alias Thorne', and direct the police towards where Le Bas is sitting, reading poetry and minding his own business.
37. Jamie Blackett, *The Enigma of Kidson*, Quiller, 2017, p. 37. At least, this is the story that Blackett tells. Upon further inspection it emerges that the boy who was said to have been flea-ridden was a boy sitting next to Mungo Mansfield in Kidson's class. When Kidson died in 2015, the other Etonian was approached for comment for his former beak's obituary and named Mungo as the victim in this tale because, as Mungo's wife Sophy Mansfield explains, 'he had a title and it would sound funnier.' The Mansfields later framed Kidson's obituary and put it in their loo at home.
38. Ibid., p. 40
39. Ibid., p. 32
40. Tim Card, *Eton Renewed*, John Murray, 1994, p. 11
41. Carrington, p. 17
42. Crewe, p. 32
43. Danziger, p. 126

44. Ibid., p. 207
45. Ibid., p. 212
46. *Vanity Fair*, November 2012
47. Those who attended Repton School in Derbyshire between 1914 and 1932 might well have a claim to have been beaten by the Archbishop of Canterbury, since its headmaster during that period, Geoffrey Fisher, was appointed to this post in 1944. Fisher's biographer Edward Carpenter claims that it is 'quite unfair . . . to regard Geoffrey Fisher as a devotee of the rod', though he accepts that 'it was a basic conviction of Geoffrey Fisher's that no school . . . could function effectively without the right degree of discipline.' (Edward Carpenter, *Archbishop Fisher: His Life and Times*, The Canterbury Press Norwich, 1991, p. 19)
48. I say 'about' since not all peers included their schooling in their *Debrett's* entry – only 81 per cent did in this edition.
49. Roger Royle, *A Few Blocks from Broadway*, Hodder & Stoughton, 1987, p. 101

11. WHEN THE GOING WAS GOOD

1. John H. Davis, *The Guggenheims: An American Epic*, William Morrow & Co., 1978, p. 381. In a later echo of such a view of the world, it is recorded that Hugh Molyneux, 7th Earl of Sefton – who died aged seventy-three in 1972 – was asked one day, while he was standing at the bar in White's, why he seemed rather 'out of sorts'. He responded that '. . . he had just had lunch upstairs and a younger member whom he had not known and who clearly did not know him had asked what he did. "What I do?", stammered Sefton . . .' with the implication that, after all, Lord Sefton did not *do* anything. (Charles Hindlip, *An Auctioneer's Lot*, Third Millennium Publishing, 2016, p. 92)
2. Bath, p. 105
3. Perrott, p. 43
4. Ibid., p. 66
5. Channon, 1943–57, p. 726
6. Ibid., p. 727
7. Jonathan Swift, *Irish Tracts, 1728–1733*, Basil Blackwell, 1964, p. 50
8. L. G. Mitchell, *Charles James Fox*, Oxford University Press, 1992, p. 96
9. *The Times*, 28 June 1950

10. In the end, Brougham Hall escaped demolition but was left roofless. It is now run by a charity.

11. *Daily Mirror*, 7 August 1953

12. John Pearson, *The Gamblers*, Arrow, 2007, pp. 24–5

13. Ibid., p. 25

14. *Gstaad Life*, 13 July 2008

15. Nigel Dempster, *Nigel Dempster's Address Book*, Weidenfeld & Nicolson, 1990, p. 169

16. She spelled her name, explains Teddy Derby, with an 'o' rather than with an 'a', though public records often state otherwise.

17. Wyatt, *Volume II*, p. 260

18. Channon, *1943–57*, p. 478. Later, in 1952, Channon reported that Isobel had 'run away' with Reginald Sheffield, the married younger brother of Sir Robert Sheffield, 7th Baronet: 'she was always a tart and always will be one.' (Ibid., p. 739) Isobel and John Derby never divorced, but she remained Sheffield's mistress. The racehorse trainer Jeremy Tree observed that the Derbys '. . . came together . . . they had a lot of ups and downs and various bad patches.' Woodrow Wyatt agreed. 'But it ended very well because basically they truly loved each other despite all her cavorting with other people.' (Wyatt, *Volume II*, p. 285)

19. Teddy Derby told me that 'I never heard him say "Oh, I think this will be a good flutter today", or "I'll have a bet on that". If he did, when he died I went through the paperwork and a bookmaker's bill or cheque would have come in, or even a statement with a zero balance on it [and it didn't].'

20. Pearson, *Gamblers*, p. 168

21. His father Edward, Lord Stanley, had been wounded in the First World War and died in October 1938, aged forty-four, from complications caused by those injuries. Channon described him as '. . . courteous, almost handsome, gentle, genial, gay, simple and loyal. He enjoyed fun and society, but was quite unmalicious, and good, stolid.' (Channon, *1938–43*, p. 10) In 1917, he married the Hon. Sibyl 'Portia' Cadogan, granddaughter of George Cadogan, 5th Earl Cadogan. Edward Stanley and three of his brothers-in-law had been caricatured in *Tatler* in 1927, their arms linked, with the caption 'Cadogan Square', since they had all married Cadogan girls. Channon observed that Edward was terrified of his wife: '[H]er biting tongue

and bullying character eclipsed and frightened him.' (Ibid., p. 11) The feeling was widespread, remembers her niece Rosemary Muir: '[W]e were terrified of her.' Portia's relationship with the Derby earldom appears, per Channon, somewhat craven. It was her habit to refer to her father-in-law Eddy Derby's future death, and the promotion she expected her husband to achieve, as 'when something happens'. (Channon, *1918–38*, p. 407) When he fell ill in December 1936, Chips reported how Portia could 'scarcely conceal her excitement'. (Ibid., p. 618) Of course, she never got as far as Countess of Derby.

22. Teddy Derby says: 'He was religious in his habits. He had a whisky and soda at 6.30 p.m. and then he would go up for a bath and to change. After he came down he would have a glass of sherry before dinner, and then he drank lemon barley water with dinner. He would sometimes have a glass of brandy after dinner if he was entertaining.'

23. The Derbys had lived in a variety of extraordinary London houses. Edward Smith-Stanley, 12th Earl of Derby, had a house on the west side of Grosvenor Square that later became the American Embassy. His grandson Edward Smith-Stanley, 14th Earl of Derby, the three-time prime minister, lived in 10 St James's Square (now Chatham House) until his death in 1869. It is thought that his son Edward Stanley, 15th Earl of Derby, who hated waste, horses, gambling and as Teddy Derby says, 'anything extravagant', downsized the family from 10 St James's Square to the more modest number 23. Two years after Eddy Derby inherited the title in 1908, he sold what was by then known as Derby House at 23 (now 33) St James's Square, having decided that it wasn't sufficient to meet his needs. In its place, he bought Stratford House, on Stratford Place off Oxford Street, now the Oriental Club. When in 1941 Christie's on King Street was bombed, their sales were moved into the empty Stratford Place for the remainder of the war; the Derbys had been clients of theirs since the eighteenth century.

24. Mark Girouard, *A Country House Companion*, Yale University Press, 1987, p. 122

25. Martin Gilbert, *Winston S. Churchill, Volume VIII: Never Despair, 1945–1965*, Houghton Mifflin, 1988, p. 984. Indeed in 2023, Teddy Derby was still employing his uncle's old valet, albeit in an adapted role. And, as Churchill is said to have put it, about Knowsley: 'it's nice to hear of a house where you can still get a left and right at a butler.' (Girouard, p.122)

26. It is wrong to suppose that John Derby made cuts to his acreage in order to pay his tax bills, in the years following his grandfather's death, because he was hard up. No, says Teddy Derby, he reduced his landholdings because in 1948, when he inherited, estate duty was so high, at 75 per cent, that it was responsible and prudent of him to reduce what was taxable. Make no mistake, he was not hard up; only half a century before, the Derbys had enjoyed among the highest incomes in the country, and had experienced little diminution in their wealth subsequently. 'If the government said "you owe us seventy per cent of everything you own", you are going to make some very big sales ... [I]n 1966 when he moved out of Knowsley, he ... cut his household staff by fourteen people – there is no suggestion that he was anything other than an extremely rich man.'

27. Equivalent to £3.9 million in May 2024, per the Bank of England.

28. Douglas Thompson, *The Hustlers*, Pan Books, 2008, p. 149

29. Equivalent to £435,000 in May 2024, per the Bank of England. Douglas Thompson points out that since John already owed Aspers a large sum, had he won he would have been set to collect only part of his winnings.

30. In 1948, Gianni Agnelli began a relationship with the Hon. Pamela Digby. Between 1939 and 1946, she had been married to Randolph Churchill, son of the prime minister, who, during the Second World War while serving with the Commandos, lost money gambling night after night. As Randolph's comrade Evelyn Waugh witheringly described to his wife Laura, the morning after it was revealed he was £800 down, having lost £400 another night that week, 'Poor Pamela will have to go to work.' (Waugh, *Letters*, p. 150)

31. Patrick Marnham, *Trail of Havoc*, Penguin, 1989, p. 14

32. Brian Masters, *The Passion of John Aspinall*, Jonathan Cape, 1988, p. 116

33. Ibid., pp. 112–13

34. Andrew Barrow, *Gossip: Fifty Years of High Society*, Pan Books, 1980, p. 228

35. Annabel Goldsmith, *Annabel: An Unconventional Life*, Weidenfeld & Nicolson, 2004, p. 191

36. Pearson, *The Gamblers*, p. 148

37. Ibid., pp. 148–9

38. Ibid., p. 167

39. Sally Moore, *Lucan*, Sidgwick & Jackson, 1987, p. 52

40. Ibid.
41. The very same as had married Margaret Whigham, future Duchess of Argyll, in 1933.
42. Moore, p. 55
43. Goldsmith, *Annabel*, p. 191
44. *New Review*, 26 May 1976
45. Scott Alexander Siskind, 'Right is the New Left', 22 April 2014; slatestarcodex.com
46. Billy Connolly, *Two Night Stand*, 1997; as seen here: youtube.com/watch?v=pRZeYHM1GzQ
47. Channon, *1943–57*, p. 320
48. Channon, *1938–43*, p. 156
49. In 1946, a twenty-one-year lease was granted to the Royal Aero Club for most of Londonderry House; Charley and Circe kept the top floor and turned it into a huge, twenty-two-room apartment, which in 1944 Jim Lees-Milne reckoned could be 'divided into five and possibly six expensive Park Lane flats' (Lees-Milne, *Prophesying Peace*, p. 123).
50. Goldsmith, *Annabel*, p. 77
51. This was Major Boyce Combe, who was rather unflatteringly nicknamed 'Boozer Combe'.
52. Goldsmith, *Annabel*, p. 77
53. Ibid., p. 78
54. Ibid., p. 89. Chips Channon would have agreed with Annabel's much later assessment of her father: 'What an aimless life; drinking himself to death,' he recorded in his diary in May 1954. (Channon, *1943–57*, p. 979)
55. Pat Strathmore, Queen Elizabeth the Queen Mother's eldest brother, was wounded in the First World War and badly shell-shocked. The fact that the Leeds were not among the wealthiest ducal families counted against Dorothy. So did the fact that even her own mother thought she was an unsuitable wife for anyone. In 1949, Channon described Pat as 'a bit cracked' (Channon, *1943–57*, p. 560) and his wife Dorothy, in 1946, as 'that mad woman'. (Ibid., p. 366)
56. Duke of Devonshire, p. 100
57. Channon, *1943–57*, p. 135
58. Duke of Devonshire, p. 101
59. Deborah Devonshire, *Wait for Me*, p. 254

60. Duke of Devonshire, p. 102
61. Marcus Scriven, *Splendour and Squalor*, Atlantic Books, 2011, p. 73
62. Ibid., p. 75
63. Waterson, *A Noble Thing*, p. 14
64. Typically, Victor's accounts of his allowance varied between £500 and £2,000. Frederick Bristol, his grandson the Hon. Robert Erskine concluded, was 'fairly peculiar', partly, he thought, as the result of Ick-worth, 'such a strange house'. His peculiarity, he reckoned, was 'the result of somebody living in the middle of a park which is nine miles in circumference'. (Scriven, p. 73)
65. Ibid., p. 84
66. Spain, debated 31 May 1937, House of Commons
67. Scriven, p. 87
68. Gerald Howson, *Arms for Spain*, St Martin's Press, 1999, p. 218
69. Scriven, p. 85
70. *Weekly Dispatch*, 9 July 1939
71. Scriven, p. 91
72. Ibid., p. 98
73. Ibid., p. 249
74. Ibid., p. 266
75. Ibid., p. 267
76. *Bury Free Press*, 10 July 1987
77. Scriven, p. 258
78. *Guardian*, 22 January 2006
79. *The Times*, 19 February 1984
80. Jessica Berens, granddaughter of Richard Yarde-Buller, 4th Baron Churston, had long suffered from depression herself. When she died in 2019, aged fifty-nine, the coroner ruled that she had taken her own life. After her close friend Lucy Ferry took hers in 2018, Berens wrote: 'To ask why a beautiful rich woman should commit suicide is to not understand either the nature of clinical depression or the experience of living with suicidal ideation. I understood her darkness, and I was not afraid of it, which is one of the reasons why we could speak to each other honestly and meaningfully.' (*Telegraph*, 27 July 2018)
81. *Tatler*, February 1990
82. *Independent*, 12 January 1999
83. John Bristol was not the only peer to die from an AIDS-related illness. Nicholas Eden, 2nd Earl of Avon, son of the former prime

minister, died from complications relating to AIDS in 1985, as did Sheridan Hamilton-Temple-Blackwood, 5th and last Marquess of Dufferin and Ava, aged forty-nine, three years later. Like John Bristol, Sheridan had inherited young – at the age of six, when his father was killed in Burma. On 30 May 1988, the *Daily Mail* headline read: 'Marquess dies of AIDS'. 'Brutes,' declared Jim Lees-Milne, a friend of Sheridan's late father, Basil Ava. (Lees-Milne, *Diaries*, p. 178)

84. A bizarre non-profit organisation founded in 1943 devoted to defending and promoting the system of constitutional monarchy. It advocated the restoration of displaced royals, and held the 'principle of monarchy against the disintegrating forces of Bolshevism and socialism'. (Scriven, p. 112) Victor was the League's chancellor from 1976.
85. Scriven, p. 238
86. *Guardian*, 22 January 2006
87. *Bury Free Press*, 10 July 1987
88. *Tatler*, February 1990
89. *Independent*, 12 January 1999
90. *Tatler*, February 1990

12. EXCURSION IN REALITY

1. They were chairman of Coutts and the first chief executive of Barclays de Zoete Wedd respectively.
2. Over half have served in the armed forces in some capacity, and twenty-three have been elected MPs, with others serving in the House of Lords, the civil service and the diplomatic service.
3. These are the twenty-six extant families of the twenty-nine-strong premier league of the 1890s: the Dukes of Bedford, Buccleuch, Devonshire, Hamilton, Norfolk, Northumberland, Richmond, Rutland, Sutherland and Westminster; the Marquesses of Anglesey, Bute, Downshire, Hertford and Londonderry; the Earls of Derby, Dudley, Pembroke, Portland, Seafield and Yarborough; the Viscounts Boyne and Portman; and the Barons Barnard, Brownlow and Leconfield.
4. *The Times*, 1 April 2011
5. Interview with Maurice FitzGerald, 9th Duke of Leinster, Irish Life and Lore archive

   The Leinsters had a troubled twentieth century. The current duke's great-uncle Maurice FitzGerald, 6th Duke of Leinster, succeeded to the dukedom in 1893 but was still in his minority when under the Wyndham Act 1903 trustees of his significant Irish estates – which had been, in 1883, as much as 73,100 acres – sold much of the land. Though the sales made a significant sum, a large proportion of the monies were required to supply trusts for members of the 4th Duke's enormous family. Maurice Leinster died in 1922, having spent time in a psychiatric institution in Edinburgh, and never married. The dukedom passed to his brother Edward, both a Gallipoli veteran and a compulsive gambler, who signed away his reversionary rights to the Leinsters' seat, Carton House, in County Kildare, to Sir Harry Mallaby-Deeley, 1st Baronet, having had no expectation that, as a younger son, he would ever inherit it. Edward Leinster was married four times; his son from his first marriage, Gerald, was brought up by his great-aunt Lady Adelaide FitzGerald at Johnstown Castle in County Wexford, and inherited the title in 1976 when his father took his own life in a Pimlico bedsit. In the 1960s Gerald moved to Oxfordshire, where his son Maurice, the current duke, lives today. He succeeded his father in 2004. His only son Thomas, Earl of Offaly, was killed in a car accident in Ireland in 1997. The duke's heir is now his nephew Edward FitzGerald.

As Marcus Scriven described in his 2009 book, *Splendour & Squalor*, Edward FitzGerald was, to members of the peerage, 'unpalatable', but nevertheless 'one of them'. And, '[M]ore galling still, he could not be dismissed as an ermined parvenu. His family had not grubbed its way into the aristocracy a couple of generations before ... nor greased its way to favour with gross, well-judged bribes to Liberal or Tory governments ... instead [the FitzGeralds were] an emblem of ancient nobility, securing status and privilege by shedding blood on the battlefield over the course of nine hundred years.' (Scriven, p. 12)

6. When compiling data on peers' professions, I have taken 'financial services' to include accountancy, asset management, straightforward merchant and high street banking, and investment banking.

7. *Guardian*, 24 May 2010

8. One of the most prominent of their number is Anthony Gifford, 6th Baron Gifford, KC, who founded the country's first law centre in North Kensington in 1970. In 1986 he chaired the Broadwater Farm Inquiry, and later served as counsel during the Guildford Four and Birmingham Six appeals. Mark Bridges, 3rd Baron Bridges, KCVO, worked as Elizabeth II's private solicitor and still acts for the Princess Royal and the

Duchy of Cornwall. Peers have served as, or are serving, police officers, and at least one heir is a serving officer. Peter St Clair-Erskine, 7th Earl of Rosslyn and from February 2023 Charles III's Lord Steward, joined the Metropolitan Police in 1980 on the recommendation of his third cousin Alistair Sutherland, then Lord Strathnaver and now 25th Earl of Sutherland, who had joined the Met in 1969 and worked as a detective. In 1994, Peter Rosslyn, then using the courtesy title Lord Loughborough, led Operation Troodos, a crackdown on drug dealers in west London, one of the targets of which was the future James Marlborough's dealer. Other policing peers include Jonathan Kemp, 3rd Viscount Rochdale, who joined the Met in 1982 and served for eleven years, beginning as a constable in Chelsea; and Simon Nelson, 10th Earl Nelson, who followed in the footsteps of his father Peter Nelson, 9th Earl Nelson, a Hertfordshire police detective. But as Peter Nelson said in 1981 of his work, 'If there were an estate to inherit, I would never be doing this.' (*People*, 21 December 1981)

9. Perrott, p. 157

10. Pete Howard de Walden's full name is Count Peter John Joseph Czernin von und zu Chudenitz, and is Czech in origin, since his father's family once held land in Bohemia. 'Over the years a lot of my friends have made Count Dracula and "undead" jokes,' he says.

11. One of, since there are two more: Hamilton and Brandon, and Richmond and Gordon, who is technically a triple duke, being Richmond, Lennox and Gordon. But it's not a competition.

12. This was a haul with twelve principal residences, most of which were 'linked together by estates so vast that it was possible for [the family] to drive from one to the other without being for any great length of time off [their] own property.' (Hamilton, p. 133)

13. Broadly equivalent in size to Bahrain and almost double the size of the whole island of Barbados. In 2016, when I first met him, he owned 240,000 acres.

14. Not far behind him are the Dukes of Westminster and Northumberland, with around 140,000 and 100,000 acres respectively, while the Lowther estate, presided over by members of the Lowther family including William Lowther, 9th Earl of Lonsdale, with 102,000 acres, is the largest aristocratic estate in England.

15. Indeed, in October 2024, land reform campaigner Andy Wightman described how, over the past twenty-five years, the Buccleuch estate has

been more successful in redistributing land than the Scottish government itself, despite there being a stated ambition to diversify landownership.

16. Hugh Montgomery-Massingberd and Christopher Simon Sykes, *Great Houses of Scotland*, Laurence King Publishing Ltd, 1997, p. 45

17. David Cannadine, *Lords and Landlords: The Aristocracy and the Towns, 1774–1967*, Leicester University Press, 1980, p. 41

18. Work on this had commenced in 1782, when Francis Moray bought a thirteen-acre plot on which stood a large townhouse called Drumsheugh House, south-east of what is now Randolph Crescent. After Francis Moray died in 1810, his son, also called Francis, 10th Earl of Moray, whose twin brother Archibald, from whom John Moray is descended, predeceased him, thought that this plot of land seemed a suitable place to build a new community. In 1822, he wrote to the architect James Gillespie and commissioned him to draw up plans to build 150 townhouses on the patch. Off-plan sales of Francis Moray's new townhouses began in August 1822. Buyers agreed to pay a build cost of between £2,000 and £3,000, and most of the plots sold quickly. The scheme was completed in 1858. Francis Moray and his second wife Margaret Ainslie's choice of street names was inspired by their family histories. Moray Place was the obvious one, named for their title and the county over which Francis Moray ruled, and Doune Terrace was in respect of his courtesy title, Lord Doune. Ainslie Place was named after Margaret's family; Great Stuart Street reflected the Morays' surname; Wemyss Place was so-called after Francis Moray's stepmother Margaret Wemyss, and Darnaway Street marked the name of the Morays' home in Moray, which retains its thousand-seater medieval banqueting hall.

19. I interviewed Duany in 2017, when he described John Moray and David Carnegie, 4th Duke of Fife, another town-building Scottish landowner, as 'touchingly concerned about doing the right thing. There is a long history of knowing that if they don't do the right thing they're not going to keep their privileges. I have had to remind them that they have to make a profit – the normal builder thinks first of the profit and then the build quality, so they have to reverse that. I'm impressed by not only the willingness to do the right thing, but how much work they are willing to do in terms of finding the experts. They don't just hand over to the experts the way that Americans do – they actually read the stuff, they're there every day, intimately

involved with every detail.' Duany added that 'these are people who have been at this for centuries, and they have a responsibility to do things as well as their ancestors did. In the United States we don't have that – we have investors and returns on investment. It's a very old way of thinking about it.'

20. Princess Louise wasn't the first royal princess to marry a commoner, nor even the first royal princess called Louise to marry a commoner – her aunt Princess Louise had married Ian Campbell, Marquess of Lorne, the future 9th Duke of Argyll, in 1871.

21. James Pope-Hennessy, *Queen Mary, 1867–1953*, George Allen & Unwin, 1959, p. 229

22. This is now a necessarily diversified estate where Caroline Fife runs a trio of self-contained apartments available to rent and the Fifes operate salmon and trout fishing on the River Southesk, and shooting across the 7,000-acre estate.

23. The Elsick estate has been owned by the Bannerman family since 1367; in 1891, Charles Carnegie, the future 10th Earl of Southesk, married Ethel Bannerman, only child and heiress of Sir Alexander Bannerman of Elsick, 9th Baronet, and Elsick came with her. David Fife is Ethel Bannerman's great-grandson.

24. But not all. Neil Rosebery did his National Service in the ranks of the Royal Electrical and Mechanical Engineers, and Merlin Sudeley joined the Scots Guards as a private soldier aged eighteen, having failed to get a commission. 'It's a period I prefer to forget,' he told me in 2022. 'I learned drill at Caterham [Guards Depot], learned how to operate a telephone, but never got as far as doing a guard duty.' Tim Willoughby de Eresby, another future peer who served as a private soldier, was with the Royal Horse Guards for two years from 1954, failed to gain a commission and subsequently became a signaller. Vere Harmsworth, from 1978 3rd Viscount Rothermere, the proprietor of the *Daily Mail*, also served as a private soldier, though he left this detail out of his *Debrett's* profile. As he told Nicholas Coleridge in the early 1990s, 'I found it extremely helpful in understanding the true nature of society. I think it gave me quite an idea about what the real world is really like for the majority of people.' (Nicholas Coleridge, *Paper Tigers*, Mandarin, 1993, p. 15) More recently, Michael Annesley, 12th Earl Annesley, born 1933, joined the Royal Air Force as an airman aged sixteen, and left in 1973 as a warrant officer.

25. Giles Romilly and Michael Alexander, *Hostages of Colditz*, Praeger, 1973, p. 109. On 12 April 1945, the order came that the Prominente were to be moved from Colditz. As they drove through Dresden towards Königstein Castle, Charlie 'snapped': 'I was round the bend. I could hear what they said to me but I could not answer.' (Henry Chancellor, *Colditz*, William Morrow & Co., 2001, p. 354) Screaming and crying, he attempted to kill a guard and had to be restrained. Once they had arrived at Königstein, John Elphinstone asked if Charlie could stay there with George 'Dawyck' Haig, later 2nd Earl Haig, who had dysentery. They befriended the commandant, Colonel Hesselmann, and his family, who asked them to take the Saxon crown jewels back to Britain as a gift to the royal family. In the confusion caused by the arrival of the Russians, the suitcases were left behind. When they arrived at an Allied airbase, the corporal, upon hearing their names, said, 'Ah. We've been looking for you all over Germany.' In October 1945, Charlie was awarded the Military Cross. (Chancellor, p. 369)

26. *Gloucester Citizen*, 9 May 1939

27. Though his younger son Lord Fred Wellesley did, serving eight years in the Blues and Royals, including with the Guards Parachute Platoon.

28. *Telegraph*, 14 March 2015

29. So few members of peerage families have become Church of England clergy since 1945 that it's worth mentioning one family that has proved an exception to the general tendency. The late Nathaniel Twisleton-Wykeham-Fiennes, 21st Baron Saye and Sele, who died aged 103 in January 2024 after an extraordinary life that included being among the first troops to reach Bergen-Belsen in 1945 and thereafter running the Broughton Castle estate in Oxfordshire, was born the eldest son of Ivo Twisleton-Wykeham-Fiennes, 20th Baron Saye and Sele. He had two brothers. The Hon. Ingelram Twisleton-Wykeham-Fiennes was killed in action in 1941, while serving with the RAF, while their younger brother, the Hon. Oliver Twisleton-Wykeham-Fiennes, went into the church, rising in 1969 to become Dean of Lincoln. As the career clergyman Trevor Beeson, a former Dean of Winchester, put it in 2002, 'There is no one very grand among today's bishops – not even an Honourable . . . for the simple reason that the aristocracy has for several decades failed to produce more than a handful of clergy.' Oliver Fiennes, along with the Hon.

Hugh Dickinson, grandson of Willoughby Dickinson, 1st Baron Dickinson, who was appointed Dean of Salisbury in 1986, became the 'last [member of the peerage] to make a mark on the Church'. (Trevor Beeson, *The Bishops*, SCM Press, 2002, p. 26)

30. Cannadine, *Decline*, p. 14
31. Forbes, p. 176
32. This, Michael Lothian told me shortly before his death in October 2024, was the right thing for his father to do, since by the mid-1980s, he and his wife Jane were unlikely to have more children. His nephew Johnnie, now Earl of Ancram, was left Peter Lothian's part of the estate, and in due course all of the Lothian estates will be reunited as they were when Peter Lothian inherited them in 1940.
33. He is not the only peer who is also a clan chief – thirty-six others also bear this responsibility.

13. REMOTE PEOPLE

1. *The Times*, 1 January 1969
2. Count Henry Bentinck, *Clogs to Clogs in Six Hundred Years*, unpublished manuscript, p. 5
3. When in 2018 he founded elderflower liqueur company St Maur with his wife Kelsey, he took the name from an ancient spelling of Seymour, and its logo from the Yarmouth crest.
4. Kelsey adds that they deliberately do not refer to their eldest son Clement by his own courtesy title, Viscount Beauchamp. 'We want for him to be Clement Seymour and to have as much freedom to just be Clement, and find out who Clement is, and what Clement wants to do.'
5. He served as a Liberal MP from 1906 to 1927 when he resigned from the Liberals, and the following year entered parliament as the Labour MP for Aberdeen North.
6. Jad Adams, *Tony Benn*, Macmillan, 1992, p. 25
7. *The Times*, 22 December 1941
8. Adams, p. 25
9. Tony Benn, *Years of Hope: Diaries, Letters and Papers, 1940–1962*, edited by Ruth Winstone, Hutchinson, 1994, p. 6
10. Adams, p. 27
11. Benn, *Years of Hope*, p. 53
12. Lord Hailsham, *A Sparrow's Flight*, Fontana, 1990, p. 262

13. Ibid., p. 73
14. Ibid., p. 262
15. Ibid., pp. 262–3
16. Lord Home, *The Way the Wind Blows*, Collins, 1976, p. 100
17. Ibid., p. 101
18. Benn, *Years of Hope*, p. 359
19. Ibid., p. 361
20. *Daily Mirror*, 24 November 1960
21. Benn, *Years of Hope*, p. 368
22. Adams, p. 176
23. Ibid., p. 177
24. Adams, p. 177
25. Benn, *Years of Hope*, p. 370
26. Adams, p. 188
27. Ibid., p. 195
28. Ibid., p. 196
29. Sir William Haley to Tony Benn, 11 December 1961, quoted in Adams, p. 196
30. Eight minutes after Tony Benn renounced his peerage he was followed by John Grigg, 2nd Baron Altrincham, who had, in 1957, described Elizabeth II's court as too upper-class.
31. Tony Benn, *Out of the Wilderness: Diaries, 1963–1967*, Hutchinson, 1987, p. 45
32. Ibid., pp. 46–7
33. Ibid., p. 47
34. Ibid.
35. *Birmingham Daily Post*, 23 March 1964
36. Sebastian Sligo adds, when we speak on a later date, that the entire process took almost four years, as he remarked to his contact at the College of Arms. In order to prove his succession, he had to prove three marriage certificates, four death certificates, three birth certificates, two wills and one affidavit.
37. *Saffron Walden Weekly News*, 26 May 1967
38. *Liverpool Daily Post*, 13 July 1967
39. Writing to him, I initially addressed him as Lord Essex. 'Just occasionally I find myself as "Paul Essex",' he says. 'I thought of using it when emailing you. I must have got out of the habit of using Paul Essex. It's quite nice, Paul Essex.'

40. Lady Morgan, *Lady Morgan's Memoirs: Autobiography, Diaries and Correspondence, Volume I*, Bernhard Tauchnitz, 1863, p. 322
41. As a young man, Alexander Pushkin was greatly influenced by Byron.
42. Nicholas Elliott, *Never Judge a Man by his Umbrella*, Michael Russell, 1991, p. 94. Elliott, who later became famous for his friendship with the British intelligence officer and Soviet double agent Kim Philby, was best man at the Chichesters' wedding in 1940. 'I have often wondered that my mother never ever mentioned him,' says John Chichester. 'I guess she didn't like him.'
43. The Palais Pannwitz was eventually sold to the German state in 1941, but not before Hermann Goering had bought six paintings from Catalina in exchange for an estimated 390,000 Dutch guilders and a Swiss visa. Catalina later claimed that the sale had not been voluntary. Today, the Palais Pannwitz is a luxury hotel.
44. Post-war Argentina was a conspicuously German environment. 'After the war Juan Perón's instincts were all fascist, and he invited a lot of ex-military and Luftwaffe personnel to the Argentine,' says John Chichester. 'The Pope was extremely helpful in getting Nazis to the Argentine, Paraguay and Chile – there was a Nazi colony in Chile, and Adolf Eichmann was in Buenos Aires.' One of Ursula's close friends was Sylvina von Dönhoff, the widow of a Wehrmacht general, who in 1954 married the former Luftwaffe pilot Adolf Galland. John Chichester adds that 'we did not much associate with Nazis.'
45. He means the life peers, of course.
46. David Cecil, *The Cecils of Hatfield House*, Constable, 1973, p. 218
47. Hatfield House was built in 1611 by Robert Cecil, 1st Earl of Salisbury, on the site of the Royal Palace of Hatfield, the childhood home of Elizabeth I. Her successor James I disliked it, and so swapped it with Salisbury in exchange for Theobalds, the Cecils' home nearby.
48. Strong, *Diaries*, p. 168

EPILOGUE

1. Nigel Winchester had inherited the marquessate in 1968 from his first cousin once removed Richard Paulet, 17th Marquess of Winchester. Richard Winchester's predecessor, Henry 'Monty' Paulet, 16th Marquess of Winchester, was adjudged bankrupt in 1930, having disclosed liabilities of over £460,000, following his ill-fated

associations with the financier Clarence Hatry, of whose companies he became a director, and who in 1929 confessed to fraud. Monty spent most of the rest of his life living abroad. As his third wife he married, in his ninetieth year, Bapsybanoo 'Bapsy' Pavry, a daughter of Khurshedji Erachji Pavry, claimed by her to be High Priest of the Parsees in Bombay, though Monty maintained that his father-in-law was the priest of a fire temple. He died in Monte Carlo in 1962, aged ninety-nine, retaining the status of the oldest ever member of the House of Lords.

2. And not, as has been previously reported, a 'pop group': 'He's very offended by that,' says Emma.

3. The five most popular Christian names among hereditary peers in 2024 were, in order: John, Charles, James, David and Richard.

4. *The Salisbury–Balfour Correspondence 1869–1892*, edited by Robin Harcourt Williams, Hertfordshire Record Society, 1988, xix, as seen in Roberts, p. 790

5. Brian Masters, *Getting Personal*, Constable, 2002, p. 183

6. Ibid., p. 185

Picture Acknowledgements

First plate section: p.1 (top) Collection of Wentworth Wood-house Preservation Trust. p. 2 (top) Heritage Images via Getty Images (middle) © The Trustees of the Bowood Archive (bottom) Fox Photos via Getty Images. p. 3 (top left) Chris Ware via Getty Images (top right) Heritage Images via Getty Images (bottom left) © Andrew Crowley (bottom right) © James McNaught. p. 4 (top) Popperfoto via Getty Images (middle) By kind permission of Lady Juliet Tadgell (bottom) Central Press via Getty Images. p. 5 (top) Pierre Manevy via Getty Images (middle) Christopher Simon Sykes via Getty Images (bottom) Tony Evans / Timelapse Library Ltd. via Getty Images. p. 6 (top left) Trinity Mirror / Mirrorpix / Alamy Stock Photo (top right) Evening Standard via Getty Images (bottom left) PA Images / Alamy Stock Photo (bottom right) Central Press via Getty Images. p. 7 (top left) By kind permission of the Countess of Mar (top right) PA Images / Alamy Stock Photo (bottom left) Homer Sykes / Alamy Stock Photo (bottom right) © Helen Cath-cart. p. 8 (top left) ullstein bild Dtl. via Getty Images (top right) Evening Standard via Getty Images (bottom left) United News / Popperfoto via Getty Images.

Second plate section: p. 1 (top three images) By kind permis-sion of the Duke of Northumberland (bottom) By kind permission of the Duke of Bedford. p. 2 (top two images) Evening Standard via Getty (bottom left) Hulton Archive via Getty Images (bottom right) Keystone via Getty Images. p. 3 (top) The Fincher Files / Popperfoto via Getty Images (bottom left) By kind permission of

Sandwell Metropolitan Borough Council – Ingestre Hall (bottom right) Patrick Robert – Corbis via Getty Images. p. 4 (top) By kind permission of the Marquess of Sligo (bottom left) Patrick Ward / Popperfoto via Getty Images (bottom right) By kind permission of the Earl of Mansfield. p. 5 (top) By kind permission of the Hon. James Stuart (middle) P. Shirley via Getty Images (bottom) By kind permission of the Lord Crathorne. p. 6 (top left) Evening Standard via Getty Images (top right) Philip Townsend via Getty Images (bottom left) L. Waldorf via Getty Images (bottom right) Trevor Jones / Popperfoto via Getty Images. p. 7 (top) Fox Photos via Getty Images (middle) WPA Pool via Getty Images (bottom) Pool via Getty Images. p. 8 (top left) Terence Spencer / Popperfoto via Getty Images (top right) United News / Popperfoto (bottom left) Tristan Fewings via Getty Images (bottom right) © Chris Watt Photography.

The author and publisher gratefully acknowledge the permission granted to reproduce the copyright material in this book. Every effort has been made to trace copyright holders and to obtain their permission. The publisher apologises for any errors or omissions and, if notified of any corrections, will make suitable acknowledgement in future reprints or editions of this book.

Index